T0181120

Lecture Notes in Artificial Intelligence   13605

Subseries of Lecture Notes in Computer Science

More information about this subseries at https://link.springer.com/bookseries/1244

Lu Fang · Daniel Povey · Guangtao Zhai ·
Tao Mei · Ruiping Wang (Eds.)

Artificial Intelligence

Second CAAI International Conference, CICAI 2022
Beijing, China, August 27–28, 2022
Revised Selected Papers, Part II

 Springer

Editors
Lu Fang 🆔
Tsinghua University
Beijing, China

Daniel Povey 🆔
Xiaomi Inc.
Beijing, China

Guangtao Zhai 🆔
Shanghai Jiao Tong University
Shanghai, China

Tao Mei 🆔
JD Explore Academy
Beijing, China

Ruiping Wang 🆔
Chinese Academy of Sciences
Beijing, China

ISSN 0302-9743   ISSN 1611-3349 (electronic)
Lecture Notes in Artificial Intelligence
ISBN 978-3-031-20499-9   ISBN 978-3-031-20500-2 (eBook)
https://doi.org/10.1007/978-3-031-20500-2

LNCS Sublibrary: SL7 – Artificial Intelligence

This Springer imprint is published by the registered company Springer Nature Switzerland AG
The registered company address is: Gewerbestrasse 11, 6330 Cham, Switzerland

Preface

The present book includes extended and revised versions of papers selected from the second CAAI International Conference on Artificial Intelligence (CICAI 2022), held in Beijing, China, during August 27–28, 2022.

CICAI is a summit forum in the field of artificial intelligence and the 2022 forum was hosted by Chinese Association for Artificial Intelligence (CAAI). CICAI aims to establish a global platform for international academic exchange, promote advanced research in AI and its affiliated disciplines, and promote scientific exchanges among researchers, practitioners, scientists, students, and engineers in AI and its affiliated disciplines in order to provide interdisciplinary and regional opportunities for researchers around the world, enhance the depth and breadth of academic and industrial exchanges, inspire new ideas, cultivate new forces, implement new ideas, integrate into the new landscape, and join the new era. The conference program included invited talks delivered by two distinguished speakers, Qiang Yang and Dacheng Tao, as well as five theme tutorials with five talks for each theme, followed by an oral session of 18 papers, a poster session of 127 papers, and a demo exhibition of 19 papers. Those papers were selected from 521 submissions using a double-blind review process, and on average each submission received 3.2 reviews. The topics covered by these selected high-quality papers span the fields of machine learning, computer vision, natural language processing, and data mining, amongst others.

This three-volume series contains 164 papers selected and revised from the proceedings of CICAI 2022. We would like to thank the authors for contributing their novel ideas and visions that are recorded in this book.

The proceeding editors also wish to thank all reviewers for their contributions and Springer for their trust and for publishing the proceedings of CICAI 2022.

September 2022

Lu Fang
Daniel Povey
Guangtao Zhai
Tao Mei
Ruiping Wang

Organization

General Chairs

Lu Fang   Tsinghua University, China
Daniel Povey   Xiaomi, China
Guangtao Zhai   Shanghai Jiao Tong University, China

Honorary Program Chair

Lina J. Karam   Lebanese American University, Lebanon

Program Chairs

Tao Mei   JD Explore Academy, China
Ruiping Wang   Chinese Academy of Sciences, China

Publication Chairs

Hui Qiao   Tsinghua University, China
Adriana Tapus   Institut Polytechnique de Paris, France

Presentation Chairs

Mengqi Ji   Beihang University, Singapore
Zhou Zhao   Zhejiang University, China
Shan Luo   King's College London, UK

Demo Chairs

Kun Li   Tianjin University, China
Fu Zhang   University of Hong Kong, China

International Liaison Chair

Feng Yang   Google Research, USA

Advisory Committee

C. L. Philip Chen	University of Macau, China
Xilin Chen	Institute of Computing Technology, Chinese Academy of Sciences, China
Yike Guo	Imperial College London, UK
Ping Ji	The City University of New York, USA
Licheng Jiao	Xidian University, China
Ming Li	University of Waterloo, Canada
Chenglin Liu	Institute of Automation, Chinese Academy of Sciences, China
Derong Liu	University of Illinois at Chicago, USA
Hong Liu	Peking University, China
Hengtao Shen	University of Electronic Science and Technology of China, China
Yuanchun Shi	Tsinghua University, China
Yongduan Song	Chongqing University, China
Fuchun Sun	Tsinghua University, China
Jianhua Tao	Institute of Automation, Chinese Academy of Sciences, China
Guoyin Wang	Chongqing University of Posts and Telecommunications, China
Weining Wang	Beijing University of Posts and Telecommunications, China
Xiaokang Yang	Shanghai Jiao Tong University, China
Changshui Zhang	Tsinghua University, China
Lihua Zhang	Fudan University, China
Song-Chun Zhu	Peking University, China
Wenwu Zhu	Tsinghua University, China
Yueting Zhuang	Zhejiang University, China

Program Committee

Abdul Rehman	Bournemouth University, UK
Biao Jie	Anhui Normal University, China
Bing Cao	Tianjin University, China
Bo Xue	University of Science and Technology of China, China
Bo Wang	Dalian University of Technology, China
Bochen Guan	OPPO US Research Center, USA
Boyun Li	Sichuan University, China
Chang Yao	East China Normal University, China
Chao Bian	Nanjing University, China

Chao Wu	Zhejiang University, China
Chaokun Wang	Tsinghua University, China
Chengyang Ying	Tsinghua University, China
Chenping Fu	Dalian University of Technology, China
Chu Zhou	Peking University, China
Chun-Guang Li	Beijing University of Posts and Telecommunications, China
Dan Guo	Hefei University of Technology, China
Daoqiang Zhang	Nanjing University of Aeronautics and Astronautics, China
Dawei Zhou	Xidian University, China
Decheng Liu	Xidian University, China
Difei Gao	National University of Singapore, Singapore
Dong Liu	University of Science and Technology of China, China
Fan Li	Xi'an Jiaotong University, China
Fan Xu	Peng Cheng Laboratory, China
Fan-Ming Luo	Nanjing University, China
Feihong Liu	Northwest University, China
Feng Bao	University of California, USA
Gang Chen	Sun Yat-sen University, China
Gaosheng Liu	Tianjin University, China
Guangchi Fang	Sun Yat-sen University, China
Guofeng Zhang	Zhejiang University, China
Guorui Feng	Shanghai University, China
Guoxin Yu	Institute of Computing Technology, Chinese Academy of Sciences, China
Hailing Wang	Shanghai University of Engineering Science, China
Haiping Ma	Anhui University, China
Hanyun Wang	Information Engineering University, China
Hao Gao	Nanjing University of Posts and Telecommunications, China
Haozhe Jia	Research and Development Institute of Northwestern Polytechnical University in Shenzhen, China
Heyou Chang	Nanjing Xiaozhuang University, China
Hengfei Cui	Northwestern Polytechnical University, Canada
Hong Chang	Chinese Academy of Sciences, China
Hong Qian	East China Normal University, China
Hongjun Li	Beijing Forestry University, China
Hongke Zhao	Tianjin University, China
Hongwei Mo	Harbin Engineering University, China

Huan Yin	Hong Kong University of Science and Technology, China
Huanjing Yue	Tianjin University, China
Hui Chen	Tsinghua University, China
Huiyu Duan	Shanghai Jiao Tong University, China
Jiajun Deng	University of Science and Technology of China, China
Jian Zhao	Institute of North Electronic Equipment, China
Jianguo Sun	Harbin Engineering University, China
Jianhui Chang	Peking University, China
Jianing Sun	Dalian University of Technology, China
Jia-Wei Chen	Xidian University, China
Jimin Pi	Baidu, China
Jing Chen	Beijing Research Institute of Precise Mechatronics and Controls, China
Jingwen Guo	Peking University Shenzhen Graduate School, China
Jingyu Yang	Tianjin University, China
Jinjian Wu	Xidian University, China
Jinsong Zhang	Tianjin University, China
Jinyu Tian	University of Macau, China
Jinyuan Liu	Dalian University of Technology, China
Jun Wang	Shanghai University, China
Jupo Ma	Xidian University, China
Kai Hu	Xiangtan University, China
Kaiqin Hu	Xi'an Jiaotong University, China
Kan Guo	Beihang University, China
Ke Xue	Nanjing University, China
Keyang Wang	Chongqing University, China
Keyu Li	Xidian University, China
Kun Cheng	Xidian University, China
Kun Zhang	Hefei University of Technology, China
Le Wang	Xi'an Jiaotong University, China
Le Wu	Hefei University of Technology, China
Lei Wang	University of Wollongong, Australia
Lei Shi	Zhengzhou University, China
Leida Li	Xidian University, China
Liansheng Zhuang	University of Science and Technology of China, China
Liguo Zhang	Harbin Engineering University, China
Likang Wu	University of Science and Technology of China, China

Lili Zhao	University of Science and Technology of China, China
Lizhi Wang	Beijing Institute of Technology, China
Longguang Wang	National University of Defense Technology, China
Meiyu Huang	China Academy of Space Technology, China
Meng Wang	Hefei University of Technology, China
Mengting Xu	Nanjing University of Aeronautics and Astronautics, China
Mengxi Jia	Peking University Shenzhen Graduate School, China
Min Wang	Hefei Comprehensive National Science Center, China
Mingkui Tan	South China University of Technology, China
Mingrui Zhu	Xidian University, China
Min-Ling Zhang	Southeast University, China
Mouxing Yang	Sichuan University, China
Ningyu Zhang	Zhejiang University, China
Peijie Sun	Tsinghua University, China
Pengfei Zhang	National University of Defense Technology, China
Pengyang Shao	Hefei University of Technology, China
Pingping Zhang	Dalian University of Technology, China
Qi Liu	University of Science and Technology of China, China
Qian Ning	Xidian University, China
Qian Xu	CILAB
Qiao Feng	Tianjin University, China
Qing Li	Beijing Normal University, China
Qingbo Wu	University of Electronic Science and Technology of China, China
Qinglin Wang	National University of Defense Technology, China
Qun Liu	Chongqing University of Posts and Telecommunications, China
Richang Hong	Hefei University of Technology, China
Rongjun Ge	Southeast University, China
Ruiping Wang	Institute of Computing Technology, Chinese Academy of Sciences, China
Ruqi Huang	Tsinghua University, China
Sheng Shen	Tianjin University, China
Shishuai Hu	Northwestern Polytechnical University, China

Shuaifeng Zhi	National University of Defense Technology, China
Shuang Yang	Institute of Computing Technology, Chinese Academy of Sciences, China
Shuang Li	The Chinese University of Hong Kong, Shenzhen, China
Shulan Ruan	University of Science and Technology of China, China
Si Liu	Beihang University, China
Sida Peng	Zhejiang University, China
Sinuo Deng	Beijing University of Technology, China
Tan Guo	Chongqing University of Posts and Telecommunications, China
Tao Huang	Xidian University, China
Tao Yue	Nanjing University, China
Tao Zhang	Tsinghua University, China
Tao He	Tsinghua University, China
Ting Shu	Shenzhen Institute of Meteorological Innovation, China
Waikeung Wong	Hong Kong Polytechnic University, China
Wangmeng Zuo	Harbin Institute of Technology, China
Wei Cao	University of Science and Technology of China, China
Wei Jia	Heifei University of Technology, China
Wei Shen	Shanghai Jiao Tong University, China
Wei Sun	Shanghai Jiao Tong University, China
Wei Pang	Beijing Information Science and Technology University, China
Wei Hu	Peking University, China
Weicheng Xie	Shenzhen University, China
Weishi Zheng	Sun Yat-sen University, China
Wenbin Wang	Institute of Computing Technology, Chinese Academy of Sciences, China
Xi Li	Zhejiang University, China
Xia Wu	Beijing Normal University, China
Xiang Ao	Institute of Computing Technology, Chinese Academy of Sciences, China
Xiang Chen	Zhejiang University and AZFT Joint Lab for Knowledge Engine, China
Xiang Gao	Jihua Laboratory, China
Xiang Bai	Huazhong University of Science and Technology, China
Xiangjun Yin	Tianjin University, China

Xiangwei Kong	Zhejiang University, China
Xianwei Zheng	Foshan University, China
Xiaodan Liang	Sun Yat-sen University, China
Xiaopeng Hong	Xi'an Jiaotong University, China
Xiaoyan Luo	Beihang University, China
Xiaoyong Lu	Northwest Normal University, China
Xiaoyun Yuan	Tsinghua University, China
Xin Yang	Dalian University of Technology, China
Xin Yuan	Westlake University, China
Xin Geng	Southeast University, China
Xin Xu	JD.com, China
Xinggang Wang	Huazhong University of Science and Technology, China
Xinglong Zhang	National University of Defense Technology, China
Xinpeng Ding	The Hong Kong University of Science and Technology, China
Xiongkuo Min	Shanghai Jiao Tong University, China
Xiongzheng Li	Tianjin University, China
Xiushan Nie	Shandong Jianzhu University, China
Xiu-Shen Wei	Nanjing University of Science and Technology, China
Xueyuan Xu	Beijing Normal University, China
Xun Chen	University of Science and Technology of China, China
Xuran Pan	Tsinghua University, China
Yang Li	Tsinghua-Berkeley Shenzhen Institute, Tsinghua University, China
Yangang Wang	Southeast University, China
Yaping Zhao	The University of Hong Kong, China
Ye Tian	Harbin Engineering University, China
Yebin Liu	Tsinghua University, China
Yi Hao	Xidian University, China
Yi Zhang	Xidian University, China
Yicheng Wu	Monash University, Australia
Yifan Zhang	National University of Defense Technology, China
Yijie Lin	Sichuan University, China
Ying Fu	Beijing Institute of Technology, China
Yingqian Wang	National University of Defense Technology, China
Yiwen Ye	Northwestern Polytechnical University, Canada
Yonghui Yang	Hefei University of Technology, China

Yu Liu	Dalian University of Technology, China
Yu Wang	Beijing Technology and Business University, China
Yuanbiao Gou	Sichuan University, China
Yuanfang Guo	Beihang University, China
Yuanman Li	Shenzhen University, China
Yuchao Dai	Northwestern Polytechnical University, China
Yucheng Zhu	Shanghai Jiao Tong University, China
Yufei Gao	Zhengzhou University, China
Yulin Cai	Tsinghua University, China
Yulun Zhang	ETH Zurich, Switzerland
Yun Tie	Zhengzhou University, China
Yunfan Li	Sichuan University, China
Zhanxiang Feng	Sun Yat-sen University, China
Zhaobo Qi	University of Chinese Academy of Sciences, China
Zhaoxiang Zhang	Chinese Academy of Sciences, China
Zhaoxin Liu	Xidian University, China
Zheng-Jun Zha	University of Science and Technology of China, China
Zhengming Zhang	Southeast University, China
Zhengyi Wang	Tsinghua University, China
Zhenya Huang	University of Science and Technology of China, China
Zhenyu Huang	Sichuan University, China
Zhenzhen Hu	National University of Defense Technology, China
Zhibo Wang	Tsinghua University, China
Zhiheng Fu	University of Western Australia, Australia
Zhiying Jiang	Dalian University of Technology, China
Zhiyuan Zhu	Western University, Canada
Zhu Liu	Dalian University of Technology, China
Ziwei Zheng	Xi'an Jiaotong University, China
Zizhao Zhang	Tsinghua University, China
Zongzhang Zhang	Nanjing University, China
Zunlei Feng	Zhejiang University, China

Contents – Part II

AI Ethics, Privacy, Fairness and Security

Saliency Map-Based Local White-Box Adversarial Attack Against Deep Neural Networks

Haohan Liu[1,2], Xingquan Zuo[1,2(✉)], Hai Huang[1], and Xing Wan[1,2]

[1] School of Computer Science, Beijing University of Posts and Telecommunications, Beijing, China
zuoxq@bupt.edu.cn
[2] Key Laboratory of Trustworthy Distributed Computing and Service, Ministry of Education, Beijing, China

Abstract. The current deep neural networks (DNN) are easily fooled by adversarial examples, which are generated by adding some small, well-designed and human-imperceptible perturbations to clean examples. Adversarial examples will mislead deep learning (DL) model to make wrong predictions. At present, many existing white-box attack methods in the image field are mainly based on the global gradient of the model. That is, the global gradient is first calculated, and then the perturbation is added into the gradient direction. Those methods usually have a high attack success rate. However, there are also some shortcomings, such as excessive perturbation and easy detection by the human's eye. Therefore, in this paper we propose a Saliency Map-based Local white-box Adversarial Attack method (SMLAA). The saliency map used in the interpretability of artificial intelligence is introduced in SMLAA. First, Gradient-weighted Class Activation Mapping (Grad-CAM) is utilized to provide a visual interpretation of model decisions to find important areas in an image. Then, the perturbation is added only to important local areas to reduce the magnitude of perturbations. Experimental results show that compared with the global attack method, SMLAA reduces the average robustness measure by 9%–24% while ensuring the attack success rate. It means that SMLAA has a high attack success rate with fewer pixels changed.

Keywords: Deep learning · Saliency map · Local white-box attack · Adversarial attack

1 Introduction

In image recognition domain, artificial intelligence has excellent capabilities and achieves human competitive results. However, risks and challenges arising from artificial intelligence cannot be ignored. Adversarial attack adds perturbations to the image without changing the model structure and parameters, so as to interfere with the decision result of a deep learning (DL) model [1]. Adversarial attack has the characteristics of strong concealment and great harm. In security-sensitive scenarios, such as unmanned driving, the attack on the DL model will be a great security threat [2].

© The Author(s), under exclusive license to Springer Nature Switzerland AG 2022
L. Fang et al. (Eds.): CICAI 2022, LNAI 13605, pp. 3–14, 2022.
https://doi.org/10.1007/978-3-031-20500-2_1

The adversarial attack in the field of image classification can be divided into white-box attacks and black-box attacks according to the amount of known information or the access rights of the target model [3, 4]. At present, most of white-box or black-box attack methods add perturbations to all pixels of a clean example to generate a globally adversarial example. However, each pixel contributes differently to causing the network model to make wrong decisions. For example, if we add perturbations to the background of an image, the decision-making of the model cannot be affected in a high probability. Figure 1(a) is a clean example, and the neural network ResNet50 predicts the example as Walker_hound with a confidence level of 44.65%. In Fig. 1(b) without the background, the model still predicts the example as Walker_hound with a confidence level of 53.21%. In Fig. 1(c) with only background information, the model predicts the example as an umbrella with a confidence level of 28.99%. That shows that not all pixels are equally important in the model prediction. That is, the DL model will pay more attention to some important areas that affect the decision.

Fig. 1. Retain and remove background examples.

Some works [5, 6] have studied attack methods based on local perturbations. Li *et al.* [5] divided the foreground and background of clean examples by training a semantic segmentation model, and performs the black-box attack by random search. Dong *et al.* [6] combined a super-pixel segmentation with class activation mapping (CAM) [7] to generate local perturbations. However, training a semantic segmentation model is very difficult, which requires massive training data, computing resources as well as training time. In addition, CAM needs to change the internal structure of the target model, which has poor universality.

In this paper, the interpretable method Grad-CAM [8] is used to obtain the saliency map of an image. Then, the saliency map is combined with a white-box attack method to form a local attack method, SMLAA. Grad-CAM consumes fewer computing resources and does not need to change the structure of the model.

The main contributions of this paper are as follows:

1) Saliency map-based interpretable method is utilized to discover locally important areas of an image. A local white-box attack method is proposed, which combines a gradient-based white-box attack method and the saliency map.
2) SMLAA is compared with some popular attack methods. Experimental results show that SMLAA can reduce the perturbation by 9%–24% while maintaining the attack success rate.

2   Related Work

2.1   Model Interpretability Methods

Model interpretability methods mainly include transparency interpretability (Ante-hoc) [9] and post-hoc interpretability (Post-hoc) [10, 11]. Robnik-Šikonja et al. [12] proposed an interpretable method to explain predictions for individual instances. It calculates the contribution of each feature to the model prediction. When the example contains a large number of features, a heuristic method is used to search. Zhou et al. [7] proposed an interpretation method, namely Class Activation Mapping (CAM). CAM uses the principle of feature map weight superposition and addition to obtain class activation maps, and finally presents visual results to show important area. Sundararajan et al. [13] proposed Integrated-Gradients (IG), a gradient-based interpretable method, and visualized the results. The main idea based on IG is to find the gradient of the prediction result for a specific category, and get the importance of each pixel point to the decision result of the category.

2.2   White-Box Adversarial Attack Methods

Goodfellow et al. [14] proposed a classic white-box attack method FGSM (Fast Gradient Sign Method). First, the gradient of the neural network loss function is solved by back-propagation. Then a single-step perturbation is added to the image in the gradient ascending direction. Madry et al. [15] improved the FGSM algorithm and proposed a strong attack method, Projected Gradient Descent algorithm (PGD). The basic idea of the PGD algorithm is to generate adversarial examples by multiple iterations. In each iteration, the perturbation is clipped to a specified range. Dong et al. [16] proposed the MIM (Momentum Iterative Method) algorithm. The difference with PGD is that the perturbation added at each iteration of MIM is related to both the current gradient and the previously computed gradient.

Furthermore, there are several studies introducing model interpretability methods into adversarial attacks. For example, Duan et al. [17] proposed a mask-guided adversarial attack method to remove the noises of semantically irrelevant regions in the backgrounds and make the adversarial noises more imperceptible. Li et al. [5] divided the foreground and background of the example through a semantic segmentation model, and implemented four black-box attack methods according to the segmentation results. However, these methods require a pre-training model for salient object detection or semantic segmentation, which consumes a lot of computing resources. Dong et al. [6] combined a super-pixel segmentation with class activation mapping (CAM) [7] to form super-pixel-guided attentional adversarial attack. The adversarial perturbations are only added to the salient areas and guaranteed to be the same within each super-pixel. However, the CAM method needs to change the network structure, such that it has poor universality. Xiang et al. [18] identified the discriminative areas of the clean example using Grad-CAM method, and produced a local pre-perturbation to improve query efficiency. In [18], instead of generating adversarial example with less perturbation, preprocessing is applied by Grad-CAM to improve the efficiency of black-box attack. In addition, SMLAA does not need to train additional surrogate models. Therefore, SMLAA consumes fewer computing resources and time.

3   Proposed Approach

Most of the existing white-box attack methods achieve the attack by adding global perturbations in the gradient direction. The global attack has a high attack success rate, but it adds a perturbation to each pixel of the image and the perturbation may be too large. Current research shows that adding local perturbations to some important pixels/areas is sufficient to achieve the attack on the DL model.

Compared with the global attack, the local attack has an additional constraint on the number of perturbed pixels. Under this constraint, the objective is to find the adversarial example with smallest perturbation. Advantage of the local attack is that only a small number of pixels require being added perturbation to complete the attack.

The interpretable method of artificial intelligence can explain the reason of model decision, and find "important" pixels that affect the decision. The saliency map method can clearly show the area that the model focuses on when making decisions. As a model interpretation method, Grad-CAM can display its interpretation results in the form of saliency map.

In this paper, the saliency map interpretation method is introduced into the white-box attack to reduce the perturbation norm while ensuring the success rate. The flow chart of the proposed method (SMLAA) is shown in Fig. 2.

SMLAA consists of two stages. The first stage is the interpretation of the saliency map. The specific operations are as follows: 1) initialize the attack parameters; 2) use Grad-CAM to interpret the clean examples and extract the matrix expression SM_{mask}; 3) binarize the interpretation results to obtain the binary matrix of the important area B_{mask}. The first stage is introduced in detail in Sect. 3.1.

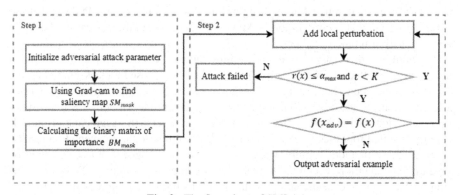

Fig. 2. The flow chart of SMLAA.

The second stage is the local attack. For an original clean example, a local perturbation is added to it based on B_{mask}. Then, it is judged whether the adversarial example can attack successfully. If the answer is not and the perturbation is not greater than a given threshold, the perturbation is increased until the attack succeeds. Single-step attack and iterative attack are adopted. The single-step attack controls the perturbation amplitude by increasing the perturbation coefficient. FGSM is used to add a global perturbation and form a local single-step attack method, namely Grad-CAM based FGSM (GC-FGSM) (see Sect. 3.2). The iterative attack controls the perturbation amplitude by increasing the number of iterations. PGD and MIM are employed to add a global perturbation, and form the local iterative attack methods, i.e., Grad-CAM based PGD (GC-PGD) and Grad-CAM based MIM (GC-MIM) (see Sect. 3.3).

3.1 Selecting Important Area by Saliency Map

The activation mapping method, Grad-CAM, is used to select important area of an image. It uses the gradient information of the last convolutional layer of CNN to calculate the weight of each feature map to determine the important area. Grad-CAM uses the back-propagated gradient to calculate the weight of each channel of the feature map.

$$\alpha_k^c = \frac{1}{Z} \sum_i \sum_j \frac{\partial y^c}{\partial A_{ij}^k} \tag{1}$$

where c represents the label. y^c is the score corresponding to the label (i.e., the value that has not passed to Softmax). A^k_{ij} denotes the value of (i, j) coordinates of the feature layer A in channel k, and Z represents the size of the feature map (i.e., length times width). Equation (1) shows that the weight of each channel k is the mean value of the feature map gradient on the channel. All channels are linearly weighted and input into the activation function ReLU.

$$L_{Grad-CAM}^c = ReLU\left(\sum_k \alpha_k^c A^k\right) \tag{2}$$

where A^k is the feature map of channel k, and output of the ReLU function is the area that has a positive influence on label c, which can be visualized through the saliency map. The saliency map can be expressed as a matrix SM_{mask} whose length and width are the size of the image, and each element in the matrix represents the importance of its corresponding pixel. Let θ be an extraction threshold, a binarized matrix B_{mask} can be obtained.

$$B_{mask}^{ij} \begin{cases} 1, & SM_{mask}^{ij} > \theta \\ 0, & SM_{mask}^{ij} \le \theta \end{cases} \tag{3}$$

Algorithm 1 is the process of important area selection based on saliency map.

Algorithm 1: Discover important areas in the image

Input: Clean example x, real label y, target model f, extraction threshold θ.
Output: B_{mask}.
Step 1: Eq. (1) is used to get the weight of each channel of the feature map;
Step 2: Eq. (2) is used to get the saliency map and its matrix SM_{mask};
Step 3: The binary matrix B_{mask} is obtained by Eq. (3) to determine the important area;
Return: B_{mask}.

3.2 Combining Saliency Map with Single-Step Attack Method

The saliency map is combined with the white-box single-step attack method FGSM to form a local single attack method GC-FGSM. FGSM is a classic white-box attack method, and generates adversarial examples by adding a single-step perturbation in the gradient direction.

$$x_{adv} = x + \alpha_F sign(g) \tag{4}$$

where x represents the clean example, g is the gradient matrix, and α_F denotes the attack parameter. FGSM generates perturbation in one step by α_F.

GC-FGSM uses the intersection of the gradient matrix g obtained by FGSM and the binarization matrix B_{mask} to obtain the gradient information of the important area. Then, local perturbation is produced according to the gradient information:

$$r = \alpha_F sign(g \wedge B_{mask}) \tag{5}$$

where $\wedge$ denotes the intersection operation. $r > \alpha_{max}$ means that the perturbation required to attack this example is too large, and the attack fails and no adversarial example is generated. If $r < \alpha_{max}$, an adversarial example x_{adv} is generated:

$$x_{adv} = x + r \tag{6}$$

If x_{adv} cannot make the target model to make a wrong decision and $r < \alpha_{max}$, then increase α_F by a step size v to generate a larger perturbation.

The pseudocode of GC-FGSM is given in Algorithm 2.

Algorithm 2: GC-FGSM

Input: Clean example x, target model f, step size v, attack parameter α_F, maximum perturbation threshold α_{max}, binary matrix of important areas B_{mask}.
Output: adversarial example x_{adv}.
1 The gradient matrix g of the model is obtained by deriving the objective function of the sample x;
2 While $f(x_{adv}) = f(x)$ do
3   Use Eq. (5) to get the perturbation r;
4   If $r > \alpha_{max}$ then
5   Break; //Algorithm 2 stops, and no adversarial example is generated.
6   End if
7   Use Eq. (6) to get adversarial example x_{adv};
8    $\alpha_F = \alpha_F + v$;
9 End while
Return x_{adv}.

3.3 Combining Saliency Map and Iterative Attack Method

The single attack adds a perturbation in the gradient direction to complete the attack, while an iterative attack includes multiple iterations. In each iteration, a small perturbation is added to the sample and the gradient information is updated. We take the

PGD attack method as an example to illustrate the iterative attack process. The example generated by PGD in $(t + 1)$-th iteration are:

$$x_{t+1} = x_t + \eta sign(g_t) \tag{7}$$

where x_t is the example in the t-th iteration, η is the step size, and g_t is the gradient matrix in the t-th iteration.

GC-PGD adjusts the direction of the gradient in the process of adding perturbation to obtain adversarial example x_{adv}. The perturbation generated by GC-PGD in the $(t+1)$-th iteration is:

$$r_{t+1} = \eta sign(g_t \wedge B_{mask}) \tag{8}$$

where B_{mask} is the binarization matrix of important area obtained in Sect. 3.1, and the gradient matrix g_t needs to be recalculated in each iteration. In each iteration, a perturbation with step size η is added to the direction of the gradient matrix g_t. The example generated in the $(t + 1)$-th iteration is:

$$x_{t+1} = x_t + r_{t+1} \tag{9}$$

The iterative attack controls the amplitude of the perturbation by increasing the number of iterations. If the perturbation is not enough to cause the target model to make a wrong decision and the maximum number of iterations has not been reached, the amplitude of perturbation is iteratively increased. If the iteration count exceeds the maximum number of iterations, the attack fails and no adversarial example is generated. The pseudocode of GC-PGD is shown in Algorithm 3.

Algorithm 3: GC-PGD

Input: Clean example x, target model f, step size η, maximum number of iterations K, maximum perturbation threshold α_{max}, binary matrix of important areas B_{mask}.
Output: adversarial example x_{adv}.
1 Set the current adversarial example $x_{adv} = x$, and current iteration count $t = 0$;
2 While $f(x_{adv}) = f(x)$ do
3   The gradient matrix g_t of the model is obtained by deriving the objective function of x_{adv};
4   Use Eq. (8) to get perturbation r_{t+1};
5   If $r_{t+1} > \alpha_{max}$ or $t \geq K$ then
6   Break; //Algorithm 3 stops, and no adversarial example is generated.
7   End if
8   Use Eq. (9) to obtain x_{t+1}, and let $x_{adv} = x_{t+1}$;
9     $t = t + 1$;
10 End while
Return x_{adv}.

Similar to GC-PGD, Grad-CAM is combined with MIM attack method to form the attack method GC-MIM. The perturbation calculation in each iteration of GC-MIM adopts the method in MIM, and the gradient g_{t+1} of GC-PGD is modified as:

$$g_{t+1} = \mu \cdot g_t + \frac{g_t}{\|g_t\|_1} \tag{10}$$

where μ is the decay factor, and the remaining steps of GC-MIM are the same as those of GC-PGD.

4 Experiments

4.1 Datasets and Networks

The ImageNet2012 dataset is used to evaluate the proposed method. This dataset contains a large amount of color image data, and is currently used by many attack methods on high-pixel images.

We select three classic neural networks, SqueezeNet1_1, MobileNet_v2, and ResNet50, and the implementation code is based on the Pytorch deep learning framework. Each network is first trained on the ImageNet2012 dataset. The prediction success rates of trained networks for clean examples are higher than 90%, and the trained networks are used as the target models of the experiment.

The proposed local attack methods (GC-FGSM, GC-PGD and GC-MIM) and their corresponding original white-box attack methods (FGSM [14], PGD [15], and MIM [16]) are used to attack the target models respectively, and their performance is compared using multiple evaluation indexes.

4.2 Evaluation Indexes

Attack Success Rate (SR) [17], Average Robustness (AR) [19], Peak Signal-to-Noise Ratio (PSNR) [20], and Structural Similarity (SSIM) [21] are selected to evaluate the attack effect. SR reflects the success rate of the attack. AR is a commonly used index for evaluating the size of the perturbation. The smaller the AR value, the less perturbation is introduced into the adversarial example. PSNR and SSIM are used to evaluate the similarity between adversarial examples and original ones. The larger the PSNR (SSIM) value, the more similar the two images are.

4.3 Hyperparameters

Through simple experiments, the appropriate hyperparameters are determined as follows: In Grad-CAM, the extraction threshold of saliency map θ is set to 0.1. In FGSM and GC-FGSM, the attack parameter α_F is set to 0.012, the perturbation threshold α_{max} is set as 0.5, and the step size v is set to 0.002. In PGD and GC-PGD, the maximum iterations K is set as 30, and the attack step size per iteration is η is set to 0.015. In MIM and GC-MIM, the maximum iterations K is set to 20, the step size per iteration η is set as 0.01, and the decay factor μ is set to 1.0.

4.4 Experimental Result

For each image in the dataset ImageNet2012, three target networks (SqueezeNet1_1, MobileNet_v2, and ResNet50) are attacked using the global attack methods (FGSM, PGD, MIM) and the local attack methods (GC-FGSM, GC-PGD, and GC-MIM) respectively to generate a series of adversarial examples. Then, three target networks are employed to classify each adversarial example. Using the labels of examples, we can judge whether adversarial examples can be correctly classified (i.e., whether the attack is successful or not). Figure 3 is an example of using FGSM and GC-FGSM to attack SqueezeNet1_1, MobileNet_v2, and ResNet50. Three examples in the first, second and third column are clean examples, global adversarial examples generated by FGSM, and local adversarial examples generated by GC-FGSM, respectively. We can see that the labels of the adversarial examples are changed for all attacks. It means that adversarial examples generated by FGSM and GC-FGSM can fool the three networks. Compared to FGSM, GC-FGSM perturbs fewer pixels and still has the same attack effect.

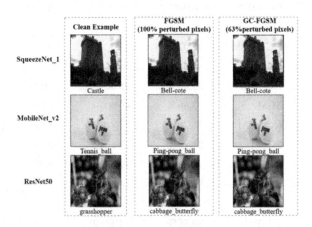

Fig. 3. FGSM and GC-FGSM attack results.

Table 1 presents the attack results of six attack methods on three target networks. For each combination of attack method and target network, we generate a set of adversarial examples. In Table 1, SR is the attack success rate for each set of adversarial examples. AR (PSNR and SSIM) means the average value of AR (PSNR and SSIM) of the all successful adversarial examples in each set. The best results are highlighted in bold font.

For the networks of SqueezeNet1_1 and ResNet50, we can see that local attack methods perform better than global attack methods in terms of AR, PSNR and SSIM. Compared with global attack methods, AR values of local attack methods are reduced by 9–24% and SR values are decreased by about 3%. That means that local attack methods can generate adversarial examples with a smaller perturbation while maintaining similar attack success rate as global attack methods. In addition, PSNR values of local attack methods are increased by about 3%, and SSIM values are also increased correspondingly.

Similar results can be observed in network of MobileNet_v2. AR values of local attack methods is decreased by 9%–23%; and PSNR values are increased by 2–3%. Note that SR values of GC-FGSM and GC-PGD are higher than those of corresponding global attack methods. For MobileNet_v2, local attack methods achieve higher attack success rate with smaller perturbation.

Table 1 shows that both global attack methods and local attack methods fool the networks with high success rate. In terms of human-imperceptible and the amount of

Table 1. Comparison of global perturbation and local perturbation on different datasets.

Network	Method	SR	AR	PSNR	SSIM
SqueezeNet1_1	FGSM	**93.00%**	5.74×10^{-3}	50.96	0.99800
	GC-FGSM	91.35%	3.97×10^{-3}	**54.28**	**0.99904**
	PGD	**80.67%**	2.36×10^{-3}	58.53	0.99954
	GC-PGD	79.38%	1.65×10^{-3}	**62.22**	**0.99978**
	MIM	**92.31%**	2.45×10^{-3}	58.15	0.99947
	GC-MIM	88.00%	1.69×10^{-3}	**61.74**	**0.99975**
MobileNet_v2	FGSM	94.31%	5.76×10^{-3}	50.83	0.99800
	GC-FGSM	**94.37%**	4.48×10^{-3}	**52.28**	**0.99862**
	PGD	81.67%	2.36×10^{-3}	58.38	0.99952
	GC-PGD	**83.00%**	1.95×10^{-3}	**60.14**	**0.99969**
	MIM	**93.66%**	2.46×10^{-3}	58.01	0.99949
	GC-MIM	91.30%	2.23×10^{-3}	**59.67**	**0.99966**
ResNet50	FGSM	**81.10%**	5.79×10^{-3}	50.88	0.99800
	GC-FGSM	79.28%	4.41×10^{-3}	**53.06**	**0.99878**
	PGD	**82.00%**	2.24×10^{-3}	58.54	0.99954
	GC-PGD	79.33%	1.67×10^{-3}	**62.65**	**0.99960**
	MIM	**90.05%**	5.34×10^{-3}	52.68	0.99871
	GC-MIM	88.65%	4.95×10^{-3}	**53.65**	**0.99906**

added perturbations, local attack method outperforms global attack methods, which means that adversarial examples generated by the proposed method are closer to the original clean example and less likely to be noticed by human.

To study the impact of the threshold θ in Eq. (3) on SR of SMLAA, we set θ to be 0.01, 0.03, 0.05, 0.1, 0.2 and 0.3, respectively, and let other parameters be the same as those in Sect. 4.3. We take the results of GC-FGSM attacking squeezenet1_1 as an example to show the effect of θ values on the SR of SMLAA, as shown in Table 2.

Table 2. Sensitivity analysis of θ.

θ	0.3	0.2	0.1	0.05	0.03	0.01
SR	87.33%	88.67%	90.00%	**92.75%**	92.35%	91.37%

Table 2 shows that if the θ value exceeds a certain threshold, the attack effect is degraded. It means that there are the most suitable local areas for attack, and higher perturbations do not necessarily achieve higher attack success rates.

5 Conclusion

This paper proposes a Saliency Map-based Local white-Box Adversarial Attack method (SMLAA). First, Grad-CAM method is used to obtain the saliency map of an image. Then, important areas in the image are identified by the saliency map, and local perturbations are added to those important areas by a single-step attack method or an iterative attack method, to generate adversarial examples with smaller perturbation.

Experiments show that compared with global attack methods, SMLAA has similar attack success rate (SR) values, the Average Robustness (AR) values of SMLAA are reduced by 9%–24%, and Peak Signal-to-Noise Ratio (PSNR) values are improved by 3%. That indicates that SMLAA can generate adversarial examples with less perturbation while maintaining a high attack success rate.

In the future, we plan to improve the attack success rate of SMLAA. In addition, we will study the local attack method based on saliency map for black-box models.

References

1. Szegedy, C., et al.: Intriguing properties of neural networks. arXiv preprint arXiv:1312.6199 (2013)
2. Duan, R., et al.: Adversarial laser beam: effective physical-world attack to DNNs in a blink. In: Proceedings of the IEEE/CVF Conference on Computer Vision and Pattern Recognition (CVPR), pp. 16062–16071 (2021)
3. Akhtar, N., Mian, A.: Threat of adversarial attacks on deep learning in computer vision: a survey. IEEE Access **6**, 14410–14430 (2018)
4. Qiu, S., Liu, Q., Zhou, S., Wu, C.: Review of artificial intelligence adversarial attack and defense technologies. Appl. Sci. **9**(5), 909 (2019)
5. Li, X., et al.: Adversarial examples versus cloud-based detectors: a black-box empirical study. IEEE Trans. Depend. Secur. Comput. **18**(4), 1933–1949 (2019)
6. Dong, X., et al.: Robust superpixel-guided attentional adversarial attack. In: Proceedings of the IEEE/CVF Conference on Computer Vision and Pattern Recognition (CVPR), pp. 2895–12904 (2020)
7. Zhou, B., Khosla, A., Lapedriza, A., Oliva, A., Torralba, A.: Learning deep features for discriminative localization. In: Proceedings of the IEEE Conference on Computer Vision and Pattern Recognition (CVPR), pp. 2921–2929 (2016)
8. Selvaraju, R.R., Cogswell, M., Das, A., Vedantam, R., Parikh, D., Batra, D.: Grad-CAM: visual explanations from deep networks via gradient-based localization. In: Proceedings of the IEEE International Conference on Computer Vision (ICCV), pp. 618–626 (2017)
9. Alvarez Melis, D., Jaakkola, T.: Towards robust interpretability with self-explaining neural networks. In: Advances in Neural Information Processing Systems 31 (2018)
10. Guidotti, R., Monreale, A., Ruggieri, S., Turini, F., Giannotti, F., Pedreschi, D.: A survey of methods for explaining black box models. ACM Comput. Surv. (CSUR) **51**(5), 1–42 (2018)
11. Baehrens, D., Schroeter, T., Harmeling, S., Kawanabe, M., Hansen, K., Mueller, K.: How to explain individual classification decisions. J. Mach. Learn. Res. **11**, 1803–1831 (2010)
12. Robnik-Šikonja, M., Kononenko, I.: Explaining classifications for individual instances. IEEE Trans. Knowl. Data Eng. **20**(5), 589–600 (2008)
13. Sundararajan, M., Taly, A., Yan, Q.: Axiomatic attribution for deep networks. In: International Conference on Machine Learning. PMLR, vol. 70, pp. 3319–3328 (2017)

14. Goodfellow, I.J., Shlens, J., Szegedy, C.: Explaining and harnessing adversarial examples. arXiv preprint arXiv:1412.6572 (2014)
15. Madry, A., Makelov, A., Schmidt, L., Tsipras, D., Vladu, A.: Towards deep learning models resistant to adversarial attacks. arXiv preprint arXiv:1706.06083 (2017)
16. Dong, Y., et al.: Boosting adversarial attacks with momentum. In: Proceedings of the IEEE Conference on Computer Vision and Pattern Recognition (CVPR), pp. 9185–9193 (2018)
17. Duan, Y., Zhou, X., Zou, J., Qiu, J., Zhang, J., Pan, Z.: Mask-guided noise restriction adversarial attacks for image classification. Comput. Secur. **100**, 102111 (2021)
18. Xiang, T., Liu, H., Guo, S., Zhang, T., Liao, X.: Local black-box adversarial attacks: a query efficient approach. arXiv preprint arXiv:2101.01032 (2021)
19. Moosavi-Dezfooli, S.M., Fawzi, A., Frossard, P.: DeepFool: a simple and accurate method to fool deep neural networks. In: Proceedings of the IEEE Conference on Computer Vision and Pattern Recognition (CVPR), pp. 2574–2582 (2016)
20. Huang, Y., et al.: AdvFilter: predictive perturbation-aware filtering against adversarial attack via multi-domain learning. In: Proceedings of the 29th ACM International Conference on Multimedia, pp. 395–403 (2021)
21. Zhou, W., Bovik, A.C., SheiKh, H.R., Simoncelli, E.P.: Image quality assessment: from error visibility to structural similarity. IEEE Trans. Image Process. **13**(4), 600–612 (2004)

Improving Adversarial Attacks with Ensemble-Based Approaches

Yapeng Ji[1,2] and Guoxu Zhou[1,3(✉)]

[1] School of Automation, Guangdong University of Technology, Guangzhou 510006, People's Republic of China
`2112004090@mail2.gdut.edu.cn`, `gx.zhou@gdut.edu.cn`
[2] Guangdong Key Laboratory of IoT information Technology, Guangzhou 510005, People's Republic of China
[3] Guangdong-HongKong-Macao Joint Laboratory for Smart Discrete Manufacturing, Guangzhou 510006, People's Republic of China

Abstract. Though Deep Neural networks (DNNs) have been applied in solving a wide variety of problems and achieved state-of-the-art performance on various vision tasks, they are vulnerable to adversarial examples which are crafted by adding human-imperceptible perturbations to legitimate inputs. However, most of the existing adversarial attacks have a low success rate under the black-box setting, where the attackers have no information about the model structure and parameters. In particular, targeted adversarial images, which are expected to predict a particular incorrect label, can hardly succeed. To address this, we propose a broad ensemble-based approach to improve the black-box attack. This method aims to find the common properties between all ensemble models. Using it in combination with Nesterov Accelerated Gradient, adversarial examples with higher transferability can be produced by a set of known models, meanwhile, keeping a higher success rate on all original models. In addition, the experiment result illustrates that, for more challenging targeted attacks, our methods exhibit higher transferability than other state-of-the-art attacks.

Keywords: Adversarial examples · Deep neural networks · Black-box attack

1 Introduction

Deep Neural networks have achieved an excellent performance on various computer vision tasks. However, in recent years the vulnerability of those models was discovered [1,2]. To be specific, DNNs will get a wrong result when the clean inputs add some imperceptible, human-imperceptible noises. In addition, adversarial examples show an intriguing transferability [1,3], where they crafted from one model can also fool other models. As a result of adversarial examples can not only evaluate the robustness of networks, but also improve the robustness of networks by adversarial training [4,9]. How to improve the transferability of adversarial examples has attracted a lot of attention (Fig. 1).

© The Author(s), under exclusive license to Springer Nature Switzerland AG 2022
L. Fang et al. (Eds.): CICAI 2022, LNAI 13605, pp. 15–29, 2022.
https://doi.org/10.1007/978-3-031-20500-2_2

(a) cock: 95.40%   (b)   (c) armadillo: 97.05%

Fig. 1. Visualization of one targeted adversarial example generated by the proposed method (EI-NI-FGSM-HAG). A original images (a) is recognized correctly as a "cock" by ResNet-50, "armadillo" is randomly selected from other wrong labels. The adversarial noises (b) crafted by ResNet-152, VGG-19, Densenet-121, Inception-v3. The adversarial images (c) is the addition of the original images (a) and the noise (b), which is recognized as a "armadillo" by ResNet-50.

With the knowledge of the network, several methods have been proposed to generate adversarial examples. Specifically, containing Optimization-based methods like box-constrained L-BFGS [1], Carlini & Wagner attack (C&W) [5], gradient-based methods like fast gradient sign (FGSM) [2] and basic iterative method (I-FGSM) [7]. Those white-box attack methods can achieve high success rates. For black-box attacks, two different kinds of approaches have been proposed to implement it: One is the query-based approach [8], which trains a surrogate model by querying the unknown model. The surrogate model has similar prediction to unknown model, then we can use white-box attack methods to generate adversarial examples. However, in practical applications, it requires a large number of queries when the unknown network is complicated, that is easily detected by the model's defense system. The other is transfer-based approach, Yinpeng Dong et al. [10] utilize white-box attack methods to attack an ensemble of multiple models to generate adversarial images with high transferability. There is no need to query unknown networks. The aim of ensemble-based approaches is to attack their common vulnerability. However, they show low efficacy for targeted attack which requires adversarial examples to be classified by a network as a targeted label [3].

In this work, we improved the transferability of the adversarial image based on the ensemble model in three aspects: ensemble schemes, gradient descent mechanisms, and optimization methods.

- We discovered that different ensemble schemes have different effects on transferability of non-targeted attacks and targeted attacks. To specific, on untarget attacks, ensemble in softmax scheme has a higher success rate than the other two schemes, and the scheme of ensemble in loss is better on targeted attacks.
- In addition, we studied different gradient descent mechanisms. The results show that pixels with higher absolute gradient values are better represented

common properties between models. By attacking common properties between models to improve the transferability of adversarial examples.

- We integrate the Nesterov Iterative Fast Gradient Sign Method (NI-FGSM) [11] to the ensemble of models to avoid falling into local optimum in the optimization process. This method has been verified to be better than Momentum Iterative Fast Gradient Sign (MI-FGSM) [10] on a single model.

Extensive experiments on the ImageNet dataset [6] demonstrate that, on black-box setting, the proposed attack methods assist to improve the success rates of both non-targeted attacks and targeted attacks on a large margin. In targeted attacks, our best attack reaches the highest success rate of 30.1% on top-5 accuracy. This makes targeted attacks possible for black-box systems.

2 Related Works

In this section, we will give a brief introduction to some related works on adversarial attack. Let x and x^{adv} be a benign input and an adversarial input, respectively. Given a classifier $f_\theta(x)$, with ground truth label y, the goal of the non-targeted attack is searching for an adversarial image x^{adv} which is predicted by classifier satisfy $f_\theta(x^{adv}) \neq y$. In targeted attack, the attacker aims to search for an adversarial image misclassified into a certain class y^{target}, that is $f_\theta(x^{adv}) = y^{target}$. To limit the distortion, the adversarial images generated by both two kinds of method should satisfy $||x^{adv} - x||_p \leq \varepsilon$, where p could be $0, 1, 2, \infty$ and ε is the maximum value of distortion.

2.1 Optimization-Based Methods

One is directly optimizing the distortion between the benign images and the adversarial images [2,5]. To be specific, for non-targeted attacking, search for an adversarial example x^{adv} by solving:

$$\underset{x^{adv}}{\arg\min} ||x^{adv} - x||_p - c \cdot J(x^{adv}, y^{true}) \tag{1}$$

where $J(x^{adv}, y^{true})$ is the loss function of prediction y^{true} and c is a constant to balance constraints the loss and distortion. Though, it is effective to find adversarial images, it is difficult to ensure the distortion between x^{adv} and x is less than ε.

2.2 Gradient-Based Methods

Fast Gradient Sign Method (FGSM): FGSM [2] find an adversarial image x^{adv} by the following equation:

$$x^{adv} = x + \varepsilon \cdot \text{sign}(\nabla_x J(x, y^{true})) \tag{2}$$

This method just needs a one-step update and ε limits the maximum distortion.

Iterative Fast Gradient Sign Method (I-FGSM): I-FGSM [7] is an iterative version of FGSM. The iteration step length is $\alpha = \varepsilon/T$, where T is the number of Iterations.It can be expressed as:

$$x_0 = x, x_{t+1}^{adv} = x_t^{adv} + \alpha \cdot \text{sign}(\nabla_x J(x_t^{adv}, y^{true})) \tag{3}$$

The performance of iterative methods is greatly greater than one-step methods in white-box setting. However, the transferability of adversarial examples is worse.

Momentum Iterative Fast Gradient Sign Method (MI-FGSM) [10]: In the optimization process, the momentum [12] is integrated into each iteration, improving the transferability of adversarial images. The broad formalization of this method is as follows:

$$g_{t+1} = \mu \cdot g_t + \frac{\nabla_x J(x_t^{adv}, y^{true})}{||\nabla_x J(x_t^{adv}, y^{true})||_1} \tag{4}$$

$$x_{t+1}^{adv} = x_t^{adv} + \alpha \cdot \text{sign}(g_{t+1}) \tag{5}$$

μ is the decay factor, and the accumulated gradient is g_t. g_t is starting with $g_0 = 0$.

Nesterov Iterative Fast Gradient Sign Method (NI-FGSM): NI-FGSM [11] considers previous accumulated gradient as a correction to avoid trapping in local optimum. Similar to MI-FGSM, g_t is starting with $g_0 = 0$. The update procedure is carried out as follows:

$$x_t^{nes} = x_t^{adv} + \alpha \cdot \mu \cdot g_t \tag{6}$$

$$g_{t+1} = \mu \cdot g_t + \frac{\nabla_x J(x_t^{nes}, y^{true})}{||\nabla_x J(x_t^{nes}, y^{true})||_1} \tag{7}$$

$$x_{t+1}^{adv} = x_t^{adv} + \alpha \cdot \text{sign}(g_{t+1}) \tag{8}$$

g_t denotes accumulated gradients [13] at the iteration t, μ denotes the decay factor.

In this paper, the distortion between x^{adv} and x measure by root mean square deviation, i.e., RMSD, Which is calculated as $d(x^{adv}, x) = \sqrt{\sum_i (x_i^{adv} - x_i)^2/N}$, Where x_i and N represent the dimensionality of x and the pixel value of the i-th dimension of x, respectively. The values for each pixel range from 0 to 255.

2.3   Targeted Attacks

The method of generating the target adversarial example is similar to the non-target adversarial example, but the goals of the attackers transform to searching for an instance x_{adv} to satisfy $f_\theta(x^{adv}) = y^{target}$. For the optimization-based methods, we have the following approximate solution to this problem.

$$\arg\min_{x^{adv}} ||x^{adv} - x||_p + c \cdot J(x^{adv}, y^{target}) \tag{9}$$

For I-FGSM, MI-FGSM and NI-FGSM, we make the following changes:

$$\boldsymbol{x}_{t+1}^{adv} = \boldsymbol{x}_t^{adv} + \alpha \cdot \text{sign}(\nabla_{\boldsymbol{x}} J(\boldsymbol{x}_t^{adv}, y^{target})) \text{(I-FGSM)}$$

$$\boldsymbol{g}_{t+1} = \mu \cdot \boldsymbol{g}_t + \frac{\nabla_{\boldsymbol{x}} J(\boldsymbol{x}_t^{adv}, y^{target})}{||\nabla_{\boldsymbol{x}} J(\boldsymbol{x}_t^{adv}, y^{target})||_1} \qquad \text{(MI-FGSM)}$$
$$\boldsymbol{x}_{t+1}^{adv} = \boldsymbol{x}_t^{adv} - \alpha \cdot \text{sign}(\boldsymbol{g}_{t+1})$$

$$\boldsymbol{x}_t^{nes} = \boldsymbol{x}_t^{adv} - \alpha \cdot \mu \cdot \boldsymbol{g}_t$$
$$\boldsymbol{g}_{t+1} = \mu \cdot \boldsymbol{g}_t + \frac{\nabla_{\boldsymbol{x}} J(\boldsymbol{x}_t^{nes}, y^{target})}{||\nabla_{\boldsymbol{x}} J(\boldsymbol{x}_t^{nes}, y^{target})||_1} \qquad \text{(NI-FGSM)}$$
$$\boldsymbol{x}_{t+1}^{adv} = \boldsymbol{x}_t^{adv} - \alpha \cdot \text{sign}(\boldsymbol{g}_{t+1})$$

3 Methodology

3.1 Motivation

In the black box case, methods using only one known model to generate adversarial samples have been shown to be effective in non-targeted attacks [3,10]. However, for targeted attacks, the adversarial samples generated by a single known model are virtually untransferable. Attacking multiple models at the same time can be beneficial to improve transferability. Intuitively, if an adversarial example is misidentified by all known models, it is likely to be misidentified by other unknown models. For targeted attacks and non-targeted attacks, there are different ensemble schemes for us to consider. In addition, the process of generating adversarial examples can be seen as an optimization problem [11], so a better optimization algorithm can also improve the transferability of adversarial examples.

3.2 Ensemble Schemes

Let $\boldsymbol{l}_k(\boldsymbol{x})$ denote the logits of k-th model, and we have k known models, the softmax cross-entropy loss of k-th model can be expressed as:

$$J_k(\boldsymbol{x}, y) = -\mathbf{1}_y \cdot \log(\text{softmax}(w_k \boldsymbol{l}_k(\boldsymbol{x}))) \qquad (10)$$

where $\mathbf{1}_y$ is the one-hot encoding of ground-truth label y, w_k is the ensemble weight. We employ three ensemble schemes for targeted and non-targeted attacks: ensemble in logits (EI-logits), ensemble in softmax (EI-softmax), ensemble in loss (EI-loss). The ensemble loss of three ensemble schemes can be represented by the following three equations:

$$J(\boldsymbol{x}, y) = -\mathbf{1}_y \cdot \log(\text{softmax}(\textstyle\sum_{k=1}^{K} w_k \boldsymbol{l}_k(\boldsymbol{x}))), \qquad (11)$$

$$J(\boldsymbol{x}, y) = -\mathbf{1}_y \cdot \log(\textstyle\sum_{k=1}^{K} \text{softmax}(w_k \boldsymbol{l}_k(\boldsymbol{x}))), \qquad (12)$$

$$J(\boldsymbol{x}, y) = \textstyle\sum_{k=1}^{K}(-\mathbf{1}_y \cdot \log(\text{softmax}(w_k \boldsymbol{l}_k(\boldsymbol{x}))), \qquad (13)$$

where $\sum_{k=1}^{K} w_k = 1$ and $w_k \geq 0$, and we have K known models. In all ensemble schemes, we set $w_1 = w_2 = ... = w_k$.

3.3   Gradient Descent Mechanisms

We discovered that some pixels did not update during the two iterations, which would affect the iteration direction of other pixels and ultimately affect the transferable of the adversarial samples. Moreover, we found that most unchanged pixels after two iterations have small absolute gradient values and those pixels with high absolute gradient values are more stable in the direction of iteration. In fact, pixels with a higher absolute gradient value have a greater impact on the loss in the white-box setting.

From the perspective of transferability, those pixels with a stable iteration direction are better represented common properties between models. Thus we can only change ones with high gradient absolute values during the iteration, so as to improve the transferability of adversarial examples under the premise of ensuring certain distortion. Based on the above analysis, we propose the higher absolute gradient method (HAG), which optimizes the adversarial perturbations over pixes with higher absolute gradient.

$$g_{t+1}^*[i] = \begin{cases} g_{t+1}[i], & \text{if} \quad i \in topk_{index} \\ 0, & \text{if} \quad i \notin topk_{index} \end{cases} \tag{14}$$

where i is the index of the corresponding element, $topk_{index}$ is computed by Eq. 15. The $topk(k, x)$ function returns the index of the first k percent of the largest elements of a given input tensor x. For MI-FGSM and NI-FGSM, the updating formulas of non-target attacks and target attacks are Eq. 16 and Eq. 17 respectively.

$$topk_{index} = topk(k, |g_{t+1}|) \tag{15}$$

$$x_{t+1}^{adv} = x_t^{adv} + \alpha \cdot sign(g_{t+1}^*) \tag{16}$$

$$x_{t+1}^{adv} = x_t^{adv} - \alpha \cdot sign(g_{t+1}^*) \tag{17}$$

3.4   Optimization Algorithm

Algorithm 1. EI-NI-FGSM-HAG

1: **Input:** A classifier f with softmax crossentopy loss function J; a real image x and ground-truth label y;
2: **Input:** The size of perturbation ε; iterations T and decay factor μ;
3: **Output:** An adversarial example x^{adv}
4: Initialize $\alpha = \varepsilon/T$; $g_0 = 0$; $x_0^{adv} = x$
5: **for** $t = 0$ to $T - 1$ **do**
6:     Get x_t^{nes} by Eq. 6
7:     Get $J(x, y)$ by Eq. 11 or Eq. 12 or Eq. 13
8:     Update g_{t+1} by Eq. 7
9:     Get g_{t+1}^* by Eq. 14
10:     Update x_{t+1}^{adv} by Eq. 16
11: **end for**
12: **return:** $x^{adv} = x_T^{adv}$

We can integrate ensemble schemes into gradient-based methods to generate adversarial examples with strong transferability. Adversarial examples crafted by one step attack method (FGSM) has higher transferability than Iterative attack methods in attacking single model. Nonetheless, when attacking ensemble models, one step method has a lower success rate on all original models so that it is failure to attack ensemble models' common vulnerability. In iterative attack methods, I-FGSM greedily searches for adversarial images in the direction of the sign of the gradient at each iteration, it easily falls into poor local optimum. MI-FGSM adopts momentum [12] which stabilizes the update direction and assists to escape from poor local optimum. NI-FGSM, more than stabilizing the update directions, gives previous accumulated gradient a correction to look ahead. Those properties are helpful to escape from poor local optimum and improve transferability of adverasial images. We merge the three ensemble schemes into NI-FGSM, where $J(x, y)$ can be calculated from Eq. 11, Eq. 12 and Eq. 13. We summarize the NI-FGSM-HAG algorithm for attacking ensemble models in Algorithm 1.

4 Experimental Results

In this section we will present experimental results to demonstrate the effectiveness of the proposed methods. We first discuss the experimental settings and implementation details in Sect. 4.1. Then we report the results of non-targeted attacks and targeted attacks for attacking a single model in Sect. 4.2. We further conduct two trials to study the effects of our methods on attacking an ensemble model on non-targeted attacks and targeted attack in Sect. 4.3.

4.1 Experimental Settings

In this section, we detail the models to be examined, the dataset to be evaluated and the hyperparameters to be used.

Models. For normally trained models, we study five networks, ResNet-50 [17] , ResNet-152 [18],VGG-19 [15], Densenet-121 [16], Inception-v3 [14].

Dataset. We use a dataset which randomly extracted an image from each category of the ILSVRC 2012 validation set, 1000 images in total, and all of them can be classified correctly by all five models in our examination. For targeted attacks, we randomly select a lable from additional lables besides the correct one.

Hyper-Parameters. For the hyper-parameters, we set number of iteration $T = 10$, and step size $\alpha = 2$. For MI-FGSM and NI-FGSM, we adopt the default decay factor $\mu = 10$.

4.2 Attacking a Single Model

We first study the transferability of attacking a single model. Table 1 presents the success rates of non-targeted attacks and Table 2 show the top-1 success

Table 1. Attack success rates (%) of non-targeted adversarial images where we attack a single network. The adversarial examples are generated by Vgg-19, Dens-121, Res-142, Inc-v3 and Res-50 respectively using I-FGSM, MI-FGSM and NI-FGSM. * indicates the white-box attacks.

	Attack	Vgg-19	Dens-121	Res-152	Inc-v3	Res-50
Vgg-19	I-FGSM	**100.0***	43.4	28.3	25.1	41.3
	MI-FGSM	**100.0***	72.0	56.1	53.0	68.5
	NI-FGSM	**100.0***	**75.5**	**58.1**	**55.2**	**71.7**
Dens-121	I-FGSM	54.5	**100.0***	56.3	35.3	67.2
	MI-FGSM	78.2	**100.0***	74.3	60.0	84.0
	NI-FGSM	**82.4**	**100.0***	**80.5**	**64.4**	**88.0**
Res-152	I-FGSM	43.1	55.6	**100.0***	30.5	69.7
	MI-FGSM	65.5	78.2	**100.0***	55.0	85.3
	NI-FGSM	**71.0**	**82.4**	**100.0***	**57.1**	**89.5**
Inc-v3	I-FGSM	22.3	19.9	18.1	**98.7***	20.0
	MI-FGSM	48.8	42.9	36.6	98.2*	40.1
	NI-FGSM	**55.4**	**49.7**	**41.3**	98.4*	**47.1**
Res-50	I-FGSM	41.1	52.3	52.1	27.1	**99.8***
	MI-FGSM	65.3	72.1	68.3	46.2	99.7*
	NI-FGSM	**71.0**	**76.4**	**77.3**	49.9	**99.8***

Table 2. Attack success rates (%) of targeted adversarial images where we attack a single network. The adversarial examples are generated by Vgg-19, Dens-121, Res-142, Inc-v3 and Res-50 respectively using I-FGSM, MI-FGSM and NI-FGSM. * indicates the white-box attacks. Results of top-5 accuracy can be found in the Table 3)

	Attack	Vgg-19	Dens-121	Res-152	Inc-v3	Res-50
Vgg-19	I-FGSM	93.2*	0.30	0.10	0.10	0.30
	MI-FGSM	99.8*	**1.50**	**0.80**	**0.20**	0.70
	NI-FGSM	**100.0***	1.10	0.50	**0.20**	**0.80**
Dens-121	I-FGSM	0.50	97.8*	0.90	0.10	1.50
	MI-FGSM	**1.90**	**100.0***	2.20	**0.60**	3.10
	NI-FGSM	1.60	**100.0***	**2.40**	**0.60**	4.00
Res-152	I-FGSM	0.30	1.60	97.5*	0.20	1.50
	MI-FGSM	**0.70**	3.60	**100.0***	**0.80**	3.40
	NI-FGSM	0.60	4.10	**100.0***	0.70	**5.20**
Inc-v3	I-FGSM	0.20	0.20	0.00	65.4*	0.20
	MI-FGSM	0.30	**0.50**	**0.60**	89.9*	**0.60**
	NI-FGSM	**0.70**	0.40	**0.60**	91.9*	**0.60**
Res-50	I-FGSM	0.30	0.60	0.60	0.10	93.1*
	MI-FGSM	0.50	1.40	**1.90**	0.60	**100.0***
	NI-FGSM	**0.90**	**2.70**	1.70	**0.70**	**100.0***

Table 3. Top-5 accuracy of targeted adversarial images where we attack a single network. The adversarial examples are generated by Vgg-19, Dens-121, Res-142, Inc-v3 and Res-50 respectively using I-FGSM, MI-FGSM and NI-FGSM. * indicates the white-box attacks.

	Attack	Vgg-19	Dens-121	Res-152	Inc-v3	Res-50
Vgg-19	I-FGSM	98.0*	1.80	0.80	0.40	2.00
	MI-FGSM	100.0*	4.50	3.10	1.50	2.70
	NI-FGSM	100.0*	4.10	2.60	1.20	3.60
Dens-121	I-FGSM	2.30	98.9*	3.20	0.60	5.50
	MI-FGSM	3.90	100.0*	4.80	2.20	8.10
	NI-FGSM	4.60	100.0*	7.50	2.80	10.5
Res-152	I-FGSM	1.90	5.00	99.3*	0.90	6.70
	MI-FGSM	2.60	9.50	100.0*	2.60	9.90
	NI-FGSM	3.40	12.0	100.0*	2.90	13.5
Inc-v3	I-FGSM	0.80	1.60	1.20	80.2*	1.40
	MI-FGSM	0.90	1.80	2.10	96.5*	2.10
	NI-FGSM	1.30	1.80	1.90	97.5*	1.80
Res-50	I-FGSM	1.10	3.60	3.10	0.70	97.3*
	MI-FGSM	2.40	5.70	5.00	1.50	100.0*
	NI-FGSM	2.30	7.80	6.20	1.70	100.0*

rates of targeted attacks. For non-targeted attacks, the success rates are the misclassification rates against the models we consider. However, for targeted attacks, the success rates are the percentage of the adversarial examples crafted for one model that are classified as the target label by the corresponding model. The adversarial images are generated for Vgg-19, Dens-121, Res-152, Ince-v3 and Res-50 respectively. We use three iterative attack methods: I-FGSM, MI-FGSM, NI-FGSM to implement attack. The diagonal blocks represent white-box attack scenario and off-diagonal ones indicate black-box attack scenario. The models that we attack are arranged in rows, and that we test on in columns.

From the table, we can see that all three iterative attack methods can attack a white-box model with an almost 100% success rate for both non-targeted attacks and targeted attacks. As for the black-box scenario, it can be observed that NI-FGSM has a higher success rate than other iterative attack methods about 60% in non-targeted attacks, indicating the effectiveness of the optimization algorithm. But for target attack in black-box scenario, despite NI-FGSM and MI-FGSM increasing the success rates than I-FGSM, the success rates are still small, less than 1% in most cases, and only ten percent in the highest cases. We show top-5 success rates in Table 3. In the black-box scenario, targeted attacks are much harder than non-targeted attacks since the black-box model needs to classify adversarial images as specific error categories. We can do this by attacking attacking an ensemble of models. We'll cover that in the next section.

4.3　Attacking an Ensemble of Models

Based on the above analysis, we focus on generating more transferable adversarial examples via attacking an ensemble of models. In this section, we display the experimental results of non-targeted attacks in Sect. 4.3 and targeted attacks in Sect. 4.3.

Table 4. The success rates (%) of non-targeted adversarial images where we attack an ensemble networks. We study five models Vgg-19, Dens-121, Res-142, Inc-v3 and Res-50 and attack the ensemble networks by MI-FGSM. "*" indicates the black-box attacks. "-" indicates the name of the hold-out model and the adversarial examples are generated for the ensemble of the other four models by three ensemble schemes: EI-logits, EI-softmax and EI-loss.

	Schemes	RMSE	Vgg-19	Dens-121	Res-152	Inc-v3	Res-50
-Vgg-19	EI-logits	13.97	80.8*	98.3	98.3	98.4	98.4
	EI-softmax	14.23	**89.7***	**100.0**	**100.0**	**99.2**	**100.0**
	EI-loss	14.04	87.9*	98.9	97.1	88.6	98.1
-Dens-121	EI-logits	13.87	95.6	86.4*	96.6	97.6	97.1
	EI-softmax	14.21	**100.0**	**94.9***	**99.9**	**99.1**	**100.0**
	EI-loss	13.97	98.2	89.9*	95.8	85.5	96.3
-Res-152	EI-logits	13.90	96.3	97.1	83.3*	97.9	97.6
	EI-softmax	14.23	**100.0**	**100.0**	**90.9***	**99.2**	**100.0**
	EI-loss	13.99	98.0	99.0	87.8*	86.6	97.1
-Inc-v3	EI-logits	13.84	96.0	97.0	96.9	71.7*	97.5
	EI-softmax	14.17	**99.9**	**100.0**	**100.0**	**83.1***	**100.0**
	EI-loss	13.93	98.5	99.1	97.0	80.6*	98.2
-Res-50	EI-logits	13.98	96.1	97.0	97.2	98.0	87.9*
	EI-softmax	14.23	**100.0**	**100.0**	**100.0**	**99.1**	**95.6***
	EI-loss	14.04	98.0	98.8	96.2	88.7	92.6*

Table 5. The second line shows the percentage of pixels that did not change after two iterations and the third line shows the probability that the absolute gradient of invariant pixels will be in the last 50% after two iterations.

Iterations	2	3	4	5	6	7	8	9	10
Unchanged	25.40	20.57	17.36	15.15	13.21	12.41	12.20	10.80	10.03
Unchanged-Lower	70.98	77.10	82.97	85.87	87.35	88.16	84.06	88.36	90.87

Non-targeted Attack. We consider five models here, which are Vgg-19, Dens-121, Res-152, Inc-v3, Res-50. Adversarial images are crafted by an ensemble of four models, and tested on the another hold-out model. Firstly, we tested the effects of different ensemble schemes on non-target attack. We compare the results of the three ensemble schemes, ensemble in logits, ensemble in softmax and ensemble in loss using the MI-FGSM attack method. The results are shown in Table 4. It can be found that the ensemble in softmax is better than the other two ensemble schemes for both the white-box and black-box attacks. For example, if adversarial examples are crafted on Vgg-19, Dense-121, Res-152, Inc-v3 has success rates of 95.6% on Res-50 and 100% on Vgg-19, while baselines like EI-logits only obtains the corresponding success rates of 87.9% and 96.1%, respectively.

In Table 5, we show the percentage of pixels whose pixel value has not altered after two iterations. We found that about 25% of pixes values are unchanged after the first two iterations, and most of them have a small absolute gradient values. Intuitively, pixels with a steady iteration direction are better represented common properties between models. So for Eq. 15, k is set to 0.5. As a result, only half of the pixes change in each iteration, which means that less perturbation is added to the adversarial examples. To compare transferability within the same disturbance range, we set the number of iterations to 13 when applying this method. We can combine HAG with EI-softmax naturally to form a much stronger non-targeted attack. We report the results in Table 6. MI-FGSM-HAG method improves the success rates on challenging black-box models and main-

Table 6. The success rates (%) of non-targeted adversarial images where we attack an ensemble networks. Using EI-softmax, we studied five models Vgg-19, Dens-121, Res-142, Inc-v3 and Res-50. "*" indicates the black-box attacks. '-"indicates the name of the hold-out model and the adversarial examples are generated for the ensemble of the other four models by MI-FGSM, MI-FGSM-HAG and NI-FGSM-HAG.

	Attacks	RMSE	Vgg-19	Dens-121	Res-152	Inc-v3	Res-50
-Vgg-19	MI-FGSM	14.23	89.7*	100.0	100.0	99.2	100.0
	MI-FGSM-HAG	13.53	90.6*	100.0	100.0	99.7	100.0
	NI-FGSM-HAG	13.69	**92.5***	100.0	100.0	**99.7**	100.0
-Dens-121	MI-FGSM	14.21	100.0	94.9*	99.9	99.1	100.0
	MI-FGSM-HAG	13.54	100.0	95.5*	100.0	99.5	100.0
	NI-FGSM-HAG	13.68	100.0	**96.4***	100.0	**99.9**	100.0
-Res-152	MI-FGSM	14.23	100.0	100.0	90.9*	99.2	100.0
	MI-FGSM-HAG	13.55	100.0	100.0	91.2*	99.4	100.0
	NI-FGSM-NAG	13.69	100.0	100.0	**93.5***	**99.8**	100.0
-Inc-v3	MI-FGSM	14.17	99.9	100.0	100.0	83.1*	100.0
	MI-FGSM-HAG	13.48	100.0	100.0	100.0	85.7*	100.0
	NI-FGSM-NAG	13.65	100.0	100.0	100.0	**87.6***	100.0
-Res-50	MI-FGSM	14.23	100.0	100.0	100.0	99.1	95.6*
	MI-FGSM-HAG	13.54	100.0	100.0	100.0	99.8	97.0*
	NI-FGSM-NAG	13.69	100.0	100.0	100.0	99.8	**97.3***

tains high success rates on white-box models. It should be noted that although we increase the number of iterations to 13 in MI-FGSM-HAG, the perturbation is still smaller than the MI-FGSM.

We then compare the success rates of NI-FGSM-HAG and MI-FGSM-HAG to see the effectiveness of optimization in Table 6. Experimental results show NI-FGSM-HAG is a stronger attack method than MI-FGSM-HAG. For the strongest attack method in the case of non-target attack NI-FGSM-HAG can fool white-box model at almost 100% and misclassify the balck-box model at almost 93% rate on average.

Targeted Attack. For more challenging targeted attack, we also examine the transferability of targeted adversarial images based on ensemble models. Table 7 presents the results for three esemble schemes using MI-FGSM methods. The results show EI-loss reaches much higher success rates than other two ensemble schemes on both black-box models and white-box models. Under the white-box setting, we see that EI-loss can reach more than 85% success rate. However, the highest success rate is only 11.7% under the black box setting.

Table 7. The success rates (%) of targeted adversarial images where we attack an ensemble networks. We study five models Vgg-19, Dens-121, Res-142, Inc-v3 and Res-50 and attack the ensemble networks by MI-FGSM. "*" indicates the black-box attacks. "-" indicates the hold-out model and the adversarial examples are generated for the ensemble of the other four models by three ensemble schemes: EI-logits, EI-softmax and EI-loss.

	Schemes	RMSE	Vgg-19	Dens-121	Res-152	Inc-v3	Res-50
-Vgg-19	EI-logits	14.44	0.9*	91.4	64.6	17.7	79.5
	EI-softmax	14.31	3.0*	10.3	80.1	31.5	80.8
	EI-loss	14.30	**3.5***	**100.0**	**99.8**	**86.1**	**100.0**
-Dens-121	EI-logits	14.45	49.4	3.0*	62.4	18.2	81.5
	EI-softmax	14.35	63.8	5.6*	3.8	37.0	75.3
	EI-loss	14.28	**98.2**	**11.0***	**99.6**	**86.5**	**100.0**
-Res-152	EI-logits	14.47	42.2	89.4	1.6*	16.3	75.8
	EI-softmax	14.35	63.9	5.6	3.9*	36.9	75.3
	EI-loss	14.31	**98.7**	**100.0**	**5.8***	**85.5**	**100.0**
-Inc-v3	EI-logits	14.51	39.5	92.6	61.4	1.1*	82.0
	EI-softmax	14.29	61.1	13.2	79.3	2.4*	81.0
	EI-loss	14.19	**99.3**	**100.0**	**99.9**	**3.7***	**100.0**
-Res-50	EI-logits	14.48	47.5	90.9	63.0	17.6	3.0 *
	EI-softmax	14.35	64.3	7.7	78.4	31.1	7.6*
	EI-loss	14.32	**98.5**	**100.0**	**99.6**	**86.3**	**11.7***

Table 8. The success rates (%) of targeted adversarial images where we attack an ensemble networks. Using EI-loss, we studied five models Vgg-19, Dens-121, Res-142, Inc-v3 and Res-50. "*" indicates the black-box attacks. "-"indicates the name of the hold-out model and the adversarial examples are generated for the ensemble of the other four models by MI-FGSM, MI-FGSM-HAG and NI-FGSM-HAG.

	Attacks	RMSE	Vgg-19	Dens-121	Res-152	Inc-v3	Res-50
-Vgg-19	MI-FGSM	14.30	3.5*	100.0	99.8	86.1	100.0
	MI-FGSM-HAG	13.58	4.1*	100.0	99.9	95.3	100.0
	NI-FGSM-HAG	13.71	**5.7***	100.0	**100.0**	**97.5**	100.0
-Dens-121	MI-FGSM	14.28	98.2	11.0*	99.6	86.5	100.0
	MI-FGSM-HAG	13.59	99.2	15.4*	**99.9**	95.0	100.0
	NI-FGSM-HAG	13.71	**99.5**	**16.0***	99.8	**97.9**	100.0
-Res-152	MI-FGSM	14.31	98.7	100.0	5.8*	**85.5**	100.0
	MI-FGSM-HAG	13.60	98.9	**100.0**	9.0*	95.0	100.0
	NI-FGSM-HAG	13.72	**99.7**	100.0	**11.5***	97.8	100.0
-Inc-v3	MI-FGSM	14.19	99.3	100.0	99.9	3.7*	100.0
	MI-FGSM-HAG	13.51	99.6	100.0	99.9	4.9*	100.0
	NI-FGSM-HAG	13.70	**100.0**	100.0	**100.0**	**6.6***	100.0
-Res-50	MI-FGSM	14.32	98.5	100.0	99.6	86.3	11.7*
	MI-FGSM-HAG	13.59	99.2	100.0	**99.9**	95.9	14.5*
	NI-FGSM-HAG	13.72	**99.8**	100.0	99.9	**98.0**	**17.3***

Table 9. Top-5 accuracy of targeted adversarial images where we attack an ensemble networks. Using EI-loss, we studied five models Vgg-19, Dens-121, Res-142, Inc-v3 and Res-50. "*" indicates the black-box attacks. "-" indicates the name of the hold-out model and the adversarial examples are generated for the ensemble of the other four models by MI-FGSM, MI-FGSM-HAG and NI-FGSM-HAG.

	Attacks	RMSE	Vgg-19	Dens-121	Res-152	Inc-v3	Res-50
-Vgg-19	MI-FGSM	14.30	8.9*	100.0	100.0	93.2	100.0
	MI-FGSM-HAG	13.58	9.8*	100.0	100.0	98.4	100.0
	NI-FGSM-HAG	13.71	**11.7***	100.0	100.0	**99.0**	100.0
-Dens-121	MI-FGSM	14.28	99.0	21.5*	99.8	93.6	100.0
	MI-FGSM-HAG	13.59	99.6	25.9*	**100.0**	98.7	100.0
	NI-FGSM-HAG	13.71	**99.7**	**29.2***	100.0	**99.7**	100.0
-Res-152	MI-FGSM	14.31	99.3	100.0	15.1*	93.7	100.0
	MI-FGSM-HAG	13.60	99.6	100.0	18.6*	98.7	100.0
	NI-FGSM-NAG	13.72	**99.9**	100.0	**22.0***	**98.9**	100.0
-Inc-v3	MI-FGSM	14.19	99.6	100.0	100.0	9.0*	100.0
	MI-FGSM-HAG	13.51	99.6	100.0	100.0	12.6*	100.0
	NI-FGSM-HAG	13.70	**100.0**	100.0	100.0	**13.4***	100.0
-Res-50	MI-FGSM	14.32	99.2	100.0	99.7	94.4	21.6*
	MI-FGSM-HAG	13.59	99.5	100.0	**100.0**	99.0	28.3*
	NI-FGSM-HAG	13.72	**99.9**	100.0	100.0	**99.5**	**30.1***

For gradient descent mechanism, we set k to 0.5 like untargeted attack. The results are summarized in Table 8. The HAG yields a maximum black-box success rate of 14.5% with lower distortion. We then conducted experiments to validate the effectiveness of the combination of NI-FGSM and HAG. As Table 8 suggests, NI-FGSM-HAG obtains a significant performance improvement. The best black-box success rate attained 17.3 %, and in white-box models, the lowest success rate reached 98.9%. We also examine targeted attacks based on top-5 accuracy, the highest success rate is 30% in balck-box setting. The results can be found in the Table 9. We found that targeted attacks also have almost the same success rate as non-target attacks in the white box setting, but a low success rate in the black-box models, which means that targeted adversarial examples have a much poor transferability.

5   Conclusion and Future Work

In this paper, we propose three methods to improve the transferability of adversarial examples based on the ensemble models. Specifically, we found that different ensemble schemes have different effects on non-targeted attacks and targeted attack, EI-softmax suitable for non-targeted attacks and EI-loss suitable for targeted attacks. Moreover, we discovered that pixels with higher absolute gradient values have better transferability. By integrating HAG with NI-FGSM, we can further improve the transferability of adversarial examples. We conduct extensive experiments to demonstrate that our methods not only yield higher success rates on untargeted attacks but also enhanced the success rates on more harder targeted attacks.

References

1. Szegedy, C., et al.: Intriguing properties of neural networks. arXiv (2013). https://arxiv.org/abs/1412.6572
2. Goodfellow, I.J., Shlens, J., Szegedy, C.: Intriguing properties of neural networks. arXiv (2014). https://arxiv.org/abs/1412.6572
3. Liu, Y., Chen, X., Liu, C., Song, D.: Delving into transferable adversarial examples and black-box attacks. arXiv (2016). https://arxiv.org/abs/1611.02770
4. Madry, A., Makelov, A., Schmidt, L., Tsipras, D., Vladu, A.: Towards deep learning models resistant to adversarial attacks. arXiv (2017). https://arxiv.org/abs/1706.06083
5. Carlini, N., Wagner, D.: Adversarial examples are not easily detected: bypassing ten detection methods, pp. 3–14. ACM (2017). https://dl.acm.org/doi/abs/10.1145/3128572.3140444
6. Russakovsky, O., et al.: ImageNet large scale visual recognition challenge. Int. J. Comput. Vision **115**(3), 211–252 (2015). https://doi.org/10.1007/s11263-015-0816-y
7. Kurakin, A., Goodfellow, I., Bengio, S., et al.: Adversarial examples in the physical world (2016). https://openreview.net/forum?id=HJGU3Rodl

8. Papernot, N., McDaniel, P., Goodfellow, I., Jha, S., Celik, Z.B., Swami, A.: Practical black-box attacks against machine learning, pp. 506–519 (2017). https://dl.acm.org/doi/abs/10.1145/3052973.3053009

9. Song, C., He, K., Wang, L., Hopcroft, J.E.: Improving the generalization of adversarial training with domain adaptation. arXiv (2018). https://arxiv.org/abs/1810.00740

10. Dong, Y., et al.: Boosting adversarial attacks with momentum. In: CVPR, pp. 9185–9193 (2018). https://openaccess.thecvf.com/content_cvpr_2018/html/Dong_Boosting_Adversarial_Attacks_CVPR_2018_paper.html

11. Lin, J., Song, C., He, K., Wang, L., Hopcroft, J.E.: Nesterov accelerated gradient and scale invariance for adversarial attacks. arXiv (2019). https://arxiv.org/abs/1810.00740

12. Polyak, B.T.: Some methods of speeding up the convergence of iteration methods. USSR Comput. Math. Math. Phys. **4**, 1–17 (1964). https://www.sciencedirect.com/science/article/abs/pii/0041555364901375

13. Nesterov, Y.: A method for unconstrained convex minimization problem with the rate of convergence O $(1/k^{\wedge} 2)$. Doklady USSR **269**, 543–547 (1983). https://cir.nii.ac.jp/crid/1570572699326076416

14. Szegedy, C., Vanhoucke, V., Ioffe, S., Shlens, J., Wojna, Z.: Rethinking the inception architecture for computer vision. In: CVPR, pp. 2818–2826 (2016). https://www.cv-foundation.org/openaccess/content_cvpr_2016/html/Szegedy_Rethinking_the_Inception_CVPR_2016_paper.html

15. Simonyan, K., Zisserman, A.: Very deep convolutional networks for large-scale image recognition. arXiv (2014). https://arxiv.org/abs/1409.1556

16. Huang, G., Liu, Z., Van Der Maaten, L., Weinberger, K.Q.: Densely connected convolutional networks. In: CVPR, pp. 4700–4708 (2017). https://openaccess.thecvf.com/content_cvpr_2017/html/Huang_Densely_Connected_Convolutional_CVPR_2017_paper.html

17. He, K., Zhang, X., Ren, S., Sun, J.: Deep residual learning for image recognition. In: CVPR, pp. 770–778 (2016). https://openaccess.thecvf.com/content_cvpr_2016/html/He_Deep_Residual_Learning_CVPR_2016_paper.html

18. He, K., Zhang, X., Ren, S., Sun, J.: Identity mappings in deep residual networks. In: Leibe, B., Matas, J., Sebe, N., Welling, M. (eds.) ECCV 2016. LNCS, vol. 9908, pp. 630–645. Springer, Cham (2016). https://doi.org/10.1007/978-3-319-46493-0_38

Applications of Artificial Intelligence

Browsing Behavioral Intent Prediction on Product Recommendation Pages of E-commerce Platform

Zebin Cai[1], Yankun Zhen[3], Mingrui He[1], Liuqing Chen[1,2(✉)], Lingyun Sun[1,2], Tingting Zhou[3], and Yichun Du[3]

[1] Zhejiang University, Hangzhou 310027, China
[2] Alibaba-Zhejiang University Joint Research Institute of Frontier Technologies, Hangzhou 310027, China
`chenlq@zju.edu.cn`
[3] Alibaba Group, Hangzhou 311121, China

Abstract. User behavior data has always been the key for e-commerce platforms to make decisions and improve experience, especially when predicting users' behavioral intent. Nowadays, the Product Recommendation Page (PRP) has played an increasingly significant role of e-commerce platforms with the popularity of recommendation systems. However, past research on predicting user behavioral intent across e-commerce platforms may not be applicable to PRPs, where users have different characteristics. In this research, users' browsing behavioral intent of PRPs is studied and predicted. A large amount of user data of PRPs is collected and processed, and the corresponding dataset is built. After that, a user interest analysis method is proposed while five browsing intent prediction models are applied and compared. The method distinguishes users with different browsing interest degrees, and the models can better predict users' browsing behavior intent within different interest groups. A validation experiment on the large-scale dataset shows that the proposed method can predict user browsing intent with a decent performance.

Keywords: E-commerce · Product recommendation page · Intent prediction · Interest analysis

1 Introduction

The key component of e-commerce business is users, their behavior data is a significant analysis resource to boost e-commercial security, profitability, and stability. In the context of big data, many studies analyzing e-commerce user behavior data have been conducted in recent years. Understanding users' purchasing intent is an essential but troublesome task. The main challenge of predicting behavioral intent is to obtain valuable information and to ensure predicted speed. It is difficult to process behavior data correctly and extract the most useful information. Real-time is also necessary for the process of user intent

L. Fang et al. (Eds.): CICAI 2022, LNAI 13605, pp. 33–45, 2022.
https://doi.org/10.1007/978-3-031-20500-2_3

prediction. If it is not fast enough to make decisions in response to user intent, it is likely to decrease user experience and even lose users. The focus of user behavioral intent prediction is also different for various scenarios in e-commerce platforms. The most common and influential intent study, user purchasing intent prediction [1] cannot be applied to all situations, especially where the purchasing intent is quite limited. In some scenarios, the main purpose is not to prompt users to make direct purchases, but to guide them in exploring products, which is typically represented by the Product Recommendation Page (PRP).

Nowadays PRPs have an increasing amount of traffic in e-commerce platforms, while the majority of research on user intent is geared towards the entire purchasing process, instead of PRPs of the platforms. In this work, users' browsing behavioral intent of PRPs is investigated and predicted. The users' behavior data are collected and then are processed to a browsing behavioral dataset. Based on this dataset, prediction models are constructed and used to predict users' browsing behavioral intent. In addition, the users' own characteristics are also modeled to distinguish different degrees of interest. Prediction models are retrained among different groups of people, which effectively improved predicted performance.

The contributions of this work are presented as follows:

1. A dataset of browsing-interactive behaviors, which contains detailed information about the path that users have browsed within PRPs. These data are easily accessible and can describe users from multiple perspectives for better users' interest analysis and browsing behavioral intent prediction.
2. A method of predicting users' browsing behavioral intent. The method requires only a small amount of easily accessible browsing behavior data, does not require building complex feature engineering to perform the prediction work, and has a fast response speed during the users' life-cycle in PRPs. Experiments are conducted on a large-scale dataset, and the results show that the model has great prediction performance.
3. A method for analyzing users' browsing interest using multiple metrics, and the results obtained contribute to improving the accuracy of browsing behavioral intent prediction.

2 Related Work

2.1 Browsing Behavior Analysis

A survey in [2] shows user web browsing behavior, keystroke behavior, network transaction behavior, and mobile terminal behavior are the most common resources to optimize the scheme for designers and modelers. Specifically, browsing behavior analysis is mainly researching user features and behaviors by applying some machine learning algorithms based on users' historical behaviors [3]. [4] presents K-means clustering algorithm used for identification of user groups on the basis of their web access log record, while [5] uses PCA to identify the most significant features from the log file before clustering users by SOM algorithm. Historical behavior data are widely collected in forms of click-stream. [6]

conducts a comparative analysis of click-stream behavior of users from different countries, research in [7] applies a collaborative filtering-based method to recommend items for different consumers, and [8] addresses the problem of user intent prediction from click-stream data of an e-commerce platform. Interest analysis is also a popular method to find users' behavioral habits. [9–14] indicate that the frequency, duration and sequence of visits on web pages reflect browsing behaviours. [34] proposes Intent Contrastive Learning to investigate the benefits of latent intents and leverage them effectively for recommendation. [35] models the comprehensive compositional coherence on both global intent contents and semantic intent contents by a Content Attentive Neural Network.

2.2   Browsing Behavioral Intent Prediction

The problem of user intent or session classification in an e-commerce setting has been heavily studied, with a variety of classic machine learning and deep learning modeling techniques employed. [15] uses Recurrent Neural Networks (RNNs) on a subset of the same dataset to predict the next session click on the user intent classification problem. [16] compares [15] to a variety of classical machine learning algorithms on multiple datasets and finds that performance varies signally by datasets. [17] extends [15] with a variant of LSTM to capture variations in dwell time between user actions. User dwell time is considered a vital factor in multiple implementations. For browsing behavior prediction, [18] uses a mixture of RNNs and treats the problem as a sequence-to-sequence translation problem, constructing a model both including prediction and recommendation. [19] shows that short sessions are very common in e-commerce datasets, moreover, a user's most recent actions are often more vital in deciphering their intent than older actions. Therefore we argue that all session lengths should be included. RNNs are used in [20] to incorporate temporal features with user preferences to improve recommendation performance, and to predict behavioral directions instead of purchase intent.

The task of browsing behavioral intent prediction is closely related to sequence classification. A brief survey by [21] categorizes the sequence classification methods into three groups: feature-based methods [22], sequence distance-based methods [23], and model-based methods [24–27]. This research is related to the model-based approach, which applies end-to-end algorithms to model the sequences and save extensive feature engineering work. The work is also related to sentence classification in natural language processing [28–30]. Text sentences and time series data are similar to each other in that they are both ordered sequences in nature. This work differs from the previous work in that the dwell time in the sequence is also concerned, while in traditional sequence classification, usually, only the data in the sequence needs to be processed.

3   Methodology

In PRPs, user browsing path and dwell time are often the most concern by researchers, and these data are also easy to obtain in many cases. Therefore, this research collects users' browsing path in the form of a sequence of pages, while each page contains detailed information about browsing behaviors and the dwell time.

The main purpose of predicting user browsing behavioral intent in this work is to predict what a user is going to browse next, i.e., to predict which page the user will go to next. However, there are many types of pages in PRPs, including not only PRPs' home page and sub-pages, but also different product pages and many other types of pages. Moreover, the naming and coding of pages are often irregular, and also unrelated to users' intent.

Based on the above, the PRPs are classified into five types by the nature of the pages, considering both the compatibility of PRPs in different e-commerce platforms and the relevance of data to user intent. The classification is helpful to make better predictions, and each type of pages has its own independent page nature rather than a name. Thus different types of pages are more likely to represent users' intent. For example, frequent browsing of the "product exploration page" can indicate that a user is more interested in a wide range of products and eager to obtain inspiration from its exploration experience. After processing the raw data, the corresponding large-scale dataset is built.

Based on the processed dataset, the browsing behavioral intent prediction in this study can be described as a sequence classification task which has five possibilities regarding output. To find the best prediction method, this work constructs five models to predict user browsing behavioral intent, that contain three deep neural network models and two traditional machine learning models. Taking into account real-time requirements of e-commerce platforms, these models are not designed to be too large and all have applicable prediction speed.

In order to improve the effectiveness of the prediction model, this work presents a deeper analysis on user behaviors and proposes a user interest analysis method. The method produces two indicators from browsing data and uses a clustering algorithm to distinguish the group of users who have a distinguishing interest in PRP. Finally, the prediction model was retrained and predicted in the different interest groups to verify the effectiveness of the proposed method. The workflow of behavior analysis and prediction are shown in Fig. 1.

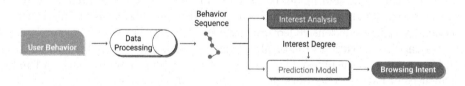

Fig. 1. Workflow diagram of user browsing behavior analysis and prediction system.

4   Experiments

4.1   Data Collection and Processing

From a mobile App of the largest e-commerce platform in China, the browsing behavior data of 284,202 users of PRPs are collected by means of end-to-end buried points. The time span of the data is one week in March 2022. The raw data of browse-interactive behaviors contain three fields, including "Scene", "Id" and "Timestamp". "Scene" and "Timestamp" identify where and when an action occurs. "Scene" also indicates the function of the page, e.g. the page is used to represent a product or advertisement. "Id" helps identify the exact page when browsing in the App.

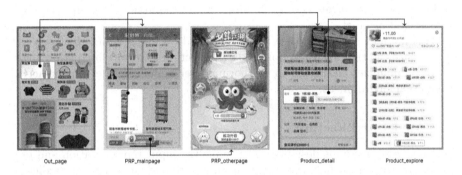

Fig. 2. An example of five types of pages and their flow directions. "PRP_mainpage", "Product_detail", "Product_explore", "Out_page", "PRP_otherpage" are indicated by yellow, red, orange, blue and green boxes respectively. (Color figure online)

Combining "Scene" and "Id", the pages are divided into five types. An example of five types of pages and their flow directions is shown in Fig. 2, where the type is indicated by bounding box with five different colors. The process of page jumping is represented by lines, of which the dots represent the clicking area that triggers the jumping of the starting page and the arrows point to the pages after the jumping. Each type contains a specific definition. The definition and distribution of five types of pages are described in Table 1. Statistics show that the two largest distributions are "Product_detail" and "PRP_otherpage", accounting for 67.9% of the pages. However, in general, there is no situation where a certain page occupies the majority of browsing activities, so we can use accuracy as the metric to evaluate the prediction performance.

To process the data into a format suitable for model recognition, pages are encoded as one-hot codes of a length of five. The dwell time between pages browsed by users is normalized within sixty seconds, as 94% of the dwell time is less than sixty seconds. Then a massive dataset is built and contains 284,202 complete user browsing behavioral sequences. [19] argues user real-time browsing intent tends to be most closely related to the most recent behaviors that

Table 1. The definition and distribution of five types of pages.

Type	PRP_mainpage	Product_detail	Product_explore	Out_page	PRP_otherpage
Definition	Recommended products page	Product detail page	Sub-page of product detail page	The off-site page of PRP, but still in the App	Within PRPs and do not belong to "PRP_mainpage", "Product_detail" and "Product_explore"
Percentage	17.3%	24.5%	11.2%	3.6%	43.4%

occurred, while behavioral actions that occurred long ago can be used to assess users' habits. Considering the applicability of historical data to current data, the model uses only five most recent occurrences in predicting user browsing intent, but the complete sequence is processed when analyzing browsing interest. So our prepared dataset for prediction consists of 2,301,388 sequences of a length of six while the first five pages and dwell time are used as input data and the sixth page is used as label.

This method just takes a few easily obtained browsing data, which can not only reduce the time consumption of data collection to ensure prediction speed but also minimize the impact on the normal operation of business in the actual production environment.

4.2   Model Architecture

The prediction model is designed to consume the input representation and predict user browsing behavioral intent in an end-to-end, sequence to prediction manner. The model in this work is not designed to be large and complex in order to ensure the speed of prediction and lightweight requirement in real online business scenarios. This research investigates two traditional machine learning models and three neural network-based models for intent prediction.

Traditional Machine Learning Models. This work tests two traditional machine learning models that can be used to handle sequence classification, namely, RF-HMM model and Compact Prediction Tree (CPT) [31] model. In the RF-HMM model, the raw data are used to train the Random Forest (RF) and Hidden Markov Model (HMM) respectively, and the HMM is used to estimate the state transfer matrix. At the prediction stage, RF is first applied to predict the probability distribution, and then the state transfer matrix of the HMM is combined to obtain the resultant values.

Neural Networks Models. Three neural network-based models are used to make browsing behavioral intent prediction. RNNs, which are good at modelling sequential data, are chosen to build the prediction model. The first neural network model uses LSTM among many RNN variants because of its ability to extract features from a long sequence. The model's main structure consists of a network of four layers with 512 LSTM neurons in each layer. Inspired by [22], considering the ability of CNN for feature extraction, the second model combines CNN and LSTM, using a one-dimensional CNN to extract the features of the sequence before applying LSTM for the prediction output. The third model is based on the Temporal Convolutional Neural (TCN), which is tiny and has achieved several SOTAs in time series tasks since it was proposed by [32] in 2018. The TCN model is consisted by a TCN layer and two hidden dense layers and a linear layer used to be output.

The dataset is split into a training set and validation set in an 80:20 ratio. During the training period, these three models are trained using the Adam optimizer, coupled with a categorical cross-entropy loss metric and a learning rate automatic controller. Training is halted after two continuous epochs of worsening validation Accuracy.

4.3   Interest Analysis Method

In this section, an interest analysis method is proposed to analyze users' interest in PRPs, and users are divided into three groups with different interest degrees. Models are trained separately in different groups of users and make predictions of them. It can improve the models' prediction accuracy utilize different preferences of different groups. Unlike the predictive models, which use only the five most recent pages, the method uses all the pages a user has browsed since entering the PRPs.

Two indicators are used which are most concerned about by real online environment to measure users' interest patterns [33].

Indicator 1: Visiting Frequency
For $user_i$, $click_i^j$ consists of the number of visits to $type_j$. Visiting frequency is defined as the ratio of type clicks to the length of the user's full browsing path. This work uses $freq_i^j$ to denote the visiting frequency to $type_j$ by $user_i$ in a session:

$$\text{freq}_i^j = \frac{\text{clicks}_i^j}{\text{len}(P_i)} \quad \left(0 \leqslant \text{freq}_i^j \leqslant 1\right) \tag{1}$$

Indicator 2: Relative Duration
In this study, the time spent browsing each page will be accumulated according to the type. Relative duration is utilized as one of the main indicators to reflect a user's interest. Relative duration $redu_i^j$ is defined as the ratio of time $user_i$ spends on $type_j$ to the entire session.

$$\text{redu}_i^j = \frac{\text{duration}_i^j}{\text{time}(P_i)} \quad \left(0 \leqslant \text{redu}_i^j \leqslant 1\right) \tag{2}$$

After processing, each user has a feature vector of shape $(2, 5)$, that is, each user has two indicators in five types. K-means algorithm is used to cluster users into different interest groups, the algorithm allows to customize the number of clusters.

The "Score" function measures the clustering effect, which is the negative number of the sum of the distance between the samples and their cluster center, and will increase with the increase of clusters. Therefore, the optimal value of the number of clusters is set according to the elbow criterion. Intuitively, the scores for the number of clusters from one to ten are mapped into (0, 1) and plotted in Fig. 3.

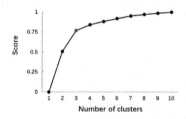

Fig. 3. Scores for different numbers of clusters.

In addition, the optimal number of clusters should also make samples evenly distributed to ensure that each model is well trained. The proportions of each group with K value of two, three and four are 1:2.10, 1:1.07:1.13 and 1:1.09:1.93:2.15, respectively. Therefore, three is the best number of clusters considering it is an elbow point and gives an even data distribution. These three groups of users are defined into high, middle, and low interest groups, which are described in detail in Sect. 4.3.

5   Results and Discussion

5.1   Prediction Results

In the testing phase, the data in the validation set are used for testing, and the prediction results for both cases with and without interest analysis are counted separately, shown in Table 2.

Without using interest analysis, models are trained by all users' data of the training set. Neutral network based models perform much better than traditional machine learning models. LSTMs model takes highest accuracy at 88.72% without using interest analysis, indicating that it can learn behavioral characteristics and habits of users better from these few and easily obtained browsing data. However, the accuracy of RF-HMM and CPT models does not exceed 70%, probably because these models are too simple to learn users' behavioral habits from little information.

Table 2. Prediction results for different groups of users of different models.

Model	Accuracy			
	Without interest analysis	High interest group	Middle interest group	Low interest group
CPT	0.6425	0.6861	0.6874	0.6682
RF-HMM	0.6632	0.7233	0.6922	0.6598
TCN	0.8734	0.8936	0.8872	0.8698
CNN-LSTM	0.8612	0.8878	0.8827	0.8606
LSTMs	**0.8872**	**0.9211**	**0.8958**	**0.8842**

To test the running speed of the models, the time consumption (milliseconds) of each prediction of the five models is shown in Table 3. The single prediction time of the five models is less than 50 ms, which is satisfactory in real application scenarios. The best model, LSTMs, predicts at 28.92 ms per session. Two traditional machine learning models are faster than the neural network models and can reach around 10 ms or less.

Table 3. Time consumption per prediction for five models.

Model	CPT	RF-HMM	TCN	CNN-LSTM	LSTMs
Time (ms)	2.38	10.93	47.29	27.90	28.92

5.2 Interest Analysis Results and Discussion

This section describes the results after using the interest analysis method, which analyzes the characteristics of three different groups of users. The prediction results with the interest analysis are also discussed.

Two indicators of a user on the same page type have a strong correlation. Their distributions for the three groups of users on the five page types are shown in Fig. 4 and these distributions are easy to distinguish.

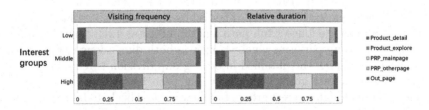

Fig. 4. Distributions of the two indicators for the three groups of users on the five pages.

According to the definition of page classification, when users spend more time visiting the "Product_detail" and "Product_explore", it means that they are more interested in products; otherwise, they just wander aimlessly in PRPs. Therefore, the group with high visiting frequency on these two types is considered the high interest group, and other two groups are considered the middle and low interest groups, respectively.

Users with different interest degrees differ greatly in the prediction results. As described in Table 2, the Accuracy of high interest group has the greatest improvement of three groups and can reach 92.11% in the best model LSTMs. The middle interest group also has better results among five models. However, there is no significant increase in the prediction results for the middle interest or even a decrease for low interest groups.

Combining the visiting frequency and duration distributions shown in Fig. 4, It can be inferred that the high interest group is more evenly distributed across the five pages and they prefer to browse pages that are directly related to the products. Delightfully, these people are often the most useful people in e-commerce because they have a higher purchase rate. In contrast, the middle interest group spends the most time on "PRP_otherpage" in PRPs, accounting for about 63.3%, but also focuses on some productive pages, so their behavioral pattern is harder to capture. The most irregular pattern is the low interest group, who barely browses the products after entering the PRPs.

Table 4. Full path length and total dwell time statistics for three groups.

Interest degree	Full path length (steps)			Total dwell time (seconds)		
	High	Middle	Low	High	Middle	Low
Mean	12.7	10.3	2.1	207.2	196.9	43.7
Median	12.0	10.0	2.0	147.9	127.0	17.8
S.D.	7.9	6.2	2.8	202.3	216.0	111.9

To further verify the division of interest groups, this research also calculates the mean, median, and standard deviation of the full path length and total dwell time of three groups. The full path length is the number of pages browsed by a user from entering the PRPs to leaving the PRPs. The total dwell time is the total time spent in this process. The results shown in Table 4 find that high interest group has the longest full path length and total dwell time, while users in low interest group performs much shorter on both dimensions than the other two groups. Therefore, the obtained interest group division is reasonable.

For middle interest group, their browsing path length and dwell time are similar to those of high interest group, but they are less likely to browse products in PRPs, so PRPs may need to help them find products they like. For low interest groups, they not only do not browse the products but also have a short browsing path and dwell time. Their irregular pattern causes the predictive Accuracy of

"Low interest group" to be worse than that "Without interest analysis". So PRPs may first consider how to retain them.

6   Conclusion

In this study, the browsing behavioral intent of online users in PRPs is investigated and predicted. This work first collects a large amount of user data in a mobile App for processing and analysis. Then five models for browsing intent prediction are proposed, while a method of analyzing users' browsing interest is further studied to boost prediction performance. Finally, the prediction models are tested and the results show that LSTMs achieved the best and it could have better performance when combined with the interest analysis method in which users are divided into different interest groups, especially in the case of high interest group who are also the most concerned by e-commerce platforms. Moreover, the prediction process of the model is speedy enough to predict the current user behavior intent by the back-office system in real-time.

Acknowledgments. This research is supported by Alibaba-Zhejiang University Joint Research Institute of Frontier Technologies.

References

1. Ben-Shimon, D., et al.: Recsys challenge 2015 and the yoochoose dataset. In: Proceedings of the 9th ACM Conference on Recommender Systems (2015)
2. Zhao, P., et al.: Behavior analysis for electronic commerce trading systems: a survey. IEEE Access **7**, 108703–108728 (2019)
3. Zhang, Y., et al.: User-click modeling for understanding and predicting search-behavior. In: Proceedings of the 17th ACM SIGKDD International Conference on Knowledge Discovery and Data Mining (2011)
4. Turčanik, M.: Web users clustering by their behaviour on the network. In: 2020 New Trends in Signal Processing (NTSP), pp. 1–5. IEEE (2020)
5. Ahmad, N.B., Alias, U.F., Mohamad, N., Yusof, N.: Principal component analysis and self-organizing map clustering for student browsing behaviour analysis. Procedia Comput. Sci. **163**, 550–559 (2019)
6. Urman, A., Makhortykh, M.: You are how (and where) you search? Comparative analysis of web search behaviour using web tracking data. arXiv preprint arXiv:2105.04961 (2021)
7. Zeng, M., Cao, H., Chen, M., Li, Y.: User behaviour modeling, recommendations, and purchase prediction during shopping festivals. Electron. Mark. **29**(2), 263–274 (2019)
8. Requena, B., Cassani, G., Tagliabue, J., Greco, C., Lacasa, L.: Shopper intent prediction from clickstream e-commerce data with minimal browsing information. Sci. Rep. **10**(1), 1–23 (2020)
9. Rathipriya, R., Thangavel, K.: A fuzzy co-clustering approach for clickstream data pattern. arXiv preprint arXiv:1109.6726 (2011)
10. Liu, H., Xing, H., Zhang, F.: Web personalized recommendation algorithm incorporated with user interest change. J. Comput. Inf. Syst. **8**(4), 1383–1390 (2012)

11. Gong, S., Cheng, G.: Mining user interest change for improving collaborative filtering. In: 2008 Second International Symposium on Intelligent Information Technology Application, vol. 3, pp. 24–27. IEEE (2008)
12. Kim, Y.S., Yum, B.-J.: Recommender system based on click stream data using association rule mining. Expert Syst. Appl. **38**(10), 13320–13327 (2011)
13. Yu, H., Luo, H.: Possibilistic fuzzy clustering algorithm based on web user access paths. J. Chin. Comput. Syst. **33**(1), 135–139 (2012)
14. Li, Y., Tan, B.-H.: Clustering algorithm of web click stream frequency pattern. Tianjin Keji Daxue Xuebao/ J. Tianjin Univ. Sci. Technol. **26**(3), 69–73 (2011)
15. Hidasi, B., et al.: Session-based recommendations with recurrent neural networks. arXiv preprint arXiv:1511.06939 (2015)
16. Xing, Z., Pei, J., Keogh, E.: Evaluation of session-based recommendation algorithms. User Model. User-Adap. Inter. **28**(4), 331–390 (2018)
17. Zhu, Y., et al.: What to do next: modeling user behaviors by time-LSTM. IJCAI **17**, 3602–3608 (2017)
18. Toth, A., et al.: Predicting shopping behavior with mixture of RNNs. In: ACM SIGIR Forum. ACM (2017)
19. Jannach, D., Ludewig, M., Lerche, L.: Session-based item recommendation in e-commerce: on short-term intents, reminders, trends and discounts. User Model. User-Adap. Inter. **27**(3), 351–392 (2017)
20. Wu, C.Y., Ahmed, A., Beutel, A., Smola, A.J., Jing, H.: Recurrent recommender networks. In: Proceedings of the Tenth ACM International Conference on Web Search and Data Mining, pp. 495–503 (2017)
21. Xing, Z., Pei, J., Keogh, E.: A brief survey on sequence classification. ACM SIGKDD Explor. Newsl. **12**(1), 40–48 (2010)
22. Ye, L., Keogh, E.: Time series shapelets: a new primitive for data mining. In: Proceedings of the 15th ACM SIGKDD International Conference on Knowledge Discovery and Data Mining, pp. 947–956 (2009)
23. Wei, L., Keogh, E.: Semi-supervised time series classification. In: Proceedings of the 12th ACM SIGKDD International Conference on Knowledge Discovery and Data Mining, pp. 748–753 (2006)
24. Sheil, H., Rana, O., Reilly, R.: Predicting purchasing intent: automatic feature learning using recurrent neural networks. In: ACM SIGIR Forum. ACM (2018)
25. Guo, L., et al.: Buying or browsing?: predicting real-time purchasing intent using attention-based deep network with multiple behavior. In: Proceedings of the 25th ACM SIGKDD International Conference on Knowledge Discovery and Data Mining (2019)
26. Sakar, C.O., et al.: Real-time prediction of online shoppers' purchasing intention using multilayer perceptron and LSTM recurrent neural networks. Neural Comput. Appl. **31**(10), 6893–6908 (2019)
27. Zhao, Y., Shen, Y., Huang, Y.: DMDP: a dynamic multi-source default probability prediction framework. Data Sci. Eng. **4**(1), 3–13 (2019)
28. Kowsari, K., et al.: Text classification algorithms: a survey. Information **10**(4), 150 (2019)
29. Guo, L., Zhang, D., Wang, L., Wang, H., Cui, B.: CRAN: a hybrid CNN-RNN attention-based model for text classification. In: Trujillo, J.C., et al. (eds.) ER 2018. LNCS, vol. 11157, pp. 571–585. Springer, Cham (2018). https://doi.org/10.1007/978-3-030-00847-5_42
30. Zhang, X., Zhao, J., LeCun, Y.: Character-level convolutional networks for text classification. In: Advances in Neural Information Processing Systems, vol. 28 (2015)

31. Gueniche, T., Fournier-Viger, P., Tseng, V.S.: Compact prediction tree: a lossless model for accurate sequence prediction. In: Motoda, H., Wu, Z., Cao, L., Zaiane, O., Yao, M., Wang, W. (eds.) ADMA 2013. LNCS (LNAI), vol. 8347, pp. 177–188. Springer, Heidelberg (2013). https://doi.org/10.1007/978-3-642-53917-6_16
32. Bai, S., Kolter, J.Z., Koltun, V.: An empirical evaluation of generic convolutional and recurrent networks for sequence modeling. arXiv preprint arXiv:1803.01271 (2018)
33. Su, Q., Chen, L.: A method for discovering clusters of e-commerce interest patterns using click-stream data. Electron. Commer. Res. Appl. **14**(1), 1–13 (2015)
34. Chen, Y., et al.: Intent contrastive learning for sequential recommendation. In: Proceedings of the ACM Web Conference 2022 (2022)
35. Li, Z., et al.: Learning the compositional visual coherence for complementary recommendations. In: IJCAI (2020)

An Optical Satellite Controller Based on Diffractive Deep Neural Network

Shaohua Liu, Hongkun Dou, Hongjue Li$^{(\boxtimes)}$, and Yue Deng

School of Astronautics, Beihang University, Beijing, China
{liushaohua,douhk,lihongjue,ydeng}@buaa.edu.cn

Abstract. Formulated as an optimal control problem, space relative trajectory planning is crucial for on-orbit servicing spacecraft on various missions. While a variety of deep-neural-network (DNN) methods have been proposed to solve the problem, they are energy-consuming and computationally consuming, which limits their on-board deployments. In this work, we proposed a kind of diffractive-deep-neural-network-based optical satellite controller, and transformed the solution of the optimal control problem into a light-field-based fine-grained regression task. Firstly, an electro-optic conversion module was designed to convert numerical relative state variables from electronic signals into light field as the input of a diffractive modulation (DM) module, the diffractive masks of which could be trained to implement complex light field transformation. We used another optic-electro conversion module to convert the light field at the output plane of DM module into electronic signals. Then, we trained the DM module to make the decoded electrical signals consistent with the desired optimal control commands. Therefore, when the light carrying input information and propagating through the well-trained diffractive masks, the DM module could perform diffract-based solution of optimal control problem. The simulation results substantiate the feasibility and effectiveness of our OC-Nets, which can achieve comparable performance to the latest classic DNN methods, except for a few acceptable errors. Different from classic models with much too energy consumption, once fabricated physically, the device of our optical controller can provide optimal control commands **at the speed of light, with fairly little computational and energy consumption**, and enable the on-board deployment on spacecraft.

Keywords: Optical computing · Diffractive deep neural network · On-orbit service · Optimal control

1 Introduction

The approach and capture of an uncontrolled spacecraft (i.e., target) is the foundation of various space missions including debris removal missions and other

This work was supported in part by the National Key Research and Development Program of China under Grant 2020AAA0105500, in part by the National Natural Science Foundation of China under Grant 61971020 and Grant 62031001.

L. Fang et al. (Eds.): CICAI 2022, LNAI 13605, pp. 46–58, 2022.
https://doi.org/10.1007/978-3-031-20500-2_4

on-orbit service [27]. At the approaching stage, a chaser spacecraft (i.e., chaser) is supposed to approach the target as fast as possible with as possible as little fuel consumption. In order to achieve this, relative trajectory planning is usually implemented to find an optimal approach trajectory. The planning problem can further be formulated as an optimal control problem whose solution is often fuel-optimal, time-optimal, or hybrid-optimal. A variety of numerical methods have been proposed to solve the optimal control problem [4,23]. However, due to the limited on-board computational resources of the chaser, numerical methods are often too **computationally costly** [9,21] and **time-consuming** to achieve optimal real-time control.

The development of machine learning makes it possible to realize **real-time optimal control**. Especially, deep learning has reached excellent standards in solving many leading-edge artificial intelligence problems like computational vision tasks [11,12], function regression tasks [7,15] as well as optimal control problems in aerospace field like landing problems [17,24,33] and trajectory planning [16,30]. In these applications, a large number of optimal state-control pairs are generated by conventional numerical approaches and regarded as training samples to be learned by deep neural network (DNN) models. After that, the well-trained DNNs can predict a trajectory and provide optimal control commands in real-time. However, **plenty of computational consumption** and **too much energy consumption** impede the on-board deployment of classic DNN algorithms on spacecraft.

Recently, a kind of all-optical diffractive deep neural network (D^2NN) has been proposed and demonstrated at the software [14,22] and hardware level [5,18,19,34]. The all-optical intelligent computing has excellent advantages including **higher parallelization capacity**, **lower power consumption** and **light-speed signal inference**. It provides a new idea for the on-board deployment of classic DNN methods with lower energy consumption, lower computational consumption and higher inference speed. The effectiveness of D^2NN-based models has been validated in many tasks such as image classification [8,10,25], pulse shaping [29], 3D object recognition [26] and saliency detection [32]. However, most applications mentioned above are coarse-grained tasks where only the location or broad outline of the region with maximum light intensity at output plane is required, but our problem is a fine-grained task requiring to convert the continuous state/control variables into the light field at the input/output plane and decode the light intensity of each region at the output plane into a continuous value of the desired control variable. Therefore, directly using the D^2NN-based models to solve the optimal control problem still faces difficulties.

To overcome the aforementioned difficulties such as computational consumption and energy consumption, we proposed a series of D^2NN-based optical satellite controller networks (OC-Nets) to achieve real-time low-energy trajectory planning and optimal control. The solution of optimal control problem was transformed into a light-field-based fine-grained regression task. Firstly, we introduced customized electro-optic (EO) conversion modules to convert the continuous state/control variables from the form of electronic signals into the light field at the input/output plane. In our diffractive modulation (DM) module, the diffractive masks with learnable parameters were trained to regress the complex mapping between light field from the input plane to the output plane. Then, propagating through multiple well-trained diffractive masks, the light carrying the input information could undergo diffract-based solution of optimal control problem. At the output plane, we used another optic-electro (OE) conversion module to obtain the continuous electronic values of the predicted control variables from the light field. Once well-trained and fabricated physically, the device of the DM module can inference by the propagation of light, with nearly no computational consumption and energy consumption. Only the conversion modules require a little computational resource, which is much less than classic DNN models. For on-orbit missions, the device of our optical controller can provide optimal control commands **at the speed of light, with fairly little computational and energy consumption**. Overall, we summarize our contributions as follows.

- To the best of our knowledge, we are the first to introduce the principles of the D^2NN to address optimal control problems. We propose a series of novel and general optical controller networks, OC-Nets, and demonstrate their effectiveness in satellite control scenarios.
- We design the EO module and OE module, which allow D^2NN-based models to perform fine-grained tasks like regressing the light field to output continuous variables.
- Experimental results show that our OC-Net can achieve comparable performance to the latest classic DNN methods and has the advantage of ultra-low energy consumption and light-speed inference, except for a few acceptable errors.

2   Methods

2.1   Problem Formulation

Figure 1 shows a common approaching stage during a chaser approaching and capturing a target. During approaching, the relative state between the two spacecraft obeys a series of dynamic equations including the relative orbit dynamic [28], relative orbit kinematics [1], relative attitude kinematics [31] and attitude dynamic equations [20]. All the dynamic equations can be uniformly described as

$$\dot{X} = f(X, U) \tag{1}$$

with 12-dimensional relative state variable $X = [\Delta r, \Delta v, \Delta \theta, \Delta \omega]$ representing relative position, relative velocity, relative Euler angular and relative Euler angular velocity between the chaser and the target, and 6-dimensional control variable U of the chaser, where $U = [U_F, U_M]$ representing 3-axes control force $U_F = [F_x, F_y, F_z]$ and 3-axes control torque $U_M = [M_x, M_y, M_z]$.

Given an initial relative state X_0 and a final relative state X_n, there exist a lot of approaching trajectories to choose. Under a goal like minimizing time

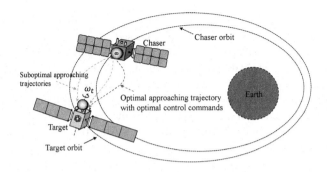

Fig. 1. Illustration of a common approaching stage mission scenario. The uncontrolled target has a spin velocity of ω_t.

consumption when approaching, the core problem of the approaching mission is to calculate the optimal approaching trajectory as quickly and accurately as possible. The trajectory planning problem can further be formulated as an optimal control problem. And the problem can be expressed to optimize the control variable $\boldsymbol{U}$, which makes the system described by dynamic equations Eq. 1 to move from $\boldsymbol{X_0}$ toward $\boldsymbol{X_n}$, under multiple constraints while keeping the objective function $\boldsymbol{L}$ optimal (i.e., minimal time to approach). Generally, the optimal control problem can be solved by the Gauss Pseudospectral Method (GPM), which can be implemented by a well-developed toolbox named GPOPS-II [21]. The optimal solutions generates by GPM has been proved to be very close to the true optimal ones [2,3]. Therefore, we chose GPM to generate training samples and took the solutions as our ground truth.

2.2   Optical Controller Framework

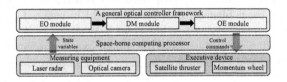

Fig. 2. A general optical controller framework with its application scenarios.

Figure 2 shows a general optical controller framework, which mainly consists of the electro-optic signal conversion module (EO module), the diffractive modulation module (DM module), and the optic-electro signal conversion module (OE module), etc.

EO Module. It plays an encoder role in the framework. The relative state variable $\boldsymbol{X} = [\Delta r_x, \Delta r_y, \Delta r_z, \Delta v_x, \Delta v_y, \Delta v_z, \Delta \theta_x, \Delta \theta_y, \Delta \theta_z, \Delta \omega_x, \Delta \omega_y, \Delta \omega_z]$ is encoded from electronic signals into the light field as the input of the DM module. In practice, the EO module is mainly composed of laser generator, expander, spatial light modulator (SLM), Digital Micromirror Device (DMD) and so on. Here, we choose the amplitude-encoding mode at the input plane. As Fig. 3(a) shows, the input plane is divided into the background region and another 12 sub-coding regions (sub-regions) corresponding to 12 components of the relative state variable X. The light intensity outside the coding region is set to zero. And the light intensity in each sub-region ranges from 0 to 1 and follows a linear mapping function:

$$I_{in,i} = (x_i - x_{i,min})/(x_{i,max} - x_{i,min}) \tag{2}$$

where $x_{i,max}$ and $x_{i,min}$ represent the maximum and minimum value of the ith component of relative state variable X (e.g., 1st, 3rd, and 7th represents Δr_x, Δr_z, and $\Delta \theta_x$, respectively) in the dataset. x_i represents the current observed value of the ith component of X. And, $I_{in,i}$ represents the light intensity of the ith sub-region corresponding to the ith component of X. For instance, the observed value of x_1 (i.e., Δr_x) is 9.7, and the $x_{1,max}$ and $x_{1,min}$ are 10.0 and 2.5, respectively. Therefore, the light intensity of the 1st sub-region (i.e., $I_{in,1}$) is 0.96 according to Eq. 2.

OE Module. It plays a decoder role. Given the specific relative state X, the light field at the output plane of the DM module can be captured and decoded into the predicted value of the specified control variable. For simplicity, we only built the predictor of the control force $U_F = [F_x, F_y, F_z]$. As Fig. 3(c) and Fig. 3(d) show, we designed two kinds of OE modules outputting 1 and 3 control variables, respectively.

Take the OE-3 module as an example, the light intensity of the whole output plane ranges from 0 to 1. Similar to the EO module, the output plane is also divided into the background region and another 3 sub-decoding regions (sub-regions) corresponding to the 3 components of control variable U_F. For each sub-region, a detector is placed to capture the light intensity $\tilde{I}_{out,i}$ at the corresponding sub-region, and generate a 256 color gray scale (8 bit quantized) image covered range of 20×20 pixels. And the global average intensity $\bar{I}_{out,i}$ can be calculated by the global average pooling (i.e., GAP) operation as Eq. 3 shows.

$$\bar{I}_{out,i} = GAP(\frac{\lfloor \tilde{I}_{out,i} \times 256 \rfloor}{255}) \tag{3}$$

Then, the desirable value of U_F can be obtained according to

$$\tilde{u}_i = \begin{cases} u_{i,max} & if \ \bar{I}_{out,i} \geq 1 \\ \bar{I}_{out,i} \times (u_{i,max} - u_{i,min}) + u_{i,min} & otherwise \end{cases} \tag{4}$$

where $u_{i,max}$ and $u_{i,min}$ represent the maximum and minimum values of the i_{th} component of U_F (e.g., 1st and 3rd represents F_x and F_z, respectively) in the dataset. $\tilde{u}_i$ is the desirable continuous value of the i_{th} component of U_F.

In practice, Charge Coupled Device (CCD) or Complementary Metal-Oxide-Semiconductor Transistor (CMOS) can be chosen as the detector.

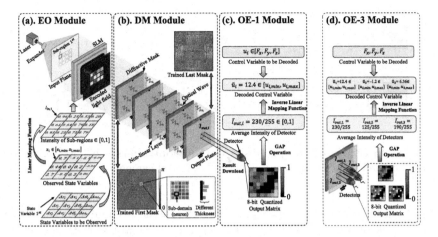

Fig. 3. Basic working mechanism of the proposed optical controller.(a) The encoding mechanism of EO module. (b)The propagation mechanism of light in DM module.(c) The decoding mechanism of OE-1 module with 1 detector. (d) The decoding mechanism of OE-3 module with 3 detectors.

DM Module. As Fig. 3(b) shows, the core of the DM module is multiple composite blocks, each of which consists of a diffractive mask and a non-linear layer. Each diffractive mask can further be divided in a number of sub-domains, and the sub-domain with different thickness can achieve different degree of phase modulation for the light field reaching it. Just like the learnable weights of neurons connecting the adjacent layers in a fully connected network, the thickness of each sub-domain is learnable. Thus we also refer to the sub-domain as neuron. The non-linear layer is typically realized by the strontium barium niobate (SBN) ferroelectric thin film [6], the refractive index of which changes with the intensity of the incident light. Similar to the activation function in a fully connected network, the SBN film can perform complex activation operations for the light field. The multiple composite blocks are spaced evenly in the free space between the input and output planes. The learnable parameters (i.e., the thickness of each neuron) of all diffractive masks can be trained to regress complex nonlinear transformations between light field of the input plane and the output.

Therefore, we can train the DM module to solve the optimal control problem in the term of a light-field-based regression task. Once well-trained, the DM module can transform the light carrying relative state variable signals into the light carrying desired optimal control signals.

2.3 Architecture of the Optical Controller

Firstly, as Fig. 4(a) shows, we combined the EO-3 module with 5 diffractive composite blocks to build a multiple-outputs optical force controller, referred to as OC-Net(m). Like other classic DNN models, the values of all the 3 components of $U_F = [F_x, F_y, F_z]$ could be obtained at once. Further, we combined the EO-1

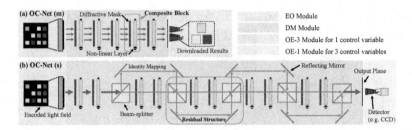

Fig. 4. Architecture of the proposed optical controllers. The OC-Net(m) can output 3 control variables at once, while the OC-Net(s) can only output one.

module with 10 composite blocks, and introduced the residual structure [8] to build a single-output optical force controller, referred to as OC-Net(s), as shown in Fig. 4(b). The OC-Net(s) can only output 1 component (e.g., F_x) of U_F at once, thus we trained 3 different OC-Net(s)s to get all the 3 components of U_F.

All optical controller networks were implemented under the wavelength of 532 nm, by setting 400×400 optical neurons at each diffractive mask with neuron size of $1\,\mu m$. The distance between adjacent composite blocks was set to $100\,\mu m$, and the distance between the non-linear layer and diffractive mask in one composite block was also set to $100\,\mu m$. The whole input plane consisted of 300×300 neurons, and each sub-region covered 20×20 neurons. The whole output plane consisted of 400×400 neurons, and each sub-region covered the range of 10×10 neurons.

2.4   Optimization of the Optical Controller

Before training, we could use the GPM to solve the optimal control problem as described in Problem Formulation, and generate a large quantity of state-control pairs (i.e., $\{X, U_F\}$ pairs) as training samples. When training the DM module, given a X, the actual light field at the output plane is labeled as $\tilde{I}_{out}$. Meanwhile, the ground truth of the regression task can be defined as the expected light field I_{out}, where the intensity of the background region is set to 0 and the expected intensity of the i_{th} sub-region can be obtained through the inverse linear mapping function:

$$I_{out,i} = (u_i - u_{i,min})/(u_{i,max} - u_{i,min}) \tag{5}$$

where u_i represents the numerical value of the i_{th} component of U_F in the $\{X, U_F\}$ pair.

Here, the mean square error (MSE) between $\tilde{I}_{out}$ and I_{out} was chosen to be the loss function, which could evaluate the training performance and guide the optimization direction of our proposed models.

3   Experiments

3.1   Dataset Description

As Fig. 1 shows, both the two spacecraft were regarded as rigid bodies flying in geostationary orbit. In this work, the chaser, which is scheduled to perform the approaching mission, is a satellite with a mass of 100 kg and all three principal axes of inertia of 100 kg·m². And the target is an 800 kg communication satellite with a principal axis of inertia of 800 kg·m². The target at an absolute angular velocity within the range of $[0.022, 0.0374]$ rad·s^{-1}. It mainly rotates its y and z axes, and simultaneously rotates around its x axis at a very low angular velocity with an uncertain direction. Under the hybrid-optimal goal about time consumption and fuel consumption, the chaser approached the target from approximately 9 m far away. Based on 97 different initial conditions randomly selected from the Table 1, 97 optimal trajectories and their corresponding optimal control commands could be obtained by GPM and the hierarchical optimization mentioned in [16]. Each trajectory consists of 249 discrete states and control variables, and together our dataset consists of $249 \times 97 = 24153\{\boldsymbol{X}, \boldsymbol{U}_F\}$ pairs. We use the first 87 trajectories as the training set, 5 trajectories for verification, and the remain 5 trajectories for test to ensure that there was no data leakage.

Table 1. Range of the initial conditions for the approaching mission.

Variable	Range	Variable	Range
$\Delta r_x, m$	$[8.0, 10.0]$	$\Delta v_x, m \cdot s^{-1}$	0.0
$\Delta r_y, m$	$[-0.5, 0.5]$	$\Delta v_y, m \cdot s^{-1}$	0.0
$\Delta r_z, m$	$[-0.5, 0.5]$	$\Delta v_z, m \cdot s^{-1}$	0.0
$\Delta \theta_x, rad$	0.0	$\Delta \omega_x, rad \cdot s^{-1}$	$[0.00, 0.04]$
$\Delta \theta_y, rad$	0.0	$\Delta \omega_y, rad \cdot s^{-1}$	$[0.00, 0.03]$
$\Delta \theta_z, rad$	0.0	$\Delta \omega_z, rad \cdot s^{-1}$	$[-0.02, 0.02]$

3.2   Experimental Settings

Evaluation Metrics. During inference, the real output of our optical controller is the numerical value decoded from the light field at the output plane of the DM module. Therefore, the normalized mean square error (NMSE) between u_i and $\tilde{u}_i$ was chosen to evaluate generalization performance of our proposed methods.

Baselines. We compare our optical controller networks(OC-Nets) with several latest DNN methods which introduced classic DNN models to solve the energy-consuming or time-consuming problems in the aerospace field, including on-orbit service mission(AUS-Net [16]), fuel-optimal powered landing guidance(PLG-Net [17]), real-time trajectory optimization for collision-free asteroid landing(AL-Net [33]) and real-time trajectory optimization hypersonic vehicles(HV-Net [30]).

Parameter Settings. Our models were implemented using Python 3.6.13 and Tensorflow 1.15.1. We used Adam [13] optimizer to train our models for 80 epochs until convergence, with an initial learning rate of 0.001 and a batch size of 10. All the baseline methods were conducted under the Python 3.7.9 and Pytorch 1.7.1 framework with the same optimizer, learning rate, training epochs and batch size as our methods. The hardware platform is a server with Intel(R) Xeon(R) Gold 6226R CPU @2.90 GHz, GeForce RTX 3090 Graphical Processing Unit GPU and 256 GB of RAM, running an Ubuntu 18.04 operating system.

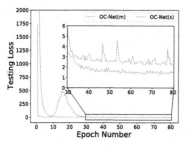

(a) Test Loss correspond to epochs during training

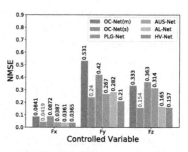

(b) NMSE of different models

Fig. 5. (a) Convergence plots of the OC-Nets and (b) performance comparisons of different models.

3.3   Experimental Results

Quantitative Analysis. Figure 5(a) shows that the proposed OC-Nets had obtained good and stable convergence after 80 epochs of training. All subsequent analyses were conducted on the test set. Under the same parameters settings, the quantitative performance of our models and baseline models is shown in Fig. 5(b). Compared with OC-Net(m), the NMSE of our OC-Net(s) decreased by nearly 50%. One reason is that, with the number of detectors at the output plane reduced from 3 to 1, the convergence of the light filed at the output plane was significantly enhanced, which effectively alleviated the dissipation of light during the propagation. The other reason is that, by introducing 5 more diffractive composite blocks and the residual structure, the further increase of depth of OC-Net(s) also brought about the effective improvement of its ability to fit complex nonlinear functions. Among baseline models, the AUS-Net, the application scenario of which is similar with that of our paper, was unable to achieve ideal results. In comparison to the HV-Net, which has the best overall performance of all baseline models reported in Fig. 5(b), our OC-Net(s) also had acceptable performance and even leaded the performance in predicting the value of the F_z.

Overall, the performance of our method was not inferior to that of the latest classic DNN methods.

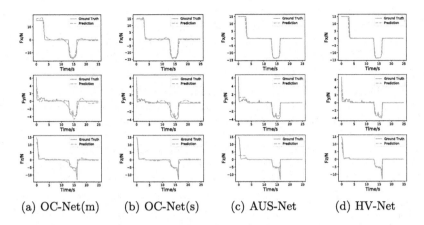

(a) OC-Net(m)   (b) OC-Net(s)   (c) AUS-Net   (d) HV-Net

Fig. 6. The visualization of the performance of our proposed models and the baselines. The optimal control commands were generated by (a) OC-Net(m), (b) OC-Net(s), (c) AUS-Net and (d)HV-Net. The ground truth belonged to the 2^{ed} trajectory of the test set (i.e., the 94th trajectory of the whole dataset)

Visualization and Qualitative Analysis. We visually compare the prediction of optimal control commands of our OC-Nets with those of baseline models in Fig. 6. Different from OC-Net(m), the prediction of OC-Net(s) became significantly better and stably, especially at the moment of sudden change in control force. And its prediction was basically consistent with the ground truth. The AUS-Net could not predict the high values of the F_y and F_z at the initial stage, and even gave relatively low outputs, as shown in Fig. 6(c). And the HV-Net still provided the nearly same visual output as the ground truth.

On the whole, OC-Net(s), the best one of our proposed optical controller models, could achieve similar performance to the HV-Net, one of the latest and best classic DNN methods, except for a few acceptable errors.

Ablation Study. We perform ablation studies to demonstrate the effectiveness of each module in our methods, and the results are shown in Table 2. Removing the non-linear layer, the significantly worse performance of the OC-Net(m) indicates that the application of non-linear layer is critical to improving the performance of the diffractive neural network in fitting nonlinear complex function scenarios. Under the condition that there was no residual structure and only 5 composite blocks, the OC-Net(s) still achieved better performance than the OC-Net(m). It may be because that the reducing the number of detectors at the output plane can significantly enhance the convergence of the light field, alleviate the dissipation of light during the propagation and strengthen the predictive capabilities of networks. However, without residual structure, simply increasing the number of composite blocks from 5 to 10, could not lead to significant performance improvements, even the prediction of F_x and F_z became worse due to more loss of light in propagation between more blocks. Only when the residual structure was introduced, the performance of the deeper OC-Net(s) with 5 more blocks could be further significantly improved. This also confirmed the importance of the residual structure to ease the dissipation of light during propagation.

Table 2. The results of ablation experiments. "NLs" means the non-linear layers, "Num of outs", means the number of outputs, "Num of CBs" means the number of composite blocks and "RS" means residual structure.

Model	NLs	Num of outs	Num of CBs	RS	NMSE ↓		
					Fx	Fy	Fz
OC-Net(m) w/o NLs	✗	3	5	✗	0.2960	1.194	0.793
OC-Net(m)	✔	3	5	✗	0.0841	0.531	0.333
OC-Net(s) w/ RS w/ 5 blocks	✔	1	5	✗	0.0769	0.449	0.246
OC-Net(s) w/o RS	✔	1	10	✗	0.0814	0.389	0.325
OC-Net(s)	✔	1	10	✔	**0.0419**	**0.240**	**0.154**

4   Conclusion

In this paper, the solution of the optimal control problem about space relative trajectory planning was transformed into a light-field-based fine-grained regression task, and we proposed a series of D^2NN-based optical satellite controller networks (OC-Nets) to achieve real-time low-energy trajectory planning and optimal control for on-orbit missions such as approaching and capturing an uncontrolled spacecraft. The simulation results of the theoretical models show that our OC-Nets can achieve comparable performance to the latest classic DNN methods, except for a few tolerable errors. Different from conventional DNN models which are facing much too computational consumption and energy consumption, once well-trained and fabricated physically, the device of our optical controller can provide optimal control commands **at the speed of light, with fairly little computational and energy consumption,** and this can enable the on-board deployment of advanced artificial intelligence algorithms on spacecraft. In the future, we will further optimize the structure of our optical network and build the hardware platform of the optical controller to verify the feasibility of its on-board application.

References

1. Bennett, T., Schaub, H.: Continuous-time modeling and control using nonsingular linearized relative-orbit elements. J. Guid. Control. Dyn. **39**(12), 2605–2614 (2016)
2. Bogacki, P., Shampine, L.F.: A 3 (2) pair of Runge-Kutta formulas. Appl. Math. Lett. **2**(4), 321–325 (1989)
3. Boyarko, G., Yakimenko, O., Romano, M.: Optimal rendezvous trajectories of a controlled spacecraft and a tumbling object. J. Guid. Control. Dyn. **34**(4), 1239–1252 (2011)

4. Bryson, A.E.: Applied Optimal Control: Optimization, Estimation and Control. CRC Press (1975)
5. Chang, J., Sitzmann, V., Dun, X., Heidrich, W., Wetzstein, G.: Hybrid optical-electronic convolutional neural networks with optimized diffractive optics for image classification. Sci. Rep. **8**(1), 1–10 (2018)
6. Christodoulides, D.N., Coskun, T.H., Mitchell, M., Segev, M.: Theory of incoherent self-focusing in biased photorefractive media. Phys. Rev. Lett. **78**(4), 646 (1997)
7. Deng, Y., Bao, F., Kong, Y., Ren, Z., Dai, Q.: Deep direct reinforcement learning for financial signal representation and trading. IEEE Trans. Neural Netw. Learn. Syst. **28**(3), 653–664 (2017). https://doi.org/10.1109/TNNLS.2016.2522401
8. Dou, H., Deng, Y., Yan, T., Wu, H., Lin, X., Dai, Q.: Residual D2NN: training diffractive deep neural networks via learnable light shortcuts. Opt. Lett. **45**(10), 2688–2691 (2020)
9. Feng, W., Han, L., Shi, L., Zhao, D., Yang, K.: Optimal control for a cooperative rendezvous between two spacecraft from determined orbits. J. Astronaut. Sci. **63**(1), 23–46 (2016)
10. Gu, Z., Gao, Y., Liu, X.: Optronic convolutional neural networks of multi-layers with different functions executed in optics for image classification. Opt. Express **29**(4), 5877–5889 (2021)
11. He, K., Zhang, X., Ren, S., Sun, J.: Deep residual learning for image recognition. In: Proceedings of the IEEE Conference on Computer Vision and Pattern Recognition, pp. 770–778 (2016)
12. Huang, G., Liu, S., Van der Maaten, L., Weinberger, K.Q.: ConDenseNet: an efficient DenseNet using learned group convolutions. In: Proceedings of the IEEE Conference on Computer Vision and Pattern Recognition, pp. 2752–2761 (2018)
13. Kingma, D.P., Ba, J.: Adam: a method for stochastic optimization. arXiv preprint arXiv:1412.6980 (2014)
14. Kulce, O., Mengu, D., Rivenson, Y., Ozcan, A.: All-optical information-processing capacity of diffractive surfaces. Light Sci. Appl. **10**(1), 1–17 (2021)
15. LeCun, Y., Bengio, Y., Hinton, G.: Deep learning. Nature **521**(7553), 436–444 (2015)
16. Li, H., Dong, Y., Li, P., Deng, Y.: Optimal real-time approach and capture of uncontrolled spacecraft. J. Spacecr. Rocket. **58**(6), 1762–1773 (2021)
17. Li, W., Gong, S.: Free final-time fuel-optimal powered landing guidance algorithm combing lossless convex optimization with deep neural network predictor. Appl. Sci. **12**(7), 3383 (2022)
18. Li, Y., Chen, R., Sensale-Rodriguez, B., Gao, W., Yu, C.: Real-time multi-task diffractive deep neural networks via hardware-software co-design. Sci. Rep. **11**(1), 1–9 (2021)
19. Lin, X., et al.: All-optical machine learning using diffractive deep neural networks. Science **361**(6406), 1004–1008 (2018)
20. Misra, G., Izadi, M., Sanyal, A., Scheeres, D.: Coupled orbit-attitude dynamics and relative state estimation of spacecraft near small solar system bodies. Adv. Space Res. **57**(8), 1747–1761 (2016)
21. Patterson, M.A., Rao, A.V.: GPOPS-II: a MATLAB software for solving multiple-phase optimal control problems using HP-adaptive Gaussian quadrature collocation methods and sparse nonlinear programming. ACM Trans. Math. Softw. (TOMS) **41**(1), 1–37 (2014)
22. Rahman, M.S.S., Li, J., Mengu, D., Rivenson, Y., Ozcan, A.: Ensemble learning of diffractive optical networks. Light Sci. Appl. **10**(1), 1–13 (2021)

23. Rao, A.V.: A survey of numerical methods for optimal control. Adv. Astronaut. Sci. **135**(1), 497–528 (2009)

24. Scorsoglio, A., D'Ambrosio, A., Ghilardi, L., Gaudet, B., Curti, F., Furfaro, R.: Image-based deep reinforcement meta-learning for autonomous lunar landing. J. Spacecr. Rocket. **59**(1), 153–165 (2022)

25. Shi, J., Chen, Y., Zhang, X.: Broad-spectrum diffractive network via ensemble learning. Opt. Lett. **47**(3), 605–608 (2022)

26. Shi, J., et al: Multiple-view D2NNs array (MDA): realizing robust 3D object recognition (2021)

27. Starek, J.A., Açıkmeşe, B., Nesnas, I.A., Pavone, M.: Spacecraft autonomy challenges for next-generation space missions. In: Feron, E. (ed.) Advances in Control System Technology for Aerospace Applications. LNCIS, vol. 460, pp. 1–48. Springer, Heidelberg (2016). https://doi.org/10.1007/978-3-662-47694-9_1

28. Vallado, D.A.: Fundamentals of Astrodynamics and Applications, vol. 12. Springer, Heidelberg (2001)

29. Veli, M., et al.: Terahertz pulse shaping using diffractive optical networks. In: CLEO: Science and Innovations, pp. SW3K-2. Optical Society of America (2021)

30. Wang, J., Wu, Y., Liu, M., Yang, M., Liang, H.: A real-time trajectory optimization method for hypersonic vehicles based on a deep neural network. Aerospace **9**(4), 188 (2022)

31. Xing, G.Q., Parvez, S.A.: Alternate forms of relative attitude kinematics and dynamics equations. In: Lynch, J.P. (ed.) 2001 Flight Mechanics Symposium, Greenbelt, MD, USA, pp. 83–97. NASA Goddard Space Flight Center (2001)

32. Yan, T., et al.: Fourier-space diffractive deep neural network. Phys. Rev. Lett. **123**(2), 023901 (2019)

33. Zhao, Y., Yang, H., Li, S.: Real-time trajectory optimization for collision-free asteroid landing based on deep neural networks. Adv. Space Res. (2022)

34. Zhou, T., et al.: Large-scale neuromorphic optoelectronic computing with a reconfigurable diffractive processing unit. Nat. Photonics **15**(5), 367–373 (2021)

Incomplete Cigarette Code Recognition via Unified SPA Features and Graph Space Constraints

Huiming Ding[1], Zhifeng Xie[1(✉)], Jundong Lai[2], Yanmin Xu[3], and Lizhuang Ma[4]

[1] Shanghai University, Shanghai, China
zhifeng_xie@shu.ed.cn
[2] Shanghai Tobacco Group Co., Ltd., Shanghai, China
[3] Shanghai Tobacco Monopoly Administration, Shanghai, China
[4] Shanghai Jiao Tong University, Shanghai, China

Abstract. Cigarette code is a 32-character string printed on a cigarette package, which can be used by tobacco administrations to determine the legality of distribution. Unfortunately, the recognition task for incomplete cigarette code often suffers from lowered recognition accuracy and the destruction of semantic context due to complex backgrounds and damaged characters. This paper proposes an end-to-end recognition network for incomplete cigarette code to improve recognition accuracy and estimate character landmarks. The proposed network first extracts multi-scale features using feature pyramid networks (FPN), then utilizes a spatial attention (SPA) mechanism to yield unified SPA features and integrates them into instance segmentation. This strengthens spatial representation ability and improves the recognition accuracy. A graph convolutional network (GCN) is introduced to construct graph space constraints and calculate character spatial correlations and accurately estimates missing character landmarks. Finally, we employ the Hungarian algorithm to align recognition characters with estimated landmarks and fill missing characters with '*' to preserve the complete semantic context, and produce the final regularized cigarette code. The experimental results demonstrate that our proposed network reduces time consumption and improves recognition accuracy, surpassing the state-of-the-art methods.

Keywords: Cigarette code recognition · Spatial attention mechanism · Graph convolutional network · Deep learning

1 Introduction

Cigarette code is a 32-character string printed onto cigarette packages, which contain information including the production date, the manufacturer, and the cigarette retail store, often used by tobacco administration to determine the

L. Fang et al. (Eds.): CICAI 2022, LNAI 13605, pp. 59–70, 2022.
https://doi.org/10.1007/978-3-031-20500-2_5

(a)   (b)   (c)   (d)

Fig. 1. Recognition task for cigarette code. (a) example incomplete cigarette code with complex background and damaged characters; (b) recognized cigarette code result without damaged characters; (c) estimated cigarette code landmarks including damaged characters; (d) final recognized result with 32 characters, where missing characters are filled by '*'.

legality of distribution [28,29]. Unfortunately, the recognition task for cigarette code suffers from many difficulties such as complex backgrounds, blurred printing, damaged characters, and even large broken areas, which greatly reduce the accuracy of character recognition. Missing character landmarks need to be estimated to produce a 32-character code with complete semantic correlation. As shown in Fig. 1, when given a source image of incomplete cigarette code, the recognition task first recognizes undamaged characters, then estimates full character landmarks, including those of damaged characters. Finally, the recognized characters and estimated landmarks are regularized to yield an 32-character cigarette code where any missing characters are filled by '*'.

The recognition of incomplete cigarette code can be divided into two subtasks: character recognition and landmark estimation. Current character recognition methods [8,15,17] have difficulty dealing with complex backgrounds and blurred printing to construct the spatial semantic context of full characters for incomplete cigarette code. Meanwhile, methods [6,22,27–31] were unable to establish the spatial correlation between characters for incomplete cigarette code in the process of landmark estimation.

To address the above problems, this paper proposes a recognition network for incomplete cigarette code based on unified spatial attention (SPA) features and graph space constraints. The network architecture is divided into four modules, as shown in Fig. 2: (1) Feature Extraction. We use the residual network (ResNet) [5] and feature pyramid network (FPN) [11] to extract multi-scale features of incomplete cigarette code. (2) Instance Segmentation. Inspired by 'SOLOv2' [24], we introduce a spatial attention mechanism to yield unified SPA features, which enhance the spatial representation for characters and backgrounds. (3) Landmark Estimation. We first estimate initial landmarks using integral regression based on the unified SPA features. We then construct graph space constraints based on graph convolutional network (GCN) [6] to optimize the spatial correlation between characters, and therefore can accurately estimate the full character landmarks. (4) Text Regularization. The Hungarian algorithm [7] is introduced to align the instance segmentation results and estimated landmarks.

In addition, we construct and execute experiments on a dataset containing 15,000 images of incomplete cigarette code, including missing characters,

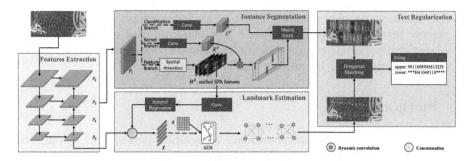

Fig. 2. The network architecture of our recognition network for incomplete cigarette code consists of four modules: (1) Features Extraction; (2) Instance Segmentation; (3) Landmark Estimation; (4) Text Regularization.

complex background, and blurred printing. The experimental results demonstrate that our proposed method can accurately recognize characters, effectively estimate the landmarks, and produce the recognized result of cigarette code with 32 characters.

2 Related Work

Some popular techniques relevant to the recognition task for incomplete cigarette code can be classified into three categories: text recognition, landmark estimation, and graph convolutional networks.

Recognition methods based on deep learning are widely used in complex scenes [1,8,15,17,28,29]. However, the performances of these methods were weak for incomplete cigarette code because of the complex backgrounds and blurred printing. Otherwise, attention mechanisms have been used in some studies [10,14,18] to draw attention to channel and spatial dimensions, which can strengthen feature representation and improve text recognition performance. To this end, inspired by SOLOv2 [25], in this paper we introduce a spatial attention mechanism to yield unified SPA features, and strengthen the spatial representation for characters and backgrounds.

Incomplete cigarette code recognition requires landmark estimation for both present and missing characters. State-of-the-art methods for landmark estimation [2,22,23,26] have been applied mainly to face localization and human pose estimation. They introduced heatmap-supervised [23], multi-stage supervised training [26], multi-scale features [2] to estimate landmarks. Notably, Sun et al. [22] reconsidered the task of human pose estimation using an integral regression perspective that can generate joint coordinates from heatmap. Inspired by this, in this study we apply integral regression to generate the initial character landmarks for further GCN-based optimization.

Character correlation can be modelled as a graph-based relationship, which can be learned using GCN [6,30]. GCN-based landmark estimation works [3,31] usually built graph neural networks through a prior graph node relationship to achieve better detection performance. Therefore, we have employed GCN to construct graph space constraints for the 32 cigarette code characters to improve landmark estimation for incomplete cigarette code.

3   Method

In this paper, we propose an end-to-end recognition network for incomplete cigarette code which can: accurately recognize characters using multi-scale SPA features; estimate full-character landmarks by constraining the character spatial correlation; and produce recognition results with semantic context. As shown in Fig. 2, the network is divided into feature extraction, instance segmentation, landmark estimation, and text regularization modules.

3.1   Features Extraction Using FPN

The FPN structure can effectively extract the multi-scale features of an incomplete cigarette code to obtain the character location and semantic information [11]. We use ResNet [5] as the bottom-up part for forwarding features from the image to the top-down part. The top-down part applies layer-by-layer upsampling and lateral connection operations to the feature maps to obtain multi-scale features from P_2 to P_5. P_2 features are the stronger of these features for locational representation and the weaker for semantic representation in the image, while P_5 behaves oppositely. The feature extraction module can effectively utilize character location and semantic information from input images to provide multi-scale features for the instance segmentation and landmark estimation modules.

3.2   Instance Segmentation via Unified SPA Features

In instance segmentation module, the multi-scale features P_i, $i \in [2, 5]$ are first distributed to classification, kernel, and feature branches. A dynamic convolutional operation is then introduced to produce masks. Lastly, we employ a matrix non-maximum suppression (Matrix NMS) [25] to produce instances of the incomplete cigarette code.

In classification branch, each feature P_i is aligned to the cell $s_i \times s_i$, where s_i is the number of x-axis and y-axis for input image, and obtain $F_i^C \in \mathbb{R}^{s_i \times s_i \times d}$, where d is the channel of the input image. After four convolutional operations, the features C_i are aligned into the category feature shape $s_i \times s_i \times n$, where n is the category number. Finally, the features C_i are concatenated from different scales into feature $C^F \in \mathbb{R}^{s^2 \times n}$, where s is the summation of s_i.

In kernel branch, we introduce the coordinate convolution [13] into feature P_i to improve the mask spatial representation. After similar operations in the classification branch, the mask kernel $K^F \in \mathbb{R}^{s^2 \times e}$ is predicted, where e is the channel number of the mask kernel.

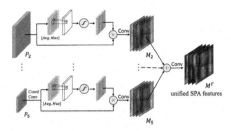

Fig. 3. Unified SPA features. Spatial attention mechanism is introduced to yield unified SPA features and strengthen the spatial representation for characters and backgrounds.

As shown in Fig. 3, we employ a spatial attention mechanism in the mask feature branch to strengthen the representation of cigarette code spatial features, and unify the multi-scale SPA features to generate the final mask features. The SPA features can be calculated as follows:

$$F_i^{spa} = \sigma(f(AvgPool(F_i^M) \odot MaxPool(F_i^M))), \tag{1}$$

where σ denotes the sigmoid function, $f(\cdot)$ is the convolutional operation, and $\odot$ denotes concatenatal operation. The input feature F_i^M is equal to P_i if $i < 5$. Since the feature P_5 lacks the location information, the coordinate convolution is added to the input feature F_5^M. The unified SPA features M^F is calculated as

$$M^F = Conv(\sum_{i=2}^{5} M_i) = Conv(\sum_{i=2}^{5}(f(F_i^{spa} \otimes F_i^M))), \tag{2}$$

where $\otimes$ denotes element-wise multiplication; $f(\cdot)$ is series upsample and convolutional operation to align the mask features shapes from multi-scales; M_i denotes mask feature result of ith scale; and $Conv$ is a convolutional operation. Equation 1 uses spatial attention to obtain SPA features from F_i^M. Equation 2 first employs an element-wise multiplication operation between F_i^M and F_i^{spa} to enhance the representation ability of character location features. Then the $f(\cdot)$ upsamples the SPA features until its shape matches that of P_2. Additionally, an element-wise summation for each feature M_i is performed to obtain the unified SPA features M^+. Finally, a $Conv$ operation is used to ascend dimension for M^+ to obtain the unified SPA mask features M_F for the landmark estimation.

When the kernel feature K^F and unified SPA mask feature M^F are calculated, a dynamic convolutional operation is introduced to produce the instance masks M. For each kernel feature K_z^F where $z \in [1, s^2]$, the instance mask M_k can be calculated as $M_k = K_z^F \circledast M^F$, where $\circledast$ denotes dynamic convolution.

For category feature C^F in the classification branch, we first filter out low confidence results using a 0.1 threshold and a 0.5 threshold to obtain C' and M respectively. Finally, Matrix NMS [25] is employed to obtain the final instance segmentation result from C' and M.

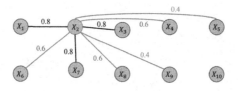

Fig. 4. Cigarette characters correlation. The black edges indicate the node's closest edge, whose weights are defined as 0.8; analogously, the weights of the green and blue edges are set to 0.6 and 0.4 respectively. If the distance between two nodes is $d \leq 3$, the value of correlation between two nodes is set to $0.2 \times (5 - d)$, otherwise is set to 0.(Color figure online)

3.3 Landmark Estimation via Graph Space Constraints

In landmark estimation module we first employ integral regression to estimate the initial landmarks of characters based on the unified SPA features, then we introduce GCN to construct graph-based space constraints that indicate the spatial correlations between individual characters.

In the integral regression process, firstly a convolutional operation is used to calculate the heatmap features from the unified SPA features M^+. Then, integral regression is performed using a discretization algorithm to generate the initial landmarks as follows:

$$X_i^{init} = \int_{p \in \Omega} (p \cdot \widetilde{F}_i^H(p)) = \sum_{x=1}^{h} \sum_{y=1}^{w} (p \cdot \widetilde{F}_i^H(p)), \tag{3}$$

where $\widetilde{F}_i^H(p)$ is the normalized heatmap feature; p is the heatmap pixel point; Ω is the heatmap pixel region of width w and height h; and X_i^{init} denotes the landmark coordinates at channel i after the discretization algorithm. As a result, the initial landmarks $X^{init} \in \mathbb{R}^{2 \times 32}$ have been calculated.

The next step is to optimize the landmarks for the graph space constraints, by introducing GCN to constrain spatial semantic correlations between the 32 characters. Firstly, we align the shape of the FPN high-level feature P_5 as $F^{sem} \in \mathbb{R}^{h'w' \times 32}$ to 32 dimensions, corresponding to 32 characters. Secondly, the feature sequence X of characters is calculated as $X = X^{init} \odot F^{sem}$, where $\odot$ denotes a concatenation operation. Finally, GCN is introduced to optimize landmarks, with a GCN operation shown as follows:

$$X' = f(X, A) = ReLU(AXW), \tag{4}$$

where X' denotes the optimized landmarks through GCN operation $f(\cdot)$; X denotes input feature sequences; A is the adjacency matrix; W denotes the GCN weights; and $ReLU$ is the activation function. The GCN weights W of GCN are updated after network training is completed. The adjacency matrix A is defined as shown in Fig. 4.

3.4 Text Regularization

The text regularization section uses the Hungarian matching algorithm to match the incomplete cigarette code recognition results with the estimated landmarks, and use '*' to fill the broken characters.

We define the mask centroids of character instances as a set X^{mask} and the estimated landmarks as a set X^{gcn}. Then our matching task is transformed into an assignment problem [20] for each $i \in X^{mask}$, $j \in X^{gcn}$. The minimization assignment between X^{mask} and X^{gcn} is expressed as:

$$R = \arg \min_{R}(\sum_{i=1}^{n} \sum_{j=1}^{n}(d_{ij} \cdot r_{ij})), i, j \in (1, 2, \cdots, n), \qquad (5)$$

where R denotes minimization matching matrix; d_{ij} is the Euclidean distance between X_i^{mask} and X_j^{gcn}; $r_{ij} \in 0, 1$ indicates the matching relationship between X_i^{mask} and X_j^{gcn}.

We introduce the Hungarian algorithm to calculate the minimization matching matrix R. Then, we use the matrix R to match outcomes from the instance segmentation and landmark estimation modules to produce the recognition result for the incomplete cigarette code. Lastly, we fill missing character locations with '*' to regularize the 32-character cigarette code recognition result.

3.5 Loss Function

In the classification branch, we introduce the Focal loss [12] to calculate the classification loss L_{cate}. In the mask kernel and mask feature branches, we employ Dice loss [19] to calculate the loss L_{mask} for the predicted mask area.

In the landmark initialization and optimization tasks, we introduce the loss function ℓ_1 loss [21] to calculate the initial landmarks loss L_{init} and optimized landmarks loss L_{opt}.

Ultimately, the overall loss function for our end-to-end recognition network is defined as:

$$L = L_{cate} + \lambda_0 L_{mask} + \lambda_1 L_{init} + \lambda_2 L_{opt}, \qquad (6)$$

where λ_0, λ_1, λ_2 denote weights of each loss function. The optimal network performance is achieved for $(\lambda_0, \lambda_1, \lambda_2)$ equal to $(3, 0.1, 1)$.

4 Experiments

In this section, we extensively evaluate the proposed recognition network for incomplete cigarette code on a dataset, containing 15,000 images of incomplete cigarette code, including missing characters, complex background, and blurred printing. Firstly, we evaluate the instance segmentation module; secondly, we evaluate the landmark estimation module; we then discuss the performance of the end-to-end network in recognizing cigarette code; in addition, we demonstrate the effectiveness of the core components through ablation experiments.

Table 1. Instance segmentation mask AP (%) on test set of incomplete cigarette code.

Method	AP	AP_{50}	AP_{75}	AP_M	AP_L
Mask R-CNN [4]	52.7	84.6	59.6	48.5	54.0
SOLOv2 [25]	53.7	83.9	59.2	48.6	54.6
Ours	**54.5**	**87.1**	**62.9**	**49.0**	**55.7**

4.1 Evaluation of Instance Segmentation

For evaluating the instance segmentation performance, we compared the Mask R-CNN [4], the SOLOv2 [25] and our method. In the instance segmentation module, we evaluated the performance metrics AP, AP_{50}, AP_{75}, AP_M, and AP_L for mask segmentation of Mask R-CNN, SOLOv2, and ours.

Table 1 shows that our instance segmentation module achieved an AP of 54.5%, which is a 1.8% and 0.8% improvement over Mask R-CNN and SOLOv2, respectively. These results demonstrate that our instance segmentation module has better performance for incomplete cigarette code.

4.2 Performance of Landmark Estimation

Our landmark estimation module introduces GCN to constrain characters in graph space and establish a spatial semantic correlation, which can effectively estimate the landmarks of incomplete cigarette code.

As shown in Fig. 5, we compared the landmark estimation performance between Wu et al. [27] and ours for multiple situations including: complex background on the first row; damaged characters on the second row; and skewed alignment on all rows. It is shown that our method obtained centered and smooth character locations.

4.3 End-to-End Performance

To evaluate the performance of our method for incomplete cigarette code, we evaluate the accuracy based on the test set. The accuracy was determined by the percentage of predicted results that correctly classified all 32 aligned characters. Our method achieves an accuracy rate of **90.2%**. Ten results of the recognition process for incomplete cigarette code are shown in Fig. 6. The results show that our network has good recognition performance for incomplete cigarette code.

As other text detection methods were incapable of recognition task for incomplete cigarette code, we used 500 images with complete cigarette code to fairly compare our method to other text recognition methods. We then evaluated each text recognition method in terms of time consumption and accuracy. The results are shown in Table 2, where time consumption is indicated by time taken to recognize one image in seconds, and accuracy by the percentage of predicted results that correctly classify 32 aligned characters. In summary, our method yields the optimal performance in both time consumption and recognition accuracy.

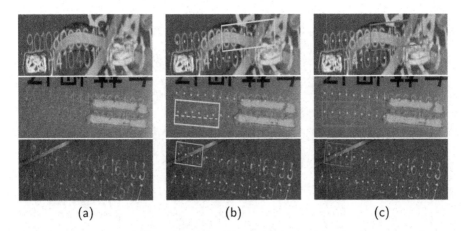

(a)   (b)   (c)

Fig. 5. Comparison of landmark estimation performance. (a) cigarette code image; (b) Wu et al. [27]; (c) ours. Locations are shown by yellow boxes for Wu et al. and green boxes for our method. Compared to Wu et al.'s method in the case of complex background, damaged characters, and skewed alignment, our method obtains centered and smooth character locations

Table 2. Comparison of recognition performance for complete cigarette code between our method and several state-of-the-art methods.

Method	Time/s	Accuracy/%
Fots [15]	0.564	69.6
Mask textspotter [9]	0.588	73.4
ABCNet [16]	0.216	71.3
Xie et al. [29]	0.636	87.4
Wu et al. [27]	0.324	90.6
Ours	**0.192**	**92.6**

4.4 Ablation Experiments

We present ablation experiments on the two key components, spatial attention mechanism and graph space constraints, to investigate the effectiveness of them.

To investigate the effectiveness of the SPA, we divided the experimental results into two cases by controlling whether to add SPA to the network, and calculated the network accuracy separately. The model achieves an accuracy of 90.2% with SPA component, while it only achieves 88.5% without SPA. The SPA component improved the character recognition accuracy by 1.7%, which proves that SPA can effectively strengthen the character representation ability.

To investigate the effectiveness of the GCN, we employed mean absolute error (MAE) and root mean square error (RMSE) to evaluate landmark estimation, and the results are shown in Table 3. The MAE and RMSE from GCN-based landmark estimation decreased by 3.978% and 2.546% respectively over

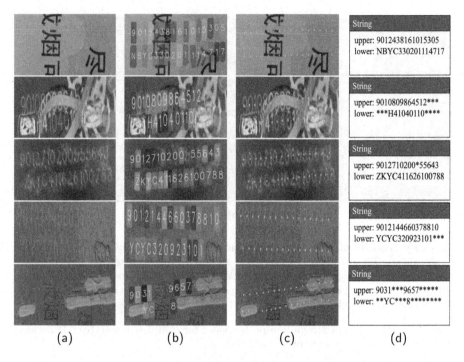

Fig. 6. Recognized results of our network. (a) cigarette code image; (b) character instances yielded from instance segmentation module; (c) character landmarks produced from landmark estimation module; (d) recognition result. Results are divided into 5 categories from top to bottom: similar color, complex background, blurred printing, damaged characters, and large broken area.

Table 3. Effectiveness of GCN.

Component	MAE	RMSE
Without GCN	0.2212	0.1807
With GCN	**0.2124**	**0.1761**

the method without GCN, indicating that GCN contributes to constructing character correlation.

5   Conclusion

In this work, we propose an end-to-end recognition network for incomplete cigarette code. The network reduces time consumption and improves recognition accuracy. Specifically, we utilize a spatial attention mechanism to yield unified SPA features, which can strengthen character and background representations, and improve the recognition accuracy; we construct graph space constraints through GCN to achieve high-accuracy landmark estimation, which can establish spatial semantic correlation between characters and estimate the land-marks effectively for incomplete cigarette code.

Acknowledgments. This work was supported by the Shanghai Natural Science Foundation of China No. 19ZR1419100.

References

1. Chen, X., Jin, L., Zhu, Y., Luo, C., Wang, T.: Text recognition in the wild: a survey. ACM Comput. Surv. **54**(2), 42:1–42:35 (2021)
2. Chen, Y., Wang, Z., Peng, Y., Zhang, Z., Yu, G., Sun, J.: Cascaded pyramid network for multi-person pose estimation. In: The IEEE Conference on Computer Vision and Pattern Recognition, pp. 7103–7112 (2018)
3. Doosti, B., Naha, S., Mirbagheri, M., Crandall, D.J.: Hope-net: a graph-based model for hand-object pose estimation. In: The IEEE Conference on Computer Vision and Pattern Recognition, pp. 6607–6616 (2020)
4. He, K., Gkioxari, G., Dollár, P., Girshick, R.B.: Mask R-CNN. In: IEEE International Conference on Computer Vision, pp. 2980–2988 (2017)
5. He, K., Zhang, X., Ren, S., Sun, J.: Deep residual learning for image recognition. In: The IEEE Conference on Computer Vision and Pattern Recognition, pp. 770–778 (2016)
6. Kipf, T.N., Welling, M.: Semi-supervised classification with graph convolutional networks. In: International Conference on Learning Representations, pp. 1–14 (2017)
7. Kuhn, H.W.: The Hungarian method for the assignment problem. In: Jünger, M., et al. (eds.) 50 Years of Integer Programming 1958-2008, pp. 29–47. Springer, Heidelberg (2010). https://doi.org/10.1007/978-3-540-68279-0_2
8. Li, H., Wang, P., Shen, C., Zhang, G.: Show, attend and read: a simple and strong baseline for irregular text recognition. In: The AAAI Conference on Artificial Intelligence, pp. 8610–8617 (2019)
9. Liao, M., Lyu, P., He, M., Yao, C., Wu, W., Bai, X.: Mask TextSpotter: an end-to-end trainable neural network for spotting text with arbitrary shapes. IEEE Trans. Pattern Anal. Mach. Intell. **43**(2), 532–548 (2021)
10. Lin, Q., Luo, C., Jin, L., Lai, S.: STAN: a sequential transformation attention-based network for scene text recognition. Pattern Recogn. **111**, 107692 (2021)
11. Lin, T., Dollár, P., Girshick, R.B., He, K., Hariharan, B., Belongie, S.J.: Feature pyramid networks for object detection. In: The IEEE Conference on Computer Vision and Pattern Recognition, pp. 936–944 (2017)
12. Lin, T., Goyal, P., Girshick, R.B., He, K., Dollár, P.: Focal loss for dense object detection. In: IEEE International Conference on Computer Vision, pp. 2999–3007 (2017)
13. Liu, R., et al.: An intriguing failing of convolutional neural networks and the CoordConv solution. In: Conference on Neural Information Processing Systems, pp. 9628–9639 (2018)
14. Liu, W., Chen, C., Wong, K.Y.K.: Char-net: a character-aware neural network for distorted scene text recognition. In: The AAAI Conference on Artificial Intelligence, pp. 7154–7161 (2018)
15. Liu, X., Liang, D., Yan, S., Chen, D., Qiao, Y., Yan, J.: FOTS: fast oriented text spotting with a unified network. In: The IEEE Conference on Computer Vision and Pattern Recognition, pp. 5676–5685 (2018)

16. Liu, Y., Chen, H., Shen, C., He, T., Jin, L., Wang, L.: ABCNet: real-time scene text spotting with adaptive Bezier-curve network. In: The IEEE Conference on Computer Vision and Pattern Recognition, pp. 9806–9815 (2020)
17. Long, S., He, X., Yao, C.: Scene text detection and recognition: the deep learning era. Int. J. Comput. Vis. **129**(1), 161–184 (2021)
18. Luo, C., Jin, L., Sun, Z.: MORAN: a multi-object rectified attention network for scene text recognition. Pattern Recogn. **90**, 109–118 (2019)
19. Milletari, F., Navab, N., Ahmadi, S.: V-net: fully convolutional neural networks for volumetric medical image segmentation. In: Fourth International Conference on 3D Vision, pp. 565–571 (2016)
20. Neumann, L., Matas, J.: A method for text localization and recognition in real-world images. In: Kimmel, R., Klette, R., Sugimoto, A. (eds.) ACCV 2010. LNCS, vol. 6494, pp. 770–783. Springer, Heidelberg (2011). https://doi.org/10.1007/978-3-642-19318-7_60
21. Shalev-Shwartz, S., Tewari, A.: Stochastic methods for l_1-regularized loss minimization. J. Mach. Learn. Res. **12**, 1865–1892 (2011)
22. Sun, X., Xiao, B., Wei, F., Liang, S., Wei, Y.: Integral human pose regression. In: Ferrari, V., Hebert, M., Sminchisescu, C., Weiss, Y. (eds.) ECCV 2018. LNCS, vol. 11210, pp. 536–553. Springer, Cham (2018). https://doi.org/10.1007/978-3-030-01231-1_33
23. Tompson, J., Goroshin, R., Jain, A., LeCun, Y., Bregler, C.: Efficient object localization using convolutional networks. In: The IEEE Conference on Computer Vision and Pattern Recognition, pp. 648–656 (2015)
24. Wang, X., Kong, T., Shen, C., Jiang, Y., Li, L.: SOLO: segmenting objects by locations. In: Vedaldi, A., Bischof, H., Brox, T., Frahm, J.-M. (eds.) ECCV 2020. LNCS, vol. 12363, pp. 649–665. Springer, Cham (2020). https://doi.org/10.1007/978-3-030-58523-5_38
25. Wang, X., Zhang, R., Kong, T., Li, L., Shen, C.: SOLOv2: dynamic and fast instance segmentation. In: Conference on Neural Information Processing Systems, pp. 1–12 (2020)
26. Wei, S., Ramakrishna, V., Kanade, T., Sheikh, Y.: Convolutional pose machines. In: The IEEE Conference on Computer Vision and Pattern Recognition, pp. 4724–4732 (2016)
27. Wu, P., Zhou, Z., Huang, J., Xie, Z., Sheng, B.: Multi-scale feature fusion for incomplete cigarette code recognition. J. Comput.-Aided Des. Comput. Graph. **33**(5), 780–788 (2021)
28. Xie, Z., Wu, J., Zhang, S., Tang, Z., Fan, J., Ma, L.: Intelligent recognition method for cigarette code based on deep neural networks. J. Comput.-Aided Des. Comput. Graph. **31**(1), 111–117 (2019)
29. Xie, Z.-F., Zhang, S.-H., Wu, P.: CNN-based erratic cigarette code recognition. In: Zhao, Y., Barnes, N., Chen, B., Westermann, R., Kong, X., Lin, C. (eds.) ICIG 2019. LNCS, vol. 11901, pp. 245–255. Springer, Cham (2019). https://doi.org/10.1007/978-3-030-34120-6_20
30. Xie, Z., Zhang, W., Sheng, B., Li, P., Chen, C.L.P.: BaGFN: broad attentive graph fusion network for high-order feature interactions. IEEE Trans. Neural Netw. Learn. Syst. Early Access 1–15 (2021)
31. Xin, M., Mo, S., Lin, Y.: EVA-GCN: head pose estimation based on graph convolutional networks. In: The IEEE Conference on Computer Vision and Pattern Recognition, pp. 1462–1471 (2021)

A Large-Scale Tobacco 3D Bin Packing Model Based on Dual-Task Learning of Group Blocks

Xudong Liu[1,2] and Haosong Wang[1,2(✉)]

[1] Faculty of Information Technology, Beijing University of Technology, Chaoyang District, Beijing 100124, People's Republic of China
`wanghs@emails.bjut.edu.cn`
[2] Key Laboratory of Computational Intelligence and Intelligent Systems, Chaoyang District, Beijing 100124, People's Republic of China

Abstract. Aiming at the large-scale and weak heterogeneity in the tobacco cargo packing problem, this paper proposes a large-scale 3D Bin Packing model based on Dual-Task Learning of Group Blocks (GB-DTL). According to the Tobacco orders and vehicle information, the group block algorithm generates the group block set of the order. GB-DTL divides tobacco cargo packing into two tasks. The first task selects the next placed group block according to the hidden state of the vehicle environment, and the second task chooses the vehicle space to place the group block based on the first task and the hidden state. The experimental results show that GB-DTL can handle the tobacco packing problem of thousands of cargoes. By comparing with the Deep Reinforcement Learning (DRL) model for single cargo placement, GB-DTL has learned a better packing strategy. The mean vehicle full load ratio increased by 13.43%, and the mean cargo gap ratio reduced by 15.13%.

Keywords: Tobacco packing problem · 3D-Bin packing problem · Deep Reinforcement Learning · Group block · Dual task

1 Introduction

The 3D bin packing problem (3D-BPP) is one of the most interesting problems in logistics and manufacturing. As a classic combinatorial optimization problem and NP-hard problem [1], the purpose of the 3D-BPP is to find an optimal placement strategy to place cubes of different sizes in a minimum number of containers. Since the 3D-BPP is NP-hard, using an exact solution algorithm such as [2] will cause the phenomenon of dimension explosion, so there is no optimal solution algorithm with polynomial time complexity [3]. Researchers mainly solve this problem by designing heuristic or meta-heuristic algorithms, including the construction heuristic algorithm based on extreme points [4], and the heuristic algorithm based on local guided search [5]. The 3D-BPP with weak heterogeneity is mainly solved by constructing walls or blocks [6–10]. [11] proposed a two-level tabu search algorithm to optimize the number of containers used and the

L. Fang et al. (Eds.): CICAI 2022, LNAI 13605, pp. 71–83, 2022.
https://doi.org/10.1007/978-3-031-20500-2_6

placement of cargoes respectively. [12] proposed a greedy randomized adaptive search algorithm to find the optimal placement space.

The above-mentioned heuristic or meta-heuristic algorithms often require experts in specific fields to manually design corresponding strategies according to different problems, and the quality of solutions is limited by the prior knowledge of experts. In contrast, learning-based methods learn optimal policies autonomously and interactively with the environment by maximizing the reward function. With the development of artificial intelligence in recent years, reinforcement learning methods have been widely used in the field of combinatorial optimization. [13] utilized pointer networks [14] to solve classical combinatorial optimization problems such as TSP and knapsack problem.

Since the quality of the solution to the 3D-BPP is mainly determined by three factors: the order, position and direction of the cargoes. [15] inspired by the pointer network, and applied the reinforcement learning algorithm based on the pointer network to optimize the placement order of different kinds of cargoes to solve the 3D-BPP, but the direction and location of the cargo needs to be determined through a heuristic algorithm. [16] proposed a multi-task learning framework to generate cargo placement order and orientation, which also requires heuristics to determine cargo location. [17] based on the self-attention mechanism to determine the order and position of cargoes, and proposed a prioritized oversampling technique for policy learning, but the training result began to decline when more than 100 cargoes were placed. [18–20] focused on the online 3D-BPP, using the Actor-Critic to learn placement policies. Among them, [18,19] used a height map to describe the container space, resulting in an exponential relationship between the size of the action space and the resolution of the height map, and the accuracy of cargo placement cannot be guaranteed. [20] used a packing configuration tree to describe the container space, which solves the problem of excessive action space. It has achieved good results in the small-scale and strong heterogeneous packing problem with the number of cargoes not exceeding 100. [21] proposed a recurrent conditional query learning model to solve the 3D-BPP. The model makes decisions on the order, position and orientation of the cargoes, 1000 cargoes can be placed by improving the encoder structure, but the mean cargo gap ratio is only 21% at best.

In this paper, a large-scale 3D Bin Packing model based on Dual-Task Learning of Group Blocks (GB-DTL) is proposed for the characteristics of large-scale and weak heterogeneity in the cargoes of tobacco companies. Unlike other learning-based 3D bin packing model, the model input is a sequence composed of single cargo. We propose a group block generation algorithm to generate a group block sequence of tobacco cargoes. The tobacco cargo packing problem is divided into two sub-tasks: selecting the group block and selecting the space for the group block to be placed. The A3C algorithm [22] is used in our model for training. To evaluate the effectiveness of GB-DTL, we designed two models. One is a DRL model based on group block placement and the other is a DRL model based on single cargo placement. Only the input data differs between the two models. The input based on group block placement model is the set of group blocks determined according to the group block generation algorithm, while the input based on single cargo placement model is the set of dimensions of each different kinds of cargo in the order in three directions. Tested with the same order in the real environment. The results show that the vehicle full load ratio is increased by 13.43% and the cargo clearance ratio is decreased by 15.13% when using the group block as input.

2   Problem Formulation

We focused on the packing problem of tobacco companies. Tobacco companies used transport vehicles to deliver orders all over the country every day. With the differentiation of orders and the expansion of the company's production and sales scale, an intelligent packing method needs to be proposed. The transporter can transport multiple destination orders at the same time, and one order may contain several different cargoes. The traditional tobacco cargo packing problem considers the restrictions of orders at different destinations, and places different types of cargoes in the order into designated vehicles in units of cigarette boxes.In this paper, under the condition of meeting the actual business constraints, the intelligent packing algorithm is used to generate the placement position and direction of each cargoes, which can effectively improve the vehicle full load ratio and tobacco transportation capacity, and reduce the cargo gap ratio and logistics cost. Different from the small-scale strong heterogeneous packing problem solved by [15–20]. The quantity of cargoes that needs to be loaded in a transport vehicle of a tobacco company is often thousands, and consists of several different kinds of cargoes, which belongs to a large-scale and weakly heterogeneous 3D-BPP.

Fig. 1. Three directions of cargoes (from left to right are dir 1, dir 2, dir 3)

Based on the on-site investigation of tobacco companies, this paper puts forward the following assumptions that meet the actual business needs. All vehicles and cargo are cubes. Orders cannot be split, and must meet the principle of last in first out (LIFO). To prevent the phenomenon of unwinding of the cargoes, there are only three directions for the cargoes to choose from.

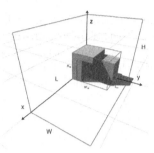

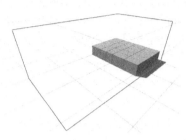

Fig. 2. Internal coordinate system of transport vehicle

Fig. 3. Group block placement diagram

The cargo direction is shown in Fig. 1. The three directions are $dir1(l_i,w_i,h_i)$, $dir2(l_i,h_i,w_i)$ and $dir3(w_i,l_i,h_i)$. A three-dimensional space coordination system is established inside the transport vehicle, with the lower-left rear corner of the vehicle as to the coordinate origin, the length, width, and height directions of the vehicle as to the x-axis, y-axis, and z-axis directions of the coordinate system. Use l_i,w_i,h_i to represent the length, width, and height of the tobacco cargo i, x_i,y_i,z_i to represent the coordinates of the lower-left corner of the tobacco cargo i placed inside the vehicle, i∈[1, j] where j represents the total number of tobacco cargoes that need to be transported by the transport vehicle. L, W, and H represent the length, width, and height of the transport vehicle, and the internal coordinate system of the transport vehicle is shown in Fig. 2.

Figure 2 L_m,W_m,H_i represent the maximum value of the cube formed by placed m pieces of cargoes inside the transport vehicle in the direction of x-axis, y-axis, z-axis. The formed cargo cube is shown in the blue frame in Fig. 2.

At the beginning of each episode, the agent gets J cargoes of size (l_i,w_i,h_i) and the size of the transport vehicle is (L, W, H). The goal of the agent is to load as many cargoes as possible by giving the placement position and direction of the cargoes in line with the actual business requirements so that the full load ratio of the transport vehicle is maximized and the cargo gap ratio is minimized. The objective function calculation formula is as follows:

$$G = \lambda \cdot \frac{\sum_{i=1}^m l_i \cdot w_i \cdot h_i}{L \cdot W \cdot H} - \omega \cdot \frac{L_m \cdot W_m \cdot H_m - \sum_{i=1}^m l_i \cdot w_i \cdot h_i}{L_m \cdot W_m \cdot H_m} \qquad (1)$$

$$S.T. \begin{cases} x_i - x_{i+1} \geq l_i \\ y_i - y_{i+1} \geq w_i \\ z_i - z_{i+1} \geq h_i \end{cases} \qquad (2)$$

In formula (1), m represents the number of cargoes loaded into the vehicle and λ and ω represents the weight of the full load ratio and the gap ratio. Formula (2) means that the cargoes cannot overlap.

3 Method

3.1 Group Block Generation Algorithm

According to the on-site investigation, when the experienced stevedores deal with the problem of placing tobacco cargoes, they will pack and place them according to the size of the cargoes. The so-called group placement is to combine and place the same kind of cargoes in different directions, which can make full use of the three-dimensional size of the transport vehicle. One layer of the group is placed, as shown in Fig. 3.

Group blocks are stacked with the same type of cargoes in the same direction, and there is no gap between the cargoes. Different from [10], the composite block traverses the three different directions of the x-axis, y-axis, and z-axis to obtain all feasible combinations (nl_i, nw_i, nh_i). The group block is traversed only in the z-axis direction, and the resulting combination can be described as (l_i, w_i, nh_i). There are only three directions for tobacco cargoes to choose from in the actual placement process, so it is necessary to generate three different directions of group blocks. The generated group block needs to satisfy the following two constraints.

Algorithm 1. Group Block Generation

Input: car_size(L,W,H); cargo_set$[(l_1, w_1, h_1, num_1), ..., (l_j, w_j, h_j, num_j)]$, $j \in [1,k]$
Output: group blockset
1: Initialize block_set=[], gap threshold=g
2: **for** each $j \in [0, len(cargo\_set)]$ **do**
3:     dir1_num = int(H / h_j);
4:     **for all** $n \in [1, dir1\_num]$ **do**
5:         **if** $n \cdot h_j \leq H$ and $n \leq num_j$ **then**
6:             add the $[l_j, w_j, n \cdot h_j]$ into block_set;
7:         **end if**
8:     **end for**
9:     dir2_num = int(H / w_j);
10:     **for all** $n \in [1, dir2\_num]$ **do**
11:         **if** $n \cdot w_j \leq H$ and $n \leq num_j$ **then**
12:             add the $[l_j, h_j, n \cdot w_j]$ into block_set;
13:         **end if**
14:     **end for**
15:     l_n=1;
16:     **while** ($l\_n \cdot w_j \leq l_j$) **do**
17:         **if** $-g \leq l\_n \cdot w_j - l_j \leq g$ **then**
18:             break;
19:         **end if**
20:         **if** $l\_n \cdot w_j \geq l_j$ **then**
21:             l_n=1 break;
22:         **end if**
23:         $l\_n = l\_n + 1$
24:     **end while**
25:     dir3_num = int(H / h_j);
26:     **for all** $n \in [1, dir3\_num]$ **do**
27:         **if** $n \cdot h_j \leq H$ and $n \cdot l\_n \leq num_j$ **then**
28:             add the $[l\_n \cdot w_j, l_j, n \cdot w_j]$ into block_set;
29:         **end if**
30:     **end for**
31: **end for**

Quantity Constraints: The quantity of cargoes required for group blocks should be less than the quantity of cargoes available.

Dimensional Constraints: The size of the group block should be smaller than the size of the transport vehicle.

The group block generation algorithm is shown in Algorithm 1. The three-direction group blocks are shown in Fig. 4.

(a) Group blocks resulting from cargoes placed in dir1   (b) Group blocks resulting from cargoes placed in dir2   (c) Group blocks resulting from cargoes placed in dir3

Fig. 4. Group Block

At the beginning of each episode, according to the size of the vehicle and the cargoes in the order, use Algorithm 1 to generate the group block of all different kinds of cargoes in the order in three directions, and store them in the group block set D. The total number of blocks is denoted as k. The group block d_i comprises the three-dimensional size of the group block and the required number of single cargoes, $i \in [1,k]$. In this way, we can get the group block sequence D=(d_1, d_2,..., d_k) required by the GB-DTL, where $d_i=(l_i, w_i, h_i, num_i)$. At each step, the agent will select a group block from D to place, and update the remaining number of cargoes in the order according to the number of single cargo required by the selected group block. If the quantity of a single cargo required by the group block is greater than the remaining quantity of same kind cargoes in the order, it will be set as unavailable through the mask.

3.2   Dual-Task Learning of Group Blocks

When the stevedores are working, the placement of cargoes is always carried out according to the following three aspects. The state in which cargoes have been placed inside the transport vehicle, the size of space left in the transport vehicle, and the size of the next placed cargo. These three aspects can completely represent the 3D-BPP of tobacco cargoes.

The tobacco cargo packing problem can be formulated as a Markov Decision Process (MDP) and solve this MDP with a DRL model. The MDP is formulated as follows.

State. In this paper, the environment state at step t consists of three parts: the set of group blocks placed inside the transport vehicle N_t. Each element n=(x_n, y_n, z_n, l_n, w_n, h_n)$\in N_t$ is composed of the coordinates of the placed group block and the size of the group block. The set of available placement spaces inside the vehicle L_t, each element $l=(x_l^s, y_l^s, z_l^s, x_l^e, y_l^e, z_l^e) \in L_t$ is composed of the starting position and ending position of the space. The EMS method introduced in [15] generates the available space set. Moreover, the set of to-be-placed group blocks D_t is generated according to the group block generation algorithm, which will be updated as the cargoes are placed. Noting that the number of elements of the N_t and L_t keeps increasing as the cargoes are placed continuously. According to the description in [20], we will fix the size of N_t and L_t store only a fixed number of elements. When the set limit is exceeded, the newly placed group block and the free space created by that group block will be added to the top of N_t and L_t, and its bottom-most element will pop up. We refer to N_t and L_t collectively as the vehicle interior environment.

Action. The action space is divided into two parts. Corresponding to the two subtasks of selecting the group block and selecting the available placement space. We use the attention mechanism to select group block $d_t \in D_t$ according to the current state $S_t^d = (N_t, L_t, D_t)$, which d_t represents its index of D_t. The attention mechanism is also used to select the placement space $l_t \in L_t$ according to the updated state $S_t^l = (N_t, L_t, d_t)$, and use the starting coordinates in l_t to mark the placement coordinates of the last lower corner of the group block. Similarly, l_t also represents the index of L_t.

Reward. According to the description of the actual situation of the tobacco company's customer orders in Sect. 2, the reward value obtained at step t is set as follows.

$$r_t = \lambda \cdot r_{vt} + \omega \cdot r_{gapt} \tag{3}$$

$$r_{vt} = \frac{\sum_{i=1}^{t} l_i \cdot w_i \cdot h_i}{L \cdot W \cdot H} \tag{4}$$

$$g_t = \begin{cases} \frac{L_t \cdot W_t \cdot H_t - \sum_{i=1}^{t} l_i \cdot w_i \cdot h_i}{L_t \cdot W_t \cdot H_t} & t > 0 \\ 0 & t = 0 \end{cases} \tag{5}$$

$$r_{gapt} = g_{t-1} - g_t \tag{6}$$

r_{vt} represents the volume ratio of the placed group blocks to the vehicle, and its cumulative reward value corresponds to the full load ratio of the vehicle, r_{gapt} which corresponds to the gap ratio between the currently placed group blocks. In formula (5) L_t, W_t, H_t is expressed in the maximum size formed by the placed group blocks in three directions at step t, as shown by the blue border in Fig. 2. Its cumulative reward value represents the gap ratio of all placed cargoes, where $\lambda = 10, \omega = 1$.

GB-DTL is trained based on the Actor-Critic method, using Actor-d and Actor-l to represent two actions, Actor-d input is S_t^d and the output policy distribution $\pi_{\theta^d}(d_t|S_t^d)$ representing the group block selection policy and its network parameters using the θ^d representation. Actor-l input is S_t^l, the output policy distribution $\pi_{\theta^l}(l_t|S_t^l)$ representing the available space selection policy and its network parameters using the θ^l representation. According S_t^l to calculated state value, the Critic predicts how much cumulative reward value can be obtained from step t to the end of the episode and guides the training of the Actor network. The network structure of GB-DTL is shown in Fig. 5. Transformer Encoder and Graph Attention Network (GAT) are respectively used to extract group block features and vehicle interior environment features. The two action networks are realized by attention mechanism, while the critic network is realized by multi-layer perceptron. The h_t^D, h_t^N and h_t^L in Fig. 5 represent the hidden states of the above three sets.

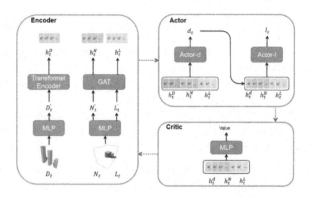

Fig. 5. Network structure of GB-DTL

At each step, the entire network uses the combined loss function shown in formula (9) for parameter update.

$$L_{actor} = (r_t + \gamma \cdot V(S_{t+1}^l) - V(S_t^l)) \cdot (log\pi_{\theta^d}(d_t|S_t^d) + log\pi_{\theta^l}(l_t|S_t^l)) \quad (7)$$

$$L_{critic} = (r_t + \gamma \cdot V(S_{t+1}^l) - V(S_t^l))^2 \quad (8)$$

$$L = L_{actor} + L_{critic} \quad (9)$$

where r_t represents the reward value obtained at time step t, which is determined according to formula (3). γ represents the discount rate, which is set to 1 in this paper. $V(S_t^l)$ represents the output value of the critic network at time step t. L_{actor} and L_{critic} are used to update Actor and Critic network parameters respectively.

4   Experiment

In order to verify the effectiveness of the DRL model based on group block placement proposed in this paper to solve the tobacco cargo packing problem, we also designed a DRL model based on single cargo placement.

In this paper, according to the actual vehicle model and cargo data provided by the tobacco company, the order is randomly generated according to the vehicle volume and the cargo volume for training. The training curves of GB-DTL are shown in Fig. 6. We mainly focus on two indicators, the mean vehicle load ratio, and the mean cargo gap ratio. It can be seen from Fig. 6, that the mean vehicle load ratio and mean cargo gap ratio curves of the group block packing model have been fluctuating before 300,000 steps. This is because the agent has been exploring different placement strategies in the early stage. After training 700,000 steps, the two curves begin to converge, the mean vehicle load ratio can be close to 90%, and the mean cargo gap ratio is close to 10%. This paper does not set the maximum number of episodes but decides when to stop training based on the effect of the training curve.

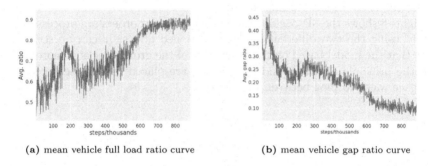

(a) mean vehicle full load ratio curve   (b) mean vehicle gap ratio curve

Fig. 6. Training curve of Group Block model

After the model training, 100 comparison experiments were conducted. The mean vehicle load ratio, maximum vehicle load ratio, minimum vehicle load ratio, and mean cargo gap ratio were calculated using the packing model based on group block placement and single cargo placement, respectively. The experimental results are shown in Fig. 7 that the DRL model based on group block placement is better than that based on single cargo placement.

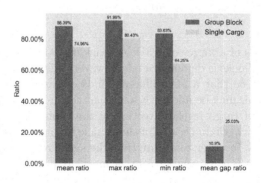

Fig. 7. The effects of the two models on different evaluation indicators. Group Block obtains much better space utilization

It shows that in the case of the same order, more cargoes can be loaded by using the group block placement, which can effectively improve the full load ratio of the vehicle and ensure better stability of the cargoes. Since the tobacco order has thousands of cargoes and is composed of several different kinds of cargoes, it is difficult to learn a packing strategy that meets the actual business needs using the DRL model based on single cargo placement because the decision sequence becomes longer. The group block is a combination of multiple cargoes in the same direction in the direction of the vehicle height. The group blocks themselves are regular, and the combination of group blocks of different sizes according to the manual packing experience can effectively utilize the inner diameter of the vehicle. Therefore, the agent only needs to select group block of different sizes for combination according to the order and the placement of the cargoes, which reduces the difficulty of training the agent and effectively improves the application effect of the packing model.

Figure 8 shows the 3D packing plots when different orders are processed separately using the two different models mentioned above. It can be seen from Fig. 8 that the model based on the placement of the group blocks is more in line with the principle of LIFO, and the cargoes are placed more closely, reducing the space waste formed between the cargoes.

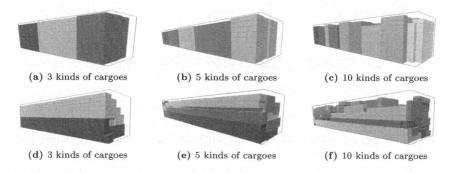

(a) 3 kinds of cargoes   (b) 5 kinds of cargoes   (c) 10 kinds of cargoes

(d) 3 kinds of cargoes   (e) 5 kinds of cargoes   (f) 10 kinds of cargoes

Fig. 8. 3D packing plot of two bin packing algorithms. (a), (b), (c) represent the boxing plots generated using the group block algorithm, (d), (e), (f) represent the boxing plots generated using the single cargo algorithm.

The effectiveness of a large-scale 3D bin packing model based on Dual-Task learning of Group Blocks is demonstrated. However, it is not difficult to see from the left side of Fig. 8c that a few different kinds of cargoes are stacked in the height direction. This may be due to the fact that the group blocks are generated by the same kind of cargo in the direction of the vehicle height, and only the combination of the length and width of the vehicle is considered. And because of the reward function, in order to ensure that the agent reduces the reward value penalty caused by the cargo gapt ratio as much as possible in each decision, and selects the larger group blocks for placement, ignoring the combination of group blocks of different sizes in the height direction. The above problem can be improved by generating group blocks with different cargoes or modifying the reward function.

Table 1. The mean ratio with different algorithms.

Algorithm name	3 kinds	5 kinds	10 kinds
Group Block	87%	91%	83%
Single Cargo	66%	76%	64%
SeaRates	90%	82%	87%
Manual Heuristic	86%	89%	85%
Genetic	85%	85%	84%

We compare our model with the SeaRates loading platform. SeaRates is the world's largest search engine for international shipping tariffs and has a container intelligent loading platform. We also compare with DRL model for single cargo placement, genetic algorithms [23], and manual-designed heuristics for tobacco packing problem. Table 1 lists the results of the above methods when processing three different orders. The results calculated by the SeaRates platform are slightly higher than ours. This is because the searates platform will split the cargoes of different orders, but this is not allowed in ours, because this will not meet the principle of LIFO. GB-DTL can achieve the computing effect comparable to the searates platform without splitting the order, it also proves the superiority of GB-DTL. Our model can perform better than manual-designed heuristics and genetic algorithm when the number of cargo types is small, but it is slightly inferior to the other two methods when the number of cargo types reaches 10. This is mainly because the group blocks are generated for the same kind of cargoes, and the grouping of various cargoes in different directions is not considered.

5 Conclusions

In order to solve the packing problem of tobacco cargoes, this paper fully considers the characteristics of large-scale and weak heterogeneity of tobacco cargoes, and proposes a large-scale 3D Bin packing model based on Dual-Task Learning of Group Blocks. We consider the actual business process of tobacco companies and use a group block generation algorithm to combine single cargoes into group blocks. The tobacco cargo packing is decomposed into two sub-tasks, the selection of the group block and the selection of the space of the group block. The selection and placement strategies of group blocks are learned through the Actor-Critic algorithm. The experimental results show that the mean full load ratio of the vehicle reaches 88.39%, and the mean cargo gap ratio reaches 10.9%. Compared with the DRL model based on single cargo placement, the two indicators are increased by 13.43% and decreased by 15.13% respectively.

References

1. Coffman, J., Edward, G., et al.: Performance bounds for level-oriented two-dimensional packing algorithms. SIAM J. Comput. **9**(4), 808–826 (1980)
2. Lysgaard, J., et al.: A new branch-and-cut algorithm for the capacitated vehicle routing problem. Math. Program. **100**(2), 423–445 (2004)
3. Martello, S., Pisinger, D., Vigo, D.: Three-dimensional bin packing problem. Oper. Res. **48**(2), 256–267 (2000)
4. Crainic, T.G., Perboli, G., Tadei, R.: Extreme point based heuristics for three-dimensional bin packing. INFORMS J. Comput. **20**(3), 368–384 (2008)
5. Faroe, O., Pisinger, D., Zachariasen, M.: Guided local search for the three-dimensional bin-packing problem. INFORMS J. Comput. **15**(3), 267–283 (2003)
6. George, J.A., Robinson, D.F.: A heuristic for packing boxes into a container. Comput. Oper. Res. **7**(3), 147–156 (1980)
7. Pisinger, D.: Heuristics for the container loading problem. Eur. J. Oper. Res. **141**(2), 382–392 (2002)
8. Eley, M.: Solving container loading problems by block arrangement. Eur. J. Oper. Res. **141**(2), 393–409 (2002)
9. Fanslau, T., Bortfeldt, A.: A tree search algorithm for solving the container loading problem. INFORMS J. Comput. **22**(2), 222–235 (2010)
10. Zhang, D.F., Peng, Y., Zhang, L.L.: A multi-layer heuristic search algorithm for three dimensional container loading problem. Chinese J. Comput. **35**(12), 2553–2561 (2012)
11. Crainic, T.G., Perboli, G., Tadei, R.: TS(2)PACK: a two-level tabu search for the three-dimensional bin packing problem. Eur. J. Oper. Res. **195**(3), 744–760 (2009)
12. Moura, A., Oliveira, J.F.: A GRASP approach to the container-loading problem. IEEE Intell. Syst. **20**(4), 50–57 (2005)
13. Bello, I., Pham, H., Le, Q.V.: Neural combinatorial optimization with reinforcement learning. In: 5th International Conference on Learning Representations (ICLR) (2017)
14. Vinyals, O., Fortunato, M., Jaitly, N.: Pointer networks. In: 29th Annual Conference on Neural Information Processing Systems (NIPS), vol. 28 (2015)
15. Hu, H., Zhang, X., Yan, X.: Solving a new 3d bin packing problem with deep reinforcement learning method. arXiv preprint arXiv:1708.05930 (2017)
16. Duan, L., Hu, H., Qian, Y.: A multi-task selected learning approach for solving 3D flexible bin packing problem. In: Proceedings of the 18th International Conference on Autonomous Agents and MultiAgent Systems (AAMAS), pp. 1386–1394 (2019)
17. Zhang, J., Zi, B., Ge, X.: Attend2Pack: bin packing through deep reinforcement learning with attention. arXiv preprint arXiv:2107.04333 (2021)
18. Zhao, H., et al.: Online 3D bin packing with constrained deep reinforcement learning. In: 35th AAAI Conference on Artificial Intelligence (2021)
19. Zhao, H., et al.: Learning practically feasible policies for online 3D bin packing. Sci. China Inf. Sci. **65**(1), 1–17 (2022)
20. Zhao, H., et al.: Learning efficient online 3D bin packing on packing configuration trees. In: 2021 International Conference on Learning Representations (ICLP) (2021)
21. Li, D.D., et al.: One model packs thousands of items with recurrent conditional query learning. Knowl.-Based Syst. **235**, 107683 (2022)

22. Mnih, V., et al. Asynchronous methods for deep reinforcement learning. In: 33rd International Conference on Machine Learning (ICML), pp. 1928–1937 (2016)
23. Korhan, K., Mustafa, M.I.: A hybrid genetic algorithm for packing in 3d with deepest bottom left with fill method. In: Third International Conference on Advances in Information Systems, pp. 441–450 (2004)

ETH-TT: A Novel Approach for Detecting Ethereum Malicious Accounts

Ziang Yuan[1], Tan Yang[1(✉)], and Jiantong Cao[2]

[1] State Key Laboratory of Networking and Switching Technology,
School of Computer Science (National Pilot Software Engineering School),
Beijing, China
tyang@bupt.edu.cn
[2] School of Economics and Management, Beijing University of Posts
and Telecommunications, Beijing, China
tony000@bupt.edu.cn

Abstract. Ethereum, as the second generation of blockchain technology, it not only brings many advantages, but also spawns various malicious incidents. Ethereum's anonymity makes it a hotbed of cybercrime, causing huge losses to users and severely disrupting the Ethereum ecosystem. To this end, this paper proposes a method for detecting malicious accounts in Ethereum based on ETH tracking tree (ETH-TT). Firstly, based on the transaction history replay mechanism, an ETH tracking algorithm for tracking the transaction amount of Ethereum is designed to obtain the ETH tracking tree, and extract sequence features from it. Then train the LSTM model to reduce the dimension of the sequence features to obtain the output features. Finally, detection is done by a machine learning classifier, fused with manual features from account transaction history. We uses 5576 malicious accounts and 4968 normal accounts as dataset for experiments. The results show that the ETH-TT method can achieve an F1-score of 95.4% with the cooperation of the XGBoost classifier, which is better than the detection method using only manual features.

Keywords: Blockchain · Ethereum · Malicious accounts detection · ETH tracking tree · LSTM · Machine learning

1 Introduction

As a representative of the blockchain 2.0, Ethereum provides a complete Turing scripting language, allowing users to deploy decentralized applications (DAPP) on Ethereum to implement user-defined methods, bringing more possibilities to the blockchain [9,15]. Based on the account model, Ethereum supports direct transactions between accounts.

While Ethereum brings more functions to users, it also brings more vulnerabilities and threats, and due to the design and implementation of Ethereum,

L. Fang et al. (Eds.): CICAI 2022, LNAI 13605, pp. 84–94, 2022.
https://doi.org/10.1007/978-3-031-20500-2_7

the vulnerabilities caused are more difficult to deal with than in the traditional mode [16]. According to the research of Chen [1], Ethereum faces 44 types of vulnerabilities and 26 types of attacks. The hackers use certain technical means to complete malicious events through accounts on the Ethereum platform, such accounts for malicious behavior are defined as Ethereum malicious account. The following are some of the major events that have occurred in recent years. In June 2016, the famous crowdfunding project The Dao [7] was stolen about US$60 million by attackers using the reentrant vulnerability in the smart contract. In July 2017, a security vulnerability occurred in Parity1.5[1] and above, 150,000 ETH were stolen, worth US$30 million. Upbit [14], one of the largest cryptocurrency exchanges in South Korea, was stolen by an unidentified attacker in November 2019. 342,000 ETH were sent to an Ethereum wallet and quickly spread to about 800 accounts. Therefore, there is an urgent need to use computer technologies such as pattern recognition, machine learning, or neural networks to detect malicious behavior on the Ethereum platform, and further detect malicious accounts in Ethereum [18]. Thereby reducing risks and bringing more security.

In the field of Ethereum malicious account detection, the current research is mainly based on the manual features extracted from the transaction history of the address, and then the machine learning classifier is constructed for training, such as the study of Kumar [8], Poursafaei [11], Farrugia [3], etc. In some papers, it also shows good F-score and Recall. However, the information contained in the manual features used in these studies is incomplete. According to our analysis, malicious accounts often quickly transfer "Black Money" ETH to multiple accounts after conducting malicious acts. This makes it difficult for official institutions to recover them to achieve money laundering purposes. Take Upbit [14] as an example. In a few days, the hacker transferred the stolen 342,000 ETH to more than 800 accounts, which were distributed in more than ten transaction levels [14]. In the end, most of the ETH flowed into the exchange to withdraw money to complete the money laundering work. There are also malicious events such as Cryptopia and Bitpoint [13], which are also similar to the above-mentioned behavior patterns. Therefore, analyzing the transfer behavior and further tracking the flow of malicious transaction ETH between accounts is of great significance for detecting malicious accounts.

Inspired by this, we propose an ETH Tracking Tree (ETH-TT) based method for detecting malicious accounts in Ethereum, and achieves good results in the final evaluation, which is better than the method that only using manual features.

2 ETH Tracking Tree Method

The whole flow of ETH-TT method proposed is shown in Fig. 1. First, determine the parameters of the limits, including the tracking time and the number of tracking tree layers. Then use the key transaction algorithm and the ETH tracking algorithm to obtain the ETH tracking tree, and further calculate the

---

[1] Multi-signature wallet version 1.5 of Parity Technologies.

traceability rate information. Next, the sequence features are parsed from the tracking tree and feed into the LSTM model to get the output vector features. Finally, the vector features and manual features are connected and input into the machine learning classifier to get the final result.

Fig. 1. ETH-TT method flow chart

2.1   ETH Tracking Tree and Traceability Rate

Before describing how to building the ETH tracking tree, we need to find the key transaction corresponding to the account and let it be the starting transaction to initiate the tracking. Specifically, we need to sort the transaction list of addresses and find the most representative transaction as the key transaction. In the research of Wu [16], they proposed that the key characteristics of a transaction are its transaction amount and timestamp. We use his formula to sort the transactions, as shown in Eq. 1.

$$P_t^{0.5} * P_a^{0.5} \tag{1}$$

Among them, P_a represents the ratio of the one transaction's ETH to the total transactions' ETH of the address, and P_t represents the position of the one transaction's timestamp in the entire transaction history time range of the address. The index is used to balance the influence of two parameters, and 0.5 is the best value [16].

The key transaction algorithm is shown in Algorithm 1. After entering an address, find all transactions for the address and sort them in reverse order according to Eq. 1. It then traverses the sorted transaction list until it finds a transaction that meets the traceability conditions, and then returns it as a key transaction. A transaction can be traced, that is, the ETH generated by the transaction has been transferred later.

The ETH tracking tree is constructed by the ETH tracking algorithm, as shown in the Algorithm 2. The algorithm is based on the transaction history replay mechanism, and first takes the ETH of the key transaction as the target ETH. Under some constraints such as tracking time and number of tracking tree layers, track the flow of the target ETH between the accounts to form a corresponding tree structure, called ETH tracking tree. Finally, calculate the traceability rate of the target ETH in the tree's nodes. The following describes the algorithm in detail in two steps.

Algorithm 1. Key Transaction Algorithm

Input: Target Address A
Output: Key Transaction of Address A
1: $Txlist=A.$getTxList().sort(key:$P_a^{0.5}*P_t^{0.5}$,reverse:True)
2: **for** each $tx \in Txlist$ **do**
3:     **if** $canBeTraced(tx)$ **then** return tx
4:     **end if**
5: **end for**

Algorithm 2. ETH Tracking Algorithm

Input: KeyTransaction Tx, Layer Limit $Layers$, Time Limit $Days$
Output: ETH Tracking Tree $Tree$
1: $Tree=$Init()
2: $PathTx=$Init()
3: $Datelist=$getDate($Tx,Days$)
4: $Tree.$root$=Tx.$toAddr
5: **for** each $date \in Datelist$ **do**
6:     $Txlist=$getTxList($date$).sort(key:timeStamp,blockNumber)
7:     **for** each $tx \in Txlist$ **do**
8:         **if** $isEligible(tx, Layers)$ and $tx.fromAddr$ $\in$ $Tree$ **then** appendToPathTx($tx, PathTx$)
9:             **if** $tx.toAddr \notin Tree$ **then** appendToTree($tx, tx.toAddr, Tree$)
10:            **end if**
11:        **end if**
12:    **end for**
13: **end for**
14: **for** $tx \in PathTx$ **do** calculateTraceabilityRate($tx,Tree$)
15: **end for**

The first part of the ETH tracking algorithm is to create the structure of the tree. Specifically, the first step is to determine the number of tracking tree layers and tracking time as the limits of the tracking algorithm. The second step is to calculate the time range according to the key transaction and time limit, and find the corresponding Ethereum transaction list based on this, and finally sort by the timestamp and transaction index (block number), that is, the actual transaction order. The third step is to add the output address of the key transaction to the tracking tree as the root node. The fourth step is to traverse the sorted transaction list after the key transaction, find the output transactions of the root node, insert the output addresses of these transactions into the tree according to the transaction order. For example, address A is already in the tree, and has transactions with address B and address C successively. Then address B and address C are regarded as the child nodes of A. Loop to find all the tree nodes' output transactions and child nodes, until find the exchange addresses, contract addresses, or reach the limit of the number of tracking tree layers. Thus ETH tracking tree is established.

In the tracking algorithm, the concept of traceability rate will be involved. The traceability rate of an account at a certain timestamp indicates the proportion of the target ETH held in its balance to the total target ETH needs to be tracked, that is, the distribution of target ETH among accounts. Which can visually show the information of the flow of ETH. When a transfer transaction occurs in an account with a traceability rate, the traceability rate will be converted accordingly. The formula for traceability rate conversion is shown in Eq. 2. Among them, $Balance_{from}$ represents the balance of the account before the transaction. $Amount$ is the ETH amount of the transaction. $Rate_{from}$ represents the traceability rate of the account before the transaction. Finally, the traceability rate conversion amount can be obtained.

$$Conversion_{rate} = (Amount/(Balance_{from})) * Rate_{from} \qquad (2)$$

After describing the concept of traceability rate and traceability rate conversion, we can carry out the remaining process of the tracking algorithm. The second part of the algorithm is to calculate the traceability rate related information of the nodes in the ETH tracking tree. Specifically, after getting the tracking tree, traverse the list of transactions encountered during the tracking process, where each transaction represents a traceability rate conversion process as described above, so the traceability rate of the node is constantly changing. By calculating each traceability rate conversion, some information related to the traceability rate are calculated, i.e., the final traceability rate of each node and the maximum traceability rate reached, and the position of the point in time when the maximum traceability rate is reached. Then we maintain these parameters on the tracking tree nodes for later calculation of sequence features.

Through the above two steps of the ETH tracking algorithm, a simple example of the finally obtained ETH tracking tree is shown in Fig. 2.

2.2 Features Extraction

Generally speaking, features extraction is divided into two parts.

- Firstly we could find the transaction history of target address, and then extract features from it. In this part, we refer to the research of Kumar [8] to extract 45 features. The features include the number of Input/Output transactions, the average handling charge, the Input/Output amount, etc.
- The second part is to use the ETH tracking tree to extract sequence features to obtain the information of the ETH flow. As shown in Fig. 3, each level of the sequence corresponds to each level in the tree. After getting the tracking tree, we first calculate the features of each node in the tree according to the traceability rate information obtained in the Algorithm 2 and some auxiliary information. See the Table 1 for details. The evaluation indicators of these features (including arithmetic mean, variance, standard deviation, mean square

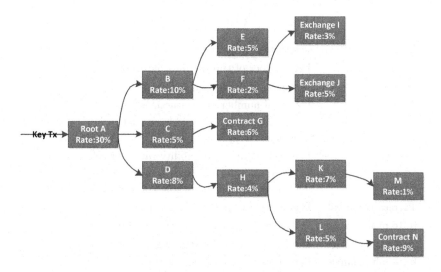

Fig. 2. ETH tracking tree

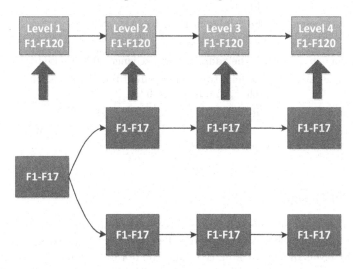

Fig. 3. Extracting sequence features from ETH tracking tree

root value, majority, median, geometric average) are then taken by layer, and the number of nodes in that layer is added as the last feature, with a total of 120 dimensions as the features of each layer. Finally the sequence features of M * N are obtained, where M represents the number of layers of the tracking tree, N stands for a fixed 120-dimensional feature.

Table 1. Tracking tree node features

Features	Descriptions
Input_tx_num	The number of transactions received
Output_tx_num	The number of transactions sent
Tx_num	The total number of transactions
Addr_num	The number of distinct addresses where transactions took place
Max_rate	The maximum of traceability rate ever achieved
Max_rate_position	The position of the time point to reach the maximum traceability rate in the whole transaction sequence
Tx_mean_interval	The average transaction time interval
Rate_mean_change	The average conversion of traceability rate
Rate_max_change	The maximum conversion of traceability rate
Rate_min_change	The minimum conversion of traceability rate
Max_tx_num	The maximum number of transactions with the same address
Max_value_num	The maximum ETH traded
Rate	The final traceability rate
Is_exchange	1 if the address is an exchange address else 0
Exchange_rate	The final traceability rate if the address is an exchange address else 0
Is_contract	1 if the address is an contract address else 0
Contract_rate	The final traceability rate if the address is an contract address else 0

2.3 Model Design

We need to extract sequence features into fixed-dimensional features to train machine learning classifiers. Considering that there is a dependency relationship between the levels of the tracking tree, and the obtained features are long-range sequences, we use Long Short Term Memory (LSTM) as the features extraction model [4,5,17].

The overall design of the model is shown in Fig. 4. We construct a bidirectional multi-layer LSTM, and feed the sequence features (which may need to be filled) into LSTM for training and getting output features. The length of LSTM sequence is determined by the restrictions on the number of tracking tree layers set in the experiment. After the output features is obtained, it is connected with the manual features of the address. Then the fusion features are feed into machine learning classifiers for training, and the final results can are obtained. In addition, the manual features will be directly feed into the machine learning classifier for comparison.

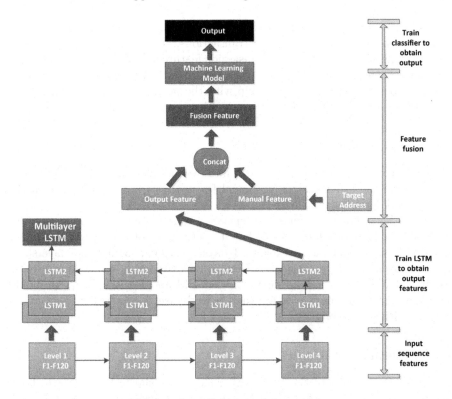

Fig. 4. Overall design of the model

3 Experiment

3.1 Dataset

First, we built a Geth Ethereum node on the server and started to synchronize the block information. Then we use the Ethereum ETL project [10] to store transaction information on the hard disk in the form of a CSV file on a daily basis.

- We need to collect malicious addresses (positive samples) and normal addresses (negative samples) of EOA. Firstly, we collected 5585 positive samples from the tag library of Etherscan [12] and Cryptoscamdb [2], GitHub [6], third-party certification bodies, etc. Including fraud, phishing, money laundering, currency theft and other types. In order to collect negative samples, We continuously randomly took addresses from senders and receivers in the transaction list and put them into the positive sample set (automatic deduplication), and cycled this process until the set size reaches 6000.

– The second step we need to take is preprocessing. First, all sample addresses were traversed, if there were no transactions, they were filtered out. Took advantage of the "create" type transaction feature of smart contract to filtered it out. Then traversed the negative samples and filtered out the ones that have direct transaction relationship with the positive samples. Finally, 5576 positive samples and 4968 negative samples were left as the final dataset.

3.2   Experimental Details

The entire control experiment is divided into two modules, one uses the ETH-TT method, and the other uses only manual features to train the model with the same kind of features as Kumar [8].

In the ETH-TT experiment, we specified four parameter combinations as control experiments to limit the tracking time (number of days) and the number of tracking tree layers, respectively [3 days, 5 layers], [3 days, 15 layers], [5 days, 15 layers], [5 days, 20 layers]. Finally, it is trained in 4 machine learning classifiers: XGBoost, Random Forest, LightGBM and Decision Tree. It should be noted that we randomly divide the entire dataset into a training-set and a test-set, with a ratio of 7:3.

3.3   Experimental Result

The evaluation results of the above experiments are shown in the Fig. 5. Each sub-graph in the Fig. 5 shows the Manual Feature method and the ETH-TT method under different parameter combinations. The indicators are Precision, Recall, F1-score, Accuracy.

F1-score can comprehensively reflect the effect of the model. Under the parameters of [5 days, 20 layers], the XGBoost model reached the optimal 95.42%. Recall can measure the ability of the model to find positive samples, XGBoost reached the best 94.69%.

3.4   Result Analysis

The results show that the ETH-TT method is effective for detecting malicious Ethereum accounts, and is better than Kumar [8], that is, the method that only uses manual features. After reaching the parameter combination of [5 days, 20 layers], all indicators are better than the method of Kumar [8] under different machine learning classifiers.

From the perspective of parameter combinations, with tracking time and the number of tracking tree layers are relaxed, the overall effect of the model is getting better and better. This shows that with the expansion of the ETH tracking tree, the contribution of the features extracted from it to the model is magnifying, which further illustrates the effectiveness of the ETH-TT method.

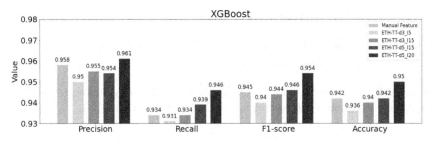

(a) Evaluation results under XGBoost model

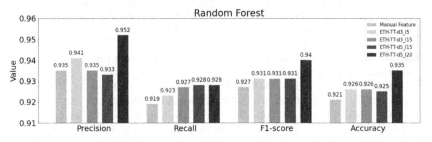

(b) Evaluation results under LightGBM model

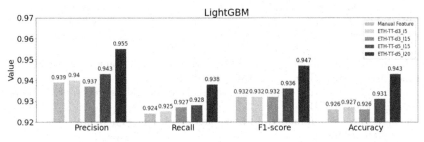

(c) Evaluation results under Random Forest model

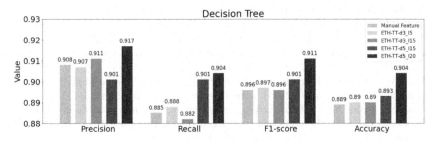

(d) Evaluation results under Decision Tree model

Fig. 5. Evaluation results

4   Availability of Data and Material

The dataset and model files mentioned in the article are available here:
https://github.com/yfzjay/ETH-TT.

Acknowledgments. This work was supported by the National Key Research and Development Program of China under grant No. 2019YFC1521101.

References

1. Chen, H., Pendleton, M., Njilla, L., Xu, S.: A survey on Ethereum systems security: vulnerabilities, attacks, and defenses. ACM Comput. Surv. (CSUR) **53**(3), 1–43 (2020)
2. Cryptoscamdb (2019). https://api.cryptoscamdb.org
3. Farrugia, S., Ellul, J., Azzopardi, G.: Detection of illicit accounts over the Ethereum blockchain. Expert Syst. Appl. **150**, 113318 (2020)
4. Graves, A.: Generating sequences with recurrent neural networks. arXiv preprint arXiv:1308.0850 (2013)
5. Hochreiter, S., Schmidhuber, J.: Long short-term memory. Neural Comput. **9**(8), 1735–1780 (1997)
6. IRMkz: Ethereum addresses-darklist. https://github.com/MyEtherWallet/ethereum-lists/blob/master/src/addresses/addresses-darklist.json (2020)
7. Jentzsch, C.: A standard decentralized autonomous organization (DAO) framework written in solidity to run on the Ethereum blockchain (2016). https://github.com/slockit/DAO/tree/v1.0
8. Kumar, N., Singh, A., Handa, A., Shukla, S.K.: Detecting malicious accounts on the Ethereum blockchain with supervised learning. In: Dolev, S., Kolesnikov, V., Lodha, S., Weiss, G. (eds.) CSCML 2020. LNCS, vol. 12161, pp. 94–109. Springer, Cham (2020). https://doi.org/10.1007/978-3-030-49785-9_7
9. Lee, X.T., Khan, A., Sen Gupta, S., Ong, Y.H., Liu, X.: Measurements, analyses, and insights on the entire Ethereum blockchain network. In: Proceedings of The Web Conference 2020, pp. 155–166 (2020)
10. Medvedev, E.: blockchain-etl/ethereum-etl (2020). https://github.com/blockchain-etl/ethereum-etl
11. Poursafaei, F., Hamad, G.B., Zilic, Z.: Detecting malicious Ethereum entities via application of machine learning classification. In: 2020 2nd Conference on Blockchain Research & Applications for Innovative Networks and Services (BRAINS), pp. 120–127. IEEE (2020)
12. Tan, M.: Ethereum blockchain explore (2015)r. https://etherscan.io
13. Tan, M.: Heist accounts (2015). https://etherscan.io/accounts/label/heist
14. Tan, M.: Upbit hack (2015). https://etherscan.io/accounts/label/upbit-hack
15. Wood, G., et al.: Ethereum: a secure decentralised generalised transaction ledger. Ethereum Proj. Yellow Pap. **151**(2014), 1–32 (2014)
16. Wu, J., et al.: Who are the phishers? Phishing scam detection on Ethereum via network embedding. arxiv prepr. arxiv:1911.09259 (2019)
17. Xingjian, S., Chen, Z., Wang, H., Yeung, D.Y., Wong, W.K., Woo, W.: Convolutional LSTM network: a machine learning approach for precipitation nowcasting. In: Advances in Neural Information Processing Systems, pp. 802–810 (2015)
18. Xu, J.J.: Are blockchains immune to all malicious attacks? Financ. Innov. **2**(1), 1–9 (2016)

Multi-objective Meta-return Reinforcement Learning for Sequential Recommendation

Yemin Yu[1,2], Kun Kuang[2(✉)], Jiangchao Yang[3], Zeke Wang[2], Kunyang Jia[3], Weiming Lu[2], Hongxia Yang[3], and Fei Wu[2,4,5]

[1] City University of Hong Kong, Hong Kong, China
yeminyu2-c@my.cityu.edu.hk
[2] Institute of Artificial Intelligence,Zhejiang University, Hangzhou, China
{kunkuang,wangzeke,luwm}@zju.edu.cn, wufei@cs.zju.edu.cn
[3] Damo Academy, Alibaba Group, Hangzhou, China
{jiangchao.yjc,kunyang.jky,yang.yhx}@alibaba-inc.com
[4] Shanghai Institute for Advanced Study of Zhejiang University, Shanghai, China
[5] Shanghai AI Laboratory, Shanghai, China

Abstract. With the demand for information filtering among big data, reinforcement learning (RL) that considers the long-term effects of sequential interactions is attracting much attention in the sequential recommendation realm. Many RL models have shown promising results on sequential recommendation; however, these methods have two major issues. First, they always apply the conventional exponential decaying summation for return calculation in the recommendation. Second, most of them are designed to optimize a single objective on the current reward or use simple scalar addition to combine heterogeneous rewards (e.g., Click Through Rate [CTR] or Browsing Depth [BD]) in the recommendation. In real-world recommender systems, we often need to simultaneously maximize multiple objectives (e.g., both CTR and BD), for which some objectives are prone to long-term effect (i.e., BD) and others focus on current effect (i.e., CTR), leading to trade-offs during optimization. To address these challenges, we propose a Multi-Objective Meta-return Reinforcement Learning ($\mathbf{M^2OR\text{-}RL}$) framework for sequential recommendation, which consists of a *meta-return network* and a *multi-objective gating network*. Specifically, the *meta-return network* is designed to adaptively capture the return of each action in an objective, while the *multi-objective gating network* coordinates trade-offs among multiple objectives. Extensive experiments are conducted on an online e-commence recommendation dataset and two benchmark datasets and have shown the superior performance of our approach.

1 Introduction

Recommender Systems, as the essential infrastructure in the era of big data, has been widely applied to different web services [1,6,8,30,36]. For the past decades,

L. Fang et al. (Eds.): CICAI 2022, LNAI 13605, pp. 95–111, 2022.
https://doi.org/10.1007/978-3-031-20500-2_8

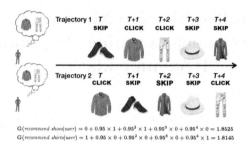

$$G(recommend\ shoes|user) = 0 + 0.95 \times 1 + 0.95^2 \times 1 + 0.95^3 \times 0 + 0.95^4 \times 0 = 1.8525$$
$$G(recommend\ shirts|user) = 1 + 0.95 \times 0 + 0.95^2 \times 0 + 0.95^3 \times 0 + 0.95^4 \times 1 = 1.8145$$

Fig. 1. An example to demonstrate the insufficiency of conventional exponential decaying reward summation in RL. Suppose we set the reward for the user's click feedback as 1 and skip as 0. Utilizing the conventional return formula defined in Eq. 3 with discount factor $\gamma = 0.95$, we calculate the returns for the first actions in both trajectories for customers with the same interest in shirts and jeans. The calculated return $G(\cdot)$ in recommendation clearly suggests a misleading strategy of recommending shoes over recommending shirts.

plenty of works in collaborative learning [33], deep learning, and sequential modeling have been developed to continuously improve the performance of sequential recommendation in many real applications. Especially with the recent focus on auxiliary tasks such as long-term revenues and user experience, deep reinforcement learning (DRL) [4,20,22,28] has drawn much attention in the sequential recommendation communities.

However, we are facing the following challenges in employing RL for recommendation: (1) **How to design a flexible and powerful return function to capture the sequential long-term effect in sequential recommendation.** Most existing RL-based recommendation methods directly apply the conventional exponential decaying summation to estimate return, resulting in a misleading and incorrect recommendations. As shown in Fig. 1, the RL agent will fail to identify the preferable strategy (recommending shirt) due to using the conventional return function with a pre-defined discount factor. Hence, it is paramount to design a suitable return function for RL in sequential recommendation. (2) **How to simultaneously optimize multiple objectives in sequential recommendation.** There are usually multiple objectives needed to be simultaneously optimized for the sake of different user engagements, such as the Click Through Rate (CTR) and Browsing Depth (BD), and each objective corresponds to a unique sequential long-term effect. Specifically, click feedback tends to be more short-termed and intermittent, while BD feedback tends to be long-termed and continuous. However, most of the existing DRL methods [42] use a single network to aggregate both instant and delayed rewards and use the same discount factor for summation, leading to underperformance in real-world recommendation applications. Therefore, it is still an open problem to efficiently capture the sequential return of each objective and jointly optimize the multiple objectives in RL for sequential recommendation.

To address these challenges, we propose a novel method, namely Multi-Objective Meta-return Reinforcement Learning (M^{2}OR-RL) for sequential recommendation. We design a meta-return network to flexibly and adaptively estimate the appropriate return of each action in sequential recommendation and propose a multi-objective gating network for jointly optimizing multiple objectives via coordinating their trade-offs. Specifically, the fundamental idea of the meta-return network is to optimize a multi-head attention network to generate step-wise return value when considering the complete trajectory information, and the key idea of the multi-objective gating network is to generate a step-wise weighting vector for each objective respectively. We perform experiments on static benchmark recommendation datasets and a pre-trained environment designed for RL recommender system. The result shows that the proposed M^{2}OR-RL method significantly improves the baselines with different discount factors.

The main contributions of this paper are:

- We investigate the problem of RL with multiple objectives in sequential recommendation, and demonstrate the limitations of using the conventional exponential decaying summation of returns calculation in previous RL methods on this problem.
- We propose a novel multi-objective Meta-return Reinforcement Learning (M^{2}OR-RL) framework, which consists a meta-return networks to flexibly and precisely estimate return of each objective and a multi-objective gating network to jointly optimize multiple objectives via coordinating their trade-offs.
- We perform extensive experiments on benchmark and real-world recommendation datasets. The result shows that our method can achieve a multi-objective optimization with different base RL algorithms.

2 Related Works

Recommender Systems. In the early age of recommeder systems, different approaches is categorized into three main classes [1]: content-based, collaborative filtering, and hybrid method. Content-based methods [26] recommend an item to a user based on the features of the items and the profile representing the user's interests. On the other hand, collaborative filtering (CF) [2,19] methods were the mainstream approach when utilizing different interactive histories for recommendation. Hybrid methods [14] combine content-based and CF methods and successfully avoid some weaknesses. However, both the content-based method and CF method have a critical drawback: they treat user behavior as static events with an underlying assumption that all of the historical interactions of a user are equally important to the user's current preference.

DRL in Recommendation. DRL algorithm in recommender systems can be divided into three categories: value-based approaches such as deep Q-learning methods [15,25,32], policy-gradient ones such as REINFORCE methods [34], and hybrid type such as actor-critic methods [18]. Value-based approaches [5,41] use a single light-weighted value network but suffer from the deadly triad problem when combining function approximation, off-policy learning, and bootstrapping together [11]. On the other hand, policy gradient methods [3,4] are comparably stable by directly applying function approximation to the policy of the RL agent but require off-policy correction approximation and a large amount of data to converge. Therefore, actor-critic methods [5,16,22,40] combine Q-learning and policy gradient to stabilize the learning process. In the meantime, DRL recommender system defines user feedback such as clicks [38,40], views [4], and ratings [22] as direct rewards for each action, depending on the specific recommendation environment. More sophisticated design [42] incorporates different metrics(instant/delayed) such as BD into the final reward calculation and achieves multi-task learning. However, none of the DRL for recommendation work addressed the significance of evaluating the accuracy of conventional return calculation when simultaneously optimizing multiple objectives.

3   Preliminaries

This section first presents a formal definition of the recommendation task as a sequential decision-making problem with Markov Decision Process (MDP). Next, we introduce the conventional return calculation with exponentially decaying summation and its limitations on recommendation tasks.

For a standard MDP tuple $M = (\mathcal{S}, \mathcal{A}, T, r, \gamma)$ under **recommendation** setting, we define:

- $\mathcal{S}$ is the **state space**. The state is at step t is represented as $s_t = \{u, I_t\}$, where u is user specific demographic information and I_t is the item history embedding sequence $\{i_0, \ldots, i_t\}$ of the user.
- $\mathcal{A}$ is the **action space**. The agent will pick an item a_t at each timestamp t according to its policy.
- $\mathcal{P}$ is the **state transition probability** $P(s'|s, a)$. Since the state is a representation of user's interaction history, the state transition is dependent on user feedbacks at each timestamp.
- $\mathcal{R}$ is the **reward**. The user will react to each recommended item with feedbacks such as clicking, purchase, ratings, etc. The agent will receive each instant reward r according to its own reward function $r(s_t, a_t)$.
- γ is the **discount factor** for calculating the return.

We define the total trajectory as $\tau = \{s_0, a_0, r_0, \ldots, s_T, a_T, r_T\}$, and the return $G(\tau)$ of a trajectory τ is conventionally computed as:

$$G(\tau) = \sum_{t=0}^{\infty} \gamma^t r_t$$

Similarly, we calculate the return for state action pair in each step as:

$$G(s_t, a_t) = \sum_{m=t}^{\infty} \gamma^{m-t} r_m.$$

Under the MDP settings, a RL algorithm is designed to learn an optimal policy π to select a action a when given state s to maximize $G(s, a)$. A policy π with parameter θ is a probability distribution on $\mathcal{A}$ given a state $s, \pi_\theta : \mathcal{S} \times \mathcal{A} \rightarrow [0, 1]$. A trajectory τ is generated under policy π_θ if all the actions along the trajectory is chosen following π_θ, i.e., $\tau \sim \pi_\theta$ means $a_t \sim \pi_\theta (\cdot \mid s_t)$ and $s_{t+1} \sim P (\cdot \mid s_t, a_t)$. The value of a state s is defined as the expected return of all trajectories when the agent starts at s and then follows π_θ:

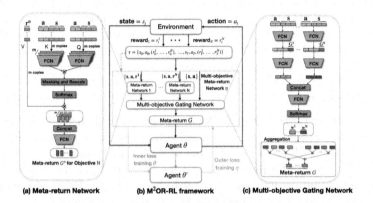

(a) Meta-return Network   **(b) M^{2}OR-RL framework**   **(c) Multi-objective Gating Network**

Fig. 2. The proposed M^{2}OR-RL framework. (a) is the design of the meta-return network for each objective; (b) represents the hierarchical architecture of the proposed M^{2}OR-RL framework; and (c) is the design of the multi-objective gating network. In addition to the inner loss training for θ in the RL agent, we use the outer loss training for M^{2}OR-Network parameters η with the updated agent θ'.

$$V^{\pi_\theta}(s) = E_\tau [G(\tau) \mid \tau (s_0) = s, \tau \sim \pi_\theta]$$

Similarly, the value of a state-action pair is defined as:

$$Q^{\pi_\theta}(s, a) = E_\tau [G(\tau) \mid \tau (s_0) = s, \tau (a_0) = a \cdot \tau \sim \pi_\theta]$$

As mentioned before, multiple objectives should be addressed differently when calculating the return according to the nature of the objective. Since the conventional return formulation has a fixed formula and is incapable of adjusting towards incoherencies and trade-off effects, we re-formulate the return calculation process by introducing a separate meta-return network, and design a multi-objective gating network for coordinating trade-offs between different objectives.

4   Approach

In this section, we first present the architecture overview of our proposed M^{2}OR-RL framework, including the design of its two main components: meta-return network and multi-objective gating network. Afterward, we give out the meta-gradient formulation for the meta-return network and present the optimization process for M^{2}OR-RL.

4.1   M²OR-RL Framework

Figure 2 demonstrates the M²OR-RL framework. We divide the meta-network into separate sub-networks according to the total number of objectives N for return calculation. Different reward networks will be aggregated at the end to generate the final Meta-return $G_\eta(s_t, a_t)$ with a state-action dependent gating network.

Meta-return Network. To generate returns for each step, we fully re-parameterize our update target with multi-head attention [35] networks. The meta-return network will take the whole trajectory τ as input. We use $(r_t^1, \ldots, r_t^n)$ to represent the rewards from different objectives at time step t, where n refers to the number of objectives. $(r_t^1, \ldots, r_t^n)$ are distributed and combined individually with the states and actions to create the downstream inputs for each sub-network.

Multi-objective Gating Network. As shown in Fig. 2 on the right, for multi-objective optimization, we utilize a novel gating network to dynamically aggregate results from each meta-return network. The fundamental idea is to generate an appropriate weight for reward aggregation based on the individual states and actions information. Intuitively, we want to use a weighted aggregation instead of the conventional return formulation for dynamic adjustments.

Let N denote the number of total optimization objectives. The gating network receives state s_t and action a_t at each step t as input. The input is copied N times and fed into separate fully connected networks (FCN) to produce embeddings, and the embeddings are concatenated respectively with the returns $\mathbf{G}^i$ for each objective i. The concatenated embeddings are passed through another FCN and a softmax activation layer to produce a weighting vector $\{w^1, \ldots, w^N\}$ with the dimension equal to the total number of optimization objectives. In the end, we perform a weighted aggregation for N objectives:

$$\mathbf{G}(s_t, a_t) = \sum_{i=0}^{N} w_i g_t^i$$

where g_t^i is the single Meta-return element in $\mathbf{G}^i = g_0^i, \ldots, g_T^i$.

M²OR-RL Base Model. We build M²OR-RL based on the actor-critic architecture. We denote the policy network (actor) as $\pi_\theta(a|s)$ and value network (critic) as $Q_\theta(s, a)$, where we use θ to denote the parameters. The actor network is responsible for generating an action a_t based on current s_t, and the critic network is designed to evaluate the quality of the action provided by the actor network. For the actor network, the state vector s is passed through a 3-layer fully-connected network (FCN) to generate $\tilde{a}$. We use $\tilde{a}$ to perform dot-product with all item embeddings and pass through a softmax layer to generate a score vector $\mathbf{v}$. Finally, we recommend the best item with ϵ-greedy exploration according to the score vector. For the critic network $Q_\theta(s, a)$, the state s and a is concatenated and passed through a 3-layer FCN to generate a scalar Q-value.

4.2   Optimization

We denote the learnable parameters in the RL agent network as θ and the parameters in the meta-return network as η. We now elaborate the meta-gradient optimization of the two networks.

We re-parameterize the update target $\mathbf{G}$ with an individual neural network by taking the full trajectory as input. Let $\mathbf{G}_\eta$ denote the meta-return network we want to adapt during the training process. We use a two-level optimization process similar to [37] by first defining a inner RL loss L_η^{inner}, where the agent will use the fixed parameters η and optimize L_η^{inner} with respect to parameters θ. After $\mathbf{M}$ episodes of the inner loss training, we can acquire a differentiable outer(meta) loss $L^{outer}(\tau_{t+M+1}, \theta_{t+M})$ with the updated θ' network using simple chain rule.

With the idea of meta-gradient, we can train the meta-return network simultaneously with the RL agent in an end-to-end two-step optimization manner. For simplicity, let $\mathbf{G}_\eta(t)$ denote the meta-return $\mathbf{G}_\eta(s_t, a_t)$ at step t. For the actor-critic method with trajectory τ, we have the **inner** loss for policy and value networks as:

$$L_{\text{value}}(\tau; \theta) = \sum_{t \in \tau} (\mathbf{G}_\eta(t) - Q_\theta(s_t, a_t))^2 \tag{1}$$

$$L_{\text{policy}}(\tau; \theta) = - \sum_{t \in \tau} \log \pi_{\theta_\pi}(a_t | s_t) (\mathbf{G}_\eta(t) - Q_\theta(s_t, a_t))) \tag{2}$$

For simplicity, we discard the summation part in later derivation since the gradient of summation is simply the summation of gradients. As stated above, we use the inner loss training to update θ with fixed $\mathbf{G}_\eta$. We denote θ'_v and θ'_π as the updated parameters for the policy network and the value network after $\mathbf{M}$ iterations, and τ' for the new trajectory used during meta-update. Intuitively, it is straightforward to set the learning objective of $\mathbf{G}_\eta(t)$ to be the performance of the updated agent θ'. Thus, we denote the **outer** loss on trajectory τ':

$$L_{\text{outer}}(\tau'; \theta', \eta) = L_{\text{value}}(\tau'; \theta', \eta) + L_{\text{policy}}(\tau'; \theta', \eta) \tag{3}$$

and the outer loss is used to train parameters η using fixed θ'. For reference, Algorithm 1 in Appx.A elaborates the complete algorithm for the M²OR-RL training.

5   Experiments

We first evaluate the performance of our proposed M²OR-RL method on an online RL environment for recommendation: **Virtual TB** [31] with multiple objectives (Subsect. 5.2). To clearly demonstrate the advantages of our proposed meta-return network in M²OR-RL, we further conduct extensive experiments on the two benchmark datasets with single objective (Subsect. 5.3) as ablation studies. Alternately, our extensive experiments intend to investigate and answer the following research questions:

1. How will the discount factor γ affects the performance of recommendation in those conventional RL models?
2. How effective is the proposed meta-return network comparing to the conventional return formulation in recommendation scenarios?
3. How can we utilize the meta-return network to improve multi-objective optimization when trade-offs happen between targets?

Table 1. Comparison on multiple objectives (i.e., CTR and BD) between RL baseline model with different discount factor γ and our M^2OR-RL framework.(Non-RL baselines has no discount factor as hyper-parameters)

	CTR					BD				
γ	0.95	0.9	0.85	0.8	**+M²OR − RL**	0.95	0.9	0.85	0.8	**+M²OR − RL**
DQN	0.492	0.497	0.507	0.511	0.552	10.2	10.2	9.1	8.5	11.9
DDPG	0.524	0.535	0.541	0.547	0.560	11.7	10.5	10.3	9.8	12.3
TD3	0.535	0.539	0.543	0.552	0.563	11.8	10.6	10.3	10.2	12.4
SAC	0.543	0.547	0.551	0.563	**0.573**	12.1	11.3	10.5	10.4	**13.3**
FM	0.519					6.3				
NCF	0.515					6.5				
GRU4Rec	0.524					7.2				
SASRec	0.548					6.9				

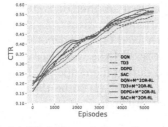 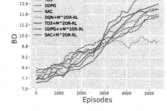

(a) Click-through Rate Curve   (b) Browse Depth Curve

Fig. 3. Average CTR and BD of 50 runs over episodes on the VirtualTB dataset. The baseline models are reported with the most suitable γ.

5.1   Experimental Setup

Datasets. We conduct our experiments on **Virtual TB** [31], **MovieLens-20M** [10] and **Amazon Games** [23].

Base Models. In order to prove the robustness of our approach, we select different types of RL base models and non-RL recommender system as baselines. Specifically, we build our M^2OR-RL framework upon **DQN** [24], **DDPG** [21], **TD3** [7], and **SAC** [9]. For non-RL recommender systems, we select **FM** [27], **NCF** [12], **GRU4Rec** [13], and **SASRec** [17] as baselines.

Evaluation Metric. In sequential recommendation, CTR and BD are two of the most important metrics for evaluation. Therefore, we set maximizing CTR and BD as the objectives to demonstrate the superiority of our method over baselines. Specifically, the CTR objective is calculated by the dividing the amount of clicked items by the total number of items in each episode. The BD objective is simply the total length of the episode.

5.2   Experiment with Multiple Objectives

Result Analysis. The results for both CTR and BD metrics are summarized in Table 1 and Fig. 3. In Table 1, we compare M²OR-RL with the base models under different discount factor, and we have the following observations and analysis:

Table 2. CTR result on MovieLens20M and Amazon Games with different discount factor

γ	MovieLens20M					Amazon Games				
	0.95	0.9	0.85	0.8	+M²OR-RL	0.95	0.9	0.85	0.8	+M²OR-RL
DQN	0.571	0.574	0.580	0.586	**0.601**	0.352	0.360	0.365	0.374	**0.397**
DDPG	0.589	0.602	0.607	0.595	**0.619**	0.397	0.405	0.415	0.412	**0.427**
TD3	0.593	0.601	0.597	0.603	**0.625**	0.409	0.411	0.422	0.427	**0.433**
SAC	0.608	0.606	0.609	0.607	**0.635**	0.394	0.402	0.413	0.415	**0.424**
FM	0.578					0.375				
NCF	0.571					0.383				
GRU4Rec	0.584					0.387				
SASRec	0.596					0.379				

- In Table 1, we can observe that non-RL baseline models performs poorly on the BD metric, which mainly due to the non-RL baseline model's incapability of capturing the long-term effect of the actions. Even though non-RL baselines can perform comparably well in the CTR metric, it is clearly not competent of multi-objective optimizations in recommendation.
- There exists an interesting trade-off effect between CTR and BD metrics for different discount factors γ for RL baseline models. For all base models, a higher γ will bring better the BD metric but worse the CTR metric. The main reason is that the reward of CTR is highly related to the short-term (current step) effect, whereas the reward of BD is related to the long-term effect as defined in Sect. 5.1 (evaluation metric).
- M²OR-RL achieved the best performance on both CTR and BD metrics compared to all of the base models. The reason is that the meta-return network in our method can dynamically capture the different effects of each objective more accurately, and the multi-objective gating network can adapt the trade-offs between CTR and BD metrics for different steps in a trajectory.

Figure 3 shows the test results of the average result of CTR and BD metrics over 50 runs on RL base models. We can observe that M²OR-RL method outperforms the other base models in both CTR and BD metrics. Another interesting observation is: At the beginning of the training process (0–2000 episode), M²OR-RL focuses more on short-term effect (i.e. click feedback), therefore achieving a better performance on the CTR metric than the base models, while the performance on BD metric, which is a long-term effect, is worse than the base models. In the middle of the training process (2000-3000 episodes), M²OR-RL focuses more on the long-term effects, leading to a significant improvement on the BD metric and a deterioration on the CTR metric. After 3000 episodes, M²OR-RL coordinates the trade-off between CTR and BD, achieving a significant improvement on both CTR and BD metrics.

5.3 Experiment with Single Objective

In this part, we target to validate the superiority of a single meta-return network over the conventional return formulation to serve as an ablation study. In order to prevent introducing negative trade-off impacts of other objectives, we constrain the experimental setting to CTR optimization.

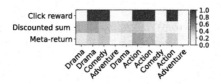

Fig. 4. Comparison of the weights calculation for the conventional return and the meta-return drawn from MovieLens20M. The x-axis labels the category of the movies in the trajectory.

Result Analysis. Table 2 illustrates the evaluation results on CTR, where the best result is marked as bold. With the addition of the Meta-return framework, M²OR-RL achieves the best CTR performance over all the base models. Typically, without the meta-return network, different algorithms achieve best result with different discount factors, proving that RL for recommendation is sensitive to the discount factor hyperparameter, and the meta-return network can implicitly adjust towards the best setting. From Fig. 4, we can observe the result from the meta-return network is more accurate in representing the preference of the user. The meta-return network is able to represent the user's preference towards "Action" movies while down-weighting the reward of the second 'Drama' movie according to the feedbacks of the complete trajectory. Specifically, we can observe that DQN benefits most from the meta-return network when comparing with the other three actor-critic method. The main reason is that DQN often suffers from a large number of state-action pairs and becomes intractable to estimate the optimal Q-value in certain stage. Using meta-return network provides a less biased return estimation compared to the conventional return.

6   Conclusion

In this paper, we propose a novel Multi-objective Meta-return Reinforcement Learning (M^{2}OR-RL) framework, consisting of a meta-return network for return calculation and a multi-objective gating network for jointly optimizing multiple objectives in sequential recommendation. Experimental results demonstrate that M^{2}OR-RL can achieve superior performance compared to different state-of-the-art methods, and it can be easily extended to other RL algorithms with few adjustments. Future work can explore distinct frameworks of the meta-return network under different circumstances in sequential recommendation.

Acknowledgement. This work was supported in part by Program of Zhejiang Province Science and Technology (2022C01044), Young Elite Scientists Sponsorship Program by CAST 2021QNRC001, the Fundamental Research Funds for the Central Universities $226 - 2022 - 00142, 226 - 2022 - 00051$, the Starry Night Science Fund of Zhejiang University Shanghai Institute for Advanced Study $SN - ZJU - SIAS - 0010$.

A   Algorithms

Algorithm 1. M^{2}OR-RL training with meta-gradient computation over AC algorithm

---

Input: M^{2}OR network $\mathbf{G}_\eta$, actor network π_θ, critic network Q_θ, inner learning rate α_θ and outer learning rate α_η

1 Randomly initialize the policy network π_θ, critic network Q_θ, and meta-return network G_η; Initialize replay buffer D

2 **for** $session = 1$ **to N do**

3   **while** $size(D) < M$ **do**

4   Sample initial state s_0 from environment

5   **while** s_t *is not terminate* **do**

6   Sample action $a_t = \pi_\theta(s_t)$ according to the current policy with ϵ-greedy exploration

7   Receive reward r_t from the environment and next state s_{t+1}

8   Store the trajectory $\tau = (s_0, a_0, r_0, \cdots, s_T, a_T, r_T)$ into replay buffer D

9   **for** $j = 1$ **to M do**

10   Sample a trajectory τ from replay buffer D

11   Compute the return $G_\eta(s_t, a_t)$ for each step using M^{2}OR network G_η

12   Update θ for π_θ by : $\theta' = \theta + \alpha_\theta \nabla_\theta \log \pi_{\theta_\pi}(a_t|s_t)(G_\eta(t) - Q_{\theta_v}(s_t, a_t))$
          Update θ for Q_θ by: $\theta' = \theta + \alpha_\theta \nabla_{\theta_v}((G_\eta(s_t, a_t) - Q_{\theta_v}(s_t, a_t))^2$

13   Compute outer loss L^{outer} and update the meta-return network G_η using Eq. 3 with trajectory τ' and learning rate α_η

Detailed Algorithm is listed in Alg. 1. In practice, we use an adaptive inner training iterations $\mathbf{M}$ with respect to the learning rate. $\mathbf{M}$ is set to 1 at start for stable learning and increases when the learning rate for η is decayed over a threshold. However, for two-step optimization with $\mathbf{M} = 1$, sampling a new trajectory under the updated policy θ' greatly increases sample complexity. Instead, we apply importance sampling approach to compute the partial derivative of the outer loss with respect to θ' on the old trajectory τ:

$$\frac{\partial L_{\text{outer}}(\tau'; \theta', \eta)}{\theta'} = \mathbf{G}_\eta(t) \nabla_{\theta'} \frac{\pi_{\theta'}(s_t|a_t)}{\pi_\theta(s_t|a_t)} \Big|_{t \in \tau, \tau = \tau'}$$

A.1   Implementation Detail

Multi-head Attention in Meta-return Network. We use Multi-Head Attention for sequential modelling, and the scaled dot-product attention is defined as:

$$\text{Attention}(\mathbf{Q}, \mathbf{K}, \mathbf{V}) = \text{softmax}\left(\frac{\mathbf{Q}\mathbf{K}^T}{\sqrt{d}}\right) \mathbf{V} \tag{4}$$

where $\mathbf{Q}$ represents the query, $\mathbf{K}$ the keys and $\mathbf{V}$ the values. The scale factor $\sqrt{d}$ is used to reduce the extreme values in inner products when the dimensionality is high. The attention network is intuitively calculating the weighted sum of all values for each query using weights according to the inner product of queries and keys. We also add a positional encoding $\mathbf{P} \in \mathcal{R}^{n \times d}$ and concatenate it to both $\mathbf{K}$ and $\mathbf{V}$. As shown in Fig. 2 on the left, we provide a general framework of the meta-return network for single objective. For Multi-Head mechanism with $\mathbf{m}$ heads, the scaled dot-product attention is applied in $\mathbf{m}$ sub-spaces. We concatenate state $\mathbf{s}$ and action $\mathbf{a}$ and use it for both queries and keys, and reward $\mathbf{r}$ for value. Due to the causality of return calculation, the model should only consider rewards $\mathbf{r}_{t \geq T}$ when calculating t-th return. Therefore, we modify the attention network by adding a masking layer to mask out the products of $\mathbf{Q}_{t=i}$ and $\mathbf{K}_{t=j}$ for $(j < i)$. For each output at step t, we use the masking mechanism to limit the softmax layer to only focus on information in steps $T \geq t$.

A.2   Implementation Details

Baselines
Non-RL models

- **FM** [27] combines the advantages of support vector machines with factorization models. It represent user-item interactions as tuples of real-valued feature vectors and numeric target variables.

- **NCF** [12] models the interaction function between each user-item pair with neural networks. It use of both linearity of factorization models and non-linearity of neural networks to enhance recommendation quality.
- **GRU4Rec** [13] utilizes Gated Recurrent Units (GRU) to learn the sequential representation of browsing history and derive the ranking score of the items.
- **SASRec** [17] uses self-attention and the Transformer architecture to encode sequences of user-item interactions.

RL Models

- **DQN** approximates a state-value function in a Q-Learning framework with a neural network. Specifically, FeedRec [39], which is regarded as a state of the art RL recommender system for multi-objective optimization, uses DQN as their value network.
- **DDPG** is an actor-critic, model-free algorithm based on the deterministic policy gradient. It has an additional policy network comparing to DQN and uses OU noise for exploration.
- **TD3** is an improved version of DDPG that uses clipped double-Q learning, target policy smoothing and delayed policy updates that alleviate Q-value over-estimations.
- **SAC** is an actor-critic model that optimizes a stochastic policy. It incorporates clipped double-Q learning similar to TD3, and uses entropy regularization that can be used to balance exploration-exploitation trade-offs.

VirtualTB is a dynamic environment for performance evaluation of different RL algorithms for recommendation. It is pre-trained with real-world e-commerce dataset from TaoBao.

MovieLens-20M is a benchmark dataset comprises of ratings from users to the recommended movies on MovieLens website.

Amazon Games consists of product reviews crawled from *amazon.com*.

VirtualTB. In Taobao, a customer enters a recommendation page with a certain profile, and the recommondation system outputs a list of items according to the query. The VirtualTB platform can provide simulated interactions, including state-transition and reward, to the RL agent. In VirtualTB, each customer has 11 static attributes as the demographic information and are encoded into a 88-dimensional space with binary values, in addition with 3-dimensional dynamic attributes. Dynamic attributes represent the customer's interests and alter during the interaction process, which represents the state transitions. An item is represented with 27-dimensional attributes indicating the price, sales volume, Click Through Rate (CTR), Browsing Depth (BD), etc. The environment contains two models, user click model and user leave model, to generate the reward and state termination signals. For our experimentin VirtualTB, the original user leave model is only associated with the initial user state (static user attributes). In order to adapt the environment to the experiment setting, we implement an additional user block that adds dependency between leave signal and each state-action pair. After that, the leave signal of each user is dependent on the static user attributes, where each user has an initial distribution for different browse depth, and dynamic user-item interactions, where each previous action can affect the current leave signal differently according to the state-action pairwise score. Essentially, we design a new leave score model with considering multiple objectives such as click and browsing depth to prevent the setting degenerating back to a single-objective optimization.

MovieLens-20M and Amazon Games. Movielens contains 20,000,263 ratings and 465,564 tag applications across 27,278 movies. The user rates the movies in the range of 0.5–5 with half-star increments. For Amazon Games, the original dataset is divided into several subsets by the categories of the products. We only selected the reviews under the category "Video Games" with ratings 1–5 only.

For both datasets, we choose 80% of the interactions in each user session as the training set, and leave the rest 10%/10% as the validation/testing set. For feedbacks, we only treat feedbacks with ratings greater or equal to 3.5 as positive and the rest as negative. Since both datasets are not featured as session-based recommendation, we sort the user behaviors by time to create session-based recommendation and select sessions that include 10 or more positive feedbacks. For simplicity, we fix the BD to 15 items to fit the single reward RL setting since BD isn't the concern in the first experiment. Moreover, in each session, we will remove the item from the candidate set once it has been selected by the agent to prevent repetitive selections.

We implement the meta-return network over the base models on the benchmark datasets for recommendation, including MovieLens-20M and Amazon Games. Since both datasets are static datasets and unable to provide feedbacks for every possible interactions similiar to RL environment for online-training, we perform **PMF** [29] to pretrain the embeddings of the users and items and use the PMF model as an RL environment model. In the end, the environment will provide the ground truth feedback if the user-item interaction exists in the dataset or otherwise a predicted feedback from the PMF model.

Hyperparameters Settings. For the CTR objective, we set the reward r_t^{CTR} at time step t as: $r_t^{CTR} = 1$ if the customer clicks the recommended commodity at time t, otherwise $r_t^{CTR} = 0$. For the BD objective, we set reward r_t^{BD} at time step t when considering the total depth of a episode M as: $r_t^{BD} = 0$ if the customer leaves the episode at time step t, and $r_t^{BD} = 1/M$ for the customers who keep browsing and remain in the episode. The rest of the hyperparameters settings are listed in Table 3.

Table 3. Hyperparameters of M^{2}OR-RL

Dataset	Parameters	Setting
MovieLens	State dimension	64
	Action dimension	8
	Hidden layer dimension	64
	Learning rate	1e–3
	Attention dimension (Q, K, V)	32
	# of heads in multi-head attention	2
	optimizer	Adam
Amazon	state dimension	32
	Action dimension	8
	Hidden layer dimension	64
	Learning rate	1e–3
	Attention dimension(Q,K,V)	32
	# of heads in multi-head attention	2
	Optimizer	Adam
VirtualTB	state dimension	91
	Action dimension	27
	Hidden layer dimension	256
	Learning rate	3e–4
	Attention dimension (Q, K, V)	32
	# of heads in multi-head attention	2
	Optimizer	Adam

References

1. Adomavicius, G., Tuzhilin, A.: Toward the next generation of recommender systems: a survey of the state-of-the-art and possible extensions. IEEE Trans. Knowl. Data Eng. **17**(6), 734–749 (2005)
2. Bu, J., Shen, X., Xu, B., Chen, C., He, X., Cai, D.: Improving collaborative recommendation via user-item subgroups. IEEE Trans. Knowl. Data Eng. **28**(9), 2363–2375 (2016)
3. Chen, H., et al.: Large-scale interactive recommendation with tree-structured policy gradient (2018)
4. Chen, M., Beutel, A., Covington, P., Jain, S., Belletti, F., Chi, E.: Top-k off-policy correction for a reinforce recommender system (2020)
5. Chen, S.Y., Yu, Y., Da, Q., Tan, J., Huang, H.K., Tang, H.H.: Stabilizing reinforcement learning in dynamic environment with application to online recommendation. In: SIGKDD (2018)
6. Cheng, H.T., et al.: Wide & deep learning for recommender systems. In: Proceedings of the 1st Workshop on Deep Learning for Recommender Systems (2016)
7. Fujimoto, S., van Hoof, H., Meger, D.: Addressing function approximation error in actor-critic methods. CoRR (2018)

8. Gu, Y., Ding, Z., Wang, S., Zou, L., Liu, Y., Yin, D.: Deep multifaceted transformers for multi-objective ranking in large-scale e-commerce recommender systems. In: CIKM 2020 (2020)
9. Haarnoja, T., Zhou, A., Abbeel, P., Levine, S.: Soft actor-critic: off-policy maximum entropy deep reinforcement learning with a stochastic actor. In: ICML (2018)
10. Harper, F.M., Konstan, J.A.: The movielens datasets: history and context. ACM Trans. Interact. Intell. Syst. **5**(4), 1–19 (2015)
11. van Hasselt, H., Doron, Y., Strub, F., Hessel, M., Sonnerat, N., Modayil, J.: Deep reinforcement learning and the deadly triad (2018)
12. He, X., Liao, L., Zhang, H., Nie, L., Hu, X., Chua, T.S.: Neural collaborative filtering. In: WWW (2017)
13. Hidasi, B., Karatzoglou, A., Baltrunas, L., Tikk, D.: Session-based recommendations with recurrent neural networks. CoRR (2016)
14. Hu, L., Cao, J., Xu, G., Cao, L., Gu, Z., Zhu, C.: Personalized recommendation via cross-domain triadic factorization. In: WWW (2013)
15. Huang, Z., et al.: Exploring multi-objective exercise recommendations in online education systems. In: CIKM 2019 (2019)
16. Huzhang, G., et al.: Validation set evaluation can be wrong: an evaluator-generator approach for maximizing online performance of ranking in e-commerce (2020)
17. Kang, W.C., McAuley, J.: Self-attentive sequential recommendation. In: 2018 IEEE International Conference on Data Mining (ICDM) (2018)
18. Konda, V.R., Tsitsiklis, J.N.: On actor-critic algorithms (2003)
19. Koren, Y., Bell, R., Volinsky, C.: Matrix factorization techniques for recommender systems. Computer **42**(8), 30–37 (2009)
20. Liebman, E., Saar-Tsechansky, M., Stone, P.: DJ-MC: a reinforcement-learning agent for music playlist recommendation (2014)
21. Lillicrap, T.P., et al.: Continuous control with deep reinforcement learning. In: ICLR (2016)
22. Liu, F., et al.: Deep reinforcement learning based recommendation with explicit user-item interactions modeling (2019)
23. McAuley, J., Targett, C., Shi, Q., Van Den Hengel, A.: Image-based recommendations on styles and substitutes. In: SIGIR (2015)
24. Mnih, V., et al.: Playing atari with deep reinforcement learning (2013)
25. Mnih, V., et al.: Human-level control through deep reinforcement learning. Nature **518**(7540), 529–533 (2015)
26. Qian, X., Feng, H., Zhao, G., Mei, T.: Personalized recommendation combining user interest and social circle. IEEE Trans. Knowl. Data Eng. **26**(7), 1763–1777 (2014)
27. Rendle, S.: Factorization machines. In: 2010 IEEE International Conference on Data Mining (2010)
28. Rojanavasu, P., Srinil, P., Pinngern, O.: New recommendation system using reinforcement learning. Spec. Issue Int. J. Comput. Internet Manag. (2005)
29. Salakhutdinov, R., Mnih, A.: Probabilistic matrix factorization. In: NIPS (2007)
30. Sarwar, B., Karypis, G., Konstan, J., Riedl, J.: Analysis of recommendation algorithms for e-commerce. In: Proceedings of the 2nd ACM Conference on Electronic Commerce (2000)
31. Shi, J.C., Yu, Y., Da, Q., Chen, S.Y., Zeng, A.X.: Virtual-taobao: virtualizing real-world online retail environment for reinforcement learning. In: Proceedings of the AAAI Conference on Artificial Intelligence (2019)

32. Stamenkovic, D., Karatzoglou, A., Arapakis, I., Xin, X., Katevas, K.: Choosing the best of both worlds: Diverse and novel recommendations through multi-objective reinforcement learning. In: WSDM 2022 (2022)
33. Su, X., Khoshgoftaar, T.M.: A survey of collaborative filtering techniques. Adv. Artif. Intell. (2009)
34. Sutton, R.S., McAllester, D., Singh, S., Mansour, Y.: Policy gradient methods for reinforcement learning with function approximation. In: NIPS (1999)
35. Vaswani, A., et al.: Attention is all you need. NIPS (2017)
36. Wang, H., Zhang, F., Xie, X., Guo, M.: DKN: deep knowledge-aware network for news recommendation. In: WWW (2018)
37. Xu, Z., van Hasselt, H., Silver, D.: Meta-gradient reinforcement learning (2018)
38. Zhao, X., Xia, L., Zhang, L., Ding, Z., Yin, D., Tang, J.: Deep reinforcement learning for page-wise recommendations. In: Proceedings of the 12th ACM Conference on Recommender Systems (2018)
39. Zhao, X., Zhang, L., Ding, Z., Xia, L., Tang, J., Yin, D.: Recommendations with negative feedback via pairwise deep reinforcement learning. In: SIGKDD (2018)
40. Zhao, X., Zhang, L., Xia, L., Ding, Z., Yin, D., Tang, J.: Deep reinforcement learning for list-wise recommendations (2019)
41. Zheng, G., et al.: DRN: a deep reinforcement learning framework for news recommendation (2018)
42. Zou, L., Xia, L., Ding, Z., Song, J., Liu, W., Yin, D.: Reinforcement learning to optimize long-term user engagement in recommender systems. In: SIGKDD (2019)

Purchase Pattern Based Anti-Fraud Framework in Online E-Commerce Platform Using Graph Neural Network

Sanpeng Wang$^{(\boxtimes)}$, Yan Liu, Chu Zheng$^{(\boxtimes)}$, and Rui Lin$^{(\boxtimes)}$

Retail Risk Management Group, JD, Beijing 100083, China
{wangsanpeng,liuyan961,zhengchu,linrui}@jd.com

Abstract. Click Farming is fraudulent behaviors sponsored by malicious merchants to increase exposure by hiring fraudulent teams to place fraudulent orders, posing a serious threat to the operation of platforms. Traditional anti-fraud strategies are no longer applicable as they analyzed fraudulent behaviors individually and only rely on static statistical characteristics. In this paper, we propose a novel graph-based fraud detection framework deployed on JD.com composed of *Dynamic Purchase Pattern learning* (DPP) and *Graph Neural Network with Similarities and Relations* (GSR). Specifically, the DPP module is a feature extractor based on user click location sequences collected from websites. And the GSR module is a neighborhood sampling and aggregation algorithm for locating more accurate fraud groups and aggregating various information encoded by different types of subgroups. We conduct graph node classification experiments on a large-scale real-world dataset to verify the effectiveness of our framework, and the experimental results show that the DPP is able to capture more discriminative user patterns. Furthermore, GSR achieves the best performance compared to several state-of-the-art methods. Our method can be easily extended to other domains with the same problems as our task.

Keywords: Fraud detection · User behavior · Graph neural networks

1 Introduction

For most online shopping platforms, sales and ratings are the two main factors that measure the quality of a product or a store [4]. Online shopping platforms are responsible for ensuring the authenticity of sales and ratings data. At the same time, there is an illegal industry called *Click Farming*. Click Farming is a fraudulent behavior that employs a group employees to place fraudulent orders and use fraudulent orders to increase the sales and ratings data. Therefore, fraudulent order detection has become an important issue for all online shopping platforms.

S. Wang and Y. Liu—Contribute equally to this work.

L. Fang et al. (Eds.): CICAI 2022, LNAI 13605, pp. 112–123, 2022.
https://doi.org/10.1007/978-3-031-20500-2_9

Currently, the are few studies on fraudulent order detection. First, since positive samples are scarce, most existing methods treat such tasks as anomaly detection problems [6,8,9,12,13,17]. Traditional methods rely on hand-designed features, which often have thousands of dimensions. They are hard to train and not robust enough. Another approach is use recurrent models for user behavior analysis, Wang et al. [19] took browsing item sequences as user behavior and achieved good performance with recurrent neural networks (RNN). The first disadvantage of this approach is that it only includes browsed products and ignores other representative behaviors, and another disadvantage is that millions of dynamically updated product embeddings are difficult to learn. The third approach are graph-based models [6,13,15]. Fraud gangs of fake orders have aggregation relationships in terms of IP address, devices ID etc. Therefore, some indistinguishable behaviors can be judged by the aggregating information. However, order networks typically behave as heterogeneous graphs in production environment, where orders are connected by various types of relationships. Therefore, there are two main challenges for further research.

Capture More Discriminative Features: Our approach innovatively adopts user behavior as features. We found that normal users and fraudulent users often have different behavioral features. Normal user always buys a suitable product by browsing product details or comparing similar products. While fraudulent users usually have another purchase pattern. Therefore, perhaps dynamic user behavior information is more effective.

Design More Effective Models: Device ID or IP are good edge-building features for building heterogeneous graph. But in heterogeneous graph, edges have different properties which can't be treated equally. Figure 1 depicts this situation.

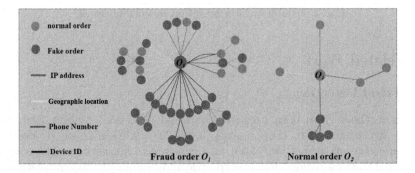

Fig. 1. Graph structure in orders network: O_1 is a fraudulent order but O_2 is a normal order, but O_1 has connections with normal orders by edge type of IP address, geographic location or phone number, O_2 has connection with fraud order by edge type of Device ID.

To address these issues, we propose a novel encoder-decoder fraud detection framework. The first part of the framework is a dynamic purchase pattern learning algorithm (DPP) which is responsible for capturing user behaviors based on click locations. We then model transactions as a heterogeneous graph and treat fraud detection as a graph node classification problem. The core of this heterogeneous graph is a sample and aggregation strategy based on neighborhood similarities and relationships. In summary, our contributions are fourfold:

- An encoder-decoder model is proposed to solve the fraudulent order detection problem. It consists of a recurrent model as an encoder and a heterogeneous graph model as a decoder (Fig. 2);
- We take the click location as user behavior and use a similarity-aware sampling strategy to avoid the negative effects of irrelevant neighbors;
- Our model outperforms other state-of-the-art models in our fraudulent order detection scenario;
- We deployed our framework on JD.com's fraudulent order detection and achieved accurate detection over 100 million online transactions per day.

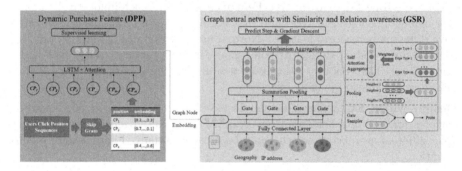

Fig. 2. Overall architecture of proposed framework.

2   Related Work

2.1   Fraud Detection

Various methods have been proposed for fraud detection, ranging from data mining algorithms [3] to deep models [5,7,8,20]. Bahnsen et al. [1] designed a feature generation method based on aggregated transactions. These hand-engineered features require domain expertise and can quickly become obsolete as fraud teams change their behavioral patterns. To bridge this gap, Wang et al. [19] elaborated user purchase behavior feature extraction by extending the item2vec algorithm [2]. However, this method only learns product embeddings but ignore the click behaviors.

2.2   Graph Representation Learning

Graph Neural Networks (GNNs) are a class of deep learning algorithms designed to perform inference on data described by graphs. Formally, GNNs follow a neighborhood aggregation and combination mechanism, the aggregator and the combinator are both trainable that optimized by a supervised, semi-supervised or unsupervised method [21]. The original Graph Convolution Networks (GCN) [11] is designed for semi-supervised learning in a transductive setting, and the algorithm requires the full graph during training. GraphSage [10] proposed a batched-training algorithm for GCN. It samples a tree rooted at each node by recursively expanding toe root node's neighbors by K steps with a fixed sample size. For each tree, it computes the root node's hidden representation by aggregating hidden representation from bottom to top hierarchically. Graph Attentional Models [18] learn to assign different edge weights at each layer based on node features and have achieved state-of-the-art results on several graph learning tasks. Pourhabibi et al. [14] made a comprehensive survey about anomaly detection in fraud detection applications based on graph, they suggested that it remains an open problem that handle graph data with nodes are not explicitly linked together.

3   Proposed Method

The fraudulent order detection problem is defined as using user behavior and the order information to determine whether the order is fraudulent. Specifically, let T denote the transaction set. It consists of user behavior B and order information S, denoted as $T = [B; S]$. A heterogeneous graph $\mathcal{G} = \langle \mathcal{V}, \mathcal{E} \rangle$ consists of node set $\mathcal{V}$ and edge set $\mathcal{E}$, where $\mathcal{E}$ is a subset of order information S.

Given any central node T_u with its neighbor nodes N_u, the neighbor nodes can be divided into z groups by their edge types, expressed as Eq. (1).

$$N_u = \bigcup_{l=1}^{z} N_u^l. \tag{1}$$

The goal of our method is to use the order information to predict the legitimacy of an order. It is modeled as a binary classification problem on graph nodes. As mentioned above, fraudulent order detection is an encoder-decoder model. The DPP module uses behavioral information to encode features F through a recurrent model. And the GSR uses the decoded features and a graph $\mathcal{G}$ to obtain predictions.

$$\begin{aligned} F &= \mathrm{DPP}(B) \\ \hat{y} &= \mathrm{GSR}(F, \mathcal{G}). \end{aligned} \tag{2}$$

3.1   Dynamic Purchase Pattern (DPP)

The browsed-products based approach [21] suffers from learning an embedding matrix from billions of products. Here we introduce a new purchase pattern called

Click Position (CP). CP is a set of clicked positions during the trading session. This model has several merits. First, click position types are less than $10,000$, which are better for training. Second, CP are more meaningful and friendly to low-frequency products.

Different user behaviors play different roles in trading session, some behaviors are distinguishable and some are not. Figure (3) illustrates some CP instances and their relative occurrence in different types of orders. We take Eq. (3) to assign weights for all behaviors, and filter out all low rate behaviors.

$$B = \left\{ B_i \Big| \max \left(\frac{CP_n \cdot All_f}{CP_f \cdot All_n}, \frac{CP_f \cdot All_n}{CP_n \cdot All_f} \right) < \theta \right\}. \tag{3}$$

where CP_n is the number of click positions in normal orders, versa CP_f in fraud orders. All_n and All_f are the number of all click positions in normal and fraud order. And θ is the threshold.

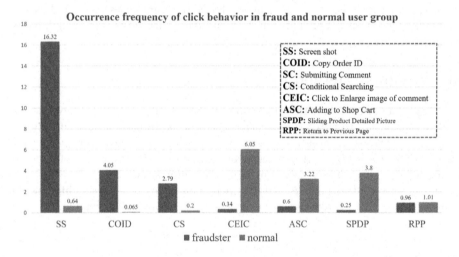

Fig. 3. Example of user click behavior difference.

Given a click positions sequence B. Our encoder consists of a combination of LSTM and self-attention, and is designed to encode the sequence of click positions. The encoding feature F is computed as Eq. (4).

$$\begin{aligned} H &= \text{LSTM}(\text{Embed}(B)) \\ F &= \text{Self-Attention}(H). \end{aligned} \tag{4}$$

At the end of the encoder, we employ a multi-layer perceptron (MLP) to obtain prediction results, aiming to learn robust encoding features.

$$\hat{y}^{\text{DPP}} = \text{MLP}(F). \tag{5}$$

DPP is trained by minimize the classification error of all click sequences, as show in Eq. (6).

$$\mathcal{L}_{\mathrm{DPP}} = -\sum_{i=1}^{n} y_i^{\mathrm{DPP}} \log \hat{y}_i^{\mathrm{DPP}}. \tag{6}$$

3.2 GNN with Similarity and Relation (GSR)

We find that DPP cannot mine the internal dependencies between different orders. Therefore, we build a heterogeneous graph and use DPP as the feature extractor. The heterogeneous graph is built based on the relationship between different nodes. If a central node and its neighbor have the same label, we call them related neighbors, otherwise they are unrelated. Furthermore, we found that different edge types plays different roles in our task. Therefore, we proposed the following neighbors sampling and aggregation strategy.

Similarity Sampler: We introduce a gate-based structure to minimize the influence of unrelated neighbors. For a central node u and its' neighbor nodes v, a similarity measure function is used to measure the similarity between them. In our proposed method, cosine similarity is adopted:

$$\mathrm{sim}(u, v) = \cos(H_u, H_v) = \frac{H_u \cdot H_v}{\|H_u\|\|H_v\|}, \tag{7}$$

where H is the sum of the central node embedding F, the embedding of in-degree nodes E_{in} and the embedding of out-degree nodes E_{out}, denoted as: $H = W \cdot F + W_{\mathrm{in}} \cdot E_{\mathrm{in}} + W_{\mathrm{out}} \cdot E_{\mathrm{out}}$. And W is the trainable weight matrix.

In our heterogeneous graph, different edge types have different properties. The difference property of edge types motivates us to use non-shareable weight matrix for them when calculating the similarity. Therefore, we apply z non-shareable and trainable weight matrices for z different edge types. Then we compute the similarity for all edge types, the neighbors' feature is updated by the product of similarities and features, as shown in Eq. (8).

$$\hat{F}_v = \mathrm{sim}(u, v) \cdot F_v. \tag{8}$$

After analyzing our dataset, we found that the number of valid neighbors is usually less than 50. Therefore we sample the neighbors to a fix number of 50, and apply zero padding for central nodes of neighbors less than 50. For each subgroup of node u, adding the embeddings of all neighbors to get the embedding of this edge type, denoted as $\hat{F}_u^l$, as in the Eq. (9).

$$\hat{F}_u^l = \sum_{v \in N_u^l} \hat{F}_v. \tag{9}$$

Relation Aggregator: And we found the importance of edge types varies with the central node. Therefore, we employ a multi-head self-attention mechanism to learn a weighted for each type, as shown in Eq. (10).

$$\alpha_u^l = \frac{\exp\left(\text{LeakyReLU}(a^T[W_a \cdot F_u \| W_b \cdot \hat{F}_u^l])\right)}{\sum_{i=1}^{z} \exp\left(\text{LeakyReLU}(a^T[W_a \cdot F_u \| W_b \cdot \hat{F}_u^i])\right)}$$

$$\hat{F}_u = \frac{1}{z}\sum_{i=1}^{z}\alpha_u^l \hat{F}_u^l. \tag{10}$$

where W_a, W_b are linear matrices of the central node and neighbor sub-groups respectively, and $[\cdot\|\cdot]$ is the concatenation function. And a residual structure is used to compute the embedding of node u, denoted as Eq. (11):

$$E_u = F_u + \hat{F}_u. \tag{11}$$

Finally, we use MLP to get the prediction result of each central node u.

$$\hat{y}_u = \text{MLP}(E_u). \tag{12}$$

Model Training: For a graph with n nodes(orders), it is optimized by minimizing the classification loss of all nodes.

$$\mathcal{L}_{\text{class}} = -\sum_{u=1}^{n} y_u \log \hat{y}_u. \tag{13}$$

Furthermore, to guide the gate structure to find irrelevant nodes and speed up convergence, w penalize those sampled irrelevant neighbors with high similarity.

$$\mathcal{L}_{\text{sim}} = -\sum_{u=1}^{n}\sum_{l=1}^{z}\sum_{v \in N_u} \delta(y_u, \hat{y}_u) \cdot \text{sim}(u, v). \tag{14}$$

where δ is an *xor* function. The final optimization objective is balanced by a penalty coefficient λ, as shown in Eq. (15).

$$\mathcal{L}_{\text{FSO}} = \mathcal{L}_{\text{class}} + \lambda\mathcal{L}_{\text{sim}}. \tag{15}$$

4   Experiments

In this section, we first evaluate the performance of our method on a large real-world dataset. Then, we conduct a case study of user purchase patterns of this model. Finally, we compare our fraudulent order detection model with some other state-of-the-art classical graph algorithms.

4.1   Dataset

This fraudulent order detection dataset comes from JD.com, and all data has been desensitized to protect business secrets and user privacy. The dataset collects many details of orders, including order IDs, IP addresses and user click positions etc. To facilitate training and validating models, we group these labeled orders by date, and 3 days ($D_1 < D_2 < D_3$) of labeled data were selected to form the dataset. Table 1 lists the statistics for the daily datasets.

Table 1. Statistics of orders datasets.

Date	Normal	Frauludent	Total
D_1	39,916	6,376	46,292
D_2	41,878	7,403	49,281
D_3	43,135	6,669	49,804

4.2 Purchase Pattern Visualization

As mentioned earlier, group fraudsters employed by the same retailer tend to exhibit similar behavior patterns during the transaction session. On the other hand, normal users have their own personalized behavior patterns. We want to provide some intuition about which patterns of our model are captured. To do this, we randomly select some orders and generate their 100-dimensional vector via DPP. We then project them into a 2-D space using t-SNE. Figure 4 reveals some important insights: First, a clear boundary between normal and fraud can be easily observed. Compare to fraudsters, the behaviors of normal users are more fragmented. Finally, there are some samples fall into the opposite space, making identification difficult. Therefore, only using behavior features without analyzing sample relationships can lead to misclassification.

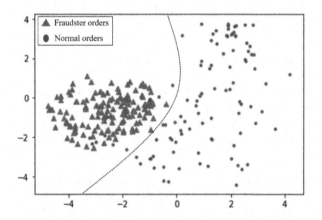

Fig. 4. Visualization of normal and fraudster group purchase behaviors using t-SNE.

Figure 5 gives an example of the classification performance of a simple linear layer with the behavior embedding as input. The x-axis represents the output risk probability. The y-axis represents the 1-dimension reduction result for each orders. As shown, it is difficult for the classifier to classify samples with probability between 0.2 and 0.8 due to ignoring the group context. Therefore, we review this part of data and use the graph model in Sect. 3.2 to identify fraudulent orders.

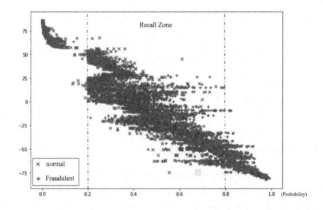

Fig. 5. Recall zone of toy classifier.

4.3 Fraudulent Order Detection Result of GSR

Orders Graph Construction: All the samples in recall zone will be used to
build the graph to facilitate our graph-based model. Equivalence relationships in
IP addresses, product IDs, phone numbers, device IDs and geography locations
are used to link edge between orders. Therefore, there is a totally one type of
node and five types of edges in the graph. Table 2 describes statistical graph
data information in the three datasets.

Table 2. Statics information of three graph datasets.

Date	Nodes	IP Address	Product ID	Phone	Device ID	Geography	Edges
D_1	20,268	9,300	268,055	2,386,941	8,345	6,299	2,678,940
D_2	20,537	7,688	249,231	2,713,310	6,509	6,612	2,983,350
D_3	23,128	7,284	349,249	3,303,950	6,568	6,741	3,673,792

Comparison Baselines: To demonstrate the effectiveness of group fraud inter-
connection, we use several basic classifiers: Random Forest (RF), Support Vector Machine (SVM), Logistic Regression (LR), Deep Neural Network (DNN) as
baselines, which ignore orders' internal dependencies, and name these models as
isolated-models. To verify the superiority of neighbor similarity and the difference in relation types, we compare our model with three supervised graph neural
networks, namely GCN [11], GraphSAGE [10], GAT [18], SCR [22] and SAGN
[16]. To demonstrate the importance of similarity and relation, two additional
baselines, GR and GS, are designed, which represent models without similarity and relation respectively. For comparison, all neighbors sampling parameters
are set to match those used in our model. All models were trained from scratch
until convergence. The initial node features are all the same dense user behavior
vector. The dimension of node embedding is uniformly set to 100.

Metrics and Performance Evaluation: Precisely identifying fraud cases is our main focus, therefore, the performances of different models is evaluated using the F1 score. To comprehensively evaluate the effect of binary classification, the area of precision-recall curve (AUC) is also provided. All networks are trained on dataset D1 and D2 respectively, and dataset D3 is used as the test set. The average of the test set evaluation results of the models trained on the two training sets is taken as the final evaluation result.

Table 3 lists the experimental results. As can be seen from the table, all isolated-models underperform graph-based models. This result suggests that neighbors are helpful in identifying ambiguous cases. And we find that the three traditional GNN methods fail to consider filtering irrelevant neighbors when aggregating features, and in addition, ignore different relation types. Finally, our model achieves about 2% improvement compare to the best baseline model. We further validate the effect of node on similarity judgement and type attention mechanism through ablation study. The comparison results show that by dynamically controlling the similarity, we can flexible mask those unrelated neighbors. Furthermore, considering the type importance weights also enhances the fraud detection capability. Therefore, we can safely conclude that the proposed method is a robust and effective fraudulent order detection system.

Table 3. Comparison results.

Type	Methods	F1	AUC
isolated	RF	68.24	72.82
	LR	70.28	73.72
	SVM	70.39	–
	DNN	69.47	72.90
Graph-based	GCN	79.22	95.72
	GraphSAGE	83.49	96.07
	GAT	79.63	95.81
	SCR	80.61	95.96
	SAGN	82.86	96.03
Proposed	GS	84.43	95.21
	GR	83.21	96.01
	GSR	**85.27**	**96.26**

5   Conclusions and Future Work

In this paper, we exploit the sequence of click position to solve the task of fraudulent order detection. We propose a two stage encoder-decoder framework for this task. First, we model the click sequence through RNN and self-attention model to generate static features. Subsequently, a GNN model based on large-scale graph is used to identify the association between transactions through the similar neighbor sampling module and the edge-type based attention module. Experiments show that our model is credible on large scale datasets and greatly improves the recall of fraudulent order detection. For future work, since the construction of real-time trade charts is a challenge for us, we will give more consideration to combine real-time charts with our methods.

References

1. Bahnsen, A.C., Aouada, D., Stojanovic, A., Ottersten, B.: Feature engineering strategies for credit card fraud detection. Expert Syst. Appl. **51**, 134–142 (2016)
2. Barkan, O., Koenigstein, N.: ITEM2VEC: neural item embedding for collaborative filtering. In: 2016 IEEE 26th International Workshop on Machine Learning for Signal Processing (MLSP), pp. 1–6. IEEE (2016)
3. Bhattacharyya, S., Jha, S., Tharakunnel, K., Westland, J.C.: Data mining for credit card fraud: a comparative study. Decis. Support Syst. **50**(3), 602–613 (2011)
4. Bickart, B., Schindler, R.M.: Internet forums as influential sources of consumer information. J. Interact. Mark. **15**(3), 31–40 (2001)
5. Chandradeva, L.S., Amarasinghe, T.M., De Silva, M., Aponso, A.C., Krishnarajah, N.: Monetary transaction fraud detection system based on machine learning strategies. In: Yang, X.-S., Sherratt, S., Dey, N., Joshi, A. (eds.) Fourth International Congress on Information and Communication Technology. AISC, vol. 1041, pp. 385–396. Springer, Singapore (2020). https://doi.org/10.1007/978-981-15-0637-6_33
6. Eberle, W., Holder, L.: Discovering structural anomalies in graph-based data. In: Seventh IEEE International Conference on Data Mining Workshops (ICDMW 2007), pp. 393–398. IEEE (2007)
7. Fei, G., Mukherjee, A., Liu, B., Hsu, M., Castellanos, M., Ghosh, R.: Exploiting burstiness in reviews for review spammer detection. In: Seventh International AAAI Conference on Weblogs and Social Media (2013)
8. Georgieva, S., Markova, M., Pavlov, V.: Using neural network for credit card fraud detection. In: AIP Conference Proceedings, vol. 2159, p. 030013. AIP Publishing LLC (2019)
9. Glover, S., Benbasat, I.: A comprehensive model of perceived risk of e-commerce transactions. Int. J. Electron. Commer. **15**(2), 47–78 (2010)
10. Hamilton, W., Ying, Z., Leskovec, J.: Inductive representation learning on large graphs. In: Advances in Neural Information Processing Systems, pp. 1024–1034 (2017)
11. Kipf, T.N., Welling, M.: Semi-supervised classification with graph convolutional networks. In: International Coference on Learning Representations (ICLR) (2017)
12. Lim, E.P., Nguyen, V.A., Jindal, N., Liu, B., Lauw, H.W.: Detecting product review spammers using rating behaviors. In: Proceedings of the 19th ACM International Conference on Information And Knowledge Management, pp. 939–948 (2010)
13. Manzoor, E., Milajerdi, S.M., Akoglu, L.: Fast memory-efficient anomaly detection in streaming heterogeneous graphs. In: Proceedings of the 22nd ACM SIGKDD International Conference on Knowledge Discovery and Data Mining, pp. 1035–1044 (2016)
14. Pourhabibi, T., Ong, K.L., Kam, B.H., Boo, Y.L.: Fraud detection: a systematic literature review of graph-based anomaly detection approaches. Decis. Support Syst. **133**, 113303 (2020)

15. Shehnepoor, S., Salehi, M., Farahbakhsh, R., Crespi, N.: Netspam: a network-based spam detection framework for reviews in online social media. IEEE Trans. Inf. Forensics Secur. **12**(7), 1585–1595 (2017)
16. Sun, C., Gu, H., Hu, J.: Scalable and adaptive graph neural networks with self-label-enhanced training. arXiv preprint arXiv:2104.09376 (2021)
17. Tao, J., Wang, H., Xiong, T.: Selective graph attention networks for account takeover detection. In: 2018 IEEE International Conference on Data Mining Workshops (ICDMW), pp. 49–54. IEEE (2018)
18. Veličković, P., Cucurull, G., Casanova, A., Romero, A., Lio, P., Bengio, Y.: Graph attention networks. In: International Conference on Learning Representations (ICLR) (2018)
19. Wang, S., Liu, C., Gao, X., Qu, H., Xu, W.: Session-based fraud detection in online e-commerce transactions using recurrent neural networks. In: Altun, Y., et al. (eds.) ECML PKDD 2017. LNCS (LNAI), vol. 10536, pp. 241–252. Springer, Cham (2017). https://doi.org/10.1007/978-3-319-71273-4_20
20. Wu, X., Dong, Y., Tao, J., Huang, C., Chawla, N.V.: Reliable fake review detection via modeling temporal and behavioral patterns. In: 2017 IEEE International Conference on Big Data (Big Data), pp. 494–499. IEEE (2017)
21. Xu, K., Hu, W., Leskovec, J., Jegelka, S.: How powerful are graph neural networks? In: International Conference on Learning Representations (ICLR) (2019)
22. Zhang, C., He, Y., Cen, Y., Hou, Z., Tang, J.: Improving the training of graph neural networks with consistency regularization. arXiv preprint arXiv:2112.04319 (2021)

Physical Logic Enhanced Network for Small-Sample Bi-layer Metallic Tubes Bending Springback Prediction

Chang Sun[1] (ORCID), Zili Wang[1,2](✉) (ORCID), Shuyou Zhang[1,2], Le Wang[1], and Jianrong Tan[1,2]

[1] State Key Laboratory of Fluid Power and Mechatronic Systems, Zhejiang University, Hangzhou 310027, China
ziliwang@zju.edu.cn
[2] Engineering Research Center for Design Engineering and Digital Twin of Zhejiang Province, Zhejiang University, Hangzhou 310027, China

Abstract. Bi-layer metallic tube (BMT) plays an extremely crucial role in engineering applications, with rotary draw bending (RDB) the high-precision bending processing can be achieved, however, the product will further springback. Due to the complex structure of BMT and the high cost of dataset acquisition, the existing methods based on mechanism research and machine learning cannot meet the engineering requirements of springback prediction. Based on the preliminary mechanism analysis, a physical logic enhanced network (PE-NET) is proposed. The architecture includes ES-NET which equivalent the BMT to the single-layer tube, and SP-NET for the final prediction of springback with sufficient single-layer tube samples. Specifically, in the first stage, with the theory-driven pre-exploration and the data-driven pretraining, the ES-NET and SP-NET are constructed, respectively. In the second stage, under the physical logic, the PE-NET is assembled by ES-NET and SP-NET and then fine-tuned with the small sample BMT dataset and composite loss function. The validity and stability of the proposed method are verified by the FE simulation dataset, the small-sample dataset BMT springback angle prediction is achieved, and the method potential in interpretability and engineering applications are demonstrated.

Keywords: Physical logic enhanced network · Mechanism analysis · Small-sample BMT dataset · Composite loss function

1 Introduction

Bent-tube is an important component for transporting gas, liquid, and even load-bearing, which plays an extremely crucial role in industrial production and application. Rotary draw bending (RDB) is the primary method for bent-tube processing, which has the advantages of high precision and well flexibility. After the bending processing, the elastic deformation recovers with the removal of the mold's constraints, which is normally called the springback phenomenon. The springback will significantly affect the accuracy of the

© The Author(s), under exclusive license to Springer Nature Switzerland AG 2022
L. Fang et al. (Eds.): CICAI 2022, LNAI 13605, pp. 124–135, 2022.
https://doi.org/10.1007/978-3-031-20500-2_10

product, making a margin necessarily to be given for compensation in the processing plan with an accurate springback prediction in advance.

Through the mechanism analysis of the bending process, the single-layer tube springback can be predicted from the angles of the bending state [1], prestress field [2], etc. With the improvement of the industry's requirements, the bi-layer metallic tube (BMT) have gradually been widely applied with advantages such as corrosion protection, wear and impact resistance, thermal and electric insulation. The material properties and interlayer coupling of BMT are incredibly complex [3], which greatly increases the difficulty of springback prediction. Therefore, different from the well-established research of the single-layer metallic tube processing, the existing springback research of the BMT mainly focuses on the influence of individual factors [4, 5]. Its processing deformation mechanism still urgently needs to be further explored.

Although it is difficult for BMT to implement the forming theory of classical single-layer tubes directly, there is a remarkable similarity in bending deformation between them. In fact, it is feasible to equivalent the bi-layer materials as one of them for simplifying, which has been verified in beams and slabs [6, 7]. Nevertheless, due to the unique cross-sectional properties, the errors in the BMT equivalence make it difficult to be used directly.

Through the unique structure and learning method, the neural network can reach the effect of a nonlinear function, and have the ability to accomplish the springback prediction based on the batch FE simulation data [8, 9]. However, when it comes to a problem with the small-sample dataset, the network can be challenging to reach an acceptable accuracy.

From the perspective of the scientific paradigm, the machine learning algorithms and the physical models are driven by data and theory, respectively. The theoretical approach is based on strict logical relationships with strong interpretability and generalization performance. Meanwhile, machine learning methods can realize the reflection of the internal relationship from dataset dimensions that are difficult to observe. Therefore, the combination of them has received more and more attention. In fact, with the guidance of physical knowledge, machine learning has been shown to benefit from plausible physically-based relationships in research and applications [10, 11]. Such methods have been initially applied and demonstrated their effectiveness in disease prediction [10, 12], geological detection [13], natural language processing [14], mechanical analysis [15], etc.

As mentioned above, the deformation mechanism of the BMT is exceptionally complicated. At the same time, since the high cost of BMT and the complex processing requirements, the scale of the dataset is limited, which makes it difficult for the network to achieve acceptable accuracy with the data-driven approach alone. However, combined with the preliminary physical analysis, the network can learn start on the basis of physical logic and existing knowledge, which can improve the training efficiency, reduce the probability of overfitting, and improve the accuracy of the network.

Therefore, the physical logic enhanced network (PE-NET) is proposed to solve the problems of the insufficient mechanism analysis and limited datasets of BMT. PE-NET includes an equivalent section network (ES-NET) and a single-layer prediction network

(SP-NET). ES-NET is used to map the equivalent shape parameters of BMT to single-layer tube, while SP-NET carries the knowledge of single-layer bending deformation for final prediction. The two are pre-trained under the data-driven and theory-driven, respectively, and then combined as PE-NET under the physical logic. After that, the parameters of PE-NET will be rationally constrained by the loss function combination of mechanism equation, and fine-tuned by the small BMT dataset.

The main contributions of this paper are as follows: (1) The equivalent section method is applied to the mechanism analysis of BMT bending. (2) A collaborative architecture of theory-driven and data-driven together is constructed based on physical logic. (3) The BMT springback angle prediction is realized by the proposed PE-NET with small-sample dataset and mechanism analysis.

2   Background Knowledge

2.1   RDB Processing of BMT

Springback is caused by residual stress after RDB processing which can be affected by multiple factors. As shown in Fig. 1, during the processing, the tube blank is deformed under the constraint and movement of molds. Specifically, under the boosting of the pressure die and the clamping of the clamp die, the tube blank is bent and rotated around the bending die, while the wiper die prevents wrinkling defect. The radius R_B and rotation angle α_B of the bending die directly determine the product shape. At the same time, the initial location L_P and boost velocity v_B of the pressure die, the processing velocity ω_B, the gap G_i and friction f_i between the tube blank and the molds also have a significant influence on the generation and distribution of residual stress.

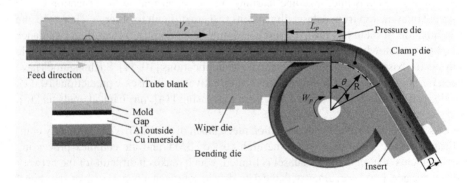

Fig. 1. RDB processing of BMT

In addition to the above processing parameters, the shape parameters are also major factor of springback to be considered. The wall thickness T and diameter D_o of the tube blank directly determine the bending properties and springback angle. For BMT, the thickness ratio T_r is also one of the decisive factors.

2.2   Equivalent Section Theory

The springback can be regarded as the recovery of the elastic deformation caused by a reverse moment M from the internal processing stress of the bent-tube before springback. Therefore, the equivalent characteristics of the material in the elastic deformation stage will be mainly analyzed.

The mechanism of tube bending is always based on the sheet bending theory. As shown in Fig. 2, take a micro-element on the section of the laminated beam. In order to simplify the analysis, the bending process satisfies the assumption of plane section and unidirectional force, and the neutral layer does not shift. For materials such as aluminum and alloy steel, the linearly strengthened elastic-plastic material model can be adopted. Assuming that there is no axial force during the processing, i.e., the pure bending condition, and normal stress can be regarded as zero. Combine with the stress distribution in the elastic deformation stage, we have

$$F_N = \int_{A_k} \sigma(x, y, z)dA = \sum_k^n \int_{A_k} E_k \frac{y}{\rho} dA = \frac{1}{\rho} \sum_k^n E_k S_{Zk} = 0 \tag{1}$$

$$M_z = \int_{A_k} \sigma(x, y, z)ydA = \sum_k^n \int_{A_k} E_k \frac{y^2}{\rho} dA = \frac{1}{\rho} \sum_k^n E_k I_{Zk} \tag{2}$$

where for the k-th material, S_{Zk} is the area moment (static moment), I_{Zk} is the moments of inertia, E_k is the distribution of the elastic modulus, and ρ is the distance from the neutral axis.

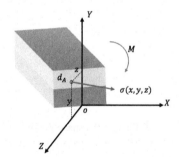

Fig. 2. Bending analysis of laminated beams

Then we have

$$\sigma_i = \frac{-E_i My}{\sum_{k=1}^n E_k I_{Zk}} = \lambda_i \frac{My}{I_{Z0}} (i = 1, 2, \dots n) \tag{3}$$

$$I_{z0} = \sum_{k=1}^n \lambda_k I_{Zk} \tag{4}$$

$$S_{Z0} = \sum_{k=1}^n \lambda_k S_{Zk} = 0 \tag{5}$$

where $\lambda_i = E_i/E_m (i = 1, 2, \ldots n)$ is the ratio of the elastic modulus, E_m is the reference elastic modulus, S_{Z0} is the total area moment of each equivalent section, and I_{z0} is the total moments of inertia of each equivalent section. For an integral region, $1/\rho$ and E_k are both constants.

As shown in Eqs. (4) and (5), the thickness of each material region will be scaled down by λ_k, the width and the circumferential centroid position will remain unchanged, and the multi-material section will be transformed into the specified material section. I_{Z0} can be obtained by the moment of inertia of the transformed section to the neutral axis, and the equivalent single-layer tube radius and thickness can be further calculated.

3   Methodology

3.1   Proposed Prediction Architecture

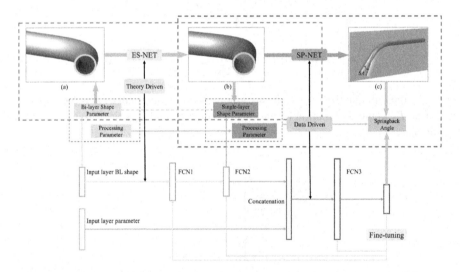

Fig. 3. The architecture of the PE-NET: (**a**) is the shape parameter of the BMT; (**b**) is the shape parameter of the single-layer tube; (**c**) is the predicted springback.

The parameter update of the traditional neural network relies on the observation of the prediction value and the label, which the parameters are able to explore in an unrestricted region. However, the small-sample of the bi-layer dataset cannot guarantee that the network parameters reach an acceptable result. Realizing domain transfer based on theory analysis, and using sufficient close domain knowledge can make up for the inferior of the small-sample dataset. On this basis, the network can be partitioned into functional modules according to physical logic, which provides very strong theoretical logic and constraints on top of the observational ones [11].

Pre-exploration of the network parameter domain and applying the guidance to the network parameters in further training is an effective way to improve training efficiency and prevent overfitting [16]. In terms of results, both theory-driven and multi-objective optimization-based parameter preselection [17] are common methods to improve network accuracy. The results of multi-objective-based methods are random, lack physical logic, and rely heavily on prior knowledge. However, theory-driven network training can achieve parameter domain pre-exploration without effective prior knowledge, and is well applied to small-sample prediction.

The proposed PE-NET architecture is shown in Fig. 3. The traditional neural network for the mapping of the parameters to the springback often adopts the data-driven method with path Fig. 3a directly to Fig. 3c. Due to the similar bending mechanism of bi-layer and single-layer materials, the close domain knowledge can be used. The PE-NET consists of two modules, namely the ES-NET which is for the equivalent mapping from the BMT to the single-layer tube, and the SP-NET which is for the final springback prediction with the single-layer tube knowledge. Specifically, at the first stage, the parameters of the ES-NET are pre-explored based on preliminary mechanism analysis, realizing the Fig. 3a,b, and the parameters of SP-NET are pretrained on the low-cost single-layer tube dataset, realizing Fig. 3b,c. In the second stage, the PE-NET is constructed by ES-NET and SP-NET based on the physical logic. Since the discrepancy of different material datasets and the error of mechanism analysis, the fine-tuning of the PE-NET is implemented. The loss function of PE-NET in the second stage is based on two parts, i.e., the rationality constraints based on the mechanism equation, and backpropagation from the small-sample dataset. The detail of their cooperation will be introduced in Sect. 3.3.

As shown in Fig. 3, benefiting from the sufficient dataset and the ability of neural networks for high-dimensional relationship mapping, a fully-connected network (FCN) can achieve acceptable accuracy for springback prediction [9]. Specifically, SP-NET and ES-NET each contain a hidden layer with 10 units. In addition, ES-NET also includes an implicit output layer (FCN2) for single-layer tube shape parameter equivalent, which is also used as an FCN with 2 units in the second stage.

3.2 Preliminary Analysis of BMT Equivalence Section

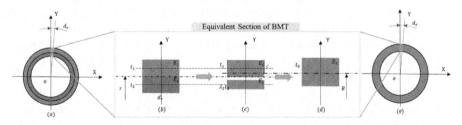

Fig. 4. Schematic diagram of equivalent section process: (**a**) is the BMT section; (**b**) is one of the microelements; (**c**) is the cross-section after the material E_2 is equivalent to E_1; (**d**) is the E_1 material section of the equivalent moment of inertia with (**c**); (**e**) is the equivalent single-layer tube section.

For the theory-driven pre-exploration of the ES-NET parameter in the first stage, the preliminary analysis based on equivalent section theory is necessary. As shown in

Fig. 4, take the elastic modulus E_1 of material on the outside as the reference, based on the calculation of area moments, the distance between the central axis and the upper edge of the micro-element c can be calculated. It can be seen from Eq. (5) that the area moments before and after are equal. Therefore, the radius R of the equivalent section is

$$R = r + e = r + \frac{(t_1 + \sqrt{\lambda_2}t_2)(t_1 - \sqrt{\lambda_2}t_2)}{2(t_1 + \lambda_2 t_2)} \tag{6}$$

where r is the radius of the junction of the BMT section, e is the centroid axis offset of the equivalent micro-element section compared with the original BMT, $t_i(i = 1, 2)$ is the thickness of the i-th material, $\lambda_2 = E_2/E_1$.

With the properties of the tube section and Eq. (6), we have

$$t_0^3 + 4R^2 t_0 - \frac{1}{R}\left[(r + t_1)^4 - (1 - \lambda_2)r^4 - \lambda_2(r - t_2)^4\right] = 0 \tag{7}$$

Combined with conditions of real numbers and engineering, the equivalent material thickness t_0 in the can be obtained.

According to R and t_0, the shape parameters of the equivalent single-layer tube can be obtained. Since the assumptions and simplifications are adopted, the error must exist. However, the above analysis ensures the equivalent result is under the basic physical laws, which can guarantee the physical rationality of the ES-NET pre-exploration in the first stage, and the fine-tuning of the PE-NET in the second stage.

3.3 Composition of the Loss Function

As shown in Fig. 3, in the first stage, the parameter updates for ES-NET and SP-NET are based on theory-driven and data-driven, respectively, as shown below.

$$L_p = MSE\left(ES - NET\left(x_s^b\right) - f_{ES-NET}\left(x_s^b\right)\right) \tag{8}$$

$$L_d = MSE\left(PE - NET\left(x^b\right) - Y_{SA}\right) \tag{9}$$

where x^b is the input of the BMT, x_s^b is the shape parameter input of the x^b, $ES - NET\left(x_s^b\right)$ reflect the shape parameter of the single-layer tube, which is also the implicit output of ES-NET and the implicit input of the PE-NET in the second stage, donated as x_s^s. Y_{SA} is the predicted springback which the output of SP-NET in the first stage and the output of the PE-NET in the second stage. f_{ES-NET} represents the theory-driven knowledge for pre-exploration of the ES-NET in the first stage.

In the second stage, the PS-NET is fine-tuned with a combination of update-driven approaches. Based on Eqs. (10) and (11), L_p can keep the ES-NET in the reasonable parameter domain and guarantee the physical plausibility of this process. However, the reliability of the loss function L_d for parameter update driven by real data will significantly be higher than L_p driven by physical equivalence theory. In order to keep their advantages in the second training stage, the integration of the two parameter update-driven approaches for better cooperation is necessary. Therefore, the dynamic weight loss function will be adopted, as follows:

$$L_{ES-NET} = zL_p + (1 - z)L_d \tag{10}$$

$$z = \begin{cases} P_{N(x_s^s,1)}(2x_s^s - f_{ES-NET}(x_s^b) \le X \le f_{ES-NET}(x_s^b)), & L_p > 2x_s^s \\ 0, & L_p \le 2x_s^s \end{cases} \qquad (11)$$

where z is the dynamic weight coefficient and N is the normal function.

Given the reasonable range of equivalence relationship result, in the second stage, when the implicit result of ES-NET is far away from the physical reasonable, L_p will guide the parameters until it is physical reasonable. When the result is within the reasonable range, L_p will no longer play a dominant role, and instead, the PE-NET parameter will be updated mainly based on L_d.

4 Case Study

As one of the most commonly used material combinations, copper-aluminum BMT has received more and more attention due to its advantages in weight and thermal properties. Their material properties vary greatly, and their elastic modulus are $E_1 = 80.7$ GPa and $E_2 = 110$ Gpa, respectively. In engineering applications, compared with the widely used aluminum tube, the data of the copper-aluminum BMT is still rare, and the research on its deformation still needs to be improved, which makes it selected as the research object.

4.1 Dataset Construction

FE simulation is an effective method to obtain engineering solutions [4, 18]. It is an important step to verify technical routes by constructing datasets that meet experimental requirements and reduce trial costs before actual applications.

With the Latin hypercube sampling, the datasets are determined. The ABAQUS 2016 platform is used for simulation analysis. The S4R shell with the specially 9th-order Simpson integration points in the thickness direction is used for the tube deformation unit, and the R3D4 rigid for the molds. The stress-strain trend of the material adopts the power hardening model. The friction constraint is applied when the tube blank is pulled. The composite material is assigned to the properties of the BMT, including the relative sampling thickness ratio. Since the velocity is one of the important factors affecting springback, the bending processing adopts explicit dynamics analysis, while static analysis is used for springback simulation. The simulated result is imported into MATLAB for post-processing to extract the springback result and build the dataset.

In order to meet the engineering practice, there is a significant order of magnitude difference between the single-layer tube and the BMT. Specifically, the single-layer tube dataset, namely Dataset1, contains 600 samples, provides sufficient single-layer tube deformation knowledge. Since the double-layer tube is a small sample, its dataset, i.e. Dataset2 has only 80 samples.

4.2 Precision Analysis of Proposed Method

As mentioned in Sect. 3.1, the training consists of two stages. The first stage is for the parameter pre-exploration of the ES-NET and the pretrain of the SP-NET, and the second stage is for the parameter fine-tuning of PE-NET. Accuracy is the median error of multiple training results. The accuracy of the two stages is the median error of 30 training sets, as shown in Table 1. Particularly, in the second stage, PE-NET is constructed based on specific SP-NET and ES-NET with the median of error.

All training is performed on MATLAB 2022a on the same GPU. All datasets will be split before training, 80% of which will be used for training, and the remaining be used for tests. The test set does not participate in the training process. The Adam optimizer is employed, and the dataset is shuffled every epoch. For the first stage, the training minibatch size is set to 5, and the initial and decay factor of the gradient are 0.005 and 0.9, respectively. For the second stage, the training minibatch size is set to 2, and the initial and decay factor of the gradient are 0.0001 and 0.8, respectively.

Table 1. The median RMSE of the two training stages

	SP-NET	ES-NET	
Stage 1	Springback angle	D_O	T
	0.7672	0.7133	0.4916
	PE-NET		
Stage 2	Springback angle		
	0.3922		

As shown in Table 1, the median error of PE-NET is 0.3922, which meets the requirements of engineering applications. It should be noted that although the second stage is fine-tuning based on the small-sample Dataset2, the accuracy is higher than that of SP-NET only based on data-driven. On the one hand, this reflects the rationality and effectiveness of the architecture proposed. On the other hand, based on the learning of multiple driving logic and datasets, the network can learn a variety of features and noise, which greatly improves the ability of generalization and overfit prevention. This can also be proved in Sect. 4.3.

4.3   Effectiveness of PE-NET

Controlled experiments are conducted to verify the effectiveness of the proposed physical logic architecture. PE-NET without ES-NET pre-exploration based on mechanism analysis, and without SP-NET pre-training are analyzed, denoted as PE-NET-WMA and PE-NET-WSP, respectively. Without any pre-operation, the PE-NET architecture and simple BPNN with 10 units hidden layer are trained based on Dataset2, denoted as BL-NET and BP-NET, respectively. All training parameters are the same. The results of multiple sets of training and corresponding average RMSE are recorded, as shown in Fig. 5 and Table 2, respectively.

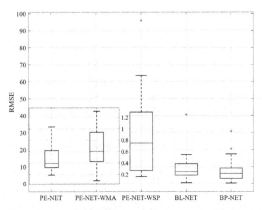

Fig. 5. Box-plot of springback prediction methods comparison

Table 2. The median RMSE of the controlled experiments

Method	RMSE
PE-NET	0.3922
PE-NET-WMA	0.6019
PE-NET-WSP	23.7527
BL-NET	6.9424
BP-NET	6.3572

Results show that PE-NET performs the best no matter of accuracy or stability. Despite the possibility of available prediction accuracy, the lack of theoretical guidance and constraints reduces the stability of PE-NET-WMA, making it less efficient than PE-NET in engineering applications. Similarly, without pre-training with close domain knowledge, the performance of PE-NET-WSP is extremely poor, making it difficult to be applied to BMT springback prediction of small samples. The above two results also prove the validation of the deformation knowledge of single-layer tube and mechanism analysis, and the effectiveness of the proposed physical logic-based PE-NET architecture has also been demonstrated. For BL-NET and BP-NET, its poor accuracy and stability make it impossible to be used in engineering applications either.

In addition, the accuracy of the mechanism analysis is also revealed. The RMSE of equivalent Dataset2 springback is 1.6164. This also proves the necessity of fine-tuning based on BMT data. On this basis, it is feasible to further improve the equivalent theory with the help of the fine-tuned ES-NET, which also demonstrates the potential of the PE-NET architecture in interpretability.

5 Conclusion

In this work, we proposed a physical logic-based architecture network PE-NET to predict the springback of BMT with small samples. The BMT was logically equivalent to the single-layer tube, and then predicted with the single-layer springback knowledge. At first, the bending deformation mechanical analysis for section equivalent was conducted. Then, with the data-driven and theory-driven methods, the ES-NET and SP-NET were built with the theory-driven parameter pre-exploration and the data-driven pretraining, respectively. Finally, the PE-NET was constructed with the combination of ES-NET and SP-NET under the physical logic and the composition of the loss function. The validation and stability of the proposed method were verified with the FE simulation platform. This work is a primary attempt to solve the engineering problems with the only small-sample and limited theory, and will be integrated into more complex prediction and interpretability research in the future.

Acknowledgments. This paper is funded by the Joint Funds of the National Natural Science Foundation of China (U20A20287), the National Natural Science Foundation of China (51905476), the Public Welfare Technology Application Projects of Zhejiang Province, China (LGG22E050008).

References

1. Zhan, M., Yang, H., Huang, L., et al.: Springback analysis of numerical control bending of thin-walled tube using numerical-analytic method. J. Mater. Process. Technol. **177**, 197–201 (2006)
2. Zhai, R.X., Ding, X.H., Yu, S.M., et al.: Stretch bending and springback of profile in the loading method of prebending and tension. Int. J. Mech. Sci. **144**, 746–764 (2018)
3. Li, W.Y., Wen, Q., Yang, X.W., et al.: Interface microstructure evolution and mechanical properties of Al/Cu bimetallic tubes fabricated by a novel friction-based welding technology. Mater. Des. **134**, 383–393 (2017)
4. Li, Y., et al.: Springback prediction of AL6061 pipe in free bending process based on finite element and analytic methods. Int. J. Adv. Manuf. Technol. **109**(7–8), 1789–1799 (2020). https://doi.org/10.1007/s00170-020-05772-2
5. Liu, J., Liu, Y., Li, L., Li, X.: Springback behaviors of bi-layered non-homogeneous bellows in hydroforming. Int. J. Adv. Manuf. Technol. **93**(5–8), 1605–1616 (2017). https://doi.org/10.1007/s00170-017-0642-1
6. Chen, W.R., Chang H.: Vibration analysis of functionally graded Timoshenko beams. Int. J. Struct. Stab. Dyn. **18**, 24 (2018)
7. He, X.T., Chen, S.F., Sun, J.Y.: Applying the equivalent section method to solve beam subjected to lateral force and bending-compression column with different moduli. Int. J. Mech. Sci. **49**, 919–924 (2007)
8. Serban, F.M., Grozav, S., Ceclan, V., et al.: Artificial neural networks model for springback prediction in the bending operations. Tehnicki Vjesnik-Technical Gazette. **27**, 868–873 (2020)
9. Zhou, H.F., Zhang, S.Y., Qiu, L.M., et al.: Springback angle prediction of circular metal tube considering the interference of cross-sectional distortion in mandrel-less rotary draw bending. Sci. Prog. **104**, 30 (2021)
10. Hsu, Y.C., Wang, J.D., Huang, P.H., et al.: Integrating domain knowledge with machine learning to detect obstructive sleep apnea: Snore as a significant bio-feature. J. Sleep Res. **31**, 10 (2022)

11. Reichstein, M., Camps-Valls, G., Stevens, B., et al.: Deep learning and process understanding for data-driven earth system science. Nature **566**, 195–204 (2019)
12. Burwinkel, H., Matz, H., Saur, S., et al.: Physics-aware learning and domain-specific loss design in ophthalmology. Med. Image Anal. **76**, 14 (2022)
13. Camps-Valls, G., Martino, L., Svendsen, D.H., et al.: Physics-aware Gaussian processes in remote sensing. Appl. Soft Comput. **68**, 69–82 (2018)
14. Sun, Y., Wang, S., Li, Y., et al.: Ernie: enhanced representation through knowledge integration. arXiv preprint arXiv:1904.09223 (2019)
15. Sun, L.N., Gao, H., Pan, S.W., et al.: Surrogate modeling for fluid flows based on physics-constrained deep learning without simulation data. Comput. Methods Appl. Mech. Eng. **361**, 25 (2020)
16. Ming, Y., Yi, L.: Model selection and estimation in regression with grouped variables. J. Roy. Stat. Soc.: Ser. B (Stat. Methodol). **68**, 49–67 (2006)
17. Trzepiecinski, T., Lemu, H.G.: Improving prediction of springback in sheet metal forming using multilayer perceptron-based genetic algorithm. Materials **13**, 16 (2020)
18. Shahabi, M., Nayebi, A.: Springback FE modeling of titanium alloy tubes bending using various hardening models. Struct. Eng. Mech. **56**, 369–383 (2015)

Blind Surveillance Image Quality Assessment via Deep Neural Network Combined with the Visual Saliency

Wei Lu, Wei Sun, Xiongkuo Min, Zicheng Zhang, Tao Wang, Wenhan Zhu, Xiaokang Yang, and Guangtao Zhai[✉]

Shanghai Jiao Tong University, Shanghai, China
{SJTU-Luwei,zhaiguangtao}@sjtu.edu.cn

Abstract. The intelligent video surveillance system (IVSS) can automatically analyze the content of the surveillance image (SI) and reduce the burden of the manual labour. However, the SIs may suffer quality degradations in the procedure of acquisition, compression, and transmission, which makes IVSS hard to understand the content of SIs. In this paper, we first conduct an example experiment (i.e. the face detection task) to demonstrate that the quality of the SIs has a crucial impact on the performance of the IVSS, and then propose a saliency-based deep neural network for the blind quality assessment of the SIs, which helps IVSS to filter the low-quality SIs and improve the detection and recognition performance. Specifically, we first compute the saliency map of the SI to select the most salient local region since the salient regions usually contain rich semantic information for machine vision and thus have a great impact on the overall quality of the SIs. Next, the convolutional neural network (CNN) is adopted to extract quality-aware features for the whole image and local region, which are then mapped into the global and local quality scores through the fully connected (FC) network respectively. Finally, the overall quality score is computed as the weighted sum of the global and local quality scores. Experimental results on the SI quality database (SIQD) show that the proposed method outperforms all compared state-of-the-art BIQA methods.

Keywords: Surveillance image · Blind quality assessment · Deep neural network · Visual saliency

1 Introduction

With the rapid development of computer vision technology and the growing demand for security, recent years have witnessed the increasing popularity of the intelligent video surveillance system (IVSS), which can automatically analyze and understand the content of surveillance videos and thus greatly reduce the burden of the manual labour. Specifically, IVSS involves analyzing the videos using algorithms that detect, track, and recognize objects of interest [1]. However, the surveillance images (SIs) may suffer different degrees of degradations

© The Author(s), under exclusive license to Springer Nature Switzerland AG 2022
L. Fang et al. (Eds.): CICAI 2022, LNAI 13605, pp. 136–146, 2022.
https://doi.org/10.1007/978-3-031-20500-2_11

(a)   (b)

Fig. 1. Examples of the SIs with low image quality, which are from the SI quality database (SIQD) [2]. The red rectangle region is the blurred face and the green rectangle region is the clear background.

in quality due to the artifacts introduced to the SI acquisition and transmission process [2,3], such as poor lighting conditions, low compression bit rates, etc. The SIs with low quality may lead to the poor performance of the computer vision tasks and thus make the IVSS difficult to effectively analyze the content of surveillance videos [4]. Hence, it is necessary to develop an effective quality assessment tool for SIs, which can help the IVSS to filter the low-quality SIs and improve the performance of the IVSS.

Objective image quality assessment (IQA), which aims to automatically predict the perceptual visual quality of images, is a hot topic in the field of image processing [5,6]. Since the reference image is not available in the surveillance system, only blind IQA (BIQA) is suitable for qualifying the quality of SIs. Existing BIQA methods can be divided into two categories, which are hand-crafted feature based and deep learning based algorithms [7,8]. Hand-crafted feature based BIQA models generally design quality-related features like natural scene statistics (NSS) features [9–12], free energy features [13,14], textures [15], etc., and then map these features into quality scores via a regression model such as support vector regression. Mittal *et al.* [9] utilized the statistical property in the spatial domain to predict the quality. Gu *et al.* [13] proposed a BIQA metric using the free-energy-based brain theory and classical human visual system (HVS)-inspired features. Deep learning based models usually adopt the convolutional neural network (CNN) to extract quality-aware features automatically and then regress them to quality scores with a fully connected (FC) network [16–19]. Sun *et al.* [16] proposed a staircase structure to hierarchically integrate the features from intermediate layers into the final quality feature representation.

However, most existing BIQA models are developed for evaluating the images with synthetic distortions such as JPEG compression, Gaussian noise, etc., and do not perform well on the SIs with authentic and diverse distortions. Moreover, the distortions in the salient regions or regions of interest (ROI) have a greater impact on the overall visual quality of the SIs than that in the inconspicuous regions, when the human visual system (HVS) or IVSS tries to extract useful information from the SIs. As depicted in Fig. 1, the SIs with a clear background and a blurred face

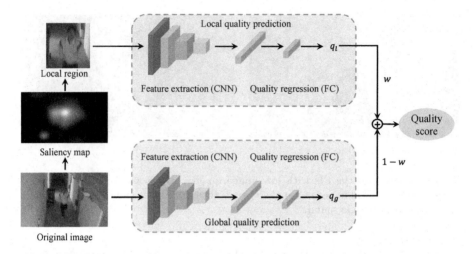

Fig. 2. The framework of the proposed method for the blind quality assessment of the SIs.

generally have poor quality since the human and IVSS cannot recognize the very blur face. However, most existing BIQA methods do not consider this characteristic and have an inferior correlation with the quality of the SIs.

In this paper, we demonstrate that the quality of the SIs has a crucial impact on the performance of the intelligent video surveillance system through an example experiment (the face detection task) on the SI quality database (SIQD) [2], and propose a visual saliency based deep neural network for the blind quality assessment of the SIs. To be more specific, we first compute the saliency map of each SI and select the local region with the maximum saliency weight. Second, the CNN is adopted to extract the quality-aware features for the whole image and the most salient local region, which are then mapped into the global quality and local quality score via the FC network respectively. Finally, the overall quality score of the SI is obtained by the weighted sum of global and local quality scores. Experimental results demonstrate that the proposed method outperforms state-of-the-art BIQA methods on the SIQD, which proves the effectiveness of the proposed method.

2   Proposed Method

In this section, the proposed blind surveillance IQA model is described in detail. As shown in Fig. 2, the framework of the proposed method mainly includes three stages: selecting the local region via the saliency map, extracting the quality-aware features for the whole image and local region, and predicting the overall quality score.

2.1 Saliency-Based Local Region Selection

According to the characteristics of the HVS, different regions of the image obtain different degrees of attention. The salient regions have a great impact on the overall quality of the SIs since the salient regions usually contain rich semantic information, which is very important for machine vision algorithms. Hence, we propose to simultaneously predict the global quality of the whole image and the local quality of the salient region.

As for the local region selection, we first compute the saliency map S for the image I using a state-of-the-art saliency model SimpleNet [20], which is pretrained on a large saliency benchmark dataset SALICON [21]. The saliency value $S(i,j)$ of the pixel (i,j) ranges in $[0,1]$, and the higher saliency value means it is more salient. Then we crop multiple image regions with the resolution of 224×224 through scanning the image I both horizontally and vertically with a stride size of 32 pixels. The overall saliency weight of each image region P is calculated as follow:

$$sw = \sum_{x}\sum_{y} S(x,y), (x,y) \in P. \tag{1}$$

Finally, the image region with the maximum saliency weight sw is selected for the local quality prediction.

2.2 Quality-Aware Feature Extraction

In recent years, CNN has demonstrated its powerful ability to solve various visual signal problems. Recent BIQA models mostly adopt the deep learning based architecture, which uses a CNN backbone to extract quality-aware features of distorted images, and then uses a fully connected network to aggregate them to quality scores. The architecture could be trained in an end-to-end manner and has become dominant in BIQA field. Compared with the handcrafted features, the features extracted by CNN contain more semantic information, which are suitable for quality assessment of SIs since a high quality of the SI means we can get exact semantic information from it.

In the proposed method, we adopt the ResNet [22], which is a commonly used backbone in existing BIQA models, to extract quality-aware features for the whole image and local region. Specifically, the ResNet18 pretrained on the ImageNet [23] is selected for the quality-aware feature extraction. First, we feed the whole image I_g or local region I_l into the CNN model and then obtain the feature map from the last convolutional layer:

$$\begin{aligned} F_g &= \mathrm{CNN}_{global}(I_g), \\ F_l &= \mathrm{CNN}_{local}(I_l), \end{aligned} \tag{2}$$

where CNN_{global}, CNN_{local} refer to the CNN models for global and local feature extraction respectively and they do not share the same parameters. F_g and F_l are respectively the feature maps extracted from the whole image and local region.

Second, the feature maps are converted into the feature vectors through the spatial global average pooling:

$$f_g = \mathrm{GAP}(F_g),$$
$$f_l = \mathrm{GAP}(F_l), \tag{3}$$

where $\mathrm{GAP}(\cdot)$ means the the spatial global average pooling, and f_g, f_l refer to the extracted feature vectors for the whole image I_g and local region I_l respectively.

2.3   Quality Prediction

With the extracted quality-aware features, we adopt two FC layers as the regression model to predict the image quality. Specifically, the features are mapped into the quality scores through two FC layers consisting of 128 and 1 neurons respectively:

$$q_g = \mathrm{FC}_{global}(f_g),$$
$$q_l = \mathrm{FC}_{local}(f_l), \tag{4}$$

where FC_{global} and FC_{local} are respectively the global quality regression model and local quality regression model. q_g means the global quality and q_l means the local quality. The overall quality score q is computed as the weighted sum of the global and local scores:

$$q = w \cdot q_l + (1 - w) \cdot q_g, \tag{5}$$

where the weight w for the local quality ranges from 0 to 1. Finally, we can train the feature extraction network and image quality regressor in an end-to-end training manner, and the euclidean distance is used as the loss function, which can be computed as:

$$L = \|q - q_{label}\|^2, \tag{6}$$

where q_{label} refer to the ground-truth quality score.

3   Experiments

In this section, we first briefly introduce the latest SI quality assessment database SIQD [2]. Next, we test a face detection algorithm on different quality of SIs selected from the SIQD, and the experimental results show that the visual quality of the SIs has a crucial impact on the face detection performance. Then we compare the proposed method and other state-of-the-art (SOTA) BIQA methods on the SIQD database. Finally, we analyze how the weight of the local quality affects the final predictive performance.

Table 1. The performance of the face detection on the SIs of different levels of quality in the SIQD database.

MOS	Precision	Recall	Accuracy
[1.0, 2.5]	0.8203	0.3477	0.3231
(2.5, 3.5]	0.7778	0.5147	0.4487
(3.5, 5.0]	0.7200	0.9403	0.6885

3.1   Test Database

The SIQD database [2] includes 500 in-the-wild SIs with different degrees of quality, which cover various scenarios and diverse illumination conditions. The objects in the SIs contain human, vehicle (license number), etc., and the database contains four different resolutions: 1920×1080, 1280×720, 704×576, and 352×288. The mean opinion scores (MOSs) of each SI range from 1 to 5, where the larger MOSs, the higher quality.

3.2   The Effect of Visual Quality on IVSS

Although there is a common consensus that the low visual quality images will lead to the performance drop of the IVSS, it is necessary to conduct the experiment to validate and quantify this impact. In the experiment, we take the face detection task as an example to investigate this impact. We first select 286 SIs which contain one or more faces from the SIQD database and annotate face regions in images with bounding boxes. Then, the pretrained MTCNN [24] network is used to detect faces for these SIs with the ground-truth bounding boxes. Finally, we compare the face detection performance on the SIs of different levels of quality. Specifically, the bounding box detected by the MTCNN network is considered to be correct if and only if its Intersection over Union (IoU) with the ground truth bounding box is more than 50%, and three common evaluation metrics are used to measure the face detection performance, which are Precision, Recall, and Accuracy.

The performance results on the SIs of different levels of quality are summarized in Table 1. From Table 1, in terms of the Recall and Accuracy metric, we first observe that the performance of high-quality SIs is significantly higher than that of low-quality SIs, which indicates that the face detection performance of the SIs is largely affected by their visual quality. Hence, it is necessary to use the BIQA metric to filter the low-quality SIs, which can help to improve the performance of face detection. In addition, we can see that the Precision value drops slightly as the visual quality increases, which may be because the misjudgments of the face detection model are more likely to occur in the background of high-quality SIs than that of low-quality SIs.

3.3   Performance Comparison with SOTA BIQA Methods

Evaluation Metrics. We adopt Pearson Linear Correlation Coefficient (PLCC), Spearman Rank Order Correlation Coefficient (SROCC), and Root Mean Squared Error (RMSE) to evaluate different BIQA methods. SROCC represents the prediction monotonicity, while PLCC and RMSE indicate the prediction accuracy. An excellent model should obtain values of SROCC and PLCC close to 1, and the value of RMSE near 0. Before calculating the PLCC and RMSE, the nonlinear four-parameter logistic function in [25] is applied to map the scores predicted by objective BIQA methods to the subjective scores.

Experiment Setup. As mentioned in Sect. 2.2, the ResNet-18 is used as the backbone for feature extraction. The proposed model is trained and tested on a server with Intel Xeon Silver 4210R CPU @ 2.40 GHz, 128 GB RAM, and NVIDIA GTX 3090 GPU. The proposed model is implemented in PyTorch. The Adam optimizer with the initial learning rate 0.0001 is used to train the proposed model. The epochs are set at 50 and the batch size is set at 8. As for the global quality prediction, we resize the resolution of the minimum dimension of images as 480 while maintaining their aspect ratios, and crop the images at the resolution of 448×448 at the center. The weight parameter w for the local quality is set as 0.2.

The proposed method is validated on the SIQD database. In the experiments, the SIQD database is divided into the training set of 80% SIs and the test set of 20% SIs. To ensure complete separation of training and testing contents, we assign the SIs belonging to the same scene to the same set. We randomly split the database for 10 times, and the average value of the above evaluation metrics is computed as the final result.

Compared Methods. We compare the proposed method with eleven popular BIQA models, including:

- Hand-crafted feature based BIQA models: BLIINDS-II [?], BRISQUE [9], CORNIA [26], DIIVINE [27], GMLF [28], HOSA [29], SISBLIM [29], and NFERM [13].
- Deep learning based BIQA models: SFA [30], DBCNN [31], and HyperIQA [32].

All compared methods are retrained on the SIQD database.

Results. The performance of the proposed method and compared BIQA models are depicted in Table 2. We can observe that the proposed method outperforms all compared BIQA models, which demonstrates the effectiveness of the proposed model in the quality prediction of the SIs. Besides, the deep learning based methods perform better than the hand-crafted feature based methods and lead by a large margin, which indicates that the features extracted by CNN are more effective and more suitable for diverse distortions in the SIs. In addition, the proposed method performs better than compared deep learning based methods which do not consider the visual saliency. It can be concluded that the introduction of the

Table 2. Performance comparison of the proposed model and eleven BIQA methods on the SIQD database.

Type	Methods	PLCC	SROCC	RMSE
Hand-craftedbased	BLIINDS-II	0.2059	0.1584	0.903
	BRISQUE	0.3256	0.3051	0.8726
	CORNIA	0.5641	0.5476	0.7619
	DIIVINE	0.2178	0.0223	0.9007
	GMLF	0.2058	0.0740	0.9030
	HOSA	0.3273	0.2871	0.8720
	SISBLIM	0.5488	0.4206	0.7714
	NFERM	0.3925	0.2576	0.8488
Deep learningbased	SFA	0.8741	0.8702	0.4153
	DBCNN	0.8785	0.8727	0.4033
	HyperIQA	0.8687	0.8631	0.4478
	Proposed	**0.9025**	**0.8973**	**0.3927**

Fig. 3. Statistical significance comparison between the proposed model and other BIQA methods on the SIQD. A black/white block (i, j) means the method at row i is statistically worse/better than the one at column j. A gray block (m, n) means the method at row m and the method at n are statistically indistinguishable. The metrics denoted by A-M are of the same order as the compared metrics in Tabel 2 (Color figure online)

Table 3. Performance comparison of different weights for the local quality.

w	PLCC	SROCC	RMSE
0	0.8768	0.8699	0.4448
0.2	**0.9025**	**0.8973**	**0.3927**
0.4	0.8960	0.8896	0.4035
0.6	0.8895	0.8778	0.4148
0.8	0.8789	0.8750	0.4334
1.0	0.8703	0.8646	0.4470

visual saliency characteristics does improve the quality predictive performance of the SIs.

To further analyze the performance of the proposed method and other BIQA models, we conduct the statistical significance test in [33] to measure the difference between the predicted quality scores and the subjective ratings. Figure 3 presents the results of the statistical significance test for the proposed method and other BIQA models on the SIQD. We can clearly observe that the performance of our proposed BIQA model is statistically superior to other compared BIQA models on the SIQD.

Ablation Study: The Importance of the Salient Region. In this section, we mainly analyze how the relative weighting between the global quality and local quality affects the final predictive performance of the proposed model. Except for the weight w for the local quality, the remaining experimental settings are set the same as that in Sect. 3.3.

The experimental results are listed in Table 3. From Table 3, we can first see that the proposed method achieves the best performance when the weight w is set as 0.2. Next, the proposed model without the global quality ($w = 1$) performs only slightly worse than that without the local quality ($w = 0$), and both of them perform worse than the proposed model with the global and local quality, which on the one hand indicates that the quality of the salient region has a great effect on the overall quality of the SIs and on the other hand indicates that it is necessary to simultaneously consider the global and local quality.

4   Conclusion

In this paper, we propose a deep neural network based BIQA model for the surveillance images, which considers the visual saliency characteristics. As the distortions in the salient regions have a great impact on the overall perceptual quality, we first select the local region with the maximum saliency weight via the saliency map. Then, the CNN model and FC network are utilized to predict the global quality for the whole image and local quality for the local region. Finally, the overall quality score is computed as the weighted sum of the global and local quality scores. Experimental results show that the proposed method is effective at predicting the visual quality of the SIs. The proposed BIQA model can help to filter the low-quality SIs and improve the performance of the intelligent video system.

References

1. Sreenu, G., Durai, M.S.: Intelligent video surveillance: a review through deep learning techniques for crowd analysis. J. Big Data **6**(1), 1–27 (2019)
2. Zhu, W., Zhai, G., Yao, C., Yang, X.: SIQD: surveillance image quality database and performance evaluation for objective algorithms. In: 2018 IEEE Visual Communications and Image Processing (VCIP). pp. 1–4. IEEE (2018)
3. Leszczuk, M., Romaniak, P., Janowski, L.: Quality assessment in video surveillance. In: Recent Developments in Video Surveillance. IntechOpen (2012)
4. Aqqa, M., Mantini, P., Shah, S.K.: Understanding how video quality affects object detection algorithms. In: VISIGRAPP (5: VISAPP), pp. 96–104 (2019)
5. Sun, W., Min, X., Zhai, G., Ma, S.: Blind quality assessment for in-the-wild images via hierarchical feature fusion and iterative mixed database training. arXiv preprint arXiv:2105.14550 (2021)
6. Sun, W., Min, X., Zhai, G., Gu, K., Duan, H., Ma, S.: MC360IQA: a multi-channel CNN for blind 360-degree image quality assessment. IEEE J. Sel. Top. Signal Proces. **14**(1), 64–77 (2019)
7. Zhai, G., Sun, W., Min, X., Zhou, J.: Perceptual quality assessment of low-light image enhancement. ACM Trans. Multimedia Comput. Commun. Appl. (TOMM) **17**(4), 1–24 (2021)
8. Zhang, Z., et al.: A no-reference deep learning quality assessment method for super-resolution images based on frequency maps. arXiv preprint arXiv:2206.04289 (2022)
9. Mittal, A., Moorthy, A.K., Bovik, A.C.: No-reference image quality assessment in the spatial domain. IEEE Trans. Image Process. **21**(12), 4695–4708 (2012)
10. Fang, Y., Ma, K., Wang, Z., Lin, W., Fang, Z., Zhai, G.: No-reference quality assessment of contrast-distorted images based on natural scene statistics. IEEE Signal Process. Lett. **22**(7), 838–842 (2014)
11. Zhang, Z., et al.: A no-reference evaluation metric for low-light image enhancement. In: 2021 IEEE International Conference on Multimedia and Expo (ICME), pp. 1–6. IEEE (2021)
12. Zhang, Z., Sun, W., Min, X., Wang, T., Lu, W., Zhai, G.: A full-reference quality assessment metric for fine-grained compressed images. In: 2021 International Conference on Visual Communications and Image Processing (VCIP), pp. 1–4. IEEE (2021)
13. Gu, K., Zhai, G., Yang, X., Zhang, W.: Using free energy principle for blind image quality assessment. IEEE Trans. Multimedia **17**(1), 50–63 (2014)
14. Zhai, G., Wu, X., Yang, X., Lin, W., Zhang, W.: A psychovisual quality metric in free-energy principle. IEEE Trans. Image Process. **21**(1), 41–52 (2011)
15. Min, X., Zhai, G., Gu, K., Liu, Y., Yang, X.: Blind image quality estimation via distortion aggravation. IEEE Trans. Broadcast. **64**(2), 508–517 (2018)
16. Sun, W., Wang, T., Min, X., Yi, F., Zhai, G.: Deep learning based full-reference and no-reference quality assessment models for compressed UGC videos. In: 2021 IEEE International Conference on Multimedia & Expo Workshops (ICMEW), pp. 1–6. IEEE (2021)

17. Wang, T., Sun, W., Min, X., Lu, W., Zhang, Z., Zhai, G.: A multi-dimensional aesthetic quality assessment model for mobile game images. In: 2021 International Conference on Visual Communications and Image Processing (VCIP), pp. 1–5. IEEE (2021)
18. Lu, W., et al.: A CNN-based quality assessment method for pseudo 4K contents. In: Zhai, G., Zhou, J., Yang, H., An, P., Yang, X. (eds.) IFTC 2021. Communications in Computer and Information Science, vol. 1560, pp. 164–176. Springer, Cham (2022). https://doi.org/10.1007/978-981-19-2266-4_13
19. Sun, W., Min, X., Lu, W., Zhai, G.: A deep learning based no-reference quality assessment model for UGC videos. arXiv preprint arXiv:2204.14047 (2022)
20. Reddy, N., Jain, S., Yarlagadda, P., Gandhi, V.: Tidying deep saliency prediction architectures. In: 2020 IEEE/RSJ International Conference on Intelligent Robots and Systems (IROS), pp. 10241–10247. IEEE (2020)
21. Jiang, M., Huang, S., Duan, J., Zhao, Q.: Salicon: saliency in context. In: Proceedings of the IEEE Conference on Computer Vision and Pattern Recognition, pp. 1072–1080 (2015)
22. He, K., Zhang, X., Ren, S., Sun, J.: Deep residual learning for image recognition. In: Proceedings of the IEEE Conference on Computer Vision and Pattern Recognition, pp. 770–778 (2016)
23. Deng, J., Dong, W., Socher, R., Li, L.J., Li, K., Fei-Fei, L.: Imagenet: a large-scale hierarchical image database. In: 2009 IEEE Conference on Computer Vision and Pattern Recognition, pp. 248–255. IEEE (2009)
24. Zhang, K., Zhang, Z., Li, Z., Qiao, Y.: Joint face detection and alignment using multitask cascaded convolutional networks. IEEE Signal Process. Lett. **23**(10), 1499–1503 (2016)
25. Seshadrinathan, K., Soundararajan, R., Bovik, A.C., Cormack, L.K.: Study of subjective and objective quality assessment of video. IEEE Trans. Image Process. **19**(6), 1427–1441 (2010)
26. Ye, P., Kumar, J., Kang, L., Doermann, D.: Unsupervised feature learning framework for no-reference image quality assessment. In: 2012 IEEE Conference on Computer Vision and Pattern Recognition, pp. 1098–1105. IEEE (2012)
27. Moorthy, A.K., Bovik, A.C.: Blind image quality assessment: from natural scene statistics to perceptual quality. IEEE Trans. Image Process. **20**(12), 3350–3364 (2011)
28. Xue, W., Mou, X., Zhang, L., Bovik, A.C., Feng, X.: Blind image quality assessment using joint statistics of gradient magnitude and Laplacian features. IEEE Trans. Image Process. **23**(11), 4850–4862 (2014)
29. Xu, J., Ye, P., Li, Q., Du, H., Liu, Y., Doermann, D.: Blind image quality assessment based on high order statistics aggregation. IEEE Trans. Image Process. **25**(9), 4444–4457 (2016)
30. Li, D., Jiang, T., Lin, W., Jiang, M.: Which has better visual quality: the clear blue sky or a blurry animal? IEEE Trans. Multimedia **21**(5), 1221–1234 (2018)
31. Zhang, W., Ma, K., Yan, J., Deng, D., Wang, Z.: Blind image quality assessment using a deep bilinear convolutional neural network. IEEE Trans. Circuits Syst. Video Technol. **30**(1), 36–47 (2018)
32. Su, S., et al.: Blindly assess image quality in the wild guided by a self-adaptive hyper network. In: Proceedings of the IEEE/CVF Conference on Computer Vision and Pattern Recognition, pp. 3667–3676 (2020)
33. Sheikh, H.R., Sabir, M.F., Bovik, A.C.: A statistical evaluation of recent full reference image quality assessment algorithms. IEEE Trans. Image Process. **15**(11), 3440–3451 (2006)

Power Grid Bus Cluster Based on Voltage Phasor Trajectory

Kaiyue Xu[1(✉)], Ying Qiao[1], and Daowei Liu[2]

[1] Institute of Software, Chinese Academy of Sciences, Beijing, China
{kaiyue2020,qiaoying}@iscas.ac.cn
[2] China Electric Power Research Institute, Beijing, China
liudaowei@epri.sgcc.com.cn

Abstract. With the continuous increase of the scale of the power system and the increasing uncertainty, mining the correlation characteristics of power grid nodes becomes increasingly essential. After the power grid fails, the voltage phasor trajectory is an important reference to reflect the impact of the bus. Based on this, we propose a bus clustering algorithm based on the voltage phasor trajectory. First, we extracted three dimensions of information for each bus: the trajectory's length, curvature, and topological distance, and then expressed the weighted sum of the distances in the three dimensions as the similarity between the buses. Secondly, based on the similarity of trajectory, we propose an improved k-means algorithm to cluster the buses. Finally, we conduct fault simulation in the IEEE 39-bus system and perform similarity analysis and clustering analysis, respectively, to reveal the propagation characteristics of faults in power grid.

Keywords: Power system · Voltage phasor trajectory · Similarity analysis · Cluster analysis

1 Introduction

As human economic activities have entered the era of an industrial economy, higher requirements have been placed on the stable operation of the power system. Various faults will inevitably occur in the actual power grid during operation. Understanding the fault propagation mechanism will help relevant personnel to respond as soon as possible, thereby avoiding huge losses. However, with the development of the power system, the spatial and temporal distribution characteristics of the power grid have become increasingly complex [1–3]. At the same time, the continuous expansion of the scale of new energy power generation [4,5] makes the power grid operating environment more complex, variable, and random [6,7], making this problem more difficult.

This work was supported by Science and Technology Project of State Grid Corporation of China: Large Power Grid Dispatch Regulation Digitization and Stability Situation Knowledge Graph Intelligent Construction based on Digital Twin (5100-202155016A-0-0-00).

The existing research on power grid faults mainly includes three parts: fault location [8,9], fault classification [10–12], and fault propagation [13,14] analysis. The research on fault location and fault classification is relatively active. Scholars have proposed two types of methods based on data-driven and model-driven, and there are many mature algorithms. However, there are few related kinds of research on fault propagation analysis. All of them are based on self-defined indicators to analyze the degree of impact of faults on each node, and there is no unified quantitative definition.

Similarity analysis is a commonly used data mining method, which can reflect the similarity between samples based on a particular metric. When the power grid fails, the voltage phasor trajectory contains a wealth of information, which is an essential basis to reflect the degree of failure of the bus [15,16]. With the wide application of wide-area measurement systems in actual power grids, we can easily obtain high-precision synchronous real-time measurements [17,18], which directly promotes the development of data mining algorithms based on voltage phasor trajectory. Therefore, we define the trajectory similarity of each bus relative to the faulted bus from three perspectives (if it is a branch fault, it can be replaced by the nearest bus) to analyze the characteristics of fault propagation to the rest of the bus. Based on the improved k-means algorithm, we perform cluster analysis on the trajectory similarity of all buses to dig deeper into the impact of faults on different areas in the power grid.

2   Propagation Mechanism of Power Grid Faults

Power systems are often affected by various fault disturbances during operation. The deviation of the local state quantity caused by the disturbance will propagate to other areas in the form of electromechanical waves, which will lead to the change of the state quantity of the power grid in other areas, thereby affecting the safe and stable operation of the power grid. In the model-driven disturbance propagation analysis, James Thorp et al. regard generators and lines as the essential components of the power grid. Under the assumption that the scale of the power grid is infinite and the distance between generators is negligible, they proposed a modeling method of the power grid continuum model. They derived the relationship between the propagation speed of electromechanical disturbance and inertia [19]:

$$v^2 = \frac{\omega U^2 \sin \theta}{2h \mid z \mid} \tag{1}$$

where v is the propagation velocity of electromechanical disturbance; ω is the generator angular frequency; U is the voltage amplitude per-unit value; θ is the line impedance angle; z is the line unit impedance per-unit value; h is the inertia per unit length.

Compared with the numerical solution, the analytical solution can better reflect the relationship between the various state quantities, reflecting fault disturbances' propagation characteristics.

However, due to the complex spatial distribution of the actual power grid parameters, it is difficult to obtain the analytical solution to the power grid fault disturbance propagation equation. Most of the existing model-driven algorithms have made some simplifications and assumptions, making it difficult for the model-based analysis results to reflect the power grid's actual situation accurately [20,21].

In recent years, various data-driven algorithms have also been gradually applied to analyzing power grid fault disturbance propagation. For example, the mature infectious disease model in biology is applied to constructing the power grid disturbance propagation dynamics model to reveal the disturbed node density after the disturbance occurs. With the development of artificial intelligence technology, many methods based on machine learning have been proposed, such as using convolutional neural networks [22] or recurrent neural networks [9,10] to achieve tasks such as location and classification of power grid faults. However, with the continuous development of large-scale power grids and increasingly complex structures, people's understanding of power grid disturbance propagation mechanisms is far from enough, and research in this field needs to be improved.

3 Trajectory-Based Similarity

When a fault occurs in the power grid, the voltage phasor trajectory of each bus reflects the propagation of the fault to other areas. To better reveal the characteristics, we comprehensively define the similarity between any bus and the faulty bus from the perspectives of the trajectory's length, curvature, and topological distance as shown in Fig. 1. The bus closest to the fault can be regarded as the central bus if it is a branch fault.

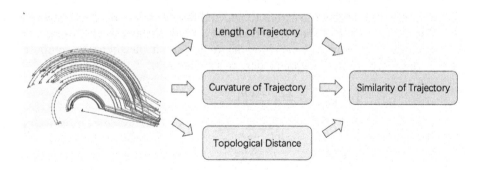

Fig. 1. The overall framework of trajectory-based similarity.

3.1 Length of Trajectory

In the actual operation of the power grid, the voltage phasor trajectory is usually a curve, and its expression is difficult to obtain. However, the sampling time

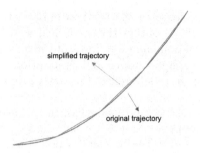

Fig. 2. Simplified schematic for the original trajectory.

interval is often tiny, so we made some simplifications and used the Euclidean distance between two adjacent points to represent the length of this trajectory, as shown in Fig. 2.

In this case, the length of the voltage phasor trajectory of the i-th bus can be defined as:

$$L^{(i)} = \sum_{k=1}^{T-1} \sqrt{(SB_{k+1}^{(i)} - SB_k^{(i)})^2 + (XB_{k+1}^{(i)} - XB_k^{(i)})^2} \tag{2}$$

where T is the total number of time sections of the trajectory, $SB_k^{(i)}$ is the real part of the voltage of the i-th bus at time k, and $XB_k^{(i)}$ is the imaginary part of the i-th bus at time k.

3.2   Curvature of Trajectory

The curvature also reflects the extent to which different buses are affected by the fault. For the curvature of the entire trajectory, we describe it as the average of the curvatures of all points. For each point, we first use its neighbors to compute the first derivative of the imaginary part to the real part:

$$\begin{cases} XB_1^{(i)\prime} = \frac{XB_2^{(i)} - XB_1^{(i)}}{SB_2^{(i)} - SB_1^{(i)}} \\ XB_k^{(i)\prime} = \frac{XB_{k+1}^{(i)} - XB_{k-1}^{(i)}}{SB_{k+1}^{(i)} - SB_{k-1}^{(i)}}, \ k = 2 \dots T-1 \\ XB_T^{(i)\prime} = \frac{XB_T^{(i)} - XB_{T-1}^{(i)}}{SB_T^{(i)} - SB_{T-1}^{(i)}} \end{cases} \tag{3}$$

where $XB_k^{(i)\prime}$ corresponds to the k-th point in the i-th trajectory.

Similarly, the second derivative of the imaginary part to the real part of any point can be expressed as:

$$
\begin{cases}
XB_1^{(i)\prime\prime} = \frac{XB_2^{(i)\prime} - XB_1^{(i)\prime}}{SB_2^{(i)} - SB_1^{(i)}} \\
XB_k^{(i)\prime\prime} = \frac{XB_{k+1}^{(i)\prime} - XB_{k-1}^{(i)\prime}}{SB_{k+1}^{(i)} - SB_{k-1}^{(i)}}, \; k = 2 \ldots T-1 \\
XB_T^{(i)\prime\prime} = \frac{XB_T^{(i)\prime} - XB_{T-1}^{(i)\prime}}{SB_T^{(i)} - SB_{T-1}^{(i)}}
\end{cases}
\tag{4}
$$

Then the curvature of the i-th trajectory can be expressed as:

$$
C^{(i)} = \frac{1}{T} \sum_{k=1}^{T} C_k^{(i)} = \frac{1}{T} \sum_{k=1}^{T} \frac{|XB_k^{(i)\prime\prime}|}{(1 + XB_k^{(i)\prime})^{3/2}}
\tag{5}
$$

3.3 Topological Distance

When the power grid fails, the parts close to the fault source are often more affected. Therefore, we introduce the property of topology distance, which represents the shortest distance from a bus to the faulty bus. We model the grid as a graph $\mathcal{G} = (\mathcal{V}, \mathcal{E}, A)$, where $\mathcal{V}$ is the set of nodes, $\mathcal{E}$ is the set of edges. The adjacency matrix is defined as $A \in R^{n \times n}$, where $A_{ij} = A_{ji}$, and $A_{ij} = 1$ if $(\mathcal{V}_i, \mathcal{V}_j) \in \mathcal{E}$, otherwise $A_{ij} = 0$.

$$
A = \begin{pmatrix}
0 & 1 & \ldots & 1 \\
1 & 0 & \ldots & 0 \\
\vdots & \vdots & \ddots & \vdots \\
1 & 0 & \ldots & 0
\end{pmatrix}
\tag{6}
$$

Then, we can use the Dijkstra algorithm to calculate the shortest distance from all buses to the faulty bus. That is, the topological distance is defined as:

$$
T^{(i)} = \min_{\mathcal{V}_j \in \mathcal{V} \wedge \mathcal{V}_j \neq \mathcal{V}_i} dist(\mathcal{V}_i, \mathcal{V}_j)
\tag{7}
$$

3.4 Similarity of Trajectories

The trajectory's length, curvature, and topological distance can be regarded as three attributes of the corresponding trajectory of a bus. To eliminate the influence of dimension, we normalize them respectively:

$$
\begin{cases}
L_{norm}^{(i)} = \frac{nL^{(i)}}{\sum_{k=1}^{n} L^{(k)}} \\
C_{norm}^{(i)} = \frac{nC^{(i)}}{\sum_{k=1}^{n} C^{(k)}} \\
T_{norm}^{(i)} = \frac{nT^{(i)}}{\sum_{k=1}^{n} T^{(k)}}
\end{cases}
\tag{8}
$$

Then, we define the similarity between the trajectories of any bus and the faulty bus as the weighted sum of three attribute distances.

$$dist(bus^{(i)}, bus^{(f)}) = \alpha \cdot |L_{norm}^{(i)} - L_{norm}^{(f)}|$$
$$+ \beta \cdot |C_{norm}^{(i)} - C_{norm}^{(f)}| + \gamma \cdot |T_{norm}^{(i)} - T_{norm}^{(f)}| \tag{9}$$

The values of α, β, and γ can be adjusted according to the actual situation of the power grid. Based on experience, we recommend setting them to 0.4, 0.4, and 0.2. On one hand, the length of the trajectory is almost as important as the curvature. On the other hand, the influence of the structure is already reflected in the properties to a large extent.

3.5   Power Grid Bus Cluster

To investigate the impact of faults on different areas in the power grid, we perform cluster analysis on all buses based on the improved k-means algorithm. The similarity between any two points can be calculated using Eq. 9. In k-means, each cluster's average value of points is taken as the new cluster center each time. The cluster center selected each time can be a point outside the sample, and in extreme cases, the result may be that a cluster is empty. To avoid this situation, in each update, we take the point in the sample that is closest to the point corresponding to the average value of the points in the cluster as the new cluster center.

The algorithm execution steps are as follows:

(1) Randomly select k bus as the initial cluster center.
(2) Calculate the distance of each point to all cluster centers using Eq. 9 and assign the point to the closest cluster center.
(3) Calculate the mean of each cluster.
(4) Calculate the distance from the sample in each cluster to the corresponding mean, and update the point with the smallest distance as the cluster center.
(5) Repeat (2)-(4) until the clusters do not change or the maximum number of iterations is reached.

4   Experiments

In this section, We take the IEEE 39-bus system as an example to show the effective of our method. Its topology diagram is shown in Fig. 3.

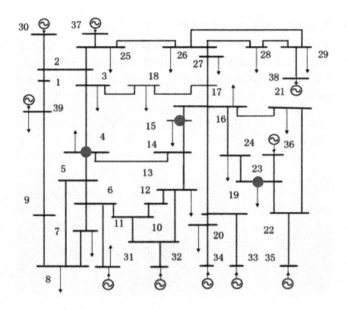

Fig. 3. IEEE 39-bus system topology.

We use transient simulation to simulate bus 3-phase short circuit faults to generate samples and apply the method in this paper to analyze. When generating samples, we selected three relatively scattered representative buses, namely 4, 15, and 23 (already marked in Fig. 3), and conducted three sets of experiments. Intercept a section of data in each group of sample faults, calculate the voltage real part and imaginary part sequence of each bus in each group of samples based on the voltage amplitude and phase angle sequence, and then draw the corresponding voltage phasor trajectory as shown in Fig. 4.

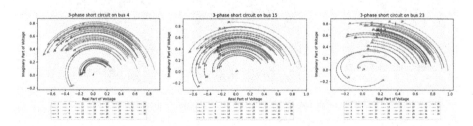

Fig. 4. Voltage phasor trajectories of three-phase short-circuit faults injected at buses 4, 15, and 23, respectively.

4.1   Visualize for Each Dimension

In this part, we first show the values of each bus in three dimensions under each fault through heat maps. Figure 5 are the heat map distributions after the three-phase short circuit faults injected at node 4, node 15, and node 23, respectively. Each small square represents the distance between the corresponding node on the horizontal axis and the corresponding node on the vertical axis in that dimension, expressed by the absolute value of the difference. Therefore, the heat maps are all symmetric matrices.

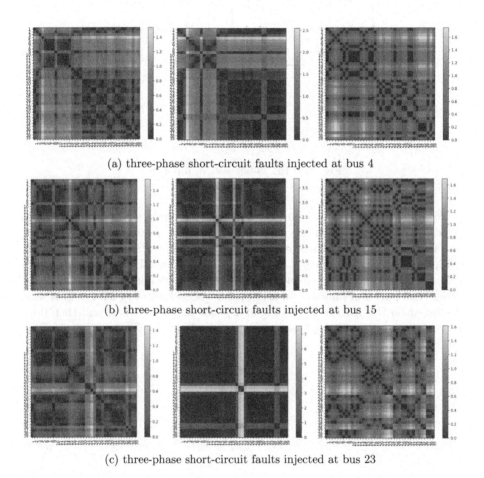

(a) three-phase short-circuit faults injected at bus 4

(b) three-phase short-circuit faults injected at bus 15

(c) three-phase short-circuit faults injected at bus 23

Fig. 5. Heat maps in three dimensions under three faults. The trajectory's length, curvature, and topological distance are indicated from left to right.

From the heat maps, we can draw the following conclusions:

(1) There are certain differences in the three dimensions, so the effects of different levels are studied separately.

(2) The length of the trajectory and the curvature of the trajectory have similar representations, which is especially evident after the failure of bus 4 and bus 23. For example, in Fig. 4(a), the 9 buses 5–8 and 10–14 are obviously different from others.

(3) The buses in the power grid are affected by faults and show obvious regional aggregation, which is reflected in three dimensions. This is consistent with the mechanism cognition of the power grid.

4.2   Trajectory Similarity Analysis

We use the methods mentioned in Sects. 3.1–3.4 to perform similarity analysis on the three samples. In the experiment, we set $\alpha = 0.4, \beta = 0.4, \gamma = 0.2$. To visualize the results, we color the top 10 most similar buses according to their similarity in the topology graph, and the colors are from dark to light (every two buses use the same color), as shown in Fig. 6). By observing Fig. 6, we can get:

(1) The area around the fault is relatively affected.

(2) Faults at different locations show different propagation effects. Affected by the complex mechanism of the power grid, the fault is not evenly propagated outward.

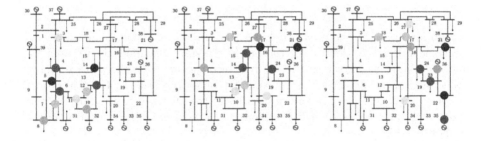

Fig. 6. Results of the similarity analysis coloring.

We take the failure of bus 4 as an example to analyze the accuracy of the results. As can be seen in Fig. 4, the lower right part of node 4 is more affected. Table 1 shows the impedance of some branches in an IEEE-39 node system. It can be seen that the impedance of bus 3 and bus 4 are significantly greater than that of bus 5 and bus 14. In addition, the impedance between bus bar 5 and bus bar 6 is also tiny, so bus 6 is also greatly affected.

Table 1. Impedance of a part of the branch.

fbus	tbus	Z
3	4	$0.0013 + j0.0213$
4	5	$0.0008 + j0.0128$
4	14	$0.0008 + j0.0129$
5	6	$0.0002 + j0.0026$

4.3   Trajectory Cluster Analysis

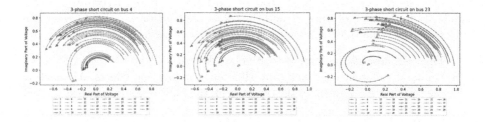

Fig. 7. Results of clustering voltage phasor trajectories into four clusters.

In addition, based on the three attributes (the trajectory's length, curvature, and topological distance) defined for the bus in the similarity analysis, we used the improved k-means algorithm to perform cluster analysis on the voltage phasor trajectories of the 39 buses. Here, the number of clusters is set to 4, 100 iterations are performed, and the phasor trajectories of the 39 buses in the four clusters under each fault are colored with different colors to show the clustering effect, as shown in Fig. 7.

To further analyze the clustering results corresponding to each fault sample, we color the bus in the four clusters with different colors in the grid topology to show the area corresponding to each cluster, as shown in Fig. 8.

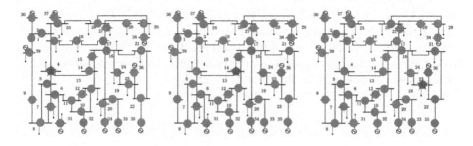

Fig. 8. Coloring results of grid topology corresponding to four clusters.

According to the results in Fig. 7 and Fig. 8, it can be seen that our method has an ideal effect on trajectory clustering, and the impact of faults gradually decreases in the order of blue cluster, orange cluster, pink cluster, and green cluster. In practical power grid applications, the dispatcher should focus on the bus in the same cluster as the faulty bus to respond to the fault as soon as possible to avoid more significant losses.

In addition, the current methods for studying the propagation characteristics of power grid faults have different goals from ours, so we cannot directly compare with these methods. For our problem, the intuitive idea is to use the sum of the Euclidean distances corresponding to each section as the distance between two trajectories. Therefore, we further compared with this method. Figure 9 shows the clustering results of this method. It is not difficult to see that under this method, there is much overlap between different clusters, so the clustering effect is terrible.

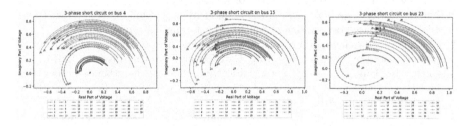

Fig. 9. Clustering results based on the sum of Euclidean distances.

5   Conclusion

In this paper, we propose a bus similarity analysis method based on voltage phasor trajectory, which fully describes the bus information from the three perspectives of the trajectory's length, curvature, and topological distance, thereby revealing the propagation characteristics of power grid faults. Furthermore, we propose a clustering algorithm to reveal the impact of grid faults on different regions. The experimental results can help the dispatcher respond in time after failure, thereby reducing the loss.

References

1. Sun, X., Si, S.: Complex Network Algorithms and Applications. National Defend Industry Press, Beijing (2015)
2. Chu, C.C., Iu, H.H.C.: Complex networks theory for modern smart grid applications: a survey. IEEE J. Emerg. Sel. Top. Circ. Syst. **7**(2), 177–191 (2017)
3. Jia, Y., Liu, R., Han, X., et al.: Risk assessment of cascading failures in power grid based on complex network theory. In 2016 14th International Conference on Control, Automation, Robotics and Vision (ICARCV), pp. 1–6. IEEE(2016)

4. Chi, Y., Liu, Y., Wang, W., et al.: Study on impact of wind power integration on power system. Power Syst. Technol. **31**(3), 77–81 (2007)
5. Du, X., Zhou, L., Guo, K., et al.: Static voltage stability analysis of large-scale photovoltaic plants. Power Syst. Technol. **39**(12), 3427–3434 (2015)
6. Liu, D., Zhang, D., Sun, H., et al.: Construction of stability situation quantitative assessment and adaptive control system for large-scale power grid in the spatio-temporal big data environment. Proc. CSEE **35**(2), 268–276 (2015)
7. Zhu, F., Zhao, H., Liu, Z., et al.: The influence of large power grid interconnected on power system dynamic stability. Proc. CSEE **27**(1), 1–7 (2007)
8. Huang, D., Liu, H., Bi, T., et al.: Rapid localization method of power grid disturbance events based on spatial and temporal correlation of disturbance propagation. Proc. CSEE **42**(06), 2045–2060 (2022)
9. Li, Z., Yao, W., Zeng, L., et al.: Power grid fault area location and fault propagation path reasoning based on long short-term memory network. Electr. Power Autom. Equipment **41**(06), 164–170+178+171-174(2021)
10. Tian, Y., Ma, W.: Power grid equipment fault text classification based on Attention-BiLSTM. Comput. Appl. **40**(S2), 24–29 (2020)
11. Lin, S.: Research on fault classification and location method of high voltage transmission line based on transients. Southwest Jiaotong University (2011)
12. Chen, G.: Research on fault classification and identification method of distribution network based on immune clustering. East China Jiaotong University (2014)
13. Cheng, R., Hua, X., Xia, C., et al.: Electromechanical disturbance propagation based on actual AC-DC interconnected large power grid. South. Power Syst. Technol. **13**(09), 49–58 (2019)
14. Wu, X., Zhang, D., Ling, X., et al.: Dynamic analysis of power grid disturbance propagation based on infectious disease model. Proc. CSEE **39**(14), 4061–4070 (2019)
15. Zheng, H., Liu, D., Li, B., et al.: Evaluation of temporal and spatial correlation characteristics of power grid nodes based on geometrical characteristics of voltage phasor trajectory. Power Syst. Technol. **44**(01), 9–18 (2020)
16. Xu, W., Xue, Y., Chen, S., et al.: Difficulties and prospects of knowledge extracting from measured trajectories. Autom. Electr. Power Syst. **33**(15), 1–7 (2009)
17. Liu, D., Song, D., Wang, H., et al.: Voltage stability online evaluation system based on WAMS and EMS. Power Syst. Technol. **38**(7), 1934–1938 (2014)
18. Wu, Q., Zhang, D., Liu, D., et al.: A method for power system steady stability situation assessment based on random matrix theory. Proc. CSEE **36**(20), 5414–5420 (2016)
19. Thorp, J, S., Seyler, C, E., Phadke, A. G.: Electromechanical wave propagation in large electric power systems. IEEE Trans. Circ. Syst. I: Fundam. Theory Appl. **45**(6), 614–622(1998)
20. Bi, T., Yan, Y., Yang, Q.: Disturbance propagation mechanism of non-uniform chained power grid based on piecewise uniform medium model. Proc. CSEE **34**(07), 1088–1094 (2014)
21. Ju, P., Liu, Y., Xue, Y., et al.: Research prospects of stochastic dynamics in power systems. Autom. Electr. Power Syst. **41**(1), 1–8 (2017)
22. Ni, C.: Rapid detection and identification of transmission line faults based on convolutional neural network. Mongolian university(2019)

Following the Lecturer: Hierarchical Knowledge Concepts Prediction for Educational Videos

Xin Zhang[1,2(✉)], Qi Liu[1,2], Wei Huang[1,2], Weidong He[1,2], Tong Xiao[1,2], and Ye Huang[1,2]

[1] Anhui Province Key Laboratory of Big Data Analysis and Application, University of Science and Technology of China, Hefei, China
{zx2020,ustc0411,hwd,xt20020109,huangyehy}@mail.ustc.edu.cn,
qiliuql@ustc.edu.cn
[2] State Key Laboratory of Cognitive Intelligence, Hefei, China

Abstract. With an irresistible trend of intelligent learning, predicting knowledge concepts for educational videos turns out to be a fundamental and essential task, which benefits personalized recommendation, retrieval, and learning. Prior studies of videos mainly focus on relatively short human actions and object recognition, while educational videos are minutes long and have heterogeneous elements such as texts, formulas, and hand-drawn graphics that serve lecturers' narration. Owing to the characteristics of education, most of the segmentation strategies for long-term videos do not apply well to educational videos. In addition, educational videos consist of progressive or referential sections and contain multimodal information. Thus, we propose a novel framework called *Spotlight Flow Network* (SFNet) to obtain hierarchical knowledge concepts for educational videos with multi-modality. Specifically, we first adopt an effective text-to-visual section segmentation strategy. Then, we model the mechanism that the viewers' spotlight follows the lecturer and leverage the associations between sections to enhance multimodal representation. We also consider explicit inter-level constraints of the hierarchical knowledge structure and associations between sections and concepts to get better predicting performance. Extensive experimental results on real-world data demonstrate the effectiveness of SFNet.

Keywords: Educational videos · Multi-modality · Hierarchical multi-label classification

1 Introduction

With the rapid development of online video platforms and intelligent educational systems like Coursera and Khan Academy [12], an enormous amount of students and knowledge seekers browse educational videos to consolidate their understanding of courses and broaden their horizons. Knowledge concepts prediction

Supplementary Information The online version contains supplementary material available at https://doi.org/10.1007/978-3-031-20500-2_13.

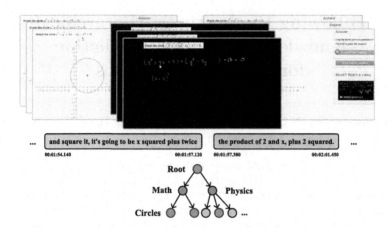

Fig. 1. An example of a math video from Khan academy and its related hierarchical knowledge concepts.

for educational videos is a fundamental task and very promising for organizing and managing educational videos with great quantity and diversity.

Figure 1 shows an example of a math video and related knowledge concepts with part of the knowledge structure. The video consists of multiple frames and a series of closed captions, and can be split into three different sections, i.e., introduction, problem solving, conclusion. In the last section, the lecturer refers to the problem and reviews the problem-solving process again, which demonstrates a common characteristic that educational videos are combined with sections (such as introduction, concept explanation, analysis, conclusion), and draws the importance of considering context of sections. As a key element of education, knowledge concepts are usually in the form of tree or Direct Acyclic Graph (DAG). As shown in Fig. 1, if we take the root node as level 0, sub-concepts are separated into two different routes from level 2, which describes Hierarchical Multi-label Classification (HMC). This type of problem has drawn more attention in industry and education with the trend of disciplinary crossover.

In the literature, prior works on video classification [3,4,22] have achieved great success. Most of these works mainly focus on relatively short video clips and recognize human actions and objects, while long-term video understanding has not been explored a lot yet. For long videos, prior studies [30] choose to evenly or randomly sample certain frames, or detect shot-boundaries [31] to break down whole videos into sections. Philip et al. [12] studied different types of educational videos and how video production decisions affect student engagement. Typical styles of educational videos include classroom lectures, slide presentations, "talking head" shots of an instructor and digital tablet drawings. Long-term content and more complex composition structure make the above strategy ineffective in educational videos. In addition, most recent HMC works [14] combine local and global approaches, and utilize hierarchical dependencies in the form of a feed-forward network. However, these studies fail to model explicit inter-level hierarchical constraints, and are currently limited to textual content.

In summary, there are the following challenges: (1) How to make use of multi-modal information from frames and subtitles. (2) How to consider finer-grained characteristics of educational videos that are relatively long, such as the section-level contexts. (3) How to effectively split educational videos. (4) How to explicitly model inter-level constraints in hierarchical knowledge structure.

To tackle the above challenges, we propose a novel framework named *Spotlight Flow Network* (SFNet). Specifically, we adopt a text-to-visual uniform segmentation strategy by utilizing progressiveness within a section and uniformity provided by timecodes of closed captions. Then, we model the mechanism of viewers' spotlight following the lecturers by leveraging different information from the preprocessing step. We also utilize explicit inter-level constraints of the hierarchical knowledge structure and associations between sections and concepts to improve the performance of knowledge concepts prediction. A real-world dataset of 7,521 educational videos is constructed and extensive experimental results address the effectiveness of our proposed method.

2   Related Work

Long-Term Video Understanding. In the literature, there have been many efforts to understand video content [2,5,6,13], including 2D and 3D CNN networks [9,26,32], two-stream methods [22], and well-known transformer-based methods [3,4] in recent years. Most of the prior works mainly focus on relatively short video clips (normally within 30 s) and recognize human actions, objects and scenes, etc., while long-term video understanding has not been explored a lot yet. Donahue et al. [8] proposed an end-to-end recurrent convolutional network for learning long-term dependencies. Wu et al. [31] proposed an object-centric transformer framework that recognizes, tracks, and represents objects and actions of long videos. In summary, most existing studies casually or equally sample certain frames from videos [17,27] or detect shot-boundaries [31] to breakdown whole videos into sections, yet they cannot apply well on educational videos due to the diversity and complexity of the contents.

Multimodal Video Representation. Aside from visual frames, videos also contain multimodal information such as audio and captions texts, which have complementary semantics and could enhance representation [15,23]. Shang et al. [19] utilized timestamps of closed captions to incorporate multimodal signals with a short-term order-sensitive attention mechanism. Gabeur et al. [11] developed a transformer-based architecture that jointly encodes different modalities' appearance by exploiting cross-modal cues. Nagrani et al. [16] added Multimodal Bottlenecks to input of transformer encoder and limited exchange of multimodal data in the middle of self-attention layers, and obtained more effective representation. For educational videos, VENet proposed by Wang et al. [28] exploited the static and incremental characteristics and modeled the fixed reading order of human, yet like other studies, is inadequate to fuse intra-section multi-modalities at a fine-grained level, which is emphatically concerned in our framework.

Hierarchical Multi-label Classification. There have been efforts for HMC in the literature [1,10]. Flat-based methods ignore the hierarchical structure and only leverage the last level. Local approaches adopt classifiers for each hierarchy, while global methods predict all classes with a single classifier. Recently, many hybrid methods that combine both the local and global manner have been proposed. Sun et al. [24] transformed the label prediction problem to optimal path prediction with structured sparsity penalties. Shimura et al. [21] addressed the data sparsity problem that data from the lower level is much sparser than that from upper levels and developed HFT-CNN to optimize. Wehrmann et al. [29] proposed a hybrid method called HMCN while penalizing hierarchical violations. Huang et al. [14] proposed HARNN, an attention-based recurrent network that models the correlation between texts and hierarchy. Recently, Shen et al. [20] presented TaxoClass that utilizes the core classes mechanism of humans. However, most prior studies are limited to texts and not adequate to capture the inter-level constraints of hierarchical structure.

3   Preliminaries

3.1   Problem Definition

The input of our task is an educational video $V = \{F, C\}$ composed of multiple frames $F = \{f_1, f_2, ..., f_n\}$ and closed captions $C = \{c_1, c_2, ..., c_m\}$, where each frame f_i is an RGB image in width W and height H, and a caption is made up with texts, start and end timecodes, i.e. $c_j = \{t_j, tc_j^{start}, tc_j^{end}\}$. Texts of captions can be described as a word sequence $t = \{w_1, w_2, ..., w_k\}$. The Hierarchical Knowledge Structure is denoted as $\gamma = (K_1, K_2, ..., K_H)$, where H represents the depth of hierarchy and $K_i = \{k_1, k_2, ...\}$ is the set of knowledge concepts of level i. The Predicted concepts are $L = \{l_1, l_2, ..., l_H\}$ where $\forall i \in \{1, 2, 3, ..., H\}$, and $l_i \subset K_i$. Given an educational video V and the hierarchical knowledge structure γ, our goal is to predict the knowledge concepts L for the video.

3.2   Text-Visual Uniform Section Segmentation

Unlike previous works [31] that detect shot boundaries of visual frames and then guide the segmentation of captions, we preprocess sequential frames and closed captions by exploiting timecodes of captions. We first complement closed captions for videos using ASR (Automatic Speech Recognition) tools. We observe that educational visual content within a section is progressive and later frames tend to contain more information. Thus, inspired by Adaptive Block Matching (ABM) [28] and Dynamic Frame Skipping [18], we develop an efficient section segmentation strategy that fits well in educational videos:

1. Select the center frames of timecode gaps as candidates of sections.
2. Merge sections. Replace adjacent candidates within t_{min} by the latter ones.
3. Calculate the difference matrix $diff$ and score σ of all adjacent candidate frames by pixel-wise value subtraction.

4. Merge sections if corresponding difference score σ is less than threshold θ_{min}.
5. Calculate all ABM scores δ for adjacent candidates if difference score σ is greater than threshold θ_{max}.
6. Select top $n_{sections}$ candidates of δ as the keyframes representing each section with uniform pairs of caption and difference matrices between sections.

It is worth noting that the ABM score is calculated by dividing two frames into patches and measuring how the latter patches cover the previous ones. The difference score σ of the k-th candidate can be expressed as:

$$\sigma(k) = \frac{1}{W * H} \sum_{i=0,j=0}^{i<W,j<H} |f_{ij}^{k+1} - f_{ij}^k|, \tag{1}$$

where f_{ij}^k denotes the scaled pixel value of the k-th candidate frame. As a result, each input video is split into fixed number of sections. Each section comprises a keyframe and several uniform pairs of difference matrix and caption texts, serving the modeling of fine-grained spotlight flow within section.

4 Spotlight Flow Network

In this section, we introduce the details of SFNet, as shown in Fig. 2. We will discuss the two main parts, especially present the modeling of the Spotlight Flow Mechanism and specify the loss function used to train the model.

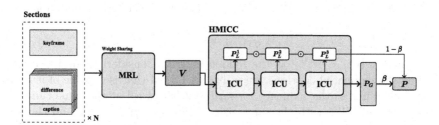

Fig. 2. The SFNet framework.

4.1 Multimodal Representation Layer

In the first stage of SFNet, we aim to represent each section by encoding multimodal data and modeling Spotlight Flow Mechanism, and obtain video-level representation. The input of each section is a keyframe and several uniform pairs of difference matrices and caption texts. We first utilize a variant of ResNet [25] to extract keyframe feature $r^f \in \mathbb{R}^{d_1}$. A base version of BERT is used to get sequential semantic vectors $r^{cs} \in \mathbb{R}^{t \times d_1}$ for all captions within the section, where t denotes the number of diff-caption pairs.

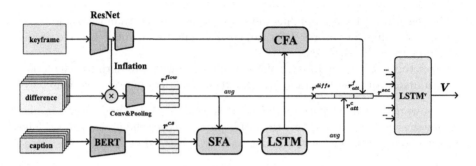

Fig. 3. Multimodal Representation Layer.

Spotlight Flow Attention (SFA). We observe that lecturers tend to conduct viewers to focus on certain visual regions. Content that periodically comes out or is regularly referenced by underlines, circle drawings, etc., strongly indicates the correlation of different time periods and connects time and moving regions. Thus, SFA is designed to model the above mechanism. Inspired by I3D [7], we inflate the feature maps from the middle of the backbone and get $r^{mid} \in \mathbb{R}^{t \times d_2 \times w \times h}$. We resize difference matrices with interpolation and apply element-wise multiplication as follows:

$$r^{flow}_{(i,j)} = r^{mid}_{(i,j)} \cdot diff_{(i,j)}, \tag{2}$$

and through the latter part of the feature extractor, we get the corresponding features of moving regions $r^{flow} \in \mathbb{R}^{t \times d_1}$. Then SFA can be formulated as:

$$r^c_{att} = SFA(r^{flow}, W_{sf}, r^{cs}) = softmax(r^{flow} \cdot W_{sf})r^{cs}, \tag{3}$$

where matrix $W_{sf} \in \mathbb{R}^{t \times d_1}$ is the hidden matrix. Considering the association between the sequential captions, we utilize Bi-LSTM that is capable of learning dependencies across the sequence forward and backward at the same time. We input $r^{c_{att}}$ and r^{flow} with the same size on temporal dimension, and the final representation of caption r^c is calculated by average pooling the hidden state.

Caption Frame Attention (CFA). We propose CFA by taking the correlation between captions and related parts of the visual content across time. We exploit CFA by using the hidden states of Bi-LSTM h as the query of attention input:

$$r^f_{att} = avg(CFA(h, r^f, r^f)) = avg(\frac{softmax(h \cdot r^f)}{\sqrt{d_k}} r^f), \tag{4}$$

where $avg()$ denotes the average pooling operation, and d_k represents the scaled factor. Therefore, the representation of the section is as follows:

$$r^{sec} = r^c \oplus avg(r^{diffs}) \oplus r^f_{att}, \tag{5}$$

and the final output of MRL is calculated by inputting all the section-level features to a video level Bi-LSTM to model the correlation among sections.

4.2   Hierarchical Multi-label Inter-level Constrained Classifier

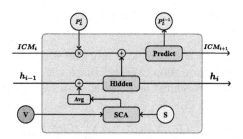

Fig. 4. Inter-level constrained unit.

Since we have obtained the multimodal representation of the video $V \in \mathbb{R}^{n \times d}$, where n is the number of sections, a Hierarchical Multi-label Inter-level Constrained Classifier (HMICC) is proposed to predict knowledge concepts for educational videos based on the feed-forward manner of current hybrid methods. The network consists of several Inter-level Constrained Units (ICU) shown in Fig. 4. Each one utilizes Section-Concept Attention (SCA) and Inter-level Constrained Matrix (ICM) to model each level's dependencies and feed the hidden information to the next unit. Specifically, $S^i \in \mathbb{R}^{C^i \times d}$ denotes the hidden representation of the i-th level and is input to SCA together with V. We apply the dot-product scores to measure the similarity of categories and video sections:

$$
\begin{aligned}
V_{att} &= softmax(S^i \cdot V) \cdot V, \\
r_{att}^v &= avg(V_{att}),
\end{aligned}
\tag{6}
$$

where we operate average pooling on temporal dimension to get r_{att}^v. Then we concatenate r_{att}^v and the previous hidden state h_{i-1} to obtain h_i by:

$$
h_i = \varphi(W_h(r_{att}^v \oplus h_{i-1}) + b_h),
\tag{7}
$$

where $\oplus$ denotes concatenation. Here we adopt the Inter-level Constrained Matrix $ICM_i \in \mathbb{R}^{C^i \times C^{i+1}}$ with each icm_{jk} representing the influence of the j-th category on the k-th one to the next level. We initialize all ICMs by calculating the conditional probabilities from the training set. The result of product between ICMs and previous prediction is added up to get the local prediction through a hidden layer, and the global output is obtained by inputting the last hidden state through a fully-connected layer:

$$
\begin{aligned}
P_L^i &= \sigma(W_L((P_L^{i-1}ICM_i) \oplus h_i) + b_L), \\
P_G &= (W_G \cdot h_H + b_G),
\end{aligned}
\tag{8}
$$

where W_h, W_L and b_H, b_L are weight matrices and bias vectors. Therefore, we can calculate the final predictions P with a parameter $\beta \in [0,1]$ for balancing the local and global outputs:

$$P = \beta \cdot P_G + (1 - \beta) \cdot (P_L^1 \oplus P_L^2 \oplus, \ldots, \oplus P_L^H), \tag{9}$$

4.3   Training SFNet

In this section, we specify a hybrid loss function for training SFNet to learn both global and local information. We calculate the global loss($\mathcal{L}_G$) and the local loss($\mathcal{L}_L$) for each hierarchical level, which can be formulated as:

$$\mathcal{L}_G = \varepsilon(P_G, Y_G), \mathcal{L}_L = \sum_{h=1}^{H} \varepsilon(P_L^h, Y_L^h), \tag{10}$$

where Y_G denotes the binary label vector for all categories of the knowledge structure and Y_L^h contains only the categories of the h-th level. We utilize the binary cross-entropy loss as $\varepsilon(\hat{Y}, Y)$ and formulate the final loss function as:

$$\mathcal{L}(\Omega) = \mathcal{L}_L + \mathcal{L}_G + \lambda ||\Omega||^2, \tag{11}$$

where Ω denotes the parameters of SFNet and λ is the hyper-parameter for L2 regularization. Thus, we can train SFNet by minimizing the loss function $\mathcal{L}(\Omega)$.

5   Experiments

5.1   Data Description

To evaluate the performance of our framework, we construct the dataset by collecting 7,521 educational videos, corresponding closed captions and hierarchical knowledge concepts from **Khan Academy**[1] The dataset involves a three-level hierarchical knowledge structure with 6, 42, 351 concepts in each level, and 399 in total. Averagely, a video is 436.4s long and has 1151 words of captions.

5.2   Baseline Approaches and Experimental Setup

We compare our proposed model with state-of-the-art works including unimodal and multimodal approaches. It is worth noting that all baseline models are pretrained on ImageNet, Kinetics dataset, etc., according to the categories, and tuned to obtain the best results.

– **R3D** [26] is a deep 3D convolution network with residual connection across layers and enables a very deep network structure while retaining performance improvement.

---

[1] All Khan Academy content is available for free at www.khanacademy.org.

- **SlowFast** [9] is a two-stream 3D CNN network that consists of two different paths that separately focus more on temporal and spatial information.
- **TimeSformer** [4] is a video transformer network that uses frame patches with positional encoding as input and exploits divided spatial and temporal self-attention.
- **R3D+BERT** is the combination of R3D and BERT. We leverage BERT to obtain the feature of captions and fuse the visual feature from frames.
- **HMCN-F** [29] is a feed-forward network that models the top-down hierarchical relationship and optimizes both local and global performance with penalties of hierarchical violations.

We implement all the methods using Pytorch. To train SFNet, we first set $n_{sections}$ as 8 and the maximum length of words for each caption as 64. We use ResNet34 and BERT-base as the feature extractor backbones and set the output dimension to 256. Hidden sizes of Bi-LSTM and HMICC are 128. We use the Adam optimizer and set up the initial learning rate to 0.0005 with cosine annealing scheduler that periodically adjust the value to 0.00005 for every 60 epochs. We also set $\beta = 0.5$, $\lambda = 0.00005$ and dropout rate as 0.5 to mitigate over-fitting. We used $Precision$, $Recall$, $F1 - score$, and mAP (mean Average Precision) as criteria for performance comparison. Whether a model considers the knowledge hierarchy or not, we calculated the performance at each hierarchical level and globally as well to further compare the differences.

Table 1. Performance Comparison on khan academy dataset. V and T denote the visual and textual modalities of the input data.

Model	Input	mAP	Precision	Micro-F1	Recall
R3D	V	0.6089	0.6745	0.5897	0.4591
SlowFast	V	0.6433	0.6936	0.6124	0.5431
TimeSformer	V	0.6799	0.7126	0.6295	0.5982
HMCN-F	T	0.7321	0.7640	0.6724	0.6213
R3D+Bert	V+T	0.8125	0.8391	0.7204	0.6428
SFNet	V+T	**0.8351**	**0.8712**	**0.7628**	**0.6787**

5.3 Experimental Results

Performance Comparison. From the results shown in Table 1 and Fig. 5, we can get several observations. First, models with textual input tend to outperform those visual-only models. In educational videos, visual content serves the lecturers' explanation. Due to the complexity and variance of visual elements such as hand-drawn graphics, it is harder to understand the semantics than textual content. It also indicates the significance of spotlight flow attention. Second, it is obvious that the performance decreases as the level gets lower. Hierarchical structure has a natural identity that higher levels have fewer categories and more

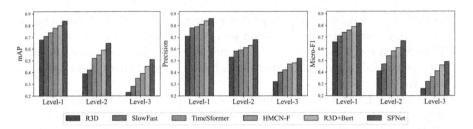

Fig. 5. Performance of SFNet and baseline models on different hierarchical levels.

data, which might explain the step down of performance. The results show that SFNet is more efficient by considering the inter-level association.

Ablation Study. To further assess how each part of our model donates to the performance, we remove each key module once at a time and construct several variants of SFNet. In Table 2, all the key modules do have contribution to better-predicting performance. The greater difference indicates more impact of the removed module. In addition, the variant without textual input has the greatest performance drop, which once again showing the above characteristics.

Table 2. The results of ablation study. V and T represent visual and textual input.

Model	mAP	Precision	Micro-F1	Recall
SFNet	0.8351	0.8712	0.7628	0.6787
V-only	0.5897	0.6528	0.5734	0.4345
T-only	0.7654	0.8133	0.7282	0.6571

6   Conclusion

In this paper, we presented Spotlight Flow Network to predict knowledge concepts for educational videos. We first adopted an effective text-to-visual section segmentation strategy for educational videos. Then, with different information paired with captions, we modeled the Spotlight Flow mechanism in which lecturers tend to conduct viewers' attention and moving regions help build up space-time connection. We also designed the HMICC to predict hierarchical knowledge concepts with implicit progressive impact and explicit inter-level constraints.

Acknowledgements. This research was partially supported by grants from the National Key Research and Development Program of China (No. 2021YFF0901003), and the National Natural Science Foundation of China (Grant No. 61922073).

References

1. Aly, R., Remus, S., Biemann, C.: Hierarchical multi-label classification of text with capsule networks. In: Proceedings of the 57th Annual Meeting of the Association for Computational Linguistics: Student Research Workshop, pp. 323–330 (2019)
2. Arandjelovic, R., Gronat, P., Torii, A., Pajdla, T., Sivic, J.: Netvlad: CNN architecture for weakly supervised place recognition. In: Proceedings of the IEEE Conference on Computer Vision and Pattern Recognition, pp. 5297–5307 (2016)
3. Arnab, A., Dehghani, M., Heigold, G., Sun, C., Lučić, M., Schmid, C.: Vivit: a video vision transformer. In: Proceedings of the IEEE/CVF International Conference on Computer Vision, pp. 6836–6846 (2021)
4. Bertasius, G., Wang, H., Torresani, L.: Is space-time attention all you need for video understanding? In: ICML, vol. 2, p. 4 (2021)
5. Bhardwaj, S., Srinivasan, M., Khapra, M.M.: Efficient video classification using fewer frames. In: Proceedings of the IEEE/CVF Conference on Computer Vision and Pattern Recognition, pp. 354–363 (2019)
6. Cao, J., Mao, D.H., Cai, Q., Li, H.S., Du, J.P.: A review of object representation based on local features. J. Zhejiang Univ. Sci. C **14**(7), 495–504 (2013). https://doi.org/10.1631/jzus.CIDE1303
7. Carreira, J., Zisserman, A.: Quo vadis, action recognition? a new model and the kinetics dataset. In: proceedings of the IEEE Conference on Computer Vision and Pattern Recognition, pp. 6299–6308 (2017)
8. Donahue, J., et al.: Long-term recurrent convolutional networks for visual recognition and description. In: Proceedings of the IEEE Conference on Computer Vision and Pattern Recognition, pp. 2625–2634 (2015)
9. Feichtenhofer, C., Fan, H., Malik, J., He, K.: Slowfast networks for video recognition. In: Proceedings of the IEEE/CVF International Conference on Computer Vision, pp. 6202–6211 (2019)
10. Feng, S., Fu, P., Zheng, W.: A hierarchical multi-label classification algorithm for gene function prediction. Algorithms **10**(4), 138 (2017)
11. Gabeur, V., Sun, C., Alahari, K., Schmid, C.: Multi-modal transformer for video retrieval. In: Vedaldi, A., Bischof, H., Brox, T., Frahm, J.-M. (eds.) ECCV 2020. LNCS, vol. 12349, pp. 214–229. Springer, Cham (2020). https://doi.org/10.1007/978-3-030-58548-8_13
12. Guo, P.J., Kim, J., Rubin, R.: How video production affects student engagement: an empirical study of MOOC videos. In: Proceedings of the first ACM Conference on Learning@ Scale Conference, pp. 41–50 (2014)
13. Herath, S., Harandi, M., Porikli, F.: Going deeper into action recognition: a survey. Image Vis. Comput. **60**, 4–21 (2017)
14. Huang, W., et al.: Hierarchical multi-label text classification: an attention-based recurrent network approach. In: Proceedings of the 28th ACM International Conference on Information and Knowledge Management, pp. 1051–1060 (2019)
15. Liang, M., Cao, X., Du, J., et al.: Dual-pathway attention based supervised adversarial hashing for cross-modal retrieval. In: 2021 IEEE International Conference on Big Data and Smart Computing (BigComp), pp. 168–171. IEEE (2021)
16. Nagrani, A., Yang, S., Arnab, A., Jansen, A., Schmid, C., Sun, C.: Attention bottlenecks for multimodal fusion. Adv. Neural. Inf. Process. Syst. **34**, 14200–14213 (2021)
17. Neimark, D., Bar, O., Zohar, M., Asselmann, D.: Video transformer network. In: Proceedings of the IEEE/CVF International Conference on Computer Vision, pp. 3163–3172 (2021)

18. Seo, J.J., Kim, H.I., De Neve, W., Ro, Y.M.: Effective and efficient human action recognition using dynamic frame skipping and trajectory rejection. Image Vis. Comput. **58**, 76–85 (2017)
19. Shang, X., Yuan, Z., Wang, A., Wang, C.: Multimodal video summarization via time-aware transformers. In: Proceedings of the 29th ACM International Conference on Multimedia, pp. 1756–1765 (2021)
20. Shen, J., Qiu, W., Meng, Y., Shang, J., Ren, X., Han, J.: Taxoclass: hierarchical multi-label text classification using only class names. In: Proceedings of the 2021 Conference of the North American Chapter of the Association for Computational Linguistics: Human Language Technologies, pp. 4239–4249 (2021)
21. Shimura, K., Li, J., Fukumoto, F.: HFT-CNN: learning hierarchical category structure for multi-label short text categorization. In: Proceedings of the 2018 Conference on Empirical Methods in Natural Language Processing, pp. 811–816 (2018)
22. Simonyan, K., Zisserman, A.: Two-stream convolutional networks for action recognition in videos. In: Advances in Neural Information Processing Systems, vol. 27 (2014)
23. Sun, C., Myers, A., Vondrick, C., Murphy, K., Schmid, C.: Videobert: a joint model for video and language representation learning. In: Proceedings of the IEEE/CVF International Conference on Computer Vision, pp. 7464–7473 (2019)
24. Sun, Z., Zhao, Y., Cao, D., Hao, H.: Hierarchical multilabel classification with optimal path prediction. Neural Process. Lett. **45**(1), 263–277 (2017). https://doi.org/10.1007/s11063-016-9526-x
25. Targ, S., Almeida, D., Lyman, K.: Resnet in resnet: generalizing residual architectures. arXiv preprint. arXiv:1603.08029 (2016)
26. Tran, D., Wang, H., Torresani, L., Ray, J., LeCun, Y., Paluri, M.: A closer look at spatiotemporal convolutions for action recognition. In: Proceedings of the IEEE Conference on Computer Vision and Pattern Recognition, pp. 6450–6459 (2018)
27. Wang, L., et al.: Temporal segment networks: towards good practices for deep action recognition. In: Leibe, B., Matas, J., Sebe, N., Welling, M. (eds.) ECCV 2016. LNCS, vol. 9912, pp. 20–36. Springer, Cham (2016). https://doi.org/10.1007/978-3-319-46484-8_2
28. Wang, X., et al.: Fine-grained similarity measurement between educational videos and exercises. In: Proceedings of the 28th ACM International Conference on Multimedia, pp. 331–339 (2020)
29. Wehrmann, J., Cerri, R., Barros, R.: Hierarchical multi-label classification networks. In: International Conference on Machine Learning, pp. 5075–5084. PMLR (2018)
30. Wu, C.Y., Feichtenhofer, C., Fan, H., He, K., Krahenbuhl, P., Girshick, R.: Long-term feature banks for detailed video understanding. In: Proceedings of the IEEE/CVF Conference on Computer Vision and Pattern Recognition, pp. 284–293 (2019)
31. Wu, C.Y., Krahenbuhl, P.: Towards long-form video understanding. In: Proceedings of the IEEE/CVF Conference on Computer Vision and Pattern Recognition, pp. 1884–1894 (2021)
32. Zhang, S., Guo, S., Huang, W., Scott, M.R., Wang, L.: V4d: 4d convolutional neural networks for video-level representation learning. arXiv preprint. arXiv:2002.07442 (2020)

Learning Evidential Cognitive Diagnosis Networks Robust to Response Bias

Jiawei Liu[1,2], Jingyi Hou[1(✉)], Na Zhang[3], Zhijie Liu[1], and Wei He[1]

[1] Institute of Artificial Intelligence, University of Science and Technology Beijing,
Beijing 100083, China
houjingyi@ustb.edu.cn
[2] Shunde Graduate School of University of Science and Technology Beijing,
Foshan 528300, China
[3] Department of Science and Technology, University of Science and Technology
Beijing, Beijing 100083, China

Abstract. As a basic task of the intelligent education system, cognitive diagnosis aims to diagnose the knowledge proficiency of students and capture the complex relationship between students and exercises. Benefiting from big data, deep learning show advantages in cognitive diagnosis tasks. However, the general deep learning-based methods are sensitive to noise, and response bias is an inevitable problem in real-world situations. To address this challenge, we propose the Evidential Cognitive Diagnosis Model (EvidentialCDM), which introduces the evidential deep learning to neural cognitive diagnostic frameworks for estimating the aleatoric and epistemic uncertainties as well as maintaining the predicting performance. In addition, this paper proposes a new dataset, named Uncertainty ASSIST (UncASSIST), in order to better deal with this problem. Experimental results show the effectiveness of our method on both the publicly available ASSIST and our proposed UncASSIST datasets.

Keywords: Neural cognitive diagnosis · Uncertainty estimation · Online education system · Response bias

1 Introduction

Educational data mining and learning analysis aim to provide learners with a high-quality and personalized learning experience. As one of the main participants in online education, students are the core research object of learning analysis. Among them, the most important research is how to mine and diagnose students' real knowledge proficiency through students' ability modelling by online education systems. Cognitive diagnosis is a technique that uses students' practice records to model their abilities and diagnose their proficiency in knowledge points. At present, researchers have proposed many cognitive diagnostic models for student assessment, such as noisy-and gate model (DINA) [5], item response theory (IRT) [8], Multidimensional IRT (MIRT) [1,15] and matrix factorization (MF) [11]. However, the above cognitive diagnosis models usually use

© The Author(s), under exclusive license to Springer Nature Switzerland AG 2022
L. Fang et al. (Eds.): CICAI 2022, LNAI 13605, pp. 171–181, 2022.
https://doi.org/10.1007/978-3-031-20500-2_14

artificially designed functions to mine students' practice processes. These functions are usually relatively simple and can hardly capture the complex relationship between students and exercises [6]. To solve this problem, Wang et al. [18] use the neural network method to learn the complex interaction between student factors and exercises, and propose NeuralCD model which utilizes a knowledge proficiency vector to represent the corresponding student and formulates the students, exercises and responses with a MIRT-like multi-layer perceptron (MLP). Although the neural networks have succeeded in many fields, such as natural language processing [4,17] and computer vision [10,12,16], with their strong fitting ability on large amounts of data, they still suffer from being sensitive and overfitting to noise. In practical applications of cognitive diagnosis, the inherent response bias of diagnostic tests will introduce noise, which is problematic for deep learning-based methods. Due to the existence of uncertainty, the accuracy of the neural network model will be extremely affected when the training data fluctuates greatly.

In the real online answer scenario, there would be more misoperation and inaccurate answers caused by the students' sloppy attitude towards questions in a relatively relaxed environment. As a result, the validity of the results of the cognitive diagnosis could be damaged. We describe the above problem as response bias. It means that there exists uncertainty in the data we obtained in the real-world cognitive diagnosis. The accidental uncertainty of data could make the deep learning based neural cognitive diagnostic model unable to accurately judge the proficiency of students in knowledge points, which reduces the accuracy of diagnostic results.

To address this challenge without any elaborate question design or manual analysis of the answers, we propose the Evidential Cognitive Diagnosis Model (EvidentialCDM) by considering the impact of inaccurate data on the diagnostic effect. Specifically, the model is based on evidential deep learning to conduct both aleatoric and epistemic uncertainty estimation according to the knowledge point proficiency vector, the knowledge point difficulty vector and the exercise discrimination. The effectiveness of EvidentialCDM is verified by experiments on real datasets. In order to simulate a more realistic response bias problem, we propose a new dataset Uncertainty-ASSIST (UncASSIST), which modifies the exercise results corresponding to a certain proportion of knowledge points with high uncertainty according to the publicly available Assitments dataset [9].

Our main contributions in this work are summarized as follows:

- We focus on the challenge of response bias in cognitive diagnosis and propose a new EvidentialCDM method to effectively deal with this problem.
- We establish a new dataset which is called UncASSIST to simulate the response bias in the real-world situation. The effectiveness of our model is verified by experiments on both off-the-shelf and our proposed datasets.

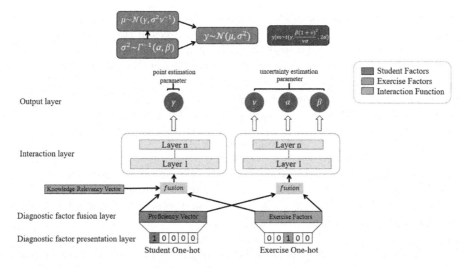

Fig. 1. The proposed evidential cognitive diagnosis model (EvidentialCDM). The colors of orange, blue and yellow indicate student factors, exercise factors and interaction function, respectively. (Color figure online)

2 Method

2.1 Problem Definition

Suppose there are N students, M exercises, and K knowledge concepts in an educational scene, which are represented as $S = \{s_1, s_2, \ldots, s_N\}$, $E = \{e_1, e_2, \ldots, e_M\}$, and $C = \{c_1, c_2, \ldots, c_K\}$, respectively. Each student s will choose a group of exercises e to practice. Therefore, the student's learning results are denoted by a triplet (s, e, r), where $s \in S$, $e \in E$, and $r \in [0, 1]$ represents the received score of the student s on exercise e. Moreover, we have the Q-matrix (often marked by experts), if the practice exercises e_i are relevant to the knowledge concept c_j then $Q_{ij} = 1$, and $Q_{ij} = 0$ if they are not relevant. Given the response scores R of the students and the matrix Q, the goal of our cognitive diagnostic task is to analyse students' proficiency to different knowledge concepts in the form of student performance prediction.

2.2 Evidential Cognitive Diagnosis Model

In order to improve the robustness of the neural cognitive diagnosis model to the uncertainty caused by te response bias, this paper proposes EvidentialCDM, which mainly contains four components: the diagnostic factor presentation layer, the diagnostic factor fusion layer, the interaction layer and the output layer. The structure of EvidentialCDM is shown in Fig. 1.

Diagnostic Factor Presentation Layer. There are many diagnostic factors considered in cognitive diagnosis research. The sources of these factors are usually divided into two aspects: students and test questions. We call them student factors and exercise factors respectively. In the aspect of students, this paper uses the knowledge point proficiency vector $\delta = [\delta_1, \delta_2, \cdots, \delta_J] \in \{0,1\}^{1 \times J}$ to denote students. We calculate δ by multiplying a one-hot vector $x \in \{0,1\}^{1 \times U}$ representing the student and a trainable matrix $A \in \mathbb{R}^{U \times J}$,

$$\delta = \text{sigmoid}(x \times A). \tag{1}$$

By multiplying the trainable matrix A, we not only obtain the proficiency vector of knowledge points δ, but also convert the sparse vector into a dense vector.

In terms of test questions, the correlation vector g of knowledge points directly comes from the Q-matrix, $Q \in \{0,1\}^{V \times J}$: $g = h \times Q$, where $g \in \{0,1\}^{1 \times J}$, and $h \in \{0,1\}^{1 \times V}$ is the one-hot vector representing the exercise. For other optional factors, this paper selects the difficulty vector of knowledge points ϕ. Different from the exercise, ϕ is a numerical variable for distinguishing between students with different knowledge proficiency degrees. $\varepsilon = [\varepsilon_1, \varepsilon_1, \cdots, \varepsilon_j]$ denotes the difficulty of each knowledge point examined by the exercise. They can be obtained by the following formula:

$$\varepsilon = \text{sigmoid}(h \times B), \quad \phi = \text{sigmoid}(h \times D), \tag{2}$$

where $\varepsilon \in \{0,1\}^{1 \times J}$, $\phi \in \{0,1\}$, $h \in \{0,1\}^{1 \times V}$, $B \in \mathbb{R}^{V \times J}$ and $D \in \mathbb{R}^{V \times 1}$ are trainable matrices.

Diagnostic Factor Fusion Layer. With the knowledge proficiency obtained above, the task of cognitive diagnosis can be formulated as an answer correctness prediction problem. This paper uses the following equation to fuse knowledge point correlation vector $g \in \{0,1\}^{1 \times J}$, the knowledge point proficiency vector δ, the knowledge point difficulty vector ε, and the exercise discrimination ϕ:

$$t = g \circ (\delta - \varepsilon) \times \phi, \tag{3}$$

where $t \in \{0,1\}^{1 \times J}$, and $\circ$ denotes the element wise multiplication.

Interaction Layer. Benefiting from the strong fitting ability of deep neural networks, we can use them to capture the relationship between students and exercises. Using neural network as an interactive function can learn from the training data, and has a wide range of applications. Mathematically, we express the output of the EvidentialCDM framework as:

$$\begin{aligned}\gamma &= \varphi_n(\ldots \varphi_1(g, \delta, \varepsilon, \phi, \theta_1)), \\ (\nu, \alpha, \beta) &= \varsigma_n(\ldots \varsigma_1(\delta, \varepsilon, \phi, \theta_2)),\end{aligned} \tag{4}$$

where φ_i and ς_i denote the mapping function of their corresponding ith MLP layers, and θ_1, θ_2 denote the learnable parameters of the corresponding interactive layers, respectively. The output $\mathbf{q} = (\gamma, \nu, \alpha, \beta)$ corresponds to a Normal-Inverse-Gamma (NIG) distribution, which will be discussed in detail in the next section. Note that there is no uncertainty of the g vector, so we use two separately networks with the same structure to output the point estimation parameters and uncertainty estimation parameters.

Output Layer. To perform uncertainty estimation, we leverage the evidential deep learning [2, 13] to train the proposed model by sampling the predicted value y from a Gaussian distribution,

$$y \sim \mathcal{N}\left(\mu, \sigma^2\right), \tag{5}$$

where the parameters of the Gaussian distribution μ and σ are drawn from the NIG distribution, the conjugate prior to the normal distribution, as described previously,

$$\mu \sim \mathcal{N}\left(\gamma, \frac{\sigma^2}{\nu}\right), \quad \sigma^2 \sim \text{Gamma}^{-1}(\alpha, \beta), \tag{6}$$

where $0 < \gamma < 1$, $\nu, \beta > 0$, $\alpha > 1$, and $\text{Gamma}^{-1}(\cdot)$ denotes the inverse-gamma distribution. Consequently, the NIG distribution is parameterized by a tuple of 4 elements, $\mathbf{q} = (\gamma, \nu, \alpha, \beta)$, which is calculated by the output layers of the EvidentialCDM. To achieve the aforementioned constraints, we apply the Sigmoid activation to derive γ and the softplus activation [7] to obtain (ν, α, β), respectively.

Given the NIG distribution above, we can obtain the student performance prediction $y* = \mathrm{E}[\mu] = \gamma$, and estimate the aleatoric uncertainty $\mathrm{E}\left[\sigma^2\right]$ and $\text{Var}[\mu]$ by the calculations:

$$\mathrm{E}\left[\sigma^2\right] = \frac{\beta}{\alpha - 1}, \quad \text{Var}[\mu] = \frac{\beta}{\nu(\alpha - 1)}. \tag{7}$$

We learn the parameters of the EvidentialCDM through maximizing a marginal likelihood w.r.t. the parameters μ and σ of the Gaussian distribution. The marginal likelihood over μ and σ is calculated by,

$$p(y \mid \mathbf{q}) = \int_0^\infty \int_{-\infty}^\infty p\left(y \mid \mu, \sigma^2\right) p\left(\mu, \sigma^2 \mid \mathbf{q}\right) d\mu d\sigma^2, \tag{8}$$

which can be drawn by a t-distribution, i.e.,

$$p(y \mid \mathbf{q}) = \mathrm{t}\left(y; \gamma, \frac{\beta(1 + \nu)}{\nu\alpha}; 2\alpha\right). \tag{9}$$

In practical learning procedure, the objective is calculated using the negative log of the marginal likelihood (NLL),

$$
\begin{aligned}
L_{NLL}(y, \mathbf{q}) = & -\log(p(y \mid \mathbf{q})) \\
= & \frac{1}{2} \log\left(\frac{\pi}{\nu}\right) - \alpha \log(2\beta(1+\nu)) \\
& + (\alpha + 0.5) \log\left((y-\gamma)^2 \nu + 2\beta(1+\nu)\right) \\
& + \log\left(\frac{\Gamma(\alpha)}{\Gamma(\alpha+0.5)}\right),
\end{aligned}
\tag{10}
$$

and minimize the NLL loss function for optimizing the model, where $\Gamma(\alpha) = \int_0^\infty t^{\alpha-1} e^{-t} dt$ is the gamma function.

Only using an NLL loss could be not sufficient enough for optimizing the proposed EvidentialCDM. Although NLL enables the model to predict appropriate point estimation γ, the model avoids lower NLL loss by increasing prediction uncertainty rather than achieving higher prediction accuracy [13]. Therefore, we employ the Lipschitz modified MSE loss function to improve the prediction accuracy of the model and alleviate the gradient conflict between multiple loss functions

$$
L_{LMSE}(y, \gamma) = \begin{cases} (y-\gamma)^2, & \text{if } (y-\gamma)^2 < U \\ 2\sqrt{U}\,|y-\gamma| - U, & \text{if } (y-\gamma)^2 \geq U \end{cases}
\tag{11}
$$

where U takes the minimum value u of the sample in the mini-batch of the training data, and $u = \min(\frac{\beta(\nu+1)}{\alpha\nu}, \frac{2\beta(\nu+1)}{\nu}(\exp(\frac{\Gamma'(\alpha+0.5)}{\Gamma(\alpha+0.5)} - \frac{\Gamma'(\alpha)}{\Gamma(\alpha)})) - 1))$.

The final loss function L_{UE} to estimate uncertainty is defined as a combination of the two losses and the regularization:

$$
L_{UE} = L_{NLL}(y, \mathbf{q}) + L_{LMSE}(y, \gamma) + c|y-\gamma|(2\nu + \alpha),
\tag{12}
$$

where the last term in the equation is the evidence regularizer and $c > 0$ is its coefficient.

In order to further enhance the point estimation ability of the model, we add a cross-entropy loss on the basis of L_{UE}, which is the cross-entropy loss between the point estimation γ and the real label r :

$$
L_{BM} = -(r \log \gamma + (1-r) \log(1-\gamma)),
\tag{13}
$$

Then we can derive the overall optimization objective:

$$
L_{total} = L_{BM} + k L_{UE},
\tag{14}
$$

where k is a hyperparameter.

2.3   Uncertainty-ASSIST (UncASSIST) Dataset

Based on the Assistments dataset [9], we use the statistical analysis to establish a new dataset, which is called Uncertainty-ASSIST (UncASSIST), to simulate the response bias in the real-world situation. Specifically, for multiple knowledge points in the assessments dataset, if the correct rate of students' answers to the exercises corresponding to some knowledge points is closer to 50%, it can be considered that students have a lower level of proficiency in the knowledge points and tend to guess randomly when answering, so the possibility of response bias in the real environment is greater for exercises corresponding to these knowledge points. The uncertainty of knowledge point ρ can be calculated by the following:

$$\rho = 1 - |Accuacy - 50\%|. \tag{15}$$

Accordingly, we rank the knowledge points according to the uncertainty from high to low, and select the knowledge points with high value of ρ in the proportions of 5%, 10%, 15%, and 20% to modify the corresponding answer results of the exercises of the knowledge points in the training set. Therefore, we have 4 subsets with data modified in the aforementioned proportions to form the entire UncASSIST dataset. The 4 subsets are named as UncASSIST-Mn, where $n \in \{5, 10, 15, 20\}$.

3 Experiments

3.1 Experimental Setup

The dimensions of all the fully connected layers are set to 100, and we use Tanh as the activation function for all layers of our model. The number of the interaciton layers is 4. We initialize the parameters with Xavier initialization. We apply the Adam optimizer for optimizing, and the learning rate is 0.001. As for the hyperparameters, the evidential regularizer factor c is set to 0.001. The size of the minibatch is 32. Our model is implemented by the PyTorch toolkit, and the experiments are conducted on a server with an RTX3090 GPU.

In order to verify the diagnostic performance of the proposed method and its ability to estimate the uncertainty of data, this paper evaluates the diagnostic effect of the model by predicting the answers to the exercises.

We evaluate the EvidentialCDM on the public cognitive diagnosis dataset, ASSISTments 2009-2010 "skill builder" (ASSIST) [9], and our modified UncAS-SIST dataset. We follow the data split setting that divides the training set and the test set of each student's answer records at the ratio of 80% and 20% on both ASSIST and UncASSIST datasets. The accuracy (Acc.), root mean square error (RMSE) [14], and area under the curve (AUC) [3] are employed as the evaluation metrics.

Our code of EvidentialCDM and Uncertainty-Assist dataset we established are publicly available at https://github.com/jasper2077/EvidentialCDM.

3.2 Main Results on the UncASSIST Dataset

We conduct extensive experiments on the 4 subsets of the proposed UncAS-SIST dataset using the EvidentialCDM and existing methods to provide several

Table 1. Comparison results on the UncASSIST-M5 and the UncASSIST-M10 datasets. Values marked in bold and with underline represent the highest scores of the BM+L$_{UE}$ and the EvidentialCDM, respectively.

Methods	UncASSIST-M5			UncASSIST-M10		
	Acc.	RMSE	AUC	Acc.	RMSE	AUC
DINA	0.614±0.02	0.507±0.02	0.662±0.02	0.613±0.02	0.510±0.02	0.657±0.02
MF	0.688±0.02	0.462±0.02	0.713±0.02	0.677±0.01	0.473±0.01	0.697±0.01
MLP	0.702±0.01	0.459±0.01	0.718±0.01	0.682±0.01	0.478±0.01	0.706±0.01
NeuralCD	0.705±0.01	0.456±0.02	0.728±0.01	0.686±0.01	0.477±0.01	0.711±0.01
BM+L$_{UE}$ (k=0.25)	0.712±0.01	0.447±0.02	<u>0.732 ± 0.01</u>	0.694±0.02	0.463±0.01	0.716±0.01
BM+L$_{UE}$ (k=0.5)	<u>0.714 ± 0.01</u>	<u>0.444 ± 0.01</u>	0.731±0.02	0.700±0.02	0.458±0.02	<u>0.717 ± 0.01</u>
BM+L$_{UE}$ (k=1)	0.709±0.01	0.450±0.01	0.728±0.01	<u>0.701 ± 0.01</u>	<u>0.453 ± 0.02</u>	0.714±0.02
BM+L$_{UE}$ (k=2)	0.699±0.02	0.459±0.02	0.716±0.01	0.695±0.02	0.462±0.02	0.716±0.01
EvidentialCDM (k=0.25)	0.710±0.01	0.447±0.02	0.731±0.01	0.696±0.02	0.462±0.02	0.716±0.01
EvidentialCDM (k=0.5)	**0.714±0.01**	**0.443±0.02**	0.731±0.02	0.701±0.01	0.454±0.02	0.717±0.01
EvidentialCDM (k=1)	0.710±0.02	0.446±0.01	**0.735±0.01**	**0.702±0.01**	**0.450±0.02**	**0.719±0.01**
EvidentialCDM (k=2)	0.686±0.02	0.460±0.02	0.730±0.01	0.691±0.02	0.459±0.01	0.718±0.01

benchmarks. The applied methods include DINA [5], MF [11], multi-layer perceptron (MLP), and NeuralCD [18], where MLP is composed of 4 fully connected layers with each layer followed by a Tanh activation function. Moreover, we also provide the results of applying the uncertainty estimation loss to the backbone model, i.e., NeuralCD, and name the method BM+L$_{UE}$. The hyperparameter k is set to $\{0.25, 0.5, 1, 2\}$. We calculate the mean and the standard deviation of the results by repeating each experiment 5 times.

Table 1 shows the comparison results of our method and other baseline methods on the UncASSIST-M5 and the UncASSIST-M10 datasets and Table 2 shows the results on the UncASSIST-M15 and the UncASSIST-M20 datasets. From the two tables, we can observe that our method extensively achieves the best performance on all the datasets. Methods using the uncertainty estimation perform better than other methods, which shows the effectiveness of the evidential learning in tackling the response bias problem. We also observe that larger k is needed with an increasing number of noisy data, which illustrates the importance of uncertainty estimation.

3.3   Analysis of the Uncertainty Estimation

We also conduct experiments to analyze the losses of uncertainty estimation and compare our method with the backbone model, NeuralCD [18]. To make a more direct analysis of the robustness of the uncertainty estimation loss, we use the ASSIST dataset by randomly modifying $\{5\%, 10\%, 15\%\}$ samples for training and provide the results of BM+L$_{UE}$ with $k \in \{0.25, 0.5, 1, 2\}$. We calculate the average of the results by repeating each experiment 5 times.

The results are shown in Table 3, respectively. From the results, we can observe that the uncertainty estimation loss makes the model more robust to

Table 2. Comparison results on the UncASSIST-M15 and the UncASSIST-M20 datasets. Values marked in bold and with underline represent the highest scores of the BM+L$_{UE}$ and the EvidentialCDM, respectively.

Methods	UncASSIST-M15			UncASSIST-M20		
	Acc.	RMSE	AUC	Acc.	RMSE	AUC
DINA	0.605±0.01	0.516±0.02	0.648±0.01	0.604±0.01	0.519±0.01	0.644±0.01
MF	0.672±0.02	0.462±0.02	0.693±0.02	0.665±0.01	0.473±0.01	0.681±0.02
MLP	0.679±0.01	0.487±0.02	0.699±0.01	0.670±0.01	0.486±0.01	0.695±0.01
NeuralCD	0.682±0.01	0.486±0.02	0.701±0.01	0.674±0.01	0.484±0.02	0.698±0.01
BM+L$_{UE}$ (k=0.25)	0.688±0.01	0.472±0.01	0.705±0.01	0.682±0.02	0.469±0.02	0.702±0.01
BM+L$_{UE}$ (k=0.5)	0.690±0.01	0.465±0.02	<u>0.706 ± 0.02</u>	0.685±0.02	0.464±0.02	<u>0.703 ± 0.02</u>
BM+L$_{UE}$ (k=1)	<u>0.692 ± 0.01</u>	<u>0.460 ± 0.01</u>	0.704±0.02	<u>0.689 ± 0.01</u>	<u>0.458 ± 0.01</u>	0.700±0.01
BM+L$_{UE}$ (k=2)	0.687±0.01	0.463±0.01	0.697±0.01	0.683±0.02	0.463±0.01	0.690±0.02
EvidentialCDM (k=0.25)	0.686±0.01	0.471±0.02	0.704±0.01	0.680±0.01	0.468±0.02	0.702±0.01
EvidentialCDM (k=0.5)	0.691±0.01	0.465±0.01	0.708±0.01	0.685±0.01	0.462±0.02	0.703±0.01
EvidentialCDM (k=1)	**0.692±0.01**	**0.458±0.01**	**0.709±0.01**	**0.690±0.01**	**0.455±0.01**	0.706±0.01
EvidentialCDM (k=2)	0.686±0.01	0.461±0.01	0.707±0.01	0.687±0.01	0.456±0.01	**0.707±0.01**

the noisy data. The results of our EvidentialCDM also gain even larger improvements compared with the methods of BM+L$_{UE}$ on ASSIST than UncASSIST. It is probably because the knowledge relevancy does not correlate with any causes of noisy data, and the learning procedure can better isolate the correlation to derive a more explainable model with diverse noisy data.

Table 3. Test results on the ASSIST dataset modified 5%, 10% and 15% of samples, respectively. Values marked in bold and with underline represent the highest scores of the BM+L$_{UE}$ and the EvidentialCDM, respectively.

Methods	Invert 5% of the data		Invert 10% of the data		Invert 15% of the data	
	RMSE	AUC	RMSE	AUC	RMSE	AUC
NeuralCD	0.472	0.719	0.472	0.719	0.488	0.708
BM+L$_{UE}$ (k=0.25)	0.460	0.731	0.463	0.720	0.472	0.714
BM+L$_{UE}$ (k=0.5)	0.455	<u>0.732</u>	0.454	<u>0.721</u>	0.467	<u>0.714</u>
BM+L$_{UE}$ (k=1)	<u>0.443</u>	0.734	<u>0.448</u>	0.719	<u>0.464</u>	0.712
BM+L$_{UE}$ (k=2)	0.448	0.723	0.449	0.712	0.470	0.704
EvidentialCDM (k=0.25)	0.453	0.735	0.454	0.722	0.476	0.709
EvidentialCDM (k=0.5)	0.445	**0.737**	0.448	**0.726**	0.466	0.712
EvidentialCDM (k=1)	0.442	0.733	**0.446**	0.725	**0.463**	**0.715**
EvidentialCDM (k=2)	**0.440**	0.734	0.449	0.719	0.469	0.709

4   Conclusion

We have proposed a new cognitive diagnosis dataset, i.e., UncASSIST, that can be used for analyzing the response bias problem in the cognitive diagnosis. Besides providing benchmarks on the proposed dataset, we have also introduced the EvidentialCDM that is robust to noisy data under the real-world online education scenario by considering the uncertainty estimation in the neural cognitive diagnosis frameworks. Experiments show that the proposed model can efficiently improve the predictive accuracy on both ASSIST and UncASSIST datasets. In the future, we look forward to developing a new mechanism to enable our model to discover text information to improve our model's interpretability on uncertainty estimation.

Acknowledgment. This work was supported in part by the National Key Research and Development Program of China under grant No. 2019YFB1703600, and the Natural Science Foundation of China under grants No. 62106021 and No. U20A20225.

References

1. Ackerman, T.A., Gierl, M.J., Walker, C.M.: Using multidimensional item response theory to evaluate educational and psychological tests. Educ. Meas. Issues Pract. **22**(3), 37–51 (2003)
2. Amini, A., Schwarting, W., Soleimany, A., Rus, D.: Deep evidential regression. In: Larochelle, H., Ranzato, M., Hadsell, R., Balcan, M., Lin, H. (eds.) Annual Conference on Neural Information Processing Systems (NeurIPS) (2020)
3. Bradley, A.P.: The use of the area under the ROC curve in the evaluation of machine learning algorithms. Pattern Recogn. **30**(7), 1145–1159 (1997)
4. Cheng, J., Dong, L., Lapata, M.: Long short-term memory-networks for machine reading. In: Su, J., Carreras, X., Duh, K. (eds.) Conference on Empirical Methods in Natural Language Processing (EMNLP), pp. 551–561 (2016)
5. De La Torre, J.: The generalized DINA model framework. Psychometrika **76**(2), 179–199 (2011). https://doi.org/10.1007/s11336-011-9207-7
6. Dibello, L.V., Roussos, L.A., Stout, W.: 31a review of cognitively diagnostic assessment and a summary of psychometric models. Handbook Statist. **26**(06), 979–1030 (2006)
7. Dugas, C., Bengio, Y., Bélisle, F., Nadeau, C., Garcia, R.: Incorporating second-order functional knowledge for better option pricing. In: Annual Conference on Neural Information Processing Systems (NIPS), pp. 472–478 (2000)
8. Embretson, S.E., Reise, S.P.: Item Response Theory. Psychology Press, London (2013)
9. Feng, M., Heffernan, N., Koedinger, K.: Addressing the assessment challenge with an online system that tutors as it assesses. User Model. User-Adap. Inter. **19**(3), 243–266 (2009). https://doi.org/10.1007/s11257-009-9063-7
10. He, K., Zhang, X., Ren, S., Sun, J.: Deep residual learning for image recognition. In: IEEE Conference on Computer Vision and Pattern Recognition (CVPR), pp. 770–778 (2016)
11. Koren, Y., Bell, R., Volinsky, C.: Matrix factorization techniques for recommender systems. Computer **42**(8), 30–37 (2009)
12. Krizhevsky, A., Sutskever, I., Hinton, G.: Imagenet classification with deep convolutional neural networks. In: Annual Conference on Neural Information Processing Systems (NIPS), vol. 25, no. 2 (2012)
13. Oh, D., Shin, B.: Improving evidential deep learning via multi-task learning. In: AAAI Conference on Artificial Intelligence (AAAI) (2021)

14. Pei, H., Yang, B., Liu, J., Dong, L.: Group sparse bayesian learning for active surveillance on epidemic dynamics. In: McIlraith, S.A., Weinberger, K.Q. (eds.) AAAI Conference on Artificial Intelligence (AAAI), pp. 800–807 (2018)
15. Reckase, M.D.: Multidimensional item response theory models. In: Multidimensional Item Response Theory, pp. 79–112. Springer, New York (2009)
16. Simonyan, K., Zisserman, A.: Very deep convolutional networks for large-scale image recognition. In: Bengio, Y., LeCun, Y. (eds.) International Conference on Learning Representations (ICLR) (2015)
17. Vaswani, A., et al.: Attention is all you need. In: Annual Conference on Neural Information Processing Systems (NIPS), pp. 5998–6008 (2017)
18. Wang, F., et al.: Neural cognitive diagnosis for intelligent education systems. In: AAAI Conference on Artificial Intelligence (AAAI), pp. 6153–6161 (2020)

An Integrated Navigation Method for UAV Autonomous Landing Based on Inertial and Vision Sensors

Kejun Shang[✉], Xixi Li, Chongliang Liu, Li Ming, and Guangfeng Hu

Beijing Institute of Automation Equipment, Beijing 100074, China
kjshang@163.com, bridge968@sina.com

Abstract. In the process of autonomous landing of unmanned aerial vehicles (UAV), the vision sensor is restricted by the field of view and UAV maneuvering process, which may make the acquired relative position/attitude parameters unstable or even odd (not unique), and there is a 'blind area' of vision measurement in the UAV rollout stage, which loses the navigation ability and seriously affects the safety of landing. In this paper, an autonomous landing navigation method based on inertial/visual sensor information fusion is proposed. When the UAV is far away from the airport and the runway imaging is complete, landing navigation parameters are determined by vision sensor based on the object image conjugate relationship of the runway sideline, and fuses with the inertial information to improve the measure performance. When the UAV is close to the airport and the runway imaging is incomplete, the measurement information of the vision sensor appears singular. The estimation of the landing navigation parameters is realized by inertial information in the aid of vision. When the UAV rollouts, the vision sensor enters the 'blind area', judges the UAV's motion state through the imaging features of two adjacent frames, and suppresses the inertial sensor error by using the UAV's motion state constraint, so as to achieve the high-precision maintenance of landing navigation parameters. The flight test shows that the lateral relative position error is less than 10m when the inertial with low accuracy and visual sensor are used, which can meet the requirement of UAV landing safely.

Keywords: Autonomous landing navigation · Deep learning semantic segmentation · Inertial/Vision data fusion

1 Introduction

Autonomous landing of UAV refers to the positioning, navigation and control of UAV relying its own flight control system and various navigation equipment. The aim is to guide the UAV to land on the runway independently and safely. It is the premise of safe recovery and reuse of UAV in complex environment. Research data indicate that the number of faults in landing process accounts for more than 80% of the total faults in UAV mission profile. For the fixed wing UAV with fast flight speed and no hovering function, the landing process is more complex and the risk is higher. Accurate measurement

L. Fang et al. (Eds.): CICAI 2022, LNAI 13605, pp. 182–193, 2022.
https://doi.org/10.1007/978-3-031-20500-2_15

of relative position/attitude between UAV and runway is the key to safe landing and navigation. At present, the main methods of radio positioning and satellite difference real-time positioning are lack of information integrity, anti-interference ability and data update frequency.

In recent years, based on the visual navigation technology, people take the runway plane as the cooperative target, determine the relative geometric relationship between the UAV and the airport runway through the visual sensor during landing, and then obtain the relative position/attitude between them. This method has a great advantage in the measurement accuracy, and has been gradually verified by the engineering application, causing extensive research internationally [1, 2]. Wand and Zhou use AprilTag markers as tracking targets for the landing navigation of rotor wing UAV [3, 4]. However, fixed wing UAVs landing on airport runways cannot use additional tracking targets except runway. Wang and Zhang propose navigation methods based on runway detection and visual-inertial fusion, when the runway features imaging integrated [5, 6]. However, the acquired relative position/attitude may be unstable or even singular due to the constraints of visual sensor's field of view, installation position, UAV's maneuver mode and flight environment. When the UAV approaches the starting line of the runway and enters the rollout stage, the runway imaging is incomplete, there is not enough feature lines for navigation due to the starting line losing and relative narrow field of view (the camera is about 1.5 m above the ground). Then the UAV enter into the 'blind area' of visual measurement, which brings a huge potential safety hazard to the landing [7–9].

To solve the above problems, this paper proposes an autonomous landing navigation method based on the information fusion of inertial/visual sensors. When the UAV is far away from the airport and the runway image is complete, the landing navigation parameters of UAV are determined based on the object image conjugate relationship of the runway characteristic line of visual sensors [10, 11]. When the UAV is close to the airport and the runway imaging is incomplete, the measurement information of the visual sensor appears singular, and the UAV landing and navigation parameters are estimated by the information of the inertial sensor assisted by the visual information. In the stage of the UAV's touchdown and rollout, the visual sensor enters the 'blind area', and judges the UAV's motion state by the imaging features of two adjacent frames in order to improve the measurement accuracy and reliability of landing navigation information.

2   Landing Process Analysis and Scheme Design

Taking a typical landing flight profile of a fixed wing UAV as an example (as shown in Fig. 1), the landing process is divided into 4 areas:

Area A: $x_l < K_1$. As shown in Fig. 2(a), the runway imaging is represented as a 'point target', so the relative position/attitude information cannot be calculated in the visual sensor coordinate system.

Area B: $K_1 \leq x_l < K_2$. As shown in Fig. 2(b), high-precision relative position/attitude measurement information can be obtained in the visual sensor coordinate system and then fuses with inertial navigation information to improve the performance.

Area C: $K_2 \leq x_l < K_3$. As shown in Fig. 2(c), it is not sufficient for visual measurement. The relative position/attitude can be acquired with the aid of inertial sensor.

Area D: $K_3 \leq x_l < K_4$. As shown in Fig. 2(d), the runway center line is clearly visible, which can be used to judge the motion state of UAV and assist to realize the inertial navigation error suppression based on motion constraints.

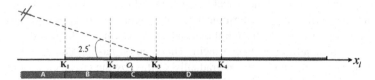

Fig. 1. The typical landing process of UAV

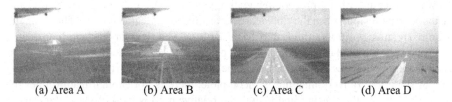

(a) Area A   (b) Area B   (c) Area C   (d) Area D

Fig. 2. Visual features during UAV's typical landing process

3   Intelligent Identification of Airport Runway Based on Deep Learning Semantic Segmentation

3.1   Runway Segmentation Network Design

The runway area is defined as the area between the left line, the right line, the start line and the end line of the runway, as shown in the quadrilateral area with A, B, E, F as the vertices in Fig. 3.

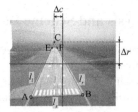

Fig. 3. Definition of runway area

When designing the segmentation network, the segmentation accuracy and multi-scale feature extraction ability of the network should also be improved while focusing on the real-time calculation.

As shown in Fig. 4, the runway segmentation network (named RunwayNet [12]) adopts an encoder-decoder structure, and the encoder consists of a backbone network and a self-attention module. The Network Backbone is a lightweight ShuffleNet V2 modified by Atrous Convolution or Dilated Convolutions, which gradually extracts abstract semantic features from the input image, and finally outputs feature map; the self-attention module performs feature transformation on the feature map output by the backbone network through two sub-modules of positional attention and channel attention to capture the similarity of feature map spatial dimension and channel dimension information to improve the receptive field and feature extraction ability of the network. The decoder module realizes the fusion of rich details and spatial location information in the shallow layer of the network with the rough and abstract semantic segmentation information in the top layer through skip connections and bilinear interpolation upsampling. Finally, use convolution to map the output feature map of the decoder into two channels (number of classification categories), and after upsampling 8 times, take the maximum value (ArgMax) in the channel dimension to obtain the final segmentation result.

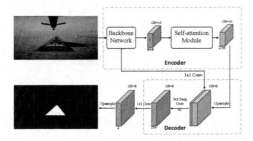

Fig. 4. RunwayNet network architecture

3.2   Runway Edge Feature Extraction

First, contour detection is performed, and the landing stage is judged according to the proportion of the runway contour. Then the spatial characteristics of the runway area are calculated, and the barycentric coordinates of the runway contour and the perimeter of the contour are calculated according to the space moment. Then the candidate line segment is fitted and run to the sideline. In order to further eliminate the wrongly classified line segments entering the runway sideline, outliers are eliminated by comparing with the reference line segments in each category. Finally, first-order polynomial fitting is performed on each type of line segment group to obtain the coordinates of the corresponding straight line equation, and minimize the squared error through iteration to get the optimal solution of the straight line equation.

4   Modeling of Visual Relative Position/Attitude Measurement Based on the Characteristics of Runway Boundary

The edge line of the airport runway mainly includes the starting line l_s, left line l_l and right line l_r. In the imaging of the visual sensor, these three lines can form a triangle

[13, 14], as shown in Fig. 3. The model based on this inherent feature can uniquely determine the relative position/attitude between the visual sensor and the runway under the condition of accurately calibrating the geographic coordinates of four points A, B, E, F and the focal length of the visual sensor [15–17].

4.1 Coordinate System and Parameters Definition

The coordinate systems involved in this paper include earth coordinate system (e system), geographical coordinate system (t system), UAV coordinate system (m system), world coordinate system (w system), runway coordinate system (l system), visual sensor coordinate system (c system), image coordinate system (i system) and inertial sensor coordinate system (b system) [18, 19]. The relationship between w system and c system is shown in Fig. 5.

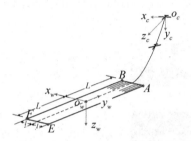

Fig. 5. The relationship between world and visual sensor coordinate system

Set the half-length and half-width of the runway as L and l, and the resolution of the visual sensor as m × n (rows × columns, unit: pixel). Define the relative attitude angles between the coordinate system of the visual sensor and the world coordinate system as the relative rolling angle γ_r, relative heading angle ψ_r and relative pitch angle θ_r, respectively. Then the rotation z_c axis $\Rightarrow y_c$ axis $\Rightarrow x_c$ axis with $-\gamma_r$, $-\psi_r$, $-\frac{\pi}{2} - \theta_r$ can match the w system. The conversion relationship between them is shown in Eq. (1) [20]

$$C_c^w = R_X\left(-\frac{\pi}{2} - \theta_r\right)R_Y(-\psi_r)R_Z(-\gamma_r) \tag{1}$$

4.2 Mathematical Modeling of Visual Relative Position/Attitude Measurement

Modeling of Object Image Conjugate Relation. Let a point P in the space in the image coordinate system be the homogeneous coordinate $P^c = [r \quad c \quad 1]^T$. The homogeneous coordinate in the world coordinate system is $P^w = \begin{bmatrix} x_w & y_w & z_w & 1 \end{bmatrix}^T$. The conjugate relationship between the object and the image is shown in Eq. (2) [21, 22]

$$P^c = s\tilde{K}\tilde{C}_w^c\tilde{T}'P^w \tag{2}$$

where $s = \frac{1}{z_c}$, and z_c is the z axis component of the space point P in the coordinate system c of the vision sensor. $\tilde{K}$ is the internal parameter array of the vision sensor. $\tilde{C}_w^c$ includes the relative attitude to be solved. $\tilde{T}'$ includes the relative position to be solved.

The process to get the relative position and attitude can be abstracted as a typical PNP problem [23, 24]. In this paper, the rectangle contour of runway composed of four vertices A, B, E and F, and the inherent features of two parallel sidelines and one starting line are used to calculate the relative position/attitude, which can avoid the problem that the measurement accuracy in the traditional solution method [5, 6] is seriously affected by the extraction error of feature point image.

Relative Attitude Solution. In the coordinate system of vision sensor, the left line l_l, the right line l_r And the starting line l_s are obtained by the feature extraction of runway. the equation can be described as

$$\begin{bmatrix} 1 & k_l & q_l \\ 1 & k_r & q_r \\ 1 & k_s & q_s \end{bmatrix} P^c = EP^c = \begin{bmatrix} 0 \\ 0 \\ 0 \end{bmatrix} \tag{3}$$

where k_i and $q_i (i = l, r, s)$ are the slope and intercept of three equations respectively.

Relative heading angle ψ_r will be reflected in the horizontal deviation Δc (unit: pixel) between and point C and the image center.

Relative rolling angle γ_r will be reflected in the slope of the starting line l_s.

Relative pitch angle θ_r will be reflected on the vertical deviation Δr (in pixels) between the C point and the image center point when imaging, so

$$\psi_r = -\arctan\left(\frac{d\Delta c}{f}\right), \ \gamma_r = \arctan(k_s), \ \theta_r = \arctan\left(\frac{d\Delta r}{f}\right) \tag{4}$$

Relative Position Solution. The equation can be sorted out as

$$\begin{bmatrix} 1 & \frac{a_3^l}{a_1^l} \\ 1 & \frac{a_3^r}{a_1^r} \end{bmatrix} \begin{bmatrix} t_x' \\ t_z' \end{bmatrix} = \begin{bmatrix} l \\ -l \end{bmatrix}, t_y' = -L - \frac{a_3^s}{a_2^s} t_z' \tag{5}$$

so the values of t_x' and t_z' and t_y' can be solved by Eq. (5).

However, when the airport runway image is incomplete or it enters the 'blind area' of visual measurement, the slope and intercept under the three characteristic edge image coordinate system of the runway cannot be obtained. The solution is singular, which brings security risks to UAV landing. The inertial/visual sensor information fusion technology presented in this paper aims to solve this problem.

5   Information Fusion Model of Inertial/Visual Sensor

The inertial/visual information fusion model used in relative position/attitude measurement during the whole landing process is shown in Fig. 6.

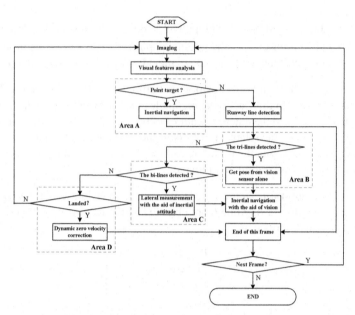

Fig. 6. Inertial/visual information fusion process

5.1 System State Equation

Select system status as

$$X = \left[\delta v^t \ \varphi^t \ \delta P^t \ \varepsilon \ \nabla \ \delta\beta_\psi \ \delta\beta_\theta \ \delta\beta_\gamma \ \delta\alpha_\theta \ \delta\alpha_\psi \right]^T \tag{6}$$

where $\delta v^t = [\delta v_N^t \ \delta v_U^t \ \delta v_E^t]$, $\varphi^t = [\varphi_N^t \ \varphi_U^t \ \varphi_E^t]$, $\delta P^t = \left[\delta\phi \ \delta\lambda \ \delta h \right]$ are velocity, attitude and position errors calculated by inertial sensor; $\varepsilon = \left[\varepsilon_x \ \varepsilon_y \ \varepsilon_z \right]$ and $\nabla = [\nabla_x \ \nabla_y \ \nabla_z]$ are the bias stability parameters of three gyros and three accelerometers; $\delta\beta_\psi, \delta\beta_\theta, \delta\beta_\gamma$ are installation error angles between inertial and visual sensor in heading, pitch and roll direction; $\delta\alpha_\theta$ and $\delta\alpha_\psi$ represent installation error angles between inertial sensor and UAV body in pitch and heading direction respectively, which can be calculated by dead reckoning in area D.

It is considered that all installation error angles are constant, and the specific form of system error equation can be seen in relevant literature [25–30].

5.2 System Observation Equation

Position Error Equation. After compensating the lever arm error between the inertial sensor and the visual sensor, the position error of the inertial information can be calculated according to the following formula

$$\begin{bmatrix} \delta L \\ \delta\lambda \\ \delta h \end{bmatrix} = \begin{bmatrix} L_{INS} \\ \lambda_{INS} \\ h_{INS} \end{bmatrix} - \left(\begin{bmatrix} \frac{1}{(R_{Mo}+h_o)} & 0 & 0 \\ 0 & \frac{1}{((R_{No}+h_o)cos(L_o))} & 0 \\ 0 & 0 & 1 \end{bmatrix} \cdot C_w^t \begin{bmatrix} t_x' \\ t_y' \\ t_z' \end{bmatrix} + \begin{bmatrix} L_o \\ \lambda_o \\ h_o \end{bmatrix} \right) \tag{7}$$

where, R_{Mo} and R_{No} are the curvature radii of the earth calculated by the coordinates of O_w points [20], $\begin{bmatrix} L_{INS} & \lambda_{INS} & h_{INS} \end{bmatrix}^T$ are the latitude, longitude and height calculated by inertial sensors. $\begin{bmatrix} L_o & \lambda_o & h_o \end{bmatrix}^T$ are the latitude, longitude and height of the central point of AB.

In area B, the relative position $\begin{bmatrix} t'_x & t'_y & t'_z \end{bmatrix}$ and relative attitude (included in C^t_w) measured by the visual sensor are directly used.

In area C, the attitude measurement information of vision sensor is singular. The installation error angle matrix C^b_c between inertial sensor and vision sensor, the matrix C^t_b and matrix C^w_t can be used to calculate the relative attitude matrix C^w_c. Then the relative position information $\begin{bmatrix} t'_x & t'_y & t'_z \end{bmatrix}$ can be obtained and used in formula (7).

$$C^w_c = C^w_t C^t_b C^b_c \tag{8}$$

Error Equation of Dynamic Zero Velocity. In area D, the image features of two adjacent frames are used to judge whether the UAV is in a straight-line rollout state. when the UAV is in this state, the velocity error of the inertial sensor is restrained by the motion constraint of zero lateral velocity and vertical velocity. The specific methods are as follows:

The output velocity of the inertial sensor is v^t, the attitude conversion matrix is C^b_t, and the attitude conversion matrix between the UAV and the inertial sensor is C^m_b. Then,

$$v^m = C^m_b C^b_t v^t, \quad v^{m'} = C^{m'}_b C^b_{t'} v^{t'} \tag{9}$$

where $v^{t'} = v^t + \delta v^t$, $v^{m'} = v^m + \delta v^m$, $C^{m'}_b = C^{m'}_m C^m_b = (I - \delta\alpha\times)C^m_b$, $C^b_{t'} = C^b_n C^n_{t'} = C^b_t(I + \phi^t\times)$. Then,

$$\delta v^m = v^{m'} - v^m = C^m_b(C^b_t \phi^t \times v^t + C^b_t \delta v^t) - \delta\alpha \times C^m_b C^b_t v^t \tag{10}$$

where $\delta\alpha = \begin{bmatrix} 0 & \delta\alpha_\theta & \delta\alpha_\psi \end{bmatrix}^T$.

Observation Equation. Based on the above analysis, the observation equation of the system is established as follows

$$Z = \begin{bmatrix} K_B \cdot \delta L & K_B \cdot \delta\lambda & K_B \cdot \delta h & K_D \cdot \delta v^m_x & K_D \cdot \delta v^m_y \end{bmatrix}^T \tag{11}$$

where

$$K_B = \begin{cases} 1 & \text{located in B or C} \\ 0 & \text{others} \end{cases}, \quad K_D = \begin{cases} 1 & \text{located in D} \\ 0 & \text{others} \end{cases} \tag{12}$$

6 Experiment Verification

6.1 Experiment Conditions

The method proposed in this paper is verified by the actual flight data of a certain UAV, the flight experiment conditions are as follows:

1. The vision sensor is installed in a forward direction, the resolution of the vision sensor is 1024×768, and the horizontal field angle is $19.2°$.
2. The performance of the inertial sensor is: the gyro bias stability is $0.5°/h$; the accelerometer bias stability is $100 \ \mu g$.
3. During landing, the UAV's track inclination is $2.5°$. $K1 = -200$ m, $K2 = -400$ m, $K3 = 750$ m, $K4 = 1500$ m. The width of the runway is 50 m.
4. During the landing process, the satellite difference positioning data are collected synchronously, which is used as the reference to evaluate the method in this paper.

The lateral position error of runway coordinate system and visual sensor coordinate system plays a decisive role in landing safety, which is the most concerned relative position component in landing control. Generally, the lateral error cannot larger than 15 m. In order to evaluate the effectiveness of this method, the lateral errors of each region in the process of UAV landing are compared, and the performance curve of this method in the whole process of UAV landing is given.

6.2 Experiment Results

1. Location error analysis of area B. The UAV's flight duration in area B is about 15 s and the flight distance is about 800 m. The pure inertial lateral error diverges to 1.50 m and the visual measurement gives a lateral error of 0.30 m, as shown in Fig. 7(a).
2. Analysis of positioning error in area C. The UAV has a continuous flight time of 30 s in area C and a flight distance of about 1150 m. The traditional method uses inertial measurement to obtain the landing navigation parameters, and the lateral position error increases rapidly to 15.76 m, exceeding the allowable range (15 m). Using the method of inertial/visual information fusion given in this paper, the error of lateral position is within 1m in the first half. Because the error of the inertial measurement is corrected by visual measurement in the first half, it can still be controlled within 3.04 m at the end of the second half, as shown in Fig. 7(b).
3. Error analysis of area D positioning. The UAV has a continuous flight time of 40 s in area D and a sliding distance of 750 m. Traditional landing visual navigation methods cannot obtain landing navigation parameters at this stage and the lateral position error generated by inertial measurement increases rapidly from 3.04 m to 51.02 m. While the maximum lateral position error is 8.24 m using the inertial/visual information fusion method given in this paper, as shown in Fig. 7(c).
4. Analysis of comprehensive positioning error in the whole landing process of UAV. Figure 7(d) shows the comparison of lateral position error curves of different landing navigation strategies during the whole landing process of UAV. The cumulative lateral

error of the traditional landing visual navigation method is 68.47 m when the UAV stops, which does not meet the requirements of safe landing. The lateral error of proposed method is 8.24 m when the UAV stops, which reduces to 12% of the traditional method, meeting the requirements of safe landing.

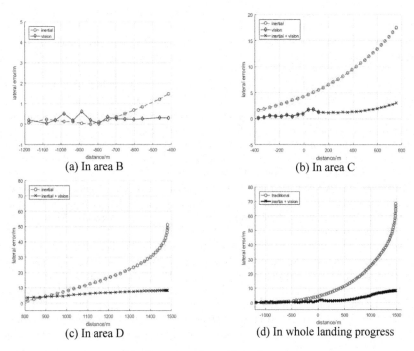

(a) In area B

(b) In area C

(c) In area D

(d) In whole landing progress

Fig. 7. Comparison of lateral errors

7 Conclusion

The vision sensor is affected by many factors during the landing process of UAV. Aiming at the instability of landing navigation parameters such as the relative position/attitude between UAV and runway, a method of autonomous landing navigation of UAV based on information fusion of inertial/vision sensor is proposed. The flight experiment shows that the lateral relative position error can reach 8.24 m under the condition of using low precision inertial and visual sensors, which can meet the requirement of UAV's safe landing. This paper provides a new low-cost strategy, fully autonomous solution for UAV landing, especially in complex electromagnetic environment.

References

1. Eitner, C., Holzapfel, F.: Development of a navigation solution for an image aided automatic landing system. In: Proceedings of the ION 2013 Pacific PNT Meeting, Honolulu, Hawaii, pp. 879–891, April 2013
2. Cai, M., et al.: Vision/INS integrated navigation for UAV autonomous landing. J. Appl. Opt. **36**(3), 343–350 (2015)
3. Wang, G., et al.: UAV autonomous landing using visual servo control based on aerostack. In: CSAE 2019, Sanya, China, October 2019
4. Zhou, H., et al.: Vision-based precision localization of UAVs for sensor payload placement and pickup for field monitoring applications. In: Proceedings Volume 10970, Sensors and Smart Structures Technologies for Civil, Mechanical, and Aerospace Systems 2019 (2019)
5. Wang, J., et al.: Integration of GPS/INS/vision sensors to navigate unmanned aerial vehicles. Int. Arch. Photogramm. Remote Sens. Spatial Inf. Sci. **37**, 963–969 (2008)
6. Zhang, L., et al.: Visual–inertial fusion-based registration between real and synthetic images in airborne combined vision system. Int. J. Adv. Robot. Syst. 1–14 (2019)
7. Wolkow, S., Angermann, M., Dekiert, A., Bestmann, U.: Model-based threshold and center-line detection for aircraft positioning during landing approach. In: Proceedings of the ION 2019 Pacific PNT Meeting, Honolulu, Hawaii, May 2019
8. Angermann, M., Wolkow, S., Dekiert, A., Bestmann, U., Hecker, P.: Fusion of dual optical position solutions for augmentation of GNSS-based aircraft landing systems. In: Proceedings of the 2019 International Technical Meeting of The Institute of Navigation, Reston, Virginia, pp. 283–295, January 2019
9. Angermann, M., Wolkow, S., Dekiert, A., Bestmann, U., Hecker, P.: Linear blend: data fusion in the image domain for image-based aircraft position during landing approach. In: Proceedings of the ION 2019 Pacific PNT Meeting, Honolulu, Hawaii, May 2019
10. Hesch, J.A., Roumeliotis, S.I.: A direct least-squares (DLS) method for PnP. In: Proceedings of 13th International Conference on Computer Vision. Barcelona, pp. 383–390 (2011)
11. Penate-Sanchez, A., Andrade-Cetto, J., Moreno-Noguer, F.: Exhaustive linearization for robust camera pose and focal length estimation. IEEE Trans. Pattern Anal. Mach. Intell. **35**(10), 2387–2400 (2013)
12. Ke-jun, S., Xin, Z., Wang Liu-jun, H., Guang-feng, L.-L.: Image semantic segmentation-based navigation method for UAV auto-landing. J. Chin. Inertial Technol. **28**(5), 1–9 (2020)
13. Li, F., Tang, D.-Q., Shen, N.: Vision-based pose estimation of UAV from line correspondences. Procedia Eng. **15**, 578–584 (2011)
14. Zhuang, L., Han, Y., Fan, Y., Cao, Y., Wang, B., Zhang, Q.: Method of pose estimation for UAV landing. Chin. Opt. Lett. **10**(s2), S20401 (2012)
15. Wolkow, S., Schwithal, A., Tonhäuser, C., Angermann, M., Hecker, P.: Image-aided position estimation based on line correspondences during automatic landing approach. In: Proceedings of the ION 2015 Pacific PNT Meeting, Honolulu, Hawaii, pp. 702–712, April 2015
16. Dosse, M.B., Kiers, H.A.L., Ten Berge, J.: Anisotropic generalized procrustes analysis. Comput. Stat. Data Anal. **55**(5):1961–1968 (2011)
17. Garro, V., Crosilla, F., Fusiello, A.: Solving the pnp problem with anisotropic orthogonal procrustes analysis. In: 2012 Second Joint 3DIM/3DPVT Conference, Zurich, pp. 262–269 (2012)
18. Cai, Y., Li, D.: AUV underwater positioning method based on monocular-vision. J. Chin. Inertial Technol. **23**(4), 489–492 (2015)
19. Zhang, H., Guo, P., Li, Z.: Vision aided alignment method for inertial navigation system on moving base. J. Chin. Inertial Technol. **22**(4), 469–473 (2014)

20. Sun, T., Xing, F., You, Z.: Accuracy measurement of star trackers based on astronomy. J Tsinghua Univ. (Sci. Tech.) **52**(4), 430–435 (2012)
21. Liu, C., Liu, L., Hu, G., et al.: A P3P problem solving algorithm for landing vision navigation. Navig. Position. Timing **5**(1), 58–61 (2018)
22. Liu, C., Yang, L., Liu, F., et al.: Navigation algorithm based on inertial/vision information fusion of UAV autonomous landing. Navig. Position. Timing **3**(6), 6–11 (2016)
23. Schwithal, A., et al.: Integrity monitoring in GNSS/INS systems by optical augmentation. In: Inertial Sensors and Systems 2017, Karlsruhe, Germany (2017)
24. Angermann, M., Wolkow, S., Schwithal, A., Tonhäuser, C., Hecker, P.: High precision approaches enabled by an optical-based navigation system. In: Proceedings of the ION 2015 Pacific PNT Meeting, Honolulu, Hawaii, pp. 694–701, April 2015
25. Kim, S.B., Bazin, J.C., Lee, H.K., et al.: Ground vehicle navigation in harsh urban conditions by integrating inertial navigation system, global positioning system, odometer and vision data. Radar Sonar Navig. **5**(8), 814–823 (2011)
26. Georgy, J., Noureldin, A., Korenberg, M.J., et al.: Modeling the stochastic drift of a MEMS-based gyroscope in gyro/odometer/GPS integrated navigation. IEEE Trans. Intell. Transp. Syst. **11**(4), 856–872 (2010)
27. Dissanayake, G., Sukkarieh, S., Nebot, E., et al.: The aiding of a low-cost strapdown inertial measurement unit using vehicle model constraints for land vehicle applications. IEEE Trans. Robot. Autom. **17**(5), 731–747 (2001)
28. Gong, J., Liang, J., Wang, Y., et al.: On-line calibration method of SINS/DVL integrated navigation system. In: 2018 25th Saint Petersburg International Conference on Integrated Navigation Systems (ICINS)
29. Guo, F., Xie, L., Chen, J., et al.: Research of SINS/DVL/OD integrated navigation system based on observability analysis. In: 2016 35th Chinese Control Conference (CCC)
30. Jiang, Y., Lin, Y.: Error estimation of INS ground alignment through observability analysis. IEEE Trans. Aerosp. Electron. Syst. **28**(1), 92–96 (1992)

An Automatic Surface Defect Detection Method with Residual Attention Network

Lei Yang[✉], Suli Bai, Hanyun Huang, and Shuyi Kong

School of Electrical and Information Engineering, Zhengzhou University,
Henan 450001, China
leiyang2019@zzu.edu.com

Abstract. Automatic defect detection is of great significance to the production process of modern industries, which will affect the product appearance and quality. And a great number of economic loss may be caused due to the defects in the industrial production process. Traditional manual defect inspection method is labor-intensive and time-consuming with subjective factors, and the detection performance is random and uncertain. Machine learning has shown a good detection ability on small-scale samples, but the detect detection task against with poor contrast, weak texture, etc., will affect the effective feature representation. To address the detection task of steel surface defects, combined with the strong context extraction ability of deep learning, an accurate deep defect classification network is proposed in the paper to provide an end-to-end detection scheme. Fused with the residual network (Resnet50) and spatial attention block, a residual attention network is proposed for effective feature representation, which could make the classification network better focus on the defect areas. Meanwhile, due to the scale information change among different defects, a multi-scale context fusion (MCF) block is proposed for effective multi-scale feature extraction, which is conducive for multi-scale object detection. Experimental results on public defect data set show that the proposed defect detection network could acquire a superior classification performance compared with some typical classification networks.

Keywords: Surface defects · Deep learning · Residual network · Multi-scale context fusion · Channel attention

1 Introduction

Surface defect detection is of great significance for the development of modern industrial manufacturing, which plays an important role in many industrial production tasks [13]. Defects may be generated in any production link in the industrial manufacturing process, and sometimes serious consequences will occur when defective products enter the market to bring the economic loss. Traditional manual defect inspection method is labor-intensive and time-consuming [16], which can not fully guarantee detection accuracy and efficiency of intelligent

L. Fang et al. (Eds.): CICAI 2022, LNAI 13605, pp. 194–205, 2022.
https://doi.org/10.1007/978-3-031-20500-2_16

manufacturing, so it is not suitable for the strict requirements of high precision and real-time detection in modern large-scale industrial production processes [3]. Therefore, an automatic defect detection method with high accuracy and good robustness is still a meaningful but challenging task for the modern industrial manufacturing.

In recent years, due to the success on effective context feature extraction, convolutional neural networks (CNNs) have achieved an excellent performance in various computer vision fields [9], which could directly process the raw images and extract high-level semantic information, and have been widely applied into different tasks, such as object detection [15], object classification [1], image segmentation [17]. And it could acquire a superior detection performance compared traditional image processing methods and machine learning methods. To improve the detection performance, different network models have been proposed, such as ResNet [6], VGG16 [10], AlexNet [8], etc. With the increasing popularity of deep learning, researchers have explored the applications of deep learning on effective and accurate non-destructive testing (NDT) [2,15,18]. In order to solve the misclassification problem caused by background chaos and structural interference, Yang et al. proposed an improved SqueezeNet network for surface defect inspection, which combined multiple convolution kernels with different kernel sizes to increase the receptive field, thus obtaining multi-scale features [12]. Faced with the fuzzy edges and unfixed shapes of weak scratches, Tao et al. proposed a new defect detection network that automatically detected weak scratches by gathering rich multidimensional features, which included a feature fusion block and a context fusion block to perform multi-scale feature fusion of high-level information and low-level information [11]. Experiments results indicated that it could well overcome the phenomenon of the long span and connectivity of weak scratches. To address the accurate detection tasks of small-scale defect detection, Geng et al. proposed a deep convolutional generative adversarial network (DCGAN) and seam carving algorithm to achieve intelligent defect detection of water wall in thermal power plants [4]. Faced with the low-quality images DCGAN was proposed to improve the image quality, and the seam carving algorithm was proposed to solve the overfitting issue of DCGAN network. On the basis, a deep CNN network was built for intelligent defect detection. Combined with the pre-trained deep network, Yang et al. proposed a welding defect detection method based on multi-scale feature fusion from X-ray welding images [14]. Due to the different feature representation ability of different network layers in the pre-trained AlexNet network, the features from different network layers were acquired as the multi-scale features. On the basis of multi-scale features, a defect detection model was proposed based on the support vector machine (SVM) classifier and Dempster-Shafer evidence theory to realize multi-scale feature fusion. Inspired by the above work, a deep defect classification network is proposed in the paper for accurate detection of steel surface defects.

Based on the above discussion on defect detection, an end-to-end defect classification scheme for steel surface defects is proposed in this paper to provide an end-to-end detection scheme, as shown in Fig. 1. Experiments on public defect data set show that the proposed defect detection network could acquire a superior detection performance compared with some typical classification networks, which could further prove the feasibility and superiority of the proposed detection scheme. The main contributions in this paper are drawn as follows:

Fig. 1. Diagram of proposed defect detection scheme.

(1) An end-to-end defect classification network is proposed in this paper for accurate defect detection.
(2) To realize effective feature representation, a residual attention network is proposed to act as the backbone network to acquire high-level contexts.
(3) Faced with the multi-scale steel surface defects, a MCF block is proposed for effective multi-scale feature extraction and fusion.

The rest part of this paper is given as follows. Section 2 gives the description of proposed defect classification network. Section 3 introduces the experimental data set and the corresponding image processing method. Section 4 is about the experimental results and analysis. The conclusions of this paper are given in Sect. 5.

2   Proposed Methodology

To address the detection task of steel surface defects, a deep defect classification network is proposed in the paper to provide an end-to-end and accurate detection scheme. This section gives the detailed description about proposed defect classification network and each network block.

2.1   Overview of Network Framework

Faced with the defects of steel surface, an end-to-end defect classification network is proposed in this paper for automatic and accurate defect detection. Figure 2 shows the whole network structure of proposed defect detection network.

As shown in Fig. 2, the whole network framework is composed of three parts: backbone network, MCF block, and classification block. Combined with the Resnet50, a residual attention network is proposed to act as the backbone network for feature representation. Here, a spatial attention block is proposed to embed into each residual block to acquire and learn the importance of feature

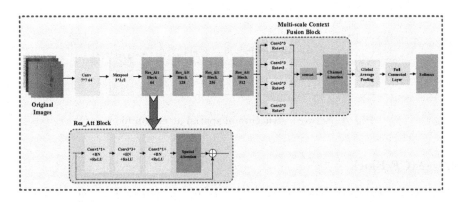

Fig. 2. Network framework of the proposed defect detection network.

maps. Combined with the atrous spatial pyramid pooling block and channel attention block, a MCF block is proposed, which could acquire different receptive fields to obtain multi-scale contexts. And the multi-scale contexts are fed into the classification block, which consists of the global average pooling layer, the fully connection layer and the softmax function.

2.2 Backbone Network

The residual network [6] is a typical deep classification network, which has been widely applied into different deep models for effective feature representation, which could effectively alleviate the problems of gradient disappearance and gradient explosion in neural network and protect the integrity of information. Due to the success of residual network, the Resnet50 network is proposed in this paper to act as the baseline network. As shown in Fig. 2, the basic structure of backbone network is divided into four main units and each unit has a similar structure, which consisting of a series of bottleneck layers contained 3, 4, 6, and 3 residual attention (Res_Att) blocks separately.

To make the classification network better focus on the defect areas, combined with the advantage of attention block, a spatial attention block [5] (see Fig. 3) is proposed to embed into each residual block to construct the residual attention block, which could capture the weight of different feature channels, thus to focus on the key attention features on defects and suppress irrelevant information.

Combined with the max-pooling layer and average pooling layer, the feature descriptors by these two pooling operations are concatenated together, which are fed into a 7 × 7 convolution layer followed by a sigmoid function to acquire the final spatial attention weight. And the final attention maps could be acquired through the element-wise multiplication with the raw feature maps.

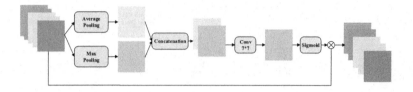

Fig. 3. Network structure of spatial attention block.

2.3 MCF Block

Faced with the defect detection task, except for the shape information, the scale information change among different defects is also a common phenomenon, which puts a strict demand on multi-scale defect detection. For the typical deep network, the high-level network layer can capture a large receptive field and has a strong ability to express abstract and high-level semantic information but a small image resolution. On the contrary, for the shallow network layer, it has a small receptive field and a relatively high resolution but a weak ability to represent effective semantic information. In order to accurately identify multi-scale steel surface defects, a MCF block is proposed in this paper to capture effective multi-scale features (see Fig. 2).

Compared with the standard convolution, the dilated convolutions with different dilated rates could well acquire different receptive fields without the increase of computing cost [19]. Due to this advantage of dilated convolution, as shown in Fig. 2, combined with the feature maps from the residual attention network, these feature maps are processed by four dilated convolutions with the convolution rates of 1, 3, 5, 7 respectively, which is equivalent to the extraction of multi-scale features. And the multi-scale feature maps are concatenated together for feature fusion.

Faced with the multi-channel feature maps generated by multiple network branches of dilated convolutions, a channel attention block is proposed to learn the important information of different channels. The sequeze-and-excitation (SE) block (see Fig. 4) is a typical channel attention block for channel calibration [7]. In order to identify steel defects more accurately and focus on the feature channels with the most information, the SE block is proposed for channel calibration to acquire the channel weights.

3   Experiment Data and Preprocessing

For the effective model evaluation, the suitable data set is the premise for the performance of proposed defect classification network. This section introduces the details about the experimental data set and the corresponding image processing method.

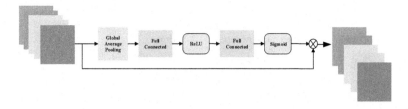

Fig. 4. Network structure of channel attention block.

3.1 Data Set

In order to verify the detection performance of the proposed defect classification network, the NEU metal surface defect data set collected by Northeast University is adopted in this paper for model evaluation, which contains of six types of defects: crazing, inclusion, patches, pitted surface, rolled-in scale and scratches. Figure 5 shows the sample images of these defects. It could be seen that these defect images are aginst with the poor contrast, weak texture, etc., which will bring a certain effect to accurate defect detection.

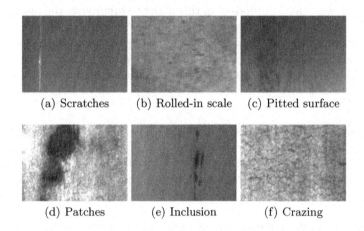

(a) Scratches   (b) Rolled-in scale   (c) Pitted surface

(d) Patches   (e) Inclusion   (f) Crazing

Fig. 5. Sample images of different defects in the NEU metal surface defect data set.

For the NEU metal surface defect data set, each defects contain 300 sample images. The detailed information of various defects in this data set is given in Table 1.

Combined with this defect data set, in order to evaluate the proposed defect classification network more accurately, the data set is divided into training set, validation set, and test set by a ratio of 7:1:2.

Table 1. Parameters about the data set and model training.

Index	Parameter	Value
1	Image size	$200 \times 200 \times 1$
2	Crazing	300
3	Inclusion	300
4	Patches	300
5	Pitted surface	300
6	Rolled-in scale	300
7	Scratches	300

3.2 Image Preprocessing

The effective model training of deep CNNs, it always relies on enough data set to support the detection performance. Data augmentation provides an effective tool for the small-scale data samples and brings great convenience to the deep learning.

In order to improve the detection performance and avoid the overfitting issue, the data augmentation is proposed in this paper to preprocess the raw images to enlarge the data set. For the training set, combined with the traditional machine vision algorithms, several typical image analysis algorithms are proposed in this paper for image preprocessing, including shear transformation, angle rotation, image brightness adjustment, contrast adjustment, saturation adjustment and chroma adjustment.

4   Experiment Results and Analysis

In this section, to effectively evaluate the proposed defect classification network, the comparative experiments and ablation experiments are carried out respectively to further illustrate the advantages of the proposed defect classification network.

Firstly, the implementation details of the proposed defect classification network is described in detail. Secondly, the ablation experiments are given to show the effectiveness of proposed each network block. Finally, the comparison experiments are provided to further illustrate the superiority of the proposed defect classification network.

4.1 Implementation Details

For the proposed defect classification network, it is built with the PaddlePaddle framework[1]. To speed up the model training and test, the related experiments are carried out in the NVIDIA Tesla V100 GPU card with 16 GB memory.

---

[1] https://www.paddlepaddle.org.cn/.

In addition, some hyper-parameters of the proposed defect classification network need to be set. Here, the Adam optimizer is adopted, and the initial learning rate is set as 0.01. With the increase of training epoches, the attenuation factor of learning rate decreases gradually. In order to avoid network overfitting, the early stop strategy is proposed. To guide the model training, the cross entropy loss is adopted to act as the loss function. Based on the memory size of GPU card, the batch size is set as 32.

To precisely evaluate the classification ability of different models, some evaluation indicators are introduced for quantitative analysis, including accuracy, precision, recall and F_1 score.

4.2 Ablation Study

In order to further verify the performance of each network block in this paper to the whole detection performance, the ablation study is carried out in this paper to show the effectiveness of proposed each network block. Here, the Resnet50 is taken as the baseline network. On the basis, combined with the spatial attention block and MCF block, the different network configuration schemes are built for the ablation study, including Baseline, Baseline+Spatial Attention, Baseline+MCF Block and Proposed method. Based on the NEU metal surface defect data set, the special experimental results are shown in Table 2. Figure 6 shows the confusion matrix for the ablation experiment.

Table 2. Experiment results of ablation study on NEU data set.

Method	Accuracy	Precision	Recall	F_1 score
Baseline	0.8883	0.8990	0.8862	0.8925
Baseline+Spatial Attention	0.9162	0.9184	0.9182	0.9183
Baseline+MCF Block	0.9353	0.9415	0.9366	0.9390
Proposed	**0.9709**	**0.9738**	**0.9715**	**0.9727**

As shown in Table 2, compared with the baseline network, due to higher evaluation indicators, it can be clearly seen that the spatial attention block and MCF block both have a positive impact on the performance improvement of the proposed defect classification network, which could prove the effectiveness of proposed each network block. Fused with the spatial attention block and MCF block to the baseline network at the same time, all evaluation indicators reach the best, which also shows the superiority of the proposed defect classification network.

Meanwhile, combined with the confusion matrix in Fig. 6, compared with other network configuration schemes, it could be seen that the proposed defect classification network exists few misclassification cases.

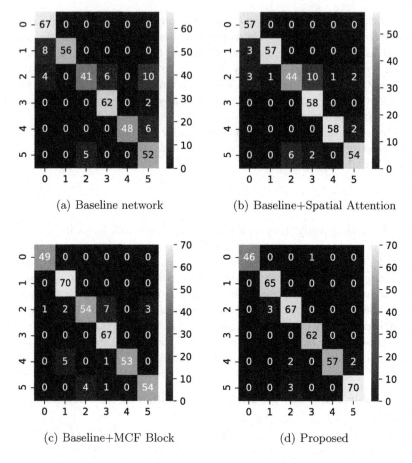

(a) Baseline network

(b) Baseline+Spatial Attention

(c) Baseline+MCF Block

(d) Proposed

Fig. 6. Confusion matrix for the ablation experiment.

4.3 Performance Comparison

In order to further illustrate the advantages of proposed defect classification network, several typical defect detection networks are selected for performance comparison, including ResNet [6], VGG16 [10], AlexNet [8]. Based on the NEU metal surface defect data set, Table 3 shows the special experimental results of different detection models, and Fig. 7 also gives the confusion matrix on different networks.

As shown in Table 3, compared with other advance detection models, the proposed defect classification network also could acquire the highest detection precision among all the comparison models. Based on the confusion matrix in Fig. 7, the proposed method also has less misclassification defects. Combined with the above results of quantitative analysis, it could further prove the superiority of proposed network.

Table 3. Experiment results of different networks on NEU data set.

Method	$Accuracy$	$Precision$	$Recall$	F_1 score
Resnet50	0.9018	0.9125	0.9009	0.9067
AlexNet	0.9028	0.9144	0.9017	0.9080
VGG16	0.8333	0.8593	0.8139	0.8360
Proposed	**0.9709**	**0.9738**	**0.9715**	**0.9727**

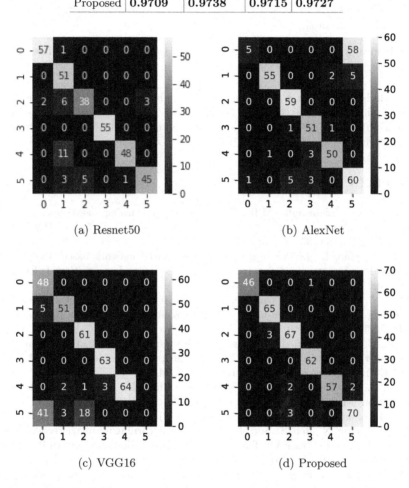

(a) Resnet50

(b) AlexNet

(c) VGG16

(d) Proposed

Fig. 7. The confusion matrix for the comparative experiment

5 Conclusion

Faced with the defect detection task against poor contrast and weak texture, a deep defect classification network is proposed in this paper for accurate and automatic defect detection. Combined with the public NEU metal surface defect data set, the proposed defect classification network could acquire a superior detection performance through the ablation study and comparative experiment. The main work of this paper is drawn as follows.

(1) An end-to-end deep classification network is proposed for accurate and automatic defect detection.
(2) A residual attention network is proposed to act as the backbone network for effective feature representation.
(3) A MCF block is proposed for effective multi-scale feature extraction from local feature maps.

In the future, we will continue to this research work and propose a defect detection network with higher detection precision and efficiency.

Acknowledgment. This work was supported by the National Natural Science Foundation of China (No. 62003309), the National Key Research & Development Project of China (2020YFB1313701) and Outstanding Foreign Scientist Support Project in Henan Province of China (No. GZS2019008).

References

1. Chen, F.C., Jahanshahi, M.R.: NB-CNN: Deep learning-based crack detection using convolutional neural network and naïve bayes data fusion. IEEE Trans. Industr. Electron. **65**(5), 4392–4400 (2017)
2. Gao, Y., Gao, L., Li, X.: A generative adversarial network based deep learning method for low-quality defect image reconstruction and recognition. IEEE Trans. Industr. Inf. **17**(5), 3231–3240 (2020)
3. Gao, Y., Gao, L., Li, X., Wang, X.V.: A multilevel information fusion-based deep learning method for vision-based defect recognition. IEEE Trans. Instrum. Meas. **69**(7), 3980–3991 (2019)
4. Geng, Z., Shi, C., Han, Y.: Intelligent small sample defect detection of water walls in power plants using novel deep learning integrating deep convolutional gan. In: IEEE Transactions on Industrial Informatics (2022)
5. Guo, C., Szemenyei, M., Yi, Y., Wang, W., Chen, B., Fan, C.: Sa-unet: Spatial attention u-net for retinal vessel segmentation. In: Proceedings of 25th International Conference on Pattern Recognition (ICPR), pp. 1236–1242. IEEE (2021)
6. He, K., Zhang, X., Ren, S., Sun, J.: Deep residual learning for image recognition. In: Proceedings of the IEEE Conference on Computer Vision and Pattern Recognition (CVPR), pp. 770–778 (2016)
7. Hu, J., Shen, L., Sun, G.: Squeeze-and-excitation networks. In: Proceedings of the IEEE Conference on Computer Vision and Pattern Recognition (CVPR), pp. 7132–7141 (2018)
8. Krizhevsky, A., Sutskever, I., Hinton, G.E.: Imagenet classification with deep convolutional neural networks. In: Advances in Neural Information Processing Systems, vol. 25 (2012)
9. Qu, Z., Cao, C., Liu, L., Zhou, D.Y.: A deeply supervised convolutional neural network for pavement crack detection with multiscale feature fusion. In: IEEE Transactions on Neural Networks and Learning Systems (2021)
10. Simonyan, K., Zisserman, A.: Very deep convolutional networks for large-scale image recognition. arXiv preprint. arXiv:1409.1556 (2014)

11. Tao, X., Zhang, D., Hou, W., Ma, W., Xu, D.: Industrial weak scratches inspection based on multifeature fusion network. IEEE Trans. Instrum. Meas. **70**, 1–14 (2020)
12. Yang, J., Fu, G., Zhu, W., Cao, Y., Cao, Y., Yang, M.Y.: A deep learning-based surface defect inspection system using multiscale and channel-compressed features. IEEE Trans. Instrum. Meas. **69**(10), 8032–8042 (2020)
13. Yang, L., Fan, J., Huo, B., Li, E., Liu, Y.: A nondestructive automatic defect detection method with pixelwise segmentation. Knowl.-Based Syst. **242**, 108338 (2022)
14. Yang, L., Fan, J., Huo, B., Liu, Y.: Inspection of welding defect based on multi-feature fusion and a convolutional network. J. Nondestr. Eval. **40**(4), 1–11 (2021). https://doi.org/10.1007/s10921-021-00823-4
15. Yang, L., Fan, J., Liu, Y., Li, E., Peng, J., Liang, Z.: Automatic detection and location of weld beads with deep convolutional neural networks. IEEE Trans. Instrum. Meas. **70**, 1–12 (2020)
16. Yang, L., Gao, G., Wu, M., Li, J.: Automatic defect recognition method of aluminium profile surface defects. In: 2021 7th International Conference on Robotics and Artificial Intelligence, pp. 21–25 (2021)
17. Yang, L., Song, S., Fan, J., Huo, B., Li, E., Liu, Y.: An automatic deep segmentation network for pixel-level welding defect detection. In: IEEE Transactions on Instrumentation and Measurement (2021)
18. Yang, L., Wang, H., Huo, B., Li, F., Liu, Y.: An automatic welding defect location algorithm based on deep learning. NDT & E Int. **120**, 102435 (2021)
19. Yu, F., Koltun, V.: Multi-scale context aggregation by dilated convolutions. arXiv preprint. arXiv:1511.07122 (2015)

Research on Intelligent Decision-Making Irrigation Model of Water and Fertilizer Based on Multi-source Data Input

Shanshan Li[1,2,3], Yisheng Miao[1,2,3], Xiao Han[1,2,3], and Wei Guo[1,2,3(✉)]

[1] National Engineering Research Center for Information Technology in Agriculture, Beijing 100097, China
`guowei@nercita.org.cn`
[2] Research Center of Information Technology, Beijing Academy of Agriculture and Forestry Sciences, Beijing 100097, China
[3] Key Laboratory of Digital Village Technology, Ministry of Agriculture and Rural Affairs, People's Republic of China, Beijing 100097, China

Abstract. At present, the integrated irrigation management and control system of water and fertilizer has met the requirements of automatic control of farmland water and fertilizer, gradually transforming the traditional manual operation into facility industrialization. However, this method has a weak use of data, and there is still a large gap between the calculation method and intelligent management and control. Taking greenhouse cabbage as the main research object, based on the cultivation environmental parameters, growth morphological parameters, water and fertilizer irrigation requirements during the growth period of cabbage, and using the efficient allocation ability of attention mechanism to data feature weights, this paper proposes the establishment of water and fertilizer intelligent decision-making management and control model integrating multi-source data input. The results showed that the prediction error of the intelligent decision-making irrigation model for water and fertilizer for greenhouse cabbage was relatively small, RMSE was $0.002447\,\mathrm{m^3}$/Day, MAE is $0.001779\,\mathrm{m^3}$/Day, and the coupling relationship between multi-source data is comprehensively analyzed, and the overall performance of model decision-making is improved through multi-feature extraction.

Keywords: Water and fertilizer · Intelligence · Multi-source data · Irrigation decision

1 Introduction

Agricultural production is the pillar of a country's economy toward self-sustainable development [1]. Over the years, water and fertilizer resource management has spanned different stages and methods in different geographical locations according to availability [2–5]. Increasing crop yield and limiting adverse environmental impacts, is a widely stated goal in agricultural science [6]. More accurate application of water and fertilizer

L. Fang et al. (Eds.): CICAI 2022, LNAI 13605, pp. 206–217, 2022.
https://doi.org/10.1007/978-3-031-20500-2_17

irrigation is regarded as one of the main means of this goal. Relative to crop demand, excessive application of nutrients will not only reduce farm profits but also degrade the environment [7]. Excessive irrigation will unsustainably deplete groundwater and streams, while excessive fertilization will rapidly reduce soil fertility, and a large number of chemical residues will endanger human health. Therefore, a large number of studies have proved that it is very important to develop a scientific decision-making and control method for water and fertilizer irrigation to better meet the needs of crops for water and nutrients at different times [8–10]. Scientific irrigation can not only effectively regulate the absorption and transfer of nutrients, but also improve the photosynthesis and transpiration of leaves, the division, and growth of plant tissues and cells, as well as the synthesis and transformation of organic substances. It can significantly promote the growth of cabbage leaf bulbs and coordinate the physiological activities of cabbage crops. To promote the healthy development of the soil micro-ecosystem, ensure the water and nutrient balance of greenhouse vegetables, and achieve high-quality production, it is very important to seek scientific irrigation and fertilization schedules.

The management and control of water and fertilizer nutrient solution have been systematically studied at home and abroad [11, 12]. At present, the regulation of nutrient solution is mainly based on the EC Value and pH value of nutrient solution at home and abroad [13], at the same time, this method is most widely used in actual production. Most studies on nutrient solution management and control system are also based on this control mode [14–18]. Some scholars use the cyclic neural network to predict the EC nutrient in the root zone of pepper in closed-loop soilless cultivation management, and have achieved good results [19]. Others use the mixed signal processing method based on the neural network to predict and analyze the ion distribution in the hydroponic solution [20]. However, the way of using multi-source data based on deep learning method to make the management decision of greenhouse cabbage nutrient solution still needs to be studied, Therefore, we propose an improved convolution neural network CNN and two-way long-term and short-term memory network AT-CNN-BiLSTM neural network model based on attention mechanism to solve this problem. The purpose is to deeply mine the existing data and accurately determine the amount of nutrient solution for water and fertilizer irrigation in real time.

2 Materials and Methods

2.1 Data Acquisition

From September 2020 to March 2021, the water and fertilizer irrigation experiment of greenhouse cabbage was carried out in the No. 14 Solar Greenhouse of Beijing National precision agriculture research demonstration base (Fig. 1). Its geographical location is 116.26 °E, 40.10 °N, with an altitude of about 50 m. The planting area belongs to a temperate continental monsoon climate, and the temperature is appropriate. The test greenhouse is 50 m long and 7.5 m wide. It is composed of an arched steel frame structure. The maximum height in the middle is about 3 m. Crops are planted in the east-west direction, and north-south direction, and covered with polyethylene trickle anti-aging film on the sunny side. A large number of intelligent control devices are set in the greenhouse. In combination with the current software and hardware configuration

Fig. 1. Location and overview of test site.

of the greenhouse, 26 ridges were built in the test area, with an average ridge spacing of 1.5 m and a ridge top width of 0.8 m. Two rows of cabbage were planted on each ridge, with a plant spacing of 0.3 m and a row spacing of 0.5 m. The planting density was 2402 plants/667 m^2.

In the experiment, according to the different water and nutrient requirements of cabbage in different growth cycles, 12 cabbage plants with basically the same growth potential were selected for observation in each plot at the cabbage seedling stage, and the data of plant height, stem diameter (rhizome), number of leaves and width of their aboveground parts were collected day by day (among them, the stem diameter was measured by electronic vernier caliper, and the plant height and width were measured by a ruler with an accuracy of 0.01 mm). 1440 groups of cabbage growth potential data were obtained. At the same time, the WS-1800 remote meteorological monitoring station is used to monitor the greenhouse micrometeorological data. The measurement parameters include air temperature, relative humidity, wind speed, and solar radiation intensity. The collection frequency is preset to 4 pieces/minute. After the meteorological station obtains the data, the data is transmitted back through the RS485 bus, and 691200 pieces of meteorological data are selected as the basis for the construction of the greenhouse meteorological data set. The current scientific daily irrigation method of a small number of times is adopted for water and fertilizer irrigation, and the daily water and fertilizer consumption is recorded through data monitoring equipment.

2.2 Identification of Influencing Factors and Coupling Verification

This study also considers the data parameters related to internal and external factors of cabbage that are constantly changing in the process of water and fertilizer irrigation in the greenhouse. It is expected to further determine the rationality of the multi-source data set by analyzing the interaction between internal and external factors and the correlation between this factor and water and fertilizer irrigation decisions and eliminate invalid data to avoid interference with the prediction effect of the model, Improve the prediction accuracy of water and fertilizer irrigation amount of greenhouse cabbage.

External Factors. The external factors affecting the irrigation amount of water and fertilizer for greenhouse cabbage mainly include air temperature, relative humidity, solar radiation intensity, EC value, pH value and temperature of nutrient solution, and potential evapotranspiration of greenhouse cabbage. Because there are two opposite physiological processes of assimilation and dissimilation in the process of crop growth, in this process, crops continuously accumulate organic matter. When the organic matter produced by assimilation is greater than dissimilation, crops show a growth trend, and temperature has an important impact on this process. Dissolving fertilizer in water to form organic nutrient solution to irrigate cabbage. At this time, the fertility of nutrient solution is the main concern of irrigation. Appropriate EC value, pH value and irrigation temperature of nutrient solution can promote the absorption and growth of cabbage nutrients, while excessive or small amount will have a negative impact on the growth of cabbage. Generally, when the fertility is too large, we need to carry out crop leaching to avoid fertilizer damage.

Internal Factors. The internal factors that affect the irrigation amount of water and fertilizer in greenhouse are the growth morphological parameters of cabbage, such as plant height, stem diameter, leaf number and plant width. Among them, cabbage plant height refers to the straight-line distance from the root of the plant to the highest part of the plant. Excessive irrigation will lead to overgrowth of the plant and unable to support the growth of leaf bulbs. Appropriate irrigation plays a positive role in plant height growth. Stem diameter refers to the diameter of the root and stems at 1cm from the ground surface, the number of leaves refers to the number of fresh leaves surviving in the growth process of cabbage, and the width refers to the span length parallel to the ridge width of cabbage.

Coupling Relationship Verification. Collect and sort out the irrigation related data in the whole growth cycle of greenhouse cabbage, and get the initial data of different indicators (Table 1). The importance of each indicator is determined by the entropy method, and the grey correlation analysis method is used to measure the correlation between the factors that change with time.

Table 1. Data indicators.

Influence factor	Input	Evaluating indicator
External factors	x_1	Air Temperature/°C
	x_2	Elative Humidity/%
	x_3	Solar Radiation Intensity/MJ $(m^2 \cdot d)$
	x_4	Nutrient Solution Conductivity/mS·cm^{-1}

(continued)

Table 1. (*continued*)

Influence factor	Input	Evaluating indicator
	x_5	pH Value of Nutrient Solution
	x_6	Nutrient Solution Temperature/°C
	x_7	Potential Evapotranspiration/mm
Internal factors	x_8	Plant Height/mm
	x_9	Stem Diameter/mm
	x_{10}	Number of Blades/leaf
	x_{11}	Plant Width/mm

During the training process of neural network model, the potential features of data are continuously extracted through the optimization and adjustment of parameters, and this process is very time-consuming. In order to avoid the negative impact of data on the model training and prediction results, the entropy method (Table 2) and grey correlation analysis method (Table 3) were used to verify the coupling relationship between the model input data, and the input variables were analyzed through entropy calculation and correlation. Entropy method is a method to reflect the disorder degree of information in information theory. The smaller the value, the lower the disorder degree and the greater the weight; On the contrary, the larger the value, the higher the degree of disorder and the smaller the weight. Grey correlation analysis judges the close relationship between data by determining the geometric similarity between the target data column and other comparison data columns. It is usually used to reflect the influence degree between data curves, and can also be used to solve the systematic analysis of comprehensive evaluation problems. Its core idea is to determine the parent sequence according to specific rules, take the object to be evaluated as a sub sequence, and solve the correlation degree between each sub sequence and the parent sequence, And draw a conclusion.

Table 2. Calculation results of entropy method.

Index	Entropy	Order
x_1	0.059456	11
x_2	0.095377	5
x_3	0.103611	3
x_4	0.081602	8

(*continued*)

Table 2. (*continued*)

Index	Entropy	Order
x_5	0.070074	10
x_6	0.075437	9
x_7	0.082517	6
x_8	0.101482	4
x_9	0.139337	1
x_{10}	0.081913	7
x_{11}	0.109193	2

When analyzing the data coupling relationship with the grey correlation degree, if the change trends of the two elements are consistent, it means that the correlation between them is very high; On the contrary, the correlation is low. When the correlation degree ranges from 0.00 to 0.35, it means that the correlation is low and the coupling effect is very weak; When the correlation degree ranges from 0.35 to 0.45, it means low correlation and weak coupling; When the correlation degree ranges from 0.45 to 0.65, it indicates medium correlation and medium coupling; When the correlation degree ranges from 0.65 to 0.85, it indicates high correlation and strong coupling; When the correlation degree ranges from 0.85 to 1.00, it means extremely high correlation and strong coupling.

Table 3. Results of grey relational analysis.

Index	Rosette stage		Heading stage		Mature period	
	Relevancy	Coupling strength	Relevancy	Coupling strength	Relevancy	Coupling strength
x_1	0.7738	Strong	0.6741	Strong	0.7482	Strong
x_2	0.6451	Secondary	0.7358	Strong	0.7838	Strong
x_3	0.8323	Strong	0.6087	Secondary	0.6847	Strong
x_4	0.5589	Secondary	0.7899	Strong	0.7983	Strong
x_5	0.6845	Strong	0.6246	Secondary	0.7341	Strong
x_6	0.7264	Strong	0.7288	Strong	0.7699	Strong
x_7	0.5811	Secondary	0.5032	Secondary	0.6320	Secondary
x_8	0.6857	Strong	0.8015	Strong	0.7859	Strong
x_9	0.6763	Strong	0.7975	Strong	0.8236	Strong
x_{10}	0.7452	Strong	0.7140	Strong	0.7664	Strong
x_{11}	0.6842	Strong	0.7923	Strong	0.7911	Strong

3   Intelligent Decision-Making Irrigation Model of Water and Fertilizer

In recent years, the use of the attention mechanism has made remarkable achievements in image recognition and document classification. It can select the information that is the most critical to the current task target from a large amount of information, capture the sequence and mark the remote dependency between the context information. For traditional convolutional neural networks and cyclic neural network, the contribution value of each eigenvector is the same, and the difference between them is ignored. In this paper, the attention mechanism is used to predict the irrigation amount of vegetable water and fertilizer. It selectively pays more attention to some important information, and assigns the corresponding weight to the output characteristics of BiLSTM neural network, to promote the model to get better prediction results. In this paper, the CNN BiLSTM greenhouse cabbage water and fertilizer intelligent decision irrigation model (AT-CNN-BiLSTM model for short) based on attention mechanism is improved. The model mainly adds an attention mechanism layer based on CNN BiLSTM model and enriches the preprocessing analysis of multi-source data and the adjustment of parameters at each layer. Its network structure is shown in Fig. 2.

After preprocessing the greenhouse multi-source irrigation data, Xi represents the ith parameter of the input sample, and T represents the time length of the sample. The processed data set is transmitted to the CNN layer, and the convolution layer is also used for convolution operation. Here, the new features generated by the convolution layer can be expressed as:

$$C_i^k = f(x_i \otimes W_k + b_k) \tag{1}$$

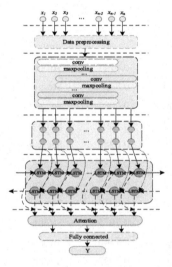

Fig. 2. AT-CNN-BiLSTM neural network structure.

Where represents the convolution operator; W is the weight vector of the convolution kernel; B is the offset term; $f(\cdot)$ represents the nonlinear excitation function. The activation function of the hidden layer adopts the relu function, which can avoid abnormal problems such as slow convergence and local maximum caused by the disappearance of the gradient. k different convolution kernels are set to promote the comprehensiveness of data feature extraction. After the convolution operation, the maximum pooling function is used for the pooling operation. The specific process can be expressed as follows:

$$C_m = [C_1, C_2, \ldots, C_{n-k+1}] \tag{2}$$

$$P_m = \max(C_m) \tag{3}$$

Taking advantage of the bi-directional feature extraction of BiLSTM, considering the interaction between each data in the greenhouse cabbage sequential growth environment data and its forward and backward data, we can use the data features at this time point to obtain the backward unit through the forward LSTM unit. In the experiment, in order to capture the long-distance dependence feature, P_m is input into the BiLSTM model, which is connected by LSTM modules in two directions and has multiple shared weights. At each time step t, each gate is represented by the output of the previous module and the input P_t at the current time. The three gates work together to complete the selection of attribute information, forgetting and updating of cell status.

In order to obtain more accurate prediction accuracy, the output results of BiLSTM are input to the attention mechanism layer. The attention mechanism can highlight the key features that affect the irrigation volume, reduce the impact of non key features on irrigation, help the BiLSTM layer make predictions, and will not increase the calculation and storage costs of the model. The weight calculation formula of the attention mechanism can be expressed as:

$$e_t = u_a \tanh(w_a h_t + b_a) \tag{4}$$

$$a_t = \frac{\exp(e_t)}{\sum_{j=1}^{t} \exp(e_j)} \tag{5}$$

where, h_t represents the hidden layer state vector of BiLSTM neural network at time t; e_t represents the attention probability distribution value; a_t indicates attention score; u_a and w_a are attention weight vectors; b_a is the attention bias vector.

4   Results and Discussion

The establishment of a model to predict the next day irrigation amount of greenhouse cabbage belongs to the category of regression problem. Therefore, root mean square error (RMSE) and mean absolute error (MAE) are selected as the model evaluation indicators, and the formulas are shown in Eqs. (6) and (7).

$$RMSE = \sqrt{\frac{\sum_{i=1}^{n} (P_i - Q_i)^2}{n}} \tag{6}$$

$$MAE = \frac{1}{n} \sum_{i=1}^{n} |P_i - Q_i| \tag{7}$$

4.1 Comparison of Prediction Performance of Different Models

It can be seen from Table 4 that when different variable factors are used as model inputs, the AT-CNN-BiLSTM model proposed in this paper has the best effect, and its RMSE and Mae values are the lowest among the three neural network models, of which the RMSE variation range is 0.0024 m³/day–0.0030 m³/The MAE range is 0.0017–0.0025 m³/Between days, it shows that the prediction accuracy of the improved model is effectively improved by using the attention mechanism method, which confirms the necessity of introducing the attention mechanism method.

Table 4. Comparison of prediction performance of the model under different input factors.

Model	Internal factor input		External factor input		All factor input	
	RMSE	MAE	RMSE	MAE	RMSE	MAE
BiLSTM	0.003020	0.002521	0.003432	0.002756	0.002731	0.002312
CNN-BiLSTM	0.003014	0.002583	0.003704	0.002938	0.002985	0.002269
AT-CNN-BiLSTM	0.002771	0.002405	0.002960	0.002474	0.002447	0.001779

4.2 Analysis of Factors Affecting the Prediction Performance of the Model

As shown in Fig. 3, three different time-series neural network models, BiLSTM, CNN BiLSTM and AT-CNN-BiLSTM, have shown good prediction effect on the irrigation amount per plant of greenhouse cabbage in the day after the prediction of the previous day's greenhouse cabbage growth environment data, and the irrigation trend is basically the same as the standard value. From the perspective of the factors affecting the prediction performance of the model, the multi-source data has a greater impact on the final water and fertilizer irrigation amount of cabbage. The model takes a variety of data variables as inputs, and the prediction effect is better than other inputs. The prediction result of internal factors is the second, and the effect of external factors is the worst. Due to the complexity of cabbage growth environment, the influencing factors on irrigation amount are complex and diverse. Under the condition of frequent farming operations, there are still defects in using external influencing factors alone to predict irrigation amount of water and fertilizer. However, prediction based on multi-source data can consider the coupling relationship between variables more, increase the amount of information and the effective basis for decision-making.

4.3 Prediction Error Analysis of Water and Fertilizer Irrigation Quantity

In the process of greenhouse irrigation decision-making and control, the size of irrigation error plays a vital role in cultivation management. The smaller the calculation error is, the more balanced the supply and demand is. Only in this way can crop growth be guaranteed, and water and fertilizer disasters are not easy to occur, which will negatively affect crop

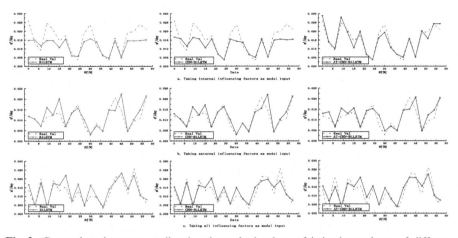

Fig. 3. Comparison between predicted and standard values of irrigation volume of different models.

production. It can be seen from Fig. 4 that the prediction accuracy of three different models with the same prediction trend and real value is more obvious. Among them, the AT-CNN-BiLSTM model proposed in this paper is better, followed by the other two models.

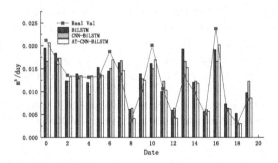

Fig. 4. Comparison of prediction accuracy of different models.

4.4 Model Stability Analysis

The AT-CNN-BiLSTM model has shown good prediction performance in the time series prediction of greenhouse cabbage irrigation. To further confirm the stability of the model and weaken the contingency of high-precision the model, BiLSTM, CNN BiLSTM and AT-CNN-BiLSTM were executed 10 times respectively, and the change range and abnormal performance of RMSE were compared. It can be seen from Fig. 5 that the RMSE variation range of the at-cnn-bilstm model is always $0.0224 \sim 0.0319$ m^3/There is no abnormal value between days, indicating that the AT-CNN-BiLSTM model has the best stability. Secondly, the RMSE of BiLSTM model varies from 0.00246 to 0.00409 m³/Day. After the CNN BiLSTM model was executed 10 times, the RMSE changed greatly and did not show good stability.

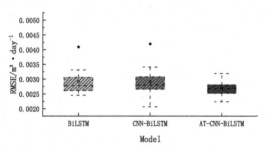

Fig. 5. Comparison of model stability.

5 Conclusion

On the premise of realizing the intelligent decision-making irrigation of water and fertilizer for greenhouse cabbage, this paper uses the front and back characteristics of original time series data and multi-scale high-level front and back characteristics to predict and analyze the irrigation amount of water and fertilizer in the joint architecture of convolution neural network and cyclic neural network, and puts forward an AT-CNN-BiLSTM neural network model with attention mechanism to predict the irrigation amount of the next day, and analyzes the application effect of the model in actual production, The validity and usability of the model are verified by experiments, which provides great help for the intelligent management of vegetable water and fertilizer.

Acknowledgements. This work was supported by Innovation 2030 Major S&T Projects of China (2021ZD0113604) and China Agriculture Research System of MOF and MARA (CARS-23-D07).

References

1. Kogo, B.K., Kumar, L., Koech, R.: Climate change and variability in Kenya: a review of impacts on agriculture and food security. Environ. Dev. Sustain. **23**(1), 23–43 (2021)
2. Zhang, Z., Yu, Z., Zhang, Y., et al.: Finding the fertilization optimization to balance grain yield and soil greenhouse gas emissions under water-saving irrigation. Soil Tillage Res. **214**, 105167 (2021).
3. Kuzman, B., Petković, B., Denić, N., et al.: Estimation of optimal fertilizers for optimal crop yield by adaptive neuro fuzzy logic. Rhizosphere **18**, 100358 (2021).
4. Zhai, L., Wang, Z., Zhai, Y, et al.: Partial substitution of chemical fertilizer by organic fertilizer benefits grain yield, water use efficiency, and economic return of summer maize. Soil and Tillage Res. **217**, 105287 (2022).
5. Xiao, H., van Es, H.M., Amsili, J.P., et al.: Lowering soil greenhouse gas emissions without sacrificing yields by increasing crop rotation diversity in the North China Plain. Field Crop. Res.**276**, 108366 (2022).

6. Bwambale, E., Abagale, F.K., Anornu, GK.: Smart irrigation monitoring and control strategies for improving water use efficiency in precision agriculture: a review. Agric. Water Manag. **260**, 107324 (2022).
7. Qin, A., Ning, D., Liu, Z., et al.: Determining threshold values for a crop water stress index-based center pivot irrigation with optimum grain yield. Agriculture **11**(10), 958 (2021)
8. Chen J, Ji X, Wu J, et al.: Review of research on irrigation decision control. In: 2021 the 3rd International Conference on Big Data Engineering and Technology (BDET), pp. 94–98 (2021)
9. Li, D., Wang, X.: Assessing irrigated water utilization to optimize irrigation schedule in the oasis-desert ecotone of Hexi Corridor of China. Agric. Ecosyst. Environ. **322**, 107647 (2021).
10. Liu, H.: Agricultural water management based on the Internet of Things and data analysis. Acta Agric. Scand. Sect. B—Soil & Plant Sci., 1–12 (2021)
11. Gallardo, M., Elia, A., Thompson, R.B.: Decision support systems and models for aiding irrigation and nutrient management of vegetable crops. Agric. Water Manag. **240**, 106209 (2020).
12. Phutthisathian, A., Pantasen, N., Maneerat, N.: Ontology-based nutrient solution control system for hydroponics. In: 2011 First International Conference on Instrumentation, Measurement, Computer, Communication and Control. IEEE, pp. 258–261 (2011)
13. Suhardiyanto, H., Seminar, K.B., Chadirin, Y., et al.: Development of a pH control system for nutrient solution in ebb and flow hydroponic culture based on fuzzy logic. IFAC Proc. Vol. **34**(11), 87–90 (2001)
14. Hyun, S., Yang, S.M., Kim, J., et al.: Development of a mobile computing framework to aid decision-making on organic fertilizer management using a crop growth model. Comput. Electron. Agric. **181**, 105936 (2021).
15. Dursun, M., Özden, S.: Optimization of soil moisture sensor placement for a PV-powered drip irrigation system using a genetic algorithm and artificial neural network. Electr. Eng. **99**(1), 407–419 (2017)
16. González Perea, R., Daccache, A., Rodríguez Díaz, J.A., et al.: Modelling impacts of precision irrigation on crop yield and in-field water management. Precis. Agric. **19**(3), 497–512 (2018)
17. Shan, B., Guo, P., Guo, S., et al.: A price-forecast-based irrigation scheduling optimization model under the response of fruit quality and price to water. Sustainability **11**(7), 2124 (2019).
18. Nguyen, D.C.H., Ascough, J.C., II., Maier, H.R., et al.: Optimization of irrigation scheduling using ant colony algorithms and an advanced cropping system model. Environ. Model. Softw. **97**, 32–45 (2017)
19. Moon, T., Ahn, T.I., Son, J.E.: Forecasting root-zone electrical conductivity of nutrient solutions in closed-loop soilless cultures via a recurrent neural network using environmental and cultivation information. Front. Plant Sci. **9**, 859 (2018).
20. Cho, W.J., Kim, H.J., Jung, D.H., et al.: Hybrid signal-processing method based on neural network for prediction of NO3, K, Ca, and Mg ions in hydroponic solutions using an array of ion-selective electrodes. Sensors **19**(24), 5508 (2019)

Interaction-Aware Temporal Prescription Generation via Message Passing Neural Network

Cong Wang, Zhi Zheng, Tong Xu$^{(\boxtimes)}$, Zikai Yin, and Enhong Chen

School of Data Science, University of Science and Technology of China, Hefei, China
{congw97,zhengzhi97,yinzikai}@mail.ustc.edu.com,
{tongxu,cheneh}@ustc.edu.com

Abstract. In recent years, deep learning techniques have been applied with great success in the healthcare industry, such as disease prediction and drug recommendation. However, existing works on drug recommendation either do not take the critical impact of doses on treatment outcomes into account, or neglect the patient's personalized history and drug-drug interactions, resulting in suboptimal recommendation results. To fill these gaps, we propose a novel Temporal Prescription Generation (TPG) model in this paper. Specifically, we first utilize a message passing neural network to capture the interaction between drugs, combined with a decomposed long and short-term memory (LSTM-DE) to characterize patient's general information. Then, we design a prescription generator based on recurrent neural network to generate drugs and estimate doses simultaneously. Experimental results on a real-world dataset clearly demonstrate that the proposed model is superior to the best existing models in terms of drug recommendation and dose estimation.

Keywords: Drug recommendation · Graph neural network

1 Introduction

Nowadays, many major hospitals have established their complete medical information systems, and Electronic Medical Records (EMRs) have been entirely popularized with the continuous advancement of medical informatization. This wealth of information provides the basis for the application of deep learning technology in the medical industry, such as disease prediction [4,10] and drug recommendation [13,15]. However, although large efforts have been made in recent years, drug recommendation models still cannot achieve satisfactory results in practical applications due to the following reasons. First, in practical applications, doctors not only need to give appropriate drugs, but also determine the appropriate dose. However, the latest studies on drug dosing can only predict the dose of a few specific drugs [1,12], which limits their application scenarios. Second, there are multiple interaction types between drugs, e.g., synergism and antagonism, and the interaction of drugs may have different effects on drug

L. Fang et al. (Eds.): CICAI 2022, LNAI 13605, pp. 218–229, 2022.
https://doi.org/10.1007/978-3-031-20500-2_18

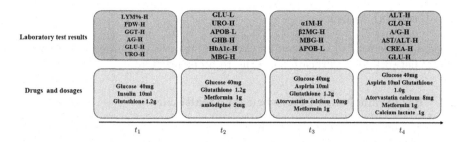

Fig. 1. An example for a patient with diabetes. Blue boxes represent laboratory test information, yellow boxes represent drug and dose information. (Color figure online)

usage and dose. However, most existing studies generally neglect the interaction between drugs or consider only a single type of interaction [8,11]. Furthermore, many EMR data contain both longitudinal information (e.g., laboratory test result sequences and drug sequences) and static information (e.g., demographics and admission records). In the example of the patient in Fig. 1, this patient has four laboratory tests and prescriptions in the hospital. However, most of the existing drug recommendation efforts are only based on static information like disease diagnosis [13,15], which is insufficient for capturing the patient condition.

To address the above challenges, we propose a Temporal Prescription Generation (TPG) model, which integrates laboratory test results and drug interactions while recommending drugs and estimating the corresponding doses. First, we construct several enhanced drug interaction graphs based on the collected drug interaction information and patient history, where each graph contains both all the drugs and the corresponding doses information. Subsequently, we combine the constructed enhanced drug interaction graphs as attribute graphs which utilize edge attribute vectors to describe the enhanced drug interaction effects based on message passing neural networks (MPNN). Then we use the decomposed long and short-term memory (LSTM-DE) [8] to describe the personalized representations of patients. Finally, we transform the prescription recommendation problem into a sequence generation process that generates drugs one by one while estimating the corresponding doses.

To summarize, the main contributions of our work are as follows:

- To the best of our knowledge, this is the first work to propose simultaneous drug recommendation and dose estimation by capturing different types of drug interactions.
- We propose to construct several enhanced drug interaction graphs based on drug interaction data and further use message passing neural networks to obtain the embedding of drugs and doses to capture drug interactions.
- We propose a combined loss function to train our TPG model, which contains maximum likelihood estimation and root mean square error to recommend the best drug and estimate the corresponding dose for the patient.
- We evaluate the performance of our model on a real-world dataset. The experiment results demonstrate that the proposed model is superior to the best existing models.

2   Related Work

Generally, the related work can be classified into two categories, i.e., recurrent neural network for healthcare and drug recommendation.

2.1   Recurrent Neural Network for Healthcare

Recurrent neural networks have achieved great success in the medical field. Choi et al. proposed an end-to-end model based on a recurrent neural network with gated recurrent units to characterize patient conditions to predict subsequent diseases and drugs [4]. Lipton et al. transformed disease prediction into a multi-label classification problem using a long-short-term memory network [10]. In order to solve the problem of unequal time intervals between patients' visits, Baytas et al. proposed a time-aware recurrent neural network to cluster patients according to different disease types [2]. Choi et al. utilized two different attention mechanisms to improve representation accuracy while maintaining model interpretability, which is widely used in the medical field [5]. Inspired by these methods, we utilize recurrent neural networks to improve drug recommendation and dose estimation accuracy.

2.2   Drug Recommendation

In the medical field, drug recommendation is a valuable research topic. Shang et al. proposed two main deep learning approaches designed for drug recommendation: instance-based and longitudinal approaches [13]. Instance-based approaches ignore the patient's longitudinal history when recommending drugs to patients. For example, zhang et al. transformed the drug recommendation problem into a multi-instance multi-label learning (MIML) problem and adopted reinforcement learning to tune the parameters [15]. Zheng et al. considered drug interactions in the drug recommendation task and proposed a drug packaging recommendation paradigm [16]. Longitudinal approaches used the temporal dependence of patient admission records to predict future drugs, Le et al. utilized external memory to model the interaction between drugs and disease [9]. Based on this, Shang et al. avoided toxicity and side effects between drugs and recommended safe drugs to patients [13]. Jin et al. developed three different LSTMs to model heterogeneous data interactions to recommend drugs [8]. Zheng et al. integrated multiple interactions between patient history and drugs and applied reinforcement learning techniques to improve the accuracy and diversity of recommended drugs [17]. However, none of them considered the estimation of dose, which was crucial for the task of drug recommendation.

3   Preliminaries

In this section, we first introduce the real-world dataset of our experiment and then propose the problem formulation for the next-time prescription recommendation task.

3.1 Dataset

In our experiments, patient admission history data are obtained from the electronic medical record database of a leading hospital in China, which contains 621,537 patients. Subsequently, we adopt the same data processing operations as LSTM-DE [8], including filtering low-frequency drugs, deleting patients with too few laboratory records and prescribing records, etc. Following Zheng et al. [16], we collect drug interaction data from two online pharmaceutical knowledge bases and construct the drug relation matrix $\mathcal{R} \in \mathbb{R}^{M \times M}$, where $\mathcal{R}_{ij}$ represents the interaction between d_i and d_j, namely 0 for no interaction, 1 for synergism, 2 for antagonism and -1 for unknown. The statistical details are as follows, our dataset contains 61,298 patients, 356 different drugs, 10 different doses, an average of 6.8 drugs per prescription, 22,986 synergistic drug pairs, 6,389 antagonistic drug pairs, and 467 drug doses that have been changed.

3.2 Problem Formulation

Here we first formulate the next time prescription recommendation problem, and then describe how patient characterization was performed.

Definition 1 (Next Time Prescription Recommendation Task). *Given a set of patients* $U = \{u_1, u_2, \ldots, u_N\}$ *with corresponding medical histories* $X = \{x^{u_1}, x^{u_2}, \ldots, x^{u_N}\}$, *the static information* $S = \{s^{u_1}, s^{u_2}, \ldots, s^{u_N}\}$ *and the drug relation matrix* $\mathcal{R}$, *the goal of next-time prescription recommendation is to get a personalized generator* g, *which can generate a candidate drug package set* $C_p = \{P_1, P_2, \ldots, P_n\}$ *and a candidate drug dose set* $C_v = \{V_1, V_2, \ldots, V_n\}$, *then it can pick out the most suitable drug package* $P \in C_p$ *and the most appropriate dose* $V \in C_v$ *based on each patient description* **u** *for the next time.*

For patient u_k, x^{u_k} is a visit sequence that comprises heterogeneous temporal sequences, such as laboratory test sequence $x_l^{u_k} = \{x_{l_1}^{u_k}, x_{l_2}^{u_k}, \ldots, x_{l_n}^{u_k}\}$, drug package sequence $x_p^{u_k} = \{x_{p_1}^{u_k}, x_{p_2}^{u_k}, \ldots, x_{p_n}^{u_k}\}$ and drug dose sequence $x_v^{u_k} = \{x_{v_1}^{u_k}, x_{v_2}^{u_k}, \ldots, x_{v_n}^{u_k}\}$, respectively. The state of patient u_k at time t can be represented by the laboratory test $\boldsymbol{x}_{l_t}^{u_k}$ and the enhanced drug graph $\boldsymbol{x}_{g_t}^{u_k}$. Each laboratory test is a one-hot vector of laboratory test item vocabulary, and each enhanced drug graph can be obtained from the drug package $x_{p_t}^{u_k} = \{d_{t_1}, d_{t_2}, \ldots, d_{t_n}\}$ and corresponding doses set $x_{v_t}^{u_k} = \{v_{t_1}, v_{t_2}, \ldots, v_{t_n}\}$, which will be described in detail in later sections.

4 Technical Details

In this section, we will introduce the technical details of TPG. As illustrated in Fig. 2, TPG consists of two components, respectively patient encoder and prescription generator. Specifically, the overall patient representation is generated by the patient encoder module. Then we use the prescription generator module to generate the drugs and estimate the corresponding doses for the next time.

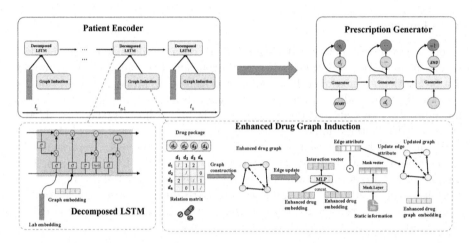

Fig. 2. A framework overview of the temporal prescription generation model.

4.1 Patient Encoder

To improve the effectiveness of the model, we recommend drugs to patients by considering the three sequences of patients' laboratory tests, drugs, and doses. First, we integrate drug and dose information to obtain the enhanced drug representation and construct several enhanced drug interaction graphs for each patient based on the collected data. After getting the enhanced drug graph representation of the patient through the MPNN framework, we feed the sequence of laboratory test result representations and the enhanced drug graph representation sequence into the LSTM-DE to obtain an overall patient representation.

Enhanced Drug Embedding. The dose range varies from drug to drug, so we first normalize the dose. In detail, we assume that each drug denoted as $\{d_1, d_2, \ldots, d_n\}$ and normalize the dose for a given drug to be within the range of [-1, 1] by the following formula: $v_{d_n}^t = \frac{2*v_{d_n}^t - (max_{d_n} + min_{d_n})}{max_{d_n} - min_{d_n}}$, where the max_{d_n} and min_{d_n} are the maximum and minimum dose during the priod of training dataset respectively. The embedding of each drug can be obtained by linear embedding $x_d^t = W_{d,x}d^t$, where $W_{d,x}$ is the embedding matrix to learn. After normalizing the doses, only a few different doses remain, and we can construct a dose vocabulary to convert the dose embedding into a one-hot vector. The enhanced drug embedding are obtained by concatenating the drug embedding and the dose embedding: $x_e^t = [x_d^t, x_v^t]$.

Temporal Enhanced Drug Interaction Graph Construction. For all drugs and doses used at time t, we define a corresponding enhanced drug interaction graph $\mathcal{G}^t = \{\mathcal{V}^t, \mathcal{E}^t\}$, where $\mathcal{V}^t$ is the node set and $\mathcal{E}^t$ is the edge set. Each specific node $v^t \in \mathcal{V}^t$ is associated with the corresponding enhanced drug embedding $\boldsymbol{x}_e^t$. Furthermore, in order to fuse the information of the drug relation matrix $\mathcal{R}$, we propose the following criterion to define the topology structure of $\mathcal{G}_t$. For nodes v^t, w^t, if $\mathcal{R}_{vw} \neq -1$, which means this drug paired has been labeled, then edge e_{vw}^t exists. Otherwise, the edge e_{vw}^t does not exist.

Enhanced Drug Interaction Graph Induction. Based on the constructed enhanced drug interaction graph, we utilize MPNN [6] to get the enhanced drug interaction graph embedding. The MPNN framework has two stages: a message passing stage and a readout stage. In the message passing stage, each node iteratively aggregates and disseminates information through neighboring nodes, corresponding to Eq. (1). In addition, the readout function summarizes any number of embedding vectors into a fixed vector representation, corresponding to Eq. (2).

$$
\begin{aligned}
\boldsymbol{m}_v^{l+1} &= \sum_{w \in \mathcal{N}_v} M_l \left(\boldsymbol{h}_v^l, \boldsymbol{h}_w^l, \boldsymbol{e}_{vw} \right), \\
\boldsymbol{h}_v^{l+1} &= U_l \left(\boldsymbol{h}_v^l, \boldsymbol{m}_v^{l+1} \right),
\end{aligned}
\tag{1}
$$

$$
\boldsymbol{h}_G = R \left(\left\{ \boldsymbol{h}_v^l \mid v \in V \right\} \right).
\tag{2}
$$

Since the temporal enhanced drug interaction graph is formed as an attributed graph, each node and edge has its corresponding attribute vector. Following Zheng et al. [16], the message passing process and the readout process can be expressed as:

$$
\begin{aligned}
\hat{\mathbf{e}}_{vw}^l &= mask \odot MLP^l \left([\mathbf{h}_w^l || \mathbf{h}_v^l] \right), \\
\mathbf{m}_v^{l+1} &= \sum_{w \in \mathcal{N}v} W_1^l \hat{\mathbf{e}}_{vw}^l, \\
\mathbf{h}_v^{l+1} &= MLP \left(W^l \mathbf{h}_v^l + \mathbf{m}_v^{l+1} \right),
\end{aligned}
\tag{3}
$$

$$
\boldsymbol{h}_G = \sum_{v \in V} \sigma(MLP([\mathbf{d}_v || \mathbf{h}_v])) \odot (MLP([\mathbf{d}_v || \mathbf{h}_v])).
\tag{4}
$$

However, patient's condition can have an impact on drug interactions, we use the patient's static features to obtain the patient's mask vector $mask = \sigma(MLP_{mask}(s))$. After l layer of the message passing process, we can get the node representation $\mathbf{h}_u^l$, edge attribute $\mathbf{e}_{vu}^l$ and multilayer perceptron MLP^l. $\mathbf{h}_u^l$ is the enhanced drug embedding for the corresponding drug d_u, i.e., $\mathbf{d}_u = \mathbf{h}_u^l$. $\mathbf{e}_{vu}^l$ is the representation for the interaction between the corresponding drugs d_u and d_v based on the interaction feature extractor MLP^l. After getting the enhanced drug graph embedding $\boldsymbol{x}_{g_t}^{u_k} = \boldsymbol{h}_G$, we can form the loss function as:

$$
\mathcal{L}_{graph} = - \sum_{v,w \in \mathcal{G}} \ln \left(softmax \left(\hat{\mathbf{e}}_{vw}^\top \mathbf{Q} \right)_{\mathcal{R}_{vw}} \right),
\tag{5}
$$

where $\mathbf{Q} \in \mathbb{R}^{D \times 3}$ is the transfer matrix to transform the edge attribute $\mathbf{e}_{vw}$ into classification probabilities, D is the dimension of $\mathbf{e}_{vw}$. We add cross entropy loss to the loss function, which aims to force the edge attribute $\mathbf{e}_{vw}$ to contain the interaction type information.

Decomposed LSTM. In order to provide personalized recommended drugs to patients, we utilize a heterogeneous decomposed LSTM (LSTM-DE) to obtain the patient's embedding, which proposes the decomposed gate that can learn the relationship between multiple sequences. Following the Jin et al.'s work [8], the detailed mathematical expressions are as follows:

$$
\begin{aligned}
s_t &= \sigma \left(W_s \left[x_{g_t}^{u_k}, h_{t-1} \right] + b_s \right), \\
d_t &= \sigma \left(W_{decomp} C_{t-1} + b_{decomp} \right), \\
\widetilde{C}_t^l &= d_t \odot \tanh \left(W_l x_{l_t}^{u_k} + b_l \right), \\
\widetilde{C}_t &= \tanh \left(W_c \left[x_{m_t}^{u_k}, h_{t-1} \right] + b_c \right), \\
C_t &= f_t \odot \left(C_{t-1} + \widetilde{C}_t^l \right) + i_t \odot \widetilde{C}_t, \\
h_t &= o_t \odot \tanh \left(C_t \right),
\end{aligned}
\tag{6}
$$

In these equations, the parameters W_s denotes the weight matrices, b_s denotes bias, symbol $\sigma(.)$, $\tanh(.)$ and $\odot$ denote the logistic function, hyperbolic tangent function, and element-wise multiplication, respectively. h_t denotes the hidden state in time t.

4.2   Prescription Generator

To obtain an end-to-end model framework, we convert the prescription recommendation problem into a sequential generation problem. The module generates the most likely drug and estimates the most appropriate dose based on personalized patient embedding. In particular, we select the t-th drug d_t based on the patient embedding $\mathbf{u} = x_n^{u_k}$ and the already selected drugs $d_1, \ldots, d_T$, the process can be represented as follows:

$$
p\left(d_1, \ldots, d_T \mid \mathbf{u} \right) = \prod_{t=1}^{T} p\left(d_t \mid d_1, \ldots, d_{t-1}, \mathbf{u} \right).
\tag{7}
$$

To transform all drugs used at a given time into a drug sequence, we first sort the drugs by the number of occurrences, with high-frequency drugs placed in the front and dose information aligned with them. Inputting a START label to the model represents the start of the drug generation process. To enable the model to generate variable-length outputs, we append an END label after each drug sequence to represent the end of drug generation. Then we choose LSTM as the sequence generation model, input $\mathbf{u}$ as the initial hidden state, and get the output probability distribution over the drug space at time step t as:

$$
p\left(d_{t+1} \right) = softmax \left(\mathbf{W}_o \mathbf{h}_t + \mathbf{M}_t \right),
\tag{8}
$$

$$(M_t)_i = \begin{cases} -\infty & \text{if the } i\text{-th drug has been predicted.} \\ 0 & \text{otherwise.} \end{cases} \qquad (9)$$

$$v_{t+1} = MLP([\mathbf{h}_t, d_{t+1}]), \qquad (10)$$

where $\mathbf{h}_t$ is the output of the LSTM cell and d_t is the predicted drug based on the conditional probability at time step t. We estimate the dose based on the predicted drug and the candidate hidden state at the current time, M_t is the mask vector which is used to prevent the LSTM model from generating repeated drugs. Finally, the loss function for drug generation with maximum likelihood estimation (MLE) loss and dose estimation with root mean square error (RMSE) loss can be formulated as follows:

$$\mathcal{L}_{MLE} = -\sum_{t=1}^{T} \log(softmax\,(\mathbf{W}_o \mathbf{h}_{t-1} + \mathbf{M}_{t-1})_{d_t^*}),$$

$$\mathcal{L}_{RMSE} = -\sqrt{\frac{1}{T} \sum_{t=1}^{T} (MLP([\mathbf{h}_{t-1}, d_t]) - v_{d_t^*}^t)^2}, \qquad (11)$$

where d_t^* is the ground-truth drug and $v_{d_t^*}^t$ is the ground-truth dose at time t.

5   Experiments

5.1   Experimental Settings

Evaluation Metrics. As a sequence generation task, we employed precision, recall and f1-value as metrics to evaluate the accuracy of the predicted drugs and utilized root mean square error to calculate the difference between estimated doses and ground truth doses.

Implementation Details. In our experiments, we used Kaiming initialization [7] to initialize all parameters and optimized the model with Adam. For the Patient Encoder module, the dimensions of drug embeddings and dose embeddings were both set to 64. The dimension of laboratory test embedding, and the hidden state dimension, were set to 64 and 512, respectively. For the Prescription Generator module, the hidden size of the LSTM was set to 32, and the dimension of MLP hidden layers was set to 128. the learning rate was set to 1×10^{-3} with decay as 0.425 every 10 epochs. The learning rate was set to 1×10^{-3} with decay as 0.425 every 10 epochs.

Baselines. To evaluate the estimated dose effect, all methods used the same MLP settings as our model. We compared our model with the following methods:

- **LSTM-FC** [8]: This method converts laboratory information and drug information and dose information into a one-hot vector combined input.

Table 1. Performance results of the baselines and proposed model on our dataset

Model	Precision ↑	Recall ↑	F1-score ↑	RMSE ↓
LSTM-FC [8]	0.4125	0.3946	0.4033	0.0556
LSTM-DE [8]	0.4532	0.4228	0.4374	0.0532
DAM [3]	0.4435	0.4028	0.4222	0.0546
GAMENet [13]	0.4812	0.4719	0.4765	0.0548
SGM [14]	0.4325	0.3928	0.4117	0.0562
TPG	**0.5128**	**0.5015**	**0.5071**	**0.0527**

- **LSTM-DE** [8]: This method enters the lab information separately into the decomposed gate to guide the prescription of medication, and the rest of the settings are the same as the above method.
- **DAM** [3]: This is the state-of-the-art model for efficiently representing multiple drug representations, leveraging attention mechanisms and a multi-task learning framework to represent all drugs used at a time.
- **GAMENet** [13]: This method uses a dynamic storage network to recommend safe drugs to others and avoid toxic and side effects.
- **SGM** [14]: This approach transforms the multi-label task into a sequence generation task, considering the relationship between the generated drugs.

5.2 Results and Analyses

Performance Comparison. Table 1 lists the results of all models on our dataset. Specifically, we can obtain the following observations. In general, compared with other baselines, our model has higher scores on the metrics in drug recommendation and lower root mean square error in dose estimation. These results suggest that our model is more suitable for drug recommendation and dose estimation tasks. Moreover, models such as GAMENet and TPG perform better than other models that do not consider the relationship between drugs, which demonstrates the importance of constructing relationships between drugs. Furthermore, TPG works better than GAMENet, suggesting the effectiveness of our constructed drug-drug interactions, which are better than co-occurrence effects.

Ablation Studies. To verify the effectiveness of each module of TPG, we designed three variants for the ablation study, namely TPG-oneday, TPG-lab, and TPG-static. The results are shown in Table 2. TPG-oneday ignores the patient's history and only considers laboratory tests and drug records on a given day. As expected, the performance of the TPG-oneday model drop significantly on the drug recommendation task, revealing the importance of the patient's admission history. Moreover, TPG-lab does not consider the laboratory test result information and only enters the patient's drug history. Since the lab information guides doctors in prescribing drugs, the effect is much reduced. Finally, TPG-static removes the mask layer of the patient in the process of drug embedding. Since the patient's static feature will affect the interaction between drugs, the performance of TPG is also better than that of TPG-static.

Table 2. Ablation studies

Model	Precision ↑	Recall ↑	F1-score ↑	RMSE ↓
TPG-oneday	0.4332	0.4126	0.4226	0.0625
TPG-lab	0.4425	0.4236	0.4328	0.0640
TPG-static	0.4648	0.4320	0.4478	0.0545
TPG	**0.5128**	**0.5015**	**0.5071**	**0.0527**

Table 3. Recommended drugs and estimated doses for a patient with two times

Period	Model	Recommended drugs and Estimated doses
	LSTM-FC	2 correcct (Aspirin:0.5, Metformin:0.3) + 5 missed
1st Time	LSTM-DE	2 correcct (Aspirin:0.5, Metformin:0.4) + 5 missed
Total glycated hemoglobin (MQ)-H	DAM	3 correcct (Aspirin:0.5, Metformin:0.4, Piracetam:0.5) + 4 missed
Glucose-H	GAMENet	3 correcct (Aspirin:0.5, Metformin:0.4, Piracetam:0.5) + 3 unseen + 4 missed
Triglycerides -H	SGM	2 correcct (Aspirin:0.5, Metformin:0.4) + 5 missed
Lipoprotein a-H	TPG	4 correcct (Aspirin:0.5, Metformin:0.4, Atorvastatin calcium:1, Piracetam:0.5) + 3 missed
	LSTM-FC	3 correct (Sodium chloride:0.5, Aspirin:0.5, Hydroclopidogrel:1) + 4 missed
2nd Time	LSTM-DE	3 correct (Sodium chloride:0.5, Aspirin:0.5, Hydroclopidogrel:1) + 4 missed
Ferritin-H	DAM	4 correct (Sodium chloride:0.5, Aspirin:0.5, Hydroclopidogrel:1, Atorvastatincalcium:1) + 2 unseen + 3 missed
Glucose -H	GAMENet	5 correct (Sodium chloride:0.5, Aspirin:0.5, Metformin:0.5, Hydroclopidogrel:1, Acarbose:1) + 1 unseen + 2 missed
Triglycerides -H	SGM	4 correcct (Sodium chloride:0.5, Aspirin:0.5, Hydroclopidogrel:1, Atorvastatincalcium:0.5,) + 3 unseen + 3 missed
Mean platelet volume -H	TPG	5 correct (Aspirin:0.5, Metformin:1, Acarbose:1, Atorvastatin calcium:1, Spironolactone:0.5) + 2 unseen + 2 missed

Case Study. We compared the recommended drugs and estimated doses for the same patient to demonstrate the effectiveness of our model. We randomly picked a patient from the test dataset with different lab results and prescribing information at two times. The patient had an acute cerebral infarction and type 2 diabetes. As shown in Table 3, Most models recommend aspirin and metformin to the patient. However, the laboratory information shows that the patient has high lipids, and TPG is the only model to recommend atorvastatin calcium to the patient to lower lipids. Compared to GAMENet, TPG can estimate a more appropriate dose of metformin in relation to the severity of the disease.

6   Conclusion

In this paper, we proposed a novel generative model called TPG to solve the prescription generation task. Specifically, we first learned the drug graph representation applying the MPNN framework for the constructed enhanced drug interaction graph and subsequently obtained the overall patient representation introducing Decomposed LSTM in combination with the information such as the laboratory representation. After that, we utilized a recurrent neural network to generate drugs one by one and estimated the corresponding doses. The experimental results demonstrated that our model had achieved substantial improvements in recommending drugs and estimating doses.

Acknowledgement. This work was supported by the grants from National Natural Science Foundation of China (No. 62072423), and the USTC Research Funds of the Double First-Class Initiative (No. YD2150002009).

References

1. Barragán-Montero, A.M.: Three-dimensional dose prediction for lung IMRT patients with deep neural networks: robust learning from heterogeneous beam configurations. Med. Phys. **46**(8), 3679–3691 (2019)
2. Baytas, I.M., Xiao, C., Zhang, X., Wang, F., Jain, A.K., Zhou, J.: Patient subtyping via time-aware lstm networks. In: Proceedings of the 23rd ACM SIGKDD international conference on knowledge discovery and data mining, pp. 65–74 (2017)
3. Chen, L., Liu, Y., He, X., Gao, L., Zheng, Z.: Matching user with item set: collaborative bundle recommendation with deep attention network. In: IJCAI, pp. 2095–2101 (2019)
4. Choi, E., Bahadori, M.T., Schuetz, A., Stewart, W.F., Sun, J.: Doctor ai: predicting clinical events via recurrent neural networks. In: Machine Learning for Healthcare Conference, pp. 301–318. PMLR (2016)
5. Choi, E., Bahadori, M.T., Sun, J., Kulas, J., Schuetz, A., Stewart, W.: Retain: an interpretable predictive model for healthcare using reverse time attention mechanism. In: Advances in Neural Information Processing Systems, vol. 29 (2016)
6. Gilmer, J., Schoenholz, S.S., Riley, P.F., Vinyals, O., Dahl, G.E.: Neural message passing for quantum chemistry. In: International Conference on Machine Learning, pp. 1263–1272. PMLR (2017)
7. He, K., Zhang, X., Ren, S., Sun, J.: Delving deep into rectifiers: surpassing human-level performance on imagenet classification. In: Proceedings of the IEEE International Conference on Computer Vision, pp. 1026–1034 (2015)
8. Jin, B., Yang, H., Sun, L., Liu, C., Qu, Y., Tong, J.: A treatment engine by predicting next-period prescriptions. In: Proceedings of the 24th ACM SIGKDD International Conference on Knowledge Discovery & Data Mining, pp. 1608–1616 (2018)
9. Le, H., Tran, T., Venkatesh, S.: Dual memory neural computer for asynchronous two-view sequential learning. In: Proceedings of the 24th ACM SIGKDD International Conference on Knowledge Discovery & Data Mining, pp. 1637–1645 (2018)
10. Lipton, Z.C., Kale, D.C., Elkan, C., Wetzel, R.: Learning to diagnose with LSTM recurrent neural networks. arXiv preprint. arXiv:1511.03677 (2015)

11. Liu, S., et al.: A hybrid method of recurrent neural network and graph neural network for next-period prescription prediction. Int. J. Mach. Learn. Cybern. **11**(12), 2849–2856 (2020)
12. Liu, Y., et al.: Dose prediction using a three-dimensional convolutional neural network for nasopharyngeal carcinoma with tomotherapy. Front. Oncol. **11**, 752007–752007 (2021)
13. Shang, J., Xiao, C., Ma, T., Li, H., Sun, J.: Gamenet: graph augmented memory networks for recommending medication combination. In: proceedings of the AAAI Conference on Artificial Intelligence, vol. 33, pp. 1126–1133 (2019)
14. Yang, P., Sun, X., Li, W., Ma, S., Wu, W., Wang, H.: SGM: sequence generation model for multi-label classification. arXiv preprint. arXiv:1806.04822 (2018)
15. Zhang, Y., Chen, R., Tang, J., Stewart, W.F., Sun, J.: Leap: learning to prescribe effective and safe treatment combinations for multimorbidity. In: proceedings of the 23rd ACM SIGKDD International Conference on Knowledge Discovery and data Mining, pp. 1315–1324 (2017)
16. Zheng, Z., et al.: Drug package recommendation via interaction-aware graph induction. In: Proceedings of the Web Conference 2021, pp. 1284–1295 (2021)
17. Zheng, Z., et al.: Interaction-aware drug package recommendation via policy gradient. In: ACM Transactions on Information Systems (TOIS) (2022)

Adversarial and Implicit Modality Imputation with Applications to Depression Early Detection

Yuzhou Nie[1], Chengyue Huang[1], Hailun Liang[2], and Hongteng Xu[3(✉)]

[1] School of Statistics, Renmin University of China, Beijing, China
[2] School of Public Administration and Policy, Renmin University of China, Beijing, China
[3] Gaoling School of Artificial Intelligence, Renmin University of China, Beijing, China
hongtengxu313@gmail.com

Abstract. Depression early detection is a significant healthcare task that heavily relies on high-quality multi-modal medical data. In practice, however, learning a robust detection model is challenging because real-world data often suffers from serious modality-level missing issues caused by imperfect data collection and strict data sharing policies. In this study, we propose an Adversarial and Implicit Modality Imputation (AIMI) method to resolve this challenge. In particular, when training multi-modal predictive models, we learn an implicit mechanism to impute the missing modalities of training data at the same time. These two learning objectives are achieved jointly in an adversarial learning framework. Based on the UK Biobank dataset, we demonstrate the effectiveness and superiority of our method on the early detection of depression. Codes are available at https://github.com/rucnyz/AIMI.

Keywords: Multi-modal learning · Adversarial learning · Implicit data imputation · Depression early detection

1 Introduction

Depression is a leading cause of disability and is a major contributor to the overall global burden of disease. According to WHO, approximately 5.0% of the adult population suffer from depression [23]. Due to the high burden of brain health disorders, depression early detection and screening are valuable, which could slow the progression of the disease through earlier access to treatment, advice and support [11,17].

Many indicators of presence or severity of depression are observable. While one single modality of indicators rarely provides complete information, the diversity of modalities brings added value. Recently, artificial intelligence-assisted techniques have been developed for the early detection of depression [5,9,14,15]. Essentially,

---

Y. Nie and C. Huang—Equal contribution.

these methods leverage a multi-modal paradigm to represent and fuse the health-care information collected by different ways (e.g., physical exams, standard questionnaire, lab tests, the medical images like CT and MRI, genetic tests, etc.) and predict the risk of depression based on the fused information. However, these methods often ignore the fact that real-world data often miss some modalities because of various reasons. For example, many patients merely do a part of lab tests or medical images because of the lack of medical insurance coverages. Even for the patients having complete modalities, their multi-modal data may be stored in different hospitals and cannot be fully-accessible because of the privacy and security issues. The above phenomena are common in the early stage of depression — the patients may just take some tests and thus only some modalities are available for disease prediction. Facing to the above modality-missing issue, most existing multi-modal learning methods often simply discard the data with missing modalities, which results in the loss of information and sub-optimal models [4, 28].

Related Work. Several methods are proposed to resolve the modality-missing issue. One direct way is to impute the missing modalities, and then adopt the on-shelf multi-modal learning algorithms. The early work in [7] simply fills the missing views with a single value (e.g. mean value based on available samples within the same class). The matrix completion methods, such as SVD imputation [20] and Bayesian principal component analysis [16], infer the missing values based on the low-rank assumption of the latent data structure. However, the missing values would simultaneously appear in one modality instead of randomly distributed, which makes the above conventional methods no longer applicable. Focusing on the imputation of missing modalities, the CRA (Cascaded Residual Autoencoder) in [19] predicts the missing modalities from the observed one. Following the same strategy, more sophisticated modality prediction mechanisms are considered, e.g. the grouping strategy in [26] and the merging strategy in [3]. More recently, deep learning-based methods [24, 25] impute missing data by adapting the well-known Generative Adversarial Network (GAN) [10], treating observed data as real data and generating missing data as fake ones. Synthetic EHR methods like medGAN [6] and its variants [2] combine GAN with an autoencoder(AE) [12] to learn the data distribution of real EHRs. However, without any feedback mechanisms, imputed modalities achieved by the above methods are unchanged and may lead to catastrophic error propagation.

To solve the above issues, we propose a novel **A**dversarial and **I**mplicit **M**odality **I**mutation method, called AIMI for short, which exploits multi-modal data with arbitrary modality-missing patterns both effectively and flexibly. As illustrated in Fig. 1, our AIMI consists of an AE [12] and a GAN [10]. For the autoencoder, its encoder projects samples with arbitrary modality-missing patterns into a common latent space and connects to a classifier, and the decoder reconstructs complete multi-view data from the latent codes. The decoder works as the generator in the framework of GAN, which imputes missing modalities via generated ones. Accordingly, besides training the encoder and the decoder to minimizes the reconstruction error of the observed modalities, we further consider two more objectives: 1) improving the classification accuracy of the associated

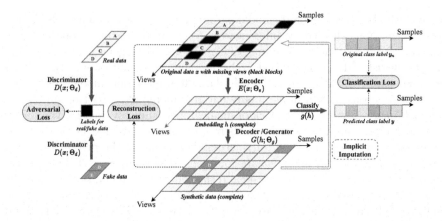

Fig. 1. An illustration of our AIMI method.

classifier; and 2) cheating a discriminator that checks whether a modality is observed or generated.

Differing from most existing data imputation methods, our method contains an implicit feedback mechanism, adjusting imputed modalities during training. In particular, after imputing the missing modalities, AIMI takes them as the input of the encoder and thus train the model under the guidance of the imputed data. This feedback mechanism achieves a new kind of data augmentation. As a result, the encoder is trained to be robust to the uncertainty of the imputation, which tends to preserve the classification accuracy of the imputed data, while the decoder also takes the imputed data into account when reconstructing modalities and cheating the discriminator.

We demonstrate the effectiveness of AIMI in the depression early detection task. based on the UK Biobank (UKB) database [18], which contains approximately 480,000 EHRs with 8 modalities, we train a multi-modal predictive model for depression early detection. Experimental results show that our AIMI is robust to the modality-missing issue and mitigates the associated problems like error propagation and over-fitting. In particular, in the experiments with missing modalities, our AIMI and its variants outperform state-of-the-art methods in both supervised and unsupervised settings.

2   Proposed Method

2.1   Learning Multi-modal Representations via Auto-encoding

Facing the data with missing modalities, we design a model with auto-encoding architecture. For the multi-modal data with V modalities, the representation model consists of V encoder-decoder pairs. For the v-th modality, its encoder is denoted as $E_v(\cdot)$, which is often parameterized by a neural network. Given the data of the v-th modality $\mathbf{x}^{(v)}$, the encoder projects it to a latent code in the d-dimensional latent space, i.e., $\mathbf{h}^{(v)} = E_v(\mathbf{x}^{(v)}) \in \mathbb{R}^d$.

We obtain a fused latent code via pooling all the modalities' latent codes:

$$\mathbf{h} = \text{Pooling}(\{\mathbf{h}^{(v)}\}_{v=1}^{V}). \tag{1}$$

Here, various pooling operations are applicable, e.g., the commonly-used mean-pooling or the attention-pooling in [8], e.g.,

$$\mathbf{h} = \sum_{v=1}^{V} \sum_{i=1}^{V} \frac{\exp(\mathbf{q}_v^T \mathbf{k}_i)}{\sqrt{d} \sum_{j=1}^{V} \exp(\mathbf{q}_v^T \mathbf{k}_j)} \mathbf{v}_i, \tag{2}$$

where $\mathbf{q}_v = f_Q(\mathbf{h}^{(v)}), \mathbf{k}_v = f_K(\mathbf{h}^{(v)}), \mathbf{v}_v = f_V(\mathbf{h}^{(v)}), \quad \forall v = 1, ..., V.$

Note that, for the data with the missed modalities, we derive the latent codes of the observed modalities and fuse them by the pooling operation in the beginning of the training process. During the training process, the missed modalities are imputed by our AIMI method and the pooling operation is applied to both observed and imputed modalities, which will be introduced in details in the following content. Accordingly, the decoder (generator) of each modality, denoted as $G_v(\cdot)$ for $v = 1, ..., V$, reconstructs the data of the v-th view from the complete latent code $\mathbf{h}$. For the missed modalities, the decoder estimates them from the complete latent code, which achieves the imputation of incomplete data.

Similar to classic autoencoders [12], given N samples of V modalities, i.e., $\{\mathbf{x}_n^{(v)}\}_{n,v=1}^{N,V}$, we can learn the model via minimizing the reconstruction error of each modality given a metric (e.g., the Euclidean distance used below):

$$\mathcal{L}_r = \sum_{n=1}^{N} \sum_{v=1}^{V} \underbrace{m_n^{(v)} \|G_v(\mathbf{h}_n) - \mathbf{x}_n^{(v)}\|^2}_{\ell_r^{(v)}(S_n; \{G_v, E_v\}_{v=1}^{V})}, \tag{3}$$

where $m_n^{(v)} \in \{0, 1\}$ is an indicator of the availability for the v-th modality of the n-th sample. Therefore, the learning problem above just considers the reconstruction of the observed modalities. It should be noted here that in the CPM-Net [27], the randomly initialized latent embedding $\mathbf{h}_n$ is directly used to represent the incomplete data (available modalities). For us, at the beginning of the training process, only available modalities are involved in feed-forward networks by considering $m_n^{(v)}$. After the first imputation, all modalities (including the synthetic parts) are trained to obtain $\mathbf{h}_n$ no matter what $m_n^{(v)}$ is, though $\mathcal{L}_r$ is still calculated by available modalities.

Besides the above reconstruction loss, we further consider the classification loss used in the CPM-Net [27]. Specifically, denote the label of the n-th multi-modal sample as y_n. The classification loss is defined as

$$\mathcal{L}_c = \sum_{n=1}^{N} \underbrace{\Delta(y_n, \arg\max_{y\in\mathcal{Y}} g(\mathbf{h}_n, y)) + \max_{y\in\mathcal{Y}} g(\mathbf{h}_n, y) - g(\mathbf{h}_n, y_n)}_{\ell_c(y_n; \{E_v\}_{v=1}^{V})}, \tag{4}$$

where $g(\mathbf{h}_n, y) = \mathbb{E}_{\mathbf{h}\sim\mathcal{T}(y)} F(\mathbf{h}, \mathbf{h}_n)$, $\mathcal{T}(y)$ is the set of latent codes from class y, $F(\mathbf{h}, \mathbf{h}_n) = \mathbf{h}^T \mathbf{h}_n$, and $\Delta(y, y_n) = 0$ if $y = y_n$ and 1 otherwise. This loss leads to a classification scheme enhancing the clustering structure of the latent codes.

Taking equations (1)∼(4) into account, we obtain the proposed multi-modal predictive model. Specifically, by jointly considering the complementary information of multi-modalities and the distribution of classes, our model makes them mutually improve each other to obtain the representation reflecting the underlying patterns, thus promoting the prediction performance.

2.2   Adversarial and Implicit Modality Imputation (AIMI)

Adversarial learning Besides the above two learning objectives, we further consider a generative adversarial loss to improve the quality of the imputed modalities. In particular, for each multi-modal sample with missing modalities, we impute the unavailable modalities by the outputs of the corresponding decoders. Given the observed real modalities and the estimated modalities, denoted as $\{\mathbf{x}_n^{(v)}\}_{v:m_n^{(v)}=1}$ and $\{G_v(\mathbf{h}_n)\}_{v:m_n^{(v)}=0}$, we would like to train a discriminator to check whether a given modality is real or fake, whose objective is

$$\mathcal{L}_a = \sum_{n=1}^{N} \sum_{v=1}^{V} \underbrace{m_n^{(v)} \log D_v(\mathbf{x}_n^{(v)}) + (1 - m_n^{(v)}) \log(1 - D_v(G_v(\mathbf{h}_n)))}_{\ell_a^{(v)}(S_n;\{G_v,D_v\}_{v=1}^{V})}, \quad (5)$$

where $D_v(\cdot)$ is the discriminator for the v-th modality.

At the same time, we train the decoder to improve the quality of the imputed modalities, which aims at cheating the discriminator. Such a generative adversarial learning strategy leads to a "min-max" game. As a result, the optimization problem of our learning task becomes

$$\mathcal{L} = \min_{\{G_v, E_v\}_{v=1}^{V}} \max_{\{D_v\}_{v=1}^{V}} \mathcal{L}_r + \lambda \mathcal{L}_c + \mu \mathcal{L}_a \quad (6)$$

where $\lambda, \mu > 0$ control the significance of different objectives. When attention-pooling is applied, the parameters of the attention layer, i.e., $\{f_Q, f_K, f_V\}$ are considered as a part of the encoder module.

Implicit Imputation with a Feedback Loop. For each missed modality $\mathbf{x}_n^{(v)}$, we fill it with the output of the corresponding decoder, i.e., $\mathbf{x}_n^{(v)} = G_v(\mathbf{h}_n; \mathbf{\Theta}_g^{(v)})$. Here, given a batch of data, both the latent code and the decoder are updated during the training progress, while their imputed modalities are fixed for the batch, which leads to sub-optimal updating of the model. Therefore, we consider an implicit imputation method, which applies several inner iterations to adjust the imputed modalities — for the t-th inner iteration, we will take the imputed modalities obtained in the previous iteration as the input of the encoders and update them by the auto-encoding architecture. Accordingly, we obtain an iterative adjustment of the imputed modalities: for the missed modality $x_n^{(v)}$, we set $\mathbf{x}_n^{(v),0} = \mathbf{0}$ and update it via

$$\mathbf{h}_n^{t-1} = \text{Pooling}(\{E_v(\mathbf{x}_n^{(v),t-1})\}_{v=1}^{V}), \quad \mathbf{x}_n^{(v),t} = G_v(\mathbf{h}_n^{t-1}) \quad \text{for } t = 1, 2, \dots \quad (7)$$

Such an iterative adjustment leverages the feedback of current model, which improve the quality of the imputations.

The rationality of this implicit imputation mechanism can be verified in both feed-forward computation and backpropagation. Firstly, this mechanism leads to iterative auto-encoding, which can be treated as an iterative function system. As a result, with the increase of the inner iterations, the imputed modalities may converge to a fixed point, which suppress the uncertainty of the imputed modalities. Secondly, when updating our model in each outer iteration, we unroll the inner iterations to compute the gradients. According to the chain rule, the gradients accumulates the gradients corresponding to the intermediate imputations, which are more robust than merely considering the gradients given one-step imputations. From this viewpoint, our implicit imputation mechanism can be treated as an augmentation method for the gradients. Taking the above implicit imputation mechanism into account, we illustrate the scheme of the proposed AIMI method in Fig. 1 and show its implementation details in Algorithm 1.

Algorithm 1: Algorithm for AIMI

Input: Multi-modal data $\{S_n, y_n\}_{n=1}^{N}$. Hyperparameters s and T
Initialize $\{E_v, G_v, D_v\}_{v=1}^{V}$ randomly.
while *not converged* **do**
    Given a batch of samples $\{S_n, y_n\}_{n \in \mathcal{B}}$.
    For $v = 1 : V$, update the discriminator D_v with gradient descent.
    For $v = 1 : V$, update the decoder G_v with gradient descent.
    For $v = 1 : V$, update the encoder E_v with gradient descent.
    If #epochs $> s$, impute missing modalities via (7) with T iterations.
end
Output: $\{E_v, G_v, D_v\}_{v=1}^{V}$.

Compared with existing partial multi-modal learning methods, e.g., the Cross Partial Multi-View Network (CPM-Net) [27], our AIMI method owns several improvements and advantages. In particular, AIMI leverages an encoder to derive latent codes of different modalities and fuse them together, whose training can be achieved by stochastic gradient descent (SGD). We do not enforce the latent codes of different modalities to have the same latent distribution, which enhances the flexibility of model. Moreover, AIMI leverages an implicit imputation mechanism to achieve robust modality adjustment with a feedback loop.

3 Experiments

3.1 Experimental Setup

We demonstrate the effectiveness of our AIMI method and apply it to depression early detection. The data in this study is derived from the UK Biobank

Table 1. Eight modalities associated with depression diagnosis.

Modalities (# of features)	Demography (4)	Sociology (6)	Lifestyle (7)	Blood (19)
Features	Age	Low income	Healthy	Red blood cell count
	Gender	Work status	Healthy diet	White blood cell count
	Screening	...	...	...
	Family history	Housing tenure	Healthy score	Lymphocytes percentage
Modalities (# of features)	**Metabolism** (7)	**Urine** (4)	**Gene** (38)	**Others** (2)
Features	Glucose	Creatinine	rs159963_ac	Non-cancerous diseases
	Total cholesterol	Microalbumin	rs1432639_ac	Medication
	...	Potassium	...	
	Apolipoprotein A	Sodium	rs5758265_ag	

(UKB) database[1]. We leverage the database consisting of the diagnoses and the multi-modal clinical records of depression, and aim to train a binary classifier to achieve the early detection of depression. In particular, we manually grouped the clinical records into 8 modalities, namely demography, sociology, lifestyle, blood, metabolism, urine, gene and others. The diagnoses are used as binary labels indicating whether the corresponding subjects are depressed or healthy. Table 1 shows the number of features in each modality.

We processed the UKB database ($UKB_{Original}$) into three parts: UKB_{All}, $UKB_{Balanced}$ and $UKB_{Complete}$. UKB_{All} is a real-world modality missing dataset (missing rate=76%), and we use it for our final evaluation. Note that we randomly select the negative samples from $UKB_{Original}$ to make the number of them equal to positive ones. We obtain $UKB_{Complete}$ dataset by removing all the "NA" values from $UKB_{Original}$ for evaluation, and $UKB_{Balanced}$ has equivalent positive and negative samples selected from $UKB_{Complete}$. The number of samples in $UKB_{Original}$, UKB_{All}, $UKB_{Complete}$ and $UKB_{Balanced}$ are 461,289, 27,616, 34,240 and 2,802 respectively. For each dataset, we choose 80% samples for training and the remaining 20% samples for testing and evaluation. Additionally, to imitate the real-world scenarios that have missed modalities, we simulate the missed modalities of each samples by setting a missing rate α and removing some modalities randomly based on the rate. The missing rate (α) is defined as $\alpha = \frac{\sum_v M_v}{V \times N}$, where M_v indicates the number of samples without the vth view. $\alpha \in \{0, 0.1, 0.3, 0.5\}$. When $\alpha = 0$, the dataset is complete without missed modalities.

For each dataset, we train a multi-modal predictive model based on our AIMI method, in which we set 400 epochs with the batch size of 800. The

---

[1] The UK Biobank is an open access resource. Data are available on application to the UK Biobank (www.ukbiobank.ac.uk/). This research has been conducted using the UK Biobank resource under application number 44430.

key hyperparameters of our method include i) the latent space dimension (d), ii) the starting epoch (s) for imputation, and iii) the number of imputation times (T). Here, we apply grid search to find the best configuration for our AIMI methods, where $d \in \{64, 128, 256\}$, $s \in \{-1, 10, 20, 30, 40, 50, 60, 100\}$, and $T \in \{0, 1, 2, 3, 4, 5\}$. s $= -1$ means we do not impute during the entire training. Additionally, we implement our AIMI method using mean-pooling and attention-pooling, denoted as **AIMI**$_{mean}$ and **AIMI**$_{att}$, respectively.

Table 2. Comparisons for various methods under different missing rates (α).

Dataset	UKB$_{Complete}$				UKB$_{Balanced}$				UKB$_{All}$
α ($\times 100\%$)	0	10	30	50	0	10	30	50	76
FeatCon	87.95	81.44	77.85	74.69	62.21	61.67	60.07	58.28	58.85
Fusion$_{mean}$	92.83	88.54	87.80	87.15	61.67	62.21	61.32	57.04	59.86
Fusion$_{att}$	90.30	89.77	88.78	82.64	62.21	61.85	60.96	55.79	59.63
DCCA	92.22	89.94	88.73	79.03	66.67	65.78	62.57	60.07	60.05
LMNN	75.70	73.08	73.16	69.75	62.92	64.17	62.38	59.89	58.12
CPM-Net	**95.83**	93.03	89.12	84.24	58.47	60.07	57.93	51.87	61.27
AIMI$_{mean}$	**95.83**	95.63	93.79	93.49	66.13	65.24	62.92	61.14	61.69
AIMI$_{att}$	95.49	**95.83**	**95.60**	**94.78**	**68.27**	**66.84**	**63.96**	**61.50**	**61.73**

3.2   Comparisons on Robust Multi-modal Depression Diagnosis

Superiority to baselines. First, the superiority of our AIMI methods are sufficiently investigated. We compare it with the following typical multi-modal representation learning methods using UKB$_{Complete}$ and UKB$_{Balanced}$ datasets under various missing rates α: (1) **FeatCon** simply concatenates multiple types of features from different modalities. (2) **DCCA** [1] (Deep Canonical Correlation Analysis) learns low-dimensional features with neural networks and concatenates them. (3) **LMNN** [22] (Large Margin Nearest Neighbors) searches a Mahalanobis distance metric to optimize the k-nearest neighbours classifier. (4) **Average-based Fusion** simply average all the modalities. (5) **Attention-based Fusion** fuse all the modalities by the attention mechanism. For the baselines, the missed modalities are filled statically with average values according to available samples within the same modality.

We report the AUC in Table 2 to verify the usefulness of our AIMI method. Specifically, we can find that

- No matter whether the dataset has missed modalities or not, our method AIMI and its variant achieve competitive performances on UKB$_{Complete}$ and outperform other baselines on UKB$_{Balanced}$.
- On UKB$_{Complete}$ dataset, our methods are relatively robust to modality-missing dataset. The degradation of the baselines' performance is much larger than ours, and the performance gaps between our methods and the baselines are widened with the increase of missing rate.

– We evaluate our algorithm on UKB_{All} dataset, and the result demonstrates our model's ability to better represent the partial modality data and stability when facing severe missing problem.

Robustness to Hyperparameters. We further check the robustness of our method to its hyperparameters (i.e., s and T) on the $UKB_{Balanced}$ dataset. In Fig. 2, we show the prediction accuracy achieved by our methods under different settings. We can find that

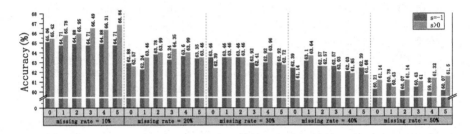

Fig. 2. Robustness analysis on the $UKB_{Balanced}$ dataset.

– With the increase of the missing rate, the performance of our method degrades monotonously, which reflects the negative influence of the missed modalities on the training of the multi-modal predictive model.
– Imputing missed modalities in the early time (i.e., $s = 1$) may bring in unstable noises because the model is not well-trained at the early stage. Therefore, we prefer imputing missed modalities after several epochs (i.e., $s > 0$) in most situations, in which the model trained in the previous epochs and with missed modalities achieves a warm-up of our AIMI method.
– Our implicit imputation method works. As Fig. 2 shows, under different missing rates α, the best performance is achieved by applying our imputation method more than once. In most cases, the prediction accuracy of our model ascends as the imputation times (T) increases.

3.3   Advantages on Modality Imputation and Representation

Apart from supervised learning scenarios, we also design experiments to validate our advantages on modality imputation and representation in unsupervised setting. For the missed modalities, besides our AIMI, we further consider the following imputation methods as baselines: (1) **Denoising Autoencoder (DAE)** [21] corrupts the data on purpose by randomly removing some of the input values. (2) **LRMC** [13] is a low-rank matrix completion method by iterative soft thresholding of singular value decomposition.

We conduct unsupervised experiments on the $UKB_{Balanced}$ dataset with different missing rates α to investigate the performance of our proposed method, especially the quality of the latent codes we learned. In particular, for the latent codes of different modalities, we evaluate their rationality and semantics by the following two measurements.

- **Imputation fidelity:** Given the latent codes, we check whether it is possible to reconstruct the corresponding missed data from the decoder. The imputation performance is evaluated by estimating the missing part of the origin data and calculating the RMSE (Root Mean Square Error [13]).
- **Clustering accuracy:** Given the latent codes, we check whether the multimodal latent codes can reflect the clustering structure of the samples. The clustering accuracy is evaluated by clustering the resulting representations and compute the accuracy(ACC).

Table 3. Comparisons on clustering accuracy and RMSE of imputed data

	Clustering accuracy (ACC)					RMSE
α ($\times 100\%$)	10	20	30	40	50	50
DAE	57.70	57.11	56.32	54.58	54.26	0.5944
LRMC	56.68	58.29	57.58	55.97	55.79	0.3961
AIMI_{mean}	**60.61**	53.48	57.04	56.86	53.30	0.1027
AIMI_{att}	59.44	**58.82**	**58.69**	**58.46**	**56.68**	**0.0947**

Table 3 shows the RMSE with $\alpha = 0.5$ and ACC with respect to different α for the unsupervised baselines and our method. We can find that the proposed AIMI and its variant outperform other methods consistently in all missing rate cases, for both ACC and RMSE. The variant using attention-pooling performs better when the missing rate is high (e.g. $\alpha = 0.4, 0.5$). We suppose the attention mechanism captures the interdependence between different modalities, thus contributing to our model's robustness and superiority.

4   Conclusion

In this work, we propose a novel multi-modal data imputation method AIMI and apply it to real-world depression early detection task. Our method imputes modalities via an adversarial network with an implicit imputation mechanism. The analytic experiments demonstrate the rationality of our method and the comparison experiments show its superiority to the baselines.

AIMI also opens the door to many interesting future directions. Firstly, justification is needed for whether adversarial learning can guarantee sufficient predictive performance for our datasets with high missing rates, since adversarial learning requires a large number of training samples and time complexity in the training phase. On the other hand, we may improve the implicit feedback mechanism to avoid the risk of repeatedly performing unnecessary (non-informative) label prediction: While the best performance is achieved by applying our imputation method more than once, the prediction accuracy does not ascend monotonously as the imputation times increases.

Acknowledgements. This work was supported in part by the National Natural Science Foundation of China (No. 62106271, 71804183); the Research Seed Funds of School of Interdisciplinary Studies, Renmin University of China; and the Research Funds of Renmin University of China (the Fundamental Research Funds for the Central Universities). Dr. Hongteng Xu also would like to thank the supports from the Beijing Key Laboratory of Big Data Management and Analysis Methods and the Public Policy and Decision-making Research Lab of Renmin University of China.

References

1. Andrew, G., Arora, R., Bilmes, J., Livescu, K.: Deep canonical correlation analysis. In: International Conference on Machine Learning, pp. 1247–1255. PMLR (2013)
2. Baowaly, M.K., Lin, C.C., Liu, C.L., Chen, K.T.: Synthesizing electronic health records using improved generative adversarial networks. J. Am. Med. Inf. Assoc. **26**(3), 228–241 (2018). https://doi.org/10.1093/jamia/ocy142
3. Boulahia, S.Y., Amamra, A., Madi, M.R., Daikh, S.: Early, intermediate and late fusion strategies for robust deep learning-based multimodal action recognition. Mach. Vis. Appl. **32**(6), 1–18 (2021). https://doi.org/10.1007/s00138-021-01249-8
4. Bzdok, D., Meyer-Lindenberg, A.: Machine learning for precision psychiatry: opportunities and challenges. Biol. Psychiatry: Cogn. Neurosci. Neuroimaging **3**(3), 223–230 (2018)
5. Cheng, B., Liu, M., Zhang, D., Shen, D.: Robust multi-label transfer feature learning for early diagnosis of Alzheimer's disease. Brain Imaging Behav. **13**(1), 138–153 (2018). https://doi.org/10.1007/s11682-018-9846-8
6. Choi, E., Biswal, S., Malin, B., Duke, J., Stewart, W.F., Sun, J.: Generating multi-label discrete patient records using generative adversarial networks. In: Machine Learning for Healthcare Conference, pp. 286–305. PMLR (2017)
7. Donders, A.R.T., van der Heijden, G.J., Stijnen, T., Moons, K.G.: Review: a gentle introduction to imputation of missing values. J. Clin. Epidemiol. **59**(10), 1087–1091 (2006). https://doi.org/10.1016/j.jclinepi.2006.01.014, https://www.sciencedirect.com/science/article/pii/S0895435606001971
8. Er, M.J., Zhang, Y., Wang, N., Pratama, M.: Attention pooling-based convolutional neural network for sentence modelling. Inf. Sci. **373**, 388–403 (2016). https://doi.org/10.1016/j.ins.2016.08.084, https://www.sciencedirect.com/science/article/pii/S0020025516306673
9. Fritsch, J., Wankerl, S., Nöth, E.: Automatic diagnosis of alzheimer's disease using neural network language models. In: ICASSP 2019–2019 IEEE International Conference on Acoustics, Speech and Signal Processing (ICASSP), pp. 5841–5845. IEEE (2019)
10. Goodfellow, I.J., et al.: Generative adversarial networks (2014)
11. Guest, F.L.: Early detection and treatment of patients with Alzheimer's disease: future perspectives. In: Guest, P.C. (ed.) Reviews on Biomarker Studies in Psychiatric and Neurodegenerative Disorders. AEMB, vol. 1118, pp. 295–317. Springer, Cham (2019). https://doi.org/10.1007/978-3-030-05542-4_15
12. Hinton, G.E., Salakhutdinov, R.R.: Reducing the dimensionality of data with neural networks. Science **313**(5786), 504–507 (2006)
13. Hotelling, H.: Relations between two sets of variates. Biometrika **28**(3/4), 321–377 (1936). http://www.jstor.org/stable/2333955

14. Kar, S., Majumder, D.D.: A novel approach of diffusion tensor visualization based neuro fuzzy classification system for early detection of Alzheimer's disease. J. Alzheimer's Dis. Rep. **3**(1), 1–18 (2019)

15. Martino-IST, I., Navarra, E.: Machine learning based analysis of fdg-pet image data for the diagnosis of neurodegenerative diseases. In: Applications of Intelligent Systems: Proceedings of the 1st International APPIS Conference 2018, vol. 310, p. 280. IOS Press (2018)

16. Oba, S., Sato, M.A., Takemasa, I., Monden, M., Matsubara, K.I., Ishii, S.: A bayesian missing value estimation method for gene expression profile data. Bioinformatics **19**(16), 2088–2096 (2003)

17. Rentz, D.M., Parra Rodriguez, M.A., Amariglio, R., Stern, Y., Sperling, R., Ferris, S.: Promising developments in neuropsychological approaches for the detection of preclinical Alzheimer's disease: a selective review. Alzheimer's Res. Ther. **5**(6), 1–10 (2013)

18. Sudlow, C.: Uk biobank: an open access resource for identifying the causes of a wide range of complex diseases of middle and old age. PLoS Med. **12**(3), e1001779 (2015)

19. Tran, L., Liu, X., Zhou, J., Jin, R.: Missing modalities imputation via cascaded residual autoencoder. In: 2017 IEEE Conference on Computer Vision and Pattern Recognition (CVPR), pp. 4971–4980 (2017). https://doi.org/10.1109/CVPR.2017.528

20. Troyanskaya, O.: Missing value estimation methods for DNA microarrays. Bioinformatics **17**(6), 520–525 (2001)

21. Vincent, P., Larochelle, H., Bengio, Y., Manzagol, P.A.: Extracting and composing robust features with denoising autoencoders. In: Proceedings of the 25th International Conference on Machine Learning, pp. 1096–1103 (2008)

22. Weinberger, K.Q., Saul, L.K.: Distance metric learning for large margin nearest neighbor classification. J. Mach. Learn. Res. **10**(2), 207–244 (2009)

23. World Health Organisation: Depression (2021). https://www.who.int/news-room/fact-sheets/detail/depression Accessed 12 Dec 2021

24. Xu, Y., Zhang, Z., You, L., Liu, J., Fan, Z., Zhou, X.: scIGANs: single-cell RNA-seq imputation using generative adversarial networks. Nucleic Acids Res. **48**(15), e85–e85 (2020). https://doi.org/10.1093/nar/gkaa506

25. Yoon, J., Jordon, J., van der Schaar, M.: GAIN: missing data imputation using generative adversarial nets. In: Dy, J., Krause, A. (eds.) Proceedings of the 35th International Conference on Machine Learning. Proceedings of Machine Learning Research, vol. 80, pp. 5689–5698. PMLR (2018). https://proceedings.mlr.press/v80/yoon18a.html

26. Yuan, L., Wang, Y., Thompson, P.M., Narayan, V.A., Ye, J.: Multi-source learning for joint analysis of incomplete multi-modality neuroimaging data. In: Proceedings of the 18th ACM SIGKDD International Conference on Knowledge Discovery and Data Mining, pp. 1149–1157 (2012)

27. Zhang, C., Han, Z., Cui, y., Fu, H., Zhou, J.T., Hu, Q.: CPM-Nets: cross partial multi-view networks. In: Wallach, H., Larochelle, H., Beygelzimer, A., d'Alché-Buc, F., Fox, E., Garnett, R. (eds.) Advances in Neural Information Processing Systems, vol. 32. Curran Associates, Inc. (2019). https://proceedings.neurips.cc/paper/2019/file/11b9842e0a271ff252c1903e7132cd68-Paper.pdf

28. Zhou, T., Thung, K.H., Liu, M., Shi, F., Zhang, C., Shen, D.: Multi-modal latent space inducing ensemble SVM classifier for early dementia diagnosis with neuroimaging data. Med. Image Anal. **60**, 101630 (2020)

EdgeVR360: Edge-Assisted Multiuser-Oriented Intelligent 360-degree Video Delivery Scheme over Wireless Networks

Zihao Chen[1], Longhao Zou[1,2], Xiaofeng Tao[1,3], Long Xu[1,4(✉)],
Gabriel-Miro Muntean[5], and Xu Wang[6]

[1] Peng Cheng Laboratory, Shenzhen 518000, China
{chenzh03,zoulh}@pcl.ac.cn

[2] Institute of Future Networks, Southern University of Science and Technology,
Shenzhen 518055, China

[3] National Engineering Laboratory for Mobile Network Technologies,
Beijing University of Posts and Telecommunications, Beijing 100876, China
taoxf@bupt.edu.cn

[4] State Key Laboratory of Space Weather, National Space Science Center,
Chinese Academy of Sciences, Beijing 100190, China
lxu@nao.cas.cn

[5] Performance Engineering Lab, Dublin City University, Dublin 9, Ireland
gabriel.muntean@dcu.ie

[6] College of Computer Science and Software Engineering, Shenzhen University,
Shenzhen 518060, China
wangxu@szu.edu.cn

Abstract. The COVID-19 situation has determined many people all over the world to experience remote work, study and play although most of them were not prepared for such a change in their lifestyle. With the coming of the high demand of virtual interaction, 360-degree Virtual Reality (VR) technologies and applications have established stronger relationships with your peers and friends if it applies. However, higher quality of VR streaming brings users deeper immersive experience which requires greater network bandwidth and latency, and more powerful computation capability for individuals. To address these issues, the proposed intelligent video delivery scheme in this paper takes advantage of the edge-assisted computational power to improve the multi-user oriented watching experience of high quality 360-degree video over wireless networks, which reduces network resource utilization, and also optimizes edge cache hit ratio and user's Field of View (FoV) quality.

Keywords: 360-degree videos · Edge computing · Deep reinforcement learning · Wireless network

ⓒ The Author(s), under exclusive license to Springer Nature Switzerland AG 2022
L. Fang et al. (Eds.): CICAI 2022, LNAI 13605, pp. 242–255, 2022.
https://doi.org/10.1007/978-3-031-20500-2_20

1   Introduction

YouTube launched its 360-degree video playback service roughly at the same time with HTC's introduction of its VIVE Head-Mounted Display (HMD) in March 2015. Google started to distribute their low-cost cardboard glasses in 2017 and following a great start with the Oculus Rift. Meta (formerly Facebook) had also been all in Metaverse applications, which started to go both wireless and stand-alone with their Oculus Quest in May 2019 and Quest 2 in September 2020. These are just some milestones in the outstanding journey Virtual Reality (VR) is making all over the world lately. Apart from Facebook and HTC, Huawei, Samsung and other major companies have released their own branded VR HMDs for the emerging and fast developing gaming and video streaming market in the past years. It is important to highlight that VR-based remote applications have been essential in 2021 as increasing number of people used them during the COVID-19 pandemic and they have continued to be fundamental in 2022 and will be so in the next few years [1]. Following the recent boost in the production and distribution of VR rich content, the 360-degree video streaming has been one of the most important VR applications, as it provides more immersive interactivity than the traditional bi-dimensional (2D) video. However, the much higher bitrate situation of 360-degree video also becomes even more challenging when considering scenarios with multiple users.

Due to the HMD Field of View (FoV) limitations (*i.e.* between 90–120°), user's real viewport is restricted to a small part of the whole 360-degree video. Unfortunately, as the real viewport projected on the 360-degree video is not generally regular, there is a need for employment of an additional warping algorithm that increases the real-time processing complexity at the server and makes difficult maintaining a smooth video playback at HMD when user's head motion is changing much.

Traditional video transmission solutions make use of cache functions only, and lack any location-specific computing-support features. Inspired by [2] that use Deep Reinforcement Learning (DRL) as part of an adaptive bitrate allocation scheme which takes delivery decisions in relation to each video chunk. Our work described in this paper employs a DRL Proximal Policy Optimization (PPO)-based algorithm [3] for global bitrate allocation scheme at the edge-side as response to video chunk requests from users in a cloud-edge-device networking context. The algorithm selects a quality level for video chunk delivery appropriate to network conditions between the cloud and edge and the edge and clients in order to improve network performance and users' viewing experience.

In this context, this paper introduces EdgeVR360, an edge-assisted multi-user intelligent scheme for 360-degree VR video delivery. EdgeVR360 is a novel scheme which employs edge-based computing to select and deliver 360° video content appropriate to user's FoV and their current networking conditions.

The major contributions of this paper are as follows:

- Introduces an edge-assisted intelligent multi-user 360-degree video delivery architecture which is proposed to enhance QoE for multiple users and the network utilization in a wireless transmission environment.

– Proposes a DRL-based global bitrate allocation scheme which applied at the edge maximizes the overall QoE for all the users. This scheme uses network state and multi-user head-motion FoV prediction information to select an appropriate quality level at each video chunk request.

The rest of this paper is organized as follows. Section 2 discusses existing research works related to 360-degree video delivery, deep reinforcement learning, cache placement policy and edge computing. Section 3 describes the system architecture of the proposed EdgeVR360 scheme. Section 4 describes in details the proposed DRL-based global bitrate allocation scheme. Section 5 presents the implementation and evaluation of the proposed EdgeVR360 solution, respectively. Finally, conclusions are drawn in Sect. 6.

2   Related Works

2.1   360-degree Video

Unlike the traditional limited FoV 2D videos, 360-degree videos provide an omni-directional view of the content in order to support an immersive user experience. Users can change the viewing direction through yaw, pitch and roll and select their region of interest. 360-degree videos are usually projected to 2D planes which also introduce distortions, and the degree of distortion depends on the projection method employed. For example, the Equirectangular Projection (ERP) is an equidistant projection makes serious distortions at the south and north poles, which results into a significant number of redundant samples [4]. Another popular method is the Cubemap Projection (CMP) which projects the 360-degree content from a sphere onto six projection planes of a cube which leads to image discontinuities [5]. In order to address these problems, an ERP-based content-aware CMP projection method [6] was proposed to preserve the integrity of most objects in six projection planes of the 360-degree content.

2.2   DRL-Based 360-degree Video Delivery

Deep Reinforcement learning is used to solve a problem by performing actions in a process of interaction between an agent and environment. The actions are performed according to a policy and are based on the feedback from environment. Solutions described in [7–11] utilize DRL to generate bitrate allocation schemes for dynamically and optimally choosing bitrates for tiles of each chunk. In order to improve the FoV-aware tile prediction ratio, Kan *et al.* proposed a scalable FoV method in [8] and Jiang *et al.* introduced a tile-based prefetch scheduling algorithm in [10], respectively. Unfortunately, most of the existing DRL-based solutions focus on individual end-user only, without considering that often more than one end-user is watching the same 360-degree VR videos. Bilal *et al.* [12] used edge computing to realize real-time multimedia interaction and transmission. However, transcoding of 360-degree video may not be possible to be performed by current network equipment due to both frequent requests and heavy computation requirements associated with tile-based encoding.

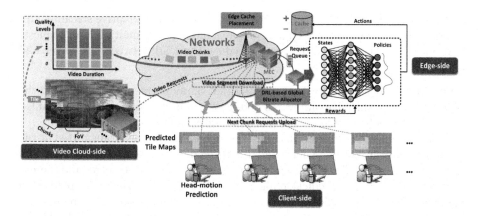

Fig. 1. Architecture of the multi-user edge-assisted 360-degree video delivery framework

Compared to the traditional content delivery architectures, the proposed EdgeVR360 scheme addresses these issues by deploying the solution at network edge and so it is friendly to the mobile devices with limited hardware characteristics. It also utilizes global delivery-related information including that about multiple users, edge cache status, and available bandwidth to optimize multi-user QoE at the same time, unlike existing solutions [13] which focus on a single viewer.

3   System Architecture

Figure 1 illustrates the system architecture of the proposed edge-assisted 360-degree video transmission framework which optimizes users' viewing QoE in a multi-user context. The architecture can be divided into three components, located at the cloud, edge and client. The architecture deploys the proposed EdgeVR360 streaming solution, a tile-based FoV-driven method, which employs ERP for the 360-degree video projection. Following Dynamic Adaptive Streaming over HTTP (DASH) [14] recommendations, the ERP 360-degree videos are segmented into multiple video chunks in the time dimension and each video chunk is re-encoded at different quality levels, and each video chunk is divided into tiles in the spatial dimension. The cloud stores all generated video chunks and tiles. The client-side consists of many users who watch the 360-degree videos from their devices.

The Cloud. In the proposed framework, the video cloud server stores DASH-based pre-processed 360-degree videos in terms of chunks and tiles. The tiles are transcoded into different quality levels, as illustrated in Fig. 1. We assume that K ERP 360-degree videos are ready for pre-processing. Each video is divided into J_k chunks, and each chunk is sliced into I tiles spatially. Finally, each tile is encoded at N different quality levels with the corresponding meta information stored in the Media Presentation Description (MPD) file, ready for adaptive streaming. In the proposed framework, the edge aggregates intelligently multiple user requests and optimizes the network delivery to reduce the load between the server and clients.

The Client. At the client, it is expected that many users are distributed in the coverage area of the edge and watch 360-degree videos from multimedia-enabled devices, such as head mounted displays, mobile phones, or computers.

Due to bandwidth limitations, only the viewpoint tiles are transmitted at the highest quality level. The client's goal is to enable user have high QoE all the time. Unfortunately, due to viewer head movement, user FoV changes and there is a need for a viewpoint prediction algorithm [7,15–18]. The viewpoint prediction algorithm we used considers past head motion to estimate some viewpoints and prefetch right video chunks and inform the edge so tile selection will also be performed at appropriate quality levels.

When the cache occupancy o^u of the u-th user is less than the maximum size of the cache occupancy o_{max}, the user actively sends a video chunk request to the edge, including the video index k, video chunk index j, user ID u, cache occupancy o^u, quality perceived by the user in the first frame of the $(j-1)$-th chunk $q^u_{k,j-1}$ and the predicted viewpoint. Following the request, the edge returns the appropriate chunk to the user.

The Edge. The edge optimizes the transmission between the cloud and clients and can be deployed at a cache-enabled base station. We use the base station's storage capacity as the edge cache, and its computing capability to support the proposed request management mechanism and DRL-based global bitrate allocation scheme. Next, the request management and edge caching will be described in details. The DRL-based global bitrate allocation scheme will be introduced in Sect. 4.

The request management controls all video chunk requests from the clients. When the edge receives a video chunk request from a user, the request management processes the video chunk request as follows. First, according to the MPD file received from the cloud and information of the prefetched chunk, the tile grid of the prefetched chunk is found. Secondly, the predicted FoV is projected into the tile grid based on the ERP format, namely the predicted tile map. We define the sets of tiles in the tile grid covered by the user's FoV as $x^u_{k,j}$ and by the predicted FoV as $\hat{x}^u_{k,j}$, respectively. Assuming that the set of all tiles in the j-th chunk of 360-degree video k is $\tilde{x}_{k,j}$, then the tile map of the u-th user's FoV $x^u_{k,j} \subseteq \tilde{x}_{k,j}$ and the tile map of u-th user's predicted FoV $\hat{x}^u_{k,j} \subseteq \tilde{x}_{k,j}$. Finally, the video chunk request stores $\hat{x}^u_{k,j}$, and waits for the next process of the DRL-based global bitrate allocation scheme.

For convenience, in the t-th execution of the DRL-based global bitrate allocation scheme, we combine those video chunk requests as a tile request $g_t = (k, \bar{o}_t, c_t, \bar{\mathbb{U}}_t, \vec{x}_t, \bar{q}_t)$. c_t is the number of chunks remaining in the k-th video. Assuming that $\mathbb{U}$ is a set of all client users, $\bar{\mathbb{U}}_t \subseteq \mathbb{U}$ indicates a set of users who need to prefetch the same video chunk. $\vec{x}_t$ is a set that contains $\hat{x}^u_{k,j}$ of each user.

$\bar{q}_{k,j-1}$ is an average quality perceived by $\bar{\mathbb{U}}_t$.

$$\bar{q}_{k,j} = \frac{\sum_{u \in \bar{\mathbb{U}}_t} q_{k,j}^u}{|\bar{\mathbb{U}}_t|} \tag{1}$$

The edge cache temporarily stores tiles downloaded from the cloud for the purpose of reusing them in order to reduce the pressure on network bandwidth resources from the cloud to the edge. However, the storage capacity of the edge cache is limited and it is unrealistic to store tiles for a long time. When the edge cache is full, new tiles should be used to replace some tiles already stored in the edge cache. Least Recently Used (LRU) and Least Frequently Used (LFU) are common legacy cache policies and often used for cache memory management.

In this paper, we propose a edge cache placement scheduling scheme for the tile-level cache management, extending existing LRU chunk-level policies. After the global bitrate allocation scheme selects an appropriate quality level according the tile request and network conditions, the corresponding tiles are retrieved from edge cache, spliced into a complete video chunk and transmitted to the client.

4   DRL-Based Global Bitrate Allocation

Extending from the DRL Proximal Policy Optimization (PPO) algorithm introduced in [3], the global DRL-based bitrate allocation scheme is proposed to select an appropriate quality level for the video tiles in order to best balance the pressure on the network bandwidth resources between the cloud and edge and between the edge and clients and improve users' viewing experience.

In the proposed framework, the agent defined in the DRL algorithm as a global bitrate allocator trains a DRL neural network with learnable parameters θ, which represents the DRL decision policy. Generally, the request g groups the information sent from the request management and contains the average cache occupancy $\bar{o}$ of each user, the number of remaining chunks c of the corresponding video, the set of the client users $\bar{\mathbb{U}}$ who need to prefetch the same video chunk, a vector-based tile map $\vec{x}$ that contains the predicted FoV $\hat{x}$ of each user and the average perceived quality $\bar{q}$ for the users $\bar{\mathbb{U}}$, computed using Eq. (1). Next the request g received by the global bitrate allocator and the average historical bandwidth $\bar{b}$ estimated by the past downloading are imported by the trained DRL network as state s. Finally, the trained DRL network outputs a quality level as an action a. Note that the client perceived quality is used as the reward r in DRL training. The details of the DRL-based bitrate allocator are introduced next.

State Space. According to the DRL-based neural network presented in Fig. 2, the environment state of the t-th request for the k-th video can be expressed as $s_t = \left(k, c_t, \bar{o}_t, \bar{q}_{k,j-1}, \vec{b}_n, \vec{d}_n, \vec{z}_t, \vec{q}_t \right)$. c_t denotes the number of chunks remaining in the video. $\bar{o}_t$ is the current cache occupancy for each user within the t-th request. $\bar{q}_{k,j-1}$ is the average perceived quality of the $(j-1)$-th chunk in the

k-th video for the set of users $\bar{\mathbb{U}}$ found in the t-th request. $\vec{b}_n$ and $\vec{d}_n$ are the average historical bandwidth and duration of the past n downloaded chunks from the edge to the client, respectively. Similarly, $\vec{z}_t$ and $\vec{q}'_t$ are the vectors that represent the available transmission sizes of quality level M and estimated quality values of the tile map $\vec{x}$ covered by the predicted FoV, respectively.

Action Space. Figure 2 illustrates how the environment makes available a set of actions from which the agent chooses one action in each state. It also shows a list of state-action pairs, where $(s_t, a_{t,m})$ indicates the m-th quality level action performed with an appropriate probability in state s_t, following the t-th request. In general, the highest action probability in a state determines the quality level for the bitrate selection of the tiles for the next chunk transmission. For example, if the action $a_{t,m}$ is made by the global bitrate allocator (i.e. agent), the predicted tiles of $\vec{x}$ encoded at the adapted bitrate ϕ_t related to the quality level m are assigned for the next chunk transmission to the relevant users. In order to improve the user perceived quality for the first chunk, a fixed action with a good quality level is selected as the input state, without considering any historical bandwidth information.

Reward. When the next action is performed by the agent, the relevant tiles with the selected quality level are stitched into a complete chunk, and then transmitted to the users who have initiated the video request. Afterwards the perceived quality of users who have watched these video chunks are collected for computation of a reward, which is fed into the DRL model training of the next request. Inspired by the general QoE metric used by MPC [19], the training reward denoted as r_t is defined as:

$$r_t = \bar{q}_{k,j} - |\bar{q}_{k,j} - \bar{q}_{k,j-1}| - \bar{\mu}_{k,j} \qquad (2)$$

The first item $\bar{q}_{k,j}$ is the average perceived quality of users who have watched the new chunks after the last action was taken. The second item $|\bar{q}_{k,j} - \bar{q}_{k,j-1}|$ presents the penalty of perceived quality variation that indicates the smoothness of chunk quality adaptation. The last item $\bar{\mu}_{k,j}$ denotes the penalty of average rebuffering time of users who have watched the new chunks. Considering that there is a certain difference in the current bandwidth of each user $u \in \bar{\mathbb{U}}_t$, the average rebuffering time $\bar{\mu}_{k,j}$ of the chunk is calculated as:

$$\bar{\mu}_{k,j} = \frac{\sum_{u \in \bar{\mathbb{U}}_t} \mu_{k,j}^u}{|\bar{\mathbb{U}}_t|}, \qquad (3)$$

where $\mu_{k,j}^u$ is the rebuffering time after the user u downloaded the new chunk.

In this work, the perceived quality of user FoV is estimated in terms of the Peak Signal to Noise Ratio (PSNR) and distortion of each tile is measured in terms of the Mean Square Error (MSE). We define the FoV quality distortion value $w_{k,j}^u$ as a weighted sum of the distortion of all I tiles.

$$w_{k,j}^u = max(\frac{1}{|x_{k,j}^u|} \sum_{i=1}^{I} \eta_{k,j,i} \times p_{k,j,i}, \zeta) \qquad (4)$$

where $\eta_{k,j,i}$ is an indicator that represents whether the i-th tile of the j-th chunk of the video k is in the user's FoV $x_{k,j}^u$. If the tile is in $x_{k,j}^u$, $\eta_{k,j,i} = 1$, otherwise $\eta_{k,j,i} = 0$. $f(k, j, i, \phi_i)$ indicates the file size of the tile, $p_{k,j,i}$ is the MSE value of the tile and ζ is the minimum MSE value in case the denominator is zero when calculating PSNR.

$q_{k,j}^u$ can be converted into a normalized PSNR as follows:

$$q_{k,j}^u = \log_{10}(\frac{255^2}{w_{k,j}^u}) \div \log_{10}(\frac{255^2}{\zeta}) \tag{5}$$

As the goal of our framework is not only to improve overall users' viewing experience, but also to make users' experience similar, we define the QoE metric for all users U as:

$$QoE = \sum_j^J \sum_u^U q_{k,j}^u - |q_{k,j}^u - q_{k,j-1}^u| - \mu_{k,j}^u. \tag{6}$$

Additionally, we use the variance of PSNR in the users' FoV in the first frame of each video chunk to quantify the fairness of the viewing experience among all users.

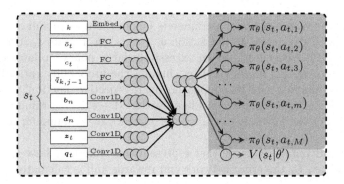

Fig. 2. Neural network of the global bitrate allocator. *Embed* indicates the word embedding layer, *FC* indicates the fully connection layer, and *Conv1D* indicates the 1-dimension convolution layer.

Neural Network. The global bitrate allocator's policy π modeling the agent's action selections associates to the parameter vector θ, which is shown in Fig. 2. As for the k-th video's name, we use a word embedding layer to convert it into a vector instead of directly inputting it into the network, which allows the network to extract possible feature vectors during the model training for expressing the semantics of the video name. In Fig. 2, $\vec{z}_t, \vec{q}_t, \vec{b}_n, \vec{d}_n$ are calculated by a 1-dimension convolution layer, $c_t, \bar{o}_t, \bar{q}_{k,j-1}$ are calculated by a fully connected layer, and then all outputs are inputted into a fully connected layer for feature fusion to obtain the current state vector. In order to avoid a too large policy update during the DRL model training, the PPO-Clip algorithm [3], an alternative heuristic way of performing lower bound optimization is adopted to constraint the policy change in a small range based on clipped surrogate objective function. While an action is made, the training network also generates a corresponding state value $V(s_t)$ and the probability distribution calculated by two fully connected layers, respectively. Finally an action $a_{t,m}$ is determined by a softmax layer according to the probability distribution.

Training. When the neural network is trained by the PPO-Clip algorithm [3], an Actor-Critic based strategy gradient method from reinforcement learning is used to predict the gradient of average discount reward value $R_t = \sum_{i=t}^{T} \gamma^{i-t} r_i$ where T is the number of requests and γ is a discount factor. During the iteration process, $(s_t, a_{t,m}, r_t, s_{t+1})$ will be stored as empirical samples in an empirical cache for updating learnable parameters of the network. Similar to [3], the loss function of the actor network that outputs action $a_{t,m}$ is defined as:

$$L_{actor}(\theta) = \mathbb{E}_t \left[\min(\hat{r}_t(\theta) A_t, \text{clip}(\hat{r}_t, 1 + \epsilon, 1 - \epsilon) A_t) \right], \tag{7}$$

where ϵ is a hyperparameter and $\hat{r}_t(\theta)$ is the probability ratio proposed by [20] for indicating the update rate of policy parameters and is calculated as:

$$\hat{r}_t(\theta) = \frac{\pi_\theta(a_{t,m}|s_t)}{\pi_{\theta'}(a_{t,m}|s_t)} = \exp\left[\log \pi_\theta(a_{t,m}|s_t) - \log \pi_{\theta'}(a_{t,m}|s_t)\right], \tag{8}$$

where θ' is the vector of policy parameters before the update and $\pi_\theta(a_{t,m}|s_t)$ is the policy with parameter θ that action $a_{t,m}$ is taken in state s_t. However, the increase of $\hat{r}_t(\theta)$ easily leads to an excessively large policy update. Hence the second term of Eq. (7) limits $\hat{r}_t(\theta)$ by clipping the probability ratio directly in the objective function with its clipped surrogate objective function, which means that the value of $\hat{r}_t(\theta)$ is only considered within $[1 + \epsilon, 1 - \epsilon]$. Finally, it finds a lower bound of the loss value of the actor network by a minimum function for updating θ.

A_t is an advantage function that represents the difference between the state values predicted by the critic network and rewards and is calculated as:

$$A_t = \delta_t + (\gamma\lambda)\delta_{t+1} + \cdots + (\gamma\lambda)^{T-t+1}\delta_{T-1} \tag{9}$$

where

$$\delta_t = r_t + \gamma V(s_{t+1}) - V(s_t) \tag{10}$$

and λ is a discount factor.

The loss function of the critic network is defined as:

$$L_{critic}(\theta) = \mathbb{E}_t \left[\max((V_\theta(s_t) - R_t)^2, (V_\theta^{clip}(s_t) - R_t)^2) \right] \tag{11}$$

where

$$V_\theta^{clip}(s_t) = \text{clip}(V_\theta(s_t), V_{\theta'}(s_t) - \epsilon, V_{\theta'}(s_t) + \epsilon) \tag{12}$$

In Eq. (12), $V_\theta(s_t)$ is limited to the interval $[V_{\theta'}(s_t) - \epsilon, V_{\theta'}(s_t) + \epsilon]$ for training steadily the critic network. Finally, we take the average squared difference of the total discount rewards R_t and the clipped $V_\theta(s_t)$ respectively to find the maximum for inspiring the critic network, which will predict the state value more accurately. Note that the critic network is used to help the actor network during training and is no longer used during testing.

In order to make the neural network to continuously explore different states during the training process, we adopt two solutions: first, instead of using the softmax layer that only chooses the index of the maximum value from the probability distribution as an action, a specific sampler with a certain randomness is employed for action selection from the probability distribution; second, an entropy regularization term is added into the loss function of the total network, defined as:

$$L_{total}(\theta) = L_{actor}(\theta) - \beta_1 L_{critic}(\theta) + \beta_2 H(\pi_\theta(\cdot|s_t)) \tag{13}$$

where β_1 and β_2 are coefficients, and $H(\pi_\theta(\cdot|s_t))$ is the entropy regularization term for encouraging the exploration of the actor network.

$$H(\pi_\theta(\cdot|s_t)) = \sum_a \pi_\theta(a_{t,m}|s_t)log\pi_\theta(a_{t,m}|s_t) \tag{14}$$

where $\pi_\theta(a_{t,m}|s_t)$ presents the policy with parameter θ for an action of the quality level m at state s_t.

5 Evaluation and Result Analysis

5.1 Implementation and Evaluation Setup

In general, it is difficult to build a real platform to serve multiple users who watch thousands of 360-degree videos at random times, and record the instant perceived quality of each video chunk from each user. Instead a simulation environment based on Python was implemented. The environment for the process of viewing 360-degree videos by multiple users is based on the public 360-degree video dataset [21] and 4G wireless bandwidth dataset [22]. In order to train the global bitrate allocator, the learning rate is set to 10^{-4} using in Adaptive Moment Estimation (Adam) that helps to optimize stochastic gradient descent [23], and the proposed neural network is trained by choosing with the batch size of 128 for 10^5 episodes. We implement this architecture using Pytorch with GPU Nvidia Titan V. As suggested by [3], $\gamma = 0.99$, $\lambda = 0.95$, $\epsilon = 0.2$, $\beta_1 = 0.5$, and $\beta_2 = 0.01$. We limit the reward to the interval $[-1, 1]$ in order to reduce learning complexity.

5.2 Evaluation Benchmarks

The proposed EdgeVR360 solution was compared to three other adaptive streaming frameworks which are briefly discussed next. A summary of the characteristics of these different adaptive solutions is shown in Table 1. **Baseline** considers

Table 1. Characteristics of evaluation benchmarks

	Baseline	Simple	Pensieve-360	EdgeVR360
Chunk-level	Yes	Yes	Yes	Yes
Tile-level	No	Yes	Yes	Yes
ABR	Throughput-based	Throughput-based	A3C	PPO-clip
Edge-assistant	No	Yes	Yes	Yes
Deployment location	Server-side	Edge-side	Client-side	Edge-side
FoV prediction at the client-side	No	LR	LR	LR

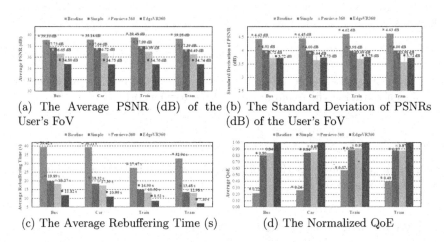

(a) The Average PSNR (dB) of the User's FoV

(b) The Standard Deviation of PSNRs (dB) of the User's FoV

(c) The Average Rebuffering Time (s)

(d) The Normalized QoE

Fig. 3. Comparisons of user perceived quality.

360-degree videos as legacy videos that are temporally divided into chunks that encoded in different quality levels [24]. **Simple** not only conducts chunk-level adaptation, but also divides a chunk into tiles, which is the same as in our proposed EdgeVR360 solution. **Pensieve – 360** is a DRL-based streaming framework for 360-degree videos assisted with edge cache, which is extended from the Pensieve [2] that conducts both chunk and tile level. **EdgeVR360** is the solution proposed in this paper. **EdgeVR360** adapts the 360-degree video at both chunk and tile levels, uses a DRL-based decision model for PPO optimization and employs a LRU-based edge cache replacement policy at the edge.

5.3   Result Analysis of User Perceived Quality

Figure 3 presents the results of user perceived quality based on the evaluation setup described above. All four solutions compared use the configurations defined in Table 1. Figure 3a shows the average PSNR results in terms of user's FoV area for all the simulated users during a 100-s video watching, and Fig. 3b illustrates the perceived quality variance in terms of the average standard PSNR deviation in each user's FoV during the whole viewing. Figure 3a demonstrates

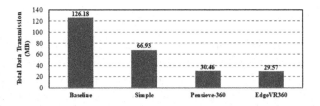

Fig. 4. Total data transmission per user

how the average PSNR values of each user's FoV when **Baseline**, **Simple** and **Pensieve − 360** are employed are all higher than that of **EdgeVR360**. The reason is that the **Baseline** and **Simple** employ a simple throughput-based ABR algorithm that considers quality level decision based on inaccurate historical throughput estimations, always transmit video to users with bitrates as high as possible or make sure that the high-quality tiles cover the users' FoV area only. However, the **Baseline** and **Simple** have worse performance on the volatility of perceived quality within the users' FoV compared against **EdgeVR360**. **EdgeVR360** reduces with about 16% the volatility of perceived quality than **Baseline** and **Simple**. These solutions find difficult to smoothen the temporal variance of perceived quality due to poor network conditions prediction. Similar to **EdgeVR360**, **Pensieve − 360** implemented the DRL-based ABR algorithm at the client and achieves good perceived. Additionally, **EdgeVR360** makes a better trade-off between the PSNR and rebuffering. Figure 3c shows how **EdgeVR360** reduces with 72%, 42%, and 38% the cumulative rebuffering time during the 100-s viewing in comparison with **Baseline**, **Simple** and **Pensieve − 360**, respectively.

5.4   Results Analysis of Network Utilization

The average received data sizes by each user during the whole 100-s transmission from the cloud to the client are illustrated in Fig. 4. During the video transmission evaluation, the four compared solutions use the settings noted in Table 1. When compared against **Baseline**, **Simple** and **Pensieve − 360**, our proposed **EdgeVR360** reduces with 77%, 56% and 3% the transmission size, respectively. In the same time, **EdgeVR360** conducts a better trade-off between the PSNR within user's FoV and rebuffering efficiency, and also maintains a higher QoE value and network utilization with the edge-assisted FoV-enabled cache policy and the global bitrate allocation scheme. Additionally, **Pensieve − 360** employs the DRL-based ABR algorithm at client-side, which requires a higher computational user-end device or hardware. It is also hard to train and update a DRL-based model on such a device and computational framework. In contrast, the edge-based framework and DRL-based application for multi-users is more powerful and flexible.

6   Conclusion

In this paper, we propose EdgeVR360, an edge-assisted intelligent 360-degree video transmission framework for multiple users in wireless network scenarios. A novel DRL-based global bitrate allocation scheme proposed in the EdgeVR360 framework utilizes the MEC-based storage and computing capacity to optimize the interaction between the client and cloud in order to improve the overall QoE of multiple users, decrease the client-side computational requirements and reduce the network bandwidth usage caused by repeated requests for content from multiple users. The experimental results show that our framework improves the QoE of multiple users and achieves higher network utilization in comparison with three alternative solutions in four different mobility scenarios and when considering four caching policies.

Acknowledgement. This research is supported by the Key-Area Research and Development Program of Guangdong Province (No. 2020B0101130006), in part by the Shenzhen Natural Science Foundation under Grants JCYJ20200109110410133, and in part by the Peng Cheng Laboratory (No. PCL2021A15). G.-M. Muntean acknowledges the support of the Science Foundation Ireland (SFI) Research Centres Programme grant number 12/RC/2289_P2 (Insight).

References

1. Alexandros, S.: Virtual Reality Has Been Boosted by Coronavirus - Here's How to Avoid It Leading Us to Dystopia, June 2020
2. Mao, H., Netravali, R., Alizadeh, M.: Neural adaptive video streaming with pensieve. In: Proceedings of the Conference of the ACM Special Interest Group on Data Communication, pp. 197–210. ACM (2017)
3. Schulman, J., Wolski, F., Dhariwal, P., Radford, A., Klimov, O.: Proximal policy optimization algorithms. CoRR, abs/1707.06347 (2017)
4. Youvalari, R.G., Aminlou, A., Hannuksela, M.M.: Analysis of regional downsampling methods for coding of omnidirectional video. In: 2016 Picture Coding Symposium (PCS), pp. 1–5 (2016)
5. Li, L., Li, Z., Ma, X., Yang, H., Li, H.: Advanced spherical motion model and local padding for 360° video compression. IEEE Trans. Image Process. **28**(5), 2342–2356 (2019)
6. Chen, Z., Wang, X., Zhou, Yu., Zou, L., Jiang, J.: Content-aware cubemap projection for panoramic image via deep Q-learning. In: Ro, Y.M., et al. (eds.) MMM 2020. LNCS, vol. 11962, pp. 304–315. Springer, Cham (2020). https://doi.org/10.1007/978-3-030-37734-2_25
7. Zhang, Y., Zhao, P., Bian, K., Liu, Y., Song, L., Li, X.: DRL360: 360-degree video streaming with deep reinforcement learning. In: IEEE INFOCOM 2019 - IEEE Conference on Computer Communications, pp. 1252–1260, April 2019
8. Kan, N., Zou, J., Tang, K., Li, C., Liu, N., Xiong, H.: Deep reinforcement learning-based rate adaptation for adaptive 360-degree video streaming. In: ICASSP 2019–2019 IEEE International Conference on Acoustics, Speech and Signal Processing (ICASSP), pp. 4030–4034, May 2019

9. Sassatelli, L., Winckler, M., Fisichella, T., Aparicio, R.: User-adaptive editing for 360 degree video streaming with deep reinforcement learning. In: Proceedings of the 27th ACM International Conference on Multimedia, pp. 2208–2210 (2019)

10. Jiang, Z., Zhang, X., Xu, Y., Ma, Z., Sun, J., Zhang, Y.: Reinforcement learning based rate adaptation for 360-degree video streaming. IEEE Trans. Broadcast. 1–15 (2020)

11. Fu, J., Chen, X., Zhang, Z., Wu, S., Chen, Z.: 360SRL: a sequential reinforcement learning approach for ABR tile-based 360 video streaming. In: 2019 IEEE International Conference on Multimedia and Expo (ICME), pp. 290–295. IEEE (2019)

12. Bilal, K., Erbad, A.: Edge computing for interactive media and video streaming. In: 2017 Second International Conference on Fog and Mobile Edge Computing (FMEC), pp. 68–73. IEEE (2017)

13. Park, S., Bhattacharya, A., Yang, Z., Dasari, M., Das, S.R., Samaras, D.: Advancing user quality of experience in 360-degree video streaming. In: 2019 IFIP Networking Conference (IFIP Networking), pp. 1–9. IEEE (2019)

14. Sodagar, I.: The MPEG-DASH standard for multimedia streaming over the internet. IEEE Multimedia **18**, 62–67 (2011)

15. Bao, Y., Wu, H., Zhang, T., Ramli, A.A., Xin, L.: Shooting a moving target: motion-prediction-based transmission for 360-degree videos. In: 2016 IEEE International Conference on Big Data (Big Data), pp. 1161–1170 (2016)

16. Guan, Y., Zheng, C., Zhang, X., Guo, Z., Jiang, J.: Pano: optimizing 360° video streaming with a better understanding of quality perception. In: Proceedings of the ACM Special Interest Group on Data Communication, pp. 394–407, August 2019

17. Qian, F., Han, B., Xiao, Q., Gopalakrishnan, V.: Flare: practical viewport-adaptive 360-degree video streaming for mobile devices. In: Proceedings of the 24th Annual International Conference on Mobile Computing and Networking, pp. 99–114 (2018)

18. Fan, C.-L., Lee, J., Lo, W.-C., Huang, C.-Y., Chen, K.-T., Hsu, C.-H.: Fixation prediction for 360∘ video streaming in head-mounted virtual reality. In: Proceedings of the 27th Workshop on Network and Operating Systems Support for Digital Audio and Video, pp. 67–72 (2017)

19. Yin, X., Jindal, A., Sekar, V., Sinopoli, B.: A control-theoretic approach for dynamic adaptive video streaming over HTTP. In: Proceedings of the 2015 ACM Conference on Special Interest Group on Data Communication, pp. 325–338 (2015)

20. Schulman, J., Levine, S., Moritz, P., Jordan, M.I., Abbeel, P.: Trust region policy optimization. CoRR, abs/1502.05477 (2015)

21. Lo, W., Fan, C., Lee, J., Huang, C., Chen, K., Hsu, C.: 360° video viewing dataset in head-mounted virtual reality. In: Proceedings of the 8th ACM on Multimedia Systems Conference, pp. 211–216, June 2017

22. Van der Hooft, J., et al.: HTTP/2-based adaptive streaming of HEVC Video Over 4G/LTE networks. IEEE Commun. Lett. **20**(11), 2177–2180 (2016)

23. Kingma, D.P., Ba, J.: Adam: a method for stochastic optimization (2017)

24. Zou, L., Trestian, R., Muntean, G.-M.: DOAS: device-oriented adaptive multimedia scheme for 3GPP LTE systems. In: 2013 IEEE 24th Annual International Symposium on Personal, Indoor, and Mobile Radio Communications (PIMRC), pp. 2180–2184 (2013)

Automatic Diagnose of Drug-Resistance Tuberculosis from CT Images Based on Deep Neural Networks

Qiuyu Du[1], Shufan Liang[2], Jixiang Guo[1], Zhang Yi[1], Weiming Li[2], Chengdi Wang[2(✉)], and Xiuyuan Xu[1(✉)]

[1] Machine Intelligence Laboratory, College of Computer Science, Sichuan University, Chengdu, China
duqiu20@stu.scu.edu.cn, {guojixiang,zhangyi,xuxiuyuan}@scu.edu.cn
[2] Department of Respiratory and Critical Care Medicine, Med-X Center for Manufacturing, West China Hospital, West China School of Medicine, Sichuan University, Chengdu, China
{weimi003,chengdi_wang}@scu.edu.cn@scu.edu.cn

Abstract. Tuberculosis was discovered about 130 years ago and has remained a persistent threat and leading cause of death worldwide. Drug therapy is currently one of the effective treatments for pulmonary tuberculosis. Tuberculosis can be divided into drug-sensitive and drug-resistant tuberculosis in terms of its drug resistance. The timely identification of drug-resistant from drug-sensitive tuberculosis is vital for effective clinical treatment and improving the cure rate of patients. The most commonly used methods of drug-resistant detection are either expensive or time-consuming (up to several months). Therefore, an effective and affordable method for early drug-resistant screening is urgently required. Automatic diagnosis using computed Tomography is one of the possible approaches for this requirement. Although there have been some applications of deep learning-based algorithms on this task, open-source datasets are lacking to support clinical significance. In this paper, a novel method is proposed to distinguish drug-resistant tuberculosis from drug-sensitive tuberculosis. First, an annotated dataset is constructed based on the clinical pathological report, in which 101 drug-sensitive cases and 304 drug-resistant cases are collected and preprocessed. Then, we employ a three-dimensional residual network as the backbone and propose a lesion slice selection strategy to train the constructed model effectively. At last, we reimplement existing methods using the constructed dataset for comparison. Extensive experimental results demonstrate that the proposed method performs the best classification with a rate of 92.21% and an AUC value of 93.50%, significantly exceeding the current baseline results.

Keywords: Neural networks · Tuberculosis · Differential diagnosis · Drug-resistance

This work was supported by the National Natural Science Foundation of China under Grant 62106163 and by the National Natural Science Foundation of China under Grant 82100119 and the CAAI-Huawei MindSpore Open Fund.

L. Fang et al. (Eds.): CICAI 2022, LNAI 13605, pp. 256–267, 2022.
https://doi.org/10.1007/978-3-031-20500-2_21

1   Introduction

Tuberculosis (TB) is an infectious disease that is one of the leading causes of death worldwide. The global number of deaths officially classified as caused by TB was 1.3 million in 2020. The drug-resistant (DR) TB cases, defined as resistance to anti-TB drugs, have been rising over the years. Approximately 2.1 million cases are resistant to the first-line anti-TB drug rifampicin [22]. Further, the COVID-19 pandemic reduced access to TB diagnosis and treatment, leading to increased TB deaths, especially in poverty areas.

There are two typical types of TB, drug-sensitive (DS) and drug-resistant (DR). The organisms resistant to two or more standard anti-TB drugs are called DR TB, while DS TB does not develop resistance to anti-TB drugs. Primary resistance occurs when a person becomes infected with a resistant strain of TB. A patient with DS TB may develop secondary (acquired) resistance during therapy because of inadequate treatment, not taking the prescribed regimen appropriately (lack of compliance), or using low-quality medication [18]. In contrast to DS TB, the DR form requires more prolonged treatment and is expensive to recover from completely. Thus, early TB detection is conductive to control DS TB from infection with resistant strain to avoid resistant strain from DR patient spread.

In clinic practice, many tests, like the sputum smear test and polymerase chain reaction, are employed for DR detection. However, some of these tests are time-consuming (up to several months) and have low efficacy rates, and others are not specific in differentiating TB types. An effective and affordable method for early DR detection is urgently required. One of the possible approaches is the utilization of radiological imaging, including X-rays and computed tomography (CT). Compared to chest X-ray (CXR), high-resolution CT is more sensitive to determining TB disease activity and characterizing subtle diseases. Cha et al. [3] confirmed the superiority of CT over CXR in characterizing the details of pulmonary TB lesions.

With the wide adoption of deep learning, significant strides have been made in the domain of medical imaging-based clinical diagnosis. In recent years, deep learning approaches have been applied in medical imaging analysis to provide immediate diagnostic support for clinicians [25,26]. However, the success of these deep learning approaches is based on extensive and high-quality datasets [21]. The current open-source CT images dataset is limited to very few TB detection tasks [15,16]. Due to the limitation of the existing dataset, deep learning is hard to be applied to the DR detection task. To solve this problem, a manually annotated dataset named TRDD (tuberculosis resistance detection dataset) is constructed in our work. The TRDD consists of 405 TB cases collected from 116 patients, including 101 DS TB cases and 304 DR TB cases. The TRDD is annotated and labeled based on the pathological reports, making each label well and truly. Besides, morphology features of lesions were labeled, such as fibrosis, miliary, and cavity, to support further research.

As abnormalities of TB are only limited to small regions, a lesion slice selection (LSS) strategy, which involves using a subset of lesion slices, is proposed. The

LSS is capable of removing redundant information from CT images while maintaining the inherent features of TB lesions. In this paper, a 3-D ResNet is applied to extract characteristics of the DR TB in CT images on the constructed TRDD, which is able to encode and extract enriched spatial information from medical image sequences. To demonstrate the effectiveness of the LSS method, extensive experiments are conducted, and the results show that the LSS method is effective in feature extraction. The results show that the LSS integrated ResNet performs better than any of the current DR detection methods with 92.21% accuracy.

In summary, the contributions of this study are as follows:

1. To further investigate DR detection, a novel dataset of 405 clinical cases is annotated and labeled manually by clinicians based on their pathological reports.
2. An effective LSS method combined with ResNet is proposed to diagnose DR TB on the CT image dataset.
3. Extensive experiments are conducted to show the state-of-the-art performance of the proposed method.

2   Related Works

Deep learning-oriented approaches have already been applied to medical images in the TB screen and detection domain and achieved promising results [13,19]. The works related to TB fall into three main categories: TB screening, tuberculosis, and lung cancer detection, and classification of TB types.

The work [15] presented 3D deep convolutional auto-encoder networks applied to the left and right lungs separately to screen TB CT images from healthy people and detect the location of TB lesions. Wong et al. [23] observed the spatial relationships between the feature vectors and proposed a novel context-aware graph neural network, which further improved the performance of classification of TB cases and healthy people with 98.93% accuracy.

Since TB and lung cancer share the same clinical as well as radiological features, which may lead to clinical misdiagnosis, Cui et al. [5] validated handcrafted radiomics features for distinguishing pulmonary TB from lung cancer based on CT images. Then, Hankare and Shirguppikar [9] proposed a more automatic threshold method allied to VGG-19 in detecting tuberculosis and lung cancer with higher accuracy.

The challenging task, automatic detection of TB types, is raised to deliver optimal treatment for TB patients. Gao et al. [6] proposed an enhanced ResNet deep learning network that injects depth information of CT images at each process block to classify the five types of TB. However, the small dataset and imbalanced data distribution make it difficult to distinguish the characteristics of some TB. To contend with smaller datasets with imbalanced distribution,

Aghajanzadeh et al. [1] used data duplication and augmentation techniques and considered variable penalties for different classes. Other tasks such as analyzing TB severity levels and generating quantitative CT reports are investigated in [7,17].

To date, only a few works have been engaged in discriminating between DS TB and DR TB. Ahmed et al. [2] proposed two different approaches based on the mean and higher-order moments and texture analysis-based features to classify tuberculosis images. However, hand-crafted features have limited representation and are usually insufficient for differentiating lesions from their hard mimics in complex environments. Further, Gao and Qian [8] proposed a 2-D patch-based deep convolutional neural network (CNN) with a support vector machine (SVM) classifier to predict multi-drug resistant TB in a more full-automatic way.

3 Data Collection

From October 2009 to January 2021, a total of 405 examinations from 116 pulmonary tuberculosis (PTB) patients were retrospectively retrieved from the imaging database of West China Hospital, Sichuan University, China. All CTs were collected via a radiology report search of CTs. To start with, the dataset was collected using DeepLNAnno, an online annotation system proposed in our preceding work [4]. After that, 25 CTs that had been incorrectly extracted were excluded from the dataset after image labeling. In this dataset, 1673 PTB lesions were collected in total, of which 784 PTB lesions from 101 cases were drug-sensitive (DS), and 889 PTB lesions from 304 cases were drug-resistant (DR). The PTB lesions were annotated and labeled by clinical physicians on collected CT images pathological reports. The dataset includes only HIV-negative patients having one of the two forms of TB, DS or DR. The DR class includes patients with rifampin resistance (RIFR) TB, multi-drug resistant (MDR), or extensively drug-resistant (XDR). Meanwhile, morphology features of lesions were labeled, such as fibrosis, miliary, and cavity. The detail of data distribution is shown in Table 1.

Table 1. Overview of numbers of data and distribution of data that collected in the TRDD.

	Patients	Examinations	Lesions
DS-TB	42	101	784
DR-TB	47	213	596
RIFR	15	46	121
MDR-TB	1	2	14
XDR-TB	11	43	158
Total	116	405	1673

4   Method

4.1   Lesion Slice Selection Method

The CT images have a difference in the number of slices and voxel size. Since the origin CT images contain much redundant information, such as bronchia and other lung parenchyma. However, abnormalities of TB occupy only limited regions, and the preprocessing technique is necessary to be applied for removing redundant pixels from CT. Thus, CT images are preprocessed first according to experimental design. Specifically, the following steps are executed. Firstly, the largest plane of each lesion in two dimensions is annotated. Since a lesion at volume level contains inner features, the depth of each lesion cube is calculated, which is half the sum of the lesion's length and width. The PTB lesions are cropped using the annotations into small cubes. The slice distance in each lesion is adjusted to $1 \times 1 \times 1$ mm to eliminate spacing differences. To obtain data consistency, lesions are resized into uniform sizes of $M \times M \times N$ with bicubic interpolation, called lesion-based patches.

There are multiple lesions of TB in each CT case, and the number of lesions varies. In order to locate and analyze all TB lesions on each CT case, the LSS strategy is introduced. Figure 1 shows a visual representation of the LSS. Furthermore, the algorithm is summarized in Algorithm 1. Firstly, the number of lesions in an individual case is counted. The given depth size N divided by the number of lesions is the partition length. The middle slices with the same length as the partition are extracted. The middle slice of the lesions is obtained by taking half of the volume depth of the lesions. All extracted lesions of an individual case are then stacked to reconstruct the desired volume, which is a depth size of N, called a patient-based patch.

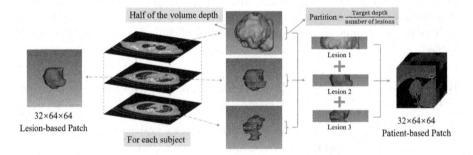

Fig. 1. Lesion slice selection method with a depth size of 32 and a width (height) size of 64.

4.2   3-D Classification Model

The applied neural network architecture implemented in this study is described in Fig. 2. The figure shows that lesion-based and patient-based patches are input

---

Algorithm 1. Lesion Slice Selection (LSS) data processing method

---

Require: A 3D volumetric image scan I; Two annotated coordinates of a lesion, (x_1, y_1) and (x_2, y_2).

Ensure: I is a rank 3 tensor; The lesion of dimension $L_w \times L_h$.

1: Compute *depth* of a lesions by $L_d = \frac{L_w + L_h}{2}$.

2: Crop lesion by two annotated coordinates with size of $L_w \times L_h \times L_d$ denoted as M_c.

3: Set constant target depth of size N and target width (height) of size M.

4: Count all tuberculosis lesions on 3D image scan of a case, denoted as n.

5: Compute partition number of slices selected for each lesion of a case by $N_s = \lceil \frac{N}{n} \rceil$.

6: Select middle N_s slices of each lesion of a case and stack all lesions in a case together with size $L_w \times L_h \times N$, denoted as M_p.

7: Resize M_p into size of $M \times M \times N$.

---

into these networks. Generally, two-dimensional(2-D) CNNs are unable to capture information that exists among slices because they take a single slice as input, and the training process is applied to each slice [12]. Thus, some of the spatial information gets lost in the process. However, 3-D kernels over height, width, and depth dimensions can directly catch the spatial features from stereo images. To this end, the DR detection model is built upon a three-dimensional (3-D) residual network (ResNet) [10] to capture the abnormalities characteristics of TB from CT images with limited regions.

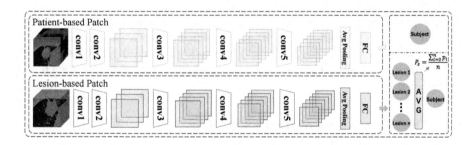

Fig. 2. Workflow of the whole model for DR detection.

4.3 Multiple Lesion-Based Patch Scoring

While each lesion-based patch can be classified into either DS or DR type, the determination of a case with multiple lesion-based patches is based on collecting all lesion-based patch scores accommodating both DS and DR clusters. All the lesion-based patches of TB in a single case are gathered to calculate the DR detection score for that case. The ensemble case score S_c is defined as,

$$S_c(x) = \frac{\sum_{i=1}^{N} \text{Prob}(x_i)}{N}, \tag{1}$$

where the classification results of each case are determined by

$$E(S_c) = \begin{cases} 0, S_c \geq th \\ 1, \text{otherwise}. \end{cases} \qquad (2)$$

5 Experiment

5.1 Implementation Details

The penalty loss function proposed in [24] is used in our ResNet to distinguish between false negative and false positive nodules by penalizing each error differently. To contend with a small dataset and avoid over-fitting, the depth of the network is set to 18. To accelerate the convergence rate of ResNet, transfer learning is utilized by first training 18-layer ResNet on the Kinetics dataset [14]. Five 5-fold cross-validations were conducted, in which four subsets were used to train the model, and the remainder was used for testing in each experiment. Each subset does not share the same patients. A model is trained for 200 epochs, and its parameters are saved at the best Area Under Curve (AUC). Stochastic gradient descent (SGD) is employed as optimization algorithm to iteratively update neural network weights based on training data. The learning rate (LR) is initialized to $1e-3$ at the beginning and is divided by ten after every 50 epochs. The batch size is set to 32. Random crop augmentation is applied to strengthen the generalization ability of the training model.

The performance is evaluated by the mean and standard deviation of accuracy (ACC), AUC, recall, precision, and specificity with a cut-off value of 0.5 and an F1 score. The experiment is conducted with one Tesla V100 (32GB) GPU using CUDA 10.1. The network was coded and built using Python 3.6 and Pytorch 1.0.0.

5.2 The Effectiveness of the LSS Strategy

To verify the effectiveness of the LSS method, the preprocessing without the LSS method is conducted with ResNet. Because TB lesions vary in size, the depth size N is set to 32 and the width (height) size M is set to 64 to accommodate the size of most lesions in this experiment. All lesions, extracted by annotations and resized into $32 \times 64 \times 64$ of an individual case, are stacked. The number of lesions of an individual case is denoted as n, and the stacked lesions of size $(32 \times n) \times 64 \times 64$ is resized directly into $32 \times 64 \times 64$. As a result, the evaluation metric of the final classification where both with LSS methods and without are listed in Table 2. As illustrated in Table 2, ResNet with the LSS method significantly performs better than without one. Figure 3 gives the confusion matrix of ResNet with the proposed LSS method, where the max accuracy result is 92.86%. Besides, as shown in Fig. 3, some DS TB is wrongly classified as DR TB, and the classification results of DR TB are better than DS TB. In clinical practice, misclassifying a DS TB as DR one may be costlier than misclassifying a DR TB as DS one, thus missing the opportunity to treat patients with DR

TB timely. Receiver operating characteristic (ROC) curves on DR detection are shown in Fig. 4, which shows that ResNet with the LSS method achieves the mean AUC of 0.935. Since the TRDD is annotated in 2-D, calculating the depth of the lesion by the length and width of the annotation box will bring in some redundant information. However, the LSS method effectively captures the slices with the most concentrated features of a lesion, which fuses all the lesions of an individual case to retain useful features as much as possible. Thus, it shows that the LSS method can help ResNet to extract the CT image features of lesions more efficiently and accurately.

Table 2. The classification results.

	Acc	AUC	Recall	Precision	Specificity	F1
With LSS	**92.21** ± 0.60	**93.50** ± 0.91	86.43 ± 1.05	**94.97** ± 0.81	**86.34** ± 2.29	**90.49** ± 0.37
Without LSS	82.76 ± 1.60	80.65 ± 0.93	**86.88** ± 1.12	87.77 ± 1.17	62.78 ± 2.04	87.12 ± 0.78

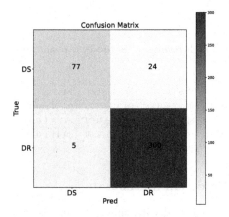

Fig. 3. Confusion matrix.   **Fig. 4.** ROC curve.

While a CNN may be considered a black box, two gradient-weighted class activation mapping (Grad-CAM) [20] of DS and DR samples are exhibited visually in Fig. 5 to present visual explanations from a ResNet integrated with the proposed LSS, which indicates that the concentrations of the ResNet focus on the lesions, as well as the micro-environment around the lesion.

(a) DS sample.   (b) DR sample.

Fig. 5. Grad-CAM.

5.3   Lesion-Based Patch vs Patient-Based Patch

On account of the number of images in the dataset is limited in the medical domain, dividing each case into smaller patches is a way to increase the amount of data [11]. In this section, we divide each CT scan into lesion-based patches to expand the dataset and explore the interrelationships between multiple lesions of TB in an individual patient. While considering a lesion-based patch, Table 3 represents a result from the LSS integrated ResNet. As shown in Table 3, the patient-based patch (92.21%) performs slightly better than the lesion-based patch (88.22%). Also, based on integrating all lesion-based patch scores of a case, the final score is computed by Eq. 1. According to the Eq. 2, a case is classified as having DS TB if the ensemble score is less than 0.4. Otherwise, this case is labeled as a DR suffering. Table 3 shows that the accuracy of the score voted for by all lesions inferior to the patient-based patch. Although the number of images is increasing when applying the lesion-based patch, multiple lesions in an individual patient are supposed to be combined to determine the type of TB.

Table 3. Lesion-based patch vs Patient-based patch results. (* is the best result and $^+$ is the second best result.)

	Acc	AUC	Recall	Precision	Specificity	F1
Patient-based case	$92.21 \pm 0.60^*$	$93.50 \pm 0.91^+$	$86.43 \pm 1.05^+$	$94.97 \pm 0.81^*$	$86.34 \pm 2.29^+$	$90.49 \pm 0.37^*$
Lesion-based patch	88.22 ± 0.23	$93.58 \pm 0.33^*$	85.21 ± 0.21	$89.99 \pm 0.74^+$	$88.73 \pm 0.92^*$	87.53 ± 0.30
Lesion-based case	$88.77 \pm 0.62^+$	88.53 ± 0.36	$92.48 \pm 0.90^*$	86.62 ± 1.13	78.81 ± 2.56	$89.44 \pm 0.26^+$

5.4   Comparison with Existing TB Detection Methods

Here we compare the results of the proposed method with those of the existing methods [2,8]. All methods were performed according to the description in the corresponding papers, including applying patch-based deep learning technique in [8], and analyzing extracted features from the bronchia and texture on the ROI of CTs using logistic regression, which is the most effective classifier in [2]. It should be noted that according to the method in [8], some cases are excluded during preprocessing phase. After that, 9604 lesion-based patches are collected to train the model constructed in [8]. Table 4 summarizes the performance of the DS detection of the proposed TRDD. With higher ACC and AUC value, our method performs better than the methods proposed by [2,8]. Compared with existing TB detection methods, the mean accuracy is shown in Fig. 6. The bar represents the mean accuracy of each method and the line represents the standard deviation. In general, the patient-based patch performs better than the lesion-based one when classifying the DR TB, since the patient-based patch contains information about all the lesions and their interrelationships. However, the lesion-based patch performs slightly better than the patient-based patch in [8]. Due to the different number of patches for each case, the patch-based method intensifies the imbalance of the constructed dataset, leading the model to tend to predict classes with large sample sizes. The proposed method is also better than the feature extraction method in [2]. The hand-crafted features are designed according to the dataset's characteristics and are not applicable to all datasets, while the CNN can mine richer features from the whole CT images and has better generalization ability.

Table 4. Experimental results with other methods.

	Acc	AUC	Recall	Precision	Specificity	F1
Ours	**92.21 ± 0.60**	**93.50 ± 0.91**	**86.43 ± 1.05**	**94.97 ± 0.81**	**86.34 ± 2.29**	**90.49 ± 0.37**
Gao and Qian [8]	80.33 ± 12.50	51.80 ± 6.57	50.13 ± 0.08	81.07 ± 12.82	52.75 ± 9.39	61.54 ± 4.15
Ahmed et al. [2]	83.00 ± 2.45	55.99 ± 3.40	82.80 ± 1.05	81.20 ± 7.36	13.17 ± 7.00	78.00 ± 3.10

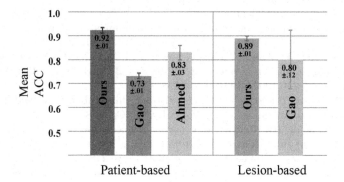

Fig. 6. The mean accuracy of existing TB detection methods.

6   Conclusion

Early detection of DR TB plays a crucial role in providing timely optimal treatment for each individual and maintaining public welfare to prevent TB proliferation. High-resolution CT images provide a non-invasive and convenient way to screen DR TB rapidly. Due to the limitation of open-source datasets in DR detection, a TB dataset annotated and labeled manually with the pathological report is constructed in this study. Moreover, the LSS method is proposed to effectively remove redundant information from CT images and capture the slices with the most concentrated features of a lesion. Finally, a ResNet with the LSS strategy is conducted to extract the TB lesions features from CT images to classify DR from DS TB disease and has achieved the best performance with 92.21% accuracy.

In the future, larger datasets with a distribution that more closely approximates the actual clinical data and more data will be established to promote deep neural networks in the clinical application of DR detection. Since patients with DS TB are far more than with DR TB in clinical, dealing with the imbalance distribution of the dataset is considered. Besides, more data acquisition of RIFP, MDR, and XDR will be collected to investigate the differentiation of the features of lesions from CT images between RIFP, MDR, and XDR. Moreover, morphology features of lesions will be used to gain a better understanding of the characteristics of CT TB images.

References

1. Aghajanzadeh, E., Shomali, B., Aminshahidi, D., Ghassemi, N.: Classification of tuberculosis type on CT scans of lungs using a fusion of 2d and 3d deep convolutional neural networks. In: CLEF (Working Notes), pp. 1133–1144 (2021)
2. Ahmed, M.S., Sk, O., Jayatilake, M., Gonçalves, T., Rato, L.: Texture analysis from 3d model and individual slice extraction for tuberculosis MDR detection, type classification and severity scoring (2018)
3. Cha, J., et al.: Radiological findings of extensively drug-resistant pulmonary tuberculosis in non-aids adults: comparisons with findings of multidrug-resistant and drug-sensitive tuberculosis. Korean J. Radiol. **10**(3), 207–216 (2009)
4. Chen, S., Guo, J., Wang, C., Xu, X., Yi, Z., Li, W.: DeepLNAnno: a web-based lung nodules annotating system for CT images. J. Med. Syst. **43**(7), 1–9 (2019). https://doi.org/10.1007/s10916-019-1258-9
5. Cui, E.N., et al.: Radiomics model for distinguishing tuberculosis and lung cancer on computed tomography scans. World J. Clin. Cases **8**(21), 5203 (2020)
6. Gao, X., Comley, R., Khan, M.H.M.: An enhanced deep learning architecture for classification of tuberculosis types from CT lung images. In: 2020 IEEE International Conference on Image Processing (ICIP), pp. 2486–2490. IEEE (2020)
7. Gao, X.W., James-Reynolds, C., Currie, E.: Analysis of tuberculosis severity levels from CT pulmonary images based on enhanced residual deep learning architecture. Neurocomputing **392**, 233–244 (2020)
8. Gao, X.W., Qian, Y.: Prediction of multidrug-resistant TB from CT pulmonary images based on deep learning techniques. Mol. Pharm. **15**(10), 4326–4335 (2017)
9. Hankare, S., Shirguppikar, S.: Detection of tuberculosis and lung cancer using CNN. In: Handbook of Smart Materials, Technologies, and Devices: Applications of Industry 4.0, pp. 1–11. Springer (2021)
10. Hara, K., Kataoka, H., Satoh, Y.: Can spatiotemporal 3d CNNS retrace the history of 2d cnns and imagenet? In: Proceedings of the IEEE Conference on Computer Vision and Pattern Recognition, pp. 6546–6555 (2018)
11. Janowczyk, A., Madabhushi, A.: Deep learning for digital pathology image analysis: a comprehensive tutorial with selected use cases. J. Pathol. Inf. **7**(1), 29 (2016)
12. Ji, S., Xu, W., Yang, M., Yu, K.: 3d convolutional neural networks for human action recognition. IEEE Trans. Pattern Anal. Mach. Intell. **35**(1), 221–231 (2012)
13. Kant, S., Srivastava, M.M.: Towards automated tuberculosis detection using deep learning. In: 2018 IEEE Symposium Series on Computational Intelligence (SSCI), pp. 1250–1253. IEEE (2018)
14. Kay, W., et al.: The kinetics human action video dataset. arXiv preprint. arXiv:1705.06950 (2017)
15. Kazlouski, S.: Tuberculosis CT image analysis using image features extracted by 3d autoencoder. In: Arampatzis, A. (ed.) CLEF 2020. LNCS, vol. 12260, pp. 131–140. Springer, Cham (2020). https://doi.org/10.1007/978-3-030-58219-7_12

16. Li, L., Huang, H., Jin, X.: AE-CNN classification of pulmonary tuberculosis based on CT images. In: 2018 9th International Conference on Information Technology in Medicine and Education (ITME), pp. 39–42. IEEE (2018)

17. Li, X., Zhou, Y., Du, P., Lang, G., Xu, M., Wu, W.: A deep learning system that generates quantitative CT reports for diagnosing pulmonary tuberculosis. Appl. Intell. **51**(6), 4082–4093 (2021). https://doi.org/10.1007/s10489-020-02051-1

18. O'Brien, R.J.: Drug-resistant tuberculosis: etiology, management and prevention. In: Seminars in respiratory infections, vol. 9, pp. 104–112 (1994)

19. Rahman, T., et al.: Reliable tuberculosis detection using chest x-ray with deep learning, segmentation and visualization. IEEE Access **8**, 191586–191601 (2020)

20. Selvaraju, R.R., Das, A., Vedantam, R., Cogswell, M., Parikh, D., Batra, D.: Grad-cam: why did you say that? arXiv preprint. arXiv:1611.07450 (2016)

21. Wang, X., Peng, Y., Lu, L., Lu, Z., Bagheri, M., Summers, R.M.: Chestx-ray8: hospital-scale chest x-ray database and benchmarks on weakly-supervised classification and localization of common thorax diseases. In: Proceedings of the IEEE Conference on Computer Vision and Pattern Recognition, pp. 2097–2106 (2017)

22. WHO, G.: Global tuberculosis report 2020. Glob. Tuberc. Rep (2020)

23. Wong, A., Lee, J.R.H., Rahmat-Khah, H., Sabri, A., Alaref, A., Liu, H.: TB-Net: a tailored, self-attention deep convolutional neural network design for detection of tuberculosis cases from chest x-ray images. Front. Artif. Intell. **5** (2022)

24. Xie, Y., et al.: Knowledge-based collaborative deep learning for benign-malignant lung nodule classification on chest CT. IEEE Trans. Med. Imaging **38**(4), 991–1004 (2018)

25. Xu, X., et al.: DeepLN: a framework for automatic lung nodule detection using multi-resolution CT screening images. Knowl.-Based Syst. **189**, 105128 (2020)

26. Zhou, K., et al.: Automatic airway tree segmentation based on multi-scale context information. Int. J. Comput. Assist. Radiol. Surg. **16**(2), 219–230 (2021). https://doi.org/10.1007/s11548-020-02293-x

Maintaining Structural Information by Pairwise Similarity for Unsupervised Domain Adaptation

Jian Liu[1,2] and Yahong Han[1,2(✉)]

[1] College of Intelligence and Computing, Tianjin University, Tianjin, China
{liujian_cic,yahong}@tju.edu.cn
[2] Tianjin Key Lab of Machine Learning, Tianjin University, Tianjin, China

Abstract. Unsupervised domain adaptation (UDA) aims to transfer the knowledge learned from the labeled source domain to the unlabeled target domain. Among them, the source domain and the target domain have the same label space, but the representation distributions of their input space are different. Mainstream approaches resort to domain adversarial training to align input distributions of two domains in the feature space. Although these methods have made remarkable progress, they have the risk of destroying discriminative structural information between different classes in the target domain. To alleviate this risk, we are inspired by the *problem reduction* method in ensemble methods and binarization techniques, and propose a novel approach Maintaining Structural Information of the target domain based on Pairwise semantic Similarity (whether two instances belong to the same class or not) (MSIPS). Specifically, We introduce Contrastive Learning to obtain feature prototypes for each category on the source domain, and then use these prototypes to predict the similarity of paired target domain samples. Finally, we restrict the target domain to maintain discriminative structural information through such weak information (i.e., pairwise similarity). Extensive experiments of various domain shift scenarios show that our method obtains competitive performance with SOTA, and qualitative visualization can demonstrate the effectiveness of our method.

Keywords: Unsupervised domain adaptation · Problem reduction · Pairwise similarity

1 Introduction

The breakthrough of convolutional neural network (CNN) [12] in the field of computer vision is inseparable from the support of massive labeled data [6]. Nevertheless, the collection and annotation of numerous data is an extremely expensive and time-consuming process. Meanwhile, In many practical scenarios, the models performed well on testing data will have serious performance degradation when predicting the data with distribution discrepancy (i.e., domain

L. Fang et al. (Eds.): CICAI 2022, LNAI 13605, pp. 268–279, 2022.
https://doi.org/10.1007/978-3-031-20500-2_22

shift). To alleviate these problems, unsupervised domain adaptation (UDA) has attracted a lot of attention, which transfers knowledge from a label-rich source domain to a fully-unlabeled target domain.

A variety of unsupervised domain adaptation methods have been proposed and have achieved significant progress [3,9,17,21,29]. The mainstream methods resort to domain adversarial training to align input distributions of two domains in the feature space, so that the model has good generalization ability in inferencing the data from different domains with domain shift. Although this method effectively reduces the distribution discrepancy in the feature space of the source domain and the target domain, it also leads to the mixing of the representation of different classes in the target domain to a certain extent. Recently, some studies [27,29,33] have begun to consider compensating or maintaining the structural information of the target domain damaged by domain adversarial training. Specifically, some of them propose fine-tuning the model using pseudo-labelled target domain data to compensate for structural information between different classes of the target domain. However, the quality of pseudo-labels is hard to control, especially when the domain shift is serious, the false pseudo-labels will cause error accumulation, and eventually lead to negative transfer [30] of the model. Another method is to learn the structural information between the classes of the source domain in the process of model training, and use it as a regularization term to guide the representations distribution of the target domain with similar structural information. However, these works are based on the assumption that the structural information of different classes of representations of the target domain and the source domain is consistent, which is difficult to fully guarantee in complex real scenes.

To effectively address the above problem, we are inspired by the *problem reduction* method, and propose a novel approach Maintaining Structural Information of the target domain based on Pairwise semantic Similarity (whether two instances belong to the same class or not) (MSIPS). The *problem reduction* method has had a long history in the literature, especially in binarization techniques and ensemble methods [7]. Its core strategy is to transform a complex task into a different and simpler task. Specifically, in domain adaptation, the ideal way to maintain structural information between classes within the target domain is to have labeled target domain data for different classes as Fig. 1(a), which is naturally not achievable in unsupervised settings. We consider transforming the above multi-classification task that requires all class labels into a simpler binary classification task. As shown in the Fig. 1(b), given a pair of target domain instances, we indirectly maintain the structural information between all classes of the target domain by predicting whether the two instances belong to the same class. That is, if two instances are predicted to be the same class, their representation is as close as possible in the feature space, and vice versa.

A direct idea is to predict whether the two samples belong to the same category by calculating the similarity of their representations, but we cannot scientifically set a reasonable threshold for the similarity. Moreover, domain adversarial training has the risk of destroying the structural information between the original classes of the target domain, which will further reduce the accuracy of our prediction of pairwise similarity. Therefore, we introduce Contrastive Learning to obtain feature prototypes for each category of the source domain, which will explicitly model the intra-class discrepancy and the inter-class discrepancy, and predict the pairwise similarity of the target domain instances by these prototype features that are far away from each other.

In summary, the main contributions of this paper are as follows:

(1) We are the first to use pairwise similarity of the target domain to maintain structural information in unsupervised domain adaptation, which is motivated by the *problem reduction* method.
(2) Contrastive Learning is introduced to obtain the category prototypes of the source domain. We use them as Category-Prototypes Bank to provide more accurate pairwise similarity for our method.
(3) We conduct careful ablation studies on benchmark UDA datasets, which demonstrate the effectiveness of our method and show competitive performance with several state-of-the-art methods

Fig. 1. Methods of maintaining structural information.

2 Related Works

2.1 Alignment Based Unsupervised Domain Adaptation

Unsupervised Domain Adaptation (UDA) generally assumes that the two domains have the same conditional distribution, but different marginal distributions (i.e., domain shift). In order to alleviate the influence of domain shift and improve the generalization ability of the trained source domain model on the target domain data, many work [19,27–29,31,33] proposed to align the representation distribution of the source domain and the target domain in the model training process. Some of them measure the degree of domain shift quantitatively by various metrics, e.g., maximum mean discrepancy (MMD) [17,18], and achieve domain-level alignment by minimizing the metrics. Another part of

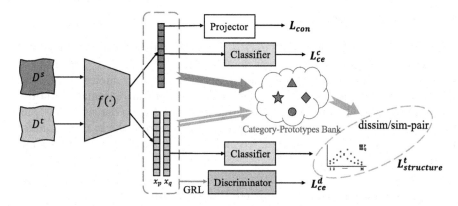

Fig. 2. Proposed method of maintaining structural information by pairwise similarity (Best viewed in color). Our method consists of a backbone, a classifier, a domain discriminator and a category prototype bank. Red and blue refer to data or representation from source domain and target domain respectively. The modules with same color have the same parameters, and GRL refers to the gradient reversal layer for domain-adversarial training. (Color figure online)

them [9,24,31,33] is to learn discriminative domain invariant features by introducing a domain discriminator for domain adversarial training. Although these methods effectively align the representation distributions of source domain and target domain, they all have the risk of damaging the structural information within the target domain, that is, the discrimination of the feature of the target domain is reduced [4]. In order to achieve class-level domain alignment, [23] introduces the class label into the domain discriminator, so that it can be aware of the classification boundary. [10] uses the pseudo-labeled target domain data to fine-tune the model to compensate for the damaged structural information between classes. [3] attempts to obtain the category centroid of different domains, forcing them to maintain consistency. Our method maintains structural information through pairwise similarity between classes inherent in the target domain, so we do not rely on the assumption that two domains have standard structural similarity.

2.2   Problem Reduction Method

Problem Reduction Method has had a long history in the literature, especially in binarization techniques and ensemble methods [1]. The most well-known strategies are "one-vs-all" [25] and "one-vs-one" [11]. The core idea of these work is to transform a more complex task into one or more simpler tasks. We are motivated by this method, and propose to maintain structural information by pairwise similarity for unsupervised domain adaptation.

3   Our Approach

Consider labeled data $\mathcal{D}^s = \{(x_i^s, y_i^s)\}_{i=1}^{N_s}$ from the source domain and unlabeled data $\mathcal{D}^t = \{(x_i^t)\}_{i=1}^{N_t}$ from the target domain, where $y^s = \{1, 2, \ldots, M\}$ is M different classes, N_s and N_t is the number of source and target samples, respectively. Unsupervised domain adaptation (UDA) assumes that source domain and target domain have shared label space $\mathcal{Y}$ but large distribution gap between $P(\mathcal{D}^s)$ and $P(\mathcal{D}^t)$. Our goal is to transfer the knowledge learned from the source domain to the target domain. In this section, we introduce our MSIPS method, as shown in Fig. (2).

3.1   Category-Prototypes Guided Pairwise Similarity

Given the representation of a pair of target domain samples x_p^t and x_q^t, the traditional method to predict whether they are similar is to measure the distance, e.g., Cosine Similarity, Euclidean Distance, between the two representations through some metrics, and compare it with the threshold. But it is hard to find such a suitable threshold, let alone the risk of domain adversarial training mixing different classes of representations in the target domain. In order to solve this problem, considering that the source domain and the target domain have the same label space, we explore to find a reference point for each category in the feature of the source domain and the target domain, which can not only be clearly distinguished from each other, but also alleviate the influence of domain shift. By comparing pairwise target domain representations with these benchmark representations, we can accurately determine whether the two samples belong to the same class. Specifically, motivated by InfoNCE [22] in Contrastive Learning, in addition to cross entropy (CE) loss, we impose a contrastive loss to make different classes of source domain representations more representative:

$$\mathcal{L}_{con} = -\log \frac{\exp\left(d\left(x^s, x^{s+}\right)/\tau\right)}{\exp\left(d\left(x^s, x^{s+}\right)/\tau\right) + \sum_{j=1}^{K-1} \exp\left(d\left(x^s, x_j^{s-}\right)/\tau\right)}, \quad (1)$$

where x^s denote any source representation output by Projector, x^{s+} is the randomly sampled positive representation with the same class label from the same batch and x_j^{s-} is the negative representation with different class labels. Moreover, $d(\cdot, \cdot)$ denotes cosine similarity and τ is a temperature factor. That is, the overall training procedure of MSIPS for labeled source domain data can be summarized as follows:

$$\mathcal{L}_{total}^s = \mathcal{L}_{ce}^c + \lambda \mathcal{L}_{con}, \quad (2)$$

where λ is trade-off parameter to balance losses. For simplicity, we set the λ to 1 based on our preliminary experiment.

Further, we calculate the mean values of the source domain features of each category as Eq. (3), and store them as the prototype of the category into the Category Prototype Bank.

$$p_m = \frac{1}{n} \sum_{i=1}^{n} (x_i^s | y_i^s = m) \quad (3)$$

For a pair of target domain representations x_p^t and x_q^t, we measure the distance between them and M prototypes, and further predict their pseudo labels y_p^t, y_q^t by softmax operation. So far, we can get their pairwise similarity label $Y_{ps} \in \{0, 1\}$. As shown in Fig. (2), if they belong to the same category, we represent it as *sim-pair* ($Y_{ps} = 1$), and vice versa as *dissim-pair* ($Y_{ps} = 0$).

3.2   Maintaining Structural Information via Pairwise Similarity

For source domain data, class labels can be used as supervised information to guide the model to learn the classification boundaries of different classes of data. We call this discriminative information between multiple classes structural information. But in unsupervised domain adaptation, there is no labeled data in the target domain, so it is difficult to learn this structural information directly. Different from the methods [3,29] maintaining structural information consistency between two domains based on the assumption of domain closeness [2], which cannot always be fully guaranteed in real scenarios, we propose to maintain structural information via pairwise similarity. In the previous subsection, for a given pair of target domain samples x_p^t and x_q^t, we have predicted their pairwise similarity, that is, whether they belong to the same class. Note that the correct probability of such two-class classification task prediction is higher than that of multi-class classification task prediction. Therefore, we are inspired by the *problem reduction* method [14] and use pairwise similarity to maintain the structural information of the target domain. If x_p^t and x_q^t are *sim-pair*, we believe that the corresponding distributions output by the source domain classifier $\mathcal{P}$ and $\mathcal{Q}$ are similar, and KL-divergence is used to measure the distance between the two distributions. We optimize the loss function as follows:

$$\mathcal{L}_{sim\_pair} = \mathcal{D}_{KL}\left(\mathcal{P}^{\star} \| \mathcal{Q}\right) + \mathcal{D}_{KL}\left(\mathcal{Q}^{\star} \| \mathcal{P}\right), \tag{4}$$

where $\mathcal{P}^{\star}$ and $\mathcal{Q}^{\star}$ are alternatively assumed to be constant, because the function for calculating KL-divergence is asymmetric. If x_p^t and x_q^t are *dissim-pair*, we optimize a hinge-loss as Eq. (5) (where the value of margin σ refers to [13]), and expect their distributions to be different.

$$\mathcal{L}_{dissim\_pair} = L_h\left(\mathcal{D}_{KL}\left(\mathcal{P}^{\star} \| \mathcal{Q}\right), \sigma\right) + L_h\left(\mathcal{D}_{KL}\left(\mathcal{Q}^{\star} \| \mathcal{P}\right), \sigma\right) \tag{5}$$

$$L_h(e, \sigma) = \max(0, \sigma - e) \tag{6}$$

Combining $\mathcal{L}_{sim\_pair}$ and $\mathcal{L}_{dissim\_pair}$, we get our structure loss. In addition, in order to further suppress the influence of pairwise similarity error caused by pseudo-label noise, we set a weight η for the structure loss based on the confidence of pseudo-label prediction as Eq. (7):

$$\eta = \sum_{m=1}^{M} P(y_p^t = m)P(y_q^t = m), \tag{7}$$

where $P(\cdot)$ is the output of softmax operation. Intuitively, if both y_p^t and y_q^t are predicted as the same class with greater confidence, the structure loss between them will be more involved in model optimization. Therefore, the total loss for maintaining structural information can be defined as follows: s

$$\mathcal{L}_{structure}^t = \eta Y_{ps} \mathcal{L}_{sim\_pair} + (1 - \eta)(1 - Y_{ps})\mathcal{L}_{dissim\_pair}. \qquad (8)$$

3.3   Combining with Domain Adversarial Training

Domain adversarial training can achieve domain-level alignment, and make the category prototype of the source domain we learn tend to be domain-invariant, thereby improving the accuracy of our prediction of pairwise similarity for the target samples. Therefore, we combine it with the proposed method. Finally, the total loss of MSIPS is as follows:

$$\mathcal{L}_{total} = \mathcal{L}_{total}^s + \mathcal{L}_{structure}^t + \mathcal{L}_{ce}^d, \qquad (9)$$

where $\mathcal{L}_{ce}^d$ is the loss of domain discriminator (a classifier that distinguishes samples from source or target domains) in domain adversarial training as [9], usually Cross Entropy loss with domain labels.

4   Experiments

4.1   Datasets

We evaluated our method in the following two standard benchmarks for UDA.

Office-31 [26] is the most popular real-world benchmark dataset for visual domain adaptation, which is made up of three distinct domains, i.e., Amazon (A), Webcam (W) and DSLR (D). It contains 4,110 images of 31 categories in three domains. We evaluated our method on six domain adaptation tasks.

Office-Home [32] is a more challenging recent dataset for UDA, which consists of 15500 images from 65 categories. There are 4 different domains in it: Art (Ar), Clip Art (Cl), Product (Pr), and Real-World (Rw). We evaluate our method in all the 12 one-source to one-target adaptation cases.

4.2   Implementation Details

Our implementation is based on [15]. Following the standard protocol for UDA, we use all labeled source data and all unlabeled target data. We use the ImageNet [6] pre-trained ResNet-50 [12] as the base network for fair comparison, where the last FC layer is replaced with the task-specific FC layer(s) to parameterize the classifier. We use mini-batch stochastic gradient descent (SGD) with a momentum of 0.9, an initial learning rate of 0.001, and a weight decay of 0.005. All reported results of mean($\pm$std) are obtained from the average of three runs.

Table 1. Accuracy (%) on Office-31 for unsupervised domain adaptation (ResNet-50). The best accuracy is indicated in bold.

Method	A→W	D→W	W→D	A→D	D→A	W→A	Avg
DANN	82.0±0.4	96.9±0.2	99.1±0.1	79.7±0.4	68.2±0.4	67.4±0.5	82.2
CCN	78.2	97.4	98.6	73.5	62.8	60.6	78.5
CCN⋆	88.5±0.4	97.4±0.5	98.6±0.1	84.5±0.7	73.5±0.2	73.4±0.3	86.0
PFAN	83.0±0.3	99.0±0.2	99.9±0.1	76.3±0.3	63.3±0.3	60.8±0.5	80.4
MDD	94.5±0.3	98.4±0.1	**100.0±0.0**	93.5±0.2	74.6±0.3	72.2±0.1	88.9
SymNets	90.8±0.1	98.8±0.3	**100.0±0.0**	93.9±0.5	74.6±0.6	72.5±0.5	88.4
CAN	94.5±0.3	99.1±0.2	99.8±0.2	95.0±0.3	**78.0±0.3**	77.0±0.3	90.6
GVB	92.0±0.3	98.7±0.0	**100.0±0.0**	91.4±0.5	74.9±0.5	73.4±0.1	88.3
SRDC	95.7±0.2	**99.2±0.1**	**100.0±0.0**	**95.8±0.2**	76.7±0.3	77.1±0.1	90.8
MSIPS	**95.9±0.3**	98.7±0.2	**100.0±0.0**	95.8±0.1	76.8±0.2	**78.6±0.5**	**91.0**

4.3 Comparison with Baselines

We select a series of popular methods as baselines to compare with MSIPS, including DANN [8] as a baseline for further analysis of our contributions and some state-of-the-art methods for performance comparisons. In particular, we compare with CCN [13] which uses pairwise similarity to perform conditional clustering on target domain data, PFAN [3] aligns the category prototypes of the target domain and source domain directly, SRDC [29] uses the structural information of source domain contained in source domain labels to guide target domain data clustering. Note that most of them are domain adaptation methods based on alignment. In addition, bridging theory based MDD [35], alignment based CAN [16], GVB [5] and SymNets [34] are also selected as baselines.

Results on **Office-31** are reported in Table 1, where results of existing methods are quoted from their respective papers or the works. CCN uses imageNet as an auxiliary dataset to learn a model for predicting pairwise similarity. On this basis, we fine-tune the model using all data outside the target data to further improve its accuracy in predicting pairwise similarity. The results are recorded as CCN⋆. We can see that MSIPS outperforms all compared methods on most of the transfer tasks, and the average performance reaches SOTA. We utilize t-SNE [20] to visualize embedded features on the source domain and the target domain by Source Model from DANN, CCN⋆, SRDC (only target domain representations) and our method. As shown in Fig. (3), we can find that the source domain features and target domain features learned by MSIPS have the characteristics of close distance within the class and long distance between classes. At the same time, the same classes of features from different domains are clustered, which fully proves that our method effectively maintains the structural information of the target domain. The results of **Office-Home** are reported in Table 2. Although the average performance of our method is slightly lower than SRDC (−0.1%), it reaches SOTA in multiple domain adaptation tasks. Especially in Ar→Cl, our method exceeds SRDC by 7.7 %, which indicates that our method is promising.

Table 2. Accuracy (%) on office-home for unsupervised domain adaptation (ResNet-50). The best accuracy is indicated in bold.

Method	Ar→Cl	Ar→Pr	Ar→Rw	Cl→Ar	Cl→Pr	Cl→Rw	Pr→Ar	Pr→Cl	Pr→Rw	Rw→Ar	Rw→Cl	Rw→Pr	Avg
DANN	45.6	59.3	70.1	47.0	58.5	60.9	46.1	43.7	68.5	63.2	51.8	76.8	57.6
SymNets	47.7	72.9	78.5	64.2	71.3	74.2	64.2	48.8	79.5	74.5	52.6	82.7	67.6
MDD	54.9	73.7	77.8	60.0	71.4	71.8	61.2	53.6	78.1	72.5	60.2	82.3	68.1
GVB	57.0	74.7	79.8	64.6	74.1	74.6	65.2	55.1	81.0	74.6	59.7	84.3	70.4
SRDC	52.3	**76.3**	81.0	**69.5**	76.2	**78.0**	**68.7**	53.8	**81.7**	76.3	57.1	**85.0**	**71.3**
MSIPS	**60.0**	75.4	**81.1**	65.7	**76.4**	75.1	65.1	**57.7**	**81.7**	72.4	**61.1**	82.7	71.2

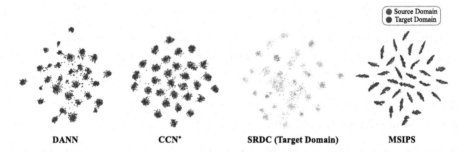

DANN   **CCN***   **SRDC (Target Domain)**   **MSIPS**

Fig. 3. The t-SNE visualization of embedded features on the task W→A (Best viewed in color). Note that for SRDC we refer to the visualization results in the original paper, in which different classes are denoted by different colors.

4.4 Ablation Studies and Discussions

For a more detailed analysis of our proposed method, we conducted ablation studies on the Office-31 dataset, and all experiments are aimed at adaptation task W→A.

Comparison of Accuracy of Predicting Pairwise Similarity. Using pairwise similarity to constrain the structure between classes has a certain history in Conditional Clustering. CCN [13] tried to use this constraint to cluster the target domain samples under cross-domain settings, but showed poor performance. The reason we analyze the failure is that although pairwise similarity has a good effect on maintaining structural information, the accuracy of predicting pairwise similarity will be severely reduced by domain shift. Instead of using the auxiliary data set to train the pairwise similarity prediction network directly, we use the data of the non-target domain from the current dataset to fine-tune the network, and further improve its accuracy in predicting the pairwise similarity (i.e., CCN*). Even so, we can observe from Fig. (4) that our method is more accurate in predicting pairwise similarity, which fully demonstrates the effectiveness of our method for predicting pairwise similarity based on category prototypes.

Effect and Error Analysis of Maintaining Structural Information. As shown in Fig. (5), our method effectively maintains the structural information of the source domain and the target domain, different classes of features are distributed in different clusters, and features with the same classes are closer

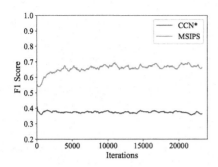
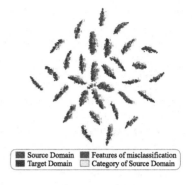

Fig. 4. F1 Score of pairwise similarity prediction (Best viewed in color).

Fig. 5. The visualization of features of misclassification (Best viewed in color).

in the feature space. However, we find that although our method has higher accuracy in predicting pairwise similarity and has adopted some strategies to suppress the impact of similarity prediction errors, there will still be some sample classification errors. We claim that further improving the accuracy of pairwise similarity prediction helps to improve the effect of domain adaptation.

5   Conclusion

In this paper, we propose a method based on pairwise similarity to maintain the structural information of the target domain for unsupervised domain adaptation. Different from the existing method of directly aligning the category structure of source domain and target domain based on domain closeness assumption, our method aims to make full use of the inherent information of whether different samples in the target domain belong to the same category, and effectively maintain the structural information of the target domain through the idea of problem reduction. The experimental results show that our method has achieved comparable performance with SOTA, and a large number of visualization results fully demonstrate the effectiveness of our method. Finally, we analyze the errors in the ablation studies and propose further research directions for improvement.

References

1. Allwein, E.L., Schapire, R.E., Singer, Y.: Reducing multiclass to binary: a unifying approach for margin classifiers. J. Mach. Learn. Res. **1**, 113–141 (2000)
2. Ben-David, S., Blitzer, J., et al.: A theory of learning from different domains. Mach. Learn. **79**(1), 151–175 (2010). https://doi.org/10.1007/s10994-009-5152-4
3. Chen, C., et al.: Progressive feature alignment for unsupervised domain adaptation. In: Proceedings of the IEEE/CVF Conference on Computer Vision and Pattern Recognition, pp. 627–636 (2019)

4. Chen, X., Wang, S., Long, M., Wang, J.: Transferability vs. discriminability: batch spectral penalization for adversarial domain adaptation. In: International Conference on Machine Learning, pp. 1081–1090. PMLR (2019)
5. Cui, S., Wang, S., Zhuo, J., Su, C., Huang, Q., Tian, Q.: Gradually vanishing bridge for adversarial domain adaptation. In: Proceedings of the IEEE/CVF Conference on Computer Vision and Pattern Recognition, pp. 12455–12464 (2020)
6. Deng, J., Dong, W., Socher, R., Li, L.J., Li, K., Fei-Fei, L.: Imagenet: a large-scale hierarchical image database. In: 2009 IEEE Conference on Computer Vision and Pattern Recognition, pp. 248–255. IEEE (2009)
7. Galar, M., Fernández, A., Barrenechea, E., Bustince, H., Herrera, F.: An overview of ensemble methods for binary classifiers in multi-class problems: experimental study on one-vs-one and one-vs-all schemes. Pattern Recogn. **44**(8), 1761–1776 (2011)
8. Ganin, Y., Lempitsky, V.: Unsupervised domain adaptation by backpropagation. In: International Conference on Machine Learning, pp. 1180–1189. PMLR (2015)
9. Ganin, Y., et al.: Domain-adversarial training of neural networks. J. Mach. Learn. Res. **17**(1), 2030–2096 (2016)
10. Gu, X., Sun, J., Xu, Z.: Spherical space domain adaptation with robust pseudo-label loss. In: Proceedings of the IEEE/CVF Conference on Computer Vision and Pattern Recognition, pp. 9101–9110 (2020)
11. Hastie, T., Tibshirani, R.: Classification by pairwise coupling. In: Advances in Neural Information Processing Systems, vol. 10 (1997)
12. He, K., Zhang, X., Ren, S., Sun, J.: Deep residual learning for image recognition. In: Proceedings of the IEEE Conference on Computer Vision and Pattern Recognition, pp. 770–778 (2016)
13. Hsu, Y.C., Lv, Z., Kira, Z.: Learning to cluster in order to transfer across domains and tasks. In: International Conference on Learning Representations (2018)
14. Hsu, Y.C., Lv, Z., Schlosser, J., Odom, P., Kira, Z.: Multi-class classification without multi-class labels. In: International Conference on Learning Representations (2018)
15. Jiang, J., Chen, B., Bo, F., Long, M.: Transfer-learning-library. https://github.com/thuml/Transfer-Learning-Library (2020)
16. Kang, G., Jiang, L., Yang, Y., Hauptmann, A.G.: Contrastive adaptation network for unsupervised domain adaptation. In: Proceedings of the IEEE/CVF Conference on Computer Vision and Pattern Recognition, pp. 4893–4902 (2019)
17. Long, M., Cao, Y., Wang, J., Jordan, M.: Learning transferable features with deep adaptation networks. In: International Conference on Machine Learning, pp. 97–105. PMLR (2015)
18. Long, M., Zhu, H., Wang, J., Jordan, M.I.: Unsupervised domain adaptation with residual transfer networks. In: Advances in Neural Information Processing Systems, vol. 29 (2016)
19. Long, M., Zhu, H., Wang, J., Jordan, M.I.: Deep transfer learning with joint adaptation networks. In: International Conference on Machine Learning, pp. 2208–2217. PMLR (2017)
20. Van der Maaten, L., Hinton, G.: Visualizing data using t-SNE. J. Mach. Learn. Res. **9**(11), 2579–2605 (2008)
21. Na, J., Jung, H., Chang, H.J., Hwang, W.: Fixbi: bridging domain spaces for unsupervised domain adaptation. In: Proceedings of the IEEE/CVF Conference on Computer Vision and Pattern Recognition, pp. 1094–1103 (2021)
22. Oord, A.V.D., Li, Y., Vinyals, O.: Representation learning with contrastive predictive coding. arXiv preprint. arXiv:1807.03748 (2018)

23. Pei, Z., Cao, Z., Long, M., Wang, J.: Multi-adversarial domain adaptation. In: 32nd AAAI Conference on Artificial Intelligence (2018)
24. Pinheiro, P.O.: Unsupervised domain adaptation with similarity learning. In: Proceedings of the IEEE Conference on Computer Vision and Pattern Recognition, pp. 8004–8013 (2018)
25. Rifkin, R., Klautau, A.: In defense of one-vs-all classification. J. Mach. Learn. Res. **5**, 101–141 (2004)
26. Saenko, K., Kulis, B., Fritz, M., Darrell, T.: Adapting visual category models to new domains. In: Daniilidis, K., Maragos, P., Paragios, N. (eds.) ECCV 2010. LNCS, vol. 6314, pp. 213–226. Springer, Heidelberg (2010). https://doi.org/10.1007/978-3-642-15561-1_16
27. Sener, O., Song, H.O., Saxena, A., Savarese, S.: Learning transferrable representations for unsupervised domain adaptation. In: Advances in Neural Information Processing Systems, vol. 29 (2016)
28. Sun, B., Feng, J., Saenko, K.: Correlation alignment for unsupervised domain adaptation. In: Csurka, G. (ed.) Domain Adaptation in Computer Vision Applications. ACVPR, pp. 153–171. Springer, Cham (2017). https://doi.org/10.1007/978-3-319-58347-1_8
29. Tang, H., Chen, K., Jia, K.: Unsupervised domain adaptation via structurally regularized deep clustering. In: Proceedings of the IEEE/CVF Conference on Computer Vision and Pattern Recognition, pp. 8725–8735 (2020)
30. Torrey, L., Shavlik, J.: Transfer learning. In: Handbook of Research on Machine Learning Applications and Trends: Algorithms Methods, and Techniques, pp. 242–264. IGI global, Hershey (2010)
31. Tzeng, E., Hoffman, J., Saenko, K., Darrell, T.: Adversarial discriminative domain adaptation. In: Proceedings of the IEEE Conference on Computer Vision and Pattern Recognition, pp. 7167–7176 (2017)
32. Venkateswara, H., Eusebio, J., Chakraborty, S., Panchanathan, S.: Deep hashing network for unsupervised domain adaptation. In: Proceedings of the IEEE Conference on Computer Vision and Pattern Recognition, pp. 5018–5027 (2017)
33. Zhang, W., Ouyang, W., Li, W., Xu, D.: Collaborative and adversarial network for unsupervised domain adaptation. In: Proceedings of the IEEE Conference on Computer Vision and Pattern Recognition, pp. 3801–3809 (2018)
34. Zhang, Y., Tang, H., Jia, K., Tan, M.: Domain-symmetric networks for adversarial domain adaptation. In: Proceedings of the IEEE/CVF Conference on Computer Vision and Pattern Recognition, pp. 5031–5040 (2019)
35. Zhang, Y., Liu, T., Long, M., Jordan, M.: Bridging theory and algorithm for domain adaptation. In: International Conference on Machine Learning, pp. 7404–7413. PMLR (2019)

Hierarchical Recurrent Contextual Attention Network for Video Question Answering

Fei Zhou[1,2] and Yahong Han[1(✉)]

[1] College of Intelligence and Computing, Tianjin University, Tianjin, China
{beiyang_flychou,yahong}@tju.edu.cn
[2] Tianjin International Engineering Institute, Tianjin University, Tianjin, China

Abstract. Video question answering (VideoQA) is a task of answering a natural language question related to the content of a video. Existing methods that utilize the fine-grained object information have achieved significant improvements, however, they rely on costly external object detectors or fail to explore the rich structure of videos. In this work, we propose to understand video from two dimensions: temporal and semantic. In semantic space, videos are organized in a hierarchical structure (pixels, objects, activities, events). In temporal space, video can be viewed as a sequence of events, which contain multiple objects and activities. Based on this insight, we propose a reusable neural unit called recurrent contextual attention (RCA). RCA receives a 2D grid feature and conditional features as input, and computes multiple high-order compositional semantic representations. We then stack these units to build our hierarchy and utilize recurrent attention to generate diverse representations for different views of each subsequence. Without the bells and whistles, our model achieves excellent performance on three VideoQA datasets: TGIF-QA, MSVD-QA, and MSRVTT-QA using only grid features. Visualization results further validate the effectiveness of our method.

Keywords: Video question answering · Video understanding · Multi-modal fusion and inference

1 Introduction

Research on video-language tasks has flourished in the past few years. Video question answering (VideoQA) is one of the most prominent as it can develop agent to communicate with the dynamic visual world through natural language. From the vision perspective, fully extracting and utilizing the information contained in the video and filtering clues according to the linguistic context is the key to video question answering. Recent advancements [1, 4, 7, 14] of VideoQA can also be mainly attributed to the exploration of finer-grained spatial information within the video frames. As a representative example, L-GCN [7] first uses an additional object detector to detect the spatial bounding boxes of important

L. Fang et al. (Eds.): CICAI 2022, LNAI 13605, pp. 280–290, 2022.
https://doi.org/10.1007/978-3-031-20500-2_23

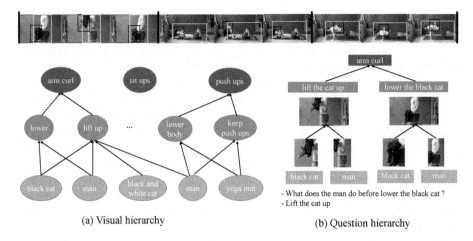

(a) Visual hierarchy

(b) Question hierarchy

Fig. 1. Hierarchy of video and question. The entire video can be divided into three events in time: curling, sit-ups, and prone; from the semantic dimension, the low-level grid forms a series of objects: cats, people; different objects interactions form different activities; all activities are organized in sequence to construct events.

objects, and then uses a graph neural network to model the relation among all objects. Objects and their relations are undoubtedly crucial for video question answering, since interactions between objects can be explicitly captured to better understand the complex content of videos.

However, it is costly to extract fine-grained object features through object detectors. Moreover, the annotation of object detection is expensive, and pre-trained object detectors can not generalize well to datasets with large domain gap. A recent study [9] compared grid-based features and object-based features in image question answering, and showed that incorporating object detector can significantly slow down the model by 4.6 to 23.8 times, but does not bring significant performance improvements compared to plain CNN features (grid features). They also concluded that the semantic content that the feature represent is more critical than the format of features. Inspired by them, we revisit grid features for VideoQA and propose a reusable unit called Recurrent Contextual Attention Network (RCAN) that encapsulates and transforms a 2D sequence into a new higher-order 1D sequence conditioned on contextual features, where the 2D sequence can represent both the temporal and semantic dimension. The flexibility of RCAN allows it to be replicated and layered to form deep hierarchical recurrent contextual attention network (HRCAN), which can temporally divide and conquer long video clips and semantically form different levels of video concepts from the bottom up.

The hierarchy of the RCANs are as follows - at the lowest level, the RCANs encode the relations between raw *grid* features (considered as the input 2D sequence) in a frame and then aggregates multiple *regions* conditioned on frame-level context and linguistic context; at the next level, we combine multiple regions of a clip to form a 2D sequence, then use RCANs to perform inter-region message passing between adjacent frames guided by motion context, and finally generate high-order *events* representation conditioned on clip-level context and linguistic context; in the final stage, the attention mechanism is used to aggregate the representations of multiple sub-events to form a compact global video representation for answer inference. As shown in Fig. 1, at the lowest level, we need to first aggregate the main objects from the original pixels: *black cat, people, yoga mat*, etc.; and then form a series of actions based on motion information: *lowering, raising, sit-ups, push-ups*, etc.; and finally arrange the different actions to form the overall event: *exercise*. Specifically, the aggregation of video elements (*objects, activities, events*) is achieved through the recurrent attention of RCANs, and the interaction of visual elements is achieved through message passing in RCANs. Therefore, our method incorporates the advantages of current grid-based [10] and object-based methods [7].

The contributions are summarized as follows: (1) We propose a Recurrent Attention (RA) to extract semantic content in grid features to further explore its potentials in VideoQA; (2) Further, we extend the operating objects of RA and propose a general neural unit RCAN, which receives a sequence of low-level video elements and outputs a compositional deep-semantic video element; (3) Finally, we construct a hierarchical network based on RCAN to divide and conquer videos in time sequence, and construct different levels of video semantics from bottom to top in semantic space. State-of-the-art results on three datasets validate the effectiveness of our method.

2   Related Work

VideoQA on Grid Features. Earlier work [8] used simple spatial and temporal attention mechanism, but did not bring much improvement. Some subsequent works [2,3,13] focuses on multimodal fusion and temporal modeling with using simple pooling in space. QueST [10] is a further attempt at the spatio-temporal attention of grids features, which decomposed the question semantics in space and time to guide the attention generation in space and time, respectively. Although obtaining the performance improvement, it only attend once per frame, resulting in the lack of richness of the features obtained from each frame and the inability to model the interactions between the attended regions. Therefore, we propose a recurrent attention mechanism to alleviate this shortcoming.

VideoQA on Object Features. Most recent methods for video question answering methods employ pretrained object detectors to extract object features and model interactions between them. L-GCN [7] proposed a location-aware graph neural network to model interactions between objects. HOSTR [1] used object detection and tracking to establish object trajectories, and then applied object-based spatio-temporal attention mechanisms to model object interactions. HAIR [14] utilized both object detection features and attribute features for visual and semantic relational reasoning. These methods generally achieve better performance than grid feature-based methods, the most notable difference being that they can extract distinct object regions and explicitly model pairwise inter-actions between objects without the influence of irrelevant backgrounds. Thus in this paper, in addition to using the recurrent attention mechanism to extract diverse regions, we also use the message passing mechanism to model the inter-actions between them. A key difference is that our region extraction method is lightweight and does not require additional object detectors.

Hierarchical Architectures. Compared to images, videos contain more com-plex structures. Thus, HCRN [12] designed and stacked conditional relation blocks to represent videos as amalgam of complementing factors including appearance, motion and relations. However, it mainly focused on reasoning about temporal relations and used simple mean-pooling to model relations. Lack of fine-grained spatial information makes it not generalizable well to scenes involv-ing multiple objects. Follow a similar design philosophy, HOSTR [1] introduced nested graphs for spatio-temporal reasoning over object trajectories to learn hierarchical video representations, and achieved better performance. However, the good performance of HOSTR relies on accurate object trajectories, which is difficult to achieve in practice. In this work, we also follow the hierarchical design principle, but do not rely on any additional object detectors and object trackers.

3   Proposed Method

3.1   Visual and Linguistic Representation

Video Representations. Given a video, we uniformly sample T frames and divide it into K clips with L frames, where $T = K \times L$. For each frame, we use pre-trained 2D ResNet [6] to extract appearance features F^a, then take this frame as the center frame and combine 8 frames before and after this frame to form a segment and use pre-trained 3D ResNeXt [5] to extract motion features F^m. Specifically, we use the output of the last convolutional layer as the grid feature representation, so $F^a \in \mathbb{R}^{K \times L \times 7 \times 7 \times 2048}$, $F^m \in \mathbb{R}^{K \times L \times 4 \times 4 \times 2048}$. Next, linear feature transformations are used to transform them into the standard d-dimensional feature space. Following [7], We add spatial position encoding and frame position encoding on grid features.

Linguistic Representation. We apply GloVe converts each question word into a 300-dimensional word representations, then feed the word representations into a bidirectional LSTM to model contextual dependencies. Then We obtain word-level question representations $F^q \in \mathbb{R}^{M \times d}$ by stacking the hidden states at each time step, and then use the output of the last hidden unit as the global question representation $q_L \in \mathbb{R}^d$, where M is the length of the question.

3.2   Recurrent Contextual Attention Network Unit

As illustrated in Fig. 3(a), RCAN consists of three operations: cross-modal attention (CMAT), intra-modal graph attention (GAT), and recurrent context

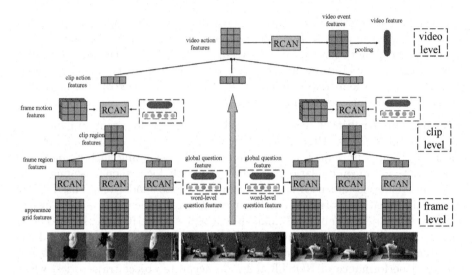

Fig. 2. Hierarchical recurrent contextual attention network (HRCAN) for VideoQA. At the frame-level, the RCAN receives grid features of a single frame as input and generates multiple frame-wise regional features in the question and frame-wise visual context. At the clip-level, we concatenate the regional features of multiple frames of a clip to generate clip-wise action features in the context of motion. Finally, we use a graph convolutional network to model the relation between video action features and generate the final video representation.

attention (RCA). The CMAT and the GAT are based on the self-attention mechanism $SAT(X, Y) = U$ [16]:

$$A = (W_1X)((W_2Y^T)/\sqrt{d} \tag{1}$$

$$H = softmax(A)(W_3Y)) \tag{2}$$

$$U = LN(X + H) \tag{3}$$

where $X \in \mathbb{R}^{N \times d}$ and $Y \in \mathbb{R}^{M \times d}$ are the inputs, $U \in \mathbb{R}^{N \times d}$ is the output, and $W_1 \sim W_3 \in \mathbb{R}^{d \times d}$ are the learned weight matrices.

RCANs takes as input a grid feature $V \in \mathbb{R}^{L_v \times d}$ ($L_v = H_v \times H_v$), which can be CNN feature map of a frame or region features of a Clip, and linguistic context $F_q \in \mathbb{R}^{M \times d}$, then produce compositional features: $R = RCAN(V, F_q) \in \mathbb{R}^{N \times d}$.

Cross-modal Attention. Through the cross-attention of word-level linguistic representation and visual features, the video elements mentioned in the question will have a stronger response.

$$\tilde{V} = CMAT(V, F^q) = SAT(V, F^q) \tag{4}$$

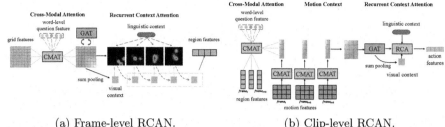

(a) Frame-level RCAN.   (b) Clip-level RCAN.

Fig. 3. Illustration of recurrent context attention unit (RCAN). Cross-modal attention (CMAT) is first used to model inter-modal interactions, then graph attention (GAT) further model intra-modal interactions, and finally recurrent contextual attention (RCA) extracts multiple higher-order representations. Additional motion information is introduced at the clip-level.

After obtaining enhanced visual features, we use graph attention (GAT) to model interactions within modalities:

$$\hat{V} = GAT(\tilde{V}, \tilde{V}) = SAT(\tilde{V}, \tilde{V}) \tag{5}$$

Graph attention enables message passing between related visual elements, such as different parts of the same object, different objects of an action, which can facilitate subsequent RCA to extract more semantic-related region features.

The detailed computation of recurrent context attention (RCA) is as follows. We first compute a guidance vector $g_t \in \mathbb{R}^d$ based on the globally average-pooled visual feature or the last attended region feature $r_{t-1} \in \mathbb{R}^d$, the l-th grid feature $\hat{v}_l$ and the linguistic context $q_L \in \mathbb{R}^d$.

$$g_{t,l} = W_{g,t}(W_{q,t}q_L + W_{r,t}r_{t-1} + W_{l,t}\hat{v}_l) + b_{g,t} \tag{6}$$

$$\alpha_{t,l} = W_{att,t}LeakyReLU(g_{t,l}) + b_{att,t} \tag{7}$$

$$\alpha_t = Softmax([\alpha_{t,1}, ..., \alpha_{t,L_v}]) \tag{8}$$

$$r_t = \sum_{l=1}^{L_v} \alpha_{t,l}\hat{v}_l \tag{9}$$

where $W_{g,t}$, $W_{q,t}$, $W_{r,t}$, $W_{l,t}$, $W_{att,t} \in \mathbb{R}^{d \times d}$ are learnable weights, and $b_{g,t}$ and $b_{att,t}$ are the biases, $a_{t,l}$ is a scale which is the weight on the l-th grid feature used to generate the t-th region. r_t is the visual context at step t, $r_0 = sumpooling(\hat{V})$. Finally, we iteratively generate N regions $R = \{r_1, ..., r_n\} \in \mathbb{R}^{N \times d}$.

3.3 Hierarchical Recurrent Contextual Attention Network

As shown in Fig. 2, at the lowest level, RCAN receives frame-level grid features F^a as input, then captures inter-modal and intra-modal interactions and finally generates a series of regional features $F^r \in R^{K \times L \times N_f \times d}$:

$$F_{k,l}^r = RCAN(F_{k,l}^a, F^q, q_L) \tag{10}$$

where, $F_{k,l}^a$ is the grid features of the l-th frame of the k-th clip, $F_{k,l}^r$ is the regional feature of the corresponding frame.

Frame-level RCAN have extracted diverse regional features from each frame and modeled intra-frame relation via GAT and RCA. The goal of clip-level RCAN is combine motion context and regional information to form different actions, such as "lower the cat, lift up the cat". As shown in Fig. 3 (b), we add a CMAT to introduce motion context into region features. Specifically, the clip-level RCAN receives the output of the frame-level RCAN R_f and the frame-level motion grid features $F^m \in R^{K \times L \times L_m \times d}$ as input, and cyclically generates a series of action representations $F^c \in \mathbb{R}^{K \times N_c \times d}$:

$$F_k^c = RCAN(F_k^r, F_k^m, F^q, q_L) \tag{11}$$

where $F_k^r \in R^{L \times N_f \times d}$ is the feature of all regions of the k-th clip, $F_k^m \in R^{L \times L_m \times d}$ is the motion feature of all frames of the k-th clip, and $F_k^c \in \mathbb{R}^{N_c \times d}$ is the action features generated by the k-th clip. Finally, we use a RCAN without RCA to model the dependencies between the clip features of the video: $F^v = RCAN(F^c, F^q) \in \mathbb{R}^{(K \times N_c) \times d}$ and use attention pooling to generate the final visual feature: $z = Attn(F^v, q_L) \in \mathbb{R}^d$.

3.4   Answer Decoder

Following the previous work [10, 12], for multiple-choice QA, we concatenate each candidate and question to form a holistic query. The global query feature q_L is fused with the final video feature z and a multilayer perceptron (MLP) is used to predict scores:

$$s = MLP([z; q_L]) \tag{12}$$

For multi-choice QA, we maximize the margin between positive and negative QA-pairs: $max(0, 1 + s^n - s^p)$. For opened QA, We treat it as a classification task on a pre-defined set of answers, then use the decoder to predict a class probability and train it using cross-entropy.

4   Experiments

4.1   Experiment Setup

Datasets. TGIF-QA [8] contains 165K QA pairs collected from 72K animated GIFs. We use action repetition (Action), state transition (Trans.), frame-level question (FrameQA) tasks for evaluation. FrameQA is an opened QA, the others are multi-choice QA. **MSVD-QA** and **MSRVTT-QA** [18] contain 50K and 243K Q&A pairs respectively, and consist of five different types of questions, including *what, who, how, when* and *where*. The task is open-ended. For all datasets, we report accuracy (percentage of correctly answered questions) as an evaluation metric according to the standard.

Table 1. Comparison with state-of-the-art methods.

Methods	TGIF-QA			MSRVTT-QA	MSVD-QA
	Action	Trans.	FrameQA		
ST-VQA [8]	62.9	69.4	49.5	30.9	31.3
PSAC [13]	70.4	76.9	55.7	–	–
QueST [10]	75.9	81.0	59.7	34.6	36.1
Co-mem [3]	68.2	74.3	51.5	31.9	31.7
HME [2]	73.9	77.8	53.8	33.0	33.7
L-GCN [7]	74.3	81.1	56.3	33.7	34.3
HGA [11]	75.4	81.0	55.1	35.5	34.7
GMIN [4]	73.0	81.7	57.5	36.1	35.4
BTA [15]	75.9	82.6	57.5	36.9	37.2
HCRN [12]	75.0	81.4	55.9	35.6	36.1
HOSTR [1]	75.0	83.0	58.0	35.9	39.4
HQGA [17]	76.9	85.6	61.3	38.6	41.2
HRCAN	**81.8**	83.6	**63.7**	**38.8**	**41.8**

Implementation Details. For each video, we uniformly sample $T = 16$ frames, then divide them into $K = 4$ clips with $L = 4$ frames per clip. We use pretrained ResNet152 from [9] to extract appearance features, and use ResNeXt101 pretrained on Kinetics to extract motion features. We set the dimension of the hidden units d to 512, and $N_f = N_c = 4$. For training details, we train our model for 50 epochs with a batch size of 32. The learning rate is set to 10^{-4}, warms up for 5 epochs, and then cosine anneals.

4.2 Comparison with Prior Work

In Table 1, we compare our method with methods involving 4 main categories: cross-attention, memory-based methods, graph-structed methods and hierarchical models. The results show that our HRCAN model consistently outperforms other models on all experimental datasets.

Specifically, both L-GCN and GMIN use graph-based methods to model object-level interactions for question answering. However, they fail to construct the hierarchical nature of the video and interactions are constructed without the guidance of language query. Through the inter-modal and inter-modal interactions in RCAN, and the semantic hierarchy of HRCAN, our model shows clear superiority on the experimental dataset. HCRN, HOSTR and HQGA are similar to us in designing hierarchical conditional architectures. However, HCRN is limited to hierarchical temporal relations between frames, which are only modeled by simple average pooling. The lack of spatial fine-grained information makes it insufficient to understand complex object interactions in space-time, which limits not only its performance in single-frame question answering, but also its temporal reasoning ability. HOSTR advances HCRN by building hierarchies on object trajectories and employing graph operations for relational reasoning. However, it lacks object-word level fine-grained matching which results in its sub-optimal results, and relies on costly object detection and trajectory tracking. Finally, the HQGA, like us, tries to aligns words in the linguistic queries with visual elements of the hierarchy in the video. However, it relies on multiple visual encoder to build different visual hierarchies, e.g., 2D & 3D CNN and Faster-RCNN, which makes it limited in practical applications.

4.3   Ablation Studies

Hierarchy. In the top section of Table 2, we layer-wisely replace the RCAN with average pooling to study the effect of the hierarchy. It can be seen that the lack of any level will cause performance degradation. And the frame-level has the greatest impact on the results, we argue that the lack of spatially fine-grained information extraction will introduce noise to subsequent levels. This show that just modeling the relation between clips is suboptimal. We also study the effect of the number of iterations in RCAN and find that increasing both N_f and N_c can lead to better overall performance.

Linguistic Conditioning. From the middle section of Table 2, the lack of language conditions jeopardize the overall performance, indicating the necessity of injecting query cues when encoding video features. Specially, we replace word-level representations F^q in cross-modal attention with global one q_L, and the performance drop shows the importance of fine-grained cross-modal matching.

Motion Conditioning. Removing the motion context at the clip level or putting the motion information before the frame level will cause performance

Table 2. Ablation studies on TGIF-QA dataset, for action repetition and frameqa tasks.

Model	Action	Frame
Hierarchy		
w/o frame-level	77.90	58.60
w/o clip-level	78.40	63.50
w/o video-level	81.70	64.01
Linguistic conditioning		
w/o linguistic cond.	78.20	62.80
w/ global linguistic cond.	80.10	63.40
Motion conditioning		
w/o motion cond. in clip-level	80.50	63.30
w motion cond. in frame-level	80.20	63.40
Full model	81.80	63.70

Model	Action	Frame
RCA(N_c and N_f)		
$N_c = 1, N_f = 1$	80.80	63.0
$N_c = 1, N_f = 2$	80.60	63.7
$N_c = 1, N_f = 4$	80.60	63.6
$N_c = 1, N_f = 1$	80.80	63.0
$N_c = 2, N_f = 1$	81.60	62.7
$N_c = 4, N_f = 1$	80.70	63.7

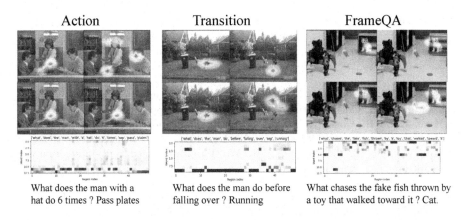

Fig. 4. Visualization of our cross-modal attention and recurrent attention in frame level. The above is the attended region heat map for recurrent attention, the below is the attention weights between grid and words in cross-modal attention.

degradation. One is that the introduction of motion context can make up for the loss of information caused by sparse sampling, and the other is that adding motion information directly to the appearance grid features may bring noise without frame-level RCAN enhancement and extraction of question-specific regions.

Qualitative Analysis. In Fig. 4, we visualize frame-level cross-modal attention and recurrent attention. It can be seen that in CMA, important objects or actions in the query are emphasized, such as "hat","passing plates", "running", "fake fish", "cat". Subsequently, the corresponding visual regions are extracted by recurrent attention. Moreover, we can observe: 1) CMA is sparse, which may be the reason that word-level supervision is better than sentence-level one. Namely, only a few query subjects in sentences need to be emphasized; 2) the attention of grid features is more flexible than that of object. Obejct features are often limited to a rectangular instance-related bounded by box, while our grid-based recurrent attention can attend flexible regions, which may only be part of the instance, *e.g.*, "plate", "legs".

5   Conclusion

In this paper, we propose a new VideoQA model termed as HRCAN, that uses a reusable attention unit RCAN to perform hierarchical reasoning on visual elements. Specifically, multimodal interactions are modeled in RCAN through inter-modal and intra-modal attention, and then low-level visual elements are aggregated into diverse high-level visual elements through recurrent attention. Our extensive experimental analysis have validated the effectiveness of the propose method. Additional visual analysis can also further validate the insights.

References

1. Dang, L.H., Le, T.M., Le, V., Tran, T.: Hierarchical object-oriented spatio-temporal reasoning for video question answering. arXiv preprint. arXiv:2106.13432 (2021)
2. Fan, C., Zhang, X., Zhang, S.: Heterogeneous memory enhanced multimodal attention model for video question answering. In: CVPR, pp. 1999–2007 (2019)
3. Gao, J., Ge, R., Chen, K.: Motion-appearance co-memory networks for video question answering. In: CVPR, pp. 6576–6585 (2018)
4. Gu, M., Zhao, Z., Jin, W., Hong, R., Wu, F.: Graph-based multi-interaction network for video question answering. IEEE Trans. Image Process. **30**, 2758–2770 (2021)
5. Hara, K., Kataoka, H., Satoh, Y.: Can spatiotemporal 3d cnns retrace the history of 2d cnns and imagenet? In: CVPR, pp. 6546–6555 (2018)
6. He, K., Zhang, X., Ren, S., Sun, J.: Deep residual learning for image recognition. In: Proceedings of the IEEE Conference on Computer Vision and Pattern Recognition, pp. 770–778 (2016)
7. Huang, D., Chen, P., Zeng, R.: Location-aware graph convolutional networks for video question answering. In: AAAI, pp. 11021–11028 (2020)
8. Jang, Y., Song, Y., Yu, Y.: Tgif-qa: toward spatio-temporal reasoning in visual question answering. In: CVPR, pp. 2758–2766 (2017)
9. Jiang, H., Misra, I., Rohrbach, M., Learned-Miller, E., Chen, X.: In defense of grid features for visual question answering. In: Proceedings of the IEEE/CVF Conference on Computer Vision and Pattern Recognition, pp. 10267–10276 (2020)
10. Jiang, J., Chen, Z.: Divide and conquer: question-guided spatio-temporal contextual attention for video question answering. In: AAAI, pp. 11101–11108 (2020)
11. Jiang, P., Han, Y.: Reasoning with heterogeneous graph alignment for video question answering. In: AAAI, pp. 11109–11116 (2020)
12. Le, T.M., Le, V., Venkatesh, S.: Hierarchical conditional relation networks for video question answering. In: CVPR, pp. 9972–9981 (2020)
13. Li, X., Song, J., Gao, L.: Beyond rnns: positional self-attention with co-attention for video question answering. In: AAAI, pp. 8658–8665 (2019)
14. Liu, F., Liu, J., Wang, W., Lu, H.: Hair: hierarchical visual-semantic relational reasoning for video question answering. In: Proceedings of the IEEE/CVF International Conference on Computer Vision, pp. 1698–1707 (2021)
15. Park, J., Lee, J., Sohn, K.: Bridge to answer: Structure-aware graph interaction network for video question answering. In: CVPR, pp. 15526–15535 (2021)
16. Vaswani, A., Shazeer, N., Parmar, N.: Attention is all you need. In: NeurIPS, pp. 5998–6008 (2017)
17. Xiao, J., Yao, A., Liu, Z., Li, Y., Ji, W., Chua, T.S.: Video as conditional graph hierarchy for multi-granular question answering. AAAI (2022)
18. Xu, D., Zhao, Z., Xiao, J.: Video question answering via gradually refined attention over appearance and motion. In: ACM MM, pp. 1645–1653 (2017)

An Intelligent Assessment System for Human Motor Functions of Stroke Patients

Jingyao Chen[1,3], Chen Wang[2], Pu Zhang[1,4], Zeng-Guang Hou[1,2(✉)],
Pingye Deng[3], Ningcun Xu[1], and Chutian Zhang[1]

[1] Faculty of Innovation Engineering, CASIA-MUST Joint Laboratory of Intelligence
Science and Technology, Macau University of Science and Technology,
Macao 999078, China
zengguang.hou@ia.ac.cn

[2] State Key Laboratory of Management and Control for Complex Systems,
Institute of Automation, Chinese Academy of Sciences, Beijing 100190, China

[3] Institute of Analysis and Testing, Beijing Academy of Science and Technology,
Beijing 100089, China

[4] Department of Rehabilitation Evaluation, Beijing Bo'ai Hospital,
China Rehabilitation Research Center, Beijing 100068, China

Abstract. Assessment is an essential part of the rehabilitation process for post-stroke patients, while due to the low accuracy and long duration of traditional rehabilitation assessment methods, as well as the fact that the assessment mainly relies on the subjective judgment of doctors, there is a lack of efficient, high-precision and objective intelligent assessment methods. Facing the above needs, this study developed a lightweight human motor function dynamic analysis system based on the Fugl-Meyer assessment scale to evaluate the different rehabilitation stages of post-stroke patients. We use a cell phone as the lightweight device to dynamically track the changes of patients' motion in multiple sensitive motion paradigms and identified motion vector centroids by sliding window convolution to perform normalization of temporal features. Based on this, we process temporal information by simulating RGB image features skillfully and use a multimodal decision fusion model consisting of a convolutional neural network (CNN) and a long and short-term memory (LSTM) network to achieve quantitative scoring of patients' rehabilitation degrees. Experimentally verified by 12 participants from the China Rehabilitation Research Center (CRRC), the system proved to be effective in assessing the rehabilitation level of stroke patients, and significantly improved the efficiency and precision of the existing assessment methods.

Keywords: Stroke · Rehabilitation assessment · Lightweight method · Multimodal fusion

1 Introduction

Stroke is an acute cerebrovascular accident (CVA) that has become the second leading cause of death worldwide [3,12]. More than 70% of surviving stroke patients are left with functional impairment, which seriously affects their physical and mental health [2,8,20]. Studies have shown that training can improve impaired motor function and reduce disability rate [10,15]. Therefore, timely rehabilitation assessment and individualized rehabilitation training guidance are becoming more and more important.

However, the rehabilitation assessment is conducted primarily by experienced rehabilitation physicians, leading to more than 30 min per session, and introducing unavoidable subjective biases. Moreover, the existing assessment method has low scoring accuracy, which makes it difficult to improve the initiative of patients. Therefore, the development of a more intelligent and quantitative lightweight assessment method for patients at different stages of rehabilitation has become an urgent need.

To achieve this purpose, we selected appropriate assessment scales and motions under the guidance of experienced rehabilitation physicians, and then used mobile phones to capture the patient's posture changes dynamically, recording 3D position coordinate information of key skeletal nodes in the human body. By combining kinematic analysis and the collateral response during rehabilitation, we acquired the joint angle and distance features. We addressed the challenge of normalizing data due to excessive variation in patient actions by identifying motion vector centroids through sliding window convolution and achieving temporal normalization of the features. We proposed a temporal data graph concept by simulating the structural properties of RGB data and using the temporal information as one of the input dimensions to achieve a dual layer fusion algorithm to process temporal data.

To validate the effectiveness of the system, 12 stroke patients have been recruited to conduct clinical trials in cooperation with the China Rehabilitation Research Center. We obtained quantitative assessment results of patients' motor dysfunction based on a lightweight data collection method and showed a high correlation with the composite scores of multiple rehabilitation physicians.

The rest of the paper is organized as follows. Section 2 describes the current relevant work, Sect. 3 describes our approach, Sect. 4 describes the experiments and results, and Sect. 5 gives the conclusion of this paper and discusses the future improvement direction.

2   Related Work

Rehabilitation is a circular type of treatment that consists of assessment, assignment, intervention, and evaluation, as shown in Fig. 1. Currently, the common methods of motor function assessment include Fugl-Meyer Assessment (FMA), Brunnstrom Staging Scale (BSS), Action Research Arm Test (ARAT), Block Box Test (BBT), and Wolf Motor Function Test (WMFT) [7]. Hou et al. [4] established a computerized adaptive testing assessment system (CAT-FM) by improving the Fugl-Meyer assessment system. E Ona et al. [9] designed an experiment based on the Box and Blocks Test (BBT) scale to assess hand motor function in patients with Parkinson's disease (PD). According to the research, the Fugl-Meyer Assessment Scale, which developed from the Brunnstrom Staging Scale,

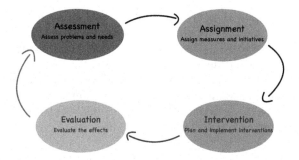

Fig. 1. Rehabilitation cycle.

contains comprehensive and quantitative assessment details for various aspects such as joint movement, coordination and motor balance, is the most commonly used assessment method [7]. In addition to the assessment system, an automated rehabilitation assessment system should also include automated motor tracking and assessment algorithms.

During human movement, the information that records the movement state can contain kinematic data, kinetic data, physiological data, etc. The basis of motor function assessment is the acquisition of human motion data, and the common methods of human posture data acquisition currently include opto-electronic measurement systems (OMSs), electromagnetic measurement systems (EMSs), image processing systems (IMSs), ultrasonic localization systems (UMSs) and inertial sensory systems (IMUs) [5], mechanical measurement systems (MMS) [19], etc. According to the research, 33.3% of the relevant studies use only vision-based sensors (IMS) for motion tracking, ranking first. 25% of the studies use only inertial sensors (IMU), 12% use only mechanical systems (MMS), 4.16% use only optoelectronic systems (OMS), and some use a combination of the above methods [7]. Therefore, we chose a vision sensor-based data acquisition method for further investigation. The current professional motion capture system such as Vicon is relatively expensive and less portable. The doctors need a lot of training before using it. These make it not conducive to patients' timely awareness of their rehabilitation state as well as doctors' timely adjustment of treatment plans. So we need to select a more lightweight and portable system to realize real-time upper limb posture tracking and functional analysis. Some studies have used wearable devices to make the measurement process more convenient [17,18,21]. Here we choose to use mobile phones as devices to further reduce the burden on patients. Mediapipe, a dynamic pose tracking tool open sourced by Google in June 2019, provides solutions for selfie segmentation, face keypoint detection, gesture tracking, human pose tracking, hair segmentation, object tracking, face detection, eye movement detection, and 3D target detection. With built-in machine learning and acceleration algorithms, it enables lightweight computational goals. Google proposed a lightweight convolutional neural network architecture for human pose estimation BlazePose designed for lightweight as well as real-time tracking on mobile devices. On a Pixel 2 phone, a recognition speed of 30 frames per second can be achieved and no depth camera is required [1]. With all this in mind, we decided to extract the coordinate points through Mediapipe.

The assessment of motor function can be achieved by relying on the collected human posture data. There are two kinds of motor function assessment systems in common use, which are actual measurement data-based evaluation systems and algorithm-based evaluation systems.

Actual Measurement Data-Based Evaluation System. Due to the different rehabilitation evaluation systems used, some assessment systems can obtain scores directly from the measurement data. Daniel Simonsen et al. [14] used a Microsoft Kinect sensor to capture subjects' experimental procedures and directly determine the subjects' motor function level by monitoring the experimental movement completion time. E Oña et al. [9] designed an experiment based on the Box and Blocks Test (BBT) scale to assess hand motor function in patients with Parkinson's disease (PD) by directly calculating the score through the maximum number of cubes that the subject could move during the one-time window.

Algorithm-Based Evaluation System. Algorithm-based assessment systems, on the other hand, generate assessment results by preprocessing the acquired human posture data to obtain feature vectors and input them into the selected algorithm. Chen Wang. et al. [16] assessed patient's motion based on multimodal fusion algorithm by acquiring participant's motion data and sEMG data. T.K.M. et al. [6] assessed patient movements based on a decision tree. Paul Otten et al. [11] used SVM and NN algorithms for automated FMA assessment by acquiring motion data with low-cost sensors. Alessandro Scanoet et al. [13] developed an automated algorithm to calculate RPS based on Kinect V2 tracking data for motor function assessment in neurological patients. In our study, we selected algorithm-based assessment systems to achieve our research objectives.

3   Methodology

3.1   Posture Tracking Actions

In collaboration with the China Rehabilitation Research Center, several post-stroke hemiplegic patients were recruited and their motor data and physiological signals were collected through different experimental movement tasks (see below for the specific experimental movement design). The 33 body key point coordinates were extracted by the Mediapipe tool, see Fig. 2. We performed experimental action selection based on Fugl-Meyer scale.

Action 1: Shoulder abduction 0–90° to the bodyside. If the patient starts with immediate arm abduction or elbow flexion, he will get 0 points; if there is a supinations or elbows flexion during movement, he will get 1 point; if he completes it successfully, as shown in the doctor's demonstration, he will get 2 points.

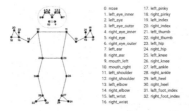

Fig. 2. Coordinate annotation of 33 human posture key points [9].

Action 2: Shoulder flexion 90°–180°. If the patient starts with immediate arm abduction or elbow flexion, he will get 0 points; if there is an abduction or elbows flexion during movement, he will get 1 point; if he can complete the shoulder flexion to 180°, without shoulder abduction or elbow flexion, he will get 2 points.

Action 3: Shoulder abduction 0–90° to the front. If the patient starts with immediate arm abduction or elbow flexion, he will get 0 points; if there is a supinations or elbows flexion during movement, he will get 1 point; if he completes it successfully, as shown in the doctor's demonstration, he will get 2 points.

Action 4: Pronation and supination while the shoulder at 0° and the elbow at 90°. If the patient has no pronation and supination, he will get 0 points; if there is a limited pronation and supination, he will get 1 point; and if he can complete the full pronation and supination, he will get 2 points.

Action 5: Pronation and supination while the shoulder at 30°–90° flexion and the elbow at 0°. If the patient has no pronation and supination, he will get 0 points; if there is a limited pronation and supination, he will get 1 point; and if he can complete the full pronation and supination, he will get 2 points.

Action 6: Knee flexion to 90° while hip at 0°. If the patient has no active motion or immediate, simultaneous hip flexion, he will get 0 points; if there is a less than 90° knee flexion and/or hip flexion during movement, he will get 1 point; and if he completes it successfully, he will get 2 points.

Action 7: Ankle dorsiflexion. If the patient has no active motion, he will get 0 points; if there is a limited dorsiflexion, he will get 1 point; and if he can complete the dorsiflexion, he will get 2 points.

3.2   Feature Extraction

We divided the video into RGB images frame by frame and extracted a total of 33 features of three-dimensional coordinate points through the Mediapipe toolkit. Since the Angle and distance between feature points such as shoulder, elbow and wrist are very important in motion evaluation, 20 joint angles and 20 related distances are selected based on the coordinate key points, in which joint reaction is also taken into account as a supplement to features, see Fig. 3.

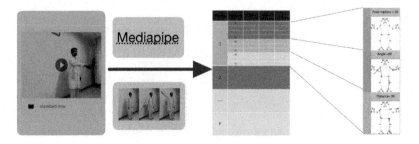

Fig. 3. Posture tracking flow chart.

Realized that the sequelae of stroke patients generally occur on one side, so the motion evaluation is also for the affected side, which means the coordinates of 33 key points are redundant. Similarly, the features of key points of the lower limbs do not need to be considered when evaluating the upper limb movements. Therefore, after feature normalization, variance filtering is carried out.

3.3 Sequence Symmetric Convolution Normalization

The next problem is that the time required for patients with different rehabilitation degrees to perform the same action varies greatly. Taking action3 as an example, some patients can complete an action in 80 frames, while others may need about 500 frames, So we did a normalized resampling.

First of all, we need to find the symmetry point of the action. So we flattened the data by each frame, And then subtracted the value of the K frame from the value of the (K+1) frame, replaced values greater than or equal to 0 with positive 1 and negative values with −1 to form a new matrix. Then, F-S segments with a length of S were selected in the form of a sliding window to calculate the column sum. The number of columns with the sum of 0 or less than a certain threshold was counted. In practice, we selected the data with the sum of columns less than or equal to 5 for statistics and then sorted it. The section with the largest number was considered the symmetry point of the action, see Fig. 4.

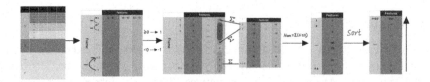

Fig. 4. Sequential symmetric convolution normalization flowchart.

Assume that the number of frames after normalization is M, using a formula (shown in Fig. 5 and Eq. 1) to calculate different sampling intervals to achieve sequence symmetric convention normalization.

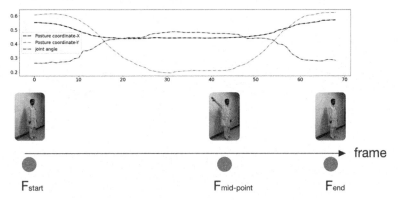

Fig. 5. Sequence symmetric convention normalization.

$$\Delta_1 = \frac{F_{mid-point} - F_{start}}{M/2} \quad \Delta_2 = \frac{F_{end} - F_{mid-point}}{M/2} \tag{1}$$

where F_{start}, $F_{mid-point}$ and F_{end} represents the first frame, the symmetry point that we calculated and the last frame. Δ_1 and Δ_2 represent the sampling intervals of the first and second-time segments.

3.4 Fusion Strategy Selection

This study proposes a Dual-channel Temporal Motion Evaluation (DTME) network that uses a two-channel fusion algorithm based on temporal convolution and long and short-term memory (LSTM) networks for motor function evaluation, as shown in Fig. 6.

Channel 1: we proposed a method of sequence diagram data set, which preprocesses the data by simulating the characteristics of RGB images and saves the timing information in the length dimension to realize the convolution algorithm based on sequence data.

Channel 2: considering the timing of data, a quantitative regression model (shown in Eq. 2) of motor dysfunction degree of upper and lower limbs was constructed based on LSTM.

$$I_t = \sigma(X_t W_{xi} + H_{t-1} W_{hi} + b_i)$$
$$F_t = \sigma(X_t W_{xf} + H_{t-1} W_{hf} + b_f)$$
$$\widetilde{C}_t = tanh(X_t W_{xc} + H_{t-1} W_{hc} + b_c)$$
$$O_t = \sigma(X_t W_{xo} + H_{t-1} W_{ho} + b_o)$$
$$C_t = F_t \odot C_{t-1} + I_t \odot \widetilde{C}_t$$
$$H_t = O_t \odot tanh(C_t) \tag{2}$$

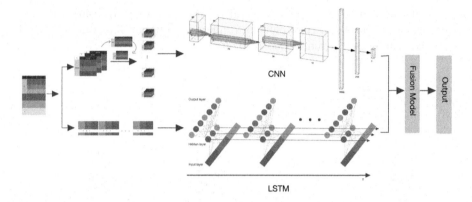

Fig. 6. Framework of DTME network.

where X_t represents the input vector, $H_{(t-1)}$ represents the hidden state of the previous time step, I_t, F_t, $\widetilde{C}_t$, and O_t represent the input gate, forgetting gate, candidate memory cell, and output gate, W and b are weight parameters, and bias parameters, H_t and C_t represent the hidden layer output and cell state of the current moment t. After all, we fuse the output results of the softmax layer of the above two channels with the fusion algorithm and output a score by analyzing motor dysfunction, ranging from 0 to 2, The closer the value is to 0, the higher the severity of the patient's motor dysfunction; the closer the value is to 2, the closer the patient's motor function is to normal, thus achieving an objective assessment of the degree of motor dysfunction in stroke patients.

4   Experiments and Results

4.1   Datasets

In this study, we created an FMA-based rehabilitation assessment dataset, named FRAction, see Fig. 7. The data were collected from stroke patients at the Chinese Rehabilitation Research Center. 18 patients were collected, and 7 assessment movements were repeated 3 times per person on the affected side, of which 6 patients' data were unavailable and 252 data segments were available. To achieve the goal of "lightweight assessment", the current acquisition method is the use of an iphone11, with the video recording format set to 1080p HD/30 fps.

Fig. 7. The FRAction dataset.

4.2   Experimental Settings

This experiment assigns 83.3% as the training set and 16.7% as the test set with 6-fold cross validation. 73 initial features (33 key points+20 angle information+20 distance information) are selected, and the number of frames is confirmed as 80 by sequence symmetric convolution normalization. Accuracy is selected as the evaluation metric.

4.3   Data Analysis

Performance Comparison of Recommendation Methods. We compared the performance of different networks. As can be seen from Table 1, the sequential symmetric convolution normalization(CCSN) can improve the performance of ordinary CNN networks, and the DTME algorithm achieves accuracies ranging from 83.3% (on action 6) to a peak of 97.1% (on action 7) on our FRAction dataset.

Table 1. Performance comparison of recommendation methods.

Networks	Action1	Action2	Action3	Action4	Action5	Action6	Action7
CNN	83.3%	77.8%	80.6%	86.1%	83.3%	75.0%	88.9%
CNN+ CCSN	88.9%	83.3%	83.3%	91.7%	88.9%	80.6%	94.4%
LSTM	86.1%	80.6%	86.1%	88.9%	83.3%	77.8%	91.7%
DTME(our method)	91.7%	86.1%	88.9%	94.4%	94.4%	83.3%	97.1%

Action Correlation Analysis. In our study, we found that there is a certain correlation between the scores of different actions. Taking action 1 and action 2 as an example for explanation, the full score of action 1 requires raising the arm to the chest, and the full score of action 2 requires raising the arm overhead, Therefore a full score for action 1 is necessary for a full score for action 2. There is a similar connection between the other actions, shown in Fig. 8, so it can be used as a kind of corrective verification to compensate for the results to some extent.

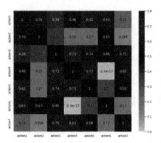

Fig. 8. Action Correlation Heat Map.

The Effect of Sequential Symmetric Convolution Normalization. The effect of using the sequential symmetric convolution normalization method on the data processing is shown in the Table 1.

Validation. Taking action 1 as an example, two participants were selected to verify the effectiveness of symmetry point location screening. As can be seen from Fig. 9, the first half of participant A's movement process is slower, while the second half is faster (Fig. 9a). After sorting the possibility of symmetry point, the most likely position was located around frame 73, which was consistent with the sequence feature diagram (Fig. 9c). On the contrary, the first half of participant B's motor process was faster and the second half was slower (Fig. 9b). The most likely location is around frame 34, which is consistent with the sequence feature diagram too (Fig. 9c).

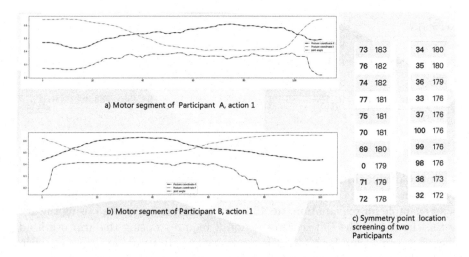

Fig. 9. Correctness Verification.

5 Conclusion

In this paper, we explored the practical problems encountered in rehabilitation assessment and proposed a light-weight human motor posture assessment solution. We selected appropriate assessment scales under the guidance of experienced physicians and completed the experimental design and data collection based on the scales. We proposed a DTME network to achieve the dynamic assessment of patients' rehabilitation degrees. In the study, we also found correlations between assessment actions, which provided ideas for further improvement of the assessment protocol. Finally, the experimental results confirmed that our method can effectively solve the problems encountered in rehabilitation assessment, greatly improve the assessment efficiency, and provide an efficient and convenient assessment method for clinical rehabilitation.

References

1. Bazarevsky, V., Grishchenko, I., Raveendran, K., Zhu, T., Grundmann, M.: Blazepose: On-device real-time body pose tracking (2020)
2. Chen, T., Zhang, B., Deng, Y., Fan, J.C., Zhang, L., Song, F.: Long-term unmet needs after stroke: systematic review of evidence from survey studies. BMJ Open 9(5) (2019)
3. Feigin, V.L., et al.: Global, regional, and national burden of stroke and its risk factors, 1990–2019: a systematic analysis for the global burden of disease study 2019. Lancet Neurol. 20(10), 795–820 (2021)
4. Hou, W.H., et al.: Development of a computerized adaptive testing system of the Fugl-Meyer motor scale in stroke patients. Arch. Phys. Med. Rehabil. 93(6), 1014–1020 (2012)
5. Kruk, E.V.D., Reijne, M.M.: Accuracy of human motion capture systems for sport applications; state-of-the-art review. Eur. J. Sport Sci. 18(6), 806–819 (2018)
6. Lee, T.K.M., Gan, S.S.W., Lim, J.G., Sanei, S.: Singular spectrum analysis of rehabilitative assessment data. In: 2013 9th International Conference on Information, Communications and Signal Processing, pp. 1–5 (2013)
7. Simbana, E.D.O., Herrera Baeza, P., Huete, J., Balaguer, C.: Review of automated systems for upper limbs functional assessment in neurorehabilitation. IEEE Access 7, 32352–32367 (2019)
8. Olver, J., et al.: Post stroke outcome: global insight into persisting sequelae using the post stroke checklist. J. Stroke Cerebrovasc. Dis. 30(4), 105612 (2021)
9. Ona, E.D., Sanchez-Herrera, P., Cuesta-Gomez, A., Martinez, S., Jardón, A., Balaguer, C.: Automatic outcome in manual dexterity assessment using colour segmentation and nearest neighbour classifier. Sensors 18(9), 2876 (2018)
10. Oosterveer, D.M., Wermer, M.J., Volker, G., Vlieland, T.P.V.: Are there differences in long-term functioning and recovery between hemorrhagic and ischemic stroke patients receiving rehabilitation? J. Stroke Cerebrovasc. Dis. 31(3), 106294 (2022)
11. Otten, P., Kim, J., Son, S.H.: A framework to automate assessment of upper-limb motor function impairment: A feasibility study. Sensors 15(8), 20097–20114 (2015)
12. Owolabi, M.O., Thrift, A.G., Mahal, A., et al.: Primary stroke prevention worldwide: translating evidence into action. Lancet Public Health 7(1), e74–e85 (2022)

13. Scano, A., Chiavenna, A., Malosio, M., Molinari Tosatti, L., Molteni, F.: Kinect v2 implementation and testing of the reaching performance scale for motor evaluation of patients with neurological impairment. Med. Eng. Phys. **56**, 54–58 (2018)
14. Simonsen, D., Nielsen, I.F., Spaich, E.G., Andersen, O.K.: Design and test of an automated version of the modified jebsen test of hand function using microsoft kinect. J. Neuroeng. Rehabil. **14**(1), 38 (2017)
15. Van Meijeren-Pont, W., et al.: Patient activation during the first 6 months after the start of stroke rehabilitation. Arch. Phys. Med. Rehabil. **103**(7), 360–1367 (2022)
16. Wang, C., Peng, L., Hou, Z.G., Li, J., Zhang, T., Zhao, J.: Quantitative assessment of upper-limb motor function for post-stroke rehabilitation based on motor synergy analysis and multi-modality fusion. IEEE Trans. Neural Syst. Rehabil. Eng. **28**(4), 943–952 (2020)
17. Wang, C., Peng, L., Hou, Z.G., Li, Y., Tan, Y., Hao, H.: A hierarchical architecture for multi-symptom assessment of early Parkinson's disease via wearable sensors. IEEE Trans. Cogn. Dev. Syst, Early Access 1–1 (2021)
18. Wang, C., Peng, L., Hou, Z.G., Zhang, P.: The assessment of upper-limb spasticity based on a multi-layer process using a portable measurement system. IEEE Trans. Neural Syst. Rehabil. Eng. **29**, 2242–2251 (2021)
19. Welch, G., Foxlin, E.: Motion tracking: no silver bullet, but a respectable arsenal. IEEE Comput. Graphics Appl. **22**(6), 24–38 (2002)
20. Wissel, J., Olver, J., Sunnerhagen, K.S.: Navigating the poststroke continuum of care. J. Stroke Cerebrovasc. Dis. **22**(1), 1–8 (2013)
21. Xu, N., Peng, X., Peng, L., Hou, Z.G.: A gait events detection algorithm based on the invariant characteristic of hip joint kinematics. In: 2021 33rd Chinese Control and Decision Conference (CCDC), pp. 861–866 (2021)

UI Layers Group Detector: Grouping UI Layers via Text Fusion and Box Attention

Shuhong Xiao[1], Tingting Zhou[4], Yunnong Chen[1], Dengming Zhang[2],
Liuqing Chen[1,3(✉)], Lingyun Sun[1,3], and Shiyu Yue[4]

[1] Zhejiang University, Hangzhou 310027, China
`chenlq@zju.edu.cn`
[2] Chongqing University of Posts and Telecommunications, Chongqing 400065, China
[3] Alibaba-Zhejiang University Joint Research Institute of Frontier Technologies,
Hangzhou 310027, China
[4] Alibaba Group, Hangzhou 311121, China

Abstract. Graphic User Interface (GUI) is facing great demand with
the popularization and prosperity of mobile apps. Automatic UI code
generation from UI design draft dramatically simplifies the development
process. However, the nesting layer structure in the design draft affects
the quality and usability of the generated code. Few existing GUI automated techniques detect and group the nested layers to improve the
accessibility of generated code. In this paper, we proposed our UI Layers
Group Detector as a vision-based method that automatically detects
images (i.e., basic shapes and visual elements) and text layers that
present the same semantic meanings. We propose two plug-in components, text fusion and box attention, that utilize text information from
design drafts as a priori information for group localization. We construct
a large-scale UI dataset for training and testing, and present a data augmentation approach to boost the detection performance. The experiment
shows that the proposed method achieves a decent accuracy regarding
layers grouping.

Keywords: UI to code · UI layers grouping · Object detection ·
Multi-modal embedding

1 Introduction

As the central intermediary of human-computer interaction, Graphic User Interface (GUI) is facing great demand with the popularization and prosperity of
mobile apps. The traditional process of designing GUI is very long-lasting. It
requires investigators to conduct user research, designers to design page materials, and then front-end engineers to code, and it is time-consuming to reach a
consensus before multi rounds of back and forth [11].

To achieve faster development and relieve engineers from heavy workloads,
some previous researchers applied intelligent methods in automatic GUI generation. Ling et al. [17] considered it a language generation task, and they utilized

© The Author(s), under exclusive license to Springer Nature Switzerland AG 2022
L. Fang et al. (Eds.): CICAI 2022, LNAI 13605, pp. 303–314, 2022.
https://doi.org/10.1007/978-3-031-20500-2_25

a language generation method to generate GUI source code from a mixed natural language. REMAUI [20] is the first work to introduce GUI screenshots as materials for code generation. They achieved a reverse process from screenshots to GUI code in seconds. Pix2code [2] then extended the use of images, and they trained an end-to-end deep learning model that generates a source code from a single design input image with 77% accuracy. More recent commercialization cases like Imgcook [12] construct a platform that allows diversified inputs including screenshots, PSDs, and Figma[1] or Sketch[2] files which contain metadata.

(a) An Example of fragmented layer in UI design.   (b) Example of grouping layers.

Fig. 1. (a) The icon with the red bounding box is formed with three basic shape layers. (b) The labeled text and image elements need to be included under the same DOM node using the "group" method by adding #group# to the target containers.

In the practice of automatic code generation, a massive gap between the design draft (created by digital tools like Sketch) and a quality product (Code and its visual presentation) is that some layers form a whole element in the design draft should be included as a single UI component in the code, while the code generated by automation is hard to reach this. In this case, design drafts should be further constrained by some specific rules to achieve UI code generation with high-quality. For instance, the state-of-art solution, Imgcook, highlights "merge" and "group" as two of the most important rules that reorganize the structure of design drafts to bridge the gap we described. The "merge" method integrates multiple fragmented layers representing basic shapes (e.g., rectangle, oval, path) and visual elements(e.g., text and image) into a single image. As illustrated in Fig. 1a, the icon with the red bounding box is formed with three basic shape layers. Without structured merging, these fragmented layers confuse the AI in understanding the semantic meaning of UI components and affect the readability and reusability of generated code. In the other case, the "group" method deals with malposed structures in the design draft. As illustrated in Fig. 1b, to ensure that generated code does not cause element loss or structural redundancy, the labeled text and image elements need to be included under the same DOM node using the "group" method by adding "#group#" to the target containers. However, Imgcook requires front-end engineers to manually locate the layers to

---

[1] https://www.figma.com/.
[2] https://www.sketch.com/.

proceed operate the "merge" or "group" method. Manual identification is time-consuming and prone to omissions because of the numerous layers and diverse nested structures. In this paper, we focus on automatically recognizing "group" problems. More specifically, we try to locate and group images (we define images as all basic shapes and visual elements) and text layers that have the same semantic meaning in the design draft. Therefore, We can optimize the design layout and obtain high-quality UI code.

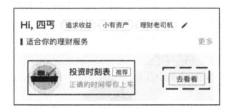 

(a) An Example of semantic consistency.   (b) An Example of various image-text group patterns

Fig. 2. (a) The clock image in blue box shares a close semantic meaning with the text "investment schedul", while the text "view it" in the red box represents another meaning. (b) The group strategy is different for the banner and small icon. We keep some background for the banner in order to avoid missing some elements (that maybe invisible) while bound the small icon group as tight as possible.

To address this issue, We proposed our UI Layers Group Detector that utilizes object detection techniques to detect the area to be grouped on real screenshot images. As multi-modal approaches have shown its great power in general UI component detection task [26], we introduce text embedding and box attention mechanism that use text-related information as extra modalities to help improve our Detector. The text layers are used as a local semantic focal, together with the global image feature to benefit generated proposals. Given an arbitrary design draft, we follow semantic consistency as the grouping criterion, i.e., not all adjacent visual elements will be integrated into a single group. As illustrated in Fig. 2a, the clock image in blue box shares a close semantic meaning with the text "investment schedule", while the text "view it" in the red box represents another meaning. Under this condition, precisely predicting the group range is challenging because of the background layer and elements around. Another challenge is that the diversified UI application scenarios result in various group patterns with different sizes and element numbers. For example, as illustrated in Fig. 2b, for the group of banner contains a thumbnail with text information like product name, price, and description, we have the empty background layer inside the bounding box to better retrieve all the banner elements in the design draft. This is because for group like banner which contains abundant elements, elements sometimes partially invisible so that they will be dropped if we apply a tight bound. While for small icon like the group only contains ">" and text

"8 items", we make the bounding box as tight as possible so that no irrelevant element will be covered.

In particular, our method solves the two challenges by following approaches. We adopt a state-of-art object detection model to achieve precise localizing of group objectives. To deploy our Group Detector as a plug-in for UI code generator like Imgcook, we choose to adopt from the Faster-RCNN because it is lightweight, delicate, and easy to modify. We collect our dataset from the Sketch files of the most frequently used mobile apps. The target groups on each image are labeled carefully by professional labelers guided by the semantic consistency we described before. The high-quality dataset allows our data-driven model to make more accurate predictions. We summarize our contributions as follows:

1. We construct a high-quality dataset containing UI screen images from widely used mobile apps. An image augmentation algorithm is introduced to boost the performance of our method.
2. We proposed our UI Layers Group Detector which takes UI screenshots and metadata from design drafts and solve the image-text grouping task. This work is designed to fill in the gap in the automatic UI code generation works.
3. We proposed the text fusion to incorporate features from text layers to the related image region. And the box attention mechanism is introduced as another plug-in component with creating an extra spatial binary image which encodes the position of each text layer inside the UI image.
4. We carry out experiments on the constructed dataset to verify that the UI Layers Group Detector achieves a decent accuracy regarding UI layers grouping.

2   Related Works

2.1   Intelligent UI Code Generation

Automation in UI code generation has become an attractive topic after the machine learning and artificial intelligence boom. Early intelligent automation research was mainly used to replace template-based UI design, where users spend time searching for suitable materials to compose their design. We can further classify these works by the level of the fidelity of the design prototype they use as input [7]. Batuhan et al. [1] use hand-drawn images to identify and generate basic buttons, text, images, and other components. Works as sketch2code [23] utilizes design drafts with more details and achieves the automatic generation of UI structure. Pix2code [2] follows a similar approach to generating textual descriptions from photographs. It takes actual UI screenshots as input and achieves a high accuracy generation. More recently, commercial platforms like Imgcook [12] takes advantage of metadata in professionally designed software and achieve a generation with high quality and reusability.

2.2   UI Design Check

With the popularization of automated UI generation technology, in practical applications, it is necessary to evaluate the generation quality and solve the problems like missing elements or components overlapping caused by hardware or software compatibility. OwlEye [19] detects GUIs with display issues and locates the detailed region of the issue based on the deep learning method. LabelDroid [4] focuses on image-based buttons and achieves a highly accurate prediction of labels by learning from large-scale commercial apps in Google Play. FSMdroid [24] uses the MCMC sampling method to analyze GUI apps dynamically and detect defects that reside on unfrequented trails.

Considering our work as an object detection task, we briefly review the recent advances in this field. Anchor-based approaches like Faster-RCNN [22] define a set of anchor boxes of different sizes and use feature maps from different convolutional layers to classify and regress anchor boxes. The following SSD [18], Yolov2 [21], and RetinaNet [15] continue this idea and achieve a state-of-art performance in natural object detection. Some achievement has also been made in using Object Detection in UI-related areas. Li et al. [13] introduce the CLAY pipeline for UI screen dataset cleaning. They address the mismatches in visual elements and metadata. Zang et al. [26] leverage object detection on recognizing UI icons and achieve good performance.

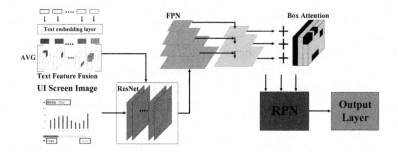

Fig. 3. The overview of proposed method.

3   Methods

In this section, we introduce the proposed approach to our UI Layers Group Detector described in Sect. 1 as shown in Fig. 3. We first introduce our work on collecting UI screen dataset based on Sketch file, which is widely used in software UI design. Image segmentation is applied considering the nature of small and regional target detection (Sect. 3.1). We then introduce our Group Detector via the order of basic setting, text fusion, and box attention. We introduce the strategy of text content and bounding boxes as extra features to help with target localization. The embedding text features are fused into the early convolution layer of our backbone (Sect. 3.2). We then introduce box attention as another way of utilizing text information. A spatial binary image is created based on text bounding boxes to guide the target detection process by revealing potential image-text group areas. We fuse the box attention with the image feature maps on all FPN output layers and feed them into the RPN for better proposals (Sect. 3.2).

3.1 Dataset

We create a high-quality UI dataset based on UI layouts developed by professional designers using Sketch. Each artboard in a Sketch file represents a UI design for Android or iOS mobile Apps. We eliminate unusual designs that placed the components without artboards as containers and convert the rest as UI screen images. A group of professional labelers was recruited to generate our target group annotation. We adapt our dataset based on COCO-style [6], including images, annotations, categories, and supplementary text consisting of text semantics and position in the images. Considering the nature of the UI screen with a large aspect ratio, while our targets are usually small and regional, image segmentation is applied to all collected UI screens. Given an arbitrary screen-shot image, we split it along the long side. To avoid distortion, we keep each piece a square shape, and only bounding boxes that are entirely inside should be recorded. To avoid some bounding boxes being separated into two samples, we leverage a sliding stride to make sure every bounding box will at least appear in one image.

We then split our dataset into training, validation, and test sets for experiments. The split is performed package-wise and image-wise, i.e., artboards in the same Sketch design file and segmented images from the same UI screen image are not shared across different splits. This approach avoids information leakage because UI screen images from the same design might have similar layouts. As a summary, the number of screen images in our dataset increases by a factor of 3 after applying the segmentation. We have 4946 screen images in the training set with 16533 labeled groups and 11617 texts. For the validation set, we have 601 screen images, 2093 labeled groups and 2093 labeled groups. And for the test set, we have 681 screen images, 2410 labeled groups and 1442 labeled groups.

3.2 UI Layers Group Detector

Usually, the placement and size of our target groups vary widely across the different UI designs. Therefore, the most crucial step in our approach is to infer the bounding boxes accurately. To achieve this goal, we utilize ResNet-50 [9] and FPN (Feature Pyramid Networks) [14] as our backbone for extracting feature maps. At the RPN (region proposal network), we use a softmax to determine positive or negative anchors and a bounding box regression to modify anchors to obtain precise proposals. Then we borrow the RoI Align [8] to replace the RoI Pooling for proposal maps extraction based on input feature maps and proposals.

Instead of quantized operations, the RoI Align utilizes linear interpolation to reduce the precision loss. At the classification stage, bounding box regression is introduced again to obtain each proposal's position offset for regressing more accurate target bounding boxes.

Text Fusion. This section introduces the text embedding features as a plug-in component to the Group Detector. As we discussed in Sect. 1, the grouping patterns varies in different application scenarios. While we also find that components with the same functionality are similar in appearance and should further apply the same grouping strategy. In this paper, together with the pixel-based UI screen image data, we further utilize the text layer information in each Sketch design, which contains the text layer position as bounding boxes and text contents. The supplementary text-level knowledge enables us to identify potential pattern-text groups and reveals the function of target groups in the UI screen.

Given a UI screen image in our dataset, let $\{bb_i\}_{i=1}^N$ be all text layer bounding boxes inside the image and $\{tt_i\}_{i=1}^N$ be all text contents. Let $I \in \mathbb{R}^{3 \times H \times W}$ as input image and $C \in \mathbb{R}^{D \times H' \times W'}$ be an intermediate feature map extracted from the first convolution layer $Conv1$ of ResNet-50. Our first step is to construct a feature map $T_i \in \mathbb{R}^{K \times H \times W}$ for every text information with the same height H and width W using the bound box $bb_i = \{x_{min}, y_{min}, x_{max}, y_{max}\}$. To achieve this, we use a text encoder to transform text content tt_i into corresponding text embedding $e_i \in \mathbb{R}^{K \times 1 \times 1}$. We let T_i fill with all 0 initially and update the text embedding e_i inside the bounding box range. Specifically, we set $T_i[:, p, q] = e_i$ where $p \in [y_{min} \times H, y_{max} \times H]$ and $q \in [x_{min} \times W, x_{max} \times W]$. In the next step, we calculate $T = avg(T_i)_{i=1}^N \in \mathbb{R}^{K \times H \times W}$ and apply the same $Conv1$ and an extra 1×1 convolution layer to get the text feature map T' with the same size of pixel feature map C. In the final step, we calculate a new feature map $F = T' \circ C$, where $\circ$ denotes the element-wise addition, and this new fused feature map is fed into the later convolution layer of Resnet-50.

Box Attention. In this section, we introduce box attention as another way of utilizing text information to improve our Group Detector. We borrow the idea of box attention from Bunian et al [3]. This mechanism was first introduced by Kolesnikov et al [10]. to model object interactions in a visual relationship detection task. Bunian et al. adopted it in their object detection pipeline. The idea of box attention is to create an extra spatial binary image encoding the position of each text layer inside the UI screen. The binary image here, is considered as a position-focal that together with the global image information to understand compositional relationship among elements.

Specifically, given an image feature map $F_i \in \mathbb{R}^{D \times H_i \times W_i}$ and text bounding box $\{bb_j\}_{j=1}^N$ where $bb_j = \{x_{min}, y_{min}, x_{max}, y_{max}\}$ corresponding to input UI screen image height H and width W, we first transform the bounding box based on H_i and W_i and create the bounding box map $B_{i,j} \in \mathbb{R}^{3 \times H_i \times W_i}$. We set $B_{i,j}[0, p, q] = 1$ where $p \in [y_{min} \times H_i, y_{max} \times H_i]$ and $q \in [x_{min} \times W_i, x_{max} \times W_i]$, $B_{i,j}[1, :, :] = 0$ and $B_{i,j}[2, :, :] = 1$. In the next step, we calculate the overall box attention map B_i for the ith image feature map as $B_i = avg(B_{i,j})_{j=1}^N$ and an extra 1×1 convolution layer is applied on it to match the image feature map dimension D. In the final step, we add the box attention map with each FPN output image feature map F_i to get the fused feature map $M_i = F_i \circ B_i$ for further proposal generating.

4 Experiments

4.1 Implementation Details

We implemente our model using MMDetection [5] codebase. We use ResNet-50 pre-trained on ImageNet together with the FPN as our backbone network. We set the anchor size [32,64,128,256,512] with anchor ratio [0.5,1.0,2.0,4.0,8.0] for the potential tiny and nonsquare target. The input UI screen images are resized into size in [800,1300] before being fed into Resnet-50. The output features of stage1-4 of ResNet-50 are fed into FPN, together with a further MaxPooling layer, giving us the five feature maps with different scales. For FPN settings, we follow the standard settings as in [14]. Proposals are computed from all five pyramid feature maps, and RoI Align is performed with bilinear interpolation.

For text embedding fusion, we first encode the text contents into vectors with length K using pre-trained transformers [25]. We set the parameter K to 16, considering the average text length of 11.4. After generating the text feature map $T \in \mathbb{R}^{K \times H' \times W'}$, we increase the channel size from K to D which is the channel size of feature map at Conv1 of stage 0 in ResNet-50. For box attention, we adopt five spatial binary images with the same size as the pyramid feature maps.

For the training details, we train our model with a mini-batch of 2 for 72 epochs using SGD optimizer with a momentum update of 0.9 and a weight decay of 0.0005; and set the initial learning rate 0.01 with a decay of factor 0.1 every 10 epochs during training. We train our model on an NVIDIA GeForce RTX 3080Ti GPU and it takes about 9 h for the model to converge.

4.2 Evaluation Metrics

In this paper, we report performance metrics used in the COCO detection evaluation criterion [16] and provide mean Average Precision (AP) across various IoU thresholds i.e. IoU=0.50:0.95,0.50,0.75 and various scales: small, medium and large. Without further specified, we refer mAP[0.50:0.95]to as AP.

4.3 Results

Detection Performance After Image Segmentation. We first test the benefits of our image segmentation algorithm. As shown in Table 1, the image segmentation contributes to a performance boost of AP by about 20%. In the UI design draft, a potential group like a banner or an icon only takes up a small area of the overall screen. Even if we have modified the anchor's size and aspect ratio accordingly, finding all targets is still challenging. With segmentation, the target becomes more prominent in the background. Furthermore, we also get an augmentation effect with an overlapping slide window that applies multiple locations for each target in image slices.

Table 1. Detection performance after image segmentation.

Method	AP	AP_{50}	AP_{75}	AP_S	AP_M	AP_L
No segmentation	0.428	0.585	0.474	0.367	0.408	0.446
Apply segmentation	**0.625**	**0.799**	**0.699**	**0.550**	**0.593**	**0.648**

Detection Models Comparison. We then compare the detection performance using recent state-of-art object detection models as shown in Table 2. All the results are tested using the segmented dataset. To deploy our Group Detector as a plug-in for UI code generator like Imgcook, we expect it to be lightweight while achieving high accuracy. "UIGD-TF" denotes our UI Layers Group Detector with the text fusion and "UIGD-BA" denotes our UI Layers Group Detector with the box attention. Here we could see that "UIGD-TF" achieves the highest AP performance of 0.658 among all the model we experimented. And "UIGD-BA" takes the second position with AP performance of 0.650. They are also lighter than other models. For example, "UIGD-TF" is 66.9% lighter on model parameters than the Sparse-RCNN while 3.7% higher on accuracy.

Table 2. Detection performance comparison.

Method	Parameters ↓	AP	AP_{50}	AP_{75}	AP_S	AP_M	AP_L
Deformable DETR	49.76M	0.603	0.751	0.670	0.439	0.558	0.635
YoloX	54.15M	0.592	0.788	0.654	0.448	0.517	0.634
Sparse-RCNN	125.21M	0.621	0.759	0.683	0.500	0.566	0.657
Faster-RCNN	41.35M	0.625	0.799	0.699	0.550	0.593	0.648
UIGD-TF	41.30M	**0.658**	**0.853**	**0.729**	**0.572**	0.643	**0.708**
UIGD-BA	41.29M	0.650	0.825	0.715	0.568	**0.651**	0.678

Performance with Text Fusion and Box Attention. We then investigate the contribution of our proposed text fusion component. As shown in Table 2, compare with the Fatser-RCNN, which got the highest accuracy in the rest of the model, we get an 3.3% AP improvement brought by the text fusion strategy suggests the necessity of the text semantic and location prior knowledge, which enriches the feature representation. The box attention also gives a 2.5%

AP improvement, indicating that concentrating on text location help captures potential group targets. Comparing the model parameters, it can be ssen that apply the text fusion and the box attention only increase the model parameters by 0.48% and 0.24% while the accuracy is significantly increased by 5.28% and 4.00%. All the results show that our proposed text fusion and box attention work effectively, and achieve our requirement of lightweight.

Detection Cases Analysis. Finally, we present some of our detection results. Figure 4a shows two cases that our Group Detector successfully localize all the target groups with highly matched bounding boxes. In these two examples, it can be seen that our model achieve a high accuracy of predicting diversified UI components with different patterns and elements number as we discussed in Sect. 1.

We also present some cases where our model fails. Figure 4b shows two typical examples that fully embody the existing shortcomings. The picture above shows that all group predictions are correct but not perfect fits. With an empty background around, our model fails to determine the boundaries of the target groups. Although this does not affect the localization of the layers in design drafts (no extra layers are included by error), the model performance is underestimated because of the low IoU. Another challenge is that our model shows weakness in distinguishing between foreground and background. As the bottom picture shows, our model mistakenly groups the address "ARK" in the background layer with the black dots in the foreground. The classic expression of this problem is that our model produces the wrong groups when faced with complex multi-level structures.

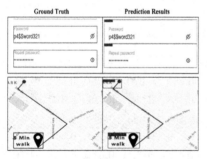
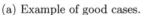

(a) Example of good cases.

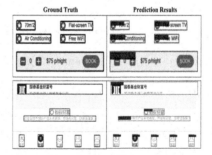

(b) Example of failure cases.

Fig. 4. (a) Our Group Detector successfully localize all the target groups with highly matched bounding boxes. (b) Our Group Detector show weakness on perfectly fit the ground truth bounding boxes on empty background around, and produces the wrong groups when faced with complex multi-level structures.

5 Conclusion

This paper investigates a novel issue about layers grouping in an automatic design draft to UI view code process, which can decrease the quality of generated code. To solve this issue, we propose our UI Layers Group Detector to locate the group accurately. By dataset segmentation, we achieve about a 20% boost in detection AP. We also propose two plug-in components to help increase the detection performance. The Text fusion introduces text semantic and location prior knowledge and achieves about a 3.3% increase in detection AP. For the box attention, the spatial binary images encoding potential text location give us a 2.5% increase in detection AP.

Acknowledgement. This research is supported by Alibaba-Zhejiang University Joint Research Institute of Frontier Technologies.

References

1. Aşıroğlu, B., et al.: Automatic html code generation from mock-up images using machine learning techniques. In: 2019 Scientific Meeting on Electrical-Electronics & Biomedical Engineering and Computer Science (EBBT), pp. 1–4 (2019)
2. Beltramelli, T.: pix2code: generating code from a graphical user interface screenshot. In: Proceedings of the ACM SIGCHI Symposium on Engineering Interactive Computing Systems, pp. 1–6 (2018)
3. Bunian, S., et al.: Visual search for mobile user interface design. In: Proceedings of the 2021 CHI Conference on Human Factors in Computing Systems, pp. 1–14 (2021)
4. Chen, J., et al.: Unblind your apps: Predicting natural-language labels for mobile GUI components by deep learning. In: 2020 IEEE/ACM 42nd International Conference on Software Engineering (ICSE), pp. 322–334. IEEE (2020)
5. Chen, K., et al.: MMDetection: Open MMLAB detection toolbox and benchmark. arXiv preprint arXiv:1906.07155 (2019)
6. Chen, X., et al.: Microsoft coco captions: data collection and evaluation server. arXiv preprint arXiv:1504.00325 (2015)
7. Dave, H., Sonje, S., Pardeshi, J., Chaudhari, S., Raundale, P.: A survey on artificial intelligence based techniques to convert user interface design mock-ups to code. In: 2021 International Conference on Artificial Intelligence and Smart Systems (ICAIS), pp. 28–33 (2021)
8. He, K., Gkioxari, G., Dollár, P., Girshick, R.: Mask r-cnn. In: Proceedings of the IEEE international conference on computer vision, pp. 2961–2969 (2017)
9. He, K., Zhang, X., Ren, S., Sun, J.: Deep residual learning for image recognition. In: Proceedings of the IEEE Conference on Computer Vision and Pattern Recognition, pp. 770–778 (2016)
10. Kolesnikov, A., Kuznetsova, A., Lampert, C., Ferrari, V.: Detecting visual relationships using box attention. In: Proceedings of the IEEE/CVF International Conference on Computer Vision Workshops (2019)
11. Kumar, A.: Automated front-end development using deep learning. https://blog. insightdatascience.com/automated-front-end-development-using-deep-learning-3169dd086e82/ (2018)

12. lab, A.: Intelligent code generation for design drafts (2021). http://www.imgcook.com/
13. Li, G., Baechler, G., Tragut, M., Li, Y.: Learning to denoise raw mobile UI layouts for improving datasets at scale. In: CHI Conference on Human Factors in Computing Systems, pp. 1–13 (2022),
14. Lin, T.Y., Dollár, P., Girshick, R., He, K., Hariharan, B., Belongie, S.: Feature pyramid networks for object detection. In: Proceedings of the IEEE Conference on Computer Vision and Pattern Recognition, pp. 2117–2125 (2017)
15. Lin, T.Y., Goyal, P., Girshick, R., He, K., Dollár, P.: Focal loss for dense object detection. In: 2017 IEEE International Conference on Computer Vision (ICCV), pp. 2999–3007 (2017)
16. Lin, T., et al.: Microsoft COCO: common objects in context. CoRR (2014), arXiv:1405.0312
17. Ling, W., et al.: Latent predictor networks for code generation. arXiv preprint arXiv:1603.06744 (2016)
18. Liu, W., et al.: SSD: Single Shot MultiBox Detector. In: Leibe, B., Matas, J., Sebe, N., Welling, M. (eds.) ECCV 2016. LNCS, vol. 9905, pp. 21–37. Springer, Cham (2016). https://doi.org/10.1007/978-3-319-46448-0_2
19. Liu, Z., Chen, C., Wang, J., Huang, Y., Hu, J., Wang, Q.: Owl eyes: spotting UI display issues via visual understanding. In: 2020 35th IEEE/ACM International Conference on Automated Software Engineering (ASE), pp. 398–409. IEEE (2020)
20. Nguyen, T.A., Csallner, C.: Reverse engineering mobile application user interfaces with remaui (t). In: 2015 30th IEEE/ACM International Conference on Automated Software Engineering (ASE), pp. 248–259 (2015)
21. Redmon, J., Farhadi, A.: Yolo9000: better, faster, stronger. In: Proceedings of the IEEE Conference on Computer Vision and Pattern Recognition, pp. 7263–7271 (2017)
22. Ren, S., He, K., Girshick, R., Sun, J.: Faster R-CNN: Towards real-time object detection with region proposal networks. IEEE Trans. Pattern Anal. Mach. Intell. **39**(6), 1137–1149 (2017)
23. Robinson, A.: Sketch2code: generating a website from a paper mockup. arXiv preprint arXiv:1905.13750 (2019)
24. Su, T.: Fsmdroid: guided GUI testing of android apps. In: 2016 IEEE/ACM 38th International Conference on Software Engineering Companion (ICSE-C), pp. 689–691 (2016)
25. Wolf, T., et al.: Transformers: state-of-the-art natural language processing. In: Proceedings of the 2020 Conference on Empirical Methods in Natural Language Processing: System Demonstrations, pp. 38–45 (2020)
26. Zang, X., Xu, Y., Chen, J.: Multimodal icon annotation for mobile applications. In: Proceedings of the 23rd International Conference on Mobile Human-Computer Interaction, pp. 1–11 (2021)

Audio-Visual Fusion Network Based on Conformer for Multimodal Emotion Recognition

Peini Guo[1,2], Zhengyan Chen[1], Yidi Li[1], and Hong Liu[1(✉)]

[1] Key Laboratory of Machine Perception, Peking University,
Shenzhen Graduate School, Shenzhen, China
guopeini@stu.pku.edu.cn, {chenzhengyan,yidili,hongliu}@pku.edu.cn
[2] Shanghai University, Shanghai, China

Abstract. Audio-visual emotion recognition aims to integrate audio and visual information for accurate emotion prediction, which is widely used in real application scenarios. However, most existing methods lack fully exploiting complementary information within modalities to obtain rich feature representations related to emotions. Recently, Transformer and CNN-based models achieve remarkable results in the field of automatic speech recognition. Motivated by this, we propose a novel audio-visual fusion network based on 3D-CNN and Convolution-augmented Transformer (Conformer) for multimodal emotion recognition. Firstly, the 3D-CNN is employed to process face sequences extracted from the video, and the 1D-CNN is used to process MFCC features of audio signals. Secondly, the visual and audio features are fed into a feature fusion module, which contains a set of convolutional layers for extracting local features and the self-attention mechanism for capturing global interactions of multimodal information. Finally, the fused features are input into linear layers to obtain the prediction results. To verify the effectiveness of the proposed method, experiments are performed on RAVDESS and a newly collected dataset named PKU-ER. The experimental results show that the proposed model achieves state-of-the-art performance in audio-only, video-only, and audio-visual fusion experiments.

Keywords: Multimodal emotion recognition · Audio-visual fusion · Convolutional Neural Network · Transformer

1 Introduction

In recent years, emotion recognition has received a great deal of attention for its robust performance and high application value, which has a wide range of applications such as intelligent transportation and human-computer interaction. Emotion recognition is a challenging task in the real world, as the way emotions

Supported by National Natural Science Foundation of China (No. 62073004), Science and Technology Plan of Shenzhen (No. JCYJ20200109140410340).

L. Fang et al. (Eds.): CICAI 2022, LNAI 13605, pp. 315–326, 2022.
https://doi.org/10.1007/978-3-031-20500-2_26

are expressed often varies across individuals and cultures [1]. Some recent works focus on multimodal emotion recognition that utilizes multiple modalities simultaneously for prediction, which can compensate for the lack of information in a single modality and has better performance than unimodal emotion recognition models. Modalities related to emotions usually include vision, audio, text, EEG, body gestures, etc. [2]. Considering that the visual and audio modalities are the most widely used due to their simplicity of sampling and good expressiveness, this paper focuses on the fusion of visual and audio modalities for emotion recognition.

Existing works of audio-visual fusion can be classified into three types according to the way features are fused: early fusion, late fusion, and model fusion [3]. Early fusion usually directly concatenates the video features and audio features after extracting them, and then feeds the fused features into fully connected layers for prediction. Deng et al. proposed a multimodal neural network structure that used Long Short-Term Memory (LSTM) to obtain time-varying visual information and performed emotional analysis by feature-level fusion of visual, audio, and textual information [4]. Kumar et al. proposed an improved multimodal emotion recognition method based on the attention mechanism and Bidirectional Gated Recurrent Unit (BiGRU) [5]. The implementation of early fusion is relatively simple, and it considers the correlation between the lower-level features of the modalities. However, it does not make full use of the complementarity of intra- and inter-modal information, resulting in little performance improvement over unimodal models. Late fusion usually models audio and visual features separately, and then joints the predictions to obtain the final predictions. Yu et al. used Convolutional Neural Network (CNN) and Deep Neural Network (DNN) to analyze textual and visual information, respectively, and then fused the prediction results of the two modalities by using the averaging strategy and weight [6]. Huang et al. firstly used image and text modalities for emotion classification separately, then proposed a multimodal model based on the fusion of two modalities, and finally fused the results of three models to obtain the final prediction results [7]. Because separate models are required to model and classify visual and audio modalities, the model structure of late fusion is more complex, and late fusion does not effectively exploit complementary information between modalities. Model fusion means that the extracted visual and audio features are fused by machine learning methods, deep neural networks, etc. Model fusion can leverage the complementary information between visual and audio modalities, which can bring significant improvement over unimodal models. In recent years, there are a lot of audio-visual fusion works based on the model fusion approach. Petridis et al. introduced a model based on residual networks and BiGRU, which is the first end-to-end audio-visual fusion model that simultaneously extracts features from raw pixels and audio waveforms and trains them on the large publicly available dataset [8]. Other methods based on model fusion using Recurrent Neural Network (RNN) for audio-visual speech recognition are proposed [9,10]. Due to the great results of the Transformer architecture based on the attention mechanism in the fields of computer vision and natural language processing,

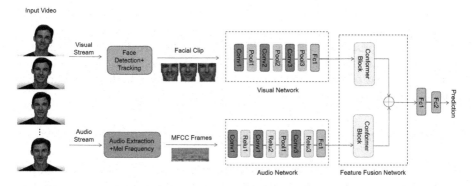

Fig. 1. The overall architecture of the proposed model, including the visual network, audio network, feature fusion network, and prediction head.

an increasing number of researchers have applied the attention mechanism in model fusion work [11]. Fu et al. proposed a feature fusion block based on the self-attention mechanism and residual structure for audio-visual fusion emotion recognition [12]. Zhang et al. proposed a feature fusion module based on the leader-follower attention mechanism [13]. The multi-modal perception attention network is proposed in [14] to learn the perception weights by using the complementarity across the audio-visual cues. Moreover, several audio-visual fusion works based on model fusion exploited the attention mechanism, with favorable results [15–17].

However, most of the existing audio-visual fusion methods focus on the design of feature fusion module, ignoring the significant impact of feature extraction on the model performance. Most existing methods only extract inter-modal complementary information, but do not effectively obtain intra-modal complementary information. Moreover, existing methods cannot guarantee the integrity of information during feature extraction and fusion, which may lose important semantic information and thus reduce the performance of the model.

Recently, models based on Transformer and CNN architectures have achieved promising results in the field of audio-visual fusion emotion recognition. To utilize the advantages of both Transformer and CNN in feature extraction, Gulati et al. proposed the Convolution-augmented Transformer (Conformer) to extract features with stronger generalization [18]. It was shown that the Conformer significantly outperformed the previous Transformer and CNN-based models, achieving state-of-the-art accuracy. Inspired by this, we propose a novel audio-visual fusion network based on Conformer architecture for emotion recognition. Specifically, the MFCC features extracted from audios are processed by 1D-CNN and the expression and action information included in consecutive frames of videos are extracted by 3D-CNN. Secondly, audio features and video features are fed into the feature fusion network, which learns location-based local features by convolution mechanism and content-based global dependencies by self-attention mechanism to effectively extract complementary information within two modalities, and achieves effective feature fusion. Finally, the fused features are fed into fully connected layers to obtain the prediction results. To verify the effectiveness of proposed method, experiments are performed on RAVDESS [19] and PKU-ER multimodal emotion recognition datasets, and the experimental results show that our model outperforms other advanced methods and achieves state-of-the-art performance.

2 Methodology

As shown in Fig. 1, a new audio-visual fusion network for emotion recognition is proposed. Firstly, 3D-CNN is used to extract features from consecutive face frames in temporal and spatial dimensions, and 1D-CNN is used to process the MFCC features extracted from original audio signals. Secondly, the audio features and visual features are further processed using Conformer to make full use of complementary information within the modalities and obtain representations with strong generalization. The features are fused as an enhanced audio-visual feature representation in this step. Finally, the fused features are fed to the fully connected layers to obtain prediction results. The process is described in detail below.

2.1 Visual Network

The input of the visual network is consecutive face frames extracted from videos. Considering the video data are time- and space-correlated, the 3D convolution is utilized that can extract face expressions and movements simultaneously. The visual modality feature extraction network mainly consists of the 3D convolution layers, the max-pooling layers and the batch normalization layers. The group mechanism is incorporated to 3D convolution layers, which can effectively reduce the number of parameters for convolution and improve the model performance. To avoid the overfitting phenomenon, dropout layers are added to the model with the probability of 0.2. The final layer of the network compresses the feature dimensions from the original five dimensions (B, C, D, H, W) to three dimensions (B, C, N), where B denotes the batch size, C denotes the number of channels, D denotes the sequence depth, H denotes the height, W denotes the width, and N denotes the compressed dimension with the size of D × H × W. For input v_i, the equations of output process in the visual network are as follows:

$$v_i' = \text{Maxpool}\left(\text{Conv}\left(v_i\right)\right), \tag{1}$$

$$v_i'' = \text{Maxpool}\left(\text{Conv}\left(v_i'\right)\right), \tag{2}$$

$$v_i''' = \text{Maxpool}\left(\text{Conv}\left(v_i''\right)\right), \tag{3}$$

$$v_o = \text{Fc}\left(v_i'''\right). \tag{4}$$

where Conv denotes the 3D convolution layer, Maxpool denotes the max-pooling layer, and Fc denotes the fully connected layer.

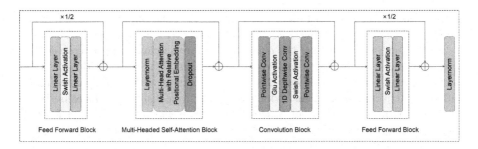

Fig. 2. Model architecture of Conformer block. It consists of two feed forward blocks sandwiching a multi-headed self-attention block and a convolution block.

2.2 Audio Network

MFCC is a kind of feature that has been proved to significantly improve the performance of speech recognition systems in recent years. MFCC is based on human auditorily perceptual characteristics, and simulates the human's audio system to the greatest extent, which is one of the most common and effective speech feature extraction algorithms. MFCC is the inverse spectral coefficient extracted in the frequency domain of the Mel scale, which describes the nonlinear nature of frequency perception by the human's ear. Therefore, the MFCC features extracted from original audios are used as the input to the network. The input passes through two 1D convolution layers to extract the local correlation of the sequence features, after which the features are compressed by a max-pooling layer to remove redundant information, and finally the features are fed to a 1D convolution layer to extract high-order semantic features. The output of intermediate layers is activated by Relu function. To avoid overfitting phenomenon, dropout layers are added to the model with the probability of 0.2. In the last layer, a linear function is used to align the last dimension of audio features with visual features to facilitate feature fusion. For input a_i, the equations of output process in the audio network are as follows:

$$a_i' = \mathrm{Conv}\left(\mathrm{Relu}\left(a_i\right)\right), \tag{5}$$

$$a_i'' = \mathrm{Conv}\left(\mathrm{Relu}\left(a_i'\right)\right), \tag{6}$$

$$a_i''' = \mathrm{Maxpool}\left(a_i''\right), \tag{7}$$

$$a_i'''' = \mathrm{Conv}\left(\mathrm{Relu}\left(a_i'''\right)\right), \tag{8}$$

$$a_o = \mathrm{Fc}\left(a_i''''\right). \tag{9}$$

where Conv denotes the 1D convolution layer, Maxpool denotes the max-pooling layer, and Fc denotes the fully connected layer.

2.3 Feature Fusion Network

A novel Conformer-based feature fusion network is introduced in this part, which aims to achieve efficient feature fusion by making full use of complementary information within multi-modalities. As shwon in Fig. 2, a Conformer block consists of two half-step feed forward blocks with a multi-headed self-attention block and a convolution block in the middle [18]. This structure is inspired by Macaron-Net, which suggests replacing the original feed forward layer in the Transformer with two half-step feed forward layers, while using half-step residual connections in both feed forward layers [20]. The Conformer utilizes both convolution and self-attention mechanisms, which can simultaneously learn location-based local dependencies and content-based global representations to extract features with stronger generalization ability. Mathematically, for Conformer block i, with input x_i, the output y_i of the block is:

$$x_i = x_i + \frac{1}{2}\text{FFN}(x_i), \tag{10}$$

$$x_i' = \tilde{x}_i + \text{MHSA}(\tilde{x}_i), \tag{11}$$

$$x_i'' = x_i' + \text{Conv}(x_i'), \tag{12}$$

$$y_i = \text{Layernorm}\left(x_i'' + \frac{1}{2}\text{FFN}(x_i'')\right), \tag{13}$$

where FFN denotes feed forward block, MHSA denotes multi-headed self-attention block, and Conv denotes convolution block.

The visual and audio features processed by Conformer are added up in the channel dimension, which ensures the integrity of the fused information. When the feature of audio modality is y_a and the feature of visual modality is y_v, the fused feature is:

$$I = y_a \oplus y_v. \tag{14}$$

where $\oplus$ denotes the element-wise addition.

2.4 Classfication

The fused features are fed into fully connected layers to obtain prediction results. The loss function is the cross-entropy function, which has great performance in multi-classification problems. The specific equations are as follows:

$$\text{prediction} = WI + b \in \mathbb{R}^N, \tag{15}$$

$$L = -\sum_i y_i \log(\hat{y}_i). \tag{16}$$

where N denotes the dimension of the output vector, I denotes the fused feature, W denotes the weight tensor, $b \in \mathbb{R}^N$ denotes the bias, $y = \{y_1, y_2, y_3 \ldots y_n\}^T$ denotes the one-hot vector of emotion labels, $\hat{y} = \{\hat{y}_1, \hat{y}_2, \hat{y}_3 \ldots \hat{y}_n\}$ denotes the probability distribution of predictions, and n denotes the number of emotion categories.

3   Experiments and Discussions

3.1   Datasets

For the emotion recognition task of audio-visual fusion, a good video emotion classification dataset is crucial. The metrics used to evaluate the dataset include

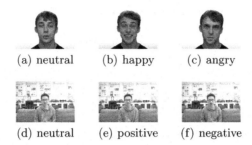

(a) neutral   (b) happy   (c) angry

(d) neutral   (e) positive   (f) negative

Fig. 3. Samples from datasets. Above: RAVDESS. Below: PKU-ER.

the clarity of the video/audio, the degree of the character's facial expression/lip movement changes, the obviousness of the pitch changes, etc. Based on the above metrics, a publicly available dataset and a self-made dataset are used to evaluate the performance of the model simultaneously.

The Ryerson Audio-Visual Database of Emotional Speech and Song (RAVDESS) contains 7356 files of utterances containing emotional polarity delivered by 24 professional actors in neutral North American accents [19]. Speechs include eight types of emotions: neutral, calm, happy, sad, angry, fearful, disgusted and surprised, and songs include five types of emotions: calm, happy, sad, angry and fearful. Each emotion contains two emotional intensities (normal, strong). All conditions are available in three formats: audio-only (16bit, 48 KHz, .wav), video-only (no sound), and audio-video (720p H.264, AAC 48 KHz, .mp4). The audio-video format of speech part is selected, with total 1440 files. The PKU-Emotion Recognition Dataset (PKU-ER) contains total 896 Chinese emotion video files recorded by 14 experimenters in human-computer interaction scenes. The emotions are classified into three categories: positive, negative, and neutral. Each emotion contains only one emotional intensity (normal). All files are in audio-video format. The above datasets facilitate the study of specific characteristics related to emotions, avoiding possible prejudices in the expression of emotions caused by cultural differences. Moreover, the number of documents corresponding to each emotion is nearly equal, obviating the problems that may result from unbalanced data samples. Some examples of the two datasets are shown in Fig. 3.

3.2 Implementation Details

For the visual modality, OpenFace [21] is utilized to extract 68 face landmarks in each frame of the video, thus cropping each frame to a face ROI with the resolution of 224×224. To alleviate the problem of small sample size of the dataset, data augmentation is performed on images, including random cropping, random horizontal flipping and normalization. For the audio modality, since there is usually no sound in the first 0.5 s, 2.45 s duration of the audio starting from the 0.5 s are extracted, with the sampling rate 44100 Hz. The first 13 MFCC features are selected for each cropped audio clip.

Table 1. Impact of model architecture on RAVDESS and PKU-ER datasets.

Model	Accuracy (on RAVDESS)	Accuracy (on PKU-ER)
Ours	78.45	90.53
w/o group convolution	77.63	89.25
w/o feature fusion block	72.57	84.61
w/o conformer encoder (A)	75.82	87.74
w/o conformer encoder (V)	74.50	86.37

The 6-fold cross-validation is performed on datasets to provide more robust results, i.e., the datasets are divided into training and validation sets in the ratio of 5:1, without dividing the separate test set. The model is trained using Adam optimizer with the initial learning rate of 0.001. The loss function is the cross-entropy function. To avoid overfitting, earlystopping is used, i.e., the accuracy is tested on validation sets after each epoch, and training is stopped in advance if the accuracy does not rise for n consecutive times, in experiments $n = 20$. All parts of the model are trained simultaneously. The training process of the model is done on a single NVIDIA RTX3090. The final accuracy reported is the average accuracy over 6 folds.

3.3   Ablation Study

Impact of Model Architecture. To verify the effectiveness of model, the impact of model architecture on performance is explored. The experimental results are shown in Table 1. When group convolution in the visual network is not used, the accuracy of the model decreases by 0.82% and 1.28% on RAVDESS and PKU-ER datasets, respectively, indicating that group convolution can effectively reduce the number of calculation parameters and improve the model performance. To verify the impact of the feature fusion network, the extracted features are stitched directly and fed into linear layers to obtain prediction results, compared with the case of using the feature fusion network. The experimental results show that when not using the feature fusion network, the classification accuracy of the model decreases by 5.88% and 5.92% on RAVDESS and PKU-ER datasets, respectively. This illustrates that feature fusion network can make full use of complementary information within and across modalities and remove redundant information, facilitating accurate predictions of emotion. When the Conformer for audio modality is removed, the classification accuracy of the model decreases by 2.63% and 2.79% on RAVDESS and PKU-ER datasets, respectively. When the Conformer for video modality is removed, the classification accuracy of the model decreases by 3.95% and 4.16% on RAVDESS and PKU-ER datasets, respectively. This indicates that Conformer can effectively learn both location-based local features and content-based global interactions to obtain representations with stronger generalization. Furthermore, Conformer has more influence on video modality than audio modality, suggesting that features within the video modality are more relevant.

Table 2. Comparison of the classification accuracy with different inputs.

Stream	Accuracy (on RAVDESS)	Accuracy (on PKU-ER)
A	62.35	56.84
V	70.03	81.58
A + V	**78.45**	**90.53**

Impact of Different Inputs. The classification accuracies of model on two datasets with different inputs (audio-only, video-only, audio-video) are shown in Table 2. When the input contains both audio and video, the accuracy of the model on datasets is 78.45% and 90.53%, respectively. When the input is only audio or video, the accuracy decreases significantly, and the accuracy is lower when the input is audio than when the input is video. This indicates that the video modality provides more information than the audio modality, in addition, audio and video modalities can effectively provide complementary information.

Impact of Noise. The random noise with Signal-to-Noise Ratios(SNR) of -5, 0, 5, 10, 15, 20 dB is added to the audio data of RAVDESS dataset to investigate the impact of different noise intensities on model performance. Figure 4 shows some visualization results of Mel-spectrogram in the case of clean and different intensities of noise. It can be seen that the features in the Mel-spectrogram become clearer as the noise intensity decreases. The experimental results are shown in Fig. 5, where the horizontal axis denotes the SNR, the vertical axis denotes the classification accuracy of the model on RAVDESS dataset, and three broken lines denote the model under three types of inputs (A for audio-only, V for video-only, and A+V for audio-video). When using video frames as input, the accuracy remains constant 70.03% as visual information is not affected by acoustic noises. In the case of high noise, the performance of audio-only model degrades dramatically, and the accuracy of audio-visual fusion model decreases more slowly, indicating that audio-visual fusion model is more robust to noise than audio-only model. In contrast, the audio-visual fusion model outperforms other models in the low-noise case, suggesting that the video and audio modalities efficiently provide complementary information which enhances the performance of audio-visual fusion model.

3.4 Comparison with the State-of-the-Art

The model is compared with the following methods:

1. MMTM [22]: A feature fusion model that allows feature fusion in convolutional layers of different spatial dimensions and feature selection using the self-attention mechanism.
2. MSAF [23]: A feature fusion model where each modal features are segmented in the channel direction into feature blocks with equal number of channels and a joint representation is created.

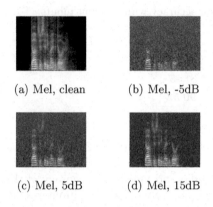

(a) Mel, clean   (b) Mel, -5dB

(c) Mel, 5dB   (d) Mel, 15dB

Fig. 4. Visualization of Mel-spectrogram under clean and different intensities of noise.

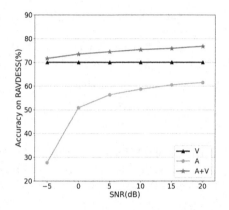

Fig. 5. The impact of noise on model.

Table 3. Comparison with state-of-the-arts on RAVDESS and PKU-ER datasets.

Model	Accuracy (on RAVDESS)	Accuracy (on PKU-ER)	Params
MMTM [22]	73.12	83.58	31.97M
MSAF [23]	74.86	83.12	25.94M
ERANNs [24]	75.23	86.94	23.60M
Ours	**78.45**	**90.53**	**18.40M**

3. ERANNs [24]: A new CNN structure proposed for audio-visual fusion emotion recognition, achieving state-of-the-art performance.

The experiment results are shown in Table 3. On both datasets, our proposed model outperforms the above methods and achieves state-of-the-art. The proposed model improves 5.33% over MMTM, 3.59% over MSAF, and 3.22% over ERANNs on the RAVDESS dataset. Moreover, the number of parameters in our model is much less than above methods, with only 18.4 millions. This indicates that the proposed model based on Conformer sufficiently obtains audio-visual features with high generalization and enables effective feature fusion and decision classification, which can achieve more advanced performance with the high parameter efficiency.

4   Conclusion

In this paper, we focus on how to extract relevant information within the audio and visual modalities and achieve effective feature fusion. To solve the problem, an audio-visual fusion network based on convolution-augmented Transformer is proposed for multimodal emotion recognition. The strategy of combining convolution with self-attention mechanism can simultaneously learn location-based local features and content-based global dependencies, obtaining sufficient complementary information within modalities. The element-wise addition operation ensures the integrity of the fused features. The experimental results on RAVDESS and PKU-ER datasets show that the proposed model achieves efficient feature extraction and fusion, achieving state-of-the-art performance. Our future work will extend the proposed method to fine-grained emotion classification, and introduce text information for multimodal emotion recognition.

References

1. Praveen, R.G., et al.: A Joint Cross-Attention Model for Audio-Visual Fusion in Dimensional Emotion Recognition. arXiv preprint arXiv:2203.14779 (2022)
2. Praveen, R.G., Granger, E., Cardinal, P.: Cross attentional audio-visual fusion for dimensional emotion recognition. In: IEEE International Conference on Automatic Face and Gesture Recognition, pp. 1–8 (2021)
3. Wu, C.H., Lin, J.C., Wei, W.L.: Survey on audio-visual emotion recognition: databases, features, and data fusion strategies. APSIPA Trans. Signal Inf. Process. **3**(1) (2014)
4. Deng, D., Zhou, Y., Pi, J., Shi, B.E.: Multimodal utterance-level affect analysis using visual, audio and text features. arXiv preprint arXiv:1805.00625 (2018)
5. Kumar, A., Vepa, J.: Gated mechanism for attention based multimodal sentiment analysis. In: IEEE International Conference on Acoustics, Speech and Signal Processing, pp. 4477–4481 (2020)
6. Yu, Y., Lin, H., Meng, J., Zhao, Z.: Visual and textual sentiment analysis of a microblog using deep convolutional neural networks. Algorithms **9**(2), 41 (2016)
7. Huang, F., Zhang, X., Zhao, Z., Xu, J., Li, Z.: Image-text sentiment analysis via deep multimodal attentive fusion. Knowl.-Based Syst. **167**, 26–37 (2019)
8. Petridis, S., Stafylakis, T., Ma, P., Cai, F.: End-to-end audiovisual speech recognition. In: IEEE International Conference on Acoustics, Speech and Signal Processing, pp. 6548–6552 (2018)
9. Liu, H., Chen, Z., Yang, B.: Lip graph assisted audio-visual speech recognition using bidirectional synchronous fusion. In: Conference of the International Speech Communication Association, pp. 3520–3524 (2020)
10. Liu, H., Xu, W., Yang, B.: Audio-visual speech recognition using a two-step feature fusion strategy. In: International Conference on Pattern Recognition, pp. 1896–1903 (2021)
11. Vaswani, A., et al.: Attention is all you need. In: Annual Conference on Neural Information Processing Systems, vol. 30, pp. 6000–6010 (2017)
12. Fu, Z., et al.: A Cross-Modal Fusion Network Based on Self-attention and Residual Structure for Multimodal Emotion Recognition. arXiv preprint arXiv:2111.02172 (2021)
13. Zhang, S., Ding, Y., Wei, Z., Guan, C.: Continuous emotion recognition with audio-visual leader-follower attentive fusion. In: Proceedings of the IEEE/CVF International Conference on Computer Vision, pp. 3567–3574 (2021)
14. Li, Y., Liu, H., Tang, H.: Multi-modal perception attention network with self-supervised learning for audio-visual speaker tracking. In: Proceedings of the AAAI Conference on Artificial Intelligence, pp. 1456–1463 (2022)

15. Serdyuk, D., Braga, O., Siohan, O.: Audio-visual speech recognition is worth $32 \times 32 \times 8$ voxels. In: IEEE Automatic Speech Recognition and Understanding Workshop, pp. 796–802 (2021)
16. Tran, M., Soleymani, M.: A pre-trained audio-visual transformer for emotion recognition. In: IEEE International Conference on Acoustics, Speech and Signal Processing, pp. 4698–4702 (2022)
17. Chang, F.J., Radfar, M., Mouchtaris, A., King, B., Kunzmann, S.: End-to-end multi-channel transformer for speech recognition. In: IEEE International Conference on Acoustics, Speech and Signal Processing, pp. 5884–5888 (2021)
18. Gulati, A., et al.: Conformer: convolution-augmented transformer for speech recognition. In: Conference of the International Speech Communication Association, pp. 5036–5040 (2020)
19. Livingstone, S.R., Russo, F.A.: The ryerson audio-visual database of emotional speech and song (RAVDESS): a dynamic, multimodal set of facial and vocal expressions in North American English. PloS Computational Linguistics, pp. 2978–2988 (2019)
20. Lu, Y., et al.: Understanding and improving transformer from a multi-particle dynamic system point of view. In: Workshop on Integration of Deep Neural Models and Differential Equations (2020)
21. Baltrusaitis, T., Zadeh, A., Lim, Y.C., Morency, L.P.: Openface 2.0: facial behavior analysis toolkit. In: IEEE International Conference on Automatic Face and Gesture Recognition, pp. 59–66 (2018)
22. Joze, H.R.V., Shaban, A., Iuzzolino, M.L., Koishida, K.: MMTM: multimodal transfer module for CNN fusion. In: Proceedings of the IEEE/CVF Conference on Computer Vision and Pattern Recognition, pp. 13289–13299 (2020)
23. Su, L., Hu, C., Li, G., Cao, D.: MSAF: Multimodal Split Attention Fusion. arXiv preprint arXiv:2012.07175 (2020)
24. Verbitskiy, S., Berikov, V., Vyshegorodtsev, V.: ERANNs: Efficient Residual Audio Neural Networks for Audio Pattern Recognition. arXiv preprint arXiv:2106.01621 (2021)

Audio-Visual Multi-person Keyword Spotting via Hybrid Fusion

Yuxin Su[1,2], Ziling Miao[1], and Hong Liu[1(✉)]

[1] Key Laboratory of Machine Perception, Peking University, Shenzhen Graduate
School, Shenzhen, China
yuxinsu@stu.pku.edu.cn, {zilingmiao,hongliu}@pku.edu.cn
[2] Xidian University, Xian, China

Abstract. As an important research method for speech recognition
tasks, audio-visual fusion has achieved good performances in improving
the robustness of keyword spotting (KWS) models, especially in a noisy
environment. However, most related studies are implemented under the
single-person scenarios, while ignoring the application in multi-person
scenarios. In this work, an audio-visual model using the hybrid fusion
is proposed for multi-person KWS. In detail, a speaker detection model
based on the attention mechanism is firstly used in the visual frontend to
select the key visual signals corresponding to the speaker. Then, semantic features of audio signals and visual signals are extracted by using
two pre-trained feature extraction networks. Finally, in order to exploit
the complementarity and independence of the signals from two modalities from the feature and decision level, the features are fed into the
proposed hybrid fusion module. In addition, the first Chinese keyword
spotting dataset named PKU-KWS is recorded. Experiments on this
dataset demonstrate the reliability of the proposed method for practical
applications. Meanwhile, the model also shows stable performance under
different noise intensities.

Keywords: Audio-visual fusion · Multi-person · Keyword spotting ·
Hybrid fusion

1 Introduction

Keyword spotting refers to spotting keywords in a continuous audio stream [1–
3]. Traditional speech-based keyword spotting has achieved good performance in
pure speech conditions [4]. However, when in complex scenes such as noisy and
reverberant environments or multi-speaker crossover, the performance of audio
model drops significantly. Therefore, visual information, which can't be affected
by audio noise, has been used to compensate for the degradation of performance
due to noise in audio models [5–8].

Supported by the National Key R&D Program of China (No. 2020AAA0108904), and
the Science and Technology Plan of Shenzhen (No. JCYJ20200109140410340).

Audio-visual fusion has been an active research area in speech recognition in recent years. However, there is little relevant work proposed on the implementation of audio-visual keyword spotting (AV-KWS) [9]. Wu et al. are the earliest to propose an AV-KWS model based on the Hidden Markov filler model (HMM-filler) [10]. In the study by Ding et al. [11], an AV-KWS model based on multidimensional convolutional neural network (MCNN) as the main architecture is built and obtains a better result. More recent research [12] has used CNN combined with long short-term memory (LSTM) for feature extraction, with a better focus on longer-term sequence correlation. What is more, the deep learning model is increasingly being used for extracting the visual features from the original speaker's face images, which seems to be the preferred approach [9].

According to recent studies, deep networks gradually replace traditional methods for keyword spotting. Most studies have been conducted on single-person scenes, while few on multi-person scenes. Moreover, most existing models based on audio-visual fusion use decision fusion, which is easy to handle asynchrony and ensures that signals from different modalities are not interfered with by each other. However, it does not make use of the correlation of the signal of the two modalities at the feature level [13].

In this paper, an audio-visual model using the hybrid fusion is proposed for multi-person keyword spotting [14]. First, a speaker detection model based on attention mechanism [15] is constructed. It enables the capture of speaker facial images in multi-person scenes and minimizes the interference of non-speakers, as well as visual background noise. Second, two pre-trained models are separately used to extract semantic features of the two modalities. Finally, the features are fed into the designed hybrid fusion network for classification. The main contributions of our work are the following:1) the first AV-KWS model which is also adapted to multi-person scenes is proposed, 2)hybrid fusion is used to exploit the complementarity and independence of visual and audio signals from the feature and decision level, 3) the first Chinese dataset PKU-KWS is recorded for multi-person keyword spotting. Eventually, experimental results on the PKU-KWS dataset show that the designed model has high reliability and stronger robustness to noise in practical applications.

2   AV-KWS Model

2.1   Architectures

As shown in Fig. 1, the designed audio-visual model using hybrid fusion for keyword spotting uses a joint learning strategy. The independence of each modality is learnt separately by the audio stream and visual stream, and the relevance between the audio modality and visual modality is focused on in the parallel feature fusion stream. Finally, hybrid fusion is used to combine the advantages of independence and relevance of the two modalities.

The model consists of three main components: speaker detection, semantic feature extraction and classification. In the speaker detection model, a bilinear attention network [16] is used to calculate match scores after extracting features

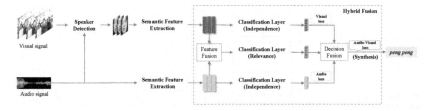

Fig. 1. The audio-visual model using hybrid fusion for muilt-person keyword spotting.

by Resnet-18. The face images with the highest match score will be selected as the output of the speaker detection model. After that, the speaker's facial images and audio signals are fed separately into the pre-trained feature extraction model to obtain high-level semantic features, and then features of the two modalities are aligned by using fully connected networks. Next, the features of the two modalities are then concatenated and fed into the posterior classification network. Meanwhile, audio features and visual features are also fed separately to two same classification networks. Finally, decision fusion is used before judgement to combine the result from the feature fusion stream and the two single modality models.

2.2 Speaker Detection

For multi-person scenes, visual background noise is very detrimental to the model, especially the facial images of non-critical speakers. In order to minimize the impact of irrelevant visual signals, a speaker detection model based on an attention mechanism is implemented in this paper [17]. In this model, the inputs are audio signals and visual signals. The speaker's original facial images will be selected as the output through the match scores between audio features and visual features. The addition of the audio signal makes the model detect the key speaker accurately through match scores even in the multi-speaker environment. The details of the model are shown in Fig. 2.

First, visual features $V \in \mathbb{R}^{B \times N \times T \times L_v}$ and auditory features $A \in \mathbb{R}^{B \times T \times L_a}$ are extracted from the inputs, where B is the batch size, N is the number of the characters, L equals 512 for the length of the feature tensor of each frame and T represents the number of time steps. For the video stream, a 3D convolutional layer with a kernel size of $5 \times 5 \times 7$ followed by a ResNet-18 [18] is used to obtain a high-level feature representation of each image stream. The audio feature is extracted by using a 1D convolutional layer with a kernel size of 80 followed by Resnet-18 [19].

A bilinear attention network is used after feature extraction to calculate the match scores S of each visual feature of each person to the audio feature. In this process, we make the attention query $Q = A$ and the attention key $K = V$. The original images corresponding to the N faces form the space to be selected.

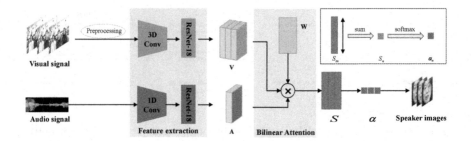

Fig. 2. The specific structure of the speaker detection model.

The match scores of each frame corresponding to the n_{th} person S_{tn} will be calculated by an additional learnable parameter matrix W:

$$S_{tn} = Q_t W V_{tn}, \ with \ S \in \mathbb{R}^{1 \times T \times N}, \tag{1}$$

where Q_t and V_{tn}, respectively, denote the audio features and the visual features of the nth person at t.

Next, all the match scores S_{tn} of each person are summed for only one person is speaking in each video.:

$$S_n = \sum_t S_{tn}. \tag{2}$$

Then, the match scores S_{tn} of each person are used to calculate the normalized attention score α_n of the n_{th} person through the softmax function:

$$\alpha_n = \frac{e^{s_n}}{\sum_m e^{s_n}}, \ with \ \alpha_n \in \mathbb{R}^{1 \times N}. \tag{3}$$

Finally, the original images of the highest match score are selected as the output of the speaker detection model.

2.3   Semantic Feature Extraction Based on Pre-trained Models

In this part, two pre-trained models are used to extract semantic features in our model. The pre-trained WavLM [20] which learns universal speech representations from massive speech data, is applied in the frontend of the audio stream to acquire semantic features. Meanwhile, the visual modality also makes use of the Audio-Visual HuBERT (AV-HuBERT) [21] model to obtain high-level visual feature representations. In addition, both of the two pre-trained models enable to extract features from indeterminate length signals.

The inputs to the above two pre-trained models are the original audio and the grey-scale face image stream which is selected in the speaker detection model. The final frame-level feature representation is obtained with a length of 768. However, due to the differences in the processing of the two modalities, the final features are not consistent in the temporal dimension. But we found that the number of the time steps of audio modality T_a with that of visual modality T_v

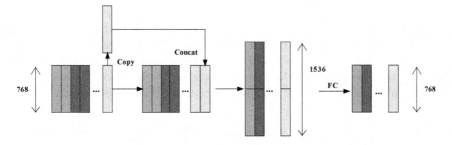

Fig. 3. Feature alignment. Align the dimension of the audio features and visual features by processing audio features. Each rectangle in this figure represents the audio feature of each frame.

always satisfies the relationship $T_a = 2T_v - 1$. It is very important for feature fusion to ensure the alignment in the time dimension between the features from two modalities. Therefore, the process shown in Fig. 3 is used to obtain audio features with the same dimension as video features. We first take the audio feature of the last time step and splice it behind the original features. Then, the audio feature of every two frames will be spliced together and fed into the fully connected network to convert the length of each splice feature to 768.

2.4 Classification Layer

First, two Bidirectional Gate Recurrent Units (BiGRUs) with a hidden layer of dimension 1,024 are used to further learn the feature representation adapted to the KWS. Then, convolutional layers and a fully connected layer are used to generate a one-dimensional vector. Finally, a softmax function is used to calculate the posterior probability of each keyword.

2.5 Hybrid Fusion

Both the feature fusion and decision fusion are used in the proposed hybrid fusion model. First, features from different modalities are concatenated together besides being fed into the classification layer directly. Before judgment, a fully connection layer is used to learn the validity of the results from each channel.

3 Experiments and Discussions

3.1 Dataset

The dataset used in our experiments, the PKU-KWS dataset, is collected in a quiet environment with controlled normal light. It contains 2,700 video segments (unequal in length) recorded in Chinese at 25 frames per second. The resolution of the video segments is 1920×1080 and the audio sample rate of 48 kHz. In each segment, 1, 2, or 3 characters with clear facial images can be seen, while only one person is speaking at the same moment. Some example frames have shown in Fig. 4. In addition, we set five keywords and select 1,040 segments to be applied to experiments where only one keyword is used. These video segments are randomly divided into three parts, 600 for the training set, 240 for the validation set, and the remaining 200 for testing. The distribution of keywords is shown in Fig. 5.

Fig. 4. Example frames from the PKU-KWS dataset.

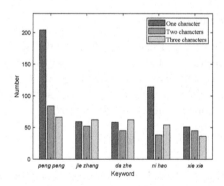

Fig. 5. The distribution of the five keywords in the PKU-KWS including *peng peng, jie zhang, da zhe, ni hao* and *xie xie.*

3.2 Preprocessing

In the visual modality, OpenCV followed by Dlib is used to detect the faces. Then the face regions in the frames are cropped down and sorted by spatial location. Finally, all the cropped images are converted to a grey-scale image with a resolution of 112×112. In addition, each group of visual images will be expanded to a three-person sample by zero-filling. A data filling example for a frame with two characters is shown in Fig. 6. After extracting the face images from each frame, a zero matrix will be added behind the grayscale images. Similar to the sample with two characters, the single-person sample will be supplemented with two additional zero matrices.

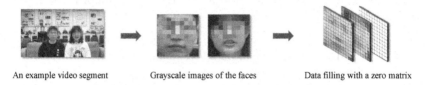

| An example video segment | Grayscale images of the faces | Data filling with a zero matrix |

Fig. 6. An example of the data filling for visual signals. A zero matrix is added behind the grayscale images arranged according to the spatial position.

For audio modality, the audio signals are extracted from the video segments at a sampling rate of 16 kHz. During training, it is worth mentioning that the audio signal will be randomly added with Gaussian white noise with different signal to noise ratio (SNR) which follows a uniform distribution between −5 dB and 15 dB.

3.3   Training

The training process can be divided into three stages: First, the speaker detection model is trained to select the speaker by learning the input. Then, two single modality models and a feature fusion based model are trained to learn the parameters of the classification network. Finally, a hybrid fusion-based model is trained to combine the judgements from different streams.

All experiments are implemented through PyTorch, using an NVIDIA Graphics RTX 3090 GPU. We use the stochastic gradient descent in all experiments to train the parameters and calculate the cross entropy loss based on the output and the label. Meanwhile, the learning rate in the hybrid fusion model is set to 0.01, while in all other training the learning rate is 0.2. As training continues, the learning rate will gradually decrease. The specific update strategy is:

$$Lr_{new} = Lr_{init} \times \frac{1}{2^{(\frac{epoch-4}{5})}} \tag{4}$$

where Lr_{new} is the updated learning rate, Lr_{init} is the initial value of the learning rate, and *epoch* represents the current training count.

3.4   Results and Analysis

Speaker Detection Model. From the examples of the distribution of attention scores shown in Fig. 7, the speaker's face images always obtain the highest match scores and more attention in each frame. The speaker is detected accurately whether in single-person or multi-speaker scenes. Experimental results of the speaker detection model are shown in Table 1. It shows that the speaker detection model has achieved recognition accuracy of 99.5% under a clean condition. Meanwhile, we find that the addition of noise has little effect on the model's recognition, which means the model is not very sensitive to audio signals. In our opinion, the reason is that there is only one character speaking in each segment, and the model prefers to detect the speaker through a simpler visual feature such as lip movement.

Table 1. Results of the speaker detection model.

SNR (dB)	Clean	15	10	5	0	−5
ACC		99.5%	99.5%	99.5%	99.5%	99.5%	99.0%

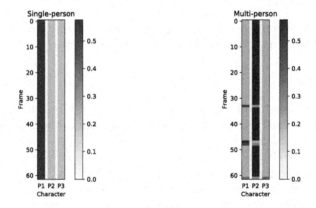

Fig. 7. Example results about distribution of match scores.

Validation of the Effectiveness of Data Enhancement Strategies. As mentioned in Sect. 3.2, data enhancement is used on the audio signals in the training set. To demonstrate the effectiveness of the data enhancement method we used, we trained the audio model separately using enhanced and unenhanced audio data. Then the two models were tested under different noise conditions and the accuracy curves with noise for both conditions are shown in Fig. 8. At low noise levels (SNR ≥ 5 dB), the difference in performance between the two models is not significant. However, as the noise continues to increase, the model using data enhancement (Red solid line) performs significantly better than the model without data enhancement (Blue solid line), showing a higher degree of robustness to noise.

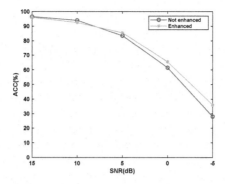

Fig. 8. Curves of recognition accuracy with noise for audio models with and without data enhanced. (Color figure online)

Validation of the Effectiveness of The Audio-Visual Model Using a Hybrid Fusion. In order to verify the contribution of the audio-visual model based hybrid fusion, the audio-visual fusion model and the single modality model are trained separately, and tested in six different noise environments. Table 2 shows the recognition accuracy of the single modality models and the fusion model in different environments. The visual model has a recognition accuracy of 82.0% and the recognition accuracy of the audio model is significantly higher than that of the visual model when the noise is not very strong (SNR $\geq$ 5 dB). As the noise is further enhanced, the original audio data is severely disturbed and the recognition accuracy decreases substantially. In an environment with clean audio, the fusion model performs slightly lower than the audio model. It is confirmed that the involvement of too much visual information leads to a decrease in recognition accuracy in the case of pure speech signals. However, with the continuous addition of noise, it can be seen that the recognition performance of the designed audio-visual fusion model obtains a better performance compared to the audio model. Especially at the SNR of -5 dB, the recognition accuracy of the audio-visual model is 71.0% which is significantly higher than that of the audio model. It means that the introduction of visual information which is not affected by audio noise compensates for the decline in recognition accuracy due to noise effectively.

Table 2. Test results of the Audio model(A), Visual model (V) and the designed Hybrid fusion based Audio-visual fusion model (AV-H) in different noise environments.

SNR (dB)	Clean	15	10	5	0	-5
A	98.5%	96.0%	92.5%	85.5%	65.5%	36.0%
V	82.0%	82.0%	82.0%	82.0%	82.0%	82.0%
AV-H	98.0%	98.0%	97.5%	96.5%	89.5%	71.0%

A Comparative Experiment for Different Modality Fusion Learning Strategies. In order to further verify the effectiveness of the designed modality synthesis learning, a comparative experiment for modality fusion learning strategies is set on the PKU-KWS dataset. The AV-KWS models with the different learning strategies methods are trained with the same database and experimental setup. As is shown in Table 3, the proposed hybrid fusion model using the modality synthesis learning obtains the best performance under both clean conditions and low noise levels (SNR $\geq$ 5 dB). It suggests that the use of the hybrid fusion makes the best use of the advantages and independence of audio-visual fusion in a low noise environment. However, as the noise increases, the recognition accuracy of the model based on feature fusion which focuses on relevance declines rapidly. Especially in the case where the SNR is -5 dB, the recognition accuracy is just 56.5% and significantly lower than that of the other two methods, while the model based on decision fusion which focuses on the independence of the two modalities performs best. It means that for KWS under high noise conditions, it may be a better choice to ensure independence between modalities than to learn relevance between features.

Table 3. Test results for the AV-KWS models focused on the independence, relevance and synthesis.

SNR (dB)	Clean	15	10	5	0	-5
Relevance	97.0%	96.0%	94.0%	89.0%	83.0%	56.5%
Independence	97.5%	97.0%	96.5%	95.0%	90.5%	73.0%
Synthesis	98.0%	98.0%	97.5%	96.5%	89.5%	71.0%

4   Conclusion

In this paper, we propose an audio-visual model based on the hybrid fusion for multi-person keyword spotting. Experiments on the PKU-KWS dataset show that the designed hybrid fusion model obtains recognition accuracy comparable to that of the audio modality model under clean conditions. Meanwhile, compared with the single modality models and the audio-visual models with other fusion methods, it achieves the best performance in low noise conditions. Even in a high noise environment, It still shows stable performance. The next step is to extend the function of the model to enable to detect the sentences with more than one keyword.

References

1. Pang, C., Liu, H., Zhang, J., Li, X.: Binaural sound localization based on reverberation weighting and generalized parametric mapping. IEEE/ACM Trans. Audio Speech Lang. Process. **25**(8), 1618–1632 (2017). https://doi.org/10.1109/TASLP. 2017.2703650

2. Wöllmer, M., Eyben, F., Keshet, J., Graves, A., Schuller, B., Rigoll, G.: Robust discriminative keyword spotting for emotionally colored spontaneous speech using bidirectional LSTM networks, pp. 3949–3952 (2009). https://doi.org/10.1109/ ICASSP.2009.4960492

3. Karakos, D., et al.: Score normalization and system combination for improved keyword spotting. In: 2013 IEEE Workshop on Automatic Speech Recognition and Understanding, pp. 210–215 (2013). https://doi.org/10.1109/ASRU.2013.6707731

4. Kim, B., Chang, S., Lee, J., Sung, D.: Broadcasted residual learning for efficient keyword spotting. arXiv preprint arXiv:2106.04140 (2021)

5. Li, Y., Liu, H., Tang, H.: Multi-modal perception attention network with self-supervised learning for audio-visual speaker tracking. In: Proceedings of the AAAI Conference on Artificial Intelligence, vol. 36, pp. 1456–1463 (2022)

6. Zheng, H., Wang, M., Li, Z.: Audio-visual speaker identification with multi-view distance metric learning, pp. 4561–4564 (2010). https://doi.org/10.1109/ICIP. 2010.5653016

7. Stewart, D., Seymour, R., Pass, A., Ming, J.: Robust audio-visual speech recognition under noisy audio-video conditions. IEEE Trans. Cybern. **44**(2), 175–184 (2014). https://doi.org/10.1109/TCYB.2013.2250954

8. Miao, Y., Gowayyed, M., Metze, F.: EESEN: end-to-end speech recognition using deep RNN models and WFST-based decoding. In: 2015 IEEE Workshop on Automatic Speech Recognition and Understanding (ASRU), pp. 167–174. IEEE (2015)

9. López-Espejo, I., Tan, Z.H., Hansen, J., Jensen, J.: Deep spoken keyword spotting: an overview. IEEE Access (2021)

10. Wu, P., Liu, H., Li, X., Fan, T., Zhang, X.: A novel lip descriptor for audio-visual keyword spotting based on adaptive decision fusion. IEEE Trans. Multimedia **18**(3), 326–338 (2016)

11. Ding, R., Pang, C., Liu, H.: Audio-visual keyword spotting based on multidimensional convolutional neural network. In: 2018 25th IEEE International Conference on Image Processing (ICIP), pp. 4138–4142. IEEE (2018)

12. Momeni, L., Afouras, T., Stafylakis, T., Albanie, S., Zisserman, A.: Seeing wake words: audio-visual keyword spotting. arXiv preprint arXiv:2009.01225 (2020)

13. Katsaggelos, A.K., Bahaadini, S., Molina, R.: Audiovisual fusion: challenges and new approaches. Proc. IEEE **103**(9), 1635–1653 (2015). https://doi.org/10.1109/ JPROC.2015.2459017

14. Liu, H., Li, W., Yang, B.: Robust audio-visual speech recognition based on hybrid fusion. In: 2020 25th International Conference on Pattern Recognition (ICPR), pp. 7580–7586 (2021). https://doi.org/10.1109/ICPR48806.2021.9412817

15. Vaswani, A., et al.: Attention is all you need. In: Advances in Neural Information Processing Systems, vol. 30 (2017)

16. Kim, J., Jun, J., Zhang, B.: Bilinear attention networks. CoRR (2018). arXiv:1805.07932

17. Braga, O., Siohan, O.: A closer look at audio-visual multi-person speech recognition and active speaker selection. In: ICASSP 2021-2021 IEEE International Conference on Acoustics, Speech and Signal Processing (ICASSP), pp. 6863–6867. IEEE (2021)

18. Afouras, T., Chung, J.S., Senior, A., Vinyals, O., Zisserman, A.: Deep audio-visual speech recognition. IEEE Trans. Pattern Anal. Mach. Intell. (2018)
19. Petridis, S., Stafylakis, T., Ma, P., Cai, F., Tzimiropoulos, G., Pantic, M.: End-to-end audiovisual speech recognition. In: 2018 IEEE International Conference on Acoustics, Speech and Signal Processing (ICASSP), pp. 6548–6552. IEEE (2018)
20. Chen, S., et al.: WavLM: large-scale self-supervised pre-training for full stack speech processing. arXiv preprint arXiv:2110.13900 (2021)
21. Shi, B., Hsu, W.N., Mohamed, A.: Robust self-supervised audio-visual speech recognition. arXiv preprint arXiv:2201.01763 (2022)

A New Adaptive TV-Based BM3D Algorithm for Image Denoising

Bo Chen[1]([⊠]), Yuru Zhang[1]([⊠]), Haoming Chen[1], Wensheng Chen[1,2], and Binbin Pan[1,2]

[1] Shenzhen Key Laboratory of Advanced Machine Learning and Applications, College of Mathematics and Statistics, Shenzhen University, Shenzhen 518060, China
{chenbo,2060201024}@szu.edu.cn
[2] Guangdong Key Laboratory of Intelligent Information Processing, Shenzhen University, Shenzhen 518060, China

Abstract. Block matching 3D filtering (BM3D) algorithm is more effective than traditional denoising methods especially for Gaussian noise. However, the traditional hard-threshold used in BM3D algorithm can not recognize the noise intensity in the process of removing additive noise with BM3D, some image details will be lost. Aiming at this problem, an improved BM3D algorithm is proposed. Firstly, the traditional hard-thresholding of the BM3D method is substituted by an adaptive filtering technique. This technique has a high capacity to acclimate and can change according to the noise intensity. Secondly, when the noise intensity is less than the threshold, the new TV model is used to replace the hard-threshold filtering, when the noise intensity exceeds the threshold, the hard and soft thresholding algorithm is used to replace the hard-threshold filtering. Through the adaptive threshold, the high noise and low noise image feature areas are screened out, targeted denoising is carried out, and the edge details are preserved. Experimental results show that the performance of the improved BM3D method is better than traditional methods.

Keywords: BM3D · Image denoising · Total variation

1 Introduction

Image denoising is very important because noise is almost everywhere. Image denoising has become a hot research spot in the field of image processing. With the continuous development of deep learning algorithms and related hardware, deep convolutional networks have applied for image noise reduction [1–3] successfully. Nevertheless, deep neural networks also have their disadvantages, such as the model is too large and the computational complexity is too high, and lack of some theoretical explanations. In order to better understand the basic principles of image denoising, it is necessary to go back and carefully study the specific ideas of some traditional algorithms, understand the basic theoretical basis used, and some clever improvement methods.

© The Author(s), under exclusive license to Springer Nature Switzerland AG 2022
L. Fang et al. (Eds.): CICAI 2022, LNAI 13605, pp. 339–349, 2022.
https://doi.org/10.1007/978-3-031-20500-2_28

There are many kinds of image noise. Impulse noise [4–6] is easier to remove than other types of noise, but some noises, such as Gaussian noise, are difficult to detect and remove. There are currently a large number of methods to deal with Gaussian white noise, in particular, the NL-means [7] and non-local mean filtering method has become a mainstream method. Subsequently, more non-local methods have been proposed [8, 9], for example, block-matching 3D (BM3D) have good performance [10].

Although BM3D filtering is one of the most popular algorithms that successfully combine block matching and 3D collaborative filtering, the algorithm still has some disadvantages. Many new methods [11–15] have been proposed to solve the problem that related noise will lead to block matching errors in BM3D. However, BM3D still has a significant problem, which will be explained as follows: in the first step of BM3D filtering, the author applies a simple hard-thresholding function to 3D collaborative filtering. Because the hard-thresholding cannot distinguish between high noise region and low noise region. A large number of real signals in the region with low noise are removed, which results in poor visual quality of the output image. Aiming at this problem, this paper improves the BM3D algorithm combined with the proposed TV model.

This paper focuses on BM3D algorithm and TV model. In order to obtain the best noise reduction performance and maintain high spatial frequency details, the hard-thresholding of BM3D filtering is replaced by the proposed adaptive filtering technique. Based on adaptive threshold, the noise image is divided into high noise region and low noise region by threshold. The proposed TV model and soft hard threshold model are employed to replace the hard-thresholding filtering in the basic estimation. Finally, experimental results show that the improved BM3D method is effective. The rest of this paper is organized as follows: Sect. 2 introduces the related work; Sect. 3 describes the method proposed in this paper; Sect. 4 for the experimental results; Sect. 5 gives the relevant conclusions.

2   Related Work

2.1   Block Matching 3D Denoising Algorithm

BM3D is a 3D collaborative filtering based on block matching. The central idea of the algorithm is to make full use of the rich self similar structures in natural images to reduce image noise. BM3D uses block matching to collect and aggregate similar structures in the image, and then performs orthogonal transformation to obtain a sparse representation of them. It makes full use of sparsity and structural similarity to filter the noise. BM3D denoising can fully preserve the structure and details of the image and obtain a good signal-to-noise ratio.

BM3D noise reduction algorithm process is divided into two steps. The first step is called basic estimation filtering, and the second step is called final estimation filtering. The flow chart of the BM3D algorithm is as follows (Fig. 1).

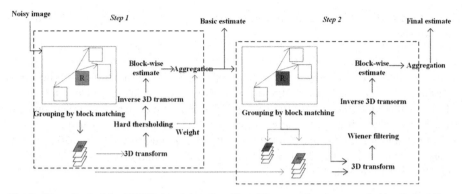

Fig. 1. Flowchart of the BM3D denoising algorithm. The operations surrounded by dashed lines are repeated for each processed block (marked with "R").

2.2 Total Variation Filter

Rudin, Osher, and Fatemi (ROF) [16] proposed the famous total variation (TV) model and TV filter is considered to be one of the most successful minimization methods to restore sharp-edged images. This section will briefly introduce the concept of TV and its application [17–19].

TV model. Let $f(x, y) : \Omega \rightarrow \Re$ denote a noisy image with Gaussian white noise of zero mean and variance σ^2, and $\Omega \in M \times N$ denote the neighborhood of the image. Then the energy functional of the TV denoising model is

$$\min_u \int_\Omega |\nabla u| dxdy + \frac{\lambda}{2} \int_\Omega |u - f|^2 dxdy \tag{1}$$

The first term $\int_\Omega |\nabla u| dxdy$ of the TV model represents the TV regularization term, and the second term $\int_\Omega |u - f|^2 dxdy$ represents the fidelity term; $\lambda > 0$ represents the regularization parameter which can balance fidelity terms and regularized terms in TV model. For the two-dimensional energy functional (1), its corresponding Euler-Lagrange equation is

$$-div\left(\frac{\nabla u}{|\nabla u|}\right) + \lambda(u - f) = 0 \tag{2}$$

There ∇u is the gradient of the original image u, and $u - f = n$, n represent noise. By gradient descent, we can get the TV denoising model.

3   A New Adaptive TV-Based BM3D Algorithm

In this paper, TV filter and a hard and soft thresholding compromise are employed to replace the hard threshold filter in original BM3D algorithm. This filter is used as the basic denoising of the 3D transform group instead of the cooperative hard threshold filter.

3.1 Hard and Soft Thresholding Compromise Denoising for Complex Texture Blocks

In the basic estimation of BM3D, since the hard-thresholding estimation is discontinuous, the literature [20] proposes to use soft-thresholding filtering to replace the hard-thresholding, but the soft threshold estimation has a certain deviation, and the application of this method is limited to a certain extent. Therefore, this paper proposes a compromise between hard thresholding and soft thresholding to improve it. Compared with the hard threshold method, the method shrinks the discontinuous points appearing at the boundary to 0, which effectively avoids the discontinuity and makes the reconstructed signal relatively smooth.

$$HS = \begin{cases} sign(X)(|X| - \varepsilon T), & \text{if}|X| > T; \\ 0, & \text{if}|X| \leq T; \end{cases} \quad (0 < \varepsilon < 1) \tag{3}$$

where X is the high-frequency coefficient, T is the threshold, and ε is any real number between 0 and 1. An appropriate ε can have a better denoising effect. In this paper, we usually choose $\varepsilon = 0.5$. This wavelet coefficient estimation model is called a compromise between hard thresholding and soft thresholding. Especially when $\varepsilon = 0$, (3) will go to the hard threshold, and if $\varepsilon = 1$, (3) will go to the soft threshold.

3.2 TV Denoising for Simple Texture Block

If the block belongs to a simple texture group, the TV model is used for denoising. Referring to [21], this paper proposes a new TV image denoising model based on energy minimization

$$\min_u E(u) = \min_u \left[\int_\Omega \varphi(|\nabla u|)dx + \frac{\alpha}{2} \int_\Omega (u_0 - u)^2 dx \right] \tag{4}$$

where $\varphi(s) = s \ln(\delta + s)$ represents the regularization term in the model, whose main function is to smooth the noise image; $\delta \geq 1$ is a positive parameter to prevent the function $\varphi(|\nabla u|)$ from being negative in the smooth region; $\alpha > 0$ represents the regularization parameter, which balances the fidelity term and the regularization term.

The energy model (4) is convex, which guarantees that a minimum solution of the model (4) exists. And it can also prove the uniqueness of the minimum solution of model (4). In this paper, the ADMM algorithm is used to minimize the energy model.

First, model (4) can be transformed into the following discretized version:

$$\min_u \left[\langle \varphi(|\nabla u|), 1 \rangle + \frac{\alpha}{2} \langle |u_0 - u|^2, 1 \rangle \right] \tag{5}$$

Second, introduce two new variables $z, d = (d_1, d_2)$, where $z = u, d = \nabla u$, , then the problem (5) can be transformed into the following linear constraint problem

$$\min_u \left[\langle \varphi(|d|), 1 \rangle + \frac{\alpha}{2} \langle |u_0 - z|^2, 1 \rangle \right] \tag{6}$$

Next, we make

$$A = \begin{bmatrix} I & 0 \\ 0 & I \end{bmatrix}, x = \begin{bmatrix} z \\ d \end{bmatrix}$$

$$B = \begin{bmatrix} -I \\ -\nabla \end{bmatrix}, y = [u], \beta = \begin{bmatrix} \beta^1 \\ \beta^2 \end{bmatrix} \tag{7}$$

Now, we let

$$f(x) = \langle \varphi|d|, 1 \rangle + \frac{\alpha}{2}\langle |u_0 - z|^2, 1 \rangle \tag{8}$$

So the Lagrange equation of problem (6) is

$$
\begin{aligned}
L_\mu(z, d, u, \beta^1, \beta^2; \mu) = {} & \langle \varphi(|d|, 1) \rangle + \frac{\alpha}{2}\langle |u_0 - z|^2, 1 \rangle \\
& - (\beta^1)^T(z - u) - (\beta^2)^T(d - \nabla u) \\
& + \frac{\mu}{2}\|z - u\|_2^2 + \frac{\mu}{2}\|d - \nabla u\|_2^2
\end{aligned}
\tag{9}
$$

According to the structure of the ADMM algorithm, problem (4) can be rewritten in the following form

$$
\begin{cases}
(z_{k+1}, d_{k+1}) = \underset{z \geq 0, d}{\arg\min}\, L_\mu(z, d, u_k, \beta_k^1, \beta_k^2; \mu) \\
u_{k+1} = \underset{d}{\arg\min}\, L_\mu(z_{k+1}, d_{k+1}, u, \beta_k^1, \beta_k^2; \mu) \\
\beta_{k+1}^1 = \beta_k^1 - k\mu(z_{k+1} - u_{k+1}) \\
\beta_{k+1}^2 = \beta_k^2 - k\mu(d_{k+1} - \nabla u_{k+1})
\end{cases}
\tag{10}
$$

Comprehensive numerical analysis, the process of using ADMM algorithm to solve the model can be abbreviated as the following steps:

Algorithm1. ADMM (TV Denoising)

1: **Initialize** $k = 0$, $\beta_0^1 = 0$, $\beta_0^2 = 0$;

2: **for** $k = 0, 1, \ldots, K$ **do**

3: $\quad z_{k+1} \leftarrow \quad (\alpha + \mu)z - \alpha u_0 - \beta_k^1 - \mu u_k = 0$;

4: $\quad d_{k+1} \leftarrow d_{k+1} = shrink(\frac{\beta_k^2}{\mu} + \nabla u_k, \frac{\varphi_i'(|d|)}{\mu})$;

5: $\quad u_{k+1} \leftarrow u_{k+1} = (I + \nabla^T\nabla)^{-1}\left(z_{k+1} - \frac{\beta_k^1}{\mu} + \nabla^T(d_{k+1} - \frac{\beta_k^2}{\mu})\right)$;

6: $\quad \beta_{k+1}^1 = \beta_k^1 - k\mu(z_{k+1} - u_{k+1})$;

7: $\quad \beta_{k+1}^2 = \beta_k^2 - k\mu(d_{k+1} - \nabla u_{k+1})$

8: **end for**

9: **return** u

3.3 Adaptive Fifiltering

In the BM3D filter, traditional hard threshold filtering is employed to obtain the base estimate. In this filter, the noise intensity is not considered. Because hard thresholding is an ineffective tool to distinguish high noise areas from low noise areas. Therefore, the algorithm proposed in this paper is designed to be able to adapt to the noise intensity. In other words, the image denoising algorithm in this paper is based on an appropriate adaptive function. Experimental results show that applying an adaptive function is more effective than traditional hard thresholding for denoising.

The adaptive filtering function proposed in this paper can be realized as follows:

$$TH(i,j) = \begin{cases} TV & \sigma < \tau; \\ HS & \sigma \geq \tau, \end{cases} \tag{11}$$

Finding the optimal value of the threshold is an extremely difficult task. A threshold that is too small leaves a lot of noise that cannot be removed, while a threshold that is too large cannot preserve important information of the image, such as edges. Therefore, the ideal value of the threshold is very important. The threshold should not be constant, so it should be adjusted and changed based on the amount of noise.

The optimal adaptive threshold of the algorithm proposed in this paper is calculated as follows:

$$\tau = \frac{\sigma^2}{\sigma_\eta^2} \tag{12}$$

where σ^2 is the variance of the noise and σ_η^2 is the clean image coefficients.

After applying an adaptive filter function to reduce noise, the following inverse transform is used to obtain a three-dimensional array of block estimates:

$$\hat{I}_{S_{xR}^{TH}}^{TH} = \mathcal{T}_{3D}^{TH^{-1}}\left(\gamma\left(\mathcal{T}_{3D}^{TH}\left(B_{S_{xR}^{TH}}\right)\right)\right) \tag{13}$$

where array $\hat{I}_{S_{xR}^{TH}}$ includes $\left|S_{xR}^{TH}\right|$ stacked block estimates $\hat{I}_x^{TH,xR}$, $\forall x \in S_{xR}^{TH}$. In $\hat{I}_x^{TH,xR}$, the subscript x represents the estimated position of this block, and the superscript xR represents the reference speed.

The algorithm flow chart proposed in this paper is as follows (Fig. 2):

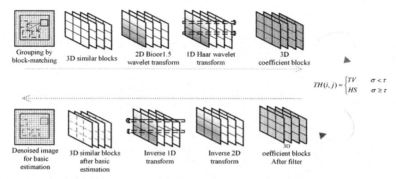

$$TH(i,j) = \begin{cases} TV & \sigma < \tau \\ HS & \sigma \geq \tau \end{cases}$$

Fig. 2. Step 1 of BM3D: Flowchart of the *basic estimation* part of the proposed improved BM3D method

4   Experiment Result and Analysis

The method in this paper is designed for gray image, and only gray images are used in the experiments. In the experiment, we test the performance under different noise variances σ. The experimental results show that the improved BM3D method is compared with the original BM3D method and TV denoising.

4.1   Parameter Setting

Many images were tested for parameter setting, and we proposed a set of parameters, as shown in Table 1.

Table 1. Improve the parameter settings of the BM3D algorithm

Basic estimate $\sigma \leq 40$	N_{pro}		N_{pro-s}	M_{pro}	τ_{pro}	λ_{3D}	λ_{2D}
	8	3	39	16	3000	2.7	0
Final estimate	N_{wie}	$N_{wie-step}$	N_{wie-s}	M_{wie}	τ_{wie}		
	8	3	39	32	400		
Basic estimate $\sigma > 40$	N_{pro}	$N_{pro-step}$	N_{pro-s}	M_{pro}	τ_{pro}	λ_{3D}	λ_{2D}
	12	4	39	16	5000	3.0	2.0
Final estimate	N_{wie}	$N_{wie-step}$	N_{wie-s}	M_{wie}	τ_{wie}		
	11	6	39	16	3500		

In the experiment, the final estimated two-dimensional linear transformation is completed by discrete cosine transform (DCT); The one-dimensional transformation is completed by "Haar" wavelet. $N_{pro-step}$ and N_{pro-s} represent the search step size and search radius respectively. The parameter settings of the improved BM3D are shown in Table 1.

4.2 Experimental Results

The effect of image denoising is evaluated by calculating the peak signal-to-noise ratio (PSNR) and structural similarity (SSIM). They are defined as follows:

$$PSNR(u, \overline{u}) = 10 \log_{10} \frac{255^2 mn}{\|u - \overline{u}\|_2^2} \tag{14}$$

$$SSIM(u, \overline{u}) = \frac{(2\mu_u \mu_{\overline{u}} + c_1)(2\sigma_{u\overline{u}} + c_2)}{(\mu_u^2 + \mu_{\overline{u}}^2 + c_1)(\sigma_u^2 + \sigma_{\overline{u}}^2 + c_2)} \tag{15}$$

where $u \in R^{m \times n}$ is the clean image, and $\overline{u} \in R^{m \times n}$ is the denoised image. μ_u and $\mu_{\overline{u}}$ are the average intensities of u, and σ_u and $\sigma_{\overline{u}}$ are the standard deviations of u and $\overline{u}$, respectively, and $\sigma_{u\overline{u}}$ is the covariance of u and $\overline{u}$. c_1 and c_2 are some stability constants.

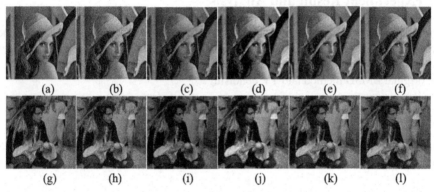

Fig. 3. Numerical result of the 'lena' and 'man' image with noise standard deviation $\sigma = 40$. (**a, g**) are Original image; (**b, h**) correspond to the noisy version; (**c, i**) are the denoising results by the BM3D model [10], PSNR = 29.86 (lena)/27.65(man);(**d, j**) are the denoising results by the TV model [21],PSNR = 27.24 (lena)/24.88(man);(**e, k**) are the denoising results by the Ali's model [12], PSNR = 29.54(lena)/27.92(man);(**f, l**) are the denoising results by the proposed model, PSNR = 30.11(lena)/28.09(man).

Figure 3 shows an example of restoring visual effects between BM3D [10], TV[21], Ali [20] and improved BM3D. Figure 4 shows when $\sigma = 30$, the detailed picture of the denoising effect of the proposed method. Obviously, the complex texture in the improved BM3D image is clearer than that in the original BM3D image. This proves that our proposed method focusing on improving the denoising effect of complex texture regions is effective.

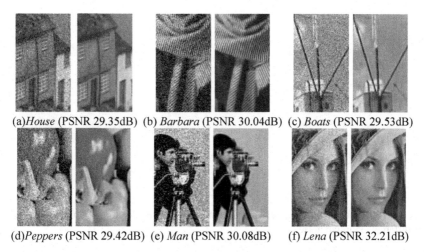

(a)*House* (PSNR 29.35dB) (b) *Barbara* (PSNR 30.04dB) (c) *Boats* (PSNR 29.53dB)

(d)*Peppers* (PSNR 29.42dB) (e) *Man* (PSNR 30.08dB)   (f) *Lena* (PSNR 32.21dB)

Fig. 4. The algorithm proposed in this paper, denoising the detail image with $\sigma = 30$.

Table 2. The PSNR and SSIM of the restored **Lena** by the different models.

σ	BM3D PSNR/SSIM	NLM [7] PSNR/SSIM	TV [21] PSNR/SSIM	Ali [20] PSNR/SSIM	Proposed PSNR/SSIM
$\sigma = 10$	35.93/0.9541	34.42/0.9092	33.00/0.9521	36.04/0.9457	36.87/0.9557
$\sigma = 15$	34.27/0.9398	32.06/0.8842	32.25/0.9376	34.77/0.9408	**35.09/0.9443**
$\sigma = 20$	33.05/0.9230	31.58/0.8473	31.43/0.9156	33.58/0.9278	**34.01/0.9325**
$\sigma = 25$	32.08/0.9053	30.79/0.8277	30.16/0.8942	32.64/0.9102	**33.11/0.9187**
$\sigma = 30$	31.26/0.8873	29.30/0.7875	29.04/0.8756	31.85/0.8907	**32.21/0.8933**
$\sigma = 35$	30.56/0.8714	28.77/0.7635	28.13/0.8433	30.77/0.8809	**30.80/0.8846**
$\sigma = 40$	29.86/0.8532	27.93/0.7442	27.24/0.8135	30.04/0.8648	**30.11/0.8746**
$\sigma = 45$	28.47/0.8447	26.78/0.7269	26.35/0.8024	28.76/0.8527	**29.38/0.8654**
$\sigma = 50$	27.39/0.8398	25.74/0.7537	25.86/0.7933	27.47/0.8477	**28.56/0.8577**

Table 2 shows that the proposed method can provide the highest PSNR and SSIM after adding different levels of noise to the same image, or after adding different levels of noise to different images. Moreover, compared with the two original algorithms, this method has stronger denoising ability. The method has good denoising stability and robustness. Although the algorithm is only suitable for low-noise phases, its implementation is quick and easy.

To more intuitively compare the performance differences between the algorithms, the data are shown in Fig. 5. Obviously, under the given conditions, the method proposed in this paper works better than other methods.

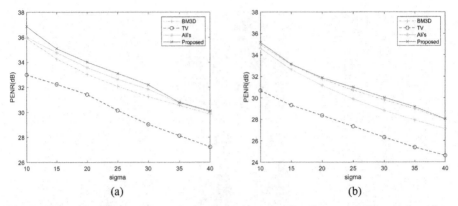

Fig. 5. (a) *Lena* and (b) *Barbara* peak signal to noise ratio (dB) diagram of different algorithms under different Gaussian noise.

5   Conclusion

In this paper, we review the BM3D image denoising algorithm and its core part, the hard-thresholding filter. Because hard-thresholding filter can not distinguish the noise intensity, this paper uses TV and soft hard threshold compromise algorithm to replace it. Through a series of experiments, it can be proved that the proposed algorithm can achieve high-quality image denoising and improve the adaptability of the algorithm when used in BM3D. The idea of this paper is suitable for removing Gaussian white noise from gray image. Our new contributions in this study are as follows: firstly, the existing image denoising methods BM3D and its components and contours are reviewed, and their shortcomings are found. Secondly, a new TV denoising algorithm based on ADMM and energy minimization method is proposed. Finally, based on the adaptive threshold, a new TV model and a soft hard threshold compromise algorithm are used to replace the hard-thresholding filter in the basic estimation of BM3D. Experimental result show that the performance of the original BM3D is significantly improved in our proposed method. In the experiment, we also found the disadvantages of the improved method: with the increase of noise intensity, the boundary effect can be seen in the smooth region after denoising. Our further research will focus on eliminating the boundary effect.

References

1. Zhang, K., Zuo, W.M., Chen, Y.J., Meng, D.Y., Zhang, L.: Beyond a Gaussian denoiser: Residual learning of deep CNN for Image denoising. IEEE Trans. Image Process. **26**(7), 3142–3155 (2017)
2. Hu, C., Zhang, Y., Zhang, W., et al.: Low-dose CT via convolutional neural network. Biomed. Opt. Express **8**(2), 679–694 (2017)
3. Tian, C.W., Fei, L.K., Zheng, W.X., et al.: Deep learning on image denoising: an overview. Neural Netw. **131**, 251–275 (2020)
4. Mafi, M., Martin, H., Cabrerizo, M., et al.: A comprehensive survey on impulse and Gaussian denoising filters for digital images. Signal Process. **157**, 236–260 (2019)

5. Mafi, M., Izquierdo, W., Cabrerizo, M., et al.: Survey on mixed impulse and Gaussian denoising filters. IET Image Process. **14**(16), 4027–4038 (2020)

6. Toygar, O., Demirel, H., Kalyoncu, C.: Interpolation-based impulse noise removal. IET Image Process. **7**(8), 777–785 (2013)

7. Buades, A., Coll, B., Morel, J.M.: A review of image denoising algorithms, with a new one. Multiscale Model. Simul. **4**(2), 490–530 (2005)

8. Bhujle, H.V., Vadavadagi, B.H.: NLM based magnetic resonance image denoising—a review. Biomed. Signal Process. Control **47**, 252–261 (2018)

9. Tounsi, Y., Kumar, M., Nassim, A., Mendoza-Santoyo, F.: Speckle noise reduction in digital speckle pattern interferometric fringes by nonlocal means and its related adaptive kernel-based methods. Appl. Opt. **57**(27), 7681–7690 (2018)

10. Dabov, K., Foi, A., Katkovnik, V., Egiazarian, K.: Image denoising by sparse 3-D transform-domain collaborative filtering. IEEE Trans. Image Process. **16**(8), 2080–2095 (2007)

11. Lebrun, M.: An analysis and implementation of the BM3D image denoising method. Image Process. Line **2**(25), 175–213 (2012)

12. Makinen, Y., Azzari, L., Foi, A.: Collaborative filtering of correlated noise: Exact transform-domain variance for improved shrinkage and patch matching. IEEE Trans. Image Process. **29**, 8339–8354 (2020)

13. Makinen, Y., Azzari, L., Foi, A.: Exact Transform-domain noise variance for collaborative filtering of stationary correlated noise. In: 2019 IEEE International Conference on Image Processing (ICIP), pp. 185–189. IEEE, Taiwan (2019)

14. Ri, G.-I., Kim, S.-J., Kim, M.-S.: Improved BM3D method with modified block-matching and multi-scaled images. Multimed. Tools Appl. **81**(9), 12661–12679 (2022). https://doi.org/10.1007/s11042-022-12270-y

15. Li, Y.J., Zhang, J.W., Wang, M.N.: Improved BM3D denoising method. IET Image Proc. **11**(12), 1197–1204 (2017)

16. Rudin, L.I., Osher, S., Fatemi, E.: Nonlinear total variation based noise removal algorithms. Physica D **60**(1–4), 259–268 (1992)

17. Chen, B., Zou, J.B., Chen, W.S., et al.: Speckle noise removal based on adaptive total variation model. In: 1st Chinese Conference on Pattern Recognition and Computer Vision (PRCV), pp. 191–202. Springer Verlag, Guang zhou (2018)

18. Chen, B., Zou, J.B., Chen, W.S., et al.: A novel energy functional minmization model for speckle noise removal. Optoelectron. Lett. **15**(5), 386–390 (2019)

19. Chen, B., Zou, J.B., Zhang, W.Q., et al.:Speckle noise removal by energy models with new regularization setting. J. Funct. Spaces (2020)

20. Yahya, A.A., et al.: BM3D image denoising algorithm based on an adaptive filtering. Multimed. Tools Appl. **79**(27–28), 20391–20427 (2020). https://doi.org/10.1007/s11042-020-08815-8

21. Chen, B., Lv, Y., Zou, J.B., et al.: A novel speckle noise removal algorithm based on ADMM and energy minimization method. J. Funct. Spaces (2020)

Data-Driven Hybrid Neural Network Under Model-Driven Supervised Learning for Structural Dynamic Impact Localization

Yingxin Luan, Teng Li[✉], Ran Song, and Wei Zhang

School of Control Science and Engineering, Shandong University, Jinan 250014, China
li.teng@sdu.edu.cn

Abstract. AI-oriented schemes, in particular deep learning schemes, provide superior capabilities of representative learning that leads to innovative estimation paradigm for structural health monitoring (SHM) applications. This paper introduces a model-driven and deep learning-enabled framework for localizing dynamic impact loads on structures. In this paper, finite element modeling (FEM) is conducted to generate enough labeled data for supervised learning. Meanwhile, a hybrid deep neural network (DNN) is established by integrating attentive and recurrent neural networks to exploit the latent features over both sensor-wise and temporal scales. The proposed DNN model is implemented to reveal the multivariate and temporal hidden correlations among complex time-series measurements and to estimate impact localization on structures. The experimental results from both numerical and physical tests demonstrate the superior performance of the proposed methodology.

Keywords: Deep learning · Attention mechanism · Structural health monitoring · Impact localization

1 Introduction

With the development of structure and infrastructure industries, more efforts have been made to detect the impact or damage to critical structural conditions [3,18]. In particular, for some severe weather conditions or natural disasters, the robustness of complex structures directly determines the safety of our human community and urban society.

Structural health monitoring (SHM) techniques refer to continuous condition monitoring of structures or structural components by measuring impact or damage-sensible data from instrumented sensors [14]. In traditional SHM applications, vibration-based approaches were able to complete damage detection of rotating machinery [11] and frame structures [4]. With superior performance

This work is supported by SGCC Laiwu, Shandong (SGSDLW00SDJS2250019).

L. Fang et al. (Eds.): CICAI 2022, LNAI 13605, pp. 350–361, 2022.
https://doi.org/10.1007/978-3-031-20500-2_29

of representative and supervised learning [17], the implementation of AI-based techniques empowers the traditional SHM field. Particularly, SHM methods combined with finite element (FE) model and machine/deep learning schemes have achieved great advantages in recent studies [5,13]. Deep neural network (DNN) prediction models trained through a large amount of model-based structural data has proven their performance of efficient operation and high accuracy [6,9].

Localization of dynamic impact is great significant to detect potential structural malfunction or damage in SHM application scenarios. Many recent work has focused on this research topic. For example, [12] investigated similarity metrics in the time domain to determine the specific locations of impact loads based on the differences in structural responses of two impact load groups. This type of time domain process generally leads to heavy computational cost for positioning estimation. Liu *et al.* [10] studied and compared a series of machine learning methods for low-velocity impact localization. Established upon DNN schemes, Zhou et al. [19] proposed a recurrent neural network to identify the time-series responses of structural impact loads, without providing the actual position of a dynamic impact load. Zargar and Yuan [16] proposed a unified CNN and RNN network architecture for impact diagnosis, which deploying a high-speed camera to collect plenty of wavefield images.

Due to the lack of on-site collections at the time instant of dynamic impacts using limited sensors, it is extremely challenging and costly to directly capture real structural data samples from physical implementation. Different from the existing vibration-based approaches, a combination of model-driven and data-driven learning methodology is proposed in this paper. Specifically, enough data samples are generated with impact load positions and corresponding structural responses through numerical simulation using structural finite element modeling (FEM). In addition, to achieve better representation of multivariate and temporal sensory measurements, an attention-based hybrid DNN model is developed to regress the structural data and provide estimation of impact locations. Summarily, the contribution of the proposed methodology are in three folds:

(1) A novel systematic workflow for structural dynamic impact localization is proposed, which integrates both model-driven FEM and data-driven deep learning approaches.
(2) An attention-based hybrid DNN model is proposed to exploit complex hidden features among temporal and multivariate time series.
(3) Both numerical and real-world experimental testing are designed and conducted to validate the estimation performance of the proposed methodology.

In the rest of the paper, Sect. 2 formulates the research problem. Section 3 presents the dataset generation using model-driven approach while proposes the data-driven DNN model for impact load localization. Experiments are given in Sect. 4 and the last section concludes the paper.

2   Problem Formulation

The research goal of this paper is to study a modeling process to generate numerical simulations of structural impact responses while establishing a DNN model to regress the responses and impact position and estimate the impact location.

The present paper focuses on the localization of dynamic impact on structures using a systematic workflow with model-driven approach and deep learning approach. First, due to the lack of on-site measurements from real structures. The training data for the proposed DNN via supervised learning is generated using finite element modeling. Afterwards, the data is utilized to train the established DNN model. Finally, the trained model is deployed to estimate impact locations.

The research motivation of the studied problem can be formulated as:

$$(x, y) = \mathcal{F}(\mathbf{A}_{1:T}^1, \mathbf{A}_{1:T}^2, \ldots, \mathbf{A}_{1:T}^M) \tag{1}$$

where $\mathbf{A}_{1:T}^m, m = 1, 2, \ldots, M$ represents the measurements of the mth instrumented sensors over T time period. (x, y) indicates the coordinates of the location of an impact load on a target structure. $\mathcal{F}$ denotes a DNN model that can accurately regress between the measurements $\mathbf{A}_{1:T}^{1:M}$ and the impact location (x, y), which is the core objective of this work.

To achieve the aforementioned motivation, the proposed methodology can be summarized as three main procedures.

(1) **Model-driven data generation:** FEM is operated to generate volumes of data samples for model-driven supervised learning. For each impact load, generating structural response $\mathbf{A}_{1:T}^{1:M}$ and its label location (x, y).
(2) **Data-driven model training:** A data-driven DNN model $\mathcal{F}$ is developed and trained using the FEM data to regress among impact locations and the corresponding multivariate time series.
(3) **Data-driven model testing:** The trained DNN model $\mathcal{F}$ is deployed for localization of dynamic impacts on structures using measurements from instrumented sensors on structures.

3   Methodology

This section introduces the main methodology of the proposed model-driven as well as deep-learning driven framework in detail, including FEM data generation and DNN model development.

3.1   FEM Data Generation

To generate sufficient training data under supervised learning, an accurate FE model of an objective structure is developed first. Depending on the scale and complexity of the target structure, different levels of modeling details should be considered, ranging from component level continuum solid elements to space rod system modeling.

With the developed model, a dynamic time history analysis is performed by applying a impact load case to any location of interest on the model. The impact load is often characterized as a triangular pulse-like loading pattern with an amplitude and a short duration in several milliseconds. The analysis will generate structural dynamic responses (e.g., displacement, velocity, acceleration, etc.) at any node and element in time domain.

The data that is generated by FEM can be formulated as:

$$m\ddot{x} + c\dot{x} + kx = p(t) \tag{2}$$

where m, c and k denote the mass, damping, and stiffness of the system, respectively. The impact load $p(t)$ can be expressed as:

$$p(t) = \begin{cases} 2p_o \frac{t}{t_d} & \text{for } t \leq \frac{1}{2}t_d \\ 2p_o \frac{t_d - t}{t_d} & \text{for } t \geq \frac{1}{2}t_d \end{cases} \tag{3}$$

where p_o is the amplitude of the triangular pulse and t_d is the pulse duration.

In this study, a large amount of loading cases with different amplitude and duration are randomly applied to the FE model. In each loading case, the location of the impact load is recorded as input data, while the acceleration responses at locations with instrumented sensors are monitored as output data.

3.2 Neural Network Design

The developed model considers both the correlationship among multi-sensor measurements and the temporal interrelationship in sequential data. The model conducts the regression process between the multivariate time-series inputs and the impact locations.

Inspired by the attention mechanism introduced in [1,15], considering the input of multivariate time series $\mathbf{A}_{1:T}^{1:M}$, a self-attention network is embedded in the proposed neural network to capture the sensor-wise dependencies within the multivariate time-series data. The attention layers can highlight the core features within the large volume of time-series data. The attentively extracted features is formulated as:

$$\begin{aligned} \mathbf{H} &= \text{softmax}(\frac{\mathbf{Q}\mathbf{K}^\mathsf{T}}{||\mathbf{Q}||||\mathbf{K}||})\mathbf{V} \\ &= \text{softmax}(\frac{(\mathbf{A}_{1:T}^{1:M}\mathbf{W}_Q)(\mathbf{A}_{1:T}^{1:M}\mathbf{W}_K)^\mathsf{T}}{||\mathbf{A}_{1:T}^{1:M}\mathbf{W}_Q||||\mathbf{A}_{1:T}^{1:M}\mathbf{W}_K||})(\mathbf{A}_{1:T}^{1:M}\mathbf{W}_V). \end{aligned} \tag{4}$$

where $\mathbf{Q}$, $\mathbf{K}$ and $\mathbf{V}$ denote the query, key, and value matrices, respectively, which are projected by the input $\mathbf{A}_{1:T}^{1:M}$ with learnable weight matrices $\mathbf{W}_Q$, $\mathbf{W}_K$, and $\mathbf{W}_V$. The dot product between the query matrix $\mathbf{Q}$ and the key matrix $\mathbf{K}$ leads to the attention matrix $\boldsymbol{\alpha}$ after normalizing by a softmax function. The resulting attention scores in the attention matrix are designated to the value matrix $\mathbf{V}$.

The final weighted output is the attentively extracted hidden feature $\mathbf{H}$, which integrates the extracted features within measurements of $\mathbf{M}$ sensors. The dot product $\|\mathbf{Q}\|\|\mathbf{K}\|$ is used to adjust a large dot-product value that may cause small gradients when operating backpropagation in neural network training.

To further extract the sequential characteristics, recurrent layers are implemented onto the attentively exploited features. This paper utilizes stacks of gated recurrent unit (GRU) [2,8] as recurrent layers in the network, updated as:

$$
\begin{aligned}
\mathbf{z}_n^{(r)} &= \mathrm{sigmoid}(\mathrm{Concat}[\mathbf{h}_{n-1}^{(r)}, \mathbf{Z}_n^{(r)}] \cdot \mathbf{W}_z^{(r)}) \\
\mathbf{r}_n^{(r)} &= \mathrm{sigmoid}(\mathrm{Concat}[\mathbf{h}_{n-1}^{(r)}, \mathbf{Z}_n^{(r)}] \cdot \mathbf{W}_z^{(r)}) \\
\tilde{\mathbf{h}}_n^{(r)} &= \tanh(\mathrm{Concat}[\mathbf{r}_n^{(r)} \odot \mathbf{h}_{n-1}^{(r)}, \mathbf{Z}_n^{(r)}] \cdot \mathbf{W}_h^{(r)}) \\
\mathbf{h}_n^{(r)} &= \left(1 - \mathbf{z}_n^{(r)}\right) \odot \mathbf{h}_{n-1}^{(r)} + \mathbf{z}_n^{(r)} \odot \tilde{\mathbf{h}}_n^{(r)}
\end{aligned}
\tag{5}
$$

where $r = 1, 2, ..., R$ denotes the rth recurrent stack in the GRU stacks. $n = 1, 2, ..., N$ denotes the nth GRU module in a GRU stack. $\mathbf{Z}_n^{(r)}$ is denoted as:

$$
\mathbf{Z}_n^{(r)} = \begin{cases} \mathbf{H}_n \subset \mathbf{H} = \mathrm{Concat}[\mathbf{H}_1, \mathbf{H}_2, ..., \mathbf{H}_N] & r = 1 \\ \mathbf{h}_n^{(r-1)} & r = 2, 3, ..., R \end{cases}
\tag{6}
$$

Finally, the estimated output is generated via fully-connected (FC) layers as:

$$
(\hat{x}, \hat{y}) = \mathrm{FC}(\mathbf{h}_N^{(R)})
\tag{7}
$$

The overall network architecture is integrated by the attention subnetwork and the recurrent subnetwork. Figure 1 shows the overall architecture of the proposed DNN model. The training of the proposed architecture is conducted using the data and labels that are generated by FEM in Sect. 3.1.

The Euclidean distance is utilized as the loss function to quantify the error distance between the estimated location and the ground truth location, i.e.:

$$
loss = \sqrt{(x - \hat{x})^2 + (y - \hat{y}^2)}
\tag{8}
$$

where $\hat{x}$ and x represent the predicted and ground truth horizontal coordinate of the impact location, respectively. $\hat{y}$ and y represent the predicted and ground truth vertical coordinate of the impact location, respectively. Adam optimizer [7] is utilized to train the proposed DNN model with the Euclidean distance as the training loss.

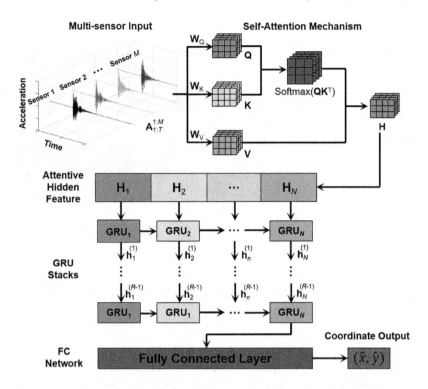

Fig. 1. Overall architecture of the proposed deep neural network.

4 Experiments

In this section, the performance of the proposed neural network is conducted and validated on real-world experiments. The structural setup of the physical experiments, the data generation setup of the dataset, the neural network setup, and the experimental performance of the proposed model are presented in detail.

4.1 Experimental Settings

Structural Setup. The experiment was conducted on an square aluminium plate structure with clamped boundary condition on two sides, as seen in Fig. 2. The plate had a dimension of 270 mm by 300 mm with a thickness of 6 mm. The density and the Young's modulus of the aluminum material were 69 GPa and 2.7 g/cm^3 with a Poisson ratio of 0.3.

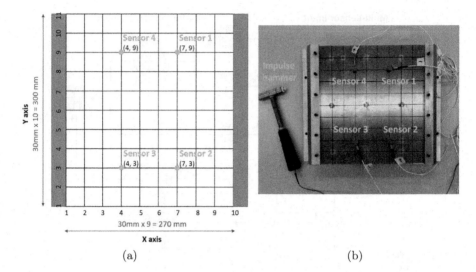

Fig. 2. Structural setup. (a) Plate specification and sensor placement. (b) Physical structure.

Considering the edge of the structural plate, the effective experimental area was divided by 9 × 10 small squares, learning to a square grid pattern. Four Brüel & Kjær type 4395 accelerometers were distributed over the plate at coordinates: Sensor 1 (7, 9), Sensor 2 (7, 3), Sensor 3 (4, 3), Sensor 4 (4, 9). The impact load was applied by using a Dytran impulse hammer. The data was transmitted using CoCo-80 acquisition system via Ethernet. All measurements were performed in a 5.76 kHz frequency range.

Data Generation Setup. To generate training dataset, the FEM of the test specimen was developed in commercial software SAP2000. The plate was modeled and meshed with thin shell element. Smaller grid tessellation can lead to higher resolution in terms of identification of impact location. In the experiment, a total of 86 grid nodes were designated in FEM, as seen in Fig. 3. Except the sensor locations and clamped edges, an impact load were randomly applied among the grid nodes with different amplitude p_o and duration t_d.

According to the actual test data, a range of 1 ms to 3 ms was assumed for t_d and the p_o was ranging from 20 N to 150 N. In total, 1,000 loading scenarios were simulated by performing dynamic time history analyses on the developed model, where the acceleration time history responses and impact locations were recorded. For each analysis, a complete loading duration was 0.5 s with a sampling rate 12800 Hz. As an illustration, Fig. 3(c) shows the acceleration time histories at four instrumented locations subjected to a loading example.

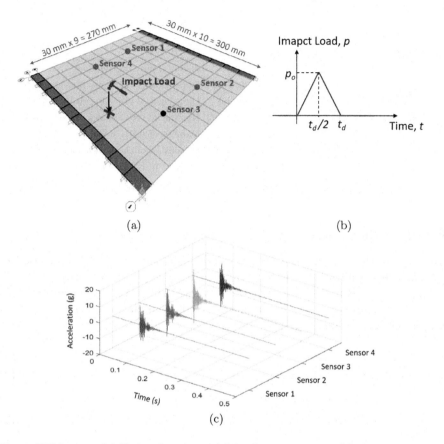

Fig. 3. FEM setup. (a) Finite element model for data generation, (b) Execution example of an impact load input, (c) Corresponding response data of acceleration time series.

Neural Network Setup. The data set is generated via FEM. The experimental data composes of training set, validation set and test set. Specifically, the dimensions of training set, validation set, test set are provided in Table 1. To train the proposed model, the batch size is set to 48 with the learning rate as 0.001. The dropout rate is set to 0.05. In addition, the hyperparameter settings are given in Table 2.

Table 1. Dataset setting.

Dataset	Source	Sample no.	Dimension
Training set	FEM	800	(800, 4, 6400)
Validation set	FEM	100	(100, 4, 6400)
Test set	FEM	100	(100, 4, 6400)

Network	Symbol	Setting	Description
Attention network	T	6400	Size of input time window
	d_q, d_k	[32, 64, 96, 128]	Dimension of the query and key state
	d_v	[20, 40, 60, 80]	Dimension of the value state
Recurrent network	N	[5, 10, 15, 20, 25]	Number of GRU blocks of each stack
	R	[1, 2, 3, 4, 5]	Number of GRU stacks
	d_r	[64, 96, 128, 256]	Dimension of the GRU hidden state
	L	[1, 2, 3, 4, 5]	Number of FC layers
	d_l	[8, 16, 32, 64]	Dimension of FC layer

4.2   Experimental Results

To evaluate the performance of the proposed model, four metrics are used to evaluate the localization accuracy. Specifically, mean absolute error of X axis (MAE of X), mean absolute error of Y axis (MAE of Y), Euclidean distance, and accuracy rate are the selected metrics in the experiments. These evaluation metrics are defined as:

$$\text{MAE of X: } e_x = \frac{1}{Total} \Sigma_{\text{test}} |x - \hat{x}| \tag{9}$$

$$\text{MAE of Y: } e_y = \frac{1}{Total} \Sigma_{\text{test}} |y - \hat{y}| \tag{10}$$

$$\text{Euclidean distance: } dis = \frac{1}{Total} \Sigma_{\text{test}} \sqrt{(x - \hat{x})^2 + (y - \hat{y}^2)} \tag{11}$$

$$\text{Accuracy rate: } acc = \frac{True}{Total} \times 100\% \tag{12}$$

where $\hat{x}$ and $\hat{y}$ represent the predicted horizontal and vertical coordinates of the impact location, respectively. x and y represent the ground-truth horizontal and vertical coordinates of the impact, respectively. $True$ and $Total$ indicate the number of the correct estimation (the estimated locations exactly match the label locations) and the total tests, respectively.

To validate the estimation performance of the proposed attention-based GRU stacks model (AttnGRUS), the experiments also implement the-state-of-the-art models for a comparative study. Specifically, covolutional neural network (CNN), long short-term memory stacks (LSTMS), GRU stacks (GRUS), CNN-LSTMS, and CNN-GRUS are chosen as the benchmark models for the comparative study. The experiments are conducted on the Pytorch framework with a 2.6 GHz Intel(R) Xeon(R) E5-2670 CPU and three GeForce GTX 1080 Ti GPUs.

The experiments are first carried out by numerical testing. Table 3 gives the experimental results on the numerical test set. For the proposed model, the network hyperparameters of AttentionGRUS are: $d_q, d_k = 64$, $d_v = 20$, $N = 10$, $R = 2$, $d_r = 256$, $L = 2$, $d_l = 16$. For the compared models, the network hyperparameters of the compared models are searched and set over grid search to achieve their best accuracy. As can be seen from the table, the proposed model AttentionGRUS achieves the best performance (highlighted gray cells)

Table 3. Numerical experimental results of the proposed and compared models.

Model	Localization Performance			
	e_x (mm)	e_y (mm)	dis (mm)	acc (%)
CNN	3.75	0.15	3.81	87
LSTMS	8.55	0.75	8.94	73
GRUS	7.2	0.75	7.86	82
CNN-LSTMS	2.1	1.2	3.12	90
CNN-GRUS	2.25	0.9	3	90
AttentionGRUS	0.15	0.3	0.45	98

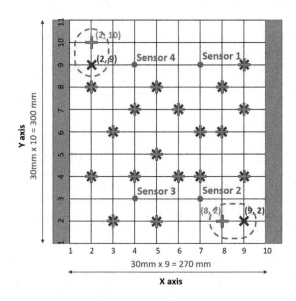

Fig. 4. Estimated locations (orange '+') and ground-truth locations (blue '×') of physical testing on structural plate. (Color figure online)

on the numerical test set in comparison with the compared models, with the accuracy rate of 98% and with the lowest estimation error regarding both X axis, Y axis, and the overall Euclidean distance. AttentionGRUS outperforms the compared benchmark models on the test set.

Figure 4 displays the experimental results of the physical testing on the structural plate using AttnGRUS. With a total of 20 randomly selected impact loads, the figure shows the estimations using AttnGRUS and the ground-truth impact locations. There are two samples not exactly matched (location (2, 9) and location (9, 2)) among the total of 20 tests. In this physical testing, the accuracy rate is 90% with e_x of 1.5 mm, e_y of 1.5 mm, and dis of 3 mm. It can be seen that the numerical localization performance of AttnGRUS in Table 3 is relatively better than the performance in the real-world testing. This difference is reasonable due to the potential noise or uncertainty between the numerical and real-world experiments. Given both the numerical and the physical tests, the experimental results validate the effectiveness and the accuracy of the proposed method.

5   Conclusion

This paper proposes a supervised learning frame that integrates both model-driven method for dataset generation and a data-driven method for localization of structural impact loads. Aiming at accurate localization of transient impact, a novel attention-based GRU stacks model is proposed. This deep neural network model can effectively handle a large scale of multivariate time-series signals and estimate the location of the excitation source accurately. In the future work, transfer learning will be implemented to finely tune the proposed model for real-world deployment. In addition, the optimization of sensor placement can be determined by further investigating the attentive importance of each structural place in a regression process.

References

1. Bahdanau, D., Cho, K., Bengio, Y.: Neural machine translation by jointly learning to align and translate. In: International Conference on Learning Representatives (2015)
2. Cho, K., et al.: Learning phrase representations using RNN encoder-decoder for statistical machine translation. arXiv preprint arXiv:1406.1078. https://doi.org/10.48550/arXiv.1406.1078 (2014)
3. Das, S., Saha, P., Patro, S.K.: Vibration-based damage detection techniques used for health monitoring of structures: a review. J. Civ. Struct. Health Monit. **6**(3), 477–507 (2016). https://doi.org/10.1007/s13349-016-0168-5
4. Fatahi, L., Moradi, S.: Multiple crack identification in frame structures using a hybrid Bayesian model class selection and swarm-based optimization methods. Struct. Health Monit. **17**(1), 39–58 (2018). https://doi.org/10.1177/1475921716683360
5. Flah, M., Nunez, I., Ben Chaabene, W., Nehdi, M.L.: Machine learning algorithms in civil structural health monitoring: a systematic review. Arch. Comput. Methods Eng. **28**(4), 2621–2643 (2020). https://doi.org/10.1007/s11831-020-09471-9
6. Kim, T., Kwon, O.S., Song, J.: Response prediction of nonlinear hysteretic systems by deep neural networks. Neural Netw. **111**, 1–10 (2019). https://doi.org/10.1016/j.neunet.2018.12.005
7. Kingma, D., Ba, J.: Adam: a method for stochastic optimization. In: International Conference on Learning Representations, December 2014. https://doi.org/10.48550/arXiv.1412.6980
8. Li, T., Pan, Y., Tong, K., Ventura, C.E., de Silva, C.W.: A multi-scale attention neural network for sensor location selection and nonlinear structural seismic response prediction. Comput. Struct. **248**, 106507 (2021). https://doi.org/10.1016/j.compstruc.2021.106507

9. Li, T., Pan, Y., Tong, K., Ventura, C.E., de Silva, C.W.: Attention-based sequence-to-sequence learning for online structural response forecasting under seismic excitation. IEEE Trans. Syst. Man Cybern. Syst. **52**(4), 2184–2200 (2022). https://doi.org/10.1109/TSMC.2020.3048696

10. Liu, Q., Wang, F., Li, J., Xiao, W.: A hybrid support vector regression with multi-domain features for low-velocity impact localization on composite plate structure. Mech. Syst. Sig. Process. **154**, 107547 (2021). https://doi.org/10.1016/j.ymssp.2020.107547

11. Obuchowski, J., Wyłomańska, A., Zimroz, R.: Selection of informative frequency band in local damage detection in rotating machinery. Mech. Syst. Sig. Process. **48**(1), 138–152 (2014). https://doi.org/10.1016/j.ymssp.2014.03.011

12. Qiu, B., Zhang, M., Xie, Y., Qu, X., Li, X.: Localisation of unknown impact loads on a steel plate using a pattern recognition method combined with the similarity metric via structural stress responses in the time domain. Mech. Syst. Sig. Process. **128**, 429–445 (2019). https://doi.org/10.1016/j.ymssp.2019.04.015

13. Seventekidis, P., Giagopoulos, D., Arailopoulos, A., Markogiannaki, O.: Structural health monitoring using deep learning with optimal finite element model generated data. Mech. Syst. Sig. Process. **145**, 106972 (2020). https://doi.org/10.1016/j.ymssp.2020.106972

14. Sony, S., Laventure, S., Sadhu, A.: A literature review of next-generation smart sensing technology in structural health monitoring. Struct. Control. Health Monit. **26**(3), e2321 (2019). https://doi.org/10.1002/stc.2321

15. Vaswani, A., et al.: Attention is all you need. In: Advances in Neural Information Processing Systems, vol. 30 (2017)

16. Zargar, S.A., Yuan, F.G.: Impact diagnosis in stiffened structural panels using a deep learning approach. Struct. Health Monit. **20**(2), 681–691 (2021). https://doi.org/10.1177/1475921720925044

17. Zhang, W., Zhang, Y., Song, R., Liu, Y., Zhang, W.: 3D layout estimation via weakly supervised learning of plane parameters from 2D segmentation. IEEE Trans. Image Process. **31**, 868–879 (2021). https://doi.org/10.1109/TIP.2021.3131025

18. Zhao, B., Cheng, C., Peng, Z., Dong, X., Meng, G.: Detecting the early damages in structures with nonlinear output frequency response functions and the CNN-LSTM model. IEEE Trans. Instrum. Meas. **69**(12), 9557–9567 (2020). https://doi.org/10.1109/TIM.2020.3005113

19. Zhou, J., Dong, L., Guan, W., Yan, J.: Impact load identification of nonlinear structures using deep recurrent neural network. Mech. Syst. Sig. Process. **133**, 106292 (2019). https://doi.org/10.1016/j.ymssp.2019.106292

Connecting Patients with Pre-diagnosis: A Multiple Graph Regularized Method for Mental Disorder Diagnosis

Tianqi Zhao[1], Ming Kong[1], Kun Kuang[1,4(✉)], Zhengxing Huang[1], Qiang Zhu[1], and Fei Wu[1,2,3]

[1] Institute of Artificial Intelligence, Zhejiang University, Hangzhou, China
{ztqwdk,zjukongming,kunkuang,zhengxinghuang,zhuq}@zju.edu.cn,
wufei@cs.zju.edu.cn
[2] Shanghai Institute for Advanced Study of Zhejiang University, Shanghai, China
[3] Shanghai AI Laboratory, Shanghai, China
[4] Key Laboratory for Corneal Diseases Research of Zhejiang Province,
Hangzhou, China

Abstract. Computer-aided diagnosis (CAD) plays an important role in medicine. But most of the previous methods only focus on the diagnosis process information like the image data for medical patterns learning, ignoring the pre-diagnosis, which is necessary and important for a doctor's decision. Besides, traditional CAD methods treat the patients as independent samples in data. To make up this gap, in this paper, we propose to connect patients with pre-diagnosis and propose a novel Multiple Graph REgularized Diagnosis (MuGRED) method for mental disorder diagnosis, which contains two main components: multi-modal representation learning and a multiple graph feature fusion module. We validated our MuGRED method on a practical dataset of children's attention deficit and hyperactivity disorder and a well-recognized ASD benchmark. Extensive experiments demonstrate that our MuGRED method can achieve a better performance than the state-of-the-art methods for mental disorder diagnosis.

Keywords: Computer-aided diagnosis · Mental disorder · Graph attention network

1 Introduction

To simplify the diagnosis process and alleviate the lack of medical resources, computer auxiliary analyses of the information generated in the process of medical diagnosis have become the focus of both academia and industry [4,12]. Most of the related works of computer-aided diagnosis focus on the doctor's diagnosis process of the patient's condition, such as analyzing the patient's medical images [5,19], or the doctor's performance when communicating with the patient [1,22]. However, most of the current computer-aided methods only focus on analyzing

L. Fang et al. (Eds.): CICAI 2022, LNAI 13605, pp. 362–374, 2022.
https://doi.org/10.1007/978-3-031-20500-2_30

the doctors' diagnosis process information for medical patterns learning, ignoring the fact that the medical diagnosis process is a comprehensive, complicated and multi-step judgment process.

Pre-diagnosis is one of the most important procedures during the diagnosis process. But how to combine the pre-diagnosis information with the computer-aided diagnosis model to obtain more accurate conclusions has not yet been paid enough attention. So we propose the *Multiple Graph Regularized Diagnosis* (MuGRED) method to generate the pre-diagnosis information with the image process diagnosis. The proposed MuGRED method consists of two main components: multimodal representation learning, which is designed to learn the representation of patients from the diagnosis process, and a multiple graph feature fusion module to fuse the information from varieties of pre-diagnosis as well as from the diagnosis process for the final diagnosis conclusion.

In this paper, we focus on the diagnosis of mental disorders. We evaluate our method's effectiveness on two datasets: a practical dataset for ADHD and a well-recognized mental disorders dataset for anxiety and depression. We introduce the pre-diagnosis results to these two multimodal behavior analysis problems and compare them with state-of-the-art methods. Experimental results show that our method can better use pre-diagnosis information to achieve a more accurate diagnosis. The main contributions of this work can be summarized as follows:

- We propose a novel end-to-end *Multiple Graph Regularized Diagnosis* model for mental disorder diagnosis. To the best of our knowledge, it is the first work of connecting the pre-diagnosis information with machine learning-based multi-modal representation learning;
- According to similar pre-diagnosis patterns, we construct multiple graphs to represent the connection between patients. The graphs can regularize the patients' representations extracted from the diagnosis process and generate the optimized feature with a feature fusion mechanism.
- Extensive experiments on two datasets of mental disorders show that our way of introducing pre-diagnosis information can effectively improve diagnostic performance, and the introduction of the pre-diagnosis information conforms to intuition and medical logic.

The rest of this paper is organized as follows. Section 2 reviews the related work. Section 3 introduces our proposed multiple graph regularized diagnosis method. Section 4 gives extensive experimental results. Finally, Sect. 5 concludes the paper.

2 Related Work

2.1 Computer-Aided Diagnosis

In recent years, deep learning has been widely used in the medical field, most of which focus on medical imaging analysis. There are also some works on mental disorder diagnosis. For example, [11] based on computer vision analysis technology to predict attention deficit and hyperactivity disorder (ADHD) and autism spectrum disorder (ASD). They considered the tester's facial expression, head position, movement, etc., and used a support vector machine (SVM) to analyze ADHD and ASD is classified. [9] build a multi-modal method using 3D facial expressions and spoken language with C-CNNs to predict PHQ scale. [18] process acceleration signal from wrist and ankle by RNN to distinguish behavior between ADHD diagnosed participants and normal ones. [2] uses clinical conversation messages to train a text-based multi-task BiLSTM network aiming at modeling both depression severity and binary health state. [17] try to diagnose the major depressive disorder or simply depression through electroencephalogram by Logistic regression, Support vector machine, and Naive Bayesian. [24] describe an intelligent auxiliary diagnosis System based on multimodal information fusion to diagnose ADHD. [26] use a cross-task approach that transfers attention from speech recognition to depression severity measurement. [3] use atrous residual temporal convolution network and temporal fusion based on visual behavior to capture depression signals. These works focus on the analysis in the diagnosis process, ignoring the integration of pre-diagnosis information, which is not enough to support a complete ADHD diagnostic logic chain.

2.2 Graph-Based Information Fusion

Constructing a graph to make feature fusion between related entities is widely applied in various applications. [20] build a multi-modal heterogeneous graph for recommendation. [23] design a heterogeneous graph neural network to jointly consider heterogeneous structural information and contents information of each node effectively. Using graph-based fusion model to simulate human logic has also been widely applied in the domain of computer-aided diagnosis. For example, [15] build the interaction between individuals and groups is established through a graph convolution network to assist in diagnosing COVID-19. [25] introduce a graph-based semi-supervised model by using partly labeled samples to diagnose dementia. [16] construct a knowledge graph to assist diagnosis based on doctor experience, case data, and other information. It proves the feasibility and research value of intelligent diagnosis assisted by graph network.

We combine the pre-diagnosis information with the diagnostic analysis process. First, the time-sequential neural network is to fuse the patient's various characteristics during the test. Then the graph neural network is established through the pre-diagnosis information, and the feature optimization is performed through the attention mechanism to improve the prediction effect.

3 Method

This paper proposed a MuGRED (Multiple Graph REgularized Diagnosis) model to solve the mental disorder diagnosis problem. The diagnosis process of the mental disorder can be summarized into two-step: Pre-diagnosis and diagnosis. During the pre-diagnosis process, patients are required to complete some questionnaires, and the doctors can get a preliminary understanding of their

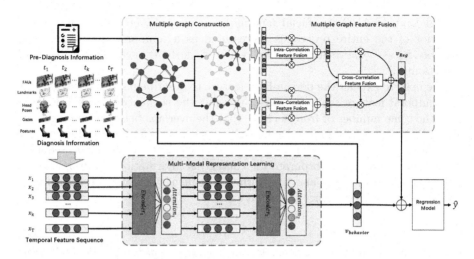

Fig. 1. Overview architecture of Multiple Graph REgularized Diagnosis (MuGRED).

psychological conditions based on the quantitative indicators. And during the diagnosis process, doctors interview patients or ask them to complete specific tasks and observe their multi-modal behaviors, such as eye movements, facial expressions, head posture, body movements, conversation content, or voice intonation. The doctors consider the patient condition of both pre-diagnosis information and performance of multi-modal behavior during the diagnosis process to draw the final diagnosis conclusion.

The proposed MuGRED model imitates the above diagnosis process of human doctors. As Fig. 1 shows, the MuGRED model consists of three modules: *Multimodal Representation Learning* module, *Multiple Graph Construction* modules, and *Multiple Graph Feature Fusion* modules. *Multimodal Representation Learning* module is to extract the behavior representation of the diagnosis process from the frame-level temporal multi-modal feature sequence. *Multiple Graph Construction* modules introduce the pre-diagnosis information to construct the correlation graph. The edges between patients are connected according to a similar pattern of pre-diagnosis results. *Multiple Graph Feature Fusion* modals firstly make a *intra-correlation feature fusion* to regularize the representation of patient behavior and then make a *cross-correlation feature fusion* to integrate the features regularized with different pre-diagnosis indicators for the final diagnosis conclusion making. In the following, we introduce the technical details of the MuGRED model.

3.1 Multi-modal Representation Learning

The inputs of the MuGRED model are from the diagnostic process. The patient behaviors are recorded as multimedia data, and we extract the patient's behavioral features according to the diagnostic logic needs, such as gaze position, facial

Action Units (FAUs) [8], facial landmarks, head pose, etc. The multi-modal behavior of the entire process is represented as a temporal feature sequence $\mathbf{X} = [\mathbf{x}_1, \mathbf{x}_2, \cdots, \mathbf{x}_T]^T$ with T frames, where $\mathbf{x}_i$ is the frame-level feature of the timestamp i.

We need to extract the person-level feature to describe patient behavior from the temporal feature sequence. First, we split the sequence into N fragments with the same number of frames (Note that the overlaps between fragments are allowed), and the temporal behavior feature sequence can be transformed into a set of fragment sequences: $\mathbf{C} = \{\mathbf{c}_1, \mathbf{c}_2, \cdots, \mathbf{c}_N\}$. For each fragment sequence $\mathbf{c}_i$, we summarize and incorporate the contextual information of a frame with a temporal neural network, and transform the sequence of frame-level features $\mathbf{c}_i$ into a hidden state sequence $\mathbf{h}_i$, noted as:

$$\mathbf{h}_i = \mathbf{\Phi}(\mathbf{c}_i, \Theta) \tag{1}$$

where $\mathbf{\Phi}$ can be any temporal encoder, such as *Temporal Convolutional Network* (TCN) [14] or *Long-Short Term Memory Network* (LSTM) [10]. Then we aggregate the hidden state of each frame with a self-attention mechanism to generate the representation of fragment feature $\mathbf{r}_i$ as:

$$\mathbf{r}_i = \frac{1}{M} \sum_{i=1}^{M} \mathbf{w}_i \mathbf{h}_i \tag{2}$$

where $\mathbf{w}_i = \frac{e^{\mathbf{h}_i}}{\sum_{i=1}^{M} e^{\mathbf{h}_i}}$ is the attention weight and M is the frame number in fragment sequences $\mathbf{c}_i$. So that we obtain the sequence of fragments $\mathbf{r} = [\mathbf{r}_1, \mathbf{r}_2, ..., \mathbf{r}_N]$. By repeating the same process of transforming the frame-level feature set $\mathbf{c}_i$ to the fragment feature $\mathbf{r}_i$, we can transform the fragment-level feature set $\mathbf{r}$ into the person-level representation $\mathbf{v}_{Behavior}$.

3.2 Multiple Graph Construction

After generating the person-level feature, we introduce the pre-diagnosis information. Given P kinds of pre-diagnosis patterns, the pre-diagnosis result of the patient i is represented as $\mathbf{R}_i = \{\mathbf{R}_i^1, \mathbf{R}_i^2, \cdots, \mathbf{R}_i^P\}$.

Suppose we've known the behavioral representation of $\hat{N}$ previous patients, we build the correlation hypergraph $G(\hat{V}, E)$ to represent the connections over the patients. Where the set of node $\hat{\mathbf{V}} = \{\hat{\mathbf{v}}_1, \hat{\mathbf{v}}_2, \cdots \hat{\mathbf{v}}_{\hat{N}}\}$ denotes the person-level feature of the previous cases. As there are P kinds of pre-diagnosis patterns, the graph includes P kinds of edges, denoted as $\mathbf{E} = \{E^1, E^2, \cdots, E^P\}$. The *p-th* kind of correlation between node $\hat{\mathbf{v}}_i$ and $\hat{\mathbf{v}}_j$ is denoted as:

$$e_{ij}^p = \begin{cases} 0 & \mathbf{R}_i^p \neq \mathbf{R}_j^p \\ 1 & \mathbf{R}_i^p = \mathbf{R}_j^p. \end{cases} \tag{3}$$

where $e_{ij}^p \in E^p$, $i, j = 1, 2, \cdots, \hat{N}$. i.e., if the node $\hat{\mathbf{v}}_i$ and $\hat{\mathbf{v}}_j$ are with the same result of the *p-th* pre-diagnosis indicator, we defined that they are with correlation in the corresponding aspect. Consequently, they are connected with the *p-th* kind of edge in the graph. For example, if two people are both with severe insomnia, we construct their correlation in the insomnia aspect. Note that the pair of nodes may contain multiple correlations, which indicates that they are with stronger correlations.

3.3 Multiple Graph Feature Fusion

In the previous section, we used the pre-diagnosis information to construct an association graph between existing cases $G(\tilde{V}, E)$. Next, we obtain the regularized patient behavior feature with a two-step operation: First, for each correlation constructed by the specific pre-diagnosis pattern, we make a *intra-correlation feature fusion* to regularize the behavior feature; and then we make a *cross-correlation feature fusion* to aggregate the set of features regularized with the single correlation.

Intra-correlation Feature Fusion. As we obtained the personal-level behavioral feature vector $\mathbf{v}_{Behavior}$ of the current patient, we regularize the feature representation with the correlation graph. By adding the node $\mathbf{v}_{Behavior}$ into the correlation graph, we connect the edges along with the above rules based on pre-diagnosis results' consistency.

For the *p-th* kind of pre-diagnosis pattern, the feature $\mathbf{v}_{Beh}$ is optimized on the sub-graph of G, denoted with $g_p = (\mathbf{V}, \mathbf{E}^p)$. We aggregate the correlated feature representation with the current case by a *graph attention network* on each pre-diagnosis indicator. The correlation and message passing that the node $\hat{\mathbf{v}}_i$ affected the node $\mathbf{v}_{Beh}$ is considered as a multi-head attention mechanism, expressed as:

$$\xi_{k,i}^p = LeakyReLU((\mathbf{W}_{self}^k \mathbf{v}_{Beh}) \cdot (\mathbf{W}_{obj}^k \hat{\mathbf{v}}_i)^T), \ \hat{e}_i^p \neq 0$$

$$\alpha_{k,i}^p = Softmax_j(\xi_{k,i}^p / s_{scale})$$

$$\mathbf{s}_i^p = \overset{K}{\underset{k=1}{\|}} \ \sigma(\Sigma_{j \in E_p} \alpha_{k,i}^p \mathbf{W}_{fea}^k v_i) \mathbf{W}^O$$

(4)

where K is the number of attention headers, $\mathbf{W}_{self}^k$, $\mathbf{W}_{obj}^k$ and $\mathbf{W}_{fea}^k$ are the linear transformation parameters of the *k-th* attention header. $\|$ represents concatenation operation, and the hyper-parameter s_{scale} is a scaled index to adjust the sensitivity of feature differences in practical applications. Finally, a dimensional attention matrix $\mathbf{W}^o$ is applied for dimensional reduction.

According to the above setting, we construct correlation graph of the previous patients through P kinds of pre-diagnosis indicators and obtain an optimized representation of the current case through each indicator. So that we get the regularized feature set $R_S = \{\mathbf{r}_s^1, \mathbf{r}_s^2, \cdots, \mathbf{r}_s^P\}$.

Cross-correlation Feature Fusion. The regularized features through various correlations of pre-diagnosis indicators describe the patient's characteristics from different aspects. To generate the pre-diagnosis-related feature of the patient, we propose a cross-correlation feature fusion with attention mechanism to fuse the features in S. The attention weight of each feature is shown as:

$$\mathbf{w}^p = \frac{1}{P} \sum_{p \in P} q^T \cdot \tanh(\mathbf{W} \cdot s^p + b) \tag{5}$$

$$\beta^p = \frac{\exp(\mathbf{w}_i^p)}{\sum_{p=1}^{P} exp(\mathbf{w}^p)} \tag{6}$$

where $\mathbf{W}$ is the weight matrix, q is the attention vector. β^p is the normalized weight. And the final feature is $\mathbf{v}_{Reg}$:

$$\mathbf{v}_{Reg} = \sum_{p=1}^{P} \beta^p \cdot s^p \tag{7}$$

Finally, we make a concatenation to the feature directly extracted from the temporal behavioral feature sequence and the optimized feature to consider both patient's direct behavior and the correlations with the pre-diagnosis-related previous diagnostic experience. So the final feature representation of making the diagnostic decisions is denoted as $\mathbf{z} = [\mathbf{v}_{Behavior} \| \mathbf{v}_{Reg}]$ for the diagnosis result prediction.

4 Experiment

4.1 Dataset Description

We evaluate the performance of our proposed method on two datasets of mental disorders: A well-recognized mental disorder benchmark *DAIC-WOZ* and a practical on attention deficit and hyperactivity disorder *ADHD*, which are described as follows:

ADHD: We cooperate with The Children's Hospital of Zhejiang University School of Medicine to collect a dataset of patients with *Attention Deficit and Hyperactive Disorder* (ADHD), including 109 children for training and 15 for testing. Before the diagnosis begins, each patient and their parents must complete various psychological assessment scales during the pre-diagnosis process. With the patients' informed consent, we record videos of these children's behaviors during their diagnosis process with multiple cameras and extract their gaze, head poses, facial action units, facial landmarks, and body movements from the videos of the diagnostic process as a sequential temporal behavioral feature. In this work, we introduce the *Conners Comprehensive Behaviour Rating Scale* (*Conners*) [6] as the pre-diagnosis information. It is a questionnaire to gain a better understanding of academic, behavioral, and social issues. The diagnostic conclusion is from the result of *SNAP-IV Teacher and Parent Rating Scale* (*SNAP-IV*) [21], which is an assessment of ADHD risk with score ranges from 0 to 3 from three main perspectives: *Inattenton* (Inatt for short), *Hyperactivity-Impulsity*(H/Imp for short) and *Oppositional Defiant Disorder* (ODD for short).

DAIC-WOZ: A well-recognized mental disorder benchmark that contains clinical interviews designed to support the diagnosis of psychological distress conditions such as anxiety [7], depression, and post-traumatic stress disorder. The participants are required to communicate with an animated virtual interview controlled by a human interviewer in another room, and their behaviors are collected as multimedia records, including video, audio and text collected. In 189 participants, 107 participants are used as training set, 35 as development set and 47 as test set. The diagnostic conclusion of DAIC-WOZ is evaluated with the depression index score Patient Health Questionnaire (PHQ-8) [13]. The questionnaire estimates the mental disorder with eight indicators: NoInterest, Depressed, Sleep, Tired, Appetite, Failure, Concentrating, and Moving. And the value of each indicator score ranges from 0 to 3 according to the severity, so the total score ranges from 0 to 24. In the experiment, we consider the multimodal behavioral features of FAUs, head poses, gazes, and 2D facial landmarks extracted from the interview videos as the input of the temporal behavioral feature sequence. We regard *gender* and each indicator in the *Patient Health Questionnaire* (PHQ-8) [13] scale as the patients' pre-diagnosis information. Since there is a strong correlation between the label and the indicators, introducing all the indicators as pre-diagnosis information is meaningless. Instead, we regard gender and randomly select several indicators as pre-diagnosis knowledge.

4.2   Implementation Details

To simplify the training process, we apply a transfer learning strategy. We first train the temporal feature extraction model to predict the label directly with 100 epochs and then transfer it to the *Temporal Feature Extraction* module of MuGRED with fixed gradient propagation to train the rest part of the model. We evaluate the diagnosis conclusion with the evaluation metrics of *Mean Absolute Error* (MAE) and *Root Mean Square Error* (RMSE).

The hyper-parameters for all the experiments are under the same setting. The model was optimized with the Adam optimizer to optimize the parameters, and we set the λ_1 to 0.9 and λ_2 to 0.999 with weight decay of 1e−4. The initialized learning rate is set to 1e−3. The final result for each experiment follows early-stop strategy and the number of train epochs is 500.

4.3   Baselines

We considered three baseline methods for multi-modal representation learning. *DepArt-Net* is one of the state-of-the-art method of on the *DAIC-WOZ* dataset problem, which applied an *atrous temporal convolutional network* to extract the multi-model sentence embedding from the multi-modal feature sequence, and then make the diagnostic decision [3], In addition, *HAN+TCN* and *HAN+LSTM* is the baselines of hierarchical attention network with two sequential encoders.

Table 1. The RMSE and MAE scores comparison of the different pre-diagnosis information aggregation methods on *DAIC-WOZ* dataset and *ADHD* dataset

Method	Concat	MuGRED	ADHD		DAIC-WOZ	
			MAE	RMSE	MAE	RMSE
DepArt-Net	✗	✗	0.507	0.613	4.665	6.004
	✓	✗	0.424	0.568	4.626	5.892
	✗	✓	0.403	0.470	2.780	3.914
	✓	✓	**0.400**	**0.465**	**2.461**	**3.171**
HAN-TCN	✗	✗	0.446	0.599	4.471	5.799
	✓	✗	0.413	0.558	2.617	3.435
	✗	✓	**0.352**	**0.461**	2.801	3.925
	✓	✓	0.363	0.472	**2.131**	**3.021**
HAN-LSTM	✗	✗	0.472	0.604	5.166	6.216
	✓	✗	0.446	0.556	2.667	3.367
	✗	✓	0.372	0.480	2.800	3.907
	✓	✓	**0.361**	**0.462**	**1.922**	**2.571**

4.4   Results

Considering that MuGRED introduced extra information of pre-diagnosis, to keep the comparison fair, we proposed another way to introduce the same information by simply concatenating the vector of pre-diagnosis indicators to the multi-model behavior embedding. We select gender and the indicator *NoInterest* as the pre-diagnosis information. The results in Table 1 compare the performance of the two kinds of pre-diagnosis information integration methods on the three kinds of temporal feature extractors. We found that for both datasets, the integration of pre-diagnosis can improve the diagnostic performance for the three kinds of feature extractors, which proves the value of introducing pre-diagnosis information. In comparing the two integration mechanisms, MuGRED leads to a more significant improvement, indicating that the model design of MuGRED plays the effectiveness of pre-diagnosis information. In addition, in most cases, integrating the pre-diagnosis information with both methods can make the best performance, which may become a practical trick of MuGRED's modification.

We then evaluate the impact of the amount of combined pre-diagnostic indicators on the diagnostic prediction performance on DAIC-WOZ dataset. As shown in Table 2, we compared the model performance in the three settings: without pre-diagnosis, with gender and 1 indicator (*NoInterest*), and with gender and 3 indicators (*NoInterest, Depressed* and *Sleep*). The results show that the richer the pre-diagnosis information introduced, the more accurate the prediction of the diagnosis conclusion.

Table 2. The RMSE and MAE scores comparison of the diagnosis results with different amounts of the pre-diagnostic indicators on *DAIC-WOZ* dataset

Method	w/o Pre-diagnosis		Gender+1 Indicator		Gender+3 Indicators	
	MAE	RMSE	MAE	RMSE	MAE	RMSE
DepArt-Net	4.665	6.004	2.780	3.914	**2.378**	**2.876**
HAN+TCN	4.471	5.799	2.801	3.925	**2.294**	**2.871**
HAN+LSTM	5.166	6.216	2.800	3.907	**2.182**	**2.855**

Table 3. The RMSE and MAE scores comparison of the diagnosis items with/without pre-diagnostic indicators on *ADHD* dataset

Method	Inatt		H/Imp		ODD	
	MAE	RMSE	MAE	RMSE	MAE	RMSE
Without pre-diagnosis						
DepArt-Net	0.507	0.591	0.648	0.758	0.366	0.454
HAN-TCN	0.425	0.562	0.665	0.802	0.277	0.342
HAN-LSTM	0.500	0.554	0.647	0.770	0.402	0.443
With pre-diagnosis of conners indicators						
DepArt-Net	0.414	0.480	0.496	0.552	0.297	0.356
HAN-TCN	0.391	0.469	0.451	0.552	0.272	0.338
HAN-LSTM	0.342	0.447	0.432	0.526	0.350	0.464

For the ADHD dataset, the ADHD risk rating is consist of three items, i.e., *Inattenton* (Inatt), *Hyperactivity-Impulsity* (H/Imp) and *Oppositional Defiant Disorder* (ODD). We wonder whether the pre-diagnosis information correlation can benefit all the performance of the predicted diagnosis items. To achieve this, we evaluate how the pre-diagnosis affects the single item of the diagnosis result. The results of comparing the prediction results of the specific three symptom index with/without pre-diagnosis information are shown in Table 3. It could be found that the performance of every single item using the same method has been improved with the help of pre-diagnosis in most cases.

5 Conclusion

In this paper, we focus on the problem of mental disorders diagnosis, where both pre-diagnosis and diagnosis process information are important for medical experts to make a diagnosis. However, most existing methods in CAD only focus on the diagnosis process information while ignoring the pre-diagnosis information. Moreover, the patients are commonly treated as independent samples in previous CAD methods, while medical experts, in real applications, always need to connect patients for comparison. Therefore, we adopted the pre-diagnosis information to connect the patients and proposed a Multiple Graph REgularized Diagnosis (MuGRED) method for mental disorders diagnosis. The proposed MuGRED method is an end-to-end learning algorithm by fusing the representation from both pre-diagnosis and diagnosis processes for final diagnosis prediction. Extensive experiments on both ASD and ADHD demonstrated the effectiveness of the proposed MuGRED method for mental disorder diagnosis.

Acknowledgement. This work was supported in part by Program of Zhejiang Province Science and Technology (2022C01044), National Natural Science Foundation of China (U20A20387), the Fundamental Research Funds for the Central Universities (226-2022-00142, 226-2022-00051), Project by Shanghai AI Laboratory (P22KS00111), and the Starry Night Science Fund of Zhejiang University Shanghai Institute for Advanced Study (SN-ZJU-SIAS-0010).

References

1. Bandini, A., Green, J.R., Taati, B., Orlandi, S., Zinman, L., Yunusova, Y.: Automatic detection of amyotrophic lateral sclerosis (ALS) from video-based analysis of facial movements: speech and non-speech tasks. In: 2018 13th IEEE International Conference on Automatic Face & Gesture Recognition (FG 2018), pp. 150–157. IEEE (2018)

2. Dinkel, H., Wu, M., Yu, K.: Text-based depression detection on sparse data. arXiv e-prints pp. arXiv-1904 (2019)

3. Du, Z., Li, W., Huang, D., Wang, Y.: Encoding visual behaviors with attentive temporal convolution for depression prediction. In: 2019 14th IEEE International Conference on Automatic Face & Gesture Recognition (FG 2019), pp. 1–7. IEEE (2019)

4. Feng, F., Wu, Y., Wu, Y., Nie, G., Ni, R.: The effect of artificial neural network model combined with six tumor markers in auxiliary diagnosis of lung cancer. J. Med. Syst. **36**(5), 2973–2980 (2012)

5. Giger, M.L.: Computer-aided diagnosis of breast lesions in medical images. Comput. Sci. Eng. **2**(5), 39–45 (2000)

6. Goyette, C.H., Conners, C.K., Ulrich, R.F.: Normative data on revised conners parent and teacher rating scales. J. Abnorm. Child Psychol. **6**(2), 221–236 (1978)

7. Gratch, J., et al.: The distress analysis interview corpus of human and computer interviews. In: LREC, pp. 3123–3128 (2014)

8. Hamm, J., Kohler, C.G., Gur, R.C., Verma, R.: Automated facial action coding system for dynamic analysis of facial expressions in neuropsychiatric disorders. J. Neurosci. Methods **200**(2), 237–256 (2011)

9. Haque, A., Guo, M., Miner, A.S., Fei-Fei, L.: Measuring depression symptom severity from spoken language and 3d facial expressions. arXiv preprint arXiv:1811.08592 (2018)
10. Hochreiter, S., Schmidhuber, J.: Long short-term memory. Neural Comput. **9**(8), 1735–1780 (1997)
11. Jaiswal, S., Valstar, M.F., Gillott, A., Daley, D.: Automatic detection of ADHD and ASD from expressive behaviour in RGBD data. In: 2017 12th IEEE International Conference on Automatic Face & Gesture Recognition (FG 2017), pp. 762–769. IEEE (2017)
12. Kaushal, C., Bhat, S., Koundal, D., Singla, A.: Recent trends in computer assisted diagnosis (cad) system for breast cancer diagnosis using histopathological images. IRBM **40**(4), 211–227 (2019)
13. Kroenke, K., Strine, T.W., Spitzer, R.L., Williams, J.B., Berry, J.T., Mokdad, A.H.: The PHQ-8 as a measure of current depression in the general population. J. Affect. Disord. **114**(1–3), 163–173 (2009)
14. Lea, C., Vidal, R., Reiter, A., Hager, G.D.: Temporal convolutional networks: a unified approach to action segmentation. In: Hua, G., Jégou, H. (eds.) ECCV 2016. LNCS, vol. 9915, pp. 47–54. Springer, Cham (2016). https://doi.org/10.1007/978-3-319-49409-8_7
15. Liang, X., Zhang, Y., Wang, J., Ye, Q., Liu, Y., Tong, J.: Diagnosis of Covid-19 pneumonia based on graph convolutional network. Front. Med. **7** (2020)
16. Liu, P., et al.: HKDP: a hybrid knowledge graph based pediatric disease prediction system. In: Xing, C., Zhang, Y., Liang, Y. (eds.) ICSH 2016. LNCS, vol. 10219, pp. 78–90. Springer, Cham (2017). https://doi.org/10.1007/978-3-319-59858-1_8
17. Mumtaz, W., Xia, L., Ali, S.S.A., Yasin, M.A.M., Hussain, M., Malik, A.S.: Electroencephalogram (EEG)-based computer-aided technique to diagnose major depressive disorder (MDD). Biomed. Signal Process. Control **31**, 108–115 (2017)
18. Muñoz-Organero, M., Powell, L., Heller, B., Harpin, V., Parker, J.: Using recurrent neural networks to compare movement patterns in ADHD and normally developing children based on acceleration signals from the wrist and ankle. Sensors **19**(13), 2935 (2019)
19. Stoitsis, J., Valavanis, I., Mougiakakou, S.G., Golemati, S., Nikita, A., Nikita, K.S.: Computer aided diagnosis based on medical image processing and artificial intelligence methods. Nucl. Instrum. Methods Phys. Res., Sect. A **569**(2), 591–595 (2006)
20. Sun, R., et al.: Multi-modal knowledge graphs for recommender systems. In: Proceedings of the 29th ACM International Conference on Information & Knowledge Management, pp. 1405–1414 (2020)
21. Swanson, J.M., et al.: Clinical relevance of the primary findings of the MTA: success rates based on severity of ADHD and odd symptoms at the end of treatment. J. Am. Acad. Child Adoles. Psychiatry **40**(2), 168–179 (2001)
22. Vyas, K., et al.: Recognition of atypical behavior in autism diagnosis from video using pose estimation over time. In: 2019 IEEE 29th International Workshop on Machine Learning for Signal Processing (MLSP), pp. 1–6. IEEE (2019)
23. Zhang, C., Song, D., Huang, C., Swami, A., Chawla, N.V.: Heterogeneous graph neural network. In: Proceedings of the 25th ACM SIGKDD International Conference on Knowledge Discovery & Data Mining, pp. 793–803 (2019)
24. Zhang, Y., Kong, M., Zhao, T., Hong, W., Zhu, Q., Wu, F.: ADHD intelligent auxiliary diagnosis system based on multimodal information fusion. In: Proceedings of the 28th ACM International Conference on Multimedia, pp. 4494–4496 (2020)

25. Zhao, M., Chan, R.H., Chow, T.W., Tang, P.: Compact graph based semi-supervised learning for medical diagnosis in Alzheimer's disease. IEEE Signal Process. Lett. **21**(10), 1192–1196 (2014)
26. Zhao, Z., Bao, Z., Zhang, Z., Cummins, N., Wang, H., Schuller, B.: Hierarchical attention transfer networks for depression assessment from speech. In: ICASSP 2020–2020 IEEE International Conference on Acoustics, Speech and Signal Processing (ICASSP), pp. 7159–7163. IEEE (2020)

A Novel Device-Free Localization Approach Based on Deep Dictionary Learning

Manman Wang, Benying Tan$^{(\boxtimes)}$, Shuxue Ding, and Yujie Li

School of Artificial Intelligence, Guilin University of Electronic Technology, Guilin 541004, China
{by-tan,sding,yujieli}@guet.edu.cn

Abstract. As an emerging technology, device-free localization (DFL) has a wide range of application scenarios in the field of the internet of things. However, most of the existing DFL methods take the mode of learning features from raw data, and then perform to achieve localization using classification, which has inferior localization performance. To improve the localization accuracy, this study proposes an accurate and effective localization technique based on deep dictionary learning with sparse representation (DDL-DFL). The method extracts the in-depth features of the data through multi-layer dictionary learning and stacks the features of each layer for classification. Furthermore, we propose a data augmentation method, which can be applied to scenarios with fewer sensor nodes to increase the data dimension and strengthen the essential features to improve the accuracy of localization. We evaluate the performance of the DDL-DFL algorithm on collected laboratory datasets, and the results are superior to existing localization algorithms. In addition, the DDL-DFL algorithm with data augmentation is conducted on the laboratory datasets with a low dimension of data, and the localization performance has been significantly improved.

Keywords: Device-free localization · Deep dictionary learning · Sparse representation · Classification · Data augmentation

1 Introduction

With the development of the new generation of information technologies, such as the internet of things and cloud computing, the demand for wireless localization is increasing daily. Smart cities, namely urban informatization and intelligence, have become an inevitable trend. Wireless localization has produced a wide range of applications in smart cities, promoting the development of smart cities.

There are already many sophisticated localization methods in the real world, such as GPS [1], ultrasonic localization [2], and radio frequency identification (RFID) localization [3]. The above current localization technology has a good performance in many application fields. However, the application requires the target be equipped with a wireless device, such as a smartphone, which may not be suitable for some scenarios. For example, it cannot usually be assumed that the target is carrying any traceable device in

© The Author(s), under exclusive license to Springer Nature Switzerland AG 2022
L. Fang et al. (Eds.): CICAI 2022, LNAI 13605, pp. 375–386, 2022.
https://doi.org/10.1007/978-3-031-20500-2_31

an emergency rescue. Therefore, device-free localization (DFL), as an emerging technology [4–7], has a broader application in indoor localization by using wireless devices to detect, track, and locate targets without carrying any additional devices. As shown in Fig. 1(a), in a DFL system, several sensors are arranged around the monitoring area. They are responsible for transmitting and receiving signals in turn, sensing the target's location by the difference of the received signals caused by the target.

Many DFL methods have been proposed, such as fingerprinting, geometric, and Radio Tomographic Imaging (RTI) methods. These techniques are widely based on compressive sensing (CS), and deep learning technology. Youssef et al. [8] first proposed the concept of device-free passive localization. Joey Wilson and Neal Patwari of the University of Utah [9] proposed using radio tomographic imaging for target localization. D. Zhang et al. [10] enhanced the robustness of the localization model by expanding the localization area and introducing more sensor nodes. K. Wu et al. [11] used radio maps constructed from channel state information (CSI) to improve the localization accuracy of single or multiple targets. X. Wang et al. [12] proposed a deep learning indoor localization method based on the CSI matrix. H. Huang et al. [6] proposed a subspace sparse coding-based algorithm for device-free localization. Zhao et al. [13] proposed to treat the location information as a picture and use a convolutional autoencoder algorithm to achieve localization. These pioneering works provided the basis for further DFL research. In addition, many device-free localization methods have been proposed to obtain higher localization accuracy and precision [14–17].

However, most of the above DFL methods are based on learning the original data features, which cannot achieve high localization accuracy. Some methods use CSI data for localization, which is not universally applicable and is only applicable to some wireless devices. Among them, there is also the use of additional sensor nodes to enrich the localization information improving the localization accuracy and increasing the construction cost. To overcome the above drawbacks, this paper proposes a wireless precise device-free localization method based on deep dictionary learning.

The contributions of this paper include the following aspects. First, we propose a wireless device-free localization precise localization method based on deep dictionary learning (DDL-DFL). We obtain a multi-level dictionary through deep dictionary learning, extracting the multi-layer depth features of the data. It is also used as an input to the sparse coding classification model for precise localization. Second, we propose a data augmentation approach that enhances essential features by overlaying data. It makes up for the drawback that the amount of data is not abundant when there are few sensor nodes. Third, to evaluate our algorithm, we use software-defined radio equipment to build a wireless location system to collect laboratory datasets, and conduct experiments on them for localization.

2   Model and Algorithm

2.1   Description of the Localization System

We designate an area of 3×3 square meters inside the laboratory as monitoring area and arrange RF sensors around it, which are responsible for transmitting and receiving signals. Each transmission and reception are simulated as a communication link and all received signal strengths form a matrix. To clearly measure each position within the area, the monitored area is discretized into grids, each grid representing a location. When a target appears at a particular place, due to the blocking and reflection of the target, the communication between the transmitting and receiving sensors will be interfered, and the received signal strength will be attenuated to a certain degree. Therefore, we can locate by studying the attenuation of the signal. For the absence of any target in the monitored area and the presence of targets in different locations, the transceiver correspondence between the sensors is different, and we obtain a different signal matrix. Therefore, when locating an object, we can treat it as a classification problem [6]. The real localization scene built by USRP is shown in Fig. 1 (b).

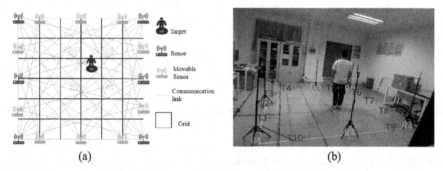

(a)   (b)

Fig. 1. DFL system built in the laboratory. (a) DFL system model in the laboratory; (b) The real localization scene made with USRP.

For the form collected data, we use the received signal strength (RSS), whose processing is more straightforward and universal compared to the literature [11, 12, 18]. In the scenario of Fig. 1, with a total of 36 locations, we set a sensor traversing 10 locations T1–T10 around the monitoring area for transmitting signals. Six sensors R1–R6 are uniformly arranged on both sides of the monitoring area for receiving signals. The received signals are Fourier transformed to select the amplitude information of the first and second harmonics. In this way, we get 12 signal strength information at each transmitting position, for a total of 10 positions, constituting a RSS matrix of size 12×10. To adapt to deep dictionary learning and sparse coding problems, we vectorize the RSS matrix and convert it into a column of size 120×1 for operation. Each location is measured 30 times, and 25 times constitute a matrix of size 120×900 as the training set. Five times the data form a matrix of size 120×180 as the test set.

2.2 Proposed Method

Unlike conventional localization methods based on sparse representation which take the mode of learning features from the original data and then use the classification method to achieve localization, as shown in Fig. 2 (a). The DDL-DFL method performs data augmentation on the training set and test set firstly. Then we obtain a multi-level dictionary through deep dictionary learning, extracting more representative multi-level features in the data. The superimposed multi-layer features are used as training set features and test set features, which are used as localization dictionaries for sparse representation and a localization matrix separately. Finding the data category in the dictionary is most similar to the localization signal with the sparse coding, which is converted to a sparse representation classification problem (SRC) [19]. The localization model is shown in Fig. 2 (b).

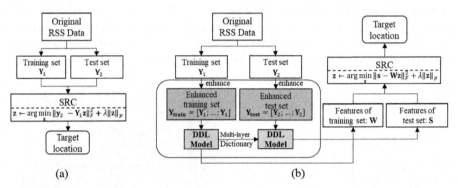

Fig. 2. Graph for localization procedures. (a) Conventional approach. (b) DDL-DFL approach.

Data Augmentation Methods for Localization. For the device-free localization problem based on radio frequency sensors, it is usually necessary to deploy more sensor nodes to enrich the location information to improve the localization accuracy, but it will cost more. This paper proposes a data augmentation method that increases the localization information and strengthens the important features by superimposing the received signal strength in the column direction. We perform the above operations on the training set and the test set separately, then obtain:

$$Y_{train} = [Y_1; ...; Y_1], Y_{test} = [Y_2; ...; Y_2]. \tag{1}$$

After superposition, the RSS information at different locations is equivalent to reinforcement for strength values with significant disparities (important features), which can promote finding an approximate representation more accurately for the last step.

The feasibility and advantages of the method are demonstrated in the experimental part of the next chapter. The method can still achieve a good localization effect even with slightly fewer sensor nodes.

Deep Dictionary Learning. This paper adopts the deep dictionary model [20], similar to the neural network's layer-by-layer learning method combined with traditional dictionary learning to perform multi-layer dictionary learning. The deep dictionary learning model is as follows:

$$Y_{train} = D_1...D_l...D_L X_L. \tag{2}$$

Here, $Y_{train} \in R^{q \times r_{train}}$ represents the observation matrix, which is composed of the training set. r_{train} represents the number of signals in Y_{train}, q donates the dimension of signals after augmentation, and the dictionary learning has L layers in total. The dictionary of each layer is represented by $D_l \in R^{m_{l-1} \times m_l}$, m_l donates the number of the dictionary atom, l donates the l-th layer, and the representation coefficient is represented by $X_l \in R^{m_l \times r_{train}}$, and Y_{train} is approximately represented by multi-layer dictionaries and representation coefficients.

The input of the first layer is Y_{train}, the output is the learned dictionary D_1 and the representation coefficient X_1. X_1 is the input of the next layer, followed by the dictionary learning of the second layer, and so on, until the L-th layer. Take two-layer dictionary learning as an example, as shown in Fig. 3.

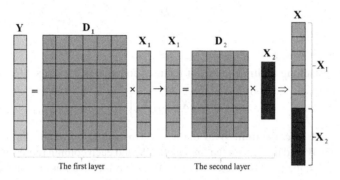

Fig. 3. Deep dictionary learning model diagram.

To solve (2), we transform the above model into the following optimization problem:

$$\min_{D_1,...,D_L,X_1,...,X_L} \|Y_{train} - D_1...D_L X_L\|_F^2 + \gamma \sum_{l=1}^{L} \|X_l\|_1, \qquad (3)$$

where $\| \cdot \|_F^2$ denotes the Frobenius-norm. The left term is the approximation error term, which is used to represent the distance between the observed and estimated signals. The right term is the regularization term, and the ℓ_1-norm is used to promote the sparsity of the coefficients in every layer of representation, and γ is a small constant that balances the error and sparsity term.

Since we integrate the layer-by-layer learning method of deep learning, we can decompose the multivariate problem into L bivariate optimization and solve the problem (4) by alternately updating. For the $l - th$ layer:

$$D_l, X_l \leftarrow \min_{D_l, X_l} \|X_{l-1} - D_l X_l\|_F^2 + \gamma \|X_l\|_1. \qquad (4)$$

We solve X_l directly by gradient descent:

$$X_l = (D_l^T D_l + \gamma I)^{-1} D_l^T X_{l-1}, \qquad (5)$$

then update D_l:

$$D_l = X_{l-1} X_l^T (X_l X_l^T)^{-1}. \qquad (6)$$

Finally, we get the dictionary $D_1, ..., D_l, ..., D_L$ and representation coefficients $X_1, ..., X_l, ..., X_L$ of each layer. To obtain richer features, we superimpose the representation coefficients obtained from each layer as the training set features W:

$$W = [X_1; ...; X_L].\tag{7}$$

Here $W \in \mathbf{R}^{m \times r_{train}}$, $m = m_1 + ... + m_L$.

The test data directly is decomposed into the representation coefficients through the above trained multi-layer dictionary:

$$X'_1, ..., X'_L \leftarrow \min_{X'_1, ..., X'_L} \|Y_{test} - D_1...D_L X'_L\|_F^2 + \gamma \sum_{l=1}^{L} \|X'_l\|_1,\tag{8}$$

where $Y_{test} \in R^{q \times r_{test}}$, $X'_l \in R^{m_l \times r_{test}}$.

Similarly, stacking multiple layers of features constitutes the test set feature S:

$$S = \left[X'_1; ...; X'_L\right].\tag{9}$$

ISTA-Based Localization. With the above two steps, we obtain the training set features matrix W and the test set features matrix S, and each column represents a signal. To realize the localization problem, we take W as the localization dictionary and S as the localization matrix. For each localization signal $\mathbf{s}$ in S, since the number of the target position is much smaller than grids, we can represent it approximately linearly sparsely by one or more columns at the same position in the training set features matrix W. The labels of the non-zero positions in the sparse representation coefficients correspond to the positions of the targets, i.e., the target is localized by the sparse representation. The classification and localization of the target are achieved using sparse representation, and the schematic diagram is shown in Fig. 4.

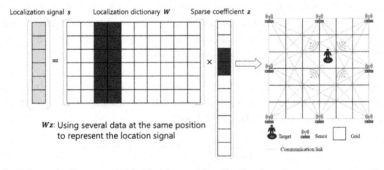

Fig. 4. Schematic diagram of classification and localization based on sparse representation.

Considering that each measured data is in a different scene, then for each localization signal, the classification model is as follows:

$$s = Wz + n,\tag{10}$$

where n denotes random noise.

For the device-free localization problem, the more data in the training set, the better, and the more similar signals to the test set can be found, which is more conducive to the realization of classification. Therefore, unlike the previous deep dictionary learning problem, the number of dictionary columns at this stage is greater than the number of rows. The dictionary is overcomplete, and its solution is not unique, so we need to consider the sparsity of z. According to the literature [21, 22], we take the ℓ_1-norm as the sparsity constraint, so we can convert problem (10) to solve:

$$z \leftarrow \min_{z} \|s - Wz\|_F^2 + \lambda\|z\|_1. \tag{11}$$

Here the first term is the approximate error term, which is used to represent the distance between the localization signal and the estimated signal, the second term is the regularization term, the ℓ_1-norm is used to promote the sparsity of the representation coefficient, and λ is a constant that trades off the error and sparsity terms.

Considering accuracy, speed, and dimensionality, we use the iterative shrinkage thresholding algorithm [23] to optimize problem (11), which is solved as follows:

$$z_{i+1} = h_\theta\left(\frac{1}{C}W^T s + \left(I - \frac{1}{C}W^T W\right)z_i\right), \tag{12}$$

where C is a constant greater than the largest eigenvalue of $W^T W$, $\theta = \lambda/C$ is the shrinkage threshold, I is a unit matrix of the same size as $W^T W$, and $h_\theta(.)$ is the shrinkage function, which is defined:

$$h_\theta(\alpha) = max(|\alpha| - \theta, 0) \bullet sign(\alpha). \tag{13}$$

Here $max(.,.)$ represents that the larger of the two items is returned, $sign(.)$ denotes a sign function.

We can also take the OMP algorithm [24] for sparse coding, which performs localization by traversing all columns of localization dictionary and finding the class corresponding to the column with the smallest representation error. In the next chapter, we add DDL and data augmentation to the OMP algorithm, and the localization effect is also well improved.

Through the above method, we can solve the problem (11). Assuming that the number of all categories is P, we let $z_p^* = \sum z_i$, $where$ $i = arg\ z_i \in class_p$, that is, the coefficients of the $p - th$ class signal are summed, then we can get:

$$z^* = \{z_1^*, \ldots, z_p^*, \ldots, z_P^*\}. \tag{14}$$

For the single-objective localization problem, the above solution contains only one non-zero term, and the corresponding index is the objective's location. The dual-objective and multi-objective localization problems can be considered based on a combination of the number of non-zero terms and the ordering of the maximum term, and their corresponding indexes are the target locations [6].

Algorithm. The localization algorithm based on deep dictionary learning (DDL-DFL) proposed in this paper is described in Algorithm 1.

Algorithm 1 DDL-DFL

Require: $Y_1 \in R^{n \times r_{train}}$, $Y_2 \in R^{n \times r_{test}}$, $D_1 \in R^{q \times m_1}$, $D_l \in R^{m_{l-1} \times m_l}$, $D_L \in R^{m_{L-1} \times m_L}$,

$\quad W \in R^{m \times r_{train}}$, $S \in R^{m \times r_{test}}$, γ, μ, $C > max\, eig(W^T W)$, $\theta = \mu/C, I = 1$.

Data augmentation: $Y_{train} = [Y_1; \ldots; Y_1], Y_{test} = [Y_2; \ldots; Y_2]$.

DDL: $D_1, \ldots, D_L, X_1, \ldots, X_L \leftarrow \underset{D_1, \ldots, D_L, X_1, \ldots, X_L}{min} \|Y_{train} - D_1 \ldots D_L X_L\|_F^2 + \gamma \sum_{l=1}^L \|X_l\|_1$,

$\quad X'_1, \ldots, X'_L \leftarrow \underset{X_1, \ldots, X_L}{min} \|Y_{test} - D_1 \ldots D_L X'_L\|_F^2 + \gamma \sum_{l=1}^L \|X'_l\|_1$.

$\quad W = [X_1; \ldots; X_L], S = [X'_1; \ldots; X'_l]$.

Localization: by solving (11).

---

3 Experimentation and Evaluation

In this section, we evaluate the localization performance of our algorithms using collected laboratory datasets. All algorithms were implemented in MATLAB R2016a and executed on a Windows 64-bit computer with 8 GB RAM and an Intel(R) Core (TM) i5 CPU.

3.1 Experimental Datasets Description

The scenario in our laboratory is six wireless sensors arranged on both sides of a 3 $\times$ 3 m^2 monitoring area for receiving signals and one wireless sensor for transmitting signals, moving through 10 edge locations [16]. We discrete the monitoring area into 36 grids; each grid is with a size of 50 $\times$ 50 cm^2. Sensor nodes are placed at 1.3 m from the ground, targeting 1.75 m of people, and the scene is arranged as shown in Fig. 1.

Each sensor node of the scenario operates in the 2.4 GHz band. Experiments were conducted to collect 30 times data at each location; 25 times data from each location were used as a training set, and five times data were used as a test for localization of the target.

3.2 Evaluation Metrics

To demonstrate the performance of our proposed algorithm, we evaluate it mainly by localization accuracy and average localization error.

The localization accuracy is calculated by: $Accuracy = C_{corret}/C_{total}$, where C_{corret}, C_{total} donates the number of correct localizations in the test data and the total number of test data, respectively.

The average localization error is calculated by the following equation:

$$ALE = \frac{\sum_{c=1}^{C} \sqrt{(x_{predict}^c - x_{true}^c)^2 + (y_{predict}^c - y_{true}^c)^2}}{C}, \tag{15}$$

where $\left(x_{predict}^c, y_{predict}^c\right)$, (x_{true}^c, y_{true}^c) denotes the coordinates of the predicted and true positions of the c-th test data. The C represents the total number of test data.

3.3   Experimental Results

The device-free localization system will inevitably suffer from various influences in real-world scenarios. To better evaluate the performance of our proposed algorithm, we add different levels of Gaussian noise to the localization signal, that is $s^* = s + n$, where n follows a Gaussian distribution. We represent the added noise level by the signal-to-noise ratio (SNR). In the specific implementation, we add SNR levels of 0 dB to 35 dB to the localization data at 5 dB signal-to-noise intervals.

To demonstrate the advantages of our proposed DDL-DFL algorithm, we compare it with original algorithms, including sparse representation classification localization via the OMP algorithm [24], the ISTA algorithm [6]. In the following, the ISTA and OMP algorithm with deep dictionary learning step are referred to as DDL-ISTA and DDL-OMP. In addition, we perform data augmentation for the above four algorithms.

DDL-DFL Localization Algorithm. We put the training set as the input into the two-layer dictionary learning model, the dimensionality of each output layer is [30,20], and γ is set to 0.5. Similarly, the final output of the two-layer representation coefficients is superimposed as the training set features, and the learned dictionary decomposes the test set with two layers of representation coefficients superimposed as the test set features. The training set features constitute the dictionary used for sparse coding, and the test set features are input to the sparse representation classification model.

The performance of our proposed algorithm and the comparison algorithm are measured on the laboratory datasets is shown in Fig. 5. When noise is added to both the training and test sets, we can see by the observation that the DDL-ISTA algorithm has an improvement over the ISTA algorithm in terms of accuracy, and a certain improvement in terms of average localization error. Similarly, for the DDL-OMP algorithm, it performs better than the OMP algorithm in both of metrics. When comparing several algorithms, the DDL-ISTA algorithm effect is the most robust to noise. When noise is added to the training sets, we also observe localization performance of the algorithm after DDL model better than original ways. Experiments on the laboratory datasets measured show that our proposed algorithm DDL-DFL has stronger anti-noise performance compared to original algorithms.

Add Data-Enhanced DDL-DFL Localization Algorithm. Since we have fewer sensor nodes in the laboratory, the data dimension of the datasets is small; the best localization effect may not be achieved. Therefore, we propose a data augmentation method. Before deep dictionary learning extracts deep features, we perform a repeated concatenation of the data to increase the row dimension of the data to strengthen the important features. In the experiment, we superimposed the data five times, and the performance comparison for several algorithms is shown in Fig. 6.

From the results, we find that the effect of adding data augmentation has improved the localization performance of all the above four algorithms by comparing with Fig. 5. Among them, the improvement is even greater for the DDL-DFL algorithm. By experiments on the laboratory datasets, we can conclude that data augmentation is more suitable to the DDL-DFL, and extraction of deep features after data augmentation is not only reduces the data dimension and enhances the real-time for localization, but also improves the localization effect to a certain extent.

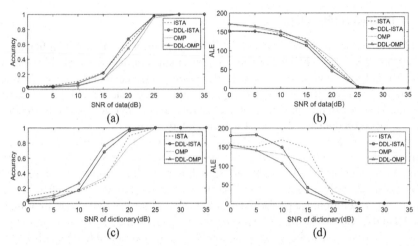

Fig. 5. Localization performance of the proposed DDL-DFL algorithm and the comparison algorithm on the laboratory datasets. (a) Accuracy after adding noise to the training and test data; (b) ALE after adding noise to the training and test data; (c) Accuracy after adding noise to the training data; (d) ALE after adding noise to the training data (unit: cm).

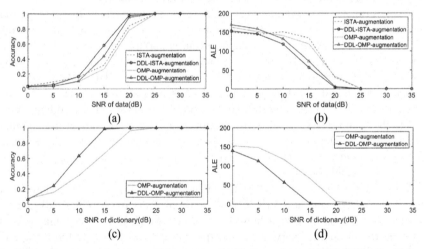

Fig. 6. Localization performance of the proposed add data-enhanced DDL-DFL algorithm and the comparison algorithm on the laboratory datasets. (a) Accuracy after adding noise to the training and test data; (b) ALE after adding noise to the training and test data; (c) Accuracy after adding noise to the training data; (d) ALE after adding noise to the training data (unit: cm).

To explore the performance of our approach, we applied our approaches to the datasets from the University of Utah [9]. In the experiments, we set the process of the DDL part to two layers, with the output dimension of each layer being [392, 196], and the parameter γ is set to 0.5. In the process of the SRC part, the parameters were fine-tuned accordingly, and the data were similarly stacked five times. The experimental results show that our proposed DDL-DFL algorithm achieves an accuracy of about 90% when the training data contains noise at 10 dB SNR level, that is, our proposed method is effective.

4   Conclusion

This study proposes an accurate localization technique based on deep dictionary learning (DDL-DFL). The in-depth features are extracted from the original data through deep dictionary learning, and the representation features of each layer are superimposed as the input of the sparse coding algorithm to realize classification and localization. Furthermore, we propose a data augmentation method applied to the scene with few sensor nodes to increase the data dimension. In this way, we can strengthen the essential features and further improve the algorithm. Experiments on real-world datasets show that the proposed method can achieve 100% localization accuracy in case of lower SNR and has certain anti-noise performance. The results are better than existing localization algorithms.

Acknowledgements. This research was partially funded by the Guangxi Postdoctoral Special Foundation and the National Natural Science Foundation of China under Grants 61903090 and 62076077, respectively.

References

1. Yucel, F., Bulut, E.: Clustered crowd GPS for privacy valuing active localization. IEEE Access **6**, 23213–23221 (2018)
2. Medina, C., Segura, J.C., De la Torre, A.J.S.: Ultrasound indoor positioning system based on a low-power wireless sensor network providing sub-centimeter accuracy. Sensors **13**, 3501–3526 (2013)
3. Pahlavan, K., Krishnamurthy, P., Geng, Y.: Localization challenges for the emergence of the smart world. IEEE Access **3**, 3058–3067 (2015)
4. Chang, L., et al.: FitLoc: fine-grained and low-cost device-free localization for multiple targets over various areas. IEEE/ACM Trans. Netw. **25**, 1994–2007 (2017)
5. Guo, Y., Huang, K., Jiang, N., Guo, X., Li, Y., Wang, G.: An exponential-Rayleigh model for RSS-based device-free localization and tracking. IEEE Trans. Mob. Comput. **14**, 484–494 (2014)
6. Huang, H., Zhao, H., Li, X., Ding, S., Zhao, L., Li, Z.: An accurate and efficient device-free localization approach based on sparse coding in subspace. IEEE Access **6**, 61782–61799 (2018)
7. Kaltiokallio, O., Yiğitler, H., Jäntti, R.: A three-state received signal strength model for device-free localization. IEEE Trans. Veh. Technol. **66**, 9226–9240 (2017)
8. Youssef, M., Mah, M., Agrawala, A.: Challenges: device-free passive localization for wireless environments. In: Proceedings of the 13th Annual ACM International Conference on Mobile Computing and Networking, pp. 222–229 (2007)
9. Wilson, J., Patwari, N.: Radio tomographic imaging with wireless networks. IEEE Trans. Mob. Comput. **9**, 621–632 (2010)

10. Zhang, D., Liu, Y., Guo, X., Ni, L.M., Systems, D.: RASS: a real-time, accurate, and scalable system for tracking transceiver-free objects. IEEE Trans. Parallel Distrib. Syst. **24**, 996–1008 (2012)
11. Wu, K., et al.: CSI-based indoor localization. IEEE Trans. Parallel Distrib. Syst. **24**, 1300–1309 (2012)
12. Wang, X., Gao, L., Mao, S., Pandey, S.: CSI-based fingerprinting for indoor localization: a deep learning approach. IEEE Trans. Veh. Technol. **66**, 763–776 (2016)
13. Zhao, L., Huang, H., Li, X., Ding, S., Zhao, H., Han, Z.: An accurate and robust approach of device-free localization with convolutional autoencoder. IEEE Internet Things J. **6**, 5825–5840 (2019)
14. Huang, H., Han, Z., Ding, S., Su, C., Zhao, L.: Improved sparse coding algorithm with device-free localization technique for intrusion detection and monitoring. Symmetry **11**, 637 (2019)
15. Li, X., Ding, S., Li, Z., Tan, B.: Device-free localization via dictionary learning with difference of convex programming. IEEE Sens. J. **17**, 5599–5608 (2017)
16. Zhang, K., Tan, B., Ding, S., Li, Y.: Device-free indoor localization based on sparse coding with nonconvex regularization and adaptive relaxation localization criteria. Int. J. Mach. Learn. Cybern., 1–15 (2022). https://doi.org/10.1007/s13042-022-01559-x
17. Zhang, K., Tan, D., Ding, S.: Device-free indoor localization based on supervised dictionary learning. In: 2021 IEEE 7th International Conference on Cloud Computing and Intelligent Systems (CCIS), pp. 438–443. IEEE (2021)
18. Wang, J., Gao, Q., Wang, H., Cheng, P., Xin, K.: Device-free localization with multidimensional wireless link information. IEEE Trans. Veh. Technol. **64**, 356–366 (2014)
19. Wright, J., Yang, A.Y., Ganesh, A., Sastry, S.S., Ma, Y.: Robust face recognition via sparse representation. IEEE Trans. Pattern Anal. Mach. Intell. **31**, 210–227 (2008)
20. Tariyal, S., Majumdar, A., Singh, R., Vatsa, M.: Deep dictionary learning. IEEE Access **4**, 10096–10109 (2016)
21. Candes, E.J., Tao, T.: Near-optimal signal recovery from random projections: universal encoding strategies. IEEE Trans. Inf. Theory **52**, 5406–5425 (2006)
22. Donoho, D.L., Elad, M.: Optimally sparse representation in general (nonorthogonal) dictionaries via $\ell 1$ minimization. Proc. Nat. Acad. Sci. USA **100**, 2197–2202 (2003)
23. Wang, J., Feng, X., Gao, Q., Zhang, X., Jin, M.: FM-based device-free localization and activity recognition via sparse representation. In: Proceedings of the 1st Workshop on Context Sensing and Activity Recognition, pp. 7–12 (2015)
24. Liu, T., Luo, X., Liang, Z., Networks, A.: Enhanced sparse representation-based device-free localization with radio tomography networks. J. Sens. Actuator Netw. **7**, 7 (2018)

Survey of Hypergraph Neural Networks and Its Application to Action Recognition

Cheng Wang[1], Nan Ma[2]([✉]), Zhixuan Wu[1], Jin Zhang[1], and Yongqiang Yao[1]

[1] Beijing Key Laboratory of Information Service Engineering, Beijing Union University, Beijing 100101, China
[2] Beijing University of Technology, Beijing 100124, China
manan123@bjut.edu.cn

Abstract. With the development of deep learning, graph neural networks have attracted ever-increasing attention due to their exciting results on handling data from non-Euclidean space in recent years. However, existing graph neural networks frameworks are designed based on simple graphs, which limits their ability to handle data with complex correlations. Therefore, in some special cases, especially when the data have interdependence, the complexity of the data poses a significant challenge to traditional graph neural networks algorithm. To overcome this challenge, researchers model the complex relationship of data by constructing hypergraph, and use hypergraph neural networks to learn the complex relationship within data, so as to effectively obtain higher-order feature representations of data. In this paper, we first review the basics of hypergraph, then provide a detailed analysis and comparison of some recently proposed hypergraph neural networks algorithm, next some applications of hypergraph neural networks for action recognition are listed, and finally propose potential future research directions of hypergraph neural networks to provide ideas for subsequent research.

Keywords: Hypergraph · Hypergraph neural network · Action recognition · Deep learning

1 Introduction

With the improvement of theories related to deep learning, artificial intelligence is flourishing in the fields of action recognition [1], object classification [2], intelligent driving [3] and so on, and more and more researchers are engaged in the research related to neural networks. Although promising results have been achieved using convolutional neural networks (CNNs) [4] for tasks such as visual recognition [5], voice recognition [6], and machine translation [7], they have not achieved the expected results when dealing with data with irregular structures.

This work was supported by Beijing Natural Science Foundation (No. 4222025), the National Natural Science Foundation of China (Nos. 61871038 and 61931012).

L. Fang et al. (Eds.): CICAI 2022, LNAI 13605, pp. 387–398, 2022.
https://doi.org/10.1007/978-3-031-20500-2_32

In the face of data with irregular structure, researchers have used recurrent neural networks (RNN) [8] to deal with them, with a significant improvement compared to CNNs. In fact, CNNs are mainly used to handle image-based data and RNNs are mainly used to handle temporal data.

Although traditional neural networks have great results in dealing with data with Euclidean structures, irregular non-Euclidean structures such as graph structures cannot be handled using traditional neural network models. Traditional algorithms tend to compress the graph-structured data into a chain structure or a tree structure which is processed using a neural network. However, there is often a loss of topological structure information in graphs, and important information may be lost in the preprocessing stage, which affects the final experimental results. Therefore, researchers have proposed graph neural networks (GNNs) [9], which are widely used due to their ability to analyze graph structured data. When dealing with information with pairwise relationships, more complete information features can be obtained by constructing graph structures and using graph neural networks for training. However, with the deep development of artificial intelligence, the problems to be solved are becoming more and more complex. In practice, in addition to pairwise relations, there exist multi-modal and multi-type data containing a large number of non-pairwise relations, and such complex relations cannot be well characterized by graph structures. Therefore, researchers have introduced the concept of hypergraph [10] to characterize complex non-pairwise relationships using hypergraph structures, and hypergraph can characterize higher-order relationships of data and feature learning through hypergraph neural networks to obtain feature representations of complex data. Compared with traditional graph neural networks, hypergraph neural networks [11] are more general representation learning frameworks capable of handling complex higher-order correlations through hypergraph structures, so as to effectively deal with multi-modal and multi-type complex data. Hypergraph learning has been widely used in tasks such as image retrieval [12], 3D object classification [13], video segmentation [14], person re-identification [15], hyperspectral image analysis [16], landmark retrieval [17], and visual tracking [18].

Action recognition is one of the representative tasks for computer vision, and accurate action recognition is an important prerequisite for intelligent interaction and human-computer collaboration, which has become a widely concerned research field in recent years, such as in the application fields of action analysis, intelligent driving, and medical control [19], and the research on body language interaction is of great significance. However, for the extraction of action features in complex environments, traditional GNN-based methods can no longer meet the practical needs, and many higher-order semantic information is ignored, thus reducing the accuracy of action recognition. Therefore, how to use hypergraph neural networks to achieve action recognition in complex environments has become a problem that has received widespread attention in recent years.

The rest of this paper is organized as follows: Sect. 2 outlines the theory related to hypergraph neural networks, and analyzes in detail hypergraph neural networks proposed in recent years. Section 3 introduces some applications of hypergraph neural networks in action recognition. Section 4 concludes the whole paper and proposes possible directions for hypergraph neural networks in the future.

2   Hypergraph Neural Networks

The hypergraph structure breaks traditional restriction that an edge can only connect two vertices in a graph structure, and expands the concept of edge into a hyperedge, which means that a hyperedge can connect multiple vertices. Complex relationships among things are connected by hyperedge, and thus can be represented using a hypergraph structure with higher-order semantics. In this subsection, we review the theory related to hypergraph in three aspects, including the definition of hypergraph, the generation methods of hypergraph, and the learning methods of hypergraph. In addition, we describe and compare the recent hypergraph neural network algorithms.

2.1   The Definition of Hypergraph

The comparison between the graph and the hypergraph is shown in Fig. 1 [20]. Similar to the definition of a simple graph, a hypergraph is defined as $\mathcal{G} = (\mathcal{V}, \mathcal{E}, \mathbf{W})$. Where $\mathcal{V}$ is the set of vertices in the hypergraph, and the element in the set are denoted as $v \in \mathcal{V}$; $\mathcal{E}$ is the set of hyperedges in the hypergraph, and the element in the set are denoted as $e \in \mathcal{E}$; $\mathbf{W}$ is the hyperedge weight matrix, which records the weight of each hyperedge, denoted as $w(e)$. The relationship between hyperedges and vertices is represented by constructing the incidence matrix $\mathbf{H}$, which is a $|\mathcal{V}| \times |\mathcal{E}|$ matrix. The elements in the incidence matrix $\mathbf{H}$ are defined as follows:

$$h(v, e) = \begin{cases} 1, v \in e \\ 0, v \notin e \end{cases} \tag{1}$$

Specifically, if the vertex v exists in the hyperedge e, then $h(v, e) = 1$, otherwise $h(v, e) = 0$. In addition, we can denote the hyperedge degree as the number of vertices contained in the hyperedge e, which can be defined as:

$$\delta(e) = \sum_{v \in v} h(v, e) \tag{2}$$

And the vertex degree as the sum of the hyperedge weights associated with the vertex v, which can be defined as:

$$d(v) = \sum_{e \in \varepsilon} w(e) h(v, e) \tag{3}$$

We also can define $\mathbf{D}_e$ and $\mathbf{D}_v$ to denote the diagonal matrix of hyperedge degree and vertex degree, respectively. Then, the standardized Laplacian matrix can be defined as:

$$\Delta = \mathbf{I} - \mathbf{D}_v^{-1/2} \mathbf{H} \mathbf{W} \mathbf{D}_e^{-1} \mathbf{H}^T \mathbf{D}_v^{-1/2} \tag{4}$$

where $\mathbf{I}$ is a Unit Matrix.

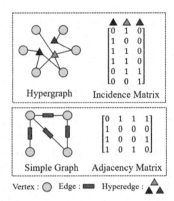

Fig. 1. Comparison of graph and hypergraph.

2.2   The Generation Methods of Hypergraph

In order to make a connection between the hypergraph and the data, it is necessary to construct a hypergraph based on the data. Since different data have different characteristics, it is crucial to choose a suitable hypergraph generation method according to the characteristics of the data. The applicability of the constructed hypergraph to the provided data directly determines the ability of the hypergraph to represent higher-order relationships among the data. The hypergraph generation methods can be generally classified into four categories, including distance-based methods [13], representation-based methods [21], attribute-based methods [22], and network-based methods [23]. Specifically, the distance-based approach is characterized as simple and effective in many applications, but is very sensitive to hyperparameter settings; the representation-based approach is characterized as avoiding the effect of noisy vertices through sparse representation, but calculating reconstruction coefficients increases network computation; the attribute-based approach is characterized as applicable to samples with specific attributes, but has the limitation of considering only single-attribute features; and the network-based approach is characterized as applicable to graphically represented data, but requires the construction of specific hypergraph.

2.3   The Learning Methods of Hypergraph

After constructing the hypergraph, the hypergraph needs to be learned to extract data features. Hypergraph learning was first introduced in [10], which allows for transductive learning [24] and can be seen as a propagation process on the hypergraph structure. Transductive learning on the hypergraph aims to make the differences in labels of the more strongly associated vertices on the hypergraph as small as possible. In recent years, hypergraph learning has been widely developed and applied in many fields. Wang et al. [20] constructed a complex hypergraph containing global and local visual features and label information to learn the relevance of images in a label-based image retrieval task. To model the functional connectivity network (FCN) of the brain, Xiao et al. [25] proposed weighted hypergraph learning, which is capable of capturing the relationships among brain regions compared to traditional graph-based methods and existing unweighted hypergraph-based methods. Inspired by deep learning, some researchers have developed hypergraph learning methods based on deep learning. For example, Feng et al. [11] proposed a hypergraph neural networks (HGNN) to model and learn complex associations in non-pairwise data. Significantly, Gao et al. [26] proposed a tensor-based dynamic hypergraph representation and learning framework that can effectively describe higher-order correlations in hypergraphs. In addition, they developed and published a toolbox called THU HyperG, which provides a collection of hypergraph generation and hypergraph learning algorithms.

2.4   Hypergraph Learning Method Based on Hypergraph Neural Networks

In order to train hypergraph and obtain higher-order semantic features of nodes by using hypergraph learning methods based on deep learning, researchers are proposing more and more neural networks suitable for extracting hypergraph features.

As the pioneer of hypergraph neural networks, Feng et al. [11] proposed a hypergraph neural network framework (HGNN) that utilizes the hypergraph structure for feature learning to effectively extract the higher-order correlations of data. HGNN extends the spectral domain-based convolution operation from the graph learning process to the hypergraph learning process by using the hypergraph Laplacian operator to convolve on the spectral domain. Specifically, the network framework uses the HGNN convolutional layer to perform a "vertex-hyperedge-vertex" transformation to iteratively update the vertex features to efficiently extract higher-order correlations on the hypergraph. The experimental results show that HGNN can extract higher-order features of vertices more effectively than traditional graph neural networks. Yadati et al. [27] proposed HyperGCN and used hypergraph-based spectral theory to train graph convolutional networks (GCNs) on hypergraph, so as to model complex relationships. HyperGCN is more effective compared to the hypergraph-based semi-supervised learning (SSL) method. And their proposed method has been applied to SSL and combinatorial optimization problems on hypergraph. Numerous experiments have shown that HyperGCN is effective for extracting features from complex data and improves the results of SSL. Jiang et al. [28] proposed a dynamic hypergraph neural network framework (DHGNN) to solve the problem that the hypergraph structure cannot be updated automatically in hypergraph neural networks, thus limiting the lack of feature representation capability of changing data. Notably, the framework consists of two important parts, dynamic hypergraph (DHG) and hypergraph convolution (HGC). Specifically, DHGNN uses the k-NN method to generate the basic hyperedges and a clustering algorithm to extend the set of adjacent hyperedges, and extracts local and global relationships by constructing the dynamic hypergraph. The experimental results demonstrate that the model has better performance, stronger robustness for different data, and significantly better than some static construction methods. Bai et al. [29] proposed two end-to-end operators, Hypergraph Convolution (HC) and Hypergraph Attention (HCA). Both operators can be inserted into most graph neural networks for model training when non-pairwise relationships are present in the data. Notably, the network uses dynamic transfer matrix instead of incidence matrix for convolutional operations. Specifically, the dynamic transfer matrix represents the importance of a vertex for a certain hyperedge, and adaptively identifies the importance of different vertices in the same hyperedge, which can more accurately describe the relationship among vertices and thus improve the performance of the neural networks. Graph embedding is a commonly used method to analyze network data. However, existing methods do not fully utilize and integrate both topology and attributes of nodes. Wu et al. [30] proposed a dual-view hypergraph neural network model for attribute graph learning, which solves the problems of inadequate modeling of nonlinear relationships among nodes in the semantic space and heterogeneity of structure and attribute information. Specifically, they address the limitations of traditional graph embedding by sharing specific hypergraph convolutional layers to model and unify the representation of different information sources. Gao et al. [31] proposed a hypergraph neural network framework (HGNN+) for hypergraph learning, which mainly consists of two processes, hypergraph modeling and hypergraph convolution, where the operational process of hypergraph convolution is performed on the spatial domain. In the process of hypergraph generation, different data use different hyperedge generation strategies to generate the hypergraph structure. In the hypergraph convolution process, a message propagation mechanism based on spatial domain, which includes two-stage hypergraph convolution. It can propose to flexibly define the convolution and aggregation operations in each stage and naturally extend it to directed hypergraph. The experimental results show that HGNN+ can obtain more gain with fewer training samples, which indicates that the proposed method can work well with limited training samples. Table 1 summarizes the classification jieg of different hypergraph neural networks on the citation dataset.

In addition, the commonly used citation datasets are summarized in this paper, as shown in Table 2.

3   Action Recognition Based on Hypergraph Neural Networks

With the continuous development of computer vision, human action recognition has shown a widespread application prospect and research value in many fields such as video surveillance, video retrieval and human-computer interaction. Methods based on deep learning have achieved excellent results in RGB data, with performance far superior to traditional methods of manually extracting

Table 1. Classification structures of different hypergraph neural networks on citation datasets.

Authors	Year	Task	Datasets	Evaluation metrics	Values(%)
HGNN	2019	Node Classification	Cora	Accuracy	81.6
			Citeseer		80.1
HyperGCN	2019	Node classification	Cora	Mean test error	32.37 ± 1.7
			Citeseer		37.35 ± 1.6
			Pubmed		25.56 ± 1.6
DHGNN	2019	Node classification	Cora	Accuracy	85.6
Bai et al. [29]	2020	Node classification	Cora	Accuracy	72.7 ± 0.3
			Citeseer		71.2 ± 0.4
			Pubmed		78.4 ± 0.3
Wu et al. [30]	2021	Node classification	Cora	Accuracy	84.63
			Citeseer		73.06
HGNN$^+$	2022	Node classification	Cora	Accuracy	73.19
			Citeseer		60.64
			Pubmed		71.38

Table 2. Overview of data statistics.

Dataset	Nodes	Edges	Features	Classes
Cora	2708	5429	1433	7
Citeseer	3327	4732	3703	6
Pubmed	19717	44338	500	3

features. In addition, the depth skeleton sequence has rich spatial and temporal information. As a result, there are many researchers who have also tried to combine deep learning and skeleton data for human behavior recognition. However, the GCN-based approach focuses only on the local physical connections among the joints and ignores the non-physical dependencies among the joints. Therefore, more and more researchers try to use hypergraph to model the human skeleton and use hypergraph neural networks to obtain a feature representation of human action for better human action recognition. This subsection will analyze and summarize the recently proposed action recognition methods based on hypergraph neural networks.

To capture the higher-order information of the skeleton and improve the accuracy of behavior recognition, Hao et al. [32] proposed a hypergraph neural networks (Hyper-GNN) framework to obtain the higher-order feature representation of the skeleton. Specifically, firstly, they divide the skeleton data into three different data input forms, including joints, bones and motion trends, and use them as vertices to construct different types of hypergraph; then, they construct hypergraphs and input them into Hyper-GNN for feature extraction to obtain higher-order feature representations of skeleton information; finally, in order to make full use of the complementarity and diversity among the three types of features, they fuse the three types of features and classify the action represented by the skeleton according to the fused features, so as to further improve the performance of action recognition. Notably, Hyper-GNN introduces a hypergraph attention mechanism and an improved residual model which has temporal convolution to extract more accurate and abundant skeleton features in the residual model. The experimental results show that the accuracy of action recognition using this method is significantly improved compared to the GCN-based method. He et al. [33] proposed a dual-stream hypergraph convolutional network (SD-HGCN) that adds a dual skeleton stream to a single skeleton stream, so as to recognize the action of interactions. Specifically, the model mainly consists of a multi-branch input adaptive fusion module (MBAFM) and a skeleton perception module (SPM). Among them, MBAFM distinguishes the input features more easily by two GCNs and an attention module; SPM adaptively learns the incidence matrix of hypergraph according to the semantic information in the skeleton sequence, identifies the relationship between skeletons, and builds the topological knowledge of human skeleton. The experimental results show that the SD-HGCN algorithm is less time-consuming, has high accuracy, and can be interacted in real time. Wei et al. [34] proposed a dynamic hypergraph convolutional network DHGCN for action recognition, which effectively extracts motion information from skeleton data, thus significantly improving the accuracy of dynamic action recognition. The algorithm constructs both static hypergraph and dynamic hypergraph based on the skeleton information, which can obtain higher-order information than a single static construction method. In this case, each joint in the dynamic hypergraph is assigned a corresponding weight according to its motion state, so as to better learn the dynamic features of the skeleton. The experimental results show that the method has better recognition ability for continuous dynamic actions. For a single skeleton data, it is not possible to adequately represent the details of human action and it is difficult to accurately identify human-object interactions. Chen et al. [35] proposed Informed Patch Enhanced HyperGCN to simultaneously learn skeleton information and local visual information, and perform multi-modal feature learning through multi-modal data fusion to obtain better behavioral features, so as to effectively improve the accuracy of action recognition. Specifically, the network framework obtains visual information near the five joints of the head, left hand, right hand, left foot, and right foot, respectively, so as to obtain part of the semantic features related to the behavior. This visual information is complemented with skeleton information to further enhance the data information required for action recognition. Experimental results show that the method reduces the computational and memory consumption of the network while improving the accuracy of action recognition.

As can be seen in Table 3, we compare recent approaches to action recognition using hypergraph neural networks on the NTU-RGB+D 60 dataset and NTU-RGB+D 120 dataset. In addition, we compare with common GCN-based approaches. It is clear that action recognition methods based on hypergraph neural networks achieve satisfactory results on different datasets, with most of the results better than the GCN-based methods. This is because hypergraphs can characterize more complex higher-order relationships and more fully exploit the complex behavioral information in real scenes. A comparison of the NTU-RGB+D 60 dataset and the NTU-RGB+D 120 dataset is shown in Table 4. With this information, hypergraph neural networks models can obtain more complete action features. It is very important to choose the right algorithm according to different features and applicability range to improve the human action recognition.

Table 3. Comparison of action recognition methods based on hypergraph neural networks and graph neural networks (Accuracy).

	Method	NTU60-XSub(%)	NTU60-XView(%)	NTU120-Xsub(%)	NTU120-XSet(%)
GCN-based	ST-GCN	81.5	88.3	70.7	73.2
	AS-GCN	86.8	94.2	78.3	79.8
	RA-GCN	87.3	93.6	81.1	82.7
	AGCN	88.5	95.1	–	–
	DGNN	89.9	96.1	–	–
	FGCN	90.2	96.3	85.4	87.4
	Shift-GCN	90.7	96.5	85.9	87.6
	DSTA-Net	91.5	96.4	86.6	89.0
	MS-G3D	91.5	96.2	86.9	88.4
HGNN-based	Hao et al. [25]	89.5	95.7	-	-
	He et al. [26]	90.9	96.7	87.0	88.2
	Wei et al. [27]	90.7	96.0	86.0	87.9
	Chen et al. [28]	**93.8**	**98.1**	**89.2**	**90.2**

Table 4. Comparison of NTU-RGB+D dataset and NTU-RGB+D 120 dataset.

Dataset	NTU-RGB+D	NTU-RGB+D 120
Number of samples	56,880	114,480
Number of action categories	60	120
Number of view angles	3	
Data Type	RGB video,depth map sequences,	
	3D skeletal data and infrared (IR) video	

4   Conclusion

This paper summarizes the research on hypergraph neural networks in recent years and discusses the design ideas of various hypergraph neural networks in detail to help researchers better understand different hypergraph neural networks. In addition, this paper aims to facilitate researchers to choose the appropriate hypergraph neural networks structure for modeling according to their practical needs.

Although various hypergraph neural networks have made promising progress in extracting features from complex data, the extraction of node features in complex environments still needs to be further explored in the future. We believe that in addition to improving a single hypergraph neural networks, it is also possible to combine hypergraph with different graph structures to model problems related to complex environments and obtain higher-order and more complete feature information. For example, Jiang et al. [28] combined dynamic graph and hypergraph to encode higher-order information and improve the accuracy of twitter sentiment prediction; Sun et al. [36] combined heterogeneous graph and hypergraph to achieve excellent results in tasks such as node classification in complex environments.

Action recognition methods based on hypergraph neural networks are the current hotspots of computer vision research, which have practical application needs and good application prospects, and related issues deserve further research. Notably, the action recognition methods based on hypergraph neural networks can be applied to the unmanned field to make self-driving vehicles into learnable and interactive wheeled robots [37, 38].

Acknowledgements. This work was supported by Beijing Natural Science Foundation (No. 4222025), the National Natural Science Foundation of China (Nos. 61871038 and 61931012).

References

1. Song, Y.F., Zhang, Z., Shan, C., Wang, L.: Constructing stronger and faster baselines for skeleton-based action recognition. IEEE Trans. Pattern Anal. Mach. Intell. (2022)
2. Xiong, J., Bi, R., Tian, Y., Liu, X., Wu, D.: Toward lightweight, privacy-preserving cooperative object classification for connected autonomous vehicles. IEEE Internet Things J. **9**(4), 2787–2801 (2021)
3. Langacker, R.W.: Interactive cognition: Toward a unified account of structure, processing, and discourse. Int. J. Cogni. Linguist. **3**(2), 95 (2012)
4. Krizhevsky, A., Sutskever, I., Hinton, G.E.: ImageNet classification with deep convolutional neural networks. In: 25th Proceedings of the Conference on Advances in Neural Information Processing Systems (2012)
5. He, K., Zhang, X., Ren, S., Sun, J.: Deep residual learning for image recognition. In: Proceedings of the IEEE conference on computer vision and pattern recognition. pp. 770–778 (2016)
6. Hinton, G., et al.: Deep neural networks for acoustic modeling in speech recognition: the shared views of four research groups. IEEE Signal Process. Mag. **29**(6), 82–97 (2012)
7. Bahdanau, D., Cho, K., Bengio, Y.: Neural machine translation by jointly learning to align and translate. arXiv preprint arXiv:1409.0473 (2014)
8. Medsker, L.R., Jain, L.: Recurrent neural networks. Des. Appl. **5**, 64–67 (2001)
9. Scarselli, F., Gori, M., Tsoi, A.C., Hagenbuchner, M., Monfardini, G.: The graph neural network model. IEEE Trans. Neural Netw. **20**(1), 61–80 (2008)
10. Bretto, A.: Hypergraph Theory. An introduction. Mathematical Engineering. Springer, Cham (2013). https://doi.org/10.1007/978-3-319-00080-0

11. Feng, Y., You, H., Zhang, Z., Ji, R., Gao, Y.: Hypergraph neural networks. In: Proceedings of the AAAI Conference on Artificial Intelligence, vol. 33, pp. 3558–3565 (2019)
12. Huang, Y., Liu, Q., Metaxas, D.:] video object segmentation by hypergraph cut. In: 2009 IEEE Conference on Computer Vision and Pattern Recognition, pp. 1738–1745. IEEE (2009)
13. Gao, Y., Wang, M., Tao, D., Ji, R., Dai, Q.: 3-d object retrieval and recognition with hypergraph analysis. IEEE Trans. Image Process. 21(9), 4290–4303 (2012)
14. Huang, Y., Liu, Q., Zhang, S., Metaxas, D.N.: Image retrieval via probabilistic hypergraph ranking. In: 2010 IEEE Computer Society Conference on Computer Vision and Pattern Recognition, pp. 3376–3383. IEEE (2010)
15. Zhao, W., et al.: Learning to map social network users by unified manifold alignment on hypergraph. IEEE Trans. Neural Netw. Learn. Syst. 29(12), 5834–5846 (2018)
16. Luo, F., Du, B., Zhang, L., Zhang, L., Tao, D.: Feature learning using spatial-spectral hypergraph discriminant analysis for hyperspectral image. IEEE Trans. Cybern. 49(7), 2406–2419 (2018)
17. Zhu, L., Shen, J., Jin, H., Zheng, R., Xie, L.: Content-based visual landmark search via multimodal hypergraph learning. IEEE Trans. Cybern. 45(12), 2756–2769 (2015)
18. Du, D., Qi, H., Wen, L., Tian, Q., Huang, Q., Lyu, S.: Geometric hypergraph learning for visual tracking. IEEE Trans. Cybern. 47(12), 4182–4195 (2016)
19. Li, Y., Ji, B., Shi, X., Zhang, J., Kang, B., Wang, L.: Tea: Temporal excitation and aggregation for action recognition. In: Proceedings of the IEEE/CVF Conference on Computer Vision and Pattern Recognition, pp. 909–918 (2020)
20. Wang, Y., Zhu, L., Qian, X., Han, J.: Joint hypergraph learning for tag-based image retrieval. IEEE Trans. Image Process. 27(9), 4437–4451 (2018)
21. Liu, Q., Sun, Y., Wang, C., Liu, T., Tao, D.: Elastic net hypergraph learning for image clustering and semi-supervised classification. IEEE Trans. Image Process. 26(1), 452–463 (2016)
22. Joslyn, C., et al.: High performance hypergraph analytics of domain name system relationships. In: HICSS 2019 Symposium on Cybersecurity Big Data Analytics (2019)
23. Zu, C., et al.: Identifying high order brain connectome biomarkers via learning on hypergraph. In: Wang, L., Adeli, E., Wang, Q., Shi, Y., Suk, H.-I. (eds.) MLMI 2016. LNCS, vol. 10019, pp. 1–9. Springer, Cham (2016). https://doi.org/10.1007/978-3-319-47157-0_1
24. Zhou, D., Huang, J., Schölkopf, B.: Learning with hypergraphs: clustering, classification, and embedding. In: 19th Proceedings of the Conference on Advances in Neural Information Processing Systems (2006)
25. Xiao, L., Stephen, J.M., Wilson, T.W., Calhoun, V.D., Wang, Y.P.: A hypergraph learning method for brain functional connectivity network construction from FMRI data. In: Medical Imaging 2020: Biomedical Applications in Molecular, Structural, and Functional Imaging, vol. 11317, pp. 254–259. SPIE (2020)
26. Gao, Y., Zhang, Z., Lin, H., Zhao, X., Du, S., Zou, C.: Hypergraph learning: methods and practices. IEEE Trans. Pattern Anal. Mach. Intell. 44, 2548–2566 (2020)
27. Yadati, N., Nimishakavi, M., Yadav, P., Nitin, V., Louis, A., Talukdar, P.: Hypergcn: a new method for training graph convolutional networks on hypergraphs. In: 32nd Proceedings of the Conference on Advances in Neural Information Processing Systems (2019)

28. Jiang, J., Wei, Y., Feng, Y., Cao, J., Gao, Y.: Dynamic hypergraph neural networks. In: IJCAI.,pp. 2635–2641 (2019)

29. Bai, S., Zhang, F., Torr, P.H.: Hypergraph convolution and hypergraph attention. Pattern Recogn. **110**, 107637 (2021)

30. Wu, L., Wang, D., Song, K., Feng, S., Zhang, Y., Yu, G.: Dual-view hypergraph neural networks for attributed graph learning. Knowl.-Based Syst. **227**, 107185 (2021)

31. Gao, Y., Feng, Y., Ji, S., Ji, R.: Hgnn $\hat{+}$: General hypergraph neural networks. IEEE Trans. Pattern Analy. Mach. Intell. (2022)

32. Hao, X., Li, J., Guo, Y., Jiang, T., Yu, M.: Hypergraph neural network for skeleton-based action recognition. IEEE Trans. Image Process. **30**, 2263–2275 (2021)

33. He, C., Xiao, C., Liu, S., Qin, X., Zhao, Y., Zhang, X.: Single-skeleton and dual-skeleton hypergraph convolution neural networks for skeleton-based action recognition. In: Mantoro, T., Lee, M., Ayu, M.A., Wong, K.W., Hidayanto, A.N. (eds.) ICONIP 2021. LNCS, vol. 13109, pp. 15–27. Springer, Cham (2021). https://doi.org/10.1007/978-3-030-92270-2_2

34. Wei, J., Wang, Y., Guo, M., Lv, P., Yang, X., Xu, M.: Dynamic hypergraph convolutional networks for skeleton-based action recognition. arXiv preprint arXiv:2112.10570 (2021)

35. Chen, Y., Li, Y., Zhang, C., Zhou, H., Luo, Y., Hu, C.: Informed patch enhanced hypergcn for skeleton-based action recognition. Inf. Processi. Manag. **59**(4), 102950 (2022)

36. Sun, X., et al.: Heterogeneous hypergraph embedding for graph classification. In: Proceedings of the 14th ACM International Conference on Web Search and Data Mining, pp. 725–733 (2021)

37. Ma, N., et al.: Future vehicles: interactive wheeled robots. Sci. China Inf. Sci. **64**(5), 1–3 (2021)

38. Li, D., Ma, N., Gao, Y.: Future vehicles: learnable wheeled robots. Sci. China Inf. Sci. **63**(9), 1–8 (2020)

Visual Perception Inference on Raven's Progressive Matrices by Semi-supervised Contrastive Learning

Aihua Yin[1,2], Weiwen Lu[1,2], Sidong Wang[1,2], Hongzhi You[5], Ruyuan Zhang[4], Dahui Wang[1,3], Zonglei Zhen[1], and Xiaohong Wan[1,2(✉)]

[1] State Key Laboratory of Cognitive Neuroscience and Learning, Beijing, China
[2] IDG/McGovern Institute for Brain Research, Beijing, China
[3] School of Systems Science, Beijing Normal University, Beijing 100875, China
xhwan@bnu.edu.cn
[4] Institute of Psychology and Behavioral Science and Shanghai Mental Health Center, Shanghai Jiao Tong University, Shanghai 200030, China
[5] School of Life Science and Technology, University of Electronic Science and Technology of China, Chengdu 611731, China

Abstract. The current deep neural networks (DNNs) in mimicking human perception remain challenges for solving visual reasoning tasks. Human perception does not merely involve a passive observer labeling sensory signals, but also contains an active inference about object attributes and their relationships towards an intended output (e.g., an action). In this work, we propose a variational autoencoder (VAE) model to discriminate the ranking relationships between object attribute values by semi-supervised contrastive learning, dubbed as SSCL-VAE. This perception-based model solves the visual reasoning task of Raven's Progressive Matrices (RPM) in three benchmarks (RAVEN, I-RAVEN and RAVEN-Fair), with high accuracy close to humans, as well as many end-to-end supervised models. The current work thus suggests that constructions of general cognitive abilities like human perception may empower the perceptron with DNN to solve high-level cognitive tasks such as abstract visual reasoning in a human-like manner.

Keywords: Perception · Inference · Contrastive learning · Semi-supervised · Autoencoder

1 Introduction

Deep neural networks (DNNs) by end-to-end supervised learning have achieved great success in visual categorizing, but are not versatile for visual reasoning [1–3]. The critical feature in abstract visual reasoning tasks, such as Raven's Progressive Matrices (RPMs) [4], is that the rules governing a sequence of entities are semantically defined by their spatiotemporal relations [5]. Learning these

---

A. Yin and W. Lu—These authors equally contributed to this study.

© The Author(s), under exclusive license to Springer Nature Switzerland AG 2022
L. Fang et al. (Eds.): CICAI 2022, LNAI 13605, pp. 399–412, 2022.
https://doi.org/10.1007/978-3-031-20500-2_33

semantic relationships by supervisions is not straightforward. Even a number of end-to-end supervised DNN models have been developed to achieve high performance in solving RPMs [1–3,6–8], these models lack interpretability and generalizability. Thus far, it remains challenging for DNNs to behave like humans in solving such visual reasoning tasks [9,10].

150 years ago, Dr. von Helmholtz addressed that the properties of the external world are not directly provided by sensory inputs, but are probably inferred through human hierarchic neural processes [11]. Perception is based on higher-order features and their relationships, rather than locally defined features, related to the stimulus. Indeed, these attributes are mixed together and must be disentangled to make explicit percepts [12,13].

Differing from the current DNN methods that need to learn from scratch the associations between the contexts and the supervised labels with a huge number of samples, humans do not rely on such domain-specific knowledge or experiences in RPMs, but their prior general cognitive abilities in recognition of object attributes and their relationships. Although humans at a very early stage of life have no such a concept of semantics and symbols, they can recognize varieties of objects [14], and comprehend simple rules governing the world and apply these rules to new contexts [15]. Importantly, the object attribute representations in the human brain are unique and invariant in different contexts [16,17], and the context-dependent relationships between attributes among the objects are implicitly inferred [11]. For instance, we recognize the same color of 'green' from different objects and further recognize that the 'green' color looks lighter than the 'red' color, but darker than the 'cyan' color.

Inspired by these insights from human perception, we move a step further towards visual reasoning ability of artificial intelligence (AI) on the basis of the general cognitive abilities in object perception as humans do. In this work, we propose a variational autoencoder (VAE) model for visual perception by semi-supervised contrastive learning (SSCL), dubbed as SSCL-VAE. The motivation of the SSCL method is to make embeddings of the same attribute from different objects are close to each other while embeddings of different attributes are separated away from each other [18]. Rule logic execution in this model follows the approach of probabilistic abduction and execution (PrAE) model [19], in which the inference engine aggregates distributed representations of a set of object attributes in the context panels to infer a posterior probabilistic representation of the target panel. Notably, the PrAE model is originally trained by supervisions of both the correct and incorrect answers, and also the ground truths of rules (metadata) contained in each RPM problem as auxiliary annotations. In this work, without these ample supervisions, SSCL-VAE merely enforces human-like perceptual abilities, in particular, the ability of qualitative comparisons between object attribute values from the different objects in the context sets, but not the answer sets. The proposed model obtains accuracies as high as humans, and many of the previous supervised models in solving RPMs in three benchmarks. Importantly, we demonstrate that constructions of human-like perception abilities on DNNs can empower AI such a capability of solving abstract visual reasoning in a human-like manner. To the best of our knowledge, this has not yet been explored in the domain of visual reasoning tasks.

2   Related Work

2.1   Object Representations

Recognition of object attributes is critical to solve visual reasoning tasks, as the latent relations, namely rules, that govern the context of instance are defined by these visual features. DNNs are believed to versatilely fit any desired function with a constraint of the loss function. However, the embeddings of latent attributes are too flexible to comply well with the semantics of object attributes that are used in these tasks, such as types, sizes, and colors in the RAVEN dataset [1–3, 6–8]. Instead, the object attributes are often blended in the latent embeddings. Recently, variational autoencoder (VAE) [20–22] and neural-vector [23] models have been proposed to build stable representations and to disentangle the blended representations of object attributes. A straightforward approach to parcel objects into desired attribute representations is to use the metadata of object attributes as auxiliary annotations to train the perception module. However, the prior annotations are needed to label by humans. In image recognitions, SSCL has been used to discover better representations by comparing the relationship representations from the same or different attributes [18, 24]. We here leverage this method in cooperation with a VAE model to shape the latent embeddings, in order to enable the model to have simple relational inference capabilities. This proposed model thus constrains the representations of the same attribute to be invariant across different objects, importantly complying with the rankings of attribute values too.

2.2   Visual Reasoning

Most of supervised models designed to solve visual reasoning tasks mainly focus on the visual reasoning process [1–3, 6–8], as the baselines of DNNs fails to solve these high-level cognitive tasks. A common motivation for visual reasoning models is to learn relational representations of latent rules by maximizing similarity between analogical relations and minimizing similarity between non-analogical relations [2, 3, 25–29]. This is achieved by comparing the relational representations with correct and incorrect answers. In striking contrast, the proposed model here embeds the relational representations in the perception module.

2.3   Neuro-symbolic Models

Unlike the monolithic DNN models, the neuro-symbolic models are composed of a perception module at the frontend and an inference module at the backend [3, 30–32]. Nonetheless, it remains challenging to train the neuro-symbolic models with the end-to-end supervised training form. Thereby, auxiliary annotations of the latent rules are additionally used to constrain the rule representations in the PrAE model [19]. Although the currently proposed model partially shares the inference engine with the PrAE model, we here use SSCL to train the visual perception module alone. Semi-supervised learning (SSL) has been also used to solve visual reasoning tasks, such as RPMs [6,33]. However, the conventional SSL combines a large number size of labeled data and a small number size of unlabeled data. In contrast, SSCL used here has no concrete labels, but the pair-wise rankings that are partially supervised. For this reason, the current method is also called semi-supervised.

3   Methods

In the RAVEN dataset [35,36], each problem consists of 9 panels in a form of 3×3 matrix with 8 context panels and a missing panel at the last panel. The goal of the task is to find out one from 8 candidate panels that completes the matrix with satisfactions of the row-wise latent rules governing the organization of object attributes Fig. 1. Besides, there are 7 configurations [Center, Left-Right (L-R), Upper-Down (U-D), 2×2 Grid, 3×3 Grid, Out-In Center (O-IC), Out-In Grid (O-IG)] in the RAVEN dataset. In different configurations, objects in panels are organized differently. We train an independent model for each configuration.

Overall, the task requires two independent cognitive abilities of object perception and rule inference. If perception on object attributes is perfect, then the process of identifying the latent rules becomes plain, an exhaustive search within the rule space in a finite set [36]. Differing from the visual perception tasks, the object attributes are also latent in visual reasoning tasks, but are conventionally required to infer from the spatiotemporal relations from the context

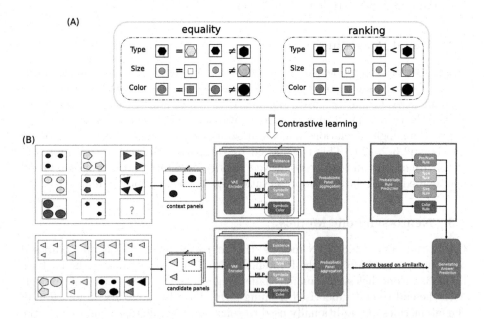

Fig. 1. Description of SSCL-VAE model. (A) The representative examples of semi-supervised contrastive learning in the equality and ranking methods, respectively. (B) A schematic of the model architecture. Please see the main text for details.

in each instance. In other words, both the object attributes and rules remain to be identified. This is hard to implement in DNNs, and also remains challenging for the neuro-symbolic models. The novelty of SSCL-VAE here mainly focuses on the learning approach, rather than the DNN architecture (Fig. 1).

3.1 Object-Based Variational Autoencoder

We use VAE as the backbone of the visual perception module. VAE consists of an encoder that maps the visual inputs to latent representations and a decoder that is required to reconstruct the input images reversely from the latent representations. We first take each object in each panel as the input and pretrain the VAE with the loss as follows,

$$Loss_{\text{VAE}} = \sum_{x} \left(||x - \hat{x}||_2 + D_{KL}\big(\mathcal{N}(\mu_x, \sigma_x^2)||\mathcal{N}(0,1)\big) \right) \tag{1}$$

$$\text{with } D_{KL}(p||q) = \sum_{i} p_i \big(log(p_i) - log(q_i)\big), \tag{2}$$

where x is the input (original) image, $\hat{x}$ is the reconstructed image, $||\cdot||$ means L2 norm, D_{KL} means Kullback-Leibler divergence, and $\mathcal{N}(\mu, \sigma^2)$ means Gaussian distribution with the mean μ and standard deviation σ.

The requirement of reconstruction ensures plenty of information in the latent embeddings of objects and also helps to stabilize the representations in later training. In the configuration such as 2×2 Grid, there may exist multiple objects in a panel. We then try to capture all the objects by selecting regions of interest, though the existence of objects in regions is not guaranteed.

3.2 Attribute Discrimination

Differing from the conventional VAE for image reconstruction, the visual perception module is additionally required to discriminate the object attributes, such as type, size and color in RPMs. To do so, we add an additional multi-layer perceptron (MLP) for each attribute to transform the latent embeddings in VAE into the distributed probabilities belonging to the separate attribute values, in which the dimension of type, size and color attribute is 5, 6 and 10, respectively. To train the MLP and finetune the encoder of VAE, we use the information of metadata of object attributes as auxiliary annotations. However, instead of the exact labels, we train the model to acquire two common-sense knowledge on these visual attributes. First, the model is trained to know whether the values of the same attribute from any pair of objects are equivalent or not. In other words, the representations of visual attributes in the model are unique and invariant across different objects. We here denote this ability of visual perception as equality. Obviously, this ability cannot discriminate the relationships between the attribute values. Second, the model is further trained to know the intrinsic orders or rankings of the values of the same attribute from two different objects. In other words, the model acquires the ability to comprehend the relationships between the attribute values. We here denote this ability of visual perception as ranking. To allow the model to acquire these abilities, we leverage contrastive learning to make pair-wise comparisons between any two objects within each RPM instance. For instance, the model is informed that two objects in an RPM instance share the same color attribute, and further which one has a lighter color, but not the exact color value in the metadata. To be specific, the corresponding loss can be formulated as:

$$Loss_a = \sum_{n=1}^{N} \sum_{i,j=1}^{16} D_{JSD}(s_{ij}^{(n,a)}, d_{ij}^{(n,a)}), \ a \in \{type, size, color\} \qquad (3)$$

$$\text{with } s_{ij}^{(n,a)} = \left\{ P(l_i^{(n,a)} > l_j^{(n,a)}), P(l_i^{(n,a)} = l_j^{(n,a)}), P(l_i^{(n,a)} < l_j^{(n,a)}) \right\}, \qquad (4)$$

$$d_{ij}^{(n,a)} = \left\{ P(y_i^{(n,a)} > y_j^{(n,a)}), P(y_i^{(n,a)} = y_j^{(n,a)}), P(y_i^{(n,a)} < y_j^{(n,a)}) \right\} \qquad (5)$$

$$D_{JSD}(p,q) = \frac{1}{2} D_{KL}\left(p\|\frac{p+q}{2}\right) + \frac{1}{2} D_{KL}\left(q\|\frac{p+q}{2}\right), \qquad (6)$$

where N is the training batch size, D_{JSD} means Jensen-Shannon divergence, $y_i^{(n,a)}, l_i^{(n,a)}$ are the predicted and ground-truth label of attribute a of the ith object in the nth RPM respectively. Here, only existing objects in each panel are used for training.

On the other hand, the input images may contain no objects, such as in the 2×2 Grid configuration. Hence, the model needs to discern the existence of objects. We add a MLP for the attribute of existence as well. For the sake of simplicity, we use negative log-likelihood loss that counts whether there exists an object. In total, the loss is expressed as follows,

$$Loss = Loss_{exist} + Loss_{type} + Loss_{size} + Loss_{color} \qquad (7)$$

3.3   Rule Inference

In the current model, the rule inference module is independent of the visual perception module. Specifically, we implement non-symbolic inference using the rule inference engine as used in the PrAE model [17], in which the probabilities of object attributes are aggregated to obtain the probabilities of panel attributes.

$$p_{panel}^a = \sum_{exist} p_{exist} \cdot \exp\left(\frac{\sum_{obj} \log(p_{obj}^a) \boldsymbol{exist}_{obj}}{\sum \boldsymbol{exist}_{obj}}\right) \qquad (8)$$

where p is a probability vector, $exist$ is a binary vector describing the existence of objects.

For each object attribute, the model calculates the probabilities of the potential rules based on the probabilities of panel attributes, and the rule with maximum normalized probability is chosen to be the predicted rule. Hence, the rule inference model cannot discover new rules, but discriminates the prior rule candidates, with an assumption that the model has full knowledge of the potential rules.

Specifically, for attribute a, the probabilistic representation of the rule can be obtained by calculating the hadamard-product of the attribute representation and the rule mask,

$$P(r) = \sum_{M \in mask(r)} \sum_{all\ elements} (p_1, p_2, p_3, ..., p_n)^T \odot M \tag{9}$$

where p is a probability vector, M is a rule mask composed of 0, 1, and each column represents the attribute representation of each panel under a certain rule.

While the normalization process of rule probabilities can be formulated as follows,

$$P_{norm}(r) = \frac{P(r)}{\sum_{r' \in E} P(r')} \tag{10}$$

where E denotes the set of potential rules.

3.4   Answer Generation

Finally, the model predicts the potential rules of each attribute containing in RAVEN through the rule inference engine and generates an aggregated probability distribution of attributes in the target panel (Fig. 1). Meanwhile, the aggregated probability distributions of attributes for the candidate panels are also computed by the visual perception module. We then compare the Jensen-Shannon divergence (JSD) between the generated attribute probability distributions with those of the candidates. The candidate with smallest divergence is then selected as the answer. This process is similar to the supervised contrastive learning approach used in the previous studies of CoPINet [3] and PrAE [19].

4   Experiments

4.1   Experimental Setup

We test SSCL-VAE in the RAVEN dataset including three benchmarks of RAVEN [36], I-RAVEN and RAVEN-Fair. The three benchmarks share the same problem contexts, but different candidate sets. We then use the same training model to test its performance in the three benchmarks. We separately train the models for the 7 different RAVEN configurations. We train our model on 6,000 samples in the training dataset and test the model on 2,000 samples in the testing dataset for each configuration, while the validation dataset is not used. The training procedure is separated into two phases. First, we pretrain VAE with 50 neurons in the latent layer to represent the visual images for 100 epochs. In order to better achieve the reconstruction effect, the learning rate of

ADAM optimizer is set to 0.001. Second, we simultaneously train both VAE and MLP to discriminate the attribute values for 100 epochs and the learning rate of the ADAM optimizer is set to 0.01. The batch size is 256 in both phases. The inputs of the object images (160×160) are resized to 32×32. Further, we also test the proposed model on the MNIST benchmark [37]. We train the model on 60,000 samples in the training dataset, and test on 10,000 samples in the testing dataset. The input size of the images is 28×28, and the batch size is also 256. All the models are implemented in PyTorch and runned with Intel(R) Xeon(R) Platinum 8272CL CPUs and NVIDIA Geforce RTX 3090 Founders Edition GPUs.

Table 1. Average accuracy (%) of different models.

	Methods	Avg	Center	2×2	3×3	L-R	U-D	O-IC	O-IG
RAVEN	Equality	39.4	37.4	61.5	33.4	37.4	32.9	28.8	34.4
	Ranking	80.1(+**40.7**)	89.3(+**51.9**)	82.3(+**20.8**)	76.3(+**42.9**)	88.8(+**51.4**)	88.3(+**55.4**)	72.0(+**43.2**)	63.9(+**19.5**)
	Full	91.9	91.8	93.4	91.2	99.8	89.0	97.4	86.6
	PrAE [19]	82.8	100.0	84.4	38.7[a]	95.2	95.9	96.0	69.5
I-RAVEN	Equality	53.4	49.9	67.8	38.8	58.3	55.8	47.3	56.0
	Ranking	85.9(+**32.5**)	92.6(+**42.7**)	85.2(+**17.4**)	81.9(+**43.1**)	92.3(+**34.0**)	91.9(+**36.1**)	84.5(+**37.2**)	72.8(+**16.8**)
	Full	94.4	95.0	95.6	95.1	100.0	92.9	99.0	90.8
	PrAE [19]	87.8	100.0	87.5	55.5[a]	97.6	98.1	98.4	78.0
RAVEN-Fair	Equality	58.5	56.2	72.7	54.3	59.2	57.0	47.4	62.9
	Ranking	88.3(+**29.8**)	94.0(+**37.8**)	87.0(+**14.3**)	84.5(+**30.2**)	94.6(+**35.4**)	93.8(+**36.8**)	83.8(+**36.4**)	80.2(+**17.3**)
	Full	95.6	96.2	95.8	95.7	100.0	94.7	99.0	93.3
	PrAE [19]	90.0	100.0	92.4	58.0[a]	98.0	98.8	98.3	84.8
	Human [36]	84.4	95.4	81.8	79.5	86.4	81.8	86.4	81.8

[a] 3×3 Grid is calculated by the training model of 2×2 Grid.

4.2 Evaluation of General Performance in Three Benchmarks

We first evaluate SSCL-VAE performance in the three benchmarks of RAVEN, I-RAVEN and RAVEN-Fair in comparison with different models that use different sources of metadata. The equality method means that the model has unique and invariant representations of attributes, and the ranking method means that the model can further infer the pair-wise relationships among the same attribute, while the full method means that the model uses the concrete labels of attribute metadata for training the model. We also compare with the PrAE model in I-RAVEN [19], as our model share the rule inference engine with PrAE. Table 1 shows the accuracies of different models. On average, the ranking method achieves accuracies 41%, 32% and 30% higher than the equality method in RAVEN, I-RAVEN and RAVEN-Fair, respectively, although lower than the full method with the detailed labels of metadata of visual attributes. In contrast, the PrAE model that alternatively uses the metadata labels of rules and the correct and incorrect answer panels as supervisions only achieves marginally better performance than the ranking method. Hence, preposition of attribute relationships in the frontend perception module, or rendering inductive inference to the perception module, makes it available for rule inference, close to humans' performance (Table 1). However, simple attribute separation in visual perception (the equality method) are insufficient to acquire such an inference ability. These results illustrate the reason why end-to-end supervised-learning DNNs are not versatile for visual reasoning tasks.

4.3   Evaluation of Attribute and Rule Representations

To appreciate the benefits of the ranking method in comparison with the equality method, we evaluate their attribute representations and rule representations. As much expected, the representations of entities of each attribute (type, size and color) do not necessarily match the actual entities, although these representations are unique and invariant across objects (Fig. 2A upper). In particular, these representations are not consistent across different configurations. In contrast, the attribute representations in the ranking method considerably align well with the ground truths of the order of attribute values in each category, even across different configurations (Fig. 2A bottom). Accordingly, the rule representations in the equality method are also inconsistent with the true rules (Fig. 2B upper). Please keep in mind that the rules are entirely defined by the attribute values. However, those representations in the ranking method largely align well with the ground truths (Fig. 2B bottom). Hence, the local rankings result in global match with the true order of attribute values, which in turn provides accurate predicted rule simply by aggregations of distributed probabilities of attributes across the context panels.

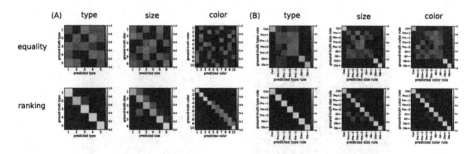

Fig. 2. The representations of object attributes and rules across all of the RAVEN configurations. (A) The confusion matrix between the predicted attribute values and ground truths. (B) The confusion matrix between the predicted rule values and ground truths.

4.4   Evaluations of Generalizability

We further evaluate the generalizability of our proposed model in solving I-RAVEN as examples. First, we evaluate cross-configuration generalizability for our model using the ranking method. The models trained in the configurations of Center, L-R, U-D and O-IC can solve the problems in the other simple configurations, but not on the configurations of the 2×2 Grid, 3×3 Grid, and O-IG. In contrast, the models trained in the configurations of the 2×2 Grid, 3×3 Grid, and O-IG can fairly transfer to solve the problems in other configurations

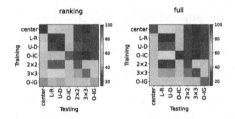

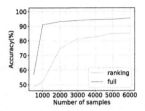

Fig. 3. Cross-configuration generalizability on I-RAVEN.

Fig. 4. The accuracy change on I-RAVEN with number of samples.

(Fig. 3). The cross-configuration generalizability using the ranking method is similar as that using the full labels of metadata (Fig. 3). Second, we examine the performance dependent on the training sample size. Figure 4 illustrates that the ranking model is not so much sensitive to the training sample sizes (red line) when the training sample size is larger than 2,000, while the metadata model remains stable until the training sample size is no less than 1,000.

4.5 MNIST

Finally, we test the proposed models also on the MNIST benchmark (Fig. 5A). The performance by the equality method is close to the chance level (10%),

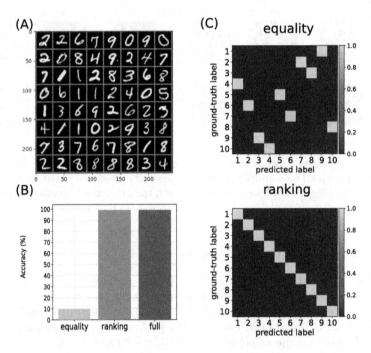

Fig. 5. The performance of the two models on the MNIST dataset. (A) Visualization of the MNIST dataset. (B) Accuracy (%) of different models. (C) The confusion matrix between the predicted attribute values and ground truths.

while that by the ranking method is as high as 99.1%, as same as the full meta-data method (Fig. 5B). Again, although the entities are uniquely and invariantly represented in the equality method, the distributed representations are not consistent with the ground truths (Fig. 5C upper). Instead, the representations by the ranking method are aligned well with the ground truths (Fig. 5C bottom). Hence, the SSCL-VAE model may have broad applications in visual perception, including both visual categorizing and visual reasoning.

5   Conclusion

In this paper we present SSCL-VAE, a semi-supervised model that obtains high performance on three RAVEN benchmarks involving abstract visual reasoning. The previous supervised learning on DNNs is dependent on the task-specific knowledge from the answers and auxiliary annotations, and also mainly focus on the rule inference module in the backend. By contrast, SSCL-VAE provides an approach to establish the general cognitive abilities in human perception, but not task-specific knowledge [9,10,38]. Thereby, it has strong robustness even for small sample size for training and generalizability for cross-configuration tests. Importantly, the current model empowers the general perception abilities, in particular, the inference on the relations between visual attributes, and enables non-symbolic inference with interpretability. The simplicity of this approach, we believe, should afford its broad applications in solving other spatiotemporal reasoning tasks [38,39].

The current model of SSCL-VAE also has some important limitations deserved to be improved. First, SSCL needs partial information of metadata, which is sometimes hard to access. It might be improved by self-supervised method, rather than semi-supervised approach. Self-supervised contrastive learning has been broadly applied in computer vision [18,24], natural language processing (NLP) [40,41], and other domains. Second, the model can be trained by independent objects and tasks to construct its general cognitive abilities in object perception including inductive inference. It remains to explore this potential by training independent tasks and testing on other independent tasks. Third, more general cognitive abilities and higher-level cognitive function can be further incorporated into the model to provide more versatile intelligent abilities in solving complex tasks.

Acknowledgments. We thank Dr. Bo Hong's discussions, inspirations and comments. This work was partially supported by grants from the National Science and Technology Innovation 2030 Project of China to Xiaohong Wan (2021ZD0203701).

References

1. Hoshen, D., Werman, M.: IQ of neural networks. arXiv preprint arXiv:1710.01692 (2017)
2. Barrett, D., Hill, F., Santoro, A., Morcos, A., Lillicrap, T.: Measuring abstract reasoning in neural networks. In: International Conference on Machine Learning, pp. 511–520. PMLR (2018)
3. Zhang, C., Jia, B., Gao, F., Zhu, Y., Lu, H., Zhu, S.-C.: Learning perceptual inference by contrasting. In: Advances in Neural Information Processing Systems, pp. 1075–1087 (2019)
4. Raven, J., Court, J., Raven, J.: Raven's Progressive Matrices. Oxford Psychologists Press, Oxford (1938)
5. Lovett, A., Forbus, K., Usher, J.: Analogy with qualitative spatial representations can simulate solving raven's progressive matrices. In: Proceedings of the Annual Meeting of the Cognitive Science Society, vol. 29, no. 29 (2007)
6. Zhuo, T., Kankanhalli, M.: Solving Raven's progressive matrices with neural networks. arXiv preprint arXiv:2002.01646 (2020)
7. Mandziuk, J., Zychowski, A.: DeepIQ: a human-inspired AI system for solving IQ test problems. In: 2019 International Joint Conference on Neural Networks (IJCNN), pp. 1–8. IEEE (2019)
8. Zhuo, T., Kankanhalli, M.: Effective abstract reasoning with dual-contrast network. In: International Conference on Learning Representations (ICLR) (2021)
9. Marcus, G., Davis, E.: Insights for AI from the human mind. Commun. ACM **64**, 38–41 (2020)
10. Fodor, A., WPylyshyn, Z., et al.: Connectionism and cognitive architecture: a critical analysis. Cognition **28**(1–2), 3–71 (1988)
11. von Helmholtz, H.: The aim and progress of physical science. In: Kahl, R. (ed.) Selected Writings of Hermann von Helmholtz, pp. 223–245. Wesleyan University Press, Middletown (Originally Published 1869) (1971)
12. Knill, D.C., Richards, W.: Perception as Bayesian inference. Cambridge University Press, Cambridge (1996)
13. DiCarlo, J.J., Cox, D.D.: Untangling invariant object recognition. Trends Cogn. Sci. **11**(8), 333–341 (2007)
14. Spelke, E.S.: Principles of object perception. Cogn. Sci. **14**(1), 29–56 (1990)
15. Gopnik, A., Glymour, C., Sobel, D.M., Schulz, L.E., Kushnir, T., Danks, D.: A theory of causal learning in children: causal maps and Bayes nets. Psychol. Rev. **111**(1), 3–32 (2004)
16. Li, N., Dicarlo, J.: Unsupervised natural experience rapidly alters invariant object representation in visual cortex. Science, 1502–1507 (2008)
17. Mansouri, F.A., Freedman, D.J., Buckley, M.J.: Emergence of abstract rules in the primate brain. Nat. Rev. Neurosci. **21**, 596–610 (2020)
18. Chen, T., Kornblith, S., Norouzi, M., Hinton, G.: A simple framework for contrastive learning of visual representations. In: International Conference on Machine Learning, pp. 1597–1607. PMLR (2020)
19. Zhang, C., Jia, B., Zhu, S.-C., Zhu, Y.: Abstract spatial-temporal reasoning via probabilistic abduction and execution. In: Proceedings of the IEEE/CVF Conference on Computer Vision and Pattern Recognition, pp. 9736–9746 (2021)
20. Kingma, D.P., Welling, M.: Auto-encoding variational Bayes. In: International Conference on Learning Representations (ICLR) (2013)

21. Higgins, I., et al.: betavae: Learning basic visual concepts with a constrained variational framework. In: International Conference on Learning Representations (ICLR) (2017)
22. Burgess, C.P., Higgins, I., Pal, A., Matthey, L., Watters, N., Desjardins, G., Lerchner, A.: Understanding disentangling in VAE. arXiv preprint arXiv:1804.03599 (2018)
23. Hersche, M., Zeqiri, M., Benini, L., Sebastian, A., Rahumi, A.: A neuro-vector-symbolic architecture for solving Raven's progressive matrices. https://arxiv.org/abs/2203.04571v1
24. He, K., Fan, H., Wu, Y., Xie, S., Girshick, R.: Momentum contrast for unsupervised visual representation learning. In: Proceedings of the IEEE/CVF Conference on Computer Vision and Pattern Recognition, pp. 9729–9738 (2020)
25. Jahrens, M., Martinetz, T.: Solving Raven's progressive matrices with multi-layer relation networks. In: 2020 International Joint Conference on Neural Networks (IJCNN), pp. 1–6. IEEE (2020)
26. Malkinski, M., Mandziuk, J.: Multi-label contrastive learning for abstract visual reasoning. arXiv preprint arXiv:2012.01944 (2020)
27. Wu, Y., Dong, H., Grosse, R., Ba, J.: The Scattering Compositional Learner: Discovering Objects, Attributes, Relationships in Analogical Reasoning. arXiv preprint arXiv:2007.04212 (2020)
28. Kiat, N.Q.W., Wang, D., Jamnik, M.: Pairwise relations discriminator for unsupervised Raven's progressive matrices. arXiv preprint arXiv:2011.01306 (2020)
29. Kim, Y., Shin, J., Yang, E., Hwang, S.J.: Few-shot visual reasoning with meta-analogical contrastive learning. In: Advances in Neural Information Processing Systems, vol. 33 (2020)
30. Yi, K., et al.: CLEVRER: collision events for video representation and reasoning. In: International Conference on Learning Representations (2020)
31. Mao, J., Gan, C., Kohli, P., Tenenbaum, J.B., Wu, J.: The neuro-symbolic concept learner: interpreting scenes, words, and sentences from natural supervision. In: International Conference on Learning Representations (ICLR) (2019)
32. Ding, M., Chen, Z., Du, T., Luo, P., Tenenbaum, J.B., Gan, C.: Dynamic visual reasoning by learning differentiable physics models from video and language. In: Advances in Neural Information Processing Systems, vol. 35 (2021)
33. Tarvainen, A., Valpola, H.: Mean teachers are better role models: weight-averaged consistency targets improve semi-supervised deep learning results. In: Advances in Neural Information Processing Systems (2017)
34. Berthelot, D., Carlini, N., Goodfellow, I., Oliver, A., Papern, N., Raffel, C.: MixMatch: a holistic approach to semi-supervised learning. In: Advances in Neural Information Processing Systems (2019)
35. Matzen, L.E., Benz, Z.O., Dixon, K.R., Posey, J., Kroger, J.K., Speed, A.E.: Recreating Raven's: software for systematically generating large numbers of ravenlike matrix problems with normed properties. Behav. Res. Methods $42(2)$, 525–541 (2010)
36. Zhang, C., Gao, F., Jia, B., Zhu, Y., Zhu, S.-C.: Raven: a dataset for relational and analogical visual reasoning. In: Proceedings of the IEEE Conference on Computer Vision and Pattern Recognition, pp. 5317–5327 (2019)
37. LeCun, Y., Bottou, L., Bengio, Y., Haffner, P.: Gradient-based learning applied to document recognition. Proc. IEEE $86(11)$, 2278–2324 (1998)
38. Chollet, F.: On the measure of intelligence. arXiv preprint arXiv:1911.01547 (2019)

39. Spratley, S., Ehinger, K., Miller, T.: A closer look at generalisation in RAVEN. In: Vedaldi, A., Bischof, H., Brox, T., Frahm, J.-M. (eds.) ECCV 2020. LNCS, vol. 12372, pp. 601–616. Springer, Cham (2020). https://doi.org/10.1007/978-3-030-58583-9_36

40. Mikolov, T., Sutskever, I., Chen, K., Corrado, G.S., Dean, J.: Distributed representations of words and phrases and their compositionality. In: Advances in Neural Information Processing Systems, vol. 26 (2013)

41. Saunshi, N., Plevrakis, O., Arora, S., Khodak, M., Khandeparkar, H.: A theoretical analysis of contrastive unsupervised representation learning. In: International Conference on Machine Learning, pp. 5628–5637. PMLR (2019)

PHN: Parallel Heterogeneous Network with Soft Gating for CTR Prediction

Ri Su⬤, Alphonse Houssou Hounye⬤, Muzhou Hou, and Cong Cao$^{(\boxtimes)}$⬤

Mathematics and Statistics School, Central South University,
Changsha 410083, China
{suricsu,hounyea,congcao}@csu.edu.cn, houmuzhou@sina.com

Abstract. The Click-though Rate (CTR) prediction task is a basic task in recommendation system. Most of the previous researches of CTR models built based on Wide & deep structure and gradually evolved into parallel structures with different modules. However, the simple accumulation of parallel structures can lead to higher structural complexity and longer training time. Based on the Sigmoid activation function of output layer, the linear addition activation value of parallel structures in the training process is easy to make the samples fall into the weak gradient interval, resulting in the phenomenon of weak gradient, and reducing the effectiveness of training. To this end, this paper proposes a Parallel Heterogeneous Network (PHN) model, which constructs a network with parallel structure through three different interaction analysis methods, and uses Soft Selection Gating (SSG) to feature heterogeneous data with different structure. Finally, residual link with trainable parameters are used in the network to mitigate the influence of weak gradient phenomenon. Furthermore, we demonstrate the effectiveness of PHN in a large number of comparative experiments, and visualize the performance of the model in training process and structure.

Keywords: Recommendation system · Click-though rate · Feature interaction

1 Introduction

The Click-through rate (CTR) prediction is one of the important basic tasks in recommendation system. By predict the click rate of user, the web or application can sort the candidate item list and push them to target user, so as to provide personalized recommendation service for users. Early CTR prediction models output CTR through Logistic Regression, and use automatic feature engineering methods such as Factorization Machine (FM) [10] and Gradient Boosting Decision Tree (GBDT) [3] for business implementation. With the development of deep learning, CTR prediction model based on neural network like PNN [9] has gradually become the mainstream application model in the real application.

Wide&deep [2] CTR predict model structure have used parallel structures of different depths to consider both memorization and generalization. In subsequent

L. Fang et al. (Eds.): CICAI 2022, LNAI 13605, pp. 413–424, 2022.
https://doi.org/10.1007/978-3-031-20500-2_34

studies, FNN [18], DeepCrossing [11], DeepFM [4], DCN [16], xDeepFM [7], DCN-V2 [17], EDCN [1], NFM [5] and other models have similar parallel structure like Wide&deep, and were utilized to analyze public embedding through different modules. Moreover, the generalization of this structure depended on the effectiveness of parallel structures.

There is no comprehensive analysis of feature interaction in previous parallel structure models. Therefore, the generalization of the model is limited. At the end of CTR model, the click rate prediction output have been achieved by linear layer with activation function. During training phase, the activation values between parallel layers tend to fall into the weak gradient interval. This phenomenon will weaken the training effect of each parallel module, and can not improve the generalization while improving the complexity of the model.

In this paper, we propose a new deep CTR model, named Parallel Heterogeneous Network (PHN). For PHN model, three parallel feature interaction structures were included to analyze CTR features from different perspectives. In order to enhance the independent analysis ability of each parallel module, Soft Select Gating module was constructed after public embedding to enhance the original embedding expression. We also added residual connections with trainable parameters to the model to reduce the weak gradient phenomenon by accumulating gradients during the back propagation process.

This paper mainly contributions are as follow:

- In order to strengthen the expression ability of CTR prediction model, this paper constructed three different linear feature interaction methods from nonlinear interaction, bite-wise interaction and vector-wise interaction based on parallel structure.
- Soft Selection Gating is constructed before the parallel structure, and the features of original embedding are enhanced by self-attention and soft gate structure while retaining the high order crossover characteristics, which improves the ability of the model to express data.
- To solve the weak gradient phenomenon in the parallel model, the residual link with trainable parameters are used in the parallel structure to reinforce the model training process.
- The effectiveness of Soft Selection Gating and the weak gradient phenomenon are visualized, and the effectiveness of PHN is verified by comparison experiments.

2   Proposed Method

The Parallel Heterogeneous Network (PHN) consists of two main structures. One of them is Soft Selection Gating (SSG) module based on self-attention to enhanced embedding features for different structures, and another one is Heterogeneous Interaction Layer (HIL), using different interaction method to analyze the enhanced features, and finally using Logistic Regression to output the confidence of sample. Figure 1(a) illustrates the main structure and the detail of model.

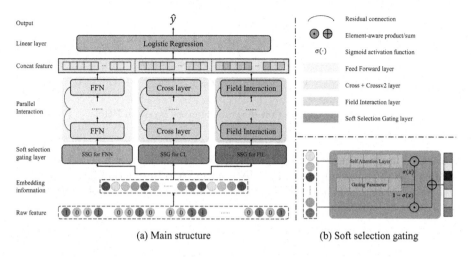

(a) Main structure   (b) Soft selection gating

Fig. 1. The overview structure of our proposed PHN model, which consists of Soft Selection Gating (SSG) module and Heterogeneous Interaction Layer (HIL)

2.1 Heterogeneous Interaction Layer

In PHN, the parallel layers use three kinds of interaction layers to improve model interaction capability: 1) cross layer is the basic part of DCN [16] and DCNV2 [17], which focuses on the element-aware feature interaction; 2) field interaction layer is the basic part of FINT [19], which focuses on the vector-aware field interaction; 3) feed forward layer is used to fitting the non-polynomial information.

Cross Interaction Layer. Feature interaction is a main key point in study of mainly CTR prediction model. As a previous study, the DCN [16] and the DCNV2 [17] proposed two kinds of explicit interaction methods, which achieved the data mode of high-order interaction by realizing the intersection of multi-layer hidden features and original features.

$$y_{dcnv2} = x_0 \odot (W \times x_i + b) + x_i \tag{1}$$

$$y_{dcn} = x_0 \odot x_i^T * w + x_i + b \tag{2}$$

where, x_0 is the input feature of the first cross layer; x_i is the output feature of the i-th cross layer, W and w represent trainable parameter vectors and matrices; $\odot$ is Hadamard product and $\times$ is matrix multiplication. In Eqs. 1 & 2 the DCN and DCNV2 used different parameter forms to interact features, but in general, it achieves element-aware feature interaction. The PHN combines the formulas of DCN and DCNV2 to construct the bit-aware interaction module. As mentioned in Fig. 2, we use the parameter part of the two crossover model and bias to construct cross layer in PHN.

Field Interaction Layer. Besides element-aware interaction, vector-aware interaction is also a key part of the model construction. Field Interaction is

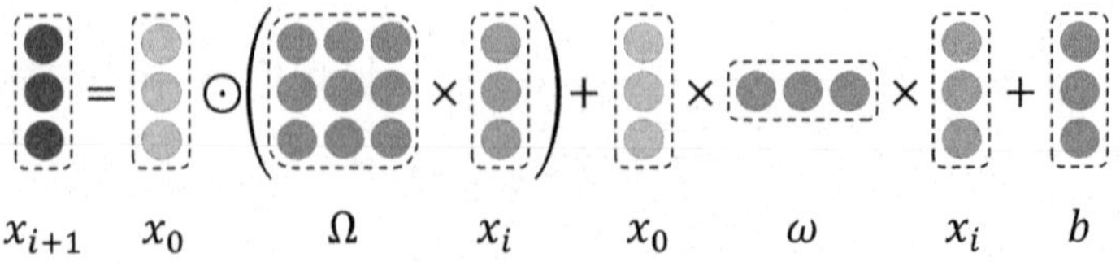

Fig. 2. The calculation diagram of cross layers in PHN

mentioned in FiBiNet [6] and FINT [19], which using the cross method to implement the vector-aware interaction. PHN use the Field Interaction layer in FRNet as a parallel part to enhance the generalization effect of the whole network on the feature crossing pattern.

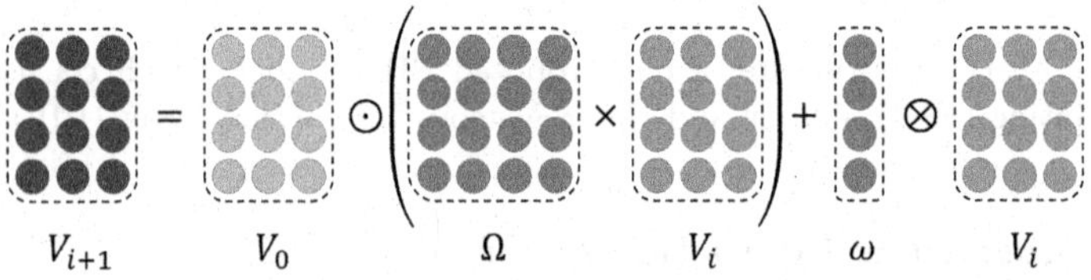

Fig. 3. The calculation diagram of field interaction layers in PHN

As shown in Fig. 3, field interaction layer uses the residual link with trainable parameter vector, which product on different fields feature to screen the output features of the upper layer. In the subsequent experiments, we will discuss and experiment residual link forms in all parallel layers.

Feed Forward Layer. The third part of parallel network is composed of Feed Forward Network. By alternating linear and nonlinear analysis of the original features, FFN complements the analysis of the previous two crossover modes to improve the overall network generalization function.

$$x_{i+1} = \sigma(\omega x_i + b) \tag{3}$$

where, σ is the activation function, which is LeakyReLU in PHN.

2.2 Soft Selection Gating

The ideal of multiple structure parallelism raise up a new question: whether different structures require different input dense feature. The traditional Multihead self-attention(MSA) mechanism [14] used weight based query vector and key vector to aggregate information in a sequence, which was an ideal method to process feature information.

$$Q_E, K_E, V_E = W_Q E, W_K E, W_V E \tag{4}$$

$$MSA(Q_E, K_E, V_E) = Softmax(\frac{Q_E K_E}{\sqrt{d_k}})V_E \qquad (5)$$

From the Eqs. 4 & 5, MSA has considered different field weights through the second-order intersection of query vector Q_E and key vector K_E. However, based on the feature interaction in the CTR prediction model, the direct using by the traditional MSA may over-focus on the feature activation value of the second-order crossover, thus losing the performance of the feature at the higher-order crossover. Inspired by the FRNet [15], an information selecting method named Soft Selection Gating (SSG) is used after the sharing embedding $E \in R^n$ in PHN. This soft-gating information selection is designed for choosing activation between MSA result and sharing raw embedding.

$$E_{sg} = G_{sg} \odot E_{sa} + [I - G_{sg}] \odot E_{se} \qquad (6)$$

where $G_{sg} \in R^n$ is the trainable gating vector, $E_{sa} \in R^n$ is the sharing self-attention embedding, $E_{se} \in R^n$ is the sharing embedding, and $I \in R^n$ is a unit vector. As the Fig. 1(b) shows, the SSG considers both sharing embedding and self-attention embedding. By using weighting parameters, the model can select the raw feature or the feature enhanced by MSA for different parallel structures. Subsequent experiments will discuss whether to share the weight of self-attention and the gating mechanism, and confirm the effectiveness of SSG.

2.3 Weak Gradient Problem

Basic on the CTR prediction task definition, the key point of improving AUC value is increasing the confidence of positive label samples and decreasing the confidence of negative label samples, which makes model more robust. In the last stage of CTR prediction model, the traditional model usually constructs confidence coefficient of click by using Sigmoid activation function.

The Fig. 4 shows that, we can think of the entire Sigmoid function as two interval, the effective gradient interval (blue) with a normal gradient, and the Weak gradient interval (red) with a gradient approaching zero. When the output value of the parallel model is accumulated at the last linear layer, it is easy to make the samples originally in the effective gradient interval to fall into the Weak gradient interval, thus weakening the learning of each part for valid samples. In this paper, this phenomenon is referred to weak gradient in parallel structures.

To mitigate this phenomenon and achieve effective training, the PHN using residual link in each substructure, enhancing the gradient accumulation of each parallel structure in the process of back propagation. To further accommodate this phenomenon, we also tried to add gating parameters to residual links and used batch normalization of different modes in the final linear layer. We will discuss this further in Sect. 3.

3   Experiments

In this section, we evaluate PHN on two benchmark data sets. We aim to answer the following research questions:

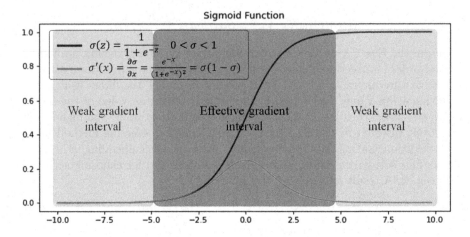

Fig. 4. Gradients of different interval in Sigmoid (Color figure online)

- **RQ1:** Will parallel structure-based PHN perform better than previous CTR prediction models over different classical data sets?
- **RQ2:** Under what circumstances can the Soft Selection Gating reasonably enhance the function of feature representation.
- **RQ3:** Is the parallel structure actually caused the weak gradient phenomenon, and the problem is effectively alleviated by residual connection or batch normalization?

3.1 Datasets Description

To evaluate the effectiveness of the model in this paper, two benchmark off-line datasets are selected for experiment: Criteo[1] and Avazu[2]. The two data sets were divided into training, validation and testing set according to the ratio of 8:1:1. Detailed information on the two benchmark datasets is shown in Table 1.

Table 1. Statistics of the benchmark datasets

Dataset	Sample size	Fields	Features	Positive ratio
Criteo	45,840,618	39	1,086,810	25.6%
Avazu	40,428,966	23	1,544,257	16.9%

For the CTR prediction task, two classical evaluation metrics such as: Logloss and AUC, were used to verify the effective generalization and robustness of the suggested model.

---

[1] https://www.kaggle.com/c/criteo-display-ad-challenge.
[2] https://www.kaggle.com/c/avazu-ctr-prediction.

3.2   Compared Models

To verify the effectiveness of the proposed PHN model, we compare it with linear model (LR, FM [10], FwFM [8], FmFM [13]), deep model (DNN, W&D [2], DeepFM [4], xDeepFM [7], AutoInt [12]), and interaction model (DCN [16], DCNV2 [17], FiBiNet [6], FINT [19]) on CTR task. All models and experiments are implemented on Huawei FuxiCTR deep learning framework [20].

3.3   Performance Comparison (RQ1)

Effectiveness of PHN. To verify the validity of the model, we followed the original structure of each comparison model, controlled the interaction layer of all models in three layers, and recorded the testing results of each model on two benchmark datasets. The specific experimental results were reported in Table 2.

Table 2. Experiment result of different CTR prediction models on Criteo and Avazu

Model	Criteo			Avazu		
	Logloss	AUC	AUC Impv.	Logloss	AUC	AUC Impv.
LR	0.457334	0.792831	–	0.382039	0.777148	–
FM	0.450260	0.801086	1.041%	0.378750	0.782448	0.681%
FwFM	0.442566	0.809314	2.079%	0.373862	0.790315	1.694%
FmFM	0.444253	0.807395	1.833%	0.376521	0.785998	1.139%
DNN	0.442271	0.809547	2.108%	0.372686	0.792553	1.982%
W&D	0.442627	0.809133	2.056%	0.372663	0.792079	1.921%
DCN	0.442382	0.809390	2.089%	0.372884	0.791767	1.881%
DCNV2	0.440825	0.811139	2.309%	0.372511	0.792352	1.956%
DeepFM	0.444391	0.807686	1.911%	0.372202	0.792856	2.021%
xDeepFM	0.444541	0.807728	1.878%	0.373387	0.791503	1.847%
AutoInt	0.442502	0.809237	2.069%	0.372830	0.791918	1.900%
FiBiNET	0.442335	0.809809	2.141%	0.371139	0.794850	2.278%
FINT	0.442471	0.808409	1.965%	0.372808	0.792043	1.917%
PHN (ours)	**0.439927**	**0.812039**	**2.383%**	**0.370481**	**0.795964**	**2.421%**

The experiment shows that, PHN achieved a good performance in both validation and testing experiments with two benchmark large datasets.

Grid Search. Figure 5 shows the grid search experiment result of PHN. With the increase of the number of cross layers, the robustness of the model also increases, which may benefit from the improvement of the expression ability of cross layers for higher-order crosses. However, as the number of layers increases, the model complexity also increase, which slow down the training process of the model. The values of AUC and Logloss shown in Fig. 5 tend to be stable when the number of cross layers is five.

3.4 Selection Information (RQ2)

Data Skew Visualization. Based on the trained PHN structure, we visualized the tensor amplification ratio after SSG output. As shown in Fig. 6, the characteristics of the three cross-layers have some similarity, such as the high proportion of field 13 and the low proportion of field 39. At the same time, the feature scaling of the three parts is somewhat different, as in field 8 and field 24.

Selection Pattern. The SSG module is designed for enhance the representation of embedding feature, which select the feature from raw embedding and self-attention embedding. Depending on the design, the selection pattern of self-attention layer and gating layer in this module can be classified as public or private. To further validate the effectiveness of SSG, we also conducted a comparison experiment. Different subscripts represent different selection patterns: *embed* (public embedding feature), *sa* (public self-attention), *sg* (public soft gating). the subscripts with a prefix "P" means that the PHN contains private layers for each parallel layer. Table 3 shows the results of comparison experiment.

This experiments show that, single self-attention layer (public of private) cannot replace the embedding feature represent, but it can help to enhance the feature by using the soft selection gating, and the AUC value of the algorithm increases by 0.123% on average. From a theoretical point of view, a feature without a high activation value in the first-order feature cannot be completely transferred, because it may show a high activation value in the high-order interaction with other features.

3.5 Weak Gradient Phenomenon (RQ3)

Efficiency Analysis. To reduce the impact of weak gradient phenomenon, there has been an attempt in PHN to enhance the data gradient flow in training through residual links (RL) or batch normalization (BN) to reduce the training pressure of each parallel part. In experiments, we tried to introduce gating parameters for RL and discussed the independence of BN in different parallel modules in the last linear layer.

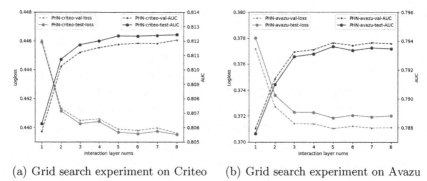

(a) Grid search experiment on Criteo   (b) Grid search experiment on Avazu

Fig. 5. The grid search performance of PHN with different interaction layers on two benchmark datasets.

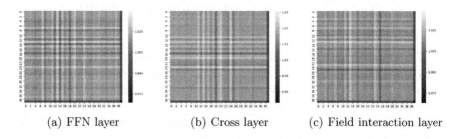

(a) FFN layer   (b) Cross layer   (c) Field interaction layer

Fig. 6. The heatmap of different parallel layers input feature scaling ratio

Different model subscripts represent different structures in PHN: *base* (basic model), *rl* (normal RL), *Prl* (parameter RL), *bn* (BN), and *pbn* (private BN). Table 4 shows the result of comparison experiments.

The experiments show that, In the back propagation process, the weak gradient problem can be improved by using gradient accumulation in the RL. In the

Table 3. Experiment result of different schemes of information selection module on Criteo and Avazu

Model	Criteo		Avazu	
	Logloss	AUC	Logloss	AUC
PHN_{embed}	0.440543	0.811647	0.371538	0.794388
PHN_{sa}	0.441301	0.810525	0.373018	0.792504
PHN_{Psa}	0.441445	0.810554	0.372369	0.792640
PHN_{sa+sg}	0.440210	0.811782	0.371608	**0.794622**
PHN_{Psa+sg}	**0.440031**	**0.811902**	**0.371351**	0.794570
PHN_{sa+Psg}	0.440256	0.811771	0.371398	0.794385
$PHN_{Psa+Psg}$	0.440692	0.811595	0.371405	0.794458

Table 4. Experiment result of different solutions to the weak gradient problem on Criteo and Avazu

Model	Criteo		Avazu	
	Logloss	AUC	Logloss	AUC
PHN_{base}	0.440034	0.811914	0.372209	0.793206
PHN_{rl}	0.439763	0.812111	0.372294	0.793044
PHN_{prl}	**0.439540**	**0.812428**	0.372084	0.793392
$PHN_{base+bn}$	0.440111	0.811879	**0.371117**	**0.795087**
PHN_{rl+bn}	0.441548	0.810359	0.372410	0.793084
PHN_{prl+bn}	0.440307	0.811711	0.371189	0.794911
$PHN_{base+pbn}$	0.443966	0.811865	0.373950	0.794839
PHN_{rl+pbn}	0.445333	0.809268	0.379022	0.791024
$PHN_{prl+pbn}$	0.444590	0.811813	0.377631	0.794621

case of parameters, the overall network can better fit the data flow in the feed forward and reverse process, and strengthen the fitting effect of different parallel structures. However, the subsequent addition of BN has not been very effective. This may be due to the uneven distribution of data flows in different parallel structures, but forced unification with normalization weakens the representation of data. This also explains to some extent that BN layer is not separable from linear layer. The last two groups of experiments also showed that the specificity of the data stream fitted was enhanced when the RL strengthened different parallel structures, while BN had certain side effects. Therefore, in PHN, the RL and BN had better be realized in an independent parallel structure.

Visualization of Activation Value. A more robust model should output more closely to the confidence of the label worthiness. Figure 7 shows the confidence curve of PHN in 200 samples after training one epoch in different configurations, to show the changes of different structures during training phase.

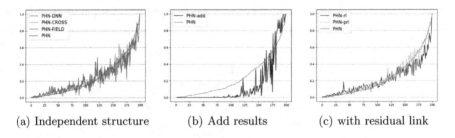

(a) Independent structure   (b) Add results   (c) with residual link

Fig. 7. Experiments on the last activation value of PHN. (Color figure online)

The red line in Fig. 7 represents the PHN model without RL and BN as the benchmark. Figure 7(a) shows that, the single interaction module showed higher negative confidence and lower positive confidence than PHN. This means that PHN is superior to partial cross structure in sample resolution. Figure 7(b) shows that, the sigmoid calculation after summing up the activation values of the parallel models can show more robustness than PHN, which means the fitting effect of a single PHN model on the data set is weakened by weak gradient phenomenon. Figure 7(c) shows that, RL can enhance the high confidence of negative samples, but also reduce the confidence of positive samples, and the RL with parameters can effectively improve the performance of the model on the PHN infrastructure.

4   Conclusion

In this paper, we described the parallel structure of the current mainstream CTR model and the weak gradient phenomenon in the parallel structure, and introduce a parallel structure model named Parallel Heterogeneous Network (PHN) in response to these phenomena. PHN model used Soft Selecting Gating (SSG) structure to isomerize features, and used Feed Forward network, cross interaction layers and field interaction layers to build the subsequent parallel part. The performance experiment results show that PHN shows the State of the Art on two large benchmark data sets, and explores the interaction layer num of the model. The comparative experimental results show that SSG can effectively improve the representation based on public embedding, and the residual link with trainable parameters can improve the representation ability of the model while maintaining the robustness of the results. Based on the overall experimental results, this work brings us to one step closer to being able to determine the optimal structure of PHN.

Acknowledgements. This study was supported by the Hunan Province Natural Science Foundation (grant number 2022JJ30673).

References

1. Chen, B., et al.: Enhancing explicit and implicit feature interactions via information sharing for parallel deep CTR models. In: Proceedings of the 30th ACM International Conference on Information and Knowledge Management, pp. 3757–3766 (2021)
2. Cheng, H.-T., et al.: Wide & deep learning for recommender systems. In: Proceedings of the 1st Workshop on Deep Learning for Recommender Systems, pp. 7–10 (2016)
3. Friedman, J.H.: Greedy function approximation: a gradient boosting machine. Ann. Stat. **2001**, 1189–1232 (2001)
4. Guo, H., Tang, R., Ye, Y., Li, Z., He, X.: DeepFM: a factorization-machine based neural network for CTR prediction. arXiv preprint arXiv:1703.04247 (2017)
5. He, X., Chua, T.-S.: Neural factorization machines for sparse predictive analytics. In: Proceedings of the 40th International ACM SIGIR conference on Research and Development in Information Retrieval, pp. 355–364 (2017)

6. Huang, T., Zhang, Z., Zhang, J.: FiBiNET: combining feature importance and bilinear feature interaction for click-through rate prediction. In: Proceedings of the 13th ACM Conference on Recommender Systems, pp. 169–177 (2019)

7. Lian, J., Zhou, X., Zhang, F., Chen, Z., Xie, X., Sun, G.: xdeepfm: Combining explicit and implicit feature interactions for recommender systems. In: Proceedings of the 24th ACM SIGKDD International Conference on Knowledge Discovery and Data Mining, pp. 1754–1763 (2018)

8. Pan, J., et al.: Field-weighted factorization machines for click-through rate prediction in display advertising. In: Proceedings of the 2018 World Wide Web Conference, pp. 1349–1357 (2018)

9. Qu, Y., et al.: Product-based neural networks for user response prediction. In: 2016 IEEE 16th International Conference on Data Mining (ICDM), pp. 1149–1154. IEEE (2016)

10. Rendle, S.: Factorization machines. In: 2010 IEEE International Conference on Data Mining, pp. 995–1000. IEEE (2010)

11. Shan, Y., Hoens, T.R., Jiao, J., Wang, H., Yu, D., Mao, J.C.: Deep crossing: web-scale modeling without manually crafted combinatorial features. In: Proceedings of the 22nd ACM SIGKDD International Conference on Knowledge Discovery and Data Mining, pp. 255–262 (2016)

12. Song, W., et al.: Autoint: automatic feature interaction learning via self attentive neural networks. In: Proceedings of the 28th ACM International Conference on Information and Knowledge Management, pp. 1161–1170 (2019)

13. Sun, Y., Pan, J., Zhang, A., Flores, A.: FM2: field-matrixed factorization machines for recommender systems. In: Proceedings of the Web Conference 2021, pp. 2828–2837 (2021)

14. Vaswani, A., et al.: Attention is all you need. In: Advances in Neural Information Processing Systems, pp. 5998–6008 (2017)

15. Wang, F., et al.: Enhancing CTR prediction with context-aware feature representation learning. arXiv preprint arXiv:2204.08758 (2022)

16. Wang, R., Fu, B., Fu, G., Wang, M.: Deep & cross network for ad click predictions. In: Proceedings of the ADKDD 2017, pp. 1–7 (2017)

17. Wang, R., et al.: DCN V2: improved deep & cross network and practical lessons for web-scale learning to rank systems. In: Proceedings of the Web Conference 2021, pp. 1785–1797 (2021)

18. Zhang, W., Du, T., Wang, J.: Deep learning over multi-field categorical data. In: Ferro, N., et al. (eds.) ECIR 2016. LNCS, vol. 9626, pp. 45–57. Springer, Cham (2016). https://doi.org/10.1007/978-3-319-30671-1_4

19. Zhao, Z., Yang, S., Liu, G., Feng, D., Xu, K.: FINT: field-aware INTeraction neural network For CTR prediction. arXiv preprint arXiv:2107.01999 (2021)

20. Zhu, J., Liu, J., Yang, S., Zhang, Q., He, X.: Fuxictr: an open benchmark for click-through rate prediction. arXiv preprint arXiv:2009.05794 (2020)

Multi-Relational Cognitive Diagnosis
for Intelligent Education

Kaifang Wu[1], Yonghui Yang[1], Kun Zhang[1], Le Wu[1,4(✉)], Jing Liu[3],
and Xin Li[2]

[1] Hefei University of Technology, Hefei, China
`lewu.ustc@gmail.com`
[2] University of Science and Technology of China, Hefei, China
`leexin@ustc.edu.cn`
[3] National Laboratory of Pattern Recognition, Institute of Automation,
Chinese Academy of Sciences, Beijing, China
`jliu@nlpr.ia.ac.cn`
[4] Institute of Artificial Intelligence, Hefei Comprehensive National Science Center,
Hefei, China

Abstract. In intelligent education, cognitive diagnosis is a fundamental but important task, which aims to discover students' mastery of different knowledge concepts. Plenty of methods have been proposed to exploit student-exercise interactions, especially graph-based methods. However, most of them treat student behaviors to exercises as a binary interaction (i.e., interacted or not), neglecting diverse behavior patterns (i.e., correct and incorrect interactions). Moreover, the number of concepts is much smaller than exercises, presenting a challenge for measuring student proficiency. Therefore, in this paper, we propose a novel *Multi-Relational Cognitive Diagnosis* (*MRCD*) framework. Specifically, we first divide students' answer behaviors into correct and incorrect interactions with exercises, and form the corresponding two student-exercise relation graphs. We then leverage Graph Convolutional Network to learn exercise-level representations of students and exercises based on different relation graphs. Since dividing operation exacerbate the data sparsity problem, we employ graph contrastive learning to enhance *MRCD* on representation learning. Moreover, considering the relatively small number of concepts, we directly employ attention mechanism to generate student and exercise representations based on relevant concepts. After that, we fuse exercise-level and concept-level representations, and send them to a cognitive diagnosis model to predict student performance. Extensive experiments over two real-world datasets demonstrate the effectiveness of our proposed model.

Keywords: Cognitive diagnosis · Graph convolutional network · Graph contrastive learning

1   Introduction

Intelligent Tutoring Systems (ITS) [4,21] have been widely applied in recent years, such as Santa and ASSISTments online education platform. These platforms provide rich exercise resources and personalized exercise suggestions [3,9] for students. The crucial task of ITS is to obtain the proficiency of students on different concepts [20], which has drawn plenty of attention.

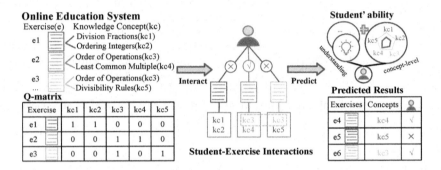

Fig. 1. The process of the cognitive diagnosis task.

Based on student-exercise historical interactions and exercise-concept correlation matrix (i.e., Q-matrix annotated by educational experts), early diagnosis models predicted student performance on exercises by handcrafted functions, such as Item Response Theory (IRT) [13,25], Deterministic Inputs, Noisy-And gate (DINA) [11], and Multidimensional IRT (MIRT) [1,26]. However, most of them only exploit shallow interactions, ignoring complex relationships among students, exercises, and concepts, which cause the performance of student prediction far from satisfaction.

With the rapid development of neural networks, many neural network-based methods have been proposed For example, [30] introduced neural network for cognitive diagnosis on the basis of traditional diagnosis methods. RCD [14] designed a relation-driven framework to learn representations by constructing the student-exercise-concept hierarchical graph, where student-exercise interactions are reduced to binary interactions. Despite the great progress, complex relations among students, exercises, and concepts are still under-exploited. One of main problems is the simplified binary processing of student-exercise interactions. As shown in Fig. 1, student-exercise interactions can be divided into correct and incorrect patterns. For the correct behavior pattern, it does not only reveal understanding to exercises, but also reflects association [37], guessing [11], and so forth. The incorrect behavior also contains different meanings, such as misunderstanding and carelessness. These phenomena demonstrate that it is useful to measure student-exercise interactions in terms of different relations. Moreover, one exercise usually contains multiple concepts, (e.g., Q-matrix in Fig. 1). However, most existing methods handle this phenomenon by treating the performance of a student in an exercise as the average capability of contained concepts [14], which ignores the potential information of student-concept interactions and is too coarse to measure the ability level of students on specific concepts.

To this end, we propose a novel *Multi-Relational Cognitive Diagnosis (MRCD)* framework. Specifically, to fully exploit student-exercise interactions, we divide answer records into correct and wrong patterns. Then, we employ Graph Convolutional Network (GCN) to learn exercise-level node representations from student-exercise relation graphs based on different behavior patterns. Meanwhile, the dividing operation will exacerbate data sparsity problem. Thus, we design a contrastive learning scheme with relational data augmentation to alleviate this problem. Moreover, considering that knowledge concepts are much less than exercises, and that student-exercise interactions are too coarse to describe the proficiency of students to concepts, we develop a self-attention module to model the relations among students, exercises, and concepts directly. Along this line, concept-level student ability and exercise characteristics can be better modeled. Next, we fuse exercise-level and concept-level representations of students and exercises, and send them into the neural diagnosis model to predict student performance. Extensive experiments over two real-world datasets demonstrate the superiority of our proposed *MRCD*.

2   Related Work

Cognitive Diagnosis Models. Cognitive diagnosis [12] focuses on assessing strengths and weaknesses regarding the student abilities. Traditionally, to overcome the limitation of Classical Test Theory [2] that evaluates student ability only by actual scores, IRT [13] leveraged a logical function to study the linear relationship between student ability and exercise characteristics (e.g., difficulty and discrimination). DINA [11] adopted discrete binary vectors to represent exercises and students. In addition, it also focused on the effect of the slip and guessing behaviors of students. MIRT [26] expanded the dimension of IRT to study the mastery levels of students in a fine-grained manner. In recent years, neural networks have been introduced for better diagnosis. For example, [30] combined neural network with the monotonicity assumptions for adaptive learning the representations of students and exercises, while ensuring the interpretability. And [10] used semantic information of exercises to obtain the difficulty and discrimination. Besides, there are also some literatures focused on the impact of educational context on students' implicit cognitive states [37], and the diagnostic task by considering both objective and subjective exercises [35].

Graph Structure Modeling. Due to the great success, graph-based modeling have attracted wide attention in many areas, which effectively improve the quality of learned representations by aggregating features from neighbors [7,16,32]. In intelligent education, graph-based methods also become one of the hot topics [14,22,29,36]. For example, [36] explored high-order relevance between exercises and concepts by aggregating node representations from exercise-concept graph. RCD [14] built a hierarchical graph consisting of three local graphs: student-exercise graph, exercise-concept graph, and concept dependency graph to learn better representations. However, these methods just mapped student-exercise interactions into binary values, ignoring the rich information hidden in different behavior patterns, which limited the performance of student prediction.

Meanwhile, Graph Contrastive learning (GCL) is one of the popular technologies on representation learning. Its core idea is to pull closer an anchor and positive samples while pushing away the anchor from negative samples in the representation space [17,18,24,31]. For alleviating the problem of data sparsity, [38] considered the original structure of graphs and node features by adopting an importance-driven approach. [33] introduced self-supervised learning as an auxiliary task to alleviate problems such as the long-tail and the robustness in recommendation. And [18] used structural neighbors and semantic neighbors to construct sample pairs. Considering two special subgraphs formed when constructing the relational graph, we construct positive and negative sample pairs from correct and wrong perspectives.

3   Problem Formulation

There are three entity sets: student set S ($|S| = M$), exercise set E ($|E| = N$), and knowledge concept set C ($|C| = K$), where M, N, K are sizes of each set. $\mathbf{Q} \in \mathbb{R}^{N \times K}$ matrix labeled by experts, describes correlations between exercise E and concept C. $q_{jk} = 1$ is that exercise e_j contains concept c_k, otherwise $q_{jk} = 0$. Besides, $\mathbf{R} \in \mathbb{R}^{M \times N}$ denotes student-exercise interactions, where $r_{ij} \in \{-1, 1, 0\}$ means that student s_i makes $\{wrong, correct, no\}$ answer to exercise e_j.

Considering the interaction type, we propose to divide $\mathbf{R}$ into two relational interactions $\mathbf{R}^+$ and $\mathbf{R}^-$, where $\mathbf{R}^+$ ($\mathbf{R}^-$) denotes correct (wrong) interactions. Taking $\mathbf{R}^+$ as an example, student-exercise interactions (i.e., correct answer and others) naturally form a bipartite graph $\mathcal{G}^+ = \{\mathbf{S} \cup \mathbf{E}, \mathbf{R}^+\}$, where the graph adjacent matrix is constructed as follows:

$$\mathbf{A}^+ = \begin{vmatrix} \mathbf{0}^{N \times M} & \mathbf{R}^+ \\ \mathbf{R}^{+T} & \mathbf{0}^{M \times N} \end{vmatrix}. \tag{1}$$

Meanwhile, the wrong relational graph $\mathcal{G}^- = \{\mathbf{S} \cup \mathbf{E}, \mathbf{R}^-\}$ is constructed similarly. The goal of cognitive diagnosis is to predict student performance on exercises, and diagnose cognitive states of students on specific knowledge concepts.

4   Multi-Relational Cognitive Diagnosis

Figure 2 shows the overall framework of *MRCD*, which consists of three main modules: *Exercise-Level Learning Module*, *Concept-Level Learning Module*, and *Diagnosis Module*. Next, we will introduce each of them in details.

4.1 Exercise-Level Learning Module

As mentioned before, complex student-exercise interactions imply a wealth of information, which requires a better utilization method than binary processing. Therefore, we propose to divide answer records into correct and wrong records, and leverage graph structure to describe student-exercise interactions.

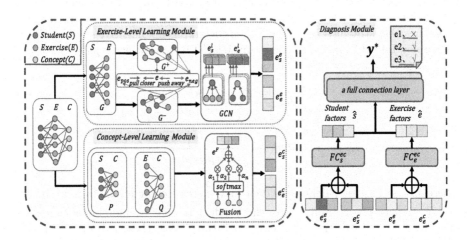

Fig. 2. The overall structure of our proposed *MRCD*. Note that the red lines indicate that students answer exercises wrong. (Color figure online)

For simplicity, in following parts, we take correct answer and other interactions $\mathbf{R}^+$ as an example to report technical details. Specifically, we leverage $\mathbf{S} \in \mathbb{R}^{M \times d}$ and $\mathbf{E} \in \mathbb{R}^{N \times d}$ to denote free embeddings of students and exercises, which are also initial values of the first layer in the graph. To obtain node embeddings at the $(t+1)^{th}$ layer based on its neighbors and its own embedding at the tth layer, we utilize graph propagation and pooling operation to update each node embedding. $A_i^+ = \{j|r_{ij}^+ = 1\}$ and $A_j^+ = \{i|r_{ij}^+ = 1\}$ denote the exercise set that student s_i has answered correctly and the student set who has answered exercise e_j correctly, the updating process can be formulated as follows:

$$s_i^{t+1} = s_i^t + \sum_{j \in A_i^+} \frac{e_j^t}{|A_i^+|}, \quad e_j^{t+1} = e_j^t + \sum_{i \in A_j^+} \frac{s_i^t}{|A_j^+|}. \tag{2}$$

Moreover, we formulate this process in matrix norm. Let $\mathbf{S}^t$ and $\mathbf{E}^t$ denote embedding matrices of students and exercises after the tth propagation, the updated embedding matrices at the $(t+1)^{th}$ propagation are calculated as follows:

$$\begin{vmatrix} \mathbf{S}^{t+1} \\ \mathbf{E}^{t+1} \end{vmatrix} = \begin{vmatrix} \mathbf{S}^t \\ \mathbf{E}^t \end{vmatrix} + (\mathbf{D}^{-1}\mathbf{A}^+) \times \begin{vmatrix} \mathbf{S}^t \\ \mathbf{E}^t \end{vmatrix}, \tag{3}$$

where $\mathbf{D}$ is a degree matrix of the $\mathbf{A}^+$, which efficiently transfers neighbor embeddings and updates fusion matrices.

Furthermore, we have noticed that dividing operation will exacerbate the data sparsity problem, which is harmful for student proficiency modeling. Thus, we employ GCL for better representation learning. Since we focus on different interactions among students and exercises, it is natural to treat node embeddings from different relational graphs as augmented embeddings. In $\mathcal{G}^+$ and $\mathcal{G}^-$, the nodes representing the same student or exercise are positive pairs of each other, while the other student(exercise) nodes in the graphs are negative samples. Then, we employ InfoNCE [8,23] to constrain $MRCD$ to pull positive pairs closer and push negative pairs away as follows:

$$
\begin{aligned}
L_s &= \sum_{s_i \in S} -log \frac{exp(sim(\mathbf{s}_i^+, \mathbf{s}_i^-)/\tau)}{\sum_{s_k \in S'} exp(sim(\mathbf{s}_i^+, \mathbf{s}_k^+)/\tau)}, \\
L_e &= \sum_{e_j \in E} -log \frac{exp(sim(\mathbf{e}_j^+, \mathbf{e}_j^-)/\tau)}{\sum_{e_k \in E'} exp(sim(\mathbf{e}_j^+, \mathbf{e}_k^+)/\tau)},
\end{aligned}
\tag{4}
$$

where $\{\mathbf{s}_i^+, \mathbf{s}_i^-, \mathbf{e}_j^+, \mathbf{e}_j^-\}$ denote student and exercise embeddings from graph $\mathcal{G}^+$ and $\mathcal{G}^-$ separately. S' and E' are the batch data that exclude anchor example of student s_i and exercise e_j. τ is temperature. With these two optimizations, $MRCD$ is able to make full use of sparse data to generate better representations.

4.2   Concept-Level Learning Module

Different from the situation that students and exercises have explicit interactions (i.e., correct, wrong, and no answers), we only obtain implicit student-concept interaction according to exercises. Meanwhile, each exercise often includes multiple concepts, and making wrong answer does not mean not mastering all included concepts in the exercise. Thus, we develop a concept-level learning module to model interactions at a fine-grained level [34].

Specifically, we first obtain student-concept interaction matrix $\mathbf{P} \in \mathbb{R}^{M \times K}$ based on $\mathbf{R}$ and $\mathbf{Q}$ matrix. $p_{ij} = 1$ means that student s_i has done exercises that contains concept c_j, Otherwise, $p_{ij} = 0$. Meanwhile, knowledge concepts are represented by $\mathbf{C} \in \mathbb{R}^{K \times d}$, where $\mathbf{c}_i$ denotes the ith concept embedding. Considering the quantitative relationship between exercises and concepts, the student-concept interaction is relatively dense. It is easy to lead to oversmoothing by using multi-layer convolution to propagate information [19]. Thus, we employ attention mechanism to measure their connections as follows:

$$
\mathbf{s}_i^c = \sum_{c_k \in C_{s_i}} \alpha_{ik} \mathbf{c}_k, \quad \alpha_{ik} = \frac{sim(\mathbf{s}_i, \mathbf{c}_k)}{\sum_{c_k \in C_{s_i}} sim(\mathbf{s}_i, \mathbf{c}_k)},
\tag{5}
$$

where $C_{s_i} = \{c_k | p_{ik} = 1\}$ denotes a set of concepts that student s_i has interacted with. $sim(\cdot)$ is cosine similarity. $\mathbf{s}_i^c$ is the concept-level representation of student s_i. Meanwhile, concept-level exercise representations are obtained similarly:

$$e_j^c = \sum_{c_l \in C_{e_j}} \beta_{jl} \mathbf{c}_l, \quad \beta_{jl} = \frac{\text{sim}(\mathbf{e}_j, \mathbf{c}_l)}{\sum_{c_l \in C_{e_j}} \text{sim}(\mathbf{e}_j, \mathbf{c}_l)}, \tag{6}$$

where $C_{e_j} = \{c_l | q_{jl} = 1\}$ denotes a set of concepts that exercise e_j contains. $\mathbf{e}_j^c$ is the concept-level representation of exercise e_j. By using this module, $MRCD$ is able to measure the different impact of concepts on students or exercises, which is helpful for better modeling grasp level of students to concepts.

4.3 Diagnosis Module

After obtaining exercise-level and concept-level representations, what we do next is to fuse these representations and predict the student performance. First of all, we leverage a Fully Connected (FC) layer with a non-negative activation function (i.e., Sigmoid function) to fuse representations as follows:

$$\hat{\mathbf{s}}_i = \sigma(FC_s([\mathbf{s}_i; \mathbf{s}_i^c])), \quad \hat{\mathbf{e}}_j = \sigma(FC_e([\mathbf{e}_j; \mathbf{e}_j^c])), \tag{7}$$

where $[;]$ denotes concatenation operation. $\sigma(\cdot)$ is Sigmoid activation function. $\{\hat{\mathbf{s}}_i, \hat{\mathbf{e}}_j\}$ are the final representations of student s_i and exercise e_j.

Secondly, similar to existing neural diagnosis models [10], we also employ expert-designed diagnosis function MIRT [26] to finish the task. Specifically, we leverage concept-level exercise representation $\mathbf{e}_j^c$ to obtain the value of exercise's discrimination with another FC layer. Then, the diagnosis result of student s_i is calculated by predicting whether exercise e_j is answered correctly as follows:

$$y_{ij}^* = \sigma(F(\mathbf{k} \times (\hat{\mathbf{s}}_i - \hat{\mathbf{e}}_j) \times \mathbf{e}_j^{disc})), \quad \mathbf{e}_j^{disc} = \sigma(FC_1(\mathbf{e}_j^c)), \tag{8}$$

where $F(\cdot)$ is the neural network with two full connected layers in which each element of the weight is restricted to be positive [30]. $\mathbf{k}$ is a one-hot vector that denotes concepts contained in exercise e_j (i.e., the j-th row in the Q matrix). $\mathbf{y}_{ij}^*$ is the predicted probability that student s_i answers exercise e_j correctly.

Loss Function. Since cognitive diagnosis is formulated as predicting whether a student do exercises correctly, Cross-Entropy is employed as the optimization:

$$L_{se} = -\sum_i \sum_j \left(y_{ij} \log y_{ij}^* + (1 - y_{ij}) \log \left(1 - y_{ij}^*\right) \right), \tag{9}$$

where y_{ij} is the ground truth whether student s_i answers exercise e_j correctly. Meanwhile, we have employed GCL to constrain $MRCD$ to learn better exercise-level representations with Eq. (4). Finally, the overall optimization target of $MRCD$ is formulated with a hyper-parameter λ as follows:

$$Loss = L_{se} + \lambda(L_s + L_e). \tag{10}$$

5   Experiments

5.1   Experimental Settings

Table 1. The statistics of the datasets.

Datasets	Students	Exercises	Concepts	Correct logs	Wrong logs	KCs per exercise
ASSISTMents0910	4,163	17,751	123	183,356	95,520	1.97
EDNET	1,000	11,760	189	734,564	353,589	2.25

Datasets. We select ASSISTMents0910[1] and EdNet[2], as the evaluation datasets. These datasets count the interaction records between students and online tutoring systems, which mainly record the data of several attributes and results of students in the exercise process. Similar to existing work [14, 28, 30, 36], we filter out exercises without concepts annotation and students who have less than 15 records. And we randomly select 1,000 students for cognitive diagnosis on EdNet dataset. The statistics of these two datasets are reported in Table 1.

Evaluation Metrics. Considering that the student ability level cannot be directly measured in cognitive diagnosis, we adopt some common indicators to evaluate the performance of the model, such as, *Root Mean Squared Error (RMSE)* [6], *Accuracy (Acc)* and *Area Under Curve (AUC)* [5].

Baselines. We compare *MRCD* with the following baselines:

- **IRT** [13]: IRT is a widely used probabilistic model based on a one-dimensional linear relationship between student ability and exercise characteristics.
- **MIRT** [26]: MIRT extends traditional IRT to model student-exercise interactions from multidimensional knowledge concepts.
- **DINA** [11]: DINA considers whether students have mastered the fine-grained knowledge concepts in a discrete manner. And the factors of student guessing and sliding are also concerned.
- **NeuralCD** [30]: NeuralCD introduces neural network to model the complex interaction relationship between students and exercises, and ensures the interpretability of student factors and exercise factors with help of the monotonicity assumption in the traditional diagnostic model.
- **RCD** [14]: RCD comprehensively models the student-exercise-concept relationship based on graph structure, especially concept dependency.

---

[1] https://sites.google.com/site/assistmentsdata/home/assistment-2009-2010-data/skill-builder-data-2009-2010.

[2] http://ednet-leaderboard.s3-website-ap-northeast-1.amazonaws.com/.

Parameter Setting. To obtain the best performance, we tune the hyper-parameters over validation set and employ Early-Stop with the patience of 6 epochs to prevent overfitting. Some common hyper-parameters are set as follows. Learning rate is set as $lr = 0.0001$. Embedding size of students, exercises, and knowledge concepts are set as the number of concepts K. The number of layer of GCN in exercise-level learning module are selected from $\{1, 2, 3, 4\}$. The temperature τ in GCL is selected from $\{0.05, 0.1, 0.15, 0.2\}$. λ in Eq. (10) is selected from $\{10^{-7}, 10^{-6}, 10^{-5}, 10^{-4}\}$. We initialize the network parameters with Xavier initialization [15].

Table 2. Overall results on student performance prediction.

Models	ASSISTMents0910			EdNet		
	ACC↑	RMSE↓	AUC↑	ACC↑	RMSE↓	AUC↑
IRT	0.67946	0.45477	0.68273	0.71707	0.43444	0.72514
DINA	0.67635	0.48847	0.71167	0.70049	0.46659	0.69111
MIRT	0.72136	0.45105	0.74283	0.72931	0.42891	0.74826
NeuralCD	0.72782	0.43374	0.75469	0.72819	0.42469	0.75792
RCD	0.73264	0.42268	0.77013	0.73246	0.42311	0.76280
MRCD	**0.74130**	**0.41862**	**0.78208**	**0.73749**	**0.41962**	**0.77040**

5.2 Experimental Results

Overall Performance. Table 2 reports the overall performance of models on student performance prediction. From the table, we observe that *MRCD* achieves the best performance on all evaluation metrics compared with other baselines, especially the state-of-the-art graph-based RCD model. This phenomenon demonstrates the effectiveness of considering different type of interactions among students and exercises and detailed measurement of students and concepts. Moreover, *MRCD* has stable performance when data becomes sparser (i.e., ASSISTMents0910 dataset), indicating the usefulness of CL framework employed in exercise-level learning module. Among all baselines, we observe that neural network-based methods have better performance than traditional cognitive diagnosis models, indicating that neural network-based methods are more powerful to measure the complex relationships among students, exercises, and concepts.

Parameter Sensitive Test. There are two important hyper-parameters to control the impact of different modules, GCN layer number D and the weight λ of CL loss. Therefore, we conduct additional experiments to verify their impacts. Results are reported in Table 3 and Fig. 3. From the results, we observe that with the increasing of GCN layers, model performance becomes better, supporting that high-order interactions are very useful for student performance prediction. Moreover, the performance increasing on ASSISTMents0910 dataset is larger

Table 3. Performance comparisons of different propagation depth D.

Depth	ASSISTMents0910			EdNet		
	ACC↑	RMSE↓	AUC↑	ACC↑	RMSE↓	AUC↑
$D = 0$	0.73004	0.43093	0.76606	0.73560	0.42052	0.76869
$D = 1$	0.73802	0.42100	0.77237	0.73512	0.42205	0.76674
$D = 2$	0.73931	0.41932	0.77855	0.73609	0.42062	0.76916
$D = 3$	**0.74130**	**0.41862**	**0.78208**	**0.73749**	0.41962	0.77040
$D = 4$	0.73890	0.41894	0.78047	0.73667	**0.41953**	**0.77058**

than EdNet. The possible reason is that more GCN layers will help $MRCD$ obtain more information for student proficiency modeling.

For the impact of CL framework, we observe from Fig. 3(a) that with the increasing of λ, the performance of $MRCD$ is first increasing and then decreasing. When λ is bigger than 0.001, the performance will have a big drop. We speculate the possible reason is that when λ is too big, $MRCD$ will be constrained to learn similar representations for all students, which will do harm to model performance. Based on three different evaluation metrics, we finally select $\lambda = 5e - 5$ and $\lambda = 1e - 6$ as best setting for two datasets separately.

Ablation Study. In this part, we make several ablation studies to verify the effectiveness of each component in $MRCD$, including *exercise-level learning module (MRCD-graph)*, *concept-level learning module (MRCD-kc)*, the consideration of *different student-exercise relations* by using RGCN [27] (*MRCD-graph-kc(rgcn)*) and *MRCD-graph-kc(t)* without the division operation. Results are illustrated in Table 4. We have to note that *Division* means whether dividing different relations. From the table, we observe that exercise-level learning module plays the most important role. Since this module focuses on high-order interactions among students and exercises, as well as employs CL framework to alleviate the sparsity problem that dividing operation introduced, it is natural that this module is very critical in our $MRCD$ model. Moreover, when treating correct and wrong answer behaviors as the same, we observe that model performance also declined somewhat, demonstrating the necessity of processing correct and wrong answer behaviors differently.

Case Study. Here we visualize the diagnostic result of a student selected from the Assistment0910 dataset as shown in Fig. 3(b). And we record the student's historical responses and exercise-concept correlation relationship in Fig. 1. Note that *Order of Operations +,−,/,* () positive reals* is abbreviated to *Order of Operations*. From Fig. 3(b), we could clearly observe that different answer behaviors have an impact on the student' mastery of corresponding knowledge concepts. And considering students' different answer behavior patterns is useful to learn the ability of students, especially in the exercises with wrong answers.

Table 4. Results of ablation experiment.

Models	Division	ASSISTMents0910			EdNet		
		ACC↑	RMSE↓	AUC↑	ACC↑	RMSE↓	AUC↑
MRCD-kc	×	0.72500	0.43450	0.75752	0.71679	0.42992	0.74397
MRCD-graph	✓	0.73840	0.41975	0.77812	0.73059	0.42227	0.76466
MRCD-grph-kc(rgcn)	✓	0.73614	0.42274	0.77334	0.73587	0.42035	0.76909
MRCD-graph-kc(t)	×	0.73849	0.42076	0.77773	0.73597	0.41980	0.76964
MRCD	✓	**0.74130**	**0.41862**	**0.78208**	**0.73749**	**0.41962**	**0.77040**

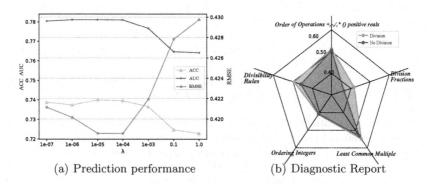

(a) Prediction performance   (b) Diagnostic Report

Fig. 3. Results of *MRCD* on ASSISTMents0910.

6   Conclusion

In this paper, we argued that different student-exercise interaction behaviors revealed different features of students, which should be considered explicitly. Thus, we proposed a novel *Multi-Relational Cognitive Diagnosis (MRCD)* framework to model student proficiency over exercises from exercise-level and concept-level perspectives simultaneously. Specifically, we first divided student-exercise interactions into correct and incorrect answer interactions and built graphs based on them. Then, we designed an exercise-level learning module, in which GCN and GCL framework are employed to learn better representations. Moreover, we developed a concept-level learning module to measure student-concept interactions and exercise-concept relationship directly. Then, we fused these two-level representations and sent them to a commonly used diagnosis model to predict student performance over exercises. Extensive experiments over two real-world datasets showed the superiority of *MRCD*. In the future, we will consider the dynamic change of student ability over time for better cognitive diagnosis.

Acknowledgments. This work was supported in part by grants from the National Key Research and Development Program of China (Grant No. 2021ZD0111802), the Fundamental Research Funds for the Central Universities (JZ2021HGTB0075), and the Open Project Program of the National Laboratory of Pattern Recognition (NLPR).

References

1. Adams, R.J., Wilson, M., Wang, W.C.: The multidimensional random coefficients multinomial logit model. Appl. Psychol. Meas. **21**(1), 1–23 (1997)
2. Allen, M.J., Yen, W.M.: Introduction to Measurement Theory. Waveland Press, Long Grove (2001)
3. Anderson, A., Huttenlocher, D., Kleinberg, J., Leskovec, J.: Engaging with massive online courses. In: WWW, pp. 687–698 (2014)
4. Anderson, J.R., Boyle, C.F., Reiser, B.J.: Intelligent tutoring systems. Science **228**(4698), 456–462 (1985)
5. Bradley, A.P.: The use of the area under the roc curve in the evaluation of machine learning algorithms. Pattern Recogn. **30**(7), 1145–1159 (1997)
6. Chai, T., Draxler, R.R.: Root mean square error (RMSE) or mean absolute error (MAE)? - arguments against avoiding RMSE in the literature. Geosci. Model Dev. **7**(3), 1247–1250 (2014)
7. Chen, L., Wu, L., Hong, R., Zhang, K., Wang, M.: Revisiting graph based collaborative filtering: a linear residual graph convolutional network approach. In: AAAI, vol. 34, pp. 27–34 (2020)
8. Chen, T., Kornblith, S., Norouzi, M., Hinton, G.: A simple framework for contrastive learning of visual representations. In: ICML, pp. 1597–1607. PMLR (2020)
9. Chen, Y., Li, X., Liu, J., Ying, Z.: Recommendation system for adaptive learning. Appl. Psychol. Meas. **42**(1), 24–41 (2018)
10. Cheng, S., et al.: Dirt: deep learning enhanced item response theory for cognitive diagnosis. In: CIKM, pp. 2397–2400 (2019)
11. De La Torre, J.: Dina model and parameter estimation: a didactic. J. Educ. Behav. Stat. **34**(1), 115–130 (2009)
12. DiBello, L.V., Roussos, L.A., Stout, W.: 31A review of cognitively diagnostic assessment and a summary of psychometric models. Handb. Stat. **26**, 979–1030 (2006)
13. Embretson, S.E., Reise, S.P.: Item Response Theory. Psychology Press, Hove (2013)
14. Gao, W., et al.: RCD: relation map driven cognitive diagnosis for intelligent education systems. In: SIGIR, pp. 501–510 (2021)
15. Glorot, X., Bengio, Y.: Understanding the difficulty of training deep feedforward neural networks. In: Proceedings of the Thirteenth International Conference on Artificial Intelligence and Statistics, pp. 249–256. JMLR Workshop and Conference Proceedings (2010)
16. He, X., Deng, K., Wang, X., Li, Y., Zhang, Y., Wang, M.: LightGCN: simplifying and powering graph convolution network for recommendation. In: SIGIR, pp. 639–648 (2020)
17. Khosla, P., et al.: Supervised contrastive learning. In: NeurIPS, vol. 33, pp. 18661–18673 (2020)
18. Lin, Z., Tian, C., Hou, Y., Zhao, W.X.: Improving graph collaborative filtering with neighborhood-enriched contrastive learning. In: WWW, pp. 2320–2329 (2022)
19. Liu, M., Shao, P., Zhang, K.: Graph-based exercise-and knowledge-aware learning network for student performance prediction. In: Fang, L., Chen, Y., Zhai, G., Wang, J., Wang, R., Dong, W. (eds.) CICAI 2021. LNCS, vol. 13069, pp. 27–38. Springer, Cham (2021). https://doi.org/10.1007/978-3-030-93046-2_3
20. Liu, Q., et al.: EKT: exercise-aware knowledge tracing for student performance prediction. IEEE Trans. Knowl. Data Eng. **33**(1), 100–115 (2019)
21. Liu, Q., et al.: Exploiting cognitive structure for adaptive learning. In: KDD, pp. 627–635 (2019)

22. Nakagawa, H., Iwasawa, Y., Matsuo, Y.: Graph-based knowledge tracing: modeling student proficiency using graph neural network. In: 2019 IEEE/WIC/ACM International Conference on Web Intelligence (WI), pp. 156–163. IEEE (2019)
23. Van den Oord, A., Li, Y., Vinyals, O.: Representation learning with contrastive predictive coding. arXiv e-prints arXiv-1807 (2018)
24. Qiu, J., et al.: GCC: graph contrastive coding for graph neural network pre-training. In: KDD, pp. 1150–1160 (2020)
25. Rasch, G.: On general laws and the meaning of measurement in psychology. In: Berkeley Symposium on Mathematical Statistics, vol. 4, pp. 321–333 (1961)
26. Reckase, M.D.: Multidimensional item response theory models. In: Reckase, M.D. (ed.) Multidimensional Item Response Theory. SSBS, pp. 79–112. Springer, New York (2009). https://doi.org/10.1007/978-0-387-89976-3_4
27. Schlichtkrull, M., Kipf, T.N., Bloem, P., van den Berg, R., Titov, I., Welling, M.: Modeling relational data with graph convolutional networks. In: Gangemi, A., et al. (eds.) ESWC 2018. LNCS, vol. 10843, pp. 593–607. Springer, Cham (2018). https://doi.org/10.1007/978-3-319-93417-4_38
28. Thai-Nghe, N., Schmidt-Thieme, L.: Multi-relational factorization models for student modeling in intelligent tutoring systems. In: 2015 Seventh International Conference on Knowledge and Systems Engineering (KSE), pp. 61–66. IEEE (2015)
29. Tong, S., et al.: Structure-based knowledge tracing: an influence propagation view. In: 2020 IEEE International Conference on Data Mining (ICDM), pp. 541–550. IEEE (2020)
30. Wang, F., et al.: Neural cognitive diagnosis for intelligent education systems. In: AAAI, vol. 34, pp. 6153–6161 (2020)
31. Wang, T., Isola, P.: Understanding contrastive representation learning through alignment and uniformity on the hypersphere. In: ICML, pp. 9929–9939. PMLR (2020)
32. Wang, X., He, X., Wang, M., Feng, F., Chua, T.S.: Neural graph collaborative filtering. In: SIGIR, pp. 165–174 (2019)
33. Wu, J., et al.: Self-supervised graph learning for recommendation. In: SIGIR, pp. 726–735 (2021)
34. Wu, L., He, X., Wang, X., Zhang, K., Wang, M.: A survey on accuracy-oriented neural recommendation: from collaborative filtering to information-rich recommendation. IEEE Trans. Knowl. Data Eng. (2022)
35. Wu, R., et al.: Cognitive modelling for predicting examinee performance. In: IJCAI (2015)
36. Yang, Y., et al.: GIKT: a graph-based interaction model for knowledge tracing. In: Hutter, F., Kersting, K., Lijffijt, J., Valera, I. (eds.) ECML PKDD 2020. LNCS (LNAI), vol. 12457, pp. 299–315. Springer, Cham (2021). https://doi.org/10.1007/978-3-030-67658-2_18
37. Zhou, Y., et al.: Modeling context-aware features for cognitive diagnosis in student learning. In: KDD, pp. 2420–2428 (2021)
38. Zhu, Y., Xu, Y., Yu, F., Liu, Q., Wu, S., Wang, L.: Graph contrastive learning with adaptive augmentation. In: WWW, pp. 2069–2080 (2021)

Clinical Phenotyping Prediction via Auxiliary Task Selection and Adaptive Shared-Space Correction

Xiao Yang[1], Ning Liu[1(✉)], Jianbo Qiao[1], Haitao Yuan[2], Teng Ma[3], Yonghui Xu[1], and Lizhen Cui[1]

[1] Shandong University, Jinan, Shandong 250100, China
liun21cs@sdu.edu.cn, clz@sdu.edu.cn
[2] Beijing University of Posts and Telecommunications, Beijing 100091, China
[3] Tsinghua University, Beijing 100084, China

Abstract. Clinical Phenotyping is a fundamental task in clinical services, which assessments whether a patient suffers a medical condition of interest. Existing works focus on learning better patients' representations. Recently, multi-task learning has been proposed to transfer knowledge from different tasks and achieved promising performance. However, the existing multi-task models still suffer from the serious negative transfer and slow convergence problem when multiple phenotype tasks are trained together. Meanwhile, phenotype relatedness is ignored, limiting to boost the performance of the multi-task learning for the phenotype prediction. To address these issues, we propose a private-shared multi-task framework with auxiliary task selection and adaptive shared-space correction for phenotype prediction (MTL_AC). To start with, we design an auxiliary task selection method to find the most compatible phenotype task against one task by using phenotype relatedness. And then, a novel adaptive shared-space correction mechanism is proposed to address the negative transfer and slow convergence problem when two tasks are jointly trained under the private-shared multitask framework. The experimental results show that the proposed method performs better on various phenotype prediction tasks.

Keywords: Clinical phenotyping · Multi-task learning · Negative transfer · Auxiliary task

1 Introduction

Clinical Phenotyping is a basic clinical process, which aims to figure out whether a patient suffers from a medical condition of interest and is commonly used as the first step to facilitate multiple medical services [19]. For example, medical experts can group the patients via predefined phenotypes for precision medicine [20]. Actually, physicians should classify the patient's phenotype via complex health records, which requires a high level of clinical experience and knowledge.

© The Author(s), under exclusive license to Springer Nature Switzerland AG 2022
L. Fang et al. (Eds.): CICAI 2022, LNAI 13605, pp. 438–449, 2022.
https://doi.org/10.1007/978-3-031-20500-2_36

With the rising complexity of patients' data collected, clinical phenotyping can be a challenging task for medical experts [24,26].

Recently, the adoption of electronic health records has collected quantities of health-related data, which offers opportunities for designing data-driven methods for automatic phenotype prediction [3,14,24].

Many works have utilized various deep learning technologies to model different aspects of the patients' data, including the recurrent neural networks [2,4,29], attention mechanism [17,22,30], graph-based methods [6,15], et al. These works are mainly focusing on learning the better representations of patients from multiple aspects. Inspired by the human learning activities, multi-task learning is designed to transfer knowledge among the tasks to improve the performance and has achieved promising performance in the clinical domain compared to training only for one task [9,21]. In spite of the success of multi-task learning in the clinical domain, they have certain limitations when performing the clinical phenotype prediction. Firstly, existing work has shown that multi-task learning may degrade the performance of some relevant tasks [7,28]. The existing multi-task models still suffer from the serious negative transfer problem caused by the multi-times updating of the shared space such that task-specific bias is introduced. Secondly, the relationship among different phenotypes is ignored, limiting to boost the performance of the multi-task learning for the phenotype prediction. In the clinical setting, one patient may suffer from different phenotypes, which may provide additional information on the phenotype relatedness.

In this paper, to boost the performance of clinical phenotype prediction, we formulate the clinical phenotype prediction task as a multi-task learning problem where each phenotype task is referred to as an independent task and propose a private-shared multitask framework with auxiliary task selection and adaptive shared-space correction for phenotype prediction (MTL_AC). Firstly, to distinguish the task-specific and task-independent information, we adopt a private-shared multi-task framework with two types of representations learned. Secondly, we propose an auxiliary task selection method to select the most compatible task with the consideration of phenotype co-occurrence. Thirdly, to diminish the negative transfer of the shared space, we design a novel adaptive shared-space correction method to adaptive change the optimization direction of the shared space. We conduct a comprehensive evaluation of real phenotype prediction tasks. Experimental results show that the proposed method outperforms the previous methods for most of the phenotype prediction tasks. In summary, the major contributions are listed as follows:

- We formulate the phenotype prediction task under the multi-task learning formulation and propose a private-shared multi-task framework with auxiliary task selection and adaptive shared-space correction.
- We design an auxiliary task section method via the co-occurrence of multiple phenotypes to select the most compatible phenotype.

- We design an adaptive shared-space correction method under the private-shared multi-task learning framework to reduce the bias introduced by the multi-times updating of the shared space.
- We conduct experiments on real clinical phenotype prediction tasks and the experimental results show the advantages of our method.

2   Related Work

2.1   Deep Learning for Clinical Phenotyping

Recently, deep learning methods have been successfully applied to clinical phenotyping. Previous works focus on learning better representations by considering the different aspects of data in electronic health data. As the information of patients is recorded sequentially in the EHR, Recurrent Neural Networks (RNN) are widely used as a temporal encoder to model the sequential information [23,27]. For example, [12] proposes an explainable deep learning system for healthcare, using RNN and attention mechanism to help medical staff to interpret, thus building a newcomer in deep learning systems. [18] propose a temporal deep learning model that performs bidirectional representation learning on EHR sequences for phenotype prediction, and can handle heterogeneous data, achieving excellent results in the prediction of chronic diseases. [1] introduced a semi-supervised learning method into phenotype prediction, using binary Markov process and Gaussian process for modeling, effectively using unlabeled EHR data to achieve high-precision prediction. These methods only focus on a single clinical phenotype task and cannot maintain the original performance in the face of multiple phenotype task predictions.

2.2   Multi-task Learning

Multi-task learning [5] is an approach that combines multiple tasks for training, aiming to exploit potential correlations and common features between tasks to improve performance. [16] proposed an adversarial sharing-private model, which uses an adversarial generation method to ensure that the information learned in the shared space and private space does not converge. In the field of clinical phenotype prediction, there is also a related study that introduces auxiliary tasks in the multi-task field into phenotype prediction. [7] proposed a method to randomly select auxiliary tasks between clinical phenotype tasks, which improved the prediction effect. [13] proposed an auxiliary task extraction method based on feature similarity, which is significantly better than random sampling.

3   Methodology

As is illustrated in Fig. 1, our proposed method MTL_AC is composed of two major components. The Auxiliary Task Selection, described in Sect. 3.1, is aimed at constructing the relatedness matrix according to the co-occurrence of multiple

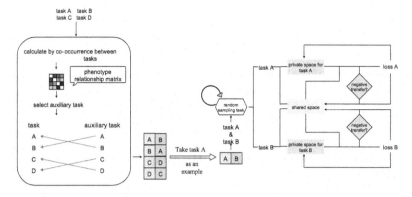

Fig. 1. MTL_AC: Taking tasks A, B, C, and D as an example, all tasks are sent to the auxiliary task selection module, each task finds the most suitable auxiliary task and then forms a task group, each group of tasks will be sent to the private-shared framework and an adaptive shared space correction mechanism is used to prevent negative transfer between tasks in task groups.

predefined phenotypes and finding the most compatible auxiliary task for each phenotype. And the Adaptive Shared-Space Correction, described in Sect. 3.2 is proposed to the re-correct bias of shared space under the private-shared multi-task framework.

3.1   Auxiliary Task Selection

Auxiliary task selection aims to find the best compatible phenotype for each phenotype. We argue that the comorbidity of phenotype plays an essential role when analyzing the patients' status, indicating the co-occurrence of phenotype may be of great help to dig out the correct phenotype with the help of the most similar phenotype task. In this section, we provide an effective way of digging out the most related phenotype task based on the intrinsic co-occurrence feature of the patients' phenotype.

Initially, we define the relationship matrix among the phenotype tasks as follows:

$$C_{ij} = \frac{\mathcal{N}(i,j)}{\mathcal{N}(i)} \tag{1}$$

where $\mathcal{N}(i,j)$ is the number of patients which suffer both of the ith and j^{th} phenotype.

In order to find the best auxiliary tasks, we need to try our best to eliminate the effects of other phenotypes. Therefore, a penalty factor is defined for each phenotype as follows:

$$P_i = \frac{\sum_j C_{ij} - 1}{N - 1} \tag{2}$$

Following Eq. 2, the penalised relationship matrix CO^p is defined as the following:

$$COMatrix_i = C_i - P_i \tag{3}$$

The final symmetrical phenotype relationship matrix reflects the degree to which tasks are suitable as auxiliary tasks. After the construction of the symmetrical phenotype relationship matrix, the auxiliary task can be selected from the relationship matrix by various distance measurements.

3.2 Private-Shared Framework with Adaptive Shared Space Correction

In this section, we first illustrate the Private-Shared Framework for phenotype prediction, and then we describe the detailed procedure of the Adaptive Shared Space Correction to reduce the bias in the shared space.

Private-Shared Framework. Given the selected auxiliary task pairs, we adopt the Private-Shared Multi-task Framework and design two layers for task-specific and task-independent feature learning.

Specifically, given the pair-wise phenotype dataset $D = \{\{D_k^i, y_k^i\}_{k=1}^{k=M}, \{D_k^j, y_k^j\}_{k=1}^{k=N}\}$, where y_k^i denotes the ground-truth label of each patient for a phenotype and $D_k^j \in R^{(T \times D)}$ is the feature matrix of kth patient for the jth phenotype with D features and T time-slots collected.

To get the representation of a patient, an encoder (e,g, LSTM, etc.) is utilized to transformer the patient's features into the embedding space, which can be obtained by:

$$x_i^k = Encoder(D_i^k; \theta) \tag{4}$$

And then, we use two different linear layers parameterized by θ^s and θ^p along with the no-linear activation functions (act) to transformer the embedding of the patient into the task-shared and task-specific space. Noted that, θ^s is shared among the tasks while θ^p is task-specific parameters. Formally, the task-specific vector $P(x_i^k)$ and the task-shared vector $S(x_i^k)$ can be computed by:

$$P(x_i^k) = f(x_i^k; \theta^p, act) \tag{5}$$

$$S(x_i^k) = f(x_i^k; \theta^s, act) \tag{6}$$

where $f(a; b, act) = act(a \cdot b)$ is the transformation function.

After that, the final patient's embedding $E(x_i^k)$ is computed by the concatenation of the two vectors, which is defined as:

$$E(x_i^k) = Concat(P(x_i^k), S(x_i^k)) \tag{7}$$

For optimization of a specific phenotype task, Binary Cross Entropy loss is adopted as the loss function.

Algorithm 1. Adaptive Shared-Space Correction

Require: Tasks: (T_i, T_j), Train data set: $x_{train} = \{x_{train}^i, x_{train}^j\}$, Validation data set:
$\quad x_{val} = \{x_{val}^i, x_{val}^j\}$, Training Parameters: $\theta = \{\theta_i \mid \theta_i = (\theta^s, \theta_i^p), i \in T\}$
Ensure: Network parameters: θ
1: **while** Not Converge **do**
2: $\quad$ Random sampling task T_i, the left task is T_j
3: $\quad$ Random sample a batch x_{batch}^i from the training set x_{train}^i of T_i
4: $\quad$ Random sample a batch x_{batch}^j from the training set x_{train}^j of T_j
5: $\quad$ Calculate the $loss_{pre}$ of T_j using θ_j and x_{batch}^j
6: $\quad$ update θ_i using x_{batch}^i
7: $\quad$ Calculate the $loss_{after}$ of T_j using θ_j and x_{batch}^j
8: $\quad$ **if** $loss_{pre} + threshold < loss_{after}$ **then**
9: $\quad\quad$ update Shared space parameters θ^s using $loss_{after}$
10: $\quad$ **end if**
11: $\quad$ **if** loss on x_{val} stop fall within limited steps **then**
12: $\quad\quad$ break;
13: $\quad$ **end if**
14: **end while**

Adaptive Shared Space Correction. As is illustrated in Sect. 3.2, the learned features can be divided into two groups, namely shared features and task-private features. However, due to the implicit separation of private and shared features when adopting the multi-task framework for phenotype prediction, the information learned in the shared space may be biased when training a task, resulting in the performance degradation of other tasks.

For any task i and j under the shared-private multi-task framework, the update process of the shared part θ^s is computed by:

$$\theta^s = \theta^s - \alpha \frac{\partial L_i(\theta^s)}{\partial \theta^s} \tag{8}$$

$$\theta^s = \theta^s - \alpha \frac{\partial L_j(\theta^s)}{\partial \theta^s} \tag{9}$$

From Eq. 8, 9, the shared parameter θ^s is updated multi-times according to the loss of the selected task while ignoring the effectiveness of other tasks, which may inject the task-specific information into the shared space. In order to separate the task-specific information during the training, we design a novel correction mechanism, namely Shared Space Correction Mechanism, to re-optimize the shared space by utilizing the information of other tasks, which is described in Algorithm 1. The aim of the Shared Space Mechanism is to ensure the correction optimization direction of the shared space. Therefore, we calculate the loss of other tasks except for the training task as an indicator to measure that the shared space is optimized in the correct direction (Algorithm 1, Line 5). If the indicator doesn't perform well on other tasks, the shared space will be re-optimized (Algorithm 1, Line 8–10).

4 Experiment

In this section, we introduce the empirical results of our MTL_AC framework on different phenotype classification tasks. And we use the area under the ROC curve (AUC) and F-score as the evaluation metrics.

4.1 Experiment Setup

Dataset. We evaluate the effectiveness of our framework on the phenotype classification tasks and report the average performance. The data set comes from a subset of the MIMIC-III database, which is open for public clinical research and covers 42276 ICU hospitalization records [11]. Following [9], a total of 17 clinical variables are selected and 25 phenotype prediction tasks are constructed. We randomly divided these data sets into training sets, validation sets, and testing sets with the proportion of 70%, 15%, and 15% respectively. We select the data within 24 h of admission for prediction.

Comparison Methods. We categorise the comparison methods as the follows:

Basic Encoder. As the data collected are sequential and multidimensional, we adopt four types of commonly-used models to capture the temporal information for clinical phenotyping.

- **LSTM:** The approach is proposed by [10], which is the standard Long-ShortLSTM [10].
- **Bi-Attention:** The approach learns the forward and backward timing information in the patient's representation vectors and predicts the patient's disease by utilizing the attention mechanism [25].
- **T-LSTM:** The approach is proposed by [2], which handles irregular time intervals in Healthcare Field by adding time decay. We modify this model into a supervised learning model.
- **SAnD:** The approach is first proposed by [22], which employs the masked, self-attention mechanism.

Phenotype Prediction Framework. We adopt three different training schemes for the phenotype prediction, which are listed as the following:

- **Baseline:** The approach formulates the phenotype prediction task as a multi-label classification problem.
- **MTNN:** A multi-task framework designed for Electronic phenotyping task [7].
- **cFSGL:** A multi-task framework designed based on accelerated gradient method (AGM) [8].

Ablation Models. In order to figure out the effectiveness of Auxiliary Task Selection and Adaptive Shared Space Correction modules, we design the ablation models as the follows:

- **SP-MTL:** The basic Shared-Private Model illustrated in Sect. 3.2.
- **MTL_AC-G:** SP-MTL with the Auxiliary Task Selection illustrated in Sect. 3.1.
- **MTL_AC-C:** SP-MTL with the Adaptive Shared Space Correction illustrated in Algorithm 1.

4.2   Experimental Settings

For the parameters in the attention mechanism in the T-LSTM model, we randomly initialize them from a uniform distribution in $(-0.1, 0.1)$. For other parameters, we adopt the default initialization strategy. And the models are trained with backpropagation using Adam optimizer. The detailed settings of hyper-parameters are shown in Table 1.

Table 1. Settings of hyper-parameters

Hyper-parameters 1	Settings
Initial learning rate	3e−4
Batch Size	32
Number of Early Stop	10
Dropout	0.5
Embedding Size of EHR data	128

4.3   Analysis of Results

Table 2. Comparison of framework MTL_AC and framework cFSGL and MTNN on basic encoders

Model	Baseline		cFSGL		MTNN		SP-MTL		MTL_AC	
	Auc	F1	Auc	F1	Auc	F1	Auc	F1	Auc	F1
LSTM	0.7054	0.5001	0.7088	0.4988	0.7081	0.4989	0.6963	0.4868	**0.7188**	**0.5166**
Bi-Attention	0.7012	0.4888	0.7029	0.4885	0.7105	0.5056	0.6981	0.4984	**0.7219**	**0.5270**
T-LSTM	0.7114	0.4978	0.7134	0.4987	0.7156	0.5049	0.7059	0.4924	**0.7264**	**0.5264**
SAnD	0.6643	0.5131	0.6796	0.5217	0.6853	0.5349	0.6681	0.5307	**0.6971**	**0.5464**

Effectiveness of the Proposed MTL_AC. Table 2 shows the prediction results of MTL_AC based on MTNN. Firstly, The predictive effect of treating phenotype as an independent task is generally better than treating phenotype as a multi-label task. There is even a situation where MTNNs prediction effect exceeds that of cFSGL. Our framework MTL_AC is based on MTNN, the accuracy has increased by 0.011 on average, and the F1 score has increased by 0.018

on average. And achieved a comprehensive and stable improvement on all models. When we use the SP-MTL model, compared with the single-task MTNN, the accuracy is reduced by 0.0128 on average, and the F1 score is reduced by 0.009 on average. It can be found that compared with the single-task, the multi-task model SP-MTL has a very serious negative transfer phenomenon.

We used T-LSTM, which achieved the best results among the four models, to show the improvement in all 25 clinical phenotype tasks, as shown in Fig. 2. The framework MTL_AC has achieved improvements in 22 phenotypes. Compared with framework cFSGL, which has only achieved improvements in 13 phenotypes, our framework has achieved very significant improvements, especially for chronic diseases. This helps to improve the difficulty of chronic disease prediction in clinical phenotype tasks.

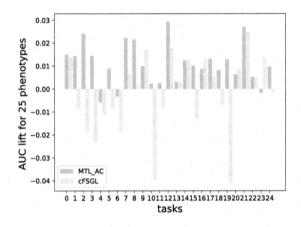

Fig. 2. Comparison of framework cFSGL and our framework MTL_AC

Table 3. Ablation of the proposed MTL_AC

Model	MTL_AC-G		MTL_AC-C	
	Auc	F1	Auc	F1
LSTM	0.7137	0.5131	0.6985	0.4855
Bi-Attention	0.7131	0.5117	0.7016	0.4993
T-LSTM	0.7224	0.5204	0.7129	0.4986
SAnD	0.6910	0.5430	0.6768	0.5275

Ablation Study. Our method is divided into finding one-to-one auxiliary tasks and a correction mechanism. We separately count the effects of each method. As shown in Table 3, after selecting auxiliary tasks (MTL_AC-G), both AUC and F1 scores are higher than MTNN. Only using Algorithm 1, Compared with SP-MTL, the accuracy is increased by 0.0535 on average, and the F1 score is increased by 0.00065 on average. The improvement effect is not as good as the one-to-one auxiliary task, and the effect is still worse than the single-task MTNN.

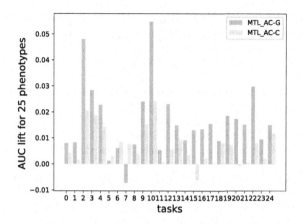

Fig. 3. Improvement of MTL_AC-G and MTL_AC-C over SP-MTL

Figure 3 shows the improvement of the two algorithms compared to the basic SP-MTL model. It can be seen that the improvement of the two algorithms for the basic multi-task model is very obvious.

5 Conclusion

In this paper, We propose the MTL_AC framework for clinical phenotypic task prediction. It exploits the co-occurrence between tasks to find the best one-to-one auxiliary phenotype task for each phenotype task, and further designs a self-correcting mechanism to prevent the negative transfer of tasks in the task-auxiliary task. Four models were tested on the MIMIC-III dataset and compared with another multi-task framework. The experimental results prove that our frameworks have produced better results. We further explore other ways of combining phenotypic tasks with other clinical tasks to gain more potential information.

Acknowledgement. This work is supported by the Fundamental Research Funds of Shandong University and partially supported by the NSFC (No. 91846205) the National Key R&D Program of China (No. 2021YFF0900800), the major Science and Technology Innovation of Shandong Province grant (No. 2021CXGC010108).

References

1. Ahuja, Y., Hong, C., Xia, Z., Cai, T.: Samgep: a novel method for prediction of phenotype event times using the electronic health record. medRxiv (2021)
2. Baytas, I.M., Xiao, C., Zhang, X., Wang, F., Jain, A.K., Zhou, J.: Patient subtyping via time-aware lstm networks. In: SIGKDD, pp. 65–74 (2017)
3. Birkhead, G.S., Klompas, M., Shah, N.R.: Uses of electronic health records for public health surveillance to advance public health. Annu. Rev. Public Health **36**, 345–359 (2015)
4. Cao, Y., et al.: Kdtnet: medical image report generation via knowledge-driven transformer. In: DASFAA, p. 117–132 (2022)
5. Caruana, R.: Multitask learning. Mach. Learn. **28**(1), 41–75 (1997)
6. Choi, E., Bahadori, M.T., Song, L., Stewart, W.F., Sun, J.: Gram: graph-based attention model for healthcare representation learning. In: SIGKDD, pp. 787–795 (2017)
7. Ding, D.Y., Simpson, C., Pfohl, S., Kale, D.C., Jung, K., Shah, N.H.: The effectiveness of multitask learning for phenotyping with electronic health records data. In: BIOCOMPUTING 2019: Proceedings of the Pacific Symposium, pp. 18–29 (2018)
8. Emrani, S., McGuirk, A., Xiao, W.: Prognosis and diagnosis of parkinson's disease using multi-task learning. In: SIGKDD, pp. 1457–1466 (2017)
9. Harutyunyan, H., Khachatrian, H., Kale, D.C., Ver Steeg, G., Galstyan, A.: Multitask learning and benchmarking with clinical time series data. Sci. Data **6**(1), 96 (2019)
10. Hochreiter, S., Schmidhuber, J.: Long short-term memory. Neural Comput. **9**(8), 1735–1780 (1997)
11. Johnson, A.E., et al.: Mimic-iii, a freely accessible critical care database. Sci. data **3**(1), 1–9 (2016)
12. Khedkar, S., Gandhi, P., Shinde, G., Subramanian, V.: Deep learning and explainable ai in healthcare using ehr. In: Deep Learning Techniques for Biomedical and Health Informatics, pp. 129–148 (2020)
13. Kung, P.N., Yin, S.S., Chen, Y.C., Yang, T.H., Chen, Y.N.: Efficient multi-task auxiliary learning: selecting auxiliary data by feature similarity. In: EMNLP, pp. 416–428 (2021)
14. Liu, N., Lu, P., Zhang, W., Wang, J.: Knowledge-aware deep dual networks for text-based mortality prediction. In: ICDE, pp. 1406–1417 (2019)
15. Liu, N., Zhang, W., Li, X., Yuan, H., Wang, J.: Coupled graph convolutional neural networks for text-oriented clinical diagnosis inference. In: DASFAA, pp. 369–385 (2020)
16. Liu, P., Qiu, X., Huang, X.: Adversarial multi-task learning for text classification. arXiv preprint arXiv:1704.05742 (2017)
17. Ma, F., Chitta, R., Zhou, J., You, Q., Sun, T., Gao, J.: Dipole: diagnosis prediction in healthcare via attention-based bidirectional recurrent neural networks. In: SIGKDD, pp. 1903–1911 (2017)
18. Meng, Y., Speier, W.F., Ong, M.K., Arnold, C.: Bidirectional representation learning from transformers using multimodal electronic health record data to predict depression. IEEE J. Biomed. Health Inform. (2021)
19. Oellrich, A., et al.: The digital revolution in phenotyping. Brief. Bioinform. **17**(5), 819–830 (2016)
20. Robinson, P.N.: Deep phenotyping for precision medicine. Hum. Mutat. **33**(5), 777–780 (2012)

21. Sadek, R.M., et al.: Parkinson's disease prediction using artificial neural network (2019)
22. Song, H., Rajan, D., Thiagarajan, J.J., Spanias, A.: Attend and diagnose: clinical time series analysis using attention models. In: AAAI (2018)
23. Wang, L., Zhang, W., He, X.: Continuous patient-centric sequence generation via sequentially coupled adversarial learning. In: DASFAA, pp. 36–52 (2019)
24. Wei, W.Q., Teixeira, P.L., Mo, H., Cronin, R.M., Warner, J.L., Denny, J.C.: Combining billing codes, clinical notes, and medications from electronic health records provides superior phenotyping performance. J. Am. Med. Inform. Assoc. 23(e1), e20–e27 (2016)
25. Yang, Y., Zheng, X., Ji, C.: Disease prediction model based on bilstm and attention mechanism. In: BIBM, pp. 1141–1148 (2019)
26. Yu, F., Cui, L., Cao, Y., Liu, N., Huang, W., Xu, Y.: Similarity-aware collaborative learning for patient outcome prediction. In: DASFAA, pp. 407–422 (2022)
27. Yu, X., Li, G., Chai, C., Tang, N.: Reinforcement learning with tree-lstm for join order selection. In: ICDE (2020)
28. Yuan, H., Li, G.: Distributed in-memory trajectory similarity search and join on road network. In: ICDE, pp. 1262–1273 (2019)
29. Yuan, H., Li, G., Bao, Z., Feng, L.: Effective travel time estimation: when historical trajectories over road networks matter. In: SIGMOD, pp. 2135–2149 (2020)
30. Yuan, H., Li, G., Bao, Z., Feng, L.: An effective joint prediction model for travel demands and traffic flows. In: ICDE (2021)

Multi-view Subspace Clustering with Joint Tensor Representation and Indicator Matrix Learning

Jing Wang[1], Xiaoqian Zhang[1,2,3], Zhigui Liu[1(✉)], Zhuang Yue[1],
and Zhengliang Huang[1]

[1] School of Information Engineering, Southwest University of Science
and Technology, Mianyang 621010, China
liuzhigui@swust.edu.cn, yuez@mails.swust.edu.cn
[2] SCII Innovation Center for Convergence and Innovation Industry Technology,
Mianyang 621010, China
[3] Tianfu Institute of Research and Innovation, Southwest University of Science
and Technology, Chengdu 610213, China

Abstract. Multi-view subspace clustering (MVSC), as an extension of single-view subspace clustering, can exploit more information and has achieved excellent performance. In particular, the MVSC methods with sparse and low-rank basing have become a research priority as they can improve the clustering effect in an effective way. However, the following problems still exist: 1) focusing only on the connections between two views, ignoring the relationship of higher-order views; 2) performing representation matrix learning and indicator matrix learning separately, unable to get the clustering result in one step and obtain the global optimal solution. To tackle these issues, a novel sparsity and low-rank based MVSC algorithm is designed. It jointly conducts tensor representation learning and indicator matrix learning. More specifically, the Tensor Nuclear Norm (TNN) is utilized to exploit the relationships among higher-order views; besides, by incorporating the subsequent spectral clustering, the indicator matrix learning is conducted during the optimization framework. An iterative algorithm, the alternating direction method of multipliers (ADMM) is derived for the solving of the proposed algorithm. Experiments over five baseline datasets prove the competitiveness and excellence of the presented method with comparisons to other eight state-of-the-art algorithms.

Keywords: Multi-view subspace clustering · Tensor nuclear norm · Spectral clustering · Higher-order correlations

---

Supported by National Natural Science Foundation of China (Grant No. 62102331, 62176125, 61772272), Natural Science Foundation of Sichuan Province (Grant No. 2022NSFSC0839), Doctoral Research Foundation of Southwest University of Science and Technology (Grant No. 22zx7110).

L. Fang et al. (Eds.): CICAI 2022, LNAI 13605, pp. 450–461, 2022.
https://doi.org/10.1007/978-3-031-20500-2_37

1   Introduction

As a typical data analysis methodology, clustering is already widely used in different fields, like artificial intelligence [1,2], biology [3], marketing [4] and so on. In general, clustering algorithms are categorized into five classes: partition-based clustering [5], hierarchical clustering [6], fuzzy clustering [7], density-based clustering [8], and model-based clustering [9,10], in which, Subspace Clustering(SC), for its validity in processing high-dimensional data, has received much public interest as a model-based clustering method. Out of different SC methods, SSC [11] and LRR [12] have made significant contributions to the growth of subspace clustering. Specifically, SSC exploits the sparse representation of data points, promoting data points represented by a linear combination of other points from the same subspace; LRR can effectively recover the subspace representation of corrupted data. Furthermore, many other variants [13,14] of SSC and LRR have also achieved superior performance. However, all these methods are intended for single-feature data and cannot handle multi-feature data.

To address above issuses, Multi-view subspace clustering methods are presented. The general MVSC methods are crudely classified as three steps. The first step is specific subspace representation learning, as with single-view subspace clustering algorithms, this step produces a coefficient matrix in each view. Two ways—self-expressiveness property [15–18] and nonnegative matrix decomposition [19] are generally adopted. The second step is multi-view correlation exploitation. After acquiring the specific representation matrices, inevitably, the shared matrix is required by merging them together. And to improve the quality of the unified representation matrix, some strategies like concatenating [20], center [21,22] and pairwise-based [17,23] regularization, and tensor singular value decomposition (t-svd) [24,25] are proposed. The last step is Spectral clustering. By inputting the shared representation matrix into the spectral clustering can obtain the final clustering results.

Although satisfactory progress has been achieved with the aforementioned methods, still there is space for enhancement. For instance, 1) Low-rank and sparsity constraints have been proved advantageous, yet few methods consider them simultaneously, and of those that do, only the relationship between two views is explored, ignoring higher-order associations. 2) Most MVSC algorithms treat the shared representation matrix as an optimization objective, which means the indicator matrix obtained from spectral clustering is not involved in the optimization process, resulting in the inability to obtain a globally optimal solution. To tackle these two problems, a new MVSC algorithm with joint tensor representation and indicator matrix learning (MVSCTI) is proposed. To illustrate our contributions more clearly, we list them as follows.

- Unlike available MVSC methods based on low-rank sparse representations that only consider the pair-wise connections of views, t-svd based TNN learning is conducted to dig the higher-order connections of multiple views.
- MVSCTI jointly pursues tensor representation and indicator matrix, which can get the indicator matrix in one step and obtain the global optimal solution.

- The effectiveness of the proposed algorithm is demonstrated by comparing it with eight advanced algorithms on five datasets.

The rest of this paper is structured as follows. The second section shows the work most relevant to this paper; The third section describes the construction of MVSCTI; For the fourth section, the superiority of MVSCTI is verified by the experimental comparison of several comparative algorithms on different datasets; The fifth section concludes the work of this paper.

2   Related Works

This section lists the related works that is most relevant to this paper.

2.1   Spectral Clustering

Spectral clustering is used extensively for the ability to deal with complex structural data and does not require any assumptions about the shape of the data. It suggests using the adjacency matrix's eigenvectors to determine the classification. The general procedure is first to generate an affinity matrix and input it into the following model to obtain the indicator matrix.

$$\min_{\mathbf{F}} Tr(\mathbf{F}^T \mathbf{L} \mathbf{F}) \quad s.t. \quad \mathbf{F}^T \mathbf{F} = \mathbf{I} \tag{1}$$

where $\mathbf{L} = \mathbf{D} - \mathbf{W}$, $\mathbf{F}$ is the indicator matrix. Each row of $\mathbf{F}$ is considered as a point, and these points are divided into groups to which they belong, employing existing algorithms such as k-means.

2.2   Multi-view Subspace Clustering

To take best benefit of multiple views information for clustering, many MVSC methods were proposed, and their general form could be elaborated as Eq. (2).

$$\min_{\mathbf{Z}^{(v)}} \sum_{v=1}^{V} \Psi\left(\mathbf{Z}^{(v)}\right) \quad s.t. \quad \mathbf{X}^{(v)} = \mathbf{X}^{(v)} \mathbf{Z}^{(v)}, \quad diag\left(\mathbf{Z}^{(v)}\right) = 0 \quad (v = 1, 2, 3...V)$$
$$\tag{2}$$

where $\mathbf{X}^{(v)}$ represents the feature matrix of the v-th view, $\Psi\left(\mathbf{Z}^{(v)}\right)$ represents the regularization term to induce the desired performance of the coefficient matrix $\mathbf{Z}^{(v)}$.

3   Model Proposal and Optimization

In this section, a MVSC method with joint tensor representation and indicator matrix learning (MVSCTI) is designed. The flowchart of MVSCTI is shown in Fig. 1.

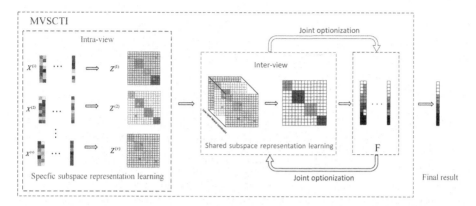

Fig. 1. Input multiple original data matrices $\mathbf{X}^{(v)}$. Then, specific subspace learning is performed using self-expressiveness property and l_1 norm constraints to obtain multiple coefficient matrices $Z^{(v)}$. Further, stack these matrices as tensor and apply low-rank constraints from lateral; after that, integrate them to a shared subspace representation matrix. Next, input it into the spectral clustering algorithm for the indicator matrix F, which is also the final optimization objective of our model. Eventually, the k-means algorithm is adopted for achieving the final results.

3.1 The Proposed Model

In consideration of the efficiency of sparse representation, a MVSC framework based on sparse representation is first proposed, as shown in Eq. (3).

$$
\min_{\mathbf{A}^{(v)}} \underbrace{\sum_{v=1}^{n_v} \frac{1}{2}\left\|\mathbf{X}^{(v)} - \mathbf{X}^{(v)}\mathbf{A}^{(v)}\right\|_F + \alpha \left\|\mathbf{A}^{(v)}\right\|_{\text{sparsity}}}_{\text{intra-views}} + \underbrace{\sum_{v \neq w, v \geqslant 1, w \leqslant n_v} corre(\mathbf{A}^{(v)}, \mathbf{A}^{(w)})}_{\text{inter-views}}
$$

$$
s.t. \ diag\left(\mathbf{A}^{(v)}\right) = 0
$$

$$(3)$$

where sparsity represents sparsity constraint and *corre* is abbreviations for correlation, which represents inter-view correlation. The formulation is divided into two terms, the first term—intra-views performs specific subspace learning within each view and the other term mines the inter-view connections. For sparsity constraints, there are many different choices, the most efficient of which is the schatten-p norm, which represents the number of non-zero elements, but it is non-convex, so we choose its convex approximate l_1 norm here, and use the TNN to dig the higher-order connections of multiple views, and the formula is shown in Eq. (4).

$$\min_{\mathbf{A}^{(v)}} \underbrace{\sum_{v=1}^{n_v} \frac{1}{2}\left\|\mathbf{X}^{(v)} - \mathbf{X}^{(v)}\mathbf{A}^{(v)}\right\|_F + \alpha_2 \left\|\mathbf{A}^{(v)}\right\|_1}_{\text{intra-views}} + \underbrace{\sum_{v \neq w, v \geqslant 1, w \leqslant n_v} \alpha_1 \|\mathcal{A}\|_\circledast}_{\text{inter - views}} \quad (4)$$

$$s.t. \ diag\left(\mathbf{A}^{(v)}\right) = 0$$

where $\|\mathcal{A}\|_\circledast$ is t-svd based TNN [24]. The above formula takes $\mathbf{A}^{(v)}$ as the final optimization objective, then, the shared similarity matrix $\mathbf{A}$ is obtained using $\sum_{v=1}^{n_v} \frac{\mathbf{A}^{(v)T} + \mathbf{A}^{(v)}}{2n_v}$, after which it is input into the spectral clustering algorithm for the indicator matrix, which is a two-step method, and the final results are not incorporated into our optimization model, implying that what is obtained in this way is not a globally optimal solution. So we further integrate the spectral clustering $Tr(\mathbf{F}^T\mathbf{L}\mathbf{F})$ into our model, and the final model is as shown in Eq. (5).

$$\min_{\mathbf{A}^{(v)}, \mathbf{F}} \sum_{v=1}^{n_v} \overbrace{(\underbrace{\frac{1}{2}\left\|\mathbf{X}^{(v)} - \mathbf{X}^{(v)}\mathbf{A}^{(v)}\right\|_F}_{\text{Self-expressiveness}} + \underbrace{\alpha_2\left\|\mathbf{A}^{(v)}\right\|_1}_{\text{Sparsity constrain}})}^{\text{Specific subspace representation learning}} + \overbrace{(\underbrace{\alpha_1\|\mathcal{A}\|_\circledast}_{\text{Low-rank tensor constrain}} + \underbrace{\lambda \operatorname{Tr}\left(\mathbf{F}^T\mathbf{L}\mathbf{F}\right)}_{\text{Spectral clustering}})}^{\text{Shared subspace representation learning}}$$

$$s.t. \ \operatorname{diag}\left(\mathbf{A}^{(v)}\right) = \mathbf{0}, \quad \mathbf{F}^T\mathbf{F} = \mathbf{I}$$

$$(5)$$

where $\mathbf{L} = \mathbf{D} - \mathbf{W}$, $\mathcal{A} = \Phi\left(\mathbf{A}^{(1)}, \cdots, \mathbf{A}^{(n_v)}\right)$, $\mathbf{W} = \sum_{v=1}^{n_v} \frac{\mathbf{A}^{(v)T} + \mathbf{A}^{(v)}}{2n_v}$, $\mathbf{F}^T\mathbf{F} = \mathbf{I}$ is set to prevent a trivial solution, $\mathbf{D} = diag\left(\sum_j [\mathbf{W}]_{1j}, \sum_j [\mathbf{W}]_{2j}, \cdots, \sum_j [\mathbf{W}]_{nj}\right)$.

This formulation is a model end-to-end, with which the global optimal solution can be obtained. The proposed model can be optimized with an efficient algorithm Alternating Direction Method of Multipliers (ADMM), and the specific optimization process and the complexity analysis is provided in the Appendix.

4   Experiment and Analysis

This section verifies the validity and superiority of MVSCTI through comparative experiments. Furthermore, the factors of excellence of the model are analyzed by conducting ablation study, parameter sensitivity and convergence analysis experiments.

4.1   Experiment Setting

Datasets. Experiments are conducted on five datasets covering different types and domains of data, such as articles, images, and biology. More details are as follows.

- **BBCsports** [26]: This dataset contains 554 articles owned by the BBC, containing five topics and two views.
- **NUS** [21]: This dataset is from NUS-WIDE. It includes 12 categories of images and 6 views, of which we have selected 2400 images.
- **Prokaryotic** [27]: This dataset contains 551 prokaryotic species with four classes and three views (textual, the proteome composition, and the gene repertoire).
- **WebKB** [22]: This dataset includes 203 web-pages with 4 categories and three views.
- **Reuters** [28]: The archive contains 1200 documents over the six labels. It comprises five views on the same documents.

Table 1 enumerates the general information of the datasets.

Table 1. Details of the five datasets.

Datasets	Views	Dimensionality	Instances	Classes
BBCsports	2	3183/3203	554	5
NUS	6	64/144/73/128/255/500	2400	12
Prokaryotic	3	438/3/393	551	4
WebKB	3	1703/230/230	203	4
Reuters	5	2000/2000/2000/2000/2000	1200	6

Baselines and Metrics. We compare the algorithm in this paper with eight advanced algorithms, which includes GBS-KO [22], SMVSC [21], LTMSC [29], Co-reg [30], DIMSC [31], FPMVS-CAG [32], CoMSC [28] and MLRSSC [27]. Three commonly used evaluation metrics are adopted for our experiment, i.e., Accuracy (ACC), Normalized Mutual Information (NMI), and Adjusted Rand Index (ARI). All comparison algorithms codes were downloaded from the URL provided by the authors. We choose the parameters provided in the original article that correspond to the optimal performance. To present a stable experimental result, we execute 20 times for every method, take the average result and its standard deviation is calculated. All experiments were run on the identical device with an Intel(R) Core(TM) i5-7400 3.00 GHz CPU.

4.2 Experimental Results and Analysis

Based on the results of the comparison experiments displayed in Table 2 as well as in Fig. 2, where - indicate that the algorithm is not applicable to the corresponding dataset. We present the following observations:

- Compared to all contrast algorithms, our method is optimal all the time, e.g., TIMVSC outperforms the second best algorithm MLRSSC by 14.4%, 18.4%, and 21.8% in ACC, NMI, and ARI, respectively, on the prokaryotic dataset.

In addition, on the Reuters dataset, TIMVSC outperforms the second best algorithm MLRSSC exceeds 27.6%, 38.4%, and 40.7% in ACC, NMI, and ARI, respectively. These show the superiority of TIMVSC.

- Figure 2 shows a two-dimensional visualization of the embedding representation F using the T-SNE algorithm. It can be observed that MVSCTI exhibits a clearer structure than most other algorithms.
- Compared with MLRSSC, our algorithm always outperforms it, while the most significant difference between them is the way of low-rank constraint, MLRSSC uses matrix svd decomposition, while MVSCTI employs t-svd decomposition, which illustrates that for multi-view clustering, adopting t-svd decomposition for low-rank constraint is able to effectively exploit the higher-order associations between views.

4.3   Model Discussion

We validate our model by performing ablation study, parameter sensitivity, run time and convergence experiments.

Ablation Study. One of the innovations of the proposed model is the joint low-rank tensor representation learning and indicator matrix learning. To further verify the advantages of this joint learning strategy, the following two experiments were designed, in which the first one eliminates the spectral clustering term (indicator matrix learning), and the second one eliminates the low-rank tensor constraint term. The experimental results are shown in Fig. 3, where No SC is eliminating spectral clustering term and No tensor is eliminating tensor learning term. Both experiments' results present a decrease compared to MVSCTI and the decrease is more significant after eliminating the tensor learning term, which illustrates the effectiveness of our joint learning strategies, and incorporating spectral clustering into the model not only reduces the clustering steps, but also improves the clustering effectiveness.

Parameter Sensitivity. For our proposed model, there are three parameters to be traded off: α_1, α_2, and λ, corresponding to the tensor term, the sparsity term, and the spectral clustering term, respectively. Figure 5 shows the parameter sensitivity experiments on NUS, where we did a logarithmic treatment of the parameter coordinate label values. One can see that the experiments can get a good results when selecting parameters in a certain range. Here we provide a parameter selection range. For all datasets, α_2 and λ can be chosen from a range of [0.01, 0.1, 1, 10] except the BBCsports dataset, whose α_2 can be chosen from a range of [0.01, 1000, 10000] and λ can be chosen from a range of [0.1, 100, 1000]; for Prokaryotic, α_1 can be chosen from a range of [0.01, 1, 10, 1000], and for the rest of datasets, α_1 can be chosen from a range of [1000, 10000, 100000].

Table 2. The experimental metrics of nine algorithms on five datasets.

Method	Metrics	BBCsports	NUS	Prokaryotic	WebKBs	Reuters
Co-reg	ACC	0.356(0.003)	0.008(0.008)	0.537(0.005)	0.613(0.016)	0.018(0.018)
	ARI	0.004(0.001)	0.141(0.003)	0.045(0.005)	0.295(0.011)	0.866(0.129)
	NMI	0.021(0.004)	0.127(0.002)	0.111(0.004)	0.258(0.005)	0.168(0.001)
LT-MSC	ACC	0.460(0.046)	0.241(0.010)	0.419(0.005)	0.538(0.003)	0.418(0.031)
	ARI	0.166(0.042)	0.012(0.000)	0.0281(0.000)	0.180(0.003)	0.151(0.018)
	NMI	0.221(0.027)	0.124(0.007)	0.130(0.006)	0.165(0.001)	0.212(0.011)
DIMSC	ACC	0.795(0.003)	0.127(0.003)	0.362(0.002)	–	–
	ARI	0.563(0.005)	0.006(0.000)	0.027(0.002)	–	–
	NMI	0.583(0.004)	0.023(0.001)	0.031(0.000)	–	–
MLRSSC	ACC	0.840(0.013)	0.294(0.008)	0.654(0.007)	0.698(0.007)	0.475(0.024)
	ARI	0.770(0.015)	0.091(0.003)	0.339(0.009)	0.476(0.013)	0.204(0.015)
	NMI	0.762(0.009)	0.157(0.003)	0.319(0.003)	0.451(0.116)	0.283(0.010)
S-MVSC	ACC	0.789(0.111)	0.295(0.009)	0.411(0.103)	0.700(0.255)	0.313(0.036)
	ARI	0.698(0.132)	0.097(0.005)	0.061(0.011)	0.501(0.021)	0.067(0.034)
	NMI	0.712(0.093)	0.164(0.004)	0.155(0.003)	0.463(0.011)	0.159(0.023)
GBS-KO	ACC	0.807(0.000)	0.165(0.000)	0.510(0.000)	0.744(0.000)	0.199(0.000)
	ARI	0.722(0.000)	0.012(0.000)	0.102(0.000)	0.368(0.000)	0.013(0.000)
	NMI	0.760(0.000)	0.122(0.000)	0.217(0.000)	0.378(0.000)	0.132(0.000)
FPMVS-CAG	ACC	0.423(0.000)	0.258(0.001)	0.523(0.000)	0.576(0.000)	0.443(0.000)
	ARI	0.132(0.000)	0.012(0.000)	0.135(0.000)	0.326(0.000)	0.169(0.000)
	NMI	0.151(0.000)	0.124(0.007)	0.154(0.000)	0.327(0.000)	0.212(0.000)
CoMSC	ACC	0.850(0.067)	0.206(0.006)	0.579(0.000)	0.735(0.030)	0.541(0.026)
	ARI	0.683(0.053)	0.041(0.003)	0.017(0.000)	0.517(0.040)	0.517(0.040)
	NMI	0.681(0.038)	0.086(0.002)	0.05(0.000)	0.492(0.022)	0.353(0.017)
MVSCTI	**ACC**	**0.939(0.047)**	**0.345(0.013)**	**0.798(0.010)**	**0.865(0.052)**	**0.751(0.006)**
	ARI	**0.890(0.042)**	**0.270(0.007)**	**0.558(0.009)**	**0.730(0.057)**	**0.611(0.012)**
	NMI	**0.890(0.025)**	**0.330(0.028)**	**0.504(0.008)**	**0.695(0.032)**	**0.667(0.010)**

Table 3. Run time of all MVC comparative algorithms on all datasets (in seconds).

Method	Co-reg	LT-MSC	DIMSC	MLRSSC	S-MVSC	GBS-KO	FPMVS-CA	CoMSC	MVSCTI
BBCsports	8.31	43.76	10.87	3.21	41.35	13.01	12.60	1.65	2.24
NUS	155.83	1939.20	1840.83	913.65	2.31	33.76	174.49	11.11	507.68
Prokaryotic	3.50	26.96	8.86	4.23	0.29	–	5.09	3.75	3.27
WebKBs	1.63	5.67	–	0.80	0.18	0.27	3.05	0.51	0.70
Reuter	25.37	493.25	–	96.55	359.40	98.23	32.99	7.76	67.47

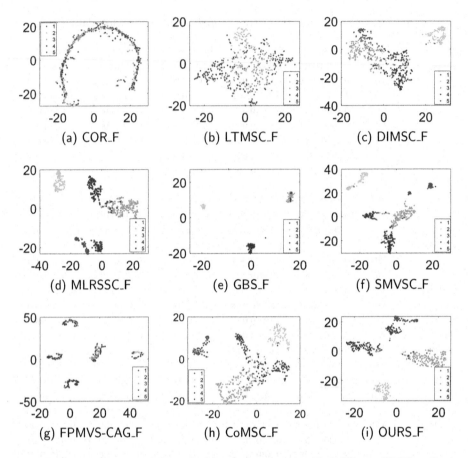

Fig. 2. The visualization of the embedding representation F of different MVC methods on BBCsports.

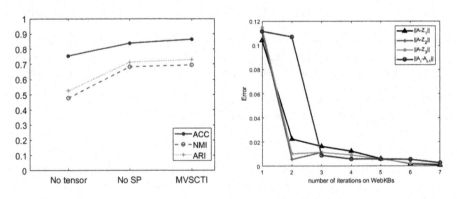

Fig. 3. Ablation study on WebKBs.   **Fig. 4.** The convergence curve on WebKBs.

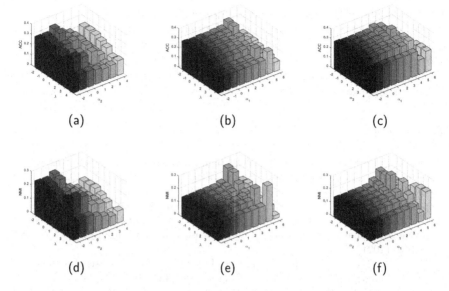

Fig. 5. Influence of parameter variation (The 1st column is about α_2 & λ with α_1 fixed as 10000; The 2nd column is about α_1 & λ with α_2 fixed as 1; The 3rd column is about α_1 & α_2 with λ fixed as 0.01) for ACC and NMI on the NUS dataset.

Run Time and Convergence. We calculated the average run time of all algorithms, and the experimental results are shown in Table 3. MVSCTI has the least run time on the BBCsports dataset in comparison with other algorithms and is in the middle on the other datasets. Furthermore, for most algorithms, it can be observed that the larger the size of the dataset, the longer the run time, except for S-MVSC, whose run time on the BBCsports dataset with a size of 554 is 41.35 s, which is the second-longest among all algorithms. Still, its run time is only 2.31 s on the NUS dataset with a size of 2400, which is much smaller than the other algorithms. This might be because it is more sensitive to data dimensionality than data size. For example, the size of NUS is twice as large as Reuter, but its dimensionality is much smaller than Reuter, which leads to its run time on Reuter (359.40 s) to be much higher than that of NUS (2.31 s). We also conduct a convergence experiment on WebKBs. As shown in Fig. 4, it can reach convergence within 7 times.

5   Conclusions

In this paper, an effective method—MVSCTI is proposed. It exploits the correlations of multiple views by low-rank tensor learning, and the global optimal solution can be gained by combining spectral clustering within the MVSC framework. In the end, we compare MVSCTI with ten advanced benchmark algorithms by experimenting on seven public datasets, and the results show the superiority of our method. Further, we validate the proposed model by conducting several general experiments. For future works, We believe the following issues remain to be explored: 1) Inter-view consistency and complementary must be exploited more effectively, which is essential for improving clustering effect; 2) Reducing the computational complexity while improving clustering performance, which is critical for large-scale data.

References

1. Cui, Z., Jing, X., Zhao, P., Zhang, W., Chen, J.: A new subspace clustering strategy for ai-based data analysis in iot system. IEEE Internet Things J. (2021)
2. He, R., et al.: A kernel-power-density-based algorithm for channel multipath components clustering. IEEE Trans. Wireless Commun. **16**(11), 7138–7151 (2017)
3. Chowdhury, H.A., Bhattacharyya, D.K., Kalita, J.K.: Uicpc: centrality-based clustering for scrna-seq data analysis without user input. Comput. Biol. Med. **137**, 104820 (2021)
4. Cheng, Y., Cheng, M., Pang, T., Liu, S.: Using clustering analysis and association rule technology in cross-marketing. Complexity **2021**, 1–11 (2021)
5. Mittal, M., Sharma, R.K., Singh, V.P., Kumar, R.: Adaptive threshold based clustering: a deterministic partitioning approach. Int. J. Inf. Syst. Modeling Des. (IJISMD) **10**(1), 42–59 (2019)
6. Murtagh, F., Contreras, P.: Algorithms for hierarchical clustering: an overview. Wiley Interdisciplinary Rev. Data Mining Knowl. Discovery **2**(1), 86–97 (2012). https://doi.org/10.1002/widm.53
7. Bagherinia, A., Minaei-Bidgoli, B., Hosseinzadeh, M., Parvin, H.: Reliability-based fuzzy clustering ensemble. Fuzzy Sets Syst. **413**, 1–28 (2021)
8. Campello, R.J., Kröger, P., Sander, J., Zimek, A.: Density-based clustering. Wiley Interdisc. Rev. Data Mining Knowl. Dis. **10**(2), e1343 (2020)
9. Bouveyron, C., Brunet-Saumard, C.: Model-based clustering of high-dimensional data: a review. Comput. Stat. Data Anal. **71**, 52–78 (2014) https://doi.org/10.1016/j.csda.2012.12.008,https://www.sciencedirect.com/science/article/pii/S0167947312004422
10. Xue, X., Zhang, X., Feng, X., Sun, H., Chen, W., Liu, Z.: Robust subspace clustering based on non-convex low-rank approximation and adaptive kernel. Inf. Sci. **513**, 190–205 (2020)
11. Elhamifar, E., Vidal, R.: Sparse subspace clustering: algorithm, theory, and applications. IEEE Trans. Pattern Anal. Mach. Intell. **35**(11), 2765–2781 (2013)
12. Liu, G., Lin, Z., Yan, S., Sun, J., Yu, Y., Ma, Y.: Robust recovery of subspace structures by low-rank representation. IEEE Trans. Pattern Anal. Mach. Intell. **35**(1), 171–184 (2012)
13. Kumar, S., Dai, Y., Li, H.: Multi-body non-rigid structure-from-motion. In: 2016 Fourth International Conference on 3D Vision (3DV), pp. 148–156. IEEE (2016)
14. Tierney, S., Gao, J., Guo, Y.: Subspace clustering for sequential data. In: Proceedings of the IEEE Conference on Computer Vision and Pattern Recognition, pp. 1019–1026 (2014)
15. Kang, Z., et al.: Partition level multiview subspace clustering. Neural Netw. **122**, 279–288 (2020)
16. Yang, Z., Xu, Q., Zhang, W., Cao, X., Huang, Q.: Split multiplicative multi-view subspace clustering. IEEE Trans. Image Process. **28**(10), 5147–5160 (2019)

17. Yu, H., Zhang, T., Lian, Y., Cai, Y.: Co-regularized multi-view subspace clustering. In: Asian Conference on Machine Learning, pp. 17–32. PMLR (2018)

18. Zhang, X., Sun, H., Liu, Z., Ren, Z., Cui, Q., Li, Y.: Robust low-rank kernel multi-view subspace clustering based on the schatten p-norm and correntropy. Inf. Sci. **477**, 430–447 (2019)

19. Tolić, D., Antulov-Fantulin, N., Kopriva, I.: A nonlinear orthogonal non-negative matrix factorization approach to subspace clustering. Pattern Recogn. **82**, 40–55 (2018)

20. Zheng, Q., Zhu, J., Li, Z., Pang, S., Wang, J., Li, Y.: Feature concatenation multi-view subspace clustering. Neurocomputing **379**, 89–102 (2020)

21. Hu, Z., Nie, F., Chang, W., Hao, S., Wang, R., Li, X.: Multi-view spectral clustering via sparse graph learning. Neurocomputing **384**, 1–10 (2020)

22. Wang, H., Yang, Y., Liu, B., Fujita, H.: A study of graph-based system for multi-view clustering. Knowl.-Based Syst. **163**, 1009–1019 (2019)

23. Tang, C., Zhu, X., Liu, X., Li, M., Wang, P., Zhang, C., Wang, L.: Learning a joint affinity graph for multiview subspace clustering. IEEE Trans. Multimed. **21**(7), 1724–1736 (2018)

24. Xie, Y., Tao, D., Zhang, W., Liu, Y., Zhang, L., Qu, Y.: On unifying multi-view self-representations for clustering by tensor multi-rank minimization. Int. J. Comput. Vision **126**(11), 1157–1179 (2018)

25. Wu, J., Lin, Z., Zha, H.: Essential tensor learning for multi-view spectral clustering. IEEE Trans. Image Process. **28**(12), 5910–5922 (2019)

26. Huang, S., Xu, Z., Lv, J.: Adaptive local structure learning for document co-clustering. Knowl.-Based Syst. **148**, 74–84 (2018)

27. Brbić, M., Kopriva, I.: Multi-view low-rank sparse subspace clustering. Pattern Recogn. **73**, 247–258 (2018)

28. Liu, J., Liu, X., Yang, Y., Guo, X., Kloft, M., He, L.: Multiview subspace clustering via co-training robust data representation. IEEE Trans. Neural Networks Learn. Syst. (2021)

29. Zhang, C., Fu, H., Liu, S., Liu, G., Cao, X.: Low-rank tensor constrained multi-view subspace clustering. In: Proceedings of the IEEE International Conference on Computer Vision, pp. 1582–1590 (2015)

30. Kumar, A., Rai, P., Daume, H.: Co-regularized multi-view spectral clustering. Adv. Neural. Inf. Process. Syst. **24**, 1413–1421 (2011)

31. Cao, X., Zhang, C., Fu, H., Liu, S., Zhang, H.: Diversity-induced multi-view subspace clustering. In: Proceedings of the IEEE Conference on Computer Vision and Pattern Recognition, pp. 586–594 (2015)

32. Wang, S., et al.: Fast parameter-free multi-view subspace clustering with consensus anchor guidance. IEEE Trans. Image Process. **31**, 556–568 (2022). https://doi.org/10.1109/TIP.2021.3131941

Weighted Competitive-Collaborative Representation Based Classifier for Imbalanced Data Classification

Yanting Li[1], Shuai Wang[1], Junwei Jin[2(✉)], and C. L. Philip Chen[3]

[1] Zhengzhou University of Light Industry, Zhengzhou, China
[2] Henan University of Technology, Zhengzhou, China
jinjunwei24@163.com
[3] South China University of Technology, Guangzhou, China
philip.chen@ieee.org

Abstract. Competitive-collaborative representation based classification (CCRC) has been widely used in pattern recognition and machine learning due to its simplicity, effectiveness, and low complexity. However, its performance is highly dependent on the data distribution. When addressing imbalanced classification issue, its classification results usually tend towards the majority classes. To solve this deficiency, a class weight learning algorithm is introduced into the framework of CCRC for imbalanced classification. The weight of each class is adaptively generated according to the representation ability of each class of training samples, in which the minority classes can be given larger weights. Our proposed model is solved with a closed-form solution and inherits the efficiency property of CCRC. Extensive experimental results show that our model outperforms the commonly used imbalanced classification methods.

Keywords: Competitive-collaborative representation · Imbalanced classification · Adaptive weight

1 Introduction

Imbalanced classification has become an important research direction in pattern recognition due to the prevalence of imbalanced datasets in the real world. Traditional classifiers generally achieve good classification results on balanced datasets but cannot work well on imbalanced datasets [14,15,18,19]. Imbalanced class distribution makes traditional classifiers more inclined to the majority classes, which results in poor overall classification accuracy [8]. In practice, the minority classes usually contain more important and valuable information than the majority classes. Once they are misjudged, there may be serious consequences. For

Supported by the National Natural Science Foundation of China under Grant 62106233 and 62106068, by the Science and Technology Research Project of Henan Province under Grant 222102210058, 222102210027, and 222102210219, and by the Grant KFJJ2020104, 2019BS032, 2020BSJJ027, and 202210463023, 202210463024.

example, judging an intrusion as a normal behavior may cause a major network security incident; misdiagnosing a cancer patient as a normal person will delay the best treatment time and threaten the patient's life. Therefore, it is necessary and urgent to improve the classification accuracy of the minority classes.

At present, there are two main aspects to improve the imbalanced classification methods [4,12]. One is from the data-level, and the other is from the algorithm-level. The former is mainly to improve the classification performance by balancing the class distribution [1,11,13]. Random under-sampling (RUS) and random oversampling (ROS) [3,9] are two commonly used sampling techniques. RUS randomly reduces the majority samples to the same number size as the minority samples, but it may lose potential information. To overcome this defect, EasyEnsemble [20,24] introduced data cleaning scheme to improve RUS. It randomly selects several subsets from the samples of the majority classes and combines them with the data of the minority classes to train and generate multiple base classifiers, which improves the learning performance. ROS is to copy the randomly selected minority class samples and add the generated selection set to the minority classes to obtain new minority class instances. Nevertheless, it may lead to overfitting. To address the overfitting problem, the authors in [6] proposed a synthetic minority over-sampling technique (SMOTE) by using interpolation theory. Afterwards, many variants of SMOTE such as adaptive synthetic sampling (ADASYN) [10], majority weighted minority oversampling technique (MWMOTE) [1], SMOTEENN [2] were provided to obtain more effective minority class instances. However, both oversampling and undersampling would destroy the relationship between the original data so that the final recognition accuracy cannot be significantly improved.

The algorithm-level is to improve the classification accuracy by enhancing the traditional classification approaches [5,23,25]. The core idea of this type is to give different weights to samples of different classes to improve the classification performance of the minority classes. Among them, the spare supervised representation-based classifier (SSRC) [21] shows excellent advantages. It introduces label information and class weights into SRC to improve the classification accuracy. But the extremely high computational complexity limits its further development and application. Inspired by this, in this paper we choose the efficient and effective CCRC [26] as the base model for imbalanced classification. We incorporate a class weight learning algorithm into CCRC according to the representation ability of each class of training samples. The algorithm adaptively obtains the weight of each class and can assign greater weights to the minority classes, so that the final classification results are more fair to the minority classes. The proposed model can be solved efficiently with a closed-form solution. Experimental results on authoritative public imbalanced datasets show that our method outperforms other commonly used imbalanced classification algorithms.

The remainder of this paper is organized as follows. Section 2 briefly introduces the related work. The proposed imbalanced classification method is described in Sect. 3. Experimental results are shown in Sect. 4. Finally, Sect. 5 draws the conclusion.

2   Related Work

This section introduces the nearest subspace classification (NSC) [19], collaborative representation based classification (CRC) [22], and CCRC [26] algorithms that are closely related to our method. First, the symbols used in the paper are given. $D = [D_1, ...D_n, ...D_N]$ represents the entire training sample set, where $D_n \in \mathbb{R}^{d \times M_n}$ represents the training sample set of class n. M_n is the number of samples in D_n, and d is the feature dimension of each sample. $M = M_1 + M_2 + ...M_N$ represents the number of all training samples. $x \in \mathbb{R}^d$ represents a test sample. $c = [c_1; ...c_n; ...c_N]$ is the coefficient vector of x over D, $c^* = [c_1^*; ...c_n^*; ...c_N^*]$ is the optimal coefficient vector of x over D. c_n is the coefficient vector of x over D_n, c_n^* is the optimal vector of x over D_n. I is the identity matrix. γ and α represent the regularization parameters. β_n represents the weight of class n.

2.1   NSC

NSC calculates the distance between the test sample x and each class of the training set and classifies x into the class of its nearest subspace. The specific model is as follows

$$c_n^* = \arg\min_{c_n} \|x - D_n c_n\|_2^2. \tag{1}$$

It has a closed-form solution

$$c_n^* = (D_n^T D_n)^{-1} D_n^T x. \tag{2}$$

According to the minimum reconstruction error criterion, the label of x is predicted as

$$\text{label}(x) = \arg\min_{n} \|x - D_n c_n^*\|_2. \tag{3}$$

2.2   CRC

NSC uses each class of training samples to represent the test samples individually. However, CRC takes all the training samples as a whole to collaboratively represent the test samples. Given a test sample x, CRC solves the minimum problem by introducing ℓ_2-norm regularization

$$c^* = \arg\min_{c} \|x - Dc\|_2^2 + \gamma \|c\|_2^2. \tag{4}$$

The above equation also has a closed-form solution

$$c^* = (D^T D + \gamma I)^{-1} D^T x. \tag{5}$$

With the optimal coefficient vector, the classification result of x is obtained

$$\text{label}(x) = \arg\min_{n} \|x - D_n c_n^*\|_2. \tag{6}$$

2.3 CCRC

CCRC introduces a competition mechanism into the CRC model, and its model is expressed as follows

$$c^* = \arg\min_c \|x - Dc\|_2^2 + \gamma\|c\|_2^2 + \alpha \sum_{n=1}^{N} \|x - D_n c_n\|_2^2, \qquad (7)$$

where $\sum_{n=1}^{N} \|x - D_n c_n\|_2^2$ reflects the competitiveness of each class. α is the regularization parameter that balances competitiveness and collaborativeness. The model can also be solved analytically

$$c^* = (1 + \alpha)(D^T D + \gamma I + \alpha G)^{-1} D^T x, \qquad (8)$$

where G is defined as

$$G = \begin{bmatrix} D_1^T D_1 & \cdots & 0 \\ \vdots & \ddots & \vdots \\ 0 & \cdots & D_n^T D_n \end{bmatrix}. \qquad (9)$$

After obtaining the optimal coefficient vector c^*, CCRC classifies the test samples x according to the same classification criterion as CRC. Here, we will not repeat it.

3 Proposed Method

This section describes the weighted competitive-collaborative representation based classifier (WCCRC) model in detail. First, a class weight learning method is introduced into the CCRC model to give different weights to different classes. Next, the proposed model is solved with a closed-form solution. Finally, the classification criterion is given.

3.1 WCCRC Model

CCRC introduces a competition mechanism between each class of samples. Assuming that the true label of a given test sample x is k, CCRC desires the intra-class loss $\|x - D_n c_n\|_2^2$ to be as small as possible and the inter-class loss $\{\|x - D_n c_n\|_2^2\}_{n=1,n\neq k}^{N}$ to be as large as possible. Since the actual label is unknown, the model minimizes the sum of all losses $\sum_{n=1}^{N} \|x - D_n c_n\|_2^2$. However, it does not consider class distribution information. When handling imbalanced classification tasks, CCRC generally makes the representation ability of the majority classes far more than the minority classes, resulting in the final classification results leaning towards the majority classes. Especially for severely imbalanced datasets, the minority classes usually have an extremely low representation for test samples. This will make their reconstruction error larger than the majority classes, which is not conducive to the final classification. In this section, we assign different weights to different classes in CCRC based on NSC. Our objective function is expressed as

$$c^* = \arg\min_c \|x - Dc\|_2^2 + \gamma\|c\|_2^2 + \alpha \sum_{n=1}^{N} \beta_n \|x - D_n c_n\|_2^2. \tag{10}$$

It is called weighted competitive-collaborative representation based classifier (WCCRC) model.

3.2   Class Weight Learning Based on NSC

We use the reconstruction error of each class in the NSC model to learn each class weight. According to Sect. 2.1, the optimal coefficient vector of x over D_n is

$$c_n^* = (D_n^T D_n)^{-1} D_n^T x. \tag{11}$$

The reconstruction error of this class to x is

$$r_n = \|x - D_n c_n^*\|_2. \tag{12}$$

We define the maximum reconstruction error as

$$r_{max} = \max\{r_n\}. \tag{13}$$

Obviously, the larger the r_n, the weaker the representation ability of D_n to x. The less likely it is that x belongs to the nth class. On the basis of this fact, the weight of the nth class is defined as

$$\beta_n = \exp(\frac{r_n - r_{max}}{\delta}), \tag{14}$$

where the scaling parameter $\delta > 0$ is to control the class weight. Taking binary-classification as an example, we can show this method can indeed give greater weights to the minority classes. Assuming that the first class is the minority class, it has a weak representation of the test sample. The reconstruction error $r_1 > r_2$, then $r_{max} = r_1$. Thus, $\beta_1 = \exp(\frac{r_1 - r_1}{\delta}) = 1$ and $\beta_2 = \exp(\frac{r_2 - r_1}{\delta}) < 1$. We get that the NSC-based class weight learning algorithm can give the minority classes greater weights for binary-classification. For multi-classification, its weighting analysis is more complicated than binary-classification. We will use experimental results in Sect. 4 to show the effectiveness of this class weight update mechanism. Algorithm 1 describes the specific steps of class weight learning.

3.3   Optimization Solution and Classification Criterion

To solve the minimization problem (10) in the WCCRC model, we first give a new matrix $\tilde{D}_n = [0, \ldots, 0, D_n, 0, \ldots, 0]$ which keeps the columns of the nth class in D and sets the other columns to zero. The theorem below can guarantee WCCRC has a closed-form solution.

Theorem 1. *Given each class weight β_n, the WCCRC model is solved as*

$$c^* = (D^T D + \alpha \sum_{n=1}^{N} \beta_n \tilde{D}_n^T \tilde{D}_n + \gamma I)^{-1} (D + \alpha \sum_{n=1}^{N} \beta_n \tilde{D}_n)^T x. \tag{15}$$

Proof. For ease of computation, the objective function in problem (10) can be written as

$$\vartheta = \|x - Dc\|_2^2 + \gamma \|c\|_2^2 + \alpha \sum_{n=1}^{N} \beta_n \|x - \tilde{D}_n c\|_2^2. \tag{16}$$

Then take the derivation of ϑ with respect to c to be zero

$$\frac{\partial \vartheta}{\partial c} = -2D^T(x - Dc) + 2\gamma c + \alpha \sum_{n=1}^{N} \beta_n [-2\tilde{D}_n^T(x - \tilde{D}_n c)]$$

$$= 0.$$

So the closed-form solution c^* can be easily obtained as

$$c^* = (D^T D + \alpha \sum_{n=1}^{N} \beta_n \tilde{D}_n^T \tilde{D}_n + \gamma I)^{-1} (D + \alpha \sum_{n=1}^{N} \beta_n \tilde{D}_n)^T x. \tag{17}$$

Thus, the proof is completed.

After obtaining the optimal coefficient vector c^*, we calculate the reconstruction error of each class

$$r_n(x) = \|x - D_n c_n^*\|_2, n = 1, 2..., N. \tag{18}$$

The minimum reconstruction error criterion determines the label of x as

$$\text{label}(x) = \arg \min_n r_n(x). \tag{19}$$

The WCCRC classification method is described in Algorithm 2

Algorithm 1. Class weight learning algorithm

Input: Training samples $D = [D_1, ...D_n, ...D_N]$, query sample x, scaling parameter δ.
    1. **for** $i = 1 : N$
    2. Calculate c_n^* by Equation (11);
    3. Calculate the residual for each class $r_n(x) = \|x - D_n c_n^*\|_2$;
    4. **end for**
    5. Find the largest residual $r_{max} = \max\{r_n\}$.
    6. Calculate the weight of each class β_n by Equation (14).
Output: All class weights $\beta_1, ...\beta_n, ...\beta_N$.

Algorithm 2. WCCRC algorithm

Input: Training set $D = [D_1, ...D_n, ...D_N]$, query sample x, regularization parameters α and γ, scaling parameter δ.
1. Normalize each column of D and x to have unit ℓ_2-norm.
2. Calculate class weights $\beta_1, ...\beta_n, ...\beta_N$ through Algorithm 1.
3. Calculate the optimal coefficient vector c^* by Equation (15).
4. Calculate the reconstruction error of each class $r_n(x)$ by Equation (18).
5. Obtain label(x) by Equation (19).
Output: label(x).

Table 1. Details of seven imbalanced datasets.

Datasets	Classes	Number	Dimension	Class distribution	IR
Wine	3	178	13	59 : 71 : 48	1.48
Newthyroid1	2	215	5	180 : 35	5.14
Newthyroid	3	215	5	150 : 35 : 30	5.00
Ecoli	8	336	7	143 : 77 : 2 : 2 : 35 : 20 : 5 : 52	71.51
Dermatology	6	366	333	111 : 60 : 71 : 48 : 48 : 20	5.55
Penbased	10	1100	16	115 : 114 : 114 : 106 : 114 : 106 : 105 : 115 : 105 : 106	1.10
Shuttle0	2	1829	9	1706 : 123	13.78

4   Experimental Results

In this section, several imbalanced datasets from UCI repository [16] are used to verify the effectiveness of the proposed method.

4.1   Datasets and Experimental Setup

During the experiments, we use two binary-class and five multi-class imbalanced datasets to test the performance of our method. The detailed feature information for these datasets is described in Table 1. The class distribution shows the number of samples of each class, and the imbalance rate (IR) indicates the ratio of the number of samples of the most majority classes to the number of samples of the least minority class. As seen from Table 1, the imbalance rates of the used datasets have a large range from 1.10 to 71.51. The higher the imbalance rate, the greater the difficulty of accurate classification.

Since the commonly used metrics in balanced classification cannot effectively evaluate imbalanced classification algorithms, we use $F - measure$ and $G - mean$ to measure imbalanced classification performance [7]. Whether binary-classification or multi-classification, the larger the $F - measure$ and $G - mean$, the better the classification performance. In the experiments, we use the five-fold cross-validation method [17]. Each dataset is randomly divided into five subsets. One subset is selected as the test set, and the remaining four are used as the training set. This method is randomly performed ten times on each dataset, and

Table 2. Comparison of F-measure (%) between WCCRC and other imbalanced classification methods on seven datasets.

Datasets	ADASYN	SMOTEENN	WELM	RUS	SMOTE	MWMOTE	EasyEnsemble	WCCRC
Wine	74.11	70.63	94.51	73.15	73.41	74.53	88.62	**100.00**
Newthyroid1	96.65	98.23	97.44	96.82	95.07	94.42	94.33	**100.00**
Newthyroid	90.53	90.42	89.91	87.23	91.74	92.43	89.14	**94.06**
Ecoli	**62.31**	46.54	38.92	36.74	60.05	60.22	33.86	50.07
Dermatology	87.32	81.43	87.25	76.13	86.34	89.73	74.14	**93.98**
Penbased	91.83	95.52	95.36	91.51	94.34	93.15	87.92	**96.35**
Shuttle0	88.42	84.62	97.41	80.43	82.72	81.32	89.41	**97.87**

Table 3. Comparison of G-mean (%) between WCCRC and other imbalanced classification methods on seven datasets.

Datasets	ADASYN	SMOTEENN	WELM	RUS	SMOTE	MWMOTE	EasyEnsemble	WCCRC
Wine	79.01	77.12	88.63	79.05	79.03	79.82	89.51	**100.00**
Newthyroid1	97.52	97.93	97.05	94.52	95.46	92.17	94.34	**100.00**
Newthyroid	92.55	92.61	90.44	93.26	91.72	92.81	93.22	**97.92**
Ecoli	29.91	38.92	30.14	35.32	33.90	34.82	27.14	**53.10**
Dermatology	92.81	89.91	91.33	92.37	92.24	92.11	78.72	**96.52**
Penbased	95.63	97.52	97.85	97.31	**98.40**	95.82	90.52	97.92
Shuttle0	87.61	97.21	97.41	97.65	84.81	85.20	92.41	**97.89**

the average is taken as the final experimental result. In specific experiments, the parameters involved in each comparison model are carefully adjusted to achieve optimal experimental results. For the proposed WCCRC, there are three parameters α, γ, δ that are important for the performance evaluation of the model. We set the candidate sets of α, γ as $\{10^{-5}, 10^{-4}, 10^{-3}, 10^{-2}, 10^{-1}\}$ and the candidate set of δ as $\{1, 2, ..., 10^1, 10^2, 10^3, 10^4, 10^5\}$. These three parameters are tuned by a grid search algorithm to obtain the optimal experimental results.

Table 4. The average classification rate (%) of all methods on seven datasets.

Methods	ADASYN	SMOTEENN	WELM	RUS	SMOTE	MWMOTE	EasyEnsemble	WCCRC
Average rate	83.30	82.76	85.26	80.82	82.80	82.75	80.23	**91.12**

4.2   Comparison with Imbalanced Classification Methods

In this section, we compare WCCRC with the commonly used imbalanced classification methods including RUS [20], ADASYN [10], SMOTE [6], MWMOTE [1], WELM [27], SMOTEENN [2], and EasyEnsemble [20]. Tables 2 and 3 show the comparison results of WCCRC and the competing algorithms in terms of $F-measure$ and $G-mean$, respectively. The best experimental results are shown in bold. It can be seen that WCCRC shows the best recognition performance on five out of seven datasets. For the severely imbalanced dataset Ecoli, although WCCRC's $F - measure$ is slightly lower than other methods, its $G - mean$ far exceeds the second best. Particularly, the accuracy of WCCRC on Wine and Newthyroid1 can reach 100%.

To comprehensively evaluate the classification performance of our method, we calculate the average classification rate of each method on all imbalanced datasets. The comparison results are reported in Table 4. We can find that two undersampling methods RUS and EasyEnsemble are relatively low. Four oversampling algorithms including SMOTE, WMMOTE, ADASYN, and SMO-TEENN have a little improvement and obtain comparable classification performance. WELM performs better than the above sampling approaches. Obviously, WCCRC outperforms all compared methods with a high average recognition rate of 91.12%. In summary, our method has great advantages in handling imbalanced classification issue.

5   Conclusion

This paper proposes a weighted competitive-collaborative representation based classifier for imbalanced classification. It solves the problem that CCRC cannot work well on imbalanced datasets. The key idea is to introduce an adaptive class weight learning scheme into the framework of CCRC. It gives greater weights to the minority classes so that the classification results are more fair to the minority classes. The proposed model is efficiently solved with a closed-form solution. Extensive experimental results on several imbalanced datasets verify the effectiveness of the proposed method. In the future, we will consider more efficient and effective weight learning approaches.

References

1. Barua, S., Islam, M.M., Yao, X., Murase, K.: MWMOTE-majority weighted minority oversampling technique for imbalanced data set learning. IEEE Trans. Knowl. Data Eng. **26**(2), 405–425 (2013)
2. Batista, G.E., Prati, R.C., Monard, M.C.: A study of the behavior of several methods for balancing machine learning training data. ACM SIGKDD Explor. Newsl. **6**(1), 20–29 (2004)
3. Cao, P., Liu, X., Zhang, J., Zhao, D., Huang, M., Zaiane, O.: l(2,1) norm regularized multi-kernel based joint nonlinear feature selection and over-sampling for imbalanced data classification. Neurocomputing **234**, 38–57 (2017)
4. Cao, P., Zhao, D., Zaiane, O.: An optimized cost-sensitive svm for imbalanced data learning. In: Pei, J., Tseng, V.S., Cao, L., Motoda, H., Xu, G. (eds.) PAKDD 2013. LNCS (LNAI), vol. 7819, pp. 280–292. Springer, Heidelberg (2013). https://doi.org/10.1007/978-3-642-37456-2_24
5. Castro, C.L., Braga, A.P.: Novel cost-sensitive approach to improve the multilayer perceptron performance on imbalanced data. IEEE Trans. Neural Netw. Learn. Syst. **24**(6), 888–899 (2013)

6. Chawla, N.V., Bowyer, K.W., Hall, L.O., Kegelmeyer, W.P.: SMOTE: synthetic minority over-sampling technique (2011)
7. Guo, H., Liu, H., Wu, C., Zhi, W., Xiao, Y., She, W.: Logistic discrimination based on G-mean and F-measure for imbalanced problem. J. Intell. Fuzzy Syst. **31**, 1155–1166 (2016)
8. He, H., Garcia, E.A.: Learning from imbalanced data (2008)
9. He, H., Garcia, E.A.: Learning from imbalanced data. IEEE Trans. Knowl. Data Eng. **21**(9), 1263–1284 (2009)
10. He, H., Yang, B., Garcia, E.A., Li, S.: ADASYN: adaptive synthetic sampling approach for imbalanced learning. In: IEEE International Joint Conference on IEEE World Congress on Computational Intelligence Neural Networks, IJCNN 2008 (2008)
11. Hernandez, J., Carrasco-Ochoa, J.A., Trinidad, J.F.M.: An empirical study of over-sampling and undersampling for instance selection methods on imbalance datasets. In: CIARP (1) (2013)
12. Huang, C., Li, Y., Loy, C.C., Tang, X.: Learning deep representation for imbalanced classification. In: 2016 IEEE Conference on Computer Vision and Pattern Recognition, CVPR 2016, Las Vegas, NV, USA, 27–30 June 2016, pp. 5375–5384. IEEE Computer Society (2016). https://doi.org/10.1109/CVPR.2016.580
13. Han, H., Wang, W.-Y., Mao, B.-H.: Borderline-SMOTE: a new over-sampling method in imbalanced data sets learning. In: Huang, D.-S., Zhang, X.-P., Huang, G.-B. (eds.) ICIC 2005. LNCS, vol. 3644, pp. 878–887. Springer, Heidelberg (2005). https://doi.org/10.1007/11538059_91
14. Jin, J., Li, Y., Chen, C.: Pattern classification with corrupted labeling via robust broad learning system. IEEE Trans. Knowl. Data Eng. **34**(10), 4959–4971 (2021)
15. Jin, J., Li, Y., Yang, T., Zhao, L., Duan, J., Chen, C.P.: Discriminative group-sparsity constrained broad learning system for visual recognition. Inf. Sci. **576**, 800–818 (2021)
16. Khan, M., Arif, R.B., Siddique, M., Oishe, M.R.: Study and observation of the variation of accuracies of KNN, SVM, LMNN, ENN algorithms on eleven different datasets from UCI machine learning repository (2018)
17. Kohavi, R.: A study of cross-validation and bootstrap for accuracy estimation and model selection. In: International Joint Conference on Artificial Intelligence (1995)
18. Li, Y., Zhang, L., Qian, T.: 2D partial unwinding-a novel non-linear phase decomposition of images. IEEE Trans. Image Process. **28**(10), 4762–4773 (2019)
19. Li, Y., Jin, J., Zhao, L., Wu, H., Sun, L., Chen, C.L.P.: A neighborhood prior constrained collaborative representation for classification. Int. J. Wavel. Multiresolut. Inf. Process. **19**, 2050073 (2020)
20. Liu, X., Wu, J., Zhou, Z., Member, S.: Exploratory undersampling for class-imbalance learning. IEEE Trans. Syst. Man Cybern. Part B **39**, 539–550 (2008)
21. Shu, T., Zhang, B., Tang, Y.Y.: Sparse supervised representation-based classifier for uncontrolled and imbalanced classification. IEEE Trans. Neural Netw. Learn. Syst. **31**, 2847–2856 (2018)
22. Wang, H., Wang, X., Chen, C., Cheng, Y.: Hyperspectral image classification based on domain adaptation broad learning. IEEE J. Sel. Top. Appl. Earth Observ. Remote Sens. **13**(99), 3006–3018 (2020)
23. Cheng, F., Zhang, J., Wen, C., Liu, Z., Li, Z.: Large cost-sensitive margin distribution machine for imbalanced data classification. Neurocomputing **224**, 45–57 (2017)

24. Yang, P., Yoo, P.D., Fernando, J., Zhou, B.B., Zhang, Z., Zomaya, A.Y.: Sample subset optimization techniques for imbalanced and ensemble learning problems in bioinformatics applications. IEEE Trans. Cybern. **44**(3), 445–455 (2013)

25. Yang, X., Kuang, Q., Zhang, W., Zhang, G.: AMDO: an over-sampling technique for multi-class imbalanced problems. IEEE Trans. Knowl. Data Eng. **30**(9), 1672–1685 (2017)

26. Yuan, H., Li, X., Xu, F., Wang, Y., Lai, L.L., Tang, Y.Y.: A collaborative-competitive representation based classifier model. Neurocomputing **275**, 627–635 (2018)

27. Zong, W., Huang, G.B., Chen, Y.: Weighted extreme learning machine for imbalance learning **101**, 229–242 (2013). https://doi.org/10.1016/j.neucom.2012.08.010

Hierarchical Graph Representation Learning with Structural Attention for Graph Classification

Bin Yu[1], Xinhang Xu[1], Chao Wen[2], Yu Xie[2], and Chen Zhang[1(✉)]

[1] School of Computer Science and Technology, Xidian University, Xi'an, China
`zhangc@xidian.edu.cn`
[2] School of Computer and Information Technology, Shanxi University,
Taiyuan, China

Abstract. Recently, graph neural networks (GNNs) exhibit strong expressive power in modeling graph structured data and have been shown to work effectively for graph classification tasks. However, existing GNN models for predicting graph categories frequently neglect the graph hierarchy information or fail to accurately capture the graph substructure, resulting in significant performance decreases. In this paper, we propose Hierarchical Graph Representation Learning (HGRL), a multi-level framework for capturing hierarchical local and global topological structures to enrich graph representations. In specific, we utilize a structural coarsening module that generates a series of coarsened graphs for an input graph instance, followed by a graph encoder to preserve the local graph structure information. Furthermore, graph convolutional networks are layered to capture high dimensional proximity in graphs, and we incorporate the attention mechanism for entire graph embedding, which enables our framework to focus on critical nodes with significant contribution to the learned low-dimensional graph representations for subsequent graph classification tasks. Experimental results on multiple benchmark datasets demonstrate that the proposed HGRL can substantially improve the classification accuracy and outperform the existing state-of-the-art graph classification approaches.

Keywords: Graph representation · Graph coarsening · Graph classification · Attention mechanism

1 Introduction

In recent years, graph networks have gained popularity for their ability to accurately represent complex interactions between composite objects, making them useful in realistic networks such as knowledge networks [1], social networks [2], and protein interaction networks [3], etc. In reality, learning high-quality representations for graphs can contribute to a variety of graph analysis tasks, including graph classification, node classification, and link prediction, among others. Graph classification, in particular, is one of the key tasks of graph analysis that

L. Fang et al. (Eds.): CICAI 2022, LNAI 13605, pp. 473–484, 2022.
https://doi.org/10.1007/978-3-031-20500-2_39

aims to predict the labels or categories of unlabeled graphs. Each node in a network is typically described as a one-hot vector, while the network is represented as a high-dimensional and sparse adjacency matrix, which is inefficient for large-scale network mining and analysis. Furthermore, the complexity of graph data makes successful graph classification difficult.

To address the above challenges, an important task is to design graph representation learning methods that can effectively characterize graph structural information. For example, DDGK [4] extends the kernel approach to graph structure data and encodes similarity mappings between graphs through unsupervised learning. In addition, Graph U-Nets [5] proposes graph pooling and unpooling operations to extend the encoder-decoder model for graph representation learning. Inspired by the success of deep neural networks [6], researchers sought to explore GNNs to address these challenges. By continually aggregating and propagating information about the nodes in the graph, GNN gathers the basic information for constructing individual node embeddings. The node embedding representations contain structural information from distant nodes, and then end-to-end training is used to obtain discriminative graph representations for classification tasks.

However, most existing works roughly exploit the global pooling to generate graph representations while ignoring the low-order topology and hierarchical characteristics of the graph structure. Therefore, a number of hierarchical representation learning methods [7–9] have recently been proposed to learn hierarchical representations in different graph networks, instead of directly concatenating features of adjacent layers.

In addition, as the number of graph convolutional layers increases, the learned node features are inclined to over-smoothing [10], which is detrimental to achieving high-quality graph classification. The self-attention mechanism [11] allows the deep learning models to focus on the key information for a specific task while avoiding noise in the rest part, which could capture the internal relevance of data or features better. Motivated by these, we propose a novel hierarchical graph representation learning framework with structural attention for graph classification. Our framework takes into consideration the rich hierarchical topological structure information and utilizes a self-attention mechanism to assign learnable weights to different levels of node representations to ultimately obtain a discriminative graph representation. The details of the method will be discussed in Sect. 3.2.

The main contributions of this paper are summarized as follows:

1. We propose a novel multi-level coarsening-based graph representation learning framework with structural attention for graph classification, named HGRL.
2. In order to extract hierarchical information of graphs, we generate a series of coarsened graphs at different scales and utilize graph encoder and stacked GCNs to characterize the hierarchical local and global graph structure.
3. The performance of our proposed framework is comprehensively evaluated on seven benchmark datasets. Extensive experimental results illustrate that in

most cases, it achieves superior performance over the state-of-the-art baseline methods on graph classification tasks.

2   Related Work

2.1   Graph Classification

The goal of graph classification is to predict the categories of graphs by analyzing the structure of graphs and the properties of nodes, which is widely used in bioinformatics, cheminformatics, traffic flow prediction, social network analysis, etc. Data-driven deep learning and graph-level representation learning [12–15] are competitive solutions to graph classification problems. Two major components of graph neural networks for graph classification are the graph convolution operator and the pooling operator. In particular, the graph convolution operator uses the topology of the graph and node property information to extract the node-level representation of the graph, while the pooling operator aggregates the node-level representation to obtain the whole graph-level representation for downstream analysis tasks. In this paper, our approach extracts structural information of graphs at multiple scales to improve the expressiveness of the learned graph-level representations for graph classification.

2.2   Graph Coarsening

As large-scale graphs become increasingly ubiquitous in various applications, they pose significant computational challenges to process, extract and analyze information. Graph coarsening methods aim to reduce the size and complexity of graphs, and allow the model to capture the information at different granularity of a graph. Numerous methodologies have been developed for graph coarsening, such as [16,17]. In this paper, we attempt to capture the hierarchical topological information of graphs, which is crucial for learning the desired deep graph representations for graph classification. Dhillon et al. [18] proposed a fast greedy clustering algorithm to coarsen graphs. During coarsening, the method first matches neighboring vertices in the (hyper) graph, and then merges the matched pairs of vertices into a single vertex to produce a coarser version of the (hyper) graph. In this paper, we utilize this method to coarsen each input graph instance and capture the hierarchical topological information of graphs.

2.3   Attention Mechanism

In the field of graph data mining, the attention mechanism [19] aims to assign different weights to different nodes in the neighborhood set of the target node, and thus to selectively process the most relevant parts of the variable input to the task. Graph Attention Network (GAT) [20] and related models [10,21–23] introduce the attention mechanism into graph neural networks, which computes attention scores between connected nodes and allows the model to process messages from the neighbors according to their attention scores. Furthermore, the attention mechanism makes the output results interpretable [24] because it reasonably balances the importance of each input component to the output results. The attention mechanism also alleviates the demand of the model on computational resources due to its smaller model complexity and fewer parameters.

3   Methodology

In this section, we provide a detailed illustration of our proposed hierarchical graph representation learning framework for graph classification.

3.1   Problem Definition and Notations

Let $G = (V, E)$ be a formal definition of a graph example for graph classification, where V is a node set with the number of nodes $|V| = N$, and E represents the edge set of G. The input feature matrix of nodes in graph G is denoted as X, and Y_G is the label of G. In addition, $A = [a_{ij}] \subseteq \mathbb{R}^{N \times N}$ denotes the adjacency matrix of G and each element $a_{ij} > 0$ of A indicates that there is an edge between nodes i and j. The purpose of graph classification is to predict the categories of graphs by analyzing available information such as graph structure information and node property features.

3.2   Framework

The basic idea of our framework is to design a creative graph representation learning method that can implement the graph classification task by extracting the hierarchical structure of each given graph instance.

Figure 1 gives the graphical illustration of our proposed hierarchical graph representation learning framework, which is composed of four components: graph coarsening, graph encoder, global graph representation and graph classification. For briefly, we first use the fast greedy clustering [18] to capture the sparse or dense structure of each coarsened graph, and obtain a sequence of increasingly coarser approximations of the original graph. Then, we design the graph encoder to map the Laplacian matrix to the latent space and merge the corresponding node attributes into the Laplacian features. Therefore, the learned low-dimensional representation after graph encoder is a characterization of both graph structure and node attributes. Although each graph example may own different feature dimensions, the graph encoder can standardize the features. Additionally, we stack graph convolutional networks to preserve the high-order neighboring structure and utilize the self-attention mechanism to discriminately aggregate different node representations to yield the entire graph representation, and a fully connected network is followed for graph classification. Overall, the entire framework allows for end-to-end training to capture graph structure at different granularity and provides greater interpretability than previous works.

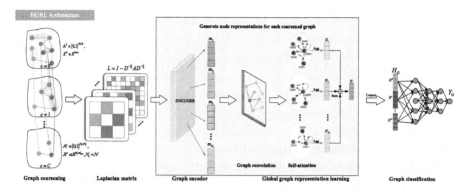

Fig. 1. The architecture of our proposed HGRL framework. The graph coarsening module generates a series of coarse-grained graphs for graph instance G and each coarsened graph is represented as a Laplacian matrix L to preserve the multi-scale topological information of G. Then, graph encoders followed by graph convolution layers are used to learn hierarchical node representations. And self-attention is applied to dynamically learn the weights of different neighboring nodes and yield all the node representations in each coarsened graph. Finally, the entire graph representation H_G generated by concating the original and C coarsened graph representations is fed to a graph classifier to predict the label Y_G.

3.3   Graph Encoder

To encode the local topological structure in each graph, we design the graph encoder, which is a deep architecture consisting of multiple nonlinear mapping functions. We use the Laplacian matrix L as input of graph encoder and map the explicit graph topology into the low-dimensional latent representation space. The Laplace matrix describes the effect of the perturbations at the nodes on the others in the graph structure, which is commonly used for graph Fourier transformation and graph convolution. In our framework, hierarchical coarsening graphs are respectively represented as Laplacian matrices of different sizes, as input to each graph encoder, denoted as

$$L^{'} = I - D^{-\frac{1}{2}}AD^{-\frac{1}{2}} \qquad (1)$$

$$L^{'}_{i,j} := \begin{cases} 1 & \text{if } i = j \text{ and } D[i] \neq 0 \\ \dfrac{-1}{\sqrt{D[i] * D[j]}} & \text{if } i \neq j \text{ and } v_i \text{ is adjacent to } v_j \\ 0 & \text{otherwise} \end{cases} \qquad (2)$$

where $L^{'} \in \mathbb{R}^{N*N}$ is the normalized Laplacian matrix based on the Laplacian matrix $L = D - A$ which preserves the graph topology in practice. D is the degree matrix, and A is the adjacency matrix of the graph with diagonal elements of 0 and $a_{ij} \in \{0, 1\}$. The normalized Laplacian matrix with element $L^{'}_{i,j}$ can preserve the graph structure and self-loop property information, as well as providing normalized input data for the graph encoder. In order to preserve structural information of graphs throughout graph coarsening completely, we utilize a matrix $\tau^{c,c+1} = [\tau_{ij}] \in \mathbb{R}^{N_c \times N_{c+1}}$ to associate the two graphs before and after coarsening, where $\tau_{ij} = 1$ indicates node v_i will be merged with node v_j at the c-th coarsen step. L' and X^{c+1} will be updated by:

$$L'^{c,c+1} = I - D^{-\frac{1}{2}}\tau^{c,c+1^T}A^c\tau^{c,c+1}D^{-\frac{1}{2}} \tag{3}$$

$$X^{c,c+1} = \tau'^{c,c+1^T}X^c \tag{4}$$

where $\tau'^{c,c+1^T}$ is columnly normalized from $\tau^{c,c+1}$, $(c = 1, ..., C)$.

In order to extract deep nonlinear latent features in the original and coarsened graphs, the number of layers in the graph encoder network is set to K. Each layer consists of a linear transformation and a nonlinear activation function. m_i^k ($k = 1, ..., K$) denotes the embedding representation of node i at k-th layer of the graph encoder, which captures the information of node i and its neighboring nodes. Given the i-th row L_i' of the normalized Laplacian matrix as the input s_i of the graph encoder, the hidden representation of node i in the k-th hidden layer is calculated as:

$$m_i^k = \sigma(W^{(k)}m_i^{(k-1)} + b^{(k)}) \tag{5}$$

where we set $m_i^0 = s_i = L_i'$ as input. $(W^{(k)}, b^{(k)})$ are the parameters in the k-th layer ($k = 1, ..., K$) of the graph encoder network, where $W^{(k)}$ is the weight matrix and $b^{(k)}$ is the bias vector. Additionally, $\sigma(\cdot)$ is an activation function such as the sigmoid function. The output $\widetilde{s}_i$ is the reconstruction result of the graph encoder with input s_i, where $\widetilde{s}_i$ is expected to remain a similar distribution consistent to s_i. Now that the normalized Laplacian matrix is transformed from the adjacency matrix of the graph that explicitly characterizes the local first-order proximities, we aim to minimize the first-order proximity loss to ensure that the original domain follows the similar distribution to the reconstruction domain, and use a standard back propagation to learn local graph representations in the middle layer by optimizing the reconstruction error.

Explicitly, optimizing the loss of graph encoder on different scales of coarsening graphs can benefit capturing the first-order topology structure and the attribute features of graphs. Through progressively training the graph encoder network, we can extract the embedding representation containing rich local information for nodes in each graph instance and its coarsened graphs.

3.4   Global Graph Representation Learning

In our framework, graph coarsening generates a series of concise versions for every graph instance while preserving the original graph structure. And the graph encoder is designed to construct a low-dimensional fixed-length embedding representations for every node, which contains the nodes' property feature and local topology information. To further preserve the global distinguishing information from the graph, graph convolutional networks are stacked to characterize the high-order neighboring structure after graph encoder, and GCNs can integrate the long-distance nodes through message propagation and neighborhood aggregation to yield a better node representation. Specifically, we adopt a multi-layer graph convolutional network with the following layered propagation rules:

$$H^{l+1} = \sigma \left(L' H^{(l)} W^{(l)} \right) \tag{6}$$

where L' with self-loops is computed by Eq. 1. $H^{(l)}$ is the output feature matrix in the l-th hidden layer ($l < \ell$) with $H^{(0)} = \left[m_i^K \right]_{i=1}^{N}$ where $[\cdot]$ represents columnly concat operator. $W^{(l)}$ is the weight matrix to be trained and $\sigma(\cdot)$ denotes a non-linear activation function, such as $ReLU(\cdot)$. To capture the distributional similarity among nearest neighbors, the self-attention mechanism is used to learn attention weights from node representations at different scales with the aim of integrating contextual information into the node representation and produce a dynamically weighted graph representation. Besides, we assign each neighboring node a weight, i.e., the inverse of degree of node i, which represents the calibrated contribution in feature aggregation. By this way, it further enhances the interpretability of attention based aggregation results and also alleviates over-smoothing to some extent caused by simply stacking deep graph convolution networks. Equation 7 describes how to yield the entire graph representation for a graph instance:

$$H_G = \left\| \prod_{c=0}^{C} \sum_{i=1}^{|V_{G^c}|} (H_i^\ell + \frac{1}{D[i]} (\sum_{j \in ner(i)} \alpha_{i,j} W H_j^\ell)) \tag{7}$$

where $\|$ represents the concatenation operation, C defines the times of graph coarsening and i represents each node in the original graph instance or its coarsened graphs. $ner(i)$ denotes the neighboring node set of node i and itself, H_j^ℓ represents the feature representation of node j obtained from the final layer of graph convolutional networks, and W represents a global learnable weight matrix. Moreover, $\alpha_{i,j}$ indicates the associated attention weight of node j to node i, which is calculated based on their latent representations:

$$\alpha_{i,j} = \frac{exp(LeakyReLU(a^T(W H_i^\ell \| W H_j^\ell)))}{\sum_{n \in ner(i)} exp(LeakyReLU(a^T(W H_i^\ell \| W H_n^\ell)))} \tag{8}$$

where W is a trainable matrix that is used to transform the latent representation of node i or j to a fixed-length vector, and a^T is a trainable vector to transform the corresponding concat vectors to values. Then, these values could be activated by $LeakyReLU$ and used to calculate the attention weights.

To achieve the graph classification task, we use a graph classifier with a fully connected layer and a Softmax layer to output an estimate of the prediction result for each graph instance, and obtain the graph label Y_G. The pseudocode of our whole HGRL framework is illustrated in Algorithm 1. All the network parameters in the proposed framework are optimized by back propagation on the cross-entropy graph classification loss coupled with $\mathcal{L}_{enc}$ until convergence.

4   Experiment

4.1   Dataset and Experimental Seetings

To probe the superiority of our framework, we validate our framework on the following datasets for graph classification, including MUTAG [25], PTC [26], D&D [27], NCI [28], PROTEINS [29] and ENZYMES [29]. For baselines, we compare the proposed method with state-of-the-art graph kernel methods (*e.g.*, LDP [30], SP [31], GK [32], WL [33]) and graph neural network methods (*e.g.*, PSCN [34], DGCNN [35], GCAPS-CNN [36]) on the graph classification task.

Algorithm 1. HGRL framework

Input:

    A graph example G

Output:

    The label Y_G of G

1: Initialize all variables

2: $G_{coarsen} = G \cup coarsen(G)$ ▷ $G_{coarsen}$ stores graph G and its coarsened graphs

3: **for** G^c in $G_{coarsen}$ **do**

4:     Calculate the normalized Laplace matrix L'_{G^c} of graph G^c

5:     Utilize graph encoder to generate the fixed-length local representation m_i^K for each node i in G^c

6:     Calculate the global representation H_i^ℓ for each node i in G^c according to Eq. 6

7: **end for**

8: Calculate the entire graph representation H_G according to Eq. 7

9: $Y_G = SoftMax(MLP(H_G))$

10: Optimize all the network parameters until convergence

11: **return** Y_G

To guarantee a fair comparison, the hyper-parameters for baselines are tuned to be optimal and we adopt a dense layer with Softmax activations to make prediction. The times of graph coarsening C is set to 3 for all datasets. The number of hidden layers in graph encoder and graph convolutional networks are settled to 3. In addition, the proposed model is optimized by the Adam algorithm and we set the learning rate as 0.001. To compare the average performance of baseline methods on the graph classification task, we perform 10-fold cross-validation, where 9-fold dataset is exploited for training and the remaining graph examples are used as the validation set. Meanwhile, we repeat the experiment 10 times on each benchmark dataset and record the average accuracy of 10-fold validation.

4.2   Experimental Results and Discussion

Graph classification is one of the most important applications in graph analysis, which attempts to predict the categories of unlabeled graphs. In order to conduct experiments, we train the proposed method and baselines on the benchmark

Table 1. Comparison of the validation average classification accuracy for nine methods on different benchmark datasets.

Algorithms	Datasets						
	MUTAG	PTC	PROTEINS	NCI1	NCI109	D&D	ENZYMES
PSCN	84.53	57.31	75.00	76.34	–	76.20	–
DGCNN	84.17	56.32	75.54	74.44	75.03	79.37	51.00
GCAPS-CNN	–	60.22	76.40	82.72	81.12	77.62	61.83
LDP	**90.10**	61.70	72.10	73.00	74.23	75.5	35.30
SP	83.32	59.21	75.07	73.00	74.34	>1 Day	40.10
GK	79.23	58.67	71.67	62.28	62.60	78.45	26.61
WL	77.30	57.48	74.68	82.19	82.46	79.78	52.22
Ours	89.13	**63.59**	**78.71**	**85.01**	**85.13**	**83.30**	**62.04**

datasets with 10-fold cross-validation. Meanwhile, we independently run each method 10 times and report the average prediction accuracy in Table 1.

From the results shown in Table 1, we can observe that the proposed method outperforms all baselines on most benchmark datasets except for MUTAG, which indicates that it can effectively capture the hierarchical topological information and generate more discriminative entire graph representations. More specifically, we observe that our method has a significant gain against the state-of-the-art graph kernel methods in graph classification on most datasets. It may be for the reason that our proposed model adopts the end-to-end supervised learning framework, which avoids separating feature extraction from classifier training and allows our method to fully use label information to promote graph representation learning. Our HGRL yields about at least 4% improvement over PSCN and DGCNN, through characterizing graph topological information in an explainable manner instead of imposing an order on nodes for entire graph embedding. When compared with GCAPS-CNN that learns high-level graph capsules of each graph, our HGRL achieves continuously higher classification accuracy in that we explicitly preserve the local features and hierarchical topological information in graphs. All the empirical evidence demonstrates that our framework can extract the hierarchical local and global information of the graph to obtain effective graph embedding representations.

4.3 Sensitivity of the Number of Coarsening Times

The important hyper-parameter C of our HGRL framework is investigated in this section. Specifically, we investigate how different coarsening times can affect the performance of graph classification. Then we report the average classification accuracy on NCI1, NCI109 and D&D since the results of different datasets show similar tends. From Fig. 2, we can observe that the performance of our proposed method improves with the increase of coarsening times. The main reason behind this may be that our proposed coarsening method can concentrate on the

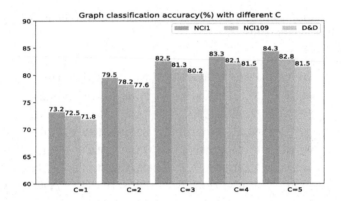

Fig. 2. Graph classification accuracy with different coarsening times C.

hierarchical topological structure, and avoid the loss of network structural information through adaptively capturing significant hierarchical topology of graphs. On the other hand, it shows that the learned graph embedding representations by our proposed graph representation learning framework can characterize more comprehensive features of the entire graph, which can effectively improve the performance of graph classification. However, with the coarsening times continuously increases, the performance tends to be stable. This may be due to the fact that most of the useful hierarchical and global information of graphs has been encoded into graph representations. It further verifies that our framework is able to extract the structural patterns of graph more effectively.

5   Conclusion

In this paper, we develop a novel graph representation learning framework for graph classification, which is capable of capturing the hierarchical global and local information of graphs. Specifically, in order to preserve the hierarchical structure of graphs, we use a coarsening module and incorporate graph encoder, graph convolutional networks and the attention mechanism to generate entire graph representations from node representations, which enforces our framework to concentrate more effectively on the crucial parts of the given graph. The effectiveness of our framework is validated on graph classification with seven benchmark datasets. Extensive experimental results demonstrate the proposed framework can outperform the state-of-the-art graph kernels and GNN based methods. In the future, we plan to extend our framework to dynamic graph classification and capture the evolution pattern of temporal-varied networks.

References

1. Zhang, Z., Li, Z., Liu, H., Xiong, N.N.: Multi-scale dynamic convolutional network for knowledge graph embedding. IEEE Trans. Knowl. Data Eng. **34**(5), 2335–2347 (2022)

2. Cai, T., Li, J., Mian, A.S., Sellis, T., Yu, J.X., et al.: Target-aware holistic influence maximization in spatial social networks. IEEE Trans. Knowl. Data Eng. **34**(4), 1993–2007 (2022)

3. Cong, Q., Anishchenko, I., Ovchinnikov, S., Baker, D.: Protein interaction networks revealed by proteome coevolution. Science **365**(6449), 185–189 (2019)

4. Al-Rfou, R., Perozzi, B., Zelle, D.: DDGK: learning graph representations for deep divergence graph kernels. In: The World Wide Web Conference, pp. 37–48 (2019)

5. Gao, H., Ji, S.: Graph U-Nets. In: International Conference on Machine Learning, pp. 2083–2092. PMLR (2019)

6. Gilmer, J., Schoenholz, S.S., Riley, P.F., Vinyals, O., Dahl, G.E.: Neural message passing for quantum chemistry. In: Proceedings of International Conference on Machine Learning, pp. 1263–1272. PMLR (2017)

7. Bianchi, F.M., Grattarola, D., Livi, L., Alippi, C.: Hierarchical representation learning in graph neural networks with node decimation pooling. IEEE Trans. Neural Netw. Learn. Syst. **33**, 2195–2207 (2020)

8. Hu, F., Zhu, Y., Wu, S., Wang, L., Tan, T.: Hierarchical graph convolutional networks for semi-supervised node classification. arXiv preprint arXiv:1902.06667 (2019)

9. Huang, J., Li, Z., Li, N., Liu, S., Li, G.: AttPool: towards hierarchical feature representation in graph convolutional networks via attention mechanism. In: Proceedings of the IEEE/CVF International Conference on Computer Vision, pp. 6480–6489 (2019)

10. Li, Q., Han, Z., Wu, X.-M.: Deeper insights into graph convolutional networks for semi-supervised learning. In: Proceedings 32nd AAAI Conference on Artificial Intelligence (2018)

11. Mnih, V., Heess, N., Graves, A., et al.: Recurrent models of visual attention. In: Advances in Neural Information Processing Systems 27 (2014)

12. Ying, Z., You, J., Morris, C., Ren, X., Hamilton, W., Leskovec, J.: Hierarchical graph representation learning with differentiable pooling. In: Advances in Neural Information Processing Systems (2018)

13. Lee, J., Lee, I., Kang, J.: Self-attention graph pooling. In: Proceedings of International Conference on Machine Learning, pp. 3734–3743. PMLR (2019)

14. Ma, Y., Wang, S., Aggarwal, C.C., Tang, J.: Graph convolutional networks with eigenpooling. In: Proceedings of the 25th ACM SIGKDD International Conference on Knowledge Discovery and Data Mining, pp. 723–731 (2019)

15. Ahmadi, A.H.K.: Memory-based graph networks. Ph.D. thesis, University of Toronto, Canada (2020)

16. Chen, H., Perozzi, B., Hu, Y., Skiena, S.: HARP: hierarchical representation learning for networks. In: Proceedings of the AAAI Conference on Artificial Intelligence, vol. 32 (2018)

17. Safro, I., Sanders, P., Schulz, C.: Advanced coarsening schemes for graph partitioning. ACM J. Exp. Algorithmics **19**, 1–24 (2015)

18. Dhillon, I.S., Guan, Y., Kulis, B.: Weighted graph cuts without eigenvectors a multilevel approach. IEEE Trans. Pattern Anal. Mach. Intell. **29**(11), 1944–1957 (2007)

19. Vaswani, A., et al.: Attention is all you need. In: Advances in Neural Information Processing Systems, vol. 30 (2017)

20. Veličković, P., Cucurull, G., Casanova, A., Romero, A., Lio, P., Bengio, Y.: Graph attention networks. In: Proceedings of International Conference on Learning Representations (2018)

21. Wang, G. Ying, R., Huang, J., Leskovec, J.: Improving graph attention networks with large margin-based constraints. In: Advances in Neural Information Processing Systems (2019)
22. Liu, Z., et al.: GeniePath: graph neural networks with adaptive receptive paths. In: Proceedings of the AAAI Conference on Artificial Intelligence, vol. 33, pp. 4424–4431 (2019)
23. Oono, K., Suzuki, T.: Graph neural networks exponentially lose expressive power for node classification. In: Proceedings of International Conference on Learning Representations (2020)
24. Bastings, J., Filippova, K.: The elephant in the interpretability room: why use attention as explanation when we have saliency methods? In: Proceedings of the 4th BlackboxNLP Workshop, EMNLP (2021)
25. Yajun, Yu., Pan, Z., Guyu, H., Ren, H.: Graph classification based on sparse graph feature selection and extreme learning machine. Neurocomputing **261**, 20–27 (2017)
26. Pan, S., Jia, W., Zhu, X., Long, G., Zhang, C.: Task sensitive feature exploration and learning for multitask graph classification. IEEE Trans. Cybern. **47**(3), 744–758 (2016)
27. Dobson, P.D., Doig, A.J.: Distinguishing enzyme structures from non-enzymes without alignments. J. Mol. Biol. **330**(4), 771–783 (2003)
28. Pan, S., Jia, W., Zhu, X.: CogBoost: boosting for fast cost-sensitive graph classification. IEEE Trans. Knowl. Data Eng. **27**(11), 2933–2946 (2015)
29. Schomburg, I., Chang, A., Ebeling, C., Gremse, M., Heldt, C., Huhn, G., Schomburg, D.: Brenda, the enzyme database: updates and major new developments. Nucleic Acids Res. **32**, 431–433 (2004)
30. Cai, C., Wang, Y.: A simple yet effective baseline for non-attributed graph classification. arXiv preprint arXiv:1811.03508 (2018)
31. Borgwardt, K.M., Kriegel, H.-P.: Shortest-path kernels on graphs. In: Proceedings of the 5th IEEE International Conference on Data Mining, pp. 74–81. IEEE (2005)
32. Shervashidze, N., Vishwanathan, S.V.N., Petri, T., Mehlhorn, K., Borgwardt, K.: Efficient graphlet kernels for large graph comparison. In: Artificial Intelligence Statistics, pp. 488–495. PMLR (2009)
33. Shervashidze, N., Schweitzer, P., Van Leeuwen, E.J., Mehlhorn, K., Borgwardt, K.M.: Weisfeiler-Lehman graph kernels. J. Mach. Learn. Res. **12**(9), 2539–2561 (2011)
34. Niepert, M., Ahmed, M., Kutzkov, K.: Learning convolutional neural networks for graphs. In: Proceedings of International Conference on Machine Learning, pp. 2014–2023. PMLR (2016)
35. Zhang, M., Cui, Z., Neumann, M., Chen, Y.: An end-to-end deep learning architecture for graph classification. In: Proceedings of the 32nd AAAI Conference on Artificial Intelligence (2018)
36. Verma, S., Zhang, Z.-L.: Graph capsule convolutional neural networks. In: Joint ICML and IJCAI Workshop on Computational Biology (2018)

Photovoltaic Hot Spots Detection Based on Kernel Entropy Component Analysis and Information Gain

Shangjun Jiang[ID] and Hui Yi[(✉)][ID]

College of Electrical Engineering and Control Science, Nanjing Tech University,
Nanjing 211816, China
shangjun@njtech.edu.cn, jsyihui@126.com

Abstract. The photovoltaic power generation is affected by many non-linear variables so, it is very difficult to detect the faults. In order to detect such faults very easily and effectively, a photovoltaic hot spot detection method based on kernel entropy component analysis (KECA) and information gain is proposed in this paper. The method first uses the kernel entropy component analysis to extract the information characteristic data of the sample, then uses the normal sample and the information gain to determine the detection threshold, and finally calculates the detection variable of the faulty sample and compares it with the detection threshold to determine whether any hot spots fault exist. Experiments show that this method can make full use of the inherent information in the data, and exhibits a good hot spot detection effect.

Keywords: KECA · Information gain · Hot spots · Fault detection

1 Introduction

The unprecedented advances in science and technology have been decreasing the cost of photovoltaic power generation over the years thereby, substantially increasing the power generation systems in the country. However, the safety of the photovoltaic power generation systems is one of the major obstacles in the deployment of photovoltaic power plants. Hot spot is one of the common faults in the photovoltaic power generation system which is mainly caused by the shadow shading [1–3], affecting not only the efficiency of the photovoltaic power generation, but even result in fire and endangers the personal safety in severe cases [4,5].

At present, the main hot spots detection methods are infrared image recognition method and electrical parameter recognition method. Traditionally, infrared image detection methods are implemented manually, but many scholars have worked on the automatic detection of hot spots based on the infrared images. For example, Henry C. proposes an automatic detection method of photovoltaic drone based modules to collect images to detect the faults by using

L. Fang et al. (Eds.): CICAI 2022, LNAI 13605, pp. 485–495, 2022.
https://doi.org/10.1007/978-3-031-20500-2_40

image processing algorithms [6]. Zhang Yiming recommends an automatic detection method based on the photovoltaic automatic detection system of walking robot [7]. Where, a robot is used to collect the infrared images of the photovoltaic modules, and the grayscale information of the images is used to complete the detection of the photovoltaic hot spots. Similarly, many researchers have also studied the photovoltaic hot spots detection based on the electrical parameters. Lazzaretti A. E. advises a fault detection method based on the artificial neural network (ANN), which uses electrical and environmental parameters to realize the identification and classification of the photovoltaic hot spots [8]. Basnet B. proposes a fault detection method based on probabilistic neural network, which uses historical data to train the model, and predicts and classifies new data [2]. Appiah A. Y. suggests an automatic feature extraction method based on long short-term memory network for photovoltaic array fault detection to solve the problem of manual feature extraction with high accuracy under noisy conditions [9].

The hot spots detection method based on the infrared image processing is too expensive for small photovoltaic power generation systems while the hot spots detection method based on electrical parameter has high computational complexity. In view of these shortcomings, an attempt is made to present a photovoltaic hot spots detection method based on kernel entropy component analysis and information gain. The method uses the kernel entropy component analysis to extract the features of the data by reducing the amount of calculation, eliminating noise, gaining the information to determine the detection variables and their thresholds, to judge hot spots occurrence according to the detection variables. Finally, it is verified by experiments that the proposed method can detect the hot spots of varying degrees.

2   Background Knowledge

2.1   Kernel Entropy Component Analysis

The concept of information entropy originates from thermal physics, which reflects the inherent uncertainty of the system. Information entropy can be used as a measure of the amount of information in data, or as an indicator of data classification and clustering. The data analysis methods based on information entropy have attracted widespread attention. Robert Jenssen introduced Renyi entropy into principal component analysis, and proposed a data feature extraction method based on the kernel entropy component analysis [10]. The Renyi entropy is defined by the following formula:

$$H(p) = -\log \int p^2(x)dx \qquad (1)$$

where, $p(x)$ represents the probability density function of the data x. Since the logarithmic function is a monotonic function, Eq. (2) can be simplified as:

$$V(p) = \int p^2(x)dx \qquad (2)$$

The Parzen window (Gaussian window) density estimator is used to estimate the value of $V(p)$, and then the estimated value of $H(p)$ is obtained. The Parzen window density estimator is given by Eq. (3).

$$\hat{p}(x) = \frac{1}{N} \sum_{xt \in D} k_\sigma(x, x_t) \tag{3}$$

where, $k_\sigma(x, x_t)$ represents the Parzen window or kernel, the kernel is centered on x_t, and the width is determined by σ. In order to make $p(x)$ an appropriate density function, the Gaussian (RBF) kernel function is usually selected. The RBF kernel function calculation formula is as follows:

$$k_\sigma(x, x_t) = \exp\left(-\frac{\|x - x_t\|}{2\sigma^2}\right) \tag{4}$$

Substituting Eq. (3), in Eq. (2) to get the estimated value of $V(p)$.

$$
\begin{aligned}
\hat{V}(p) &= \int p^2(x)dx \\
&= \frac{1}{N^2} \sum_{i=1}^{N} \sum_{j=1}^{N} \int K_\sigma(x, x_i) \\
&= \frac{1}{N^2} \sum_{i=1}^{N} \sum_{j=1}^{N} \int K_{\sqrt{2}\sigma}(x_i, x_j) \\
&= \frac{1}{N^2} I K I^T
\end{aligned}
\tag{5}
$$

where, K is an $N \times N$ kernel matrix and I is an $N \times 1$ row vector (each value in the vector is 1). It can be seen from Eq. (5) that Renyi entropy can be expressed by the kernel matrix, which can be calculated by eigenvalue and eigenvector $K = EDE^T$. Among them, $D = diag(\lambda_1, \lambda_2...\lambda_N)$ is the diagonal matrix composed of the eigenvalues of the kernel matrix, $E = (e_1, e_2...e_N)$ is the eigen-matrix composed of the corresponding eigenvectors. Combining the eigenvalue matrix and eigenvector matrix into Eq. (5), we get the estimated value of $V(p)$.

$$
\begin{aligned}
\hat{V}(p) &= \frac{1}{N^2} 1 K 1^T \\
&= \frac{1}{N^2} 1 E D E 1^T \\
&= \frac{1}{N^2} \sum_{i=1}^{N} \left(\sqrt{\lambda_i} e_i^T 1\right)^2
\end{aligned}
\tag{6}
$$

Equation (6) is the Renyi entropy value where, each eigenvalue and eigenvector contributes to the Renyi entropy value [11]. The goal of KECA is to utilize the fewest features to guarantee the least loss in the Renyi entropy value of the input sample dataset. The KECA algorithm makes full use of the information entropy theory in the feature extraction process, and reveals the internal structure of the entropy in the original feature set, and at the same time effectively mines the low-dimensional manifold features embedded in the high-dimensional feature data [12]. Compared with the traditional feature extraction algorithm KPCA, KECA does not need to assume that the data obeys the Gaussian distribution; KECA uses the Renyi entropy value to select principal components, which can retain more informative features and non-Gaussian feature information of the extracted samples [13]. At present, KECA algorithm has been widely used in image recognition [14,15], fault diagnosis [16–19], data analysis [20,21]and other fields due to its advantages.

2.2   Information Gain and Detection Variables

The feature map of KECA can be expressed as:

$$\boldsymbol{\Phi}_{\text{eca}} = \mathbf{U}_d{}^T \boldsymbol{\Phi} = \mathbf{D}_d{}^{\frac{1}{2}} \mathbf{E}_d{}^T \tag{7}$$

where, D_d is the diagonal matrix composed of the first d eigenvalues in D, and E_d is composed of the corresponding eigenvectors. The projection of a new sample in the feature space can be expressed as:

$$\begin{aligned} H_{\text{new}} &= U_d^T \Phi\left(x_{new}\right) \\ &= D_d^{-\frac{1}{2}} E_d^T \Phi^T \Phi\left(x_{new}\right) \\ &= D_d^{-\frac{1}{2}} E_d^T K\left(x, x_{new}\right) \end{aligned} \tag{8}$$

The spatial projection of formula (8) can be simplified as:

$$H = UX \tag{9}$$

KECA can reveal the inherent cluster characteristics of the data, and the extracted data is a feature data with an angular structure. The distance-based statistic detection methods T^2 and SPE cannot be applied to KECA-based fault detection [22]. Considering that KECA is a feature extraction method based on Renyi entropy, this paper introduces information gain as a detection variable for fault detection. The information entropy of data D is $H(D)$, and the conditional entropy of data D in feature A is $H(D|A)$, then the information gain is represented by:

$$G(D, A) = H(D) - H(D \mid A) \tag{10}$$

The information gain represents the degree to which the uncertainty of the information is reduced under the condition A is established. Similarly, we can define the information gain under hot spots fault conditions as:

$$G_f = H_{normal} - H_{fault} \tag{11}$$

The trace of the matrix can describe the characteristic information of the matrix, and G is not necessarily a square matrix, so the detection variable of the normal

sample is defined as: The trace of the matrix describes the characteristic information of the matrix where, G_f is not necessarily a square matrix hence, the
detection variable of the normal sample is defined as:

$$F = \mathrm{tr}\left((G)^T G\right) \tag{12}$$

Similarly, when the test sample is a normal sample, the information gain of the
normal sample is:

$$G_n = H_{normal} - H_{test} \tag{13}$$

According to the information gain between normal samples, the detection thresh-
old of hot spots can be determined as $F_m = \max \mathrm{tr}\left((G_n)^T G_n\right)$, If $F > F_m$, it
can be considered that hot spots fault has occurred.

3   Hot Spots Detection Algorithm

A photovoltaic hot spot detection algorithm based on kernel entropy component
analysis and information gain is proposed to detect accurate and timely hot spot
faults in photovoltaic modules. The algorithm consists of two parts: training
and testing, in the training phase, the normal samples are standardized and
high-dimensional projection is performed on them using the Gaussian kernel
function, and the information gain is used to determine the detection threshold;
whereas, in the testing phase, the test samples are projected in the direction of
the projection matrix, and the fault sample information entropy and detection
variables are calculated. The detection variable of the faulty sample is compared
with the detection threshold to determine the occurrence of the hot spots. The
algorithm flow is displayed in Fig. 1.

The hot spots detection steps based on the kernel entropy component analysis
are described below.

Step 1: Data preprocessing. Calculate the mean and the variance of the test
sample and the training sample, making it standard data with a mean of 0 and
a variance of 1.

Step 2: High-dimensional projection. Select the kernel function as a Gaussian
kernel function, determine the parameters of the function, and use formula (4)
to project the test sample into a high-dimensional space.

Step 3: Eigen decomposition. The kernel matrix is eigen decomposed to
obtain the eigenvalue D and the eigenvector E, the entropy value is calculated
using formula (6), and the principal components are selected according to the
size of the entropy value.

Step 4: Determine the detection threshold. Using formula (8) to calculate the
feature and using formula (13) to calculate the information gain and determine
the detection threshold.

Step 5: Extract feature data. Carry out high-dimensional projection on the
test samples, perform feature decomposition on the kernel matrix, and use Eq. (8)
to obtain the information feature data of the test data.

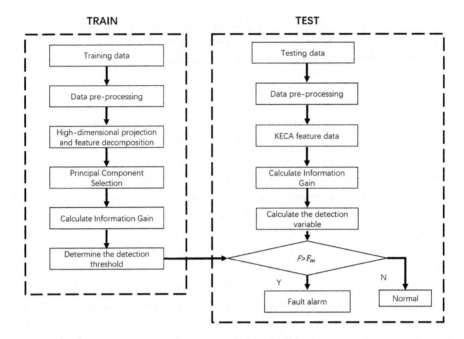

Fig. 1. Hot spots detection process.

Step 6: Detect variables. Using Eq. (11) to calculate the information gain of the test sample, and use Eq. (12) to obtain the detection variable of the fault sample.

Step 7: Hot spot detection. Compare the detection variables of the test samples with the detection threshold, and judge the hot spots when the detection threshold exceeds.

These steps are used in order to prove the effectiveness of the proposed algorithm through experimental verification in the next section.

4 Experiment and Analysis

4.1 Experiment Data

The experimental data is collected from the National Energy and Solar Energy Center of China Electric Power Research Institute on eight characteristic variables namely, open circuit voltage (V), short circuit current (A), maximum power point voltage (V), maximum power point current (A), temperature (°C), irradiance (W/m^2), maximum power (W) and fill factor F. The experiments consists of 1 normal condition experiment and 15 different hot spots experiments. The specific experiments method of hot spots is depicted in Fig. 2.

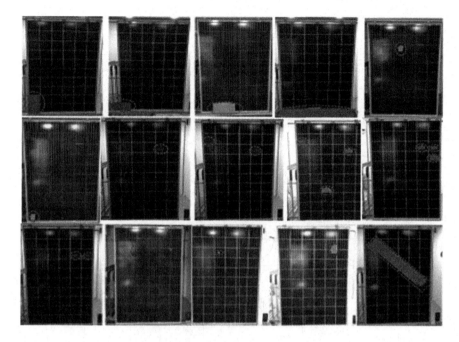

Fig. 2. Hot spots experiments 1–15.

4.2 Experimental Results and Comparison

The paper uses 15 sets of hot spots data to verify the proposed algorithm. The detection threshold $F = 1.13 \times 10^{-4}$ is obtained by using the normal samples. The specific fault detection results are shown in Fig. 3.

It is seen from Fig. 3 that the photovoltaic hot spot faults detection algorithm based on the kernel entropy component analysis can effectively realize the hot spots fault detection. The proposed algorithm can detect both large and small hot spots, such as hot spot 4 and hot spot 13; it can also detect the faults caused by the line occlusion, such as hot spot 12. The proposed algorithm can detect all 15 hot spot faults indicating that the detection effect is excellent.

In order to verify the superiority of the proposed algorithm, the proposed algorithm is compared with the traditional linear dimensionality reduction algorithm PCA and the latest manifold learning algorithm Neighborhood Preserving Embedding (NPE) algorithm [23]. The comparison results are shown in Fig. 4 and Fig. 5.

Figure 4 shows the detection results of 15 hot spots by PCA algorithm. Compared with the proposed algorithm, the fault diagnosis method based on PAC is not ideal. It can be seen from the Fig. 3 that the proposed algorithm can detect these two kinds of tiny hot spot faults, but the detection effect of PCA is very unsatisfactory. In case of hot spot 12 and hot spot 13, PCA cannot detect hot spot fault.

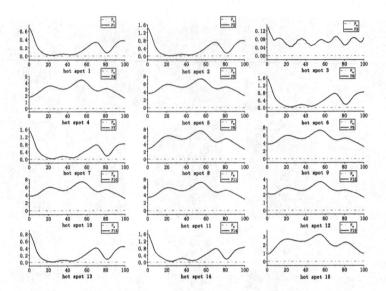

Fig. 3. KECA hot spots detection results.

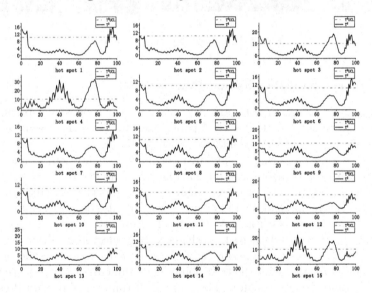

Fig. 4. Comparisons with PCA.

Figure 5 shows the fault diagnosis results of 15 hot spots based on NPE algorithm. It can be seen from the Fig. 5 that the fault diagnosis algorithm based on NPE can detect most hot spots, however, for small hot spots, NPE algorithm can not detect. In particular, for hot spot 13, NPE algorithm can not realize hot spot detection at all.

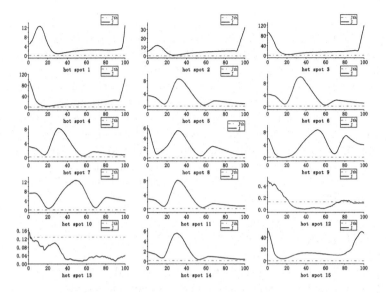

Fig. 5. Comparisons with NPE.

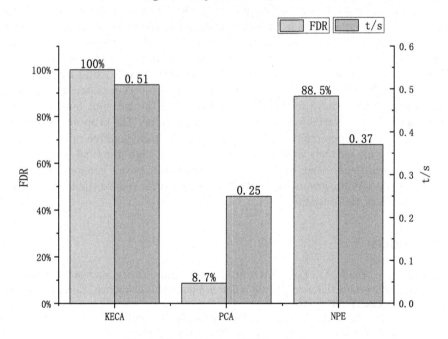

Fig. 6. Comparison of FDR and time.

The comparison of the detection time and the fault detection rate (FDR) of the three algorithms is shown in Fig. 6.

It is seen from Fig. 6 that the proposed algorithm (KECA) has a high fault recognition rate, and the FDR is 100%, which is higher than the other two algorithms, and can detect each hot spot fault. Although, the proposed algorithm takes little more detection time but detects the hot spots in all the experiments and therefore more acceptable, feasible and superior to the linear dimensionality reduction algorithm PCA and the popular learning algorithm NPE.

The effectiveness of the proposed algorithm is verified by experiments, and the proposed algorithm can detect all 15 kinds of hot spots in the experiment. The superiority of the proposed algorithm is verified by comparative experiments. The proposed method has great advantages in small hot spots fault, and is superior to the PCA-based fault detection algorithm and the NPE-based fault detection algorithm.

5   Conclusion

In view of the problems of the erstwhile methods based on the infrared processing and electric parameter method of photovoltaic hot spots detection, an attempt is made in this paper to present and test a method based on the kernel entropy component analysis. In this technique, the sample data is projected into a high-dimensional space, and then the eigenvectors and eigenvalues are obtained by eigen decomposition to calculate the sample data. The entropy value and the eigenvalues are sorted in the descending order according to the entropy value. The entropy value is used to determine the projection matrix and the test data is then projected according to the direction of the projection matrix to calculate the hot spots detection variable. The occurrence of the hot spot fault is judged when the detection variable exceeds the threshold value. The proposed algorithm improves the fault detection ability and reduces the false positive rate. The algorithm effectively extracts fault information and is of high practical value. In the future, we will study other fault types of photovoltaic power generation system, such as short circuit, grounding and aging, and further realize the identification and location of these faults.

References

1. Fadhel, S., Diallo, D., Delpha, C., et al.: Maximum power point analysis for partial shading detection and identification in photovoltaic systems. Energy Convers. Manag. **224**, 113374 (2020)
2. Basnet, B., Chun, H., Bang, J.: An intelligent fault detection model for fault detection in photovoltaic systems. J. Sens. **2020**, 1–11 (2020)
3. Appiah, A.Y., Zhang, X., Ayawli, B.B.K., et al.: Review and performance evaluation of photovoltaic array fault detection and diagnosis techniques. Int. J. Photoenergy, 1–19 (2019)
4. Wu, Z., Hu, Y., Wen, J.X., et al.: A review for solar panel fire accident prevention in large-scale PV applications. IEEE Access **8**, 132466–132480 (2020)

5. Karimi, M., Samet, H., Ghanbari, T., et al.: A current based approach for hotspot detection in photovoltaic strings. Int. Trans. Electr. Energy Syst. **30**(9), e12517 (2020)
6. Henry, C., Poudel, S., Lee, S., et al.: Automatic detection system of deteriorated PV modules using drone with thermal camera. Appl. Sci. **10**(11), 3802 (2020)
7. Zhang, Y.M.: Research and implementation of photovoltaic panel hot spots detection robot. Tianjin University of Technology (2020)
8. Lazzaretti, A.E., Costa, C.H.D., Rodrigues, M.P., et al.: A monitoring system for online fault detection and classification in photovoltaic plants. Sensors **20**(17), 4688 (2020)
9. Appiah, A.Y., Xinghua, Z., Ben, B.K.A.A., et al.: Long short-term memory networks based automatic feature extraction for photovoltaic array fault diagnosis. IEEE Access **7**, 30089–30101 (2017)
10. Jenssen, R.: Kernel entropy component analysis. IEEE Trans. Pattern Anal. Mach. Intell. **32**(5), 847–860 (2010)
11. Deng, M.Y., Liu, J.C., Xu, P., et al.: New fault detection and diagnosis strategy for nonlinear industrial process based on KECA. CIESC J. **71**(05), 2151–2163 (2020)
12. Zhou, H.D.: Research on condition recognition methods of rolling bearings based on kernel entropy component analysis. Huazhong University of Science and Technology (2017)
13. Chen, J., Yu, J.: Independent component analysis mixture model based dissimilarity method for performance monitoring of non-Gaussian dynamic processes with shifting operating conditions. Ind. Eng. Chem. Res. **53**(13), 5055–5066 (2014)
14. Gomez-Chova, L., Jenssen, R., Camps-Valls, G.: Kernel entropy component analysis for remote sensing image clustering. IEEE Geosci. Remote Sens. Lett. **9**(2), 312–316 (2012)
15. Shekar, B.H., Sharmila, K.M., Mestetskiy, L.M., et al.: Face recognition using kernel entropy component analysis. Neurocomputing **74**(6), 1053–1057 (2011)
16. Xia, Y., Ding, Q., Jiang, A., et al.: Incipient fault diagnosis for centrifugal chillers using kernel entropy component analysis and voting based extreme learning machine. Korean J. Chem. Eng. **39**(3), 504–514 (2022)
17. Zhou, H., Zhong, F., Shi, T., et al.: Class-information-incorporated kernel entropy component analysis with application to bearing fault diagnosis. J. Vib. Control **27**(5-6), 543–555 (2021)
18. Xia, Y., Ding, Q., Li, Z., et al.: Fault detection for centrifugal chillers using a Kernel Entropy Component Analysis (KECA) method. Build. Simul. **14**(1), 53–61 (2021)
19. Xu, P., Liu, J., Shang, L., et al.: Industrial process fault detection and diagnosis framework based on enhanced supervised kernel entropy component analysis. Meas. J. Int. Meas. Confed. **196**, 111181 (2022)
20. Li, Y., Wang, Y., Wang, Y., et al.: Quantum clustering using kernel entropy component analysis. Neurocomput. (Amst.) **202**, 36–48 (2016)
21. Shi, J., Jiang, Q., Zhang, Q., et al.: Sparse kernel entropy component analysis for dimensionality reduction of biomedical data. Neurocomput. (Amst.) **168**, 930–940 (2015)
22. Qi, Y.S., Zhang, H.L., Wang, L., et al.: Fault detection and diagnosis for chillers using MSPCA-KECA. CIESC J. **68**(04), 1499–1508 (2017)
23. Chen, H., Yi, H., Jiang, B., et al.: Data-driven detection of hot spots in photovoltaic energy systems. IEEE Trans. Syst. Man Cybern. Syst. **49**(8), 1731–1738 (2019)

Second-Order Global Attention Networks for Graph Classification and Regression

Fenyu Hu[1,2(✉)], Zeyu Cui[3], Shu Wu[1,2], Qiang Liu[1,2], Jinlin Wu[1,2], Liang Wang[1,2], and Tieniu Tan[1,2]

[1] National Laboratory of Pattern Recognition, Institute of Automation, Chinese Academy of Sciences, Beijing, China
fenyu.hu@cripac.ia.ac.cn,
{shu.wu,qiang.liu,jinlin.wu,wangliang,tnt}@nlpr.ia.ac.cn
[2] University of Chinese Academy of Sciences, Beijing, China
[3] DAMO Academy, Alibaba Group, Hangzhou, China

Abstract. Graph Neural Networks (GNNs) are powerful to learn representation of graph-structured data, which fuse both attributive and topological information. Prior researches have investigated the expressive power of GNNs by comparing it with Weisfeiler-Lehman algorithm. In spite of having achieved promising performance for the isomorphism test, existing methods assume overly restrictive requirement, which might hinder the performance on other graph-level tasks, e.g., graph classification and graph regression. In this paper, we argue the rationality of adaptively emphasizing important information. We propose a novel global attention module from two levels: channel level and node level. Specifically, we exploit second-order channel correlation to extract more discriminative representations. We validate the effectiveness of the proposed approach through extensive experiments on eight benchmark datasets. The proposed method performs better than the other state-of-the-art methods in graph classification and graph regression tasks. Notably, It achieves 2.7% improvement on DD dataset for graph classification and 7.1% absolute improvement on ZINC dataset for graph regression.

Keywords: Graph classification · Graph regression · Graph neural networks · Attention mechanism

1 Introduction

Graph Neural Networks (GNNs) have proved to be powerful in learning representation of graph data and have attracted a surge of interests [1,3,7,8,25,28–32]. Recently, numerous approaches have been proposed to quantify such representation power of GNNs [18,20,27]. These approaches try to bridge a theoretical connection with the Weisfeiler-Lehman (WL) algorithm [24] when judging the graph isomorphism. We term these approaches as WL-GNNs. In general, WL-GNNs

---

S. Wu—To whom correspondence should be addressed.

© The Author(s), under exclusive license to Springer Nature Switzerland AG 2022
L. Fang et al. (Eds.): CICAI 2022, LNAI 13605, pp. 496–507, 2022.
https://doi.org/10.1007/978-3-031-20500-2_41

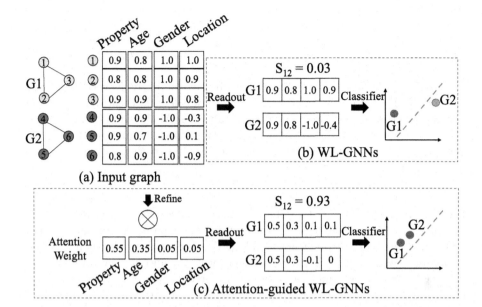

Fig. 1. A toy example of predicting the debt-paying ability of different companies. $G1$ and $G2$ show the shareholder relationships of two companies, which should be classified as the same class. (a) Each node represents a shareholder of the company and consists of four numerical attributes. These two graphs are quite similar in the first two important attributes but have vast difference in the latter two trivial attributes. (b) $G1$ and $G2$ are distinguished by WL-GNNs and may be misclassified into different classes. S_{12} refers the cosine similarity of $G1$ and $G2$. (c) Attention-guided WL-GNNs yield much closer distance in latent space.

aim to distinguish non-isomorphic graphs by approximating an injective hash function. More specifically, if two graphs are non-isomorphic, they are expected to have different embeddings through WL-GNNs. Owing to the superior performance of WL-GNNs in distinguishing graphs with regard to isomorphism test, there are also approaches that apply WL-GNNs in graph classification and graph regression tasks [18,20,21,27].

Although WL-GNNs have shown strong advantages in above graph analytical tasks, a deficiency is that graph isomorphism property is an overly restrictive requirement for other graph-level tasks. Specifically, *since any difference between two graphs can lead to the non-isomorphism, WL-GNNs do not need to consider feature importance.* However, this makes WL-GNNs inadequate to discover determinative signals that indicate the graph characteristics in some graph-level tasks. Figure 1 illustrates how WL-GNNs limit the performance in these tasks, where we consider a toy problem of predicting the debt-paying ability of different companies. Suppose $G1$ and $G2$ are two small companies, where nodes denote shareholders and the edges denote partnership. Given four dimensions representing the *property, age, gender* and *location* of the shareholders, it is commonly accepted that the rich and the middle-aged will have a higher chance to repay a loan than the poor and the young. Therefore, personal property and age features should contribute relatively more than the other two features in estimating the solvency. Correspondingly, in Fig. 1(a), $G1$ and $G2$ with similar property and age features are expected to behave similarly. Nevertheless, since $G1$ and $G2$ have obvious difference in gender and location features, the cosine similarity between these two companies is only 0.03. As shown in Fig. 1(b), when applying conventional WL-GNNs with injective multiset function [27], $G1$ and $G2$ may be far away from each other in the latent representation space and be misclassified into different classes.

A simple way to infer the global channel attention weights of graphs is employing an average pooling aggregator at each channel, and then apply some learning mechanisms to obtain the attention weights (illustrated in Fig. 1(c)). However, the global average pooling operation only explores first-order statistics, ignoring channel interdependencies. Taking Fig. 1 as an example, there might be strong interdependencies between personal property and age, because one usually needs decades of years to accumulate its fortune. Hence, we need adequately considering graph channel interdependencies. Recent works in computer vision have also shown that deep neural networks with such second-order statistics can improve classification performance [16,17,26]. To this end, we are inspired to develop a novel second-order global channel attention network to fully exploit the channel interdependencies. Similarly, global node attention also helps extract important information (please refer to Sect. 3.2 for more details).

On this basis, we propose a *Second-order Global Channel Attention* (SoGCA) mechanism for better channel correlation and importance learning. Our SoGCA adaptively learns important information by exploiting second-order channel statistics, extracting more discriminative representations. Moreover, a *Global Attention-guided Structure* (GAS) is presented to highlight important information from two levels: channel level and node level. By stacking GAS after each graph isomorphism aggregator, we obtain a *Second-order Global Attention Network* (SGAN) which is compatible with existing WL-GNNs. In order to evaluate the generality of SGAN, we devise three variants based on GIN [27], 3WLGNN [18] and PNA [2], respectively. We conduct comprehensive experiments on eight public datasets and achieve state-of-the-art results on all benchmark tasks.

2   Preliminaries

2.1   Notations and Problem Definition

Consider a graph $G(\mathcal{V}, \mathcal{E}, \mathbf{X})$ with $N = |\mathcal{V}|$ nodes and $|\mathcal{E}|$ edges. $\mathbf{X} \in \mathbb{R}^{N \times d_0}$ denotes the node feature matrix, where d_0 is the number of input attributes. Given a collection of graphs $\{G_1, ..., G_N\}$ and their corresponding labels $\{y_1, ..., y_N\}$, the task of graph classification or graph regression is to learn a mapping $f : \mathcal{G} \rightarrow \mathcal{Y}$, where $\mathcal{G}$ is the set of input graphs and $\mathcal{Y}$ is the set of labels associated with each graph.

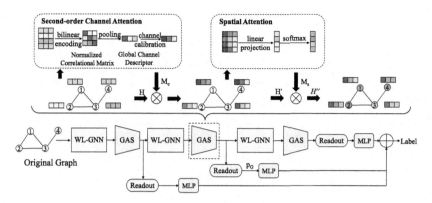

Fig. 2. The architecture of SGAN (best view in color). The WL-GNN block indicates a layer of the general WL-GNNs, which can be instantiated by GIN, 3WLGNN layers, etc. GAS block consists of a SoGCA module and a node attention module. SoGCA module uses second-order information to perform channel-wise attention, giving each dimension of hidden embeddings different weight. Node attention module obtain the importance of nodes. (Color figure online)

2.2 Graph Isomorphism Networks

Graph Isomorphism Networks [27] (GIN) is an architecture based on the Weisfeiler-Lehman Isomorphism test, which can quantify the expressive power of GNNs. GIN is as powerful as 1-WL algorithm owing to injective update and aggregation functions as:

$$\hat{\mathbf{H}}^{\ell+1} = (1 + \epsilon)\,\mathbf{H}^{\ell} + \mathbf{A}\mathbf{H}^{\ell}, \tag{1}$$

$$\mathbf{H}^{\ell+1} = \mathrm{ReLU}\left(\,\mathrm{ReLU}\left(\,\mathrm{BN}(\hat{\mathbf{H}}^{\ell+1}\,\mathbf{V}^{\ell})\,\right)\mathbf{U}^{\ell}\,\right), \tag{2}$$

where ϵ can be a learnable parameter or a fixed scalar, $\mathbf{H}^{\ell} \in \mathbb{R}^{N \times d}$ is the embedding representation of all nodes derived from the ℓth layer, $\mathbf{V}^{\ell}, \mathbf{U}^{\ell} \in \mathbb{R}^{d \times d}$ are learnable matrices for layer ℓ, BN represents Batch Normalization [10], $\mathrm{ReLU}(x) = \max(0, x)$ is the non-linear activation function, and A is the adjacency matrix of the graph.

3   Proposed Method: SGAN

In the following section, we consider the intermediate graph representation $\mathbf{H} \in \mathbb{R}^{N \times d}$ resulting from the layer of WL-GNNs, which can be instantiated by GIN, 3WLGNN layers [18], etc. Following the concept of channel in Convolutional Neural Networks (CNNs), we define each column of $\mathbf{H}$ as a **channel**.

3.1   Second-Order Global Channel Attention (SoGCA)

Existing WL-GNNs do not consider the importance of different channels for graph isomorphism test. However, for other graph-level tasks, we have analyzed the necessity of modeling feature importance in Sect. 1. Besides, recent studies in computer vision [16,17] have shown that channel interdependencies in deep CNNs are helpful for extracting more discriminative representations. Inspired by this observation, we propose a SoGCA module that incorporates channel interdependencies. As illustrated in Fig. 2, the SoGCA consists of three parts: bilinear encoding, global correlation pooling, and channel calibration.

Bilinear Encoding. The first step is to model channel interdependencies by utilizing a correlation matrix. We calculate the inner product between each pair of channels to generate a channel correlation matrix $\mathbf{D}$ as:

$$\mathbf{D} = \mathbf{H}^T\mathbf{H}, \tag{3}$$

where $\mathbf{D} \in \mathbb{R}^{d \times d}$ and each element $\mathbf{D}_{ij} = \sum_{k=1}^{N} \mathbf{H}_{ik}\mathbf{H}_{kj}$ measures the degree of second-order interdependency between two channels. A large value of $\mathbf{D}_{ij}$ indicates the ith channel and the jth channel are highly related.

To further improve feature representation, we normalize the channel correlation matrix $\mathbf{D}$. Following the practice in [16], we adopt signed square-root and ℓ_2 normalization, which yields

$$\mathbf{D}_{norm} = sign(\mathbf{D})\frac{\sqrt{|\mathbf{D}|}}{\|\sqrt{|\mathbf{D}|}\|_2}. \tag{4}$$

Note that the above operations are piecewise differentiable, so they can be used for end-to-end training.

Global Correlation Pooling. Then, we apply global average pooling function over the normalized correlation matrix D_{norm}. We obtain a global channel descriptor $\mathbf{z} = (\mathbf{z}_1, \mathbf{z}_2, ..., \mathbf{z}_d) \in \mathbb{R}^{1 \times d}$ as:

$$\mathbf{z} = \frac{1}{d}\sum_m (\mathbf{D}_{norm})_m. \tag{5}$$

Compared with directly applying global average pooling over $\mathbf{H}$, global correlation pooling captures more useful information. Each element $\mathbf{z}_i$ encodes the second-order interdependencies between the ith channel and all the other channels. So the global channel descriptor $\mathbf{z}$ can be used for learning more discriminative representation. We validate the effectiveness of global correlation pooling in Sect. 4.4.

Channel Calibration. In order to learn the attention weights and fully exploit channel interdependencies, we apply 2-layer MLPs as:

$$\mathbf{M}_c = \sigma(\text{ReLU}(\mathbf{z}\mathbf{W}_0)\mathbf{W}_1), \tag{6}$$

where $\mathbf{W}_0 \in \mathbb{R}^{d \times r}$, $\mathbf{W}_1 \in \mathbb{R}^{r \times d}$ are learnable weights, r is a hyper-parameter which controls capacity of the attention module. Finally, we obtain the channel attention map $\mathbf{M}_c$ to rescale the graph representation as:

$$\mathbf{H}' = \mathbf{M}_c \otimes \mathbf{H}. \tag{7}$$

3.2   Node Attention Module

Apart from channel attention, node attention is also important for extracting informative signals. For example, in molecular chemistry, the functional groups are usually related to a lot of chemical properties, while many other nodes do not influence the properties. So we also generate a node attention map, which can focus on important nodes and provides complementary information to channel attention.

If we apply the above bilinear encoding to calculate node attention, we would get a node correlation matrix of $\mathbb{R}^{N \times N}$. As a result, it would be intractable to handle this matrix in large graphs. For simplicity, we use a linear projection followed by a softmax function to calculate the node attention score as:

$$\mathbf{M}_n = softmax(\sigma(\mathbf{H}'\mathbf{W}_2)), \tag{8}$$

where $\mathbf{W}_2 \in \mathbb{R}^{d \times 1}$ are the trainable weight matrix for node attention, $softmax(\mathbf{x}) = e^{\mathbf{x}}/\sum e^{\mathbf{x}}$ is used for normalization.

After that, $\mathbf{M}_n$ is applied to obtain the refined graph representation $\mathbf{H}''$, which is fed into the follow-up layers of WL-GNNs:

$$\mathbf{H}'' = \mathbf{M}_n \otimes \mathbf{H}'. \tag{9}$$

In fact, the above second-order channel attention resemble that in SOPOOL [23]. However, SGAN is distinct from SOPOOL in both motivation and technique. On the one hand, SGAN points out the limitations of directly applying WL-GNNs to graph classification and graph regression tasks, while SOPOOL only focuses on strenthen important features. On the other hand, SGAN also considers the node importance via node attention.

4   Experiments

Datasets. For a comprehensive evaluation of our proposed method, we use eight benchmark datasets in benchmark-GNNs [4] and OGB [9] for graph analytical tasks, including classification, regression, and graph isomorphism test. For graph classification task, two widely used protein datasets [12], ENZYMES and DD are used. We also conduct experiments on larger datasets of MNIST and CIFAR10. These two datasets convert the original images into graphs using super-pixels. For graph regression task, we use a subset of ZINC molecular graphs dataset [11] to regress the constrained solubility of a molecule. We also apply another two molecular graphs, OGBG-molesol and OGBG-molfreesolv in OGB [9] dataset for regression. Furthermore, we use the Circular Skip Link (CSL) dataset [21] for graph isomorphism test. The statistics of these datasets are summarized in Table 1.

4.1 Experimental Setup

Compared Methods. We compare SGAN with four widely used message passing-based GNNs: GCN [14], GraphSage [6], GAT [22] and MoNet [19]. For attention-guided GNNs, we compare with SAGPool [15] and cGAO [5]. For WL-GNNs, we select GIN [27], 3WLGNN [18] and PNA [2] as baselines.

Implementation Details. We closely follow benchmark-GNNs to set hyperparameters. We perform grid-search to select the initial learning rate from a range of $1e^{-3}$ to $7e^{-5}$. The learning rate decay factor is 0.5 and the model is optimized with Adam [13] optimizer. We use classification accuracy as evaluation metric for all datasets except ZINC. For the regression task on ZINC, we measure the performance by using Mean Absolute Error (MAE). We report the average results of MNIST, CIFAR10 and ZINC over 4 runs with 4 different seeds. The results on CSL dataset are obtained by running 20 times with different seeds. All baselines on all benchmark-GNNs datasets are trained with a budget of 100k parameters. Following experimental protocols of OGB, we use edge features and report the Root Mean Squared Error (RMSE). Notably, we implement our baselines on Huawei Mindspore platform.

4.2 Performance Comparison

We compare the performance of SGAN with baseline methods on four graph classification datasets and one graph regression dataset. The results are shown in Table 2. We find that:

– **Traditional WL-GNNs perform relatively poor.** Although provably powerful in terms of graph isomorphism test, GIN and 3WLGNN do not outperform GCN or GAT obviously. This indicates that graph isomorphism property is not sufficient to yield satisfactory results in graph classification and regression tasks.

Table 1. Statistics of all datasets in experiments.

Dataset	#Graphs	#Classes	Tasks
ENZYMES	600	6	Classification
DD	1178	2	Classification
MNIST	70k	10	Classification
CIFAR10	60k	10	Classification
ZINC	12k	–	Regression
OGBG-molesol	1128	–	Regression
OGBG-molfreesolv	642	–	Regression
CSL	150	10	Isomorphism

Table 2. Results of graph classification/regression with the best performances highlighted in bold. Classification accuracies (%) are reported for all datasets except ZINC. ↓ indicates lower is better for the regression loss. OOM represents out of memory.

Method	ENZYMES	DD	MNIST	CIFAR10	ZINC (↓)
GCN	65.833	72.758	90.705	55.710	0.459
GraphSage	65.000	73.433	97.312	65.767	0.468
MoNet	63.000	71.736	90.805	54.655	0.397
GAT	**68.500**	75.900	95.535	64.223	0.475
SAGPool	66.833	75.354	92.375	57.032	0.425
cGAO	63.833	73.685	91.833	54.824	0.468
GIN	65.333	71.910	96.485	55.255	0.387
3WLGNN	61.000	OOM	95.075	59.175	0.407
PNA	–	–	97.190	**70.210**	**0.320**
SGAN(GIN)	**68.333**	**78.010**	**97.500**	58.750	**0.267**
SGAN(3WLGNN)	62.000	OOM	96.212	63.125	**0.384**
SGAN(PNA)	–	–	**97.650**	**70.340**	**0.249**

Table 3. Ablation study of SGAN(GIN) on benchmark-GNNs datasets. We investigate the effectiveness of SoGCA and node attention (NA), respectively. The first line is the results of GIN.

SoGCA	NA	ENZYMES	DD	MNIST	CIFAR10	ZINC (↓)	Isomorphism test
✗	✗	65.333	71.910	96.485	55.255	0.387	99.333
✗	✓	65.167	77.428	97.205	58.403	0.272	99.333
✓	✗	67.500	72.147	97.410	58.126	0.291	99.333
✓	✓	**68.000**	**78.010**	**97.500**	**58.750**	**0.267**	**99.333**

- **Global attention mechanisms improves the performance.** SAGPool achieves better performance than GCN in most cases. We attribute this improvement to capturing important nodes. However, neither SAGPool nor cGAO can obtain state-of-the-art results, because they only consider one kind of attention. Besides, since both SAGPool and cGAO employ GCN as base neighborhood aggregator, their performances may also be dragged down by GCN. Furthermore, cGAO may even degrades the performance on some datasets, which might be caused by lacking learnable parameters in attention process.
- **SGAN consistently achieves the best performance on all datasets.** SGAN improves the performance over GIN and 3WLGNN by remarkable margins, which verifies the necessity of modeling graph-level channel attention and node attention. Specifically, even compared with the very recent state-of-the-art PNA method, the proposed SGAN yields better results. The reason

is that PNA only focuses on capturing the **local** neighborhood distributions, while SGAN(PNA) can extract additional important **global** information.

4.3   Ablation Study of Attention Modules

In this subsection, we investigate the contributions of SoGCA and node attention module (NA) to the performance. We conduct experiments based on SGAN(GIN) by removing all SoGCA modules and NA modules, respectively. The results are shown in Table 3 and Table 4. We have the following observations:

Table 4. Ablation study of SGAN(GIN) on OGB datasets for regression. The first line is the results of GIN.

SoGCA	NA	OGBG-molesol ($\downarrow$)	OGBG-molfreesolv ($\downarrow$)
$\times$	$\times$	0.998	2.151
$\times$	$\checkmark$	1.087	2.709
$\checkmark$	$\times$	**0.875**	**1.872**
$\checkmark$	$\checkmark$	1.028	2.424

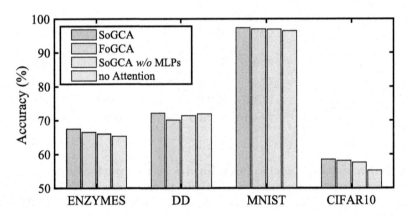

Fig. 3. The performance of different channel attention variants on graph classification. We plot the classification accuracy for the four datasets. Higher are better for these histograms. *w/o* is the abbreviation of without.

- **The characteristics of datasets influence the performance on different modules.** Interestingly, SoGCA brings more improvement on ENZYMES while NA performs better on DD and ZINC dataset. We guess these discrepancies are due to different characteristics of datasets. For instance, the input node features contain continuous values ranging from −10 to around 300 in ENZYMES. In contrast, the input node attributes in DD and ZINC dataset follow one-hot encoding, where most of the numbers in attribute vectors equal to zero. As a result, SoGCA performs better on ENZYMES because channel interdependencies might be more important to this dataset.

- **Compared to NA, the proposed SoGCA achieves more stable improvements in most cases.** Applying NA decreases the performance on some datasets, such as ENZYMES in Table 3 and the two OGB datasets in Table 4. We conjecture that most of the nodes in these datasets are important and NA neglects this information. By contrast, SoGCA still has satisfactory improvements in these datasets, which therefore verifies the necessity of modeling channel attention.
- **The combination of SoGCA and NA usually achieves better performance.** Except for the situation when NA fails, the combination of these two attention modules usually produces better performance. Since these two modules focuses on different aspects of node embedding, they provide complementary information to each other. Therefore, it is reasonable to combine them.
- **SGAN can retain the expressive power of vanilla WL-GNNs.** We conduct experiments on graph isomorphism task to study the expressive power of SGAN(GIN). For isomorphism test, it is required to strictly distinguishing these two graphs. Therefore, it might be natural that attention modules degrade the performance for graph isomorphism task. However, we find that removing SoGCA or NA makes no difference to the performance. This demonstrates that SoGCA and NA can learn adaptively according to the task. When the attention weights are near uniform distribution, SGAN(GIN) degenerates to GIN and keeps the same accuracy as GIN.

4.4   Study on Channel Interdependencies

In this subsection, we make a deeper study on the effect of modeling channel interdependencies. As presented in Sect. 3.1, our SoGCA module consists of three parts: Bilinear Encoding, Global Correlation Pooling (GCP) and Channel Calibration. Both of the first two parts and the third part can model channel interdependencies. We remove these parts respectively, yielding two model variants. The first variant is called First-order Graph Channel Attention method (**FoGCA**). The second variant is abbreviated as **SoGCA *w/o* MLPs**, which removes the 2-layer MLPs and uses the global channel descriptor $\mathbf{z}$ as channel attention map. We compare the results of these models based on GIN (i.e., no attention variant), which are shown in Fig. 3. It can be found that modeling channel attention can generally improve the performance of GIN. Either removing second-order modeling or MLPs degrades the overall performance, which verifies the necessity of modeling channel interdependencies and channel attention.

5   Conclusion

In this paper, we have proposed a novel second-order global attention networks for graph classification and regression tasks. The key of SGAN is the newly proposed SoGCA layer, which can capture second-order channel interdependencies and highlight important information. Compared with other previous WL-GNNs which focus on graph isomorphism property, our proposed SGAN can highlight determinative information from both channel level and node level. Comprehensive experiments have demonstrated the rationality and necessity of modeling channel attention and capturing second-order statistics of features for GNNs.

Acknowledgements. This work is jointly supported by National Natural Science Foundation of China (62141608, U19B2038) and CAAI Huawei MindSpore Open Fund.

References

1. Chen, F., Chen, X., Meng, F., Li, P., Zhou, J.: GoG: relation-aware graph-over-graph network for visual dialog. arXiv preprint arXiv:2109.08475 (2021)
2. Corso, G., Cavalleri, L., Beaini, D., Liò, P., Veličković, P.: Principal neighbourhood aggregation for graph nets. In: Advances in Neural Information Processing Systems (2020)
3. Cui, Z., et al.: DyGCN: dynamic graph embedding with graph convolutional network. IEEE Trans. Neural Netw. Learn. Syst. (2022)
4. Dwivedi, V.P., Joshi, C.K., Laurent, T., Bengio, Y., Bresson, X.: Benchmarking graph neural networks. arXiv preprint arXiv:2003.00982 (2020)
5. Gao, H., Ji, S.: Graph representation learning via hard and channel-wise attention networks. In: Proceedings of the 25th ACM SIGKDD International Conference on Knowledge Discovery and Data Mining (2019)
6. Hamilton, W., Ying, Z., Leskovec, J.: Inductive representation learning on large graphs. In: Advances in Neural Information Processing Systems (2017)
7. Hu, F., Liping, W., Qiang, L., Wu, S., Wang, L., Tan, T.: GraphDIVE: graph classifcation by mixture of diverse experts. In: Proceedings of the 31st International Joint Conference on Artificial Intelligence (2022)
8. Hu, F., Zhu, Y., Wu, S., Huang, W., Wang, L., Tan, T.: GraphAIR: graph representation learning with neighborhood aggregation and interaction. Pattern Recogn. **112**, 107745 (2021)
9. Hu, W., et al.: Open graph benchmark: datasets for machine learning on graphs. arXiv preprint arXiv:2005.00687 (2020)
10. Ioffe, S., Szegedy, C.: Batch normalization: accelerating deep network training by reducing internal covariate shift. In: International Conference on Machine Learning (2015)
11. Irwin, J.J., Sterling, T., Mysinger, M.M., Bolstad, E.S., Coleman, R.G.: ZINC: a free tool to discover chemistry for biology. J. Chem. Inf. Model. **52**, 1757–1768 (2012)
12. Kersting, K., Kriege, N.M., Morris, C., Mutzel, P., Neumann, M.: Benchmark data sets for graph kernels (2016)
13. Kingma, D.P., Ba, J.: Adam: a method for stochastic optimization. arXiv preprint arXiv:1412.6980 (2014)
14. Kipf, T.N., Welling, M.: Semi-supervised classification with graph convolutional networks. In: International Conference on Learning Representations (ICLR) (2017)
15. Lee, J., Lee, I., Kang, J.: Self-attention graph pooling. In: Proceedings of the 36th International Conference on Machine Learning (2019)
16. Li, P., Xie, J., Wang, Q., Zuo, W.: Is second-order information helpful for large-scale visual recognition? In: Proceedings of the IEEE International Conference on Computer Vision (2017)

17. Lin, T.Y., RoyChowdhury, A., Maji, S.: Bilinear CNN models for fine-grained visual recognition. In: Proceedings of the IEEE International Conference on Computer Vision (2015)
18. Maron, H., Ben-Hamu, H., Serviansky, H., Lipman, Y.: Provably powerful graph networks. In: Advances in Neural Information Processing Systems (2019)
19. Monti, F., Boscaini, D., Masci, J., Rodola, E., Svoboda, J., Bronstein, M.M.: Geometric deep learning on graphs and manifolds using mixture model CNNs. In: Proceedings of the IEEE Conference on Computer Vision and Pattern Recognition (2017)
20. Morris, C., et al.: Weisfeiler and Leman go neural: higher-order graph neural networks. In: Proceedings of the AAAI Conference on Artificial Intelligence (2019)
21. Murphy, R.L., Srinivasan, B., Rao, V., Ribeiro, B.: Relational pooling for graph representations. In: Proceedings of the 36th International Conference on Machine Learning (2019)
22. Veličković, P., Cucurull, G., Casanova, A., Romero, A., Liò, P., Bengio, Y.: Graph attention networks. In: International Conference on Learning Representations (2018)
23. Wang, Z., Ji, S.: Second-order pooling for graph neural networks. IEEE Trans. Pattern Anal. Mach. Intell. (2020)
24. Weisfeiler, B., Lehman, A.A.: A reduction of a graph to a canonical form and an algebra arising during this reduction. Nauchno-Technicheskaya Informatsia (1968)
25. Wu, J., Liu, Q., Xu, W., Wu, S.: Bias mitigation for evidence-aware fake news detection by causal intervention. In: Proceedings of the 45th International ACM SIGIR Conference on Research and Development in Information Retrieval (2022)
26. Xia, B.N., Gong, Y., Zhang, Y., Poellabauer, C.: Second-order non-local attention networks for person re-identification. In: Proceedings of the IEEE International Conference on Computer Vision (2019)
27. Xu, K., Hu, W., Leskovec, J., Jegelka, S.: How powerful are graph neural networks? In: International Conference on Learning Representations (2019)
28. Xu, W., Wu, J., Liu, Q., Wu, S., Wang, L.: Evidence-aware fake news detection with graph neural networks. In: Proceedings of the ACM Web Conference 2022 (2022)
29. Zhang, D., Chen, X., Xu, S., Xu, B.: Knowledge aware emotion recognition in textual conversations via multi-task incremental transformer. In: Proceedings of the 28th International Conference on Computational Linguistics (2020)
30. Zhang, M., Wu, S., Gao, M., Jiang, X., Xu, K., Wang, L.: Personalized graph neural networks with attention mechanism for session-aware recommendation. IEEE Trans. Knowl. Data Eng. 34, 3946–3957 (2022)
31. Zhang, M., Wu, S., Yu, X., Liu, Q., Wang, L.: Dynamic graph neural networks for sequential recommendation. IEEE Trans. Knowl. Data Eng. (2022)
32. Zhang, Y., Yu, X., Cui, Z., Wu, S., Wen, Z., Wang, L.: Every document owns its structure: inductive text classification via graph neural networks. In: Proceedings of the 58th Annual Meeting of the Association for Computational Linguistics (2020)

Aero-Engine Remaining Useful Life Prediction via Tensor Decomposition Method

JinCen Jiang, XiTing Wang, and ZhongZhi Hu[✉]

Institute for Aero Engine, Tsinghua University, Beijing 100084, China
huzhongzhi@tsinghua.edu.cn

Abstract. Aiming at the problems of low accuracy and long calculation time of remaining useful life (RUL) prediction of aero-engine by the data-driven method, a method for mining aero-engine information in tensor mode is proposed in this paper. Different from the traditional vector mode of data feature extraction, the tensor form of data can reflect the structure and correlation information among data. It has certain advantages when dealing with data that has strong coupling such as aero-engine signals. A large turbofan engine degradation simulation dataset (C-MAPSS dataset) with strong coupling provided by NASA is used to validate the method proposed in this paper. The results show that the data extracted by tensor decomposition method has better training effect than the unprocessed data in convolutional neural network (CNN), with the average prediction accuracy improved by 28.39%, and the average learning time shortened by 24.25%.

Keywords: Aero-engine remaining useful life prediction · Tensor mode · Tensor decomposition · Convolutional neural network

1 Introduction

Since the 21st century, in order to meet the growing demand for aviation operations and travel, new concept aero-engine such as adaptive cycle engine and hydrogen engine have been introduced. While meeting the performance, economy and environmental protection requirements, the new generation of aero-engine also makes the working environment of aero-engine harsher, with a more coupled and more complex structure, and it is more likely to lead to safety problems. Thus, improving the reliability, availability, and safety of aero-engine is the common goal pursued by various aviation powers [1]. The United States, the United Kingdom, Russia, and other countries that can develop their own aero-engine have put the Prognostics and Health Management (PHM) in an important position. As an important part of the aero-engine failure prediction and health management system, the remaining useful life Prediction is of significant importance to reduce the operation and maintenance cost of the engine, maintain its operational safety, and reduce the number of invalid replacements of parts [2].

At present, the commonly used methods for predicting the remaining useful life of aero-engine are roughly divided into three categories: model-based, empirical, and data-driven [2]. Among them, the data-driven remaining useful life prediction method does

© The Author(s), under exclusive license to Springer Nature Switzerland AG 2022
L. Fang et al. (Eds.): CICAI 2022, LNAI 13605, pp. 508–519, 2022.
https://doi.org/10.1007/978-3-031-20500-2_42

not rely on specific models, is not limited by experience, and only needs the data when the engine is working to achieve accurate remaining useful life prediction, which has attracted widespread attention. Li X, Ding Q, and Sun J Q [3] used deep convolutional neural network to predict the remaining useful life of aero-engine. H. Zhao, N. Zheng, and T. Chen et al. [4] attempted to predict the remaining useful life of aero-engine using the particle swarm algorithm of the support vector regression machine. Li H, Li Y, and Wang Z et al. [5] attempted to use the principal component long short-term memory neural network method to predict the remaining useful life of an aero-engine. In addition, there are many artificial intelligence methods used in this field [6–13].

However, the above researchers usually innovate in data training methods, and few people innovate in data processing methods. As a mechanical system with complex structure, aero-engine has a wide variety of signals and can form a complex multidimensional data. When processing multidimensional data, the traditional data processing method generally expands the multidimensional data into 2-D matrices or 1-D vectors through matrixing (or flattening), and then analyzes and processes the expanded data with the help of existing matrix analysis theory [14]. The monitored signals tend to behave as one-dimensional signals in the time or frequency domain, influenced only by time or frequency [15]. This treatment has its rationality, but there are also inherent defects that cannot be overcome by itself, which will lead to the loss of structural information between the original data, and the resulting error may also lead to the loss of useful information in the original data, which will affect the subsequent remaining useful life prediction results [16].

In fact, the signals of the aircraft engine are not independent of each other. During normal operation, aero-engine signals are extremely nonlinear and coupled. Many signal sources can be represented as multidimensional data, that is, tensors, when data is processed. As the most natural form of multidimensional data, tensors can maintain the inherent structural characteristics of the data, and can better characterize the essential properties of things in practical problems, and can obtain a more accurate data model. The tucker decomposition in the tensor decomposition method, also known as the higher-order singular value decomposition, is a multilinear generalization of the concept of singular value decomposition, which can dig out the potential structural information of the tensor and more accurately characterize the characteristics of the data after removing the redundant information. Tensor and tensor decomposition theory is currently widely used in data compression, pattern recognition, image processing and other fields [17–19], and tensor decomposition is rarely reported in the application of aero-engine life prediction.

In this paper, a method for mining aero-engine information in tensor mode is used, which can increase the accuracy of aero-engine remaining useful life prediction and reduce the training time of CNN model. The method was validated on the turbofan engine degradation dataset in NASA's C-MAPSS.

2   Introduction to Twin-Rotor Split Turbofan Engine

Figure 1 is a screenshot of a two-rotor row turbofan engine simulated by the C-MAPSS simulator, which is composed of fans, low-pressure compressors, high-pressure compressors, combustion chambers, high-pressure turbines, low-pressure turbines and other components compose.

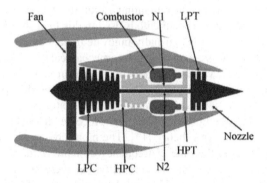

Fig. 1. Screenshot of a turbofan engine simulated by the C-MAPSS simulator [20]

Figure 2 shows the structure of the turbofan engine in Fig. 1, from which it can be seen that the signals of the components are not independent of each other, but are coupled and mutual associated.

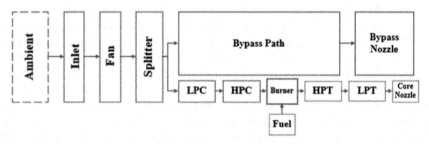

Fig. 2. Turbofan engine structure diagram

3   Remaining Useful Life Prediction of Turbofan Engine Based on Tensor Model

3.1   Method Flow

The process of predicting the remaining useful life of turbofan engine based on tensor mode proposed in this paper is shown in Fig. 3. Firstly, the C-MAPSS dataset of large turbofan engine with strong coupling provided by NASA was constructed in tensor space, and based on the tucker tensor decomposition method and the idea of alternating projection, using the high-order singular value decomposition (HOSVD) and the high-order orthogonal iterative (HOOI) joint solution algorithm, the constructed tensor samples are approximated at low rank, and the characteristics of aero-engine degradation data are obtained. Then, the powerful fitting ability of convolutional neural network is used to train the processed training set, obtain the learning model, and then test the test set, and finally realize the prediction of the remaining life of aero-engine.

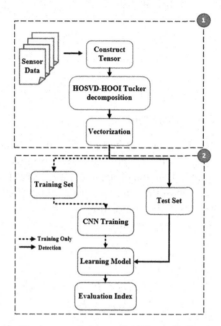

Fig. 3. Engine remaining useful life prediction process

3.2 Turbofan Engine States Sample Construction Based on Tensor

When constructing a state sample of a turbofan engine in a tensor space, each order of the tensor can be seen as a factor that affects the state of the engine, and each element in the tensor can be seen as the result of the interaction of various influencing factors.

The turbofan engine status sample constructed in this paper is a third-order tensor $X \in R^{I \times J \times K}$, and the first-order influencing factor is the sensor signal class, such as total temperature and total pressure of each component outlet, core speed, fan speed, etc. The second-order of the influencing factor is the operating cycle, that is, the change of the sample signal with the operating cycle; The third-order influencing factor is the flight condition, that is, the sample signal changes with the flight condition. This completes the construction of a third-order tensor turbofan engine status sample of a "signal class × operating cycle × flight conditions", the structure of which is shown in Fig. 4. Each element in the sample has a practical physical significance, for example, the element x_{ijk}

(where, $i \in I, j \in J, k \in K$) represents the parameter value of the i sensor signal under the k flight condition, when running to the j cycle.

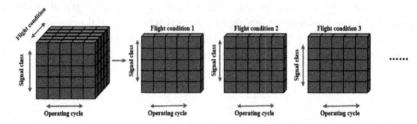

Fig. 4. Sample structure diagram of the turbofan engine state based on three-order tensor

3.3   Tensor Decomposition Algorithm

The tucker decomposition of tensors can be seen as a multilinear generalization of the SVD concept, the essence of which is to approximate the original tensor with the product of a kernel tensor and several orthogonal projection matrices [21]. The core tensor retains the most important information of the original tensor, which is smaller than the original tensor at each order. The tucker decomposition problem of tensors can be expressed specifically to solve the following problems:

$$\left.\begin{array}{ll} \max & \|X \times U_1^T \times U_2^T \times U_3^T\| \\ s.t. & X \in R^{I \times J \times K} \\ & U_1 \in R^{1 \times L}, U_2 \in R^{j \times M}, U_3 \in R^{K \times N} \\ & L \leqslant I, M \leqslant J, N \leqslant K \end{array}\right\} \tag{1}$$

where the tensor X is a sample of the state of the constructed turbofan engine; G is the nuclear tensor; Matrices U_1, U_2 and U_3 all are orthogonal projection matrices. Based on the properties of tucker tensor decomposition and tensor norm, the maximum problem described in Eq. (1) can be equivalent to the minimum problem as follows:

$$\left.\begin{array}{ll} \min & \|X - G \times U_1 \times U_2 \times U_3\| \\ s.t. & X \in R^{I \times J \times K}, G \in R^{L \times M \times N} \\ & U_1 \in R^{1 \times L}, U_2 \in R^{j \times M}, U_3 \in R^{K \times N} \\ & L \leqslant I, M \leqslant J, N \leqslant K \end{array}\right\} \tag{2}$$

Common methods for minimum value problems in solving Eq. (2) are HOSVD [22] and HOOI [23]. The basic idea of HOSVD is to use the singular value decomposition algorithm in matrix analysis to decompose each slice in the tensor once, using low-order approximation processing to filter out some smaller singular values. The basic idea of HOOI is to use the method of alternating projection to iterate multiple times to obtain the optimal result. In order to speed up the iteration speed of the HOOI algorithm, the result of the HOSVD algorithm is taken as the initial iterative value of the HOOI algorithm [24].

3.4 Convolutional Neural Network

The remaining useful life prediction algorithm used in this paper is the convolutional neural network model algorithm [25–29], the model network structure is shown in Fig. 5, the blue color represents the Conv2D layer, the yellow represents the Dropout layer, the white represents the Flatten layer, and the red represents the Dense layer. The model consists of 5 Conv2D layers, adding Dropout layers after the third, fourth and fifth Conv2D layers, adding flatten layers after the third Dropout layer, continuing to add Dropout layers, and finally adding 2 Dense layers.

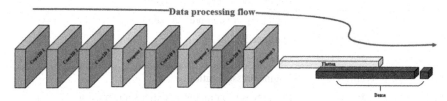

Fig. 5. Schematic diagram of the CNN model network structure (Color figure online)

Of the five Conv2D layers in the model, except for the last Conv2D layer filter with a number of 1 and a convolutional kernel shape of (10, 1) and a step size of (1, 1), the other four Conv2D layers have 10 filters, convolutional kernel shapes of (10, 1), and a step size of (1, 1). The Dropout layer parameters used are all set to 0.5, the number of neurons in the penultimate Dense layer is 100, the activation function is set to 'tanh', and the last Dense layer is the output layer, the number of neurons is 1, and the remaining useful life prediction of the output model is output. After several tests, the learning rate is set to 0.01 and the loss function is selected as mean squared error (MSE).

4   Introduction to the Experimental Dataset

The proposed method for predicting the remaining useful life of turbofan engine based on tensor model was verified by using the turbofan engine degradation simulation dataset provided by NASA [20]. The dataset was obtained by NASA's commercial modular aerial propulsion simulation system (C-MAPSS) to simulate the operation of turbofan engine under different operating conditions. The simulation generated full-period state monitoring data of turbofan engine was taken as the training set, and the non-full-period state monitoring data of turbofan engine obtained by artificial truncation was used as the test set, and the real remaining useful life data corresponding to each engine in the test set is used as supplementary reference data.

In the C-MAPSS dataset, there are twenty-six columns of data. Among them, the first column is the serial number of the turbofan engine, the second column is the corresponding operating cycle of each serial engine, the third column to the fifth column is the flight status parameter, which indicates the flight altitude, Mach number and throttle lever angle, and the sixth column to the twenty-sixth column is the status monitoring parameters of various sensors [20], and the specific information is shown in Table 1.

Table 1. Description table of twenty-one condition monitoring parameters

Serial Number	Symbol	Description	Unit
1	T2	Fan inlet total temperature	°C
2	T24	Low pressure compressor outlet total temperature	°C
3	T30	High pressure compressor outlet total temperature	°C
4	T50	Low pressure turbine outlet total temperature	°C
5	P2	Fan inlet total pressure	Pa
6	P15	Bypass duct outlet total pressure	Pa
7	P30	High pressure compressor outlet total pressure	Pa
8	Nf	Fan speed	r/min
9	Nc	Core speed	r/min
10	epr	Engine pressure ratio	–
11	Ps30	High pressure compressor outlet static pressure	Pa
12	phi	Fuel flow ratio	pps/psi
13	NRf	Fan corrected speed	r/min
14	NRc	Core corrected speed	r/min
15	BPR	Bypass ratio	–
16	farB	Combustor fuel-air ratio	–
17	htBleed	Bleed air enthalpy	–
18	Nf_dmd	Fan speed demands	r/min
19	PcNfR_dmd	Fan corrected speed demands	r/min
20	W31	High pressure turbine cooling air flow	lbm/s
21	W32	Low pressure turbine cooling air flow	lbm/s

The C-MAPSS dataset can be divided into four sub-datasets according to different working conditions and the number of aero-engine failures, namely FD001-FD004. Each sub-dataset consists of a training set and a test set, and records the condition monitoring data of the engine from normal state to performance failure state, and the details of each sub-dataset are shown in Table 2.

Table 2. Details of each sub-dataset

Dataset	FD001	FD002	FD003	FD004
Training set	100	260	100	248
Test set	100	259	100	248
Operation modes	1	6	1	6
Failures number	1	1	2	2

As can be seen from Table 1, there are twenty-one sensor status parameters. Since the values of each measurement parameter are not on a scale and the dimensions are not the same, the subsequent turbofan engine life prediction may bring calculation errors, so it needs to be standardized, and the processing formula is:

$$x_i' = \frac{x_i - \mu_i}{\sigma_i} \tag{3}$$

where x_i is the data point, μ_i is the mean value of the measurement parameter and σ_i is the standard deviation of the measurement parameter.

5   Test Results and Analysis

The training set in the 4 datasets is trained 100 times, and the test set is fed into the CNN model to obtain the remaining useful life of the turbofan engine. Figure 6 shows the relative error in the prediction of the remaining service life of the turbofan engine of different numbers in the test set of the four datasets, calculated as:

$$relative\_error = \frac{X_t - X_p}{X_t} \tag{4}$$

Among them, X_t is the real remaining useful life of the turbofan engine, X_p is the predicted remaining useful life.

In Fig. 6, the red line is the result of the test training after being processed by the Tucker tensor decomposition method, and the blue line is the result of the direct training test. It can be seen that the remaining useful life prediction accuracy of the four datasets has increased after being processed by the tucker tensor decomposition method. Among them, the accuracy improvement of FD002 and FD004 is particularly significant, because the two datasets have a large number of operating modes, and if direct training is carried out, the correlation between sensor data and flight conditions will be ignored. The tensor takes this into account better, retains the structural characteristics and correlation between the data, and can use more effective information for training.

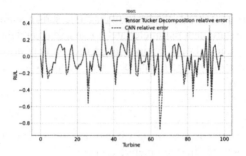

(1) FD001 dataset result comparison

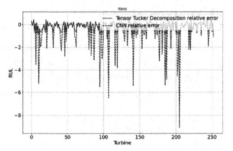

(2) FD002 dataset result comparison

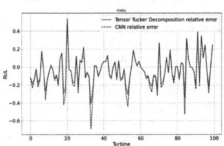

(3) FD003 dataset result comparison

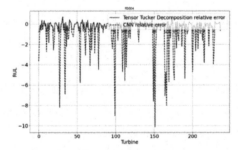

(4) FD004 dataset result comparison

Fig. 6. Comparison of the relative error of the training test result using the data that is processed by the tucker tensor decomposition method and the result using unprocessed data.

In order to further quantify the degree of improvement of the tucker tensor decomposition method on the training effect of CNN, this paper also compares the average relative error and relative error distribution of the model training and testing time and remaining useful life prediction results of the two methods.

The comparison results of the model training and testing time are shown in Table 3. It can be seen that after the tucker tensor decomposition, the CNN model training and testing time of the four datasets will be reduced, which will be reduced by 7.36%, 44.70%, 12.54% and 32.41% respectively, which indicates that the training and testing time of the model for the complex dataset will be reduced more. This is because the HOSVD and HOOI algorithms filter out factors that have little impact on the prediction results, reducing the amount of data in the training and test sets and extracting more valid information.

Table 3. Model training and testing time

Data processing\dataset	Test and training time(s)			
	FD001	FD002	FD003	FD004
Tucker tensor decomposition	623.0	1002.6	667.3	4073.1
No feature extraction	672.5	1813.0	763.0	6026.2
Reduced relative time (%)	7.36	44.70	12.54	35.41

The average relative error and the standard deviation of the remaining useful life prediction result are shown in Table 4, and the average relative error will be reduced, the relative error distribution will be more concentrated for the four datasets after being treated by the tucker tensor decomposition method. The average relative error of the four sub-datasets decreased by 2.21%, 41.46%, 2.07%, and 67.83%, respectively. In contrast, it is found that the accuracy of the remaining useful life prediction of the complex dataset after being processed by the tucker tensor decomposition method will increase more obviously. This is because the more complex the dataset contains and the more correlated it is, the more valid information can be extracted by the tucker tensor decomposition method.

Table 4. The average relative error and its standard deviation of the remaining useful life prediction results

Data processing\dataset	FD001		FD002		FD003		FD004	
	Mean	Standard deviation	Mean	Standard deviation	Mean	Standard deviation	Mean	Standard deviation
Tucker tensor decomposition	0.1305	0.1059	0.2816	0.2291	0.1277	0.1030	0.3102	0.3596
No feature extraction	0.1526	0.1461	0.6962	1.2152	0.1484	0.1311	0.9885	1.7536
Reduced average relative error (%)	2.21		41.46		2.07		67.83	

6 Conclusion

In this paper, a method for mining aero-engine data information in tensor mode is proposed and used in the prediction of the remaining useful life of aero-engine. Experimental verification was carried out on the C-MAPSS dataset and the following conclusions were obtained:

The data extracted from aero-engine data by tensor method of tucker decomposition has better training effect in CNN than the data that not be processed, with an average prediction accuracy increased by 28.39% and an average learning time shortened by 24.25%. For structurally complex dataset, the data extracted by the tensor tucker decomposition method will reduce more time of model training and testing in CNN than the data that is not processed, and the prediction accuracy will be improved more.

This paper only uses the convolutional neural network of the structure shown in Fig. 5 for data training, and it can be seen that the accuracy of CNN directly training and testing the C-MPASS training set is not enough. In future studies, it is possible to compare other remaining useful life prediction methods in tensor mode to further illustrate the superiority of this method.

References

1. Jaw, L.C., Mattingly, J.D.: Aircraft Engine Controls: Design, System Analysis, and Health Monitoring, pp. 136–138 (2009)
2. Vachtsevanos, G.J., Vachtsevanos, G.J.: Intelligent Fault Diagnosis and Prognosis for Engineering Systems. Wiley Online Library (2006)
3. Li, X., Ding, Q., Sun, J.-Q.: Remaining useful life estimation in prognostics using deep convolution neural networks. Reliab. Eng. Syst. Saf. **172**, 1–11 (2018)
4. Zhao, H., Zheng, N., Chen, T., Wei, K.: Aero engine rul prediction based on the combination of similarity and PSO-SVR (2021)
5. Li, H., Li, Y., Wang, Z., Li, Z.: Remaining useful life prediction of aero-engine based on PCA-LSTM. In: 7th International Conference on Condition Monitoring of Machinery in Non-Stationary Operations (CMMNO), pp. 63–66. IEEE (2021)
6. Wang, T., Guo, D., Sun, X.-M.: Remaining useful life predictions for turbofan engine degradation based on concurrent semi-supervised model. Neural Comput. Appl. **34**(7), 5151–5160 (2021). https://doi.org/10.1007/s00521-021-06089-1
7. Wu, B., Shi, H., Zeng, J., Shi, G., Qin, Y.: Multi-sensor information fusion-based remaining useful life prediction with nonlinear wiener process. Meas. Sci. Technol. **33**, 105106 (2022)
8. Yuan, M., Wu, Y., Lin, L.: Fault diagnosis and remaining useful life estimation of aero engine using LSTM neural network. In: IEEE International Conference on Aircraft Utility Systems (AUS), pp. 135–140. IEEE (2016)
9. Zhang, X., et al.: Remaining useful life estimation using CNN-XGB with extended time window. IEEE Access **7**, 154386–154397 (2019)
10. Al-Dulaimi, A., Zabihi, S., Asif, A., Mohammadi, A.: Hybrid deep neural network model for remaining useful life estimation. In: ICASSP 2019–2019 IEEE International Conference on Acoustics, Speech and Signal Processing (ICASSP), pp. 3872–3876. IEEE (2019)
11. Ge, Y., Zhang, F.: Remaining useful life estimation for aero-engine with multiple working conditions via an improved generative adversarial network. J. Braz. Soc. Mech. Sci. Eng. **44**(5), 1–12 (2022)

12. Jing, C., Li, Z., Ping, D.: Remaining useful life prediction for Aero-Engines combining sate space model and KF algorithm. Trans. Nanjing Univ. Aeronaut. Astronaut. **34**(03), 265–271 (2017)
13. da Costa, P.R.d.O., Akçay, A., Zhang, Y., Kaymak, U.: Remaining useful lifetime prediction via deep domain adaptation. Reliab. Eng. Syst. Saf. **195**, 106682 (2020)
14. Xianda, Z.: Matrix Analysis and Application. Tsinghua University Press Co., Ltd., Beijing (2004)
15. Cichocki, A., et al.: Tensor Decompositions for Signal Processing Applications: from two-way to multiway component analysis. IEEE Signal Process. Mag. **32**(2), 145–163 (2015)
16. Hou, C., Nie, F., Zhang, C., Yi, D., Wu, Y.: Multiple rank multi-linear SVM for matrix data classification. Pattern Recogn. **47**(1), 454–469 (2014)
17. Cammoun, L., et al.: A review of tensors and tensor signal processing. In: Aja-Fernández, S., de Luis García, R., Tao, D., Li, X. (eds.) Tensors in Image Processing and Computer Vision, pp. 1–32. Springer, London (2009). https://doi.org/10.1007/978-1-84882-299-3_1
18. Sidiropoulos, N.D., De Lathauwer, L., Fu, X., Huang, K., Papalexakis, E.E., Faloutsos, C.: Tensor decomposition for signal processing and machine learning. IEEE Trans. Signal Process. **65**(13), 3551–3582 (2017)
19. Kolda, T.G., Bader, B.W.: Tensor decompositions and applications. SIAM Rev. **51**(3), 455–500 (2009)
20. Saxena, A., Goebel, K., Simon, D., Eklund, N.: Damage propagation modeling for aircraft engine run-to-failure simulation. In: 2008 International Conference on Prognostics and Health Management, pp. 1–9. IEEE (2008)
21. Che, M., Wei, Y.: Randomized algorithms for the approximations of Tucker and the tensor train decompositions. Adv. Comput. Math. **45**(1), 395–428 (2018). https://doi.org/10.1007/s10444-018-9622-8
22. Zeng, C., Ng, M.K.: Decompositions of third-order tensors: HOSVD, T-SVD, and Beyond. Numer. Linear Algebra Appl. **27**(3), e2290 (2020)
23. Sheehan, B.N., Saad, Y.: Higher order orthogonal iteration of tensors (HOOI) and its relation to PCA and GLRAM. In: Proceedings of the 2007 SIAM International Conference on Data Mining, pp. 355–365. SIAM (2007)
24. Sun, J., Tao, D., Papadimitriou, S., Yu, P.S., Faloutsos, C.: Incremental tensor analysis: Theory and applications. ACM Trans. Knowl. Disc. Data (TKDD) **2**(3), 1–37 (2008)
25. Zhong, M., Jiansheng, G., Taoyong, G., Sheng, M.: Remaining useful life prediction of aero-engine based on improved convolutional neural network. J. Air Force Eng. Univ. (Nat. Sci. Ed.) **21**(06), 19–25 (2020)
26. Albawi, S., Mohammed, T.A., Al-Zawi, S.: Understanding of a convolutional neural network. In: 2017 International Conference on Engineering and Technology (ICET), pp. 1–6. IEEE (2017)
27. Wu, J.: Introduction to convolutional neural networks. National Key Lab for Novel Software Technology. Nanjing University, China, vol. 5, no. 23, p. 495 (2017)
28. Li, Z., Liu, F., Yang, W., Peng, S., Zhou, J.: A survey of convolutional neural networks: analysis, applications, and prospects. IEEE Trans. Neural Netw. Learn. Syst. (2021)
29. Jogin, M., Madhulika, M., Divya, G., Meghana, R., Apoorva, S.: Feature extraction using convolution neural networks (CNN) and deep learning. In: 2018 3rd IEEE International Conference on Recent Trends in Electronics, Information and Communication Technology (RTEICT), pp. 2319–2323. IEEE (2018)

FIGCI: Flow-Based Information-Geometric Causal Inference

Shengyuan Zhang[1], Jingyu Wu[1], Zejian Li[1(✉)], Li Liu[2], Jun Liao[2], and Lingyun Sun[1,3]

[1] Alibaba-Zhejiang University Joint Institute of Frontier Technologies, Zhejiang University, Hangzhou 310027, China
{zhangshengyuan,wujingyu,zejianlee,sunly}@zju.edu.cn
[2] The School of Big Data & Software Engineering, Chongqing University, Chongqing 400044, China
{dcsliuli,liaojun}@cqu.edu.cn
[3] Zhejiang-Singapore Innovation and AI Joint Research Lab, Hangzhou 310027, China

Abstract. This paper is concerned with causal discovery between two random variables X and Y with observational data. Information-Geometric Causal Inference (IGCI) is a well-established method to identify the causal direction between two variables. It assumes the cause distribution and causal mechanism are independent. However, IGCI requires the causal mechanism to be a diffeomorphism function. Fortunately, flow-based models are designed to be differentiable and have a differentiable inverse with a large capacity. We propose Flow-based IGCI (FIGCI). First, the flow-based model fits an invertible mapping between X and Y with two proposed training strategies. Second, FIGCI predicts the causal direction according to the estimated covariances between X as well as Y and the invertible mapping. Empirical studies exemplify the efficacy of FIGCI.

Keywords: Causal discovery · Flow-based models · Information-geometric causal inference

1 Introduction

Discovering the causal relationship behind different objects is one of the main spiritual activities of mankind. In the field of artificial intelligence, identifying the causal structure is also crucial to understanding the mechanisms behind observational data. Traditional causal discovery models recover a Markov equivalence class of the causal structure of observed data with independence tests if the causal Markov and faithfulness assumptions are satisfied [8,26,27]. In addition, improved methods are proposed to effectively recover the complete causal structure [6,7,12,14,25,29,31].

This study focuses on causal discovery between observed data of two variables. Given two random variables X and Y, the goal is to identify whether X

© The Author(s), under exclusive license to Springer Nature Switzerland AG 2022
L. Fang et al. (Eds.): CICAI 2022, LNAI 13605, pp. 520–531, 2022.
https://doi.org/10.1007/978-3-031-20500-2_43

causes Y or Y causes X. It cannot be solved by methods such as conditional independence tests but should resort to other priors or assumptions. Many methods have been proposed to discover bivariate causality, such as additive noise model (ANM) [13], post-non-linear model (PNL) [30], information-geometric causal inference (IGCI) [16], regression error based causal inference (RECI) [2]. The assumptions behind includes the linear relationship between cause and effect [13], the limitation of dimension [30], the noise distribution [24] and the Independent Causal Mechanisms [23].

IGCI [16] is a well-established bivariate causal discovery method. It is based on the assumption of independence between the cause distribution and the causal function. However, IGCI has several limitations. First, IGCI requires the causal function to be diffeomorphism[1]. Second, diffeomorphism functions are difficult to construct in high-dimensional space. Third, when only the observational data is available, the causal function should be learned from a predefined diffeomorphism family. The original IGCI [16] bypasses the need to learn the diffeomorphism causal mapping and approximating the covariances indirectly.

We propose Flow-based IGCI (FIGCI) to directly learn the diffeomorphism mapping and estimate the covariances. The key motivation behind is that flow-based models are designed to be diffeomorphism with well-defined Jacobian and can fit the observational data effectively [9,10,18]. Such property of flow-based models coincidentally resolves IGCI's limitations. The causal discovery process of FIGCI has two stages. The first stage is to learn the diffeomorphism mapping between X and Y. In the learning, we build the diffeomorphism mapping with multi-layer perception, Smooth Maximum Unit [1] (an invertible nonlinear function), and RealNVP [10] (a typical flow-based model). Besides, we introduce two fitting methods to train the mapping, termed FIGCI-R and FIGCI-J. The second stage is to calculate the covariances of two directions and predict the causal direction accordingly.

The main contributions of this paper are the proposed FIGCI method. To the best of our knowledge, we are the first to adopt the invertible property of flow-based models to solve the limitation of IGCI. It boasts three advantages. First, it does not presume the causal order in advance [17] but infers the direction after fitting. Second, it not only identifies the causal direction but also learns the causal mapping function. The mapping function can be used for further relational analysis. Third, the learned mapping is a neural network with a high capacity to fit high-dimensional data with complex relations compared with linear functions.

2   Related Work

The tasks of causal discovery often aim at discovering causal mechanisms behind data in order to overcome the shortcomings of artificial intelligence techniques in terms of abstraction, reasoning, and interpretability.

---

[1] A function is called a diffeomorphism if it is differentiable and bijective and it has a differentiable inverse.

Multivariate causal discovery can be divided into three categories. PC algorithm [26] is a typical constraint-based method. It uses the conditional independence test to find the skeleton and the V-structure and then orients the remaining edges by additional criteria. It is improved to have a faster speed [26] and deal with missing values [8]. Linear non-Gaussian acyclic models (LiNGAM) is a function-based method that assumes that the generative function between variables is linear and the noise is non-Gaussian distributed. It is also improved to be faster [25] and to deal with confounders [6,7,14]. Continuous optimization [31] can also uncover the causal structure with GNN [29], the independence assumption [12], and an entropy-based loss [5].

Different from multivariate causal discovery, the main principle in binary causal discovery is to find information asymmetry between X and Y [15,17,19, 21,22,24]. Most of these methods are based on the Additive Noise Models (ANM) [13]. Unsupervised inverse GP regression estimates $P(X|Y)$ and $P(Y|X)$ respectively by the unsupervised learning method, and then compares the accuracy of these two models to determine the causal direction [24]. Moreover, causal autoregressive flow (CAF) uses the flow-based model to generate the variables [17]. It calculates the likelihood ratio of one variable with a flow-based model determined by the other variable. The one with a larger likelihood is viewed as the effect. Different from this process, FIGCI fits the data with a flow-based model, which is conceptually clear. Besides, the prediction is based on IGCI.

3   Information-Geometric Causal Inference

IGCI [16] identifies the causal relationship between random variables X and Y. It is based on the Independent Causal Mechanism [23] and requires the mapping function between X and Y to be diffeomorphism. Namely, $Y = f(X)$ and $X = f^{-1}(Y)$. Without loss of generality, we assume X causes Y. We begin with the one-dimensional case and then naturally extend to the multi-dimensional case.

Definition 1 (Information-Geometric   Causal   Inference   (one-dimension) [28]). *If a model satisfies an IGCI model from X to Y, it should hold the following conditions: $Y = f(X)$ for a diffeomorphism function f of $[0,1]$ that is strictly monotonic and satisfies $f(0) = 0$ and $f(1) = 1$. Moreover, P_X should have a strictly positive continuous density p_X. Then the following condition holds:*

$$\mathrm{cov}\left[\log f', p_X\right] = 0 \tag{1}$$

$\log f'$ and p_X are both the measurable function of $X \in [0,1]$, which can be regarded as random variables on the same probability space $[0,1]$. Therefore, their covariance can be calculated. The covariance can be expanded as

$$\begin{aligned}
\mathrm{cov}\left[\log f', p_X\right] &= \int_0^1 \log f'(x) p_X(x) dx - \int_0^1 \log f'(x) dx \int_0^1 p_X(x) dx \\
&= \int_0^1 \log f'(x) p_X(x) dx - \int_0^1 \log f'(x) dx = 0
\end{aligned} \tag{2}$$

The zero covariance between $\log f'$ and p_X means the causal mechanism f is independent to the input distribution p_X. This independence implies the dependence between f^{-1} and p_Y, because p_Y contains information about f^{-1}.

Definition 2 (Identifiability of IGCI models [28]). *Given f that satisfies an IGCI model from X to Y, the inverse function f^{-1} satisfies*

$$\operatorname{cov}\left[\log f^{-1'}, p_Y\right] \geq 0 \tag{3}$$

and the equality holds if and only if f is the identity.

Figure 1 visualizes the intuition of Definition 2. P_X does not show any relation with f, while P_Y has a high density where f^{-1} has a large gradient. When the gradient of f is low, a large probability mass of X is aggregated by f to a small area of Y, and a high density of Y is formed. Then the density of P_Y is correlated to the gradient of f. On the opposite, as an input, P_X is not aware of f so P_X is not correlated to the gradient of f. As a result, the causal direction is implied by the asymmetry of covariances, and the direction can be discovered.

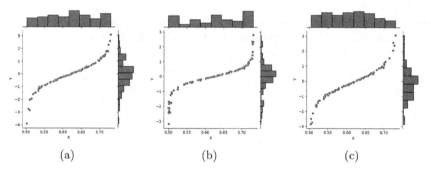

(a)   (b)   (c)

Fig. 1. The density of X the cause is not correlated with the slope of f when $X \to Y$.

Definition 3 (Information-Geometric   Causal   Inference   (multi-dimension) [28]). *If a model satisfies an IGCI model from X to Y, it should hold the following conditions: $Y = f(X)$ for some diffeomorphism function f of $B = [0,1]^d$. P_X should have a strictly positive continuous density p_X. then the following condition holds:*

$$\operatorname{cov}\left[\log|\det J_f|, p_X\right] = \int_B \log\left|\det \frac{\partial f(x)}{\partial x^T}\right| dP_X - \int_B \log\left|\det \frac{\partial f(x)}{\partial x^T}\right| dU_X = 0 \tag{4}$$

U_X is a uniform distribution on $B = [0,1]^d$. Definition 3 is a natural extension to IGCI in multi-dimensional cases.

To perform causal discovery, IGCI needs to know the causal diffeomorphism function in advances. However, only observed data is available in reality. The original IGCI [16] bypasses the need by estimating local gradients or reference measures with entropy [20]. Though effective, it fails to infer the causal function and requires extra assumptions. Our method steps further to uncover the causal function directly as introduced in the following section.

4   FIGCI Model

In order to alleviate the limitations of IGCI, we propose Flow-based Information-Geometric Causal Inference (FIGCI). Firstly, a flow-based model fits the observational data to obtain the mapping between variables. Then, the gradients or Jacobians in both directions are obtained according to the learned mapping. Finally, the IGCI covariances are calculated and compared to determine the causal direction. In this section, we first briefly introduce flow-based models and then describe detailed implementations of FIGCI.

4.1   Flow-Based Models

The flow-based model is a powerful generative model. A generative model can fit observed samples and generate new samples from the learned distribution. The flow-based model boasts a stable training process and directly maximizes the log-likelihood of observed samples. In the training, the log-likelihood is formulated.

Definition 4 (*Change of Variable [10]*). *Given a observed variable X with distribution P_X, a bijection function $g\colon X \mapsto Z$ maps X to a latent variable Z subject to a predefined P_Z, the change of variable formula is:*

$$p_X(x) = p_Z(g(x))\,|\det J_g| = p_Z(g(x))\left|\det \frac{\partial g(x)}{\partial x^T}\right| \tag{5}$$

Here J_g is the Jacobian matrix of the function g.

Notice that the latent P_Z is a predefined distribution, and thus $p_Z(g(x))$ can be calculated. When generating samples, a latent z is sampled and transformed into a new sample with $x = g^{-1}(z)$. Therefore, g is required to be diffeomorphism with an explicit invertible mapping. Besides, it should have both enough capacity and a tractable Jacobian determinant.

The coupling layers proposed in RealNVP [10] satisfy the above requirements. With little notation abuse, for an input $x \in \mathbb{R}^D$ and an output $y \in \mathbb{R}^D$, a coupling layer divide x, y from the dimension $d \in (1, D)$ and calculates

$$
\begin{aligned}
y_{1:d} &= x_{1:d} \\
y_{d+1:D} &= x_{d+1:D} \odot \exp\left(s\left(x_{1:d}\right)\right) + t\left(x_{1:d}\right)
\end{aligned}
\tag{6}
$$

Here $s(\cdot)$ and $t(\cdot)$ are the adaptive scale and translation functions. $\odot$ is the element-wise multiplication operation. Accordingly, the Jacobian matrix is

$$\frac{\partial y}{\partial x^T} = \begin{bmatrix} I_d & \mathbf{0} \\ \frac{\partial y_{d+1:D}}{\partial x_{1:d}^T} & \operatorname{diag}\left(\exp(s(x_{1:d}))\right) \end{bmatrix} \tag{7}$$

Here I_d is an identity matrix of $d \times d$. $\operatorname{diag}\left(\exp\left(s\left(x_{1:d}\right)\right)\right)$ is a diagonal matrix of $s\left(x_{1:d}\right)$. Thus the Jacobian determinant is $\exp(\sum_{i=d+1}^{D} s((x_{1:d})_i))$, while the inverse Jacobian determinant is $\exp(\sum_{i=d+1}^{D} -s(y_{1:d})_i)$. The computation involves only forward pass of s and t, so they are defined as multi-layer percep-tions (MLP) to have more flexibility.

The coupling layer leaves some components unchanged during the transfor-mation. This is solved by composing coupling layers alternately, so the compo-nents unchanged in one coupling layer are updated in the next. A binary mask $m \in \{0,1\}^D$ indicates two parts of the input. Thus, y is calculated by:

$$y = m \odot x + (1 - m) \odot (x \odot \exp(s(m \odot x)) + t(m \odot x)) \tag{8}$$

In this case, s and t are extended to mappings from R^D to R^D. Specifically, $m_i = 1$ for $i \in [1, D]$ means the value of x_i remains unchanged in this layer, while $m_i = 0$ means x_i is updated. The mask is reversed once after each coupling layer. With the mask, the Jacobian determinants of the forward direction is

$$\log \left| \det \frac{\partial y}{\partial x^T} \right| = (1 - m)^T s(m \odot x) = \sum_{i:m_i=0} s(m \odot x)_i \tag{9}$$

Apparently, $\log \left| \det \frac{\partial x}{\partial y^T} \right| = -\log \left| \det \frac{\partial y}{\partial x^T} \right|$. Equation 9 is an extension of Eq. 7. The structure of coupling layers facilitates the calculation of Jacobian determi-nants.

For high-dimensional data with $D > 1$, we use the coupling layer [10] as the base structure of the FIGCI model. The whole model consists of coupling layers and mask-reversing layers as shown in Fig. 2 and 3. For one-dimensional data, we build the FIGCI model with one-dimensional MLPs with Smooth Maximum Unit (SMU) [1] as non-linear activations. In the linear transformation, the forward pass is $y = w \times x + b$ while the backward is $x = \frac{y-b}{w}$. In the non-linear activation, we adopt a smooth and differentiable approximation of LeakyReLU.

$$y = \frac{(1 + \alpha)x + \sqrt{(1 - \alpha)^2 x^2 + \mu^2}}{2}$$
$$x = \frac{(1 + \alpha)y - \sqrt{(1 - \alpha)^2 y^2 + \alpha\mu^2}}{2\alpha} \tag{10}$$

Here α is the negative slope in LeakyReLU while μ controls the smoothness. As $\mu \to 0$, the functions goes to LeakyReLU. We stack three MLP layers with two SMU layers inbetween.

4.2   FIGCI-R Model

In this part, we introduce the combined training and causal discovering process, FIGCI-R. It has two stages. The first is to fit observed data with the designed flow-based model and thus the second is to infer the causal direction. We assume only n observed sample pairs $\{(x_i, y_i) \mid i = 1, \dots, n\}$ are available.

Step One: Fitting Causal Mechanism. The fitting is to maximize log-likelihood.

$$\arg\max_f \sum_{x_i,y_i} \log p(y_i \mid x_i; f) \propto -\frac{1}{n} \sum_{i=1}^{n} (y_i - f(x_i))^2. \tag{11}$$

This assumes $P(Y \mid X; f)$ is a Gaussian $\mathcal{N}(f(X), I)$. For multi-dimensional data, we construct a FIGCI-R shown in Fig. 2.

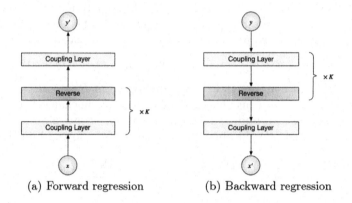

(a) Forward regression   (b) Backward regression

Fig. 2. The structure of FIGCI-R. Here $y' = f(x), x' = f^{-1}(y)$.

During the training, the fitting is performed in both directions. Therefore, the final optimization is

$$\arg \min_f \frac{1}{n} \sum_{i=1}^{n} \left[(y_i - f(x_i))^2 + (x_i - f^{-1}(y_i))^2 \right] \tag{12}$$

Step two: Identifying Causal Direction by IGCI. After fitting the function, we obtain the forward and backward Jacobian determinants to estimate IGCI covariances.

$$IGCI_{x \to y} = \mathrm{cov}\left[\log |\det J_f|, p_X\right], \quad IGCI_{y \to x} = \mathrm{cov}\left[\log |\det J_{f^{-1}}|, p_Y\right] \tag{13}$$

The covariances are estimated by Monte-Carlo estimator on real samples from P_X and synthetic samples from U_X. Finally, the causal direction is predicted by comparing the IGCI score of both directions. Namely, $|IGCI_{x \to y}| < |IGCI_{y \to x}|$ means $X \to Y$ and $|IGCI_{x \to y}| > |IGCI_{y \to x}|$ means $Y \to X$.

4.3 FIGCI-J Model

In this part, we introduce another training strategy FIGCI-J. Instead of viewing the flow-based model as a mapping between X and Y, FIGCI-J encodes X and Y to a shared latent code Z. The intuition behind is based on the diffeomorphism assumption. If there exists a bijection between X and Y, there tends to be another intermediate variable Z having bijections to both X and Y. As a result, in the forward direction, X is transformed to Z at first and then Z to Y. This is similar to the backward direction. Z acts like a virtual confounder determining X and Y at the same time to show their relation.

Based on the structure above, the core idea is to train two generative models which fit the joint distribution of X and Y with one latent Z. The two generative models are flow-based models as diffeomorphism functions. As flow-based models are neural networks with strong capacity, Z is subject to a predefined distribution such as standard Gaussian.

Step One: Fitting Causal Mechanism. In this stage, two generative models fits P_X and P_Y by maximizing the log-likelihood as Eq. 5 (Fig. 3).

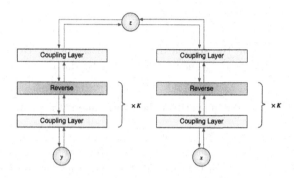

Fig. 3. The structure of FIGCI-J model.

The training of flow-based models is to maximize log-likelihood directly. We assume f_X maps X to Z and f_Y maps Y to Z. The two flow-based models should not be trained separately, because (x_i, y_i) should be mapped to a single latent code z_i. Hence, we adopt a dual decomposition strategy [4]. Given $z_{x_i} = f_X(x_i)$ and $z_{y_i} = f_Y(y_i)$, we formulate the training process as:

$$\arg\max_{f_X, f_Y} \sum_{(x_i, y_i)} [\log p_X(x_i) + \log p_Y(y_i)]$$

$$\text{s.t. } z_{x_i} = z_{y_i} \text{ for } i \in [1, \ldots, n] \tag{14}$$

With Lagrange multiplier [3], the optmization problem is reformulated as

$$\arg\max_{f_X, f_Y} \sum_{(x_i, y_i)} [\log p_X(x_i) + \log p_Y(y_i)] + \beta \frac{1}{n} \sum_{i=1}^{n} (z_{x_i} - z_{y_i})^2 \tag{15}$$

Here β controls the regularization strength.

Step two: Identifying Causal Direction by IGCI. Similar to FIGCI-R, the causal direction is predicted by the IGCI scores of the directions $X \to Y$ and $Y \to X$. The two generative models from Z are both bijections and thus the computation of both directions is tractable. The overall structure is visualized in Fig. 3. The blue arrow shows the computational path from X to Y and the red shows the path from Y to X.

5   Experiments

5.1   Experiments with Different Dimensional Data

We compare the performance of FIGCI on synthetic data with those of several existing binary causal discovery methods: the ANM [13], RECI [2] and CAF [17]. Firstly, we construct a series of synthetic data to compare the accuracy of causal direction identification of our FIGCI model with these existing methods with the process of data generation based on the SEM:

$$\mathbf{x}_1 = \mathbf{z}_1, \quad \mathbf{x}_i = f_i(\mathbf{x}_{i-1}, \mathbf{z}_i) \quad i > 1 \tag{16}$$

Here $\mathbf{z}_i$ is the noise from the standard Laplace distribution. We use the method in CAF [17] to design f_i and generate the synthetic data.

Table 1. The results of synthetic data with different amount of noise.

Noise	$\lambda = 0.001$					$\lambda = 0.01$					$\lambda = 0.1$				
Dim	25	40	60	75	100	25	40	60	75	100	25	40	60	75	100
ANM	0.50	0.51	0.54	0.51	0.49	0.50	0.51	0.53	0.48	0.49	0.50	0.52	0.52	0.52	0.45
RECI	1.00	1.00	1.00	1.00	1.00	1.00	1.00	1.00	1.00	1.00	1.00	1.00	1.00	1.00	1.00
CAF	1.00	1.00	1.00	0.98	0.99	1.00	1.00	1.00	0.98	0.99	1.00	1.00	1.00	0.98	0.99
FIGCI-R	0.95	0.99	0.87	0.66	0.60	0.93	0.90	0.80	0.68	0.60	0.94	0.93	0.82	0.63	0.61
FIGCI-J	1.00	1.00	1.00	1.00	1.00	1.00	1.00	1.00	1.00	1.00	1.00	1.00	1.00	1.00	1.00

Experiments are conducted on data with different dimensions. The number of samples $n = 100$ and each experiment is repeated 100 times to get an average accuracy (Table 1), λ represents the degree of noise. FIGCI-R achieves relatively high accuracy with relatively low dimensions, but its performance gradually decays as the dimension increases. We attribute decay to the inability of l_2 loss to measure similarity in high-dimensional space because of its sensitivity to outliers. FIGCI-J achieves state-of-the-art performance under different dimensions, and its performance does not decrease with the increase of noise.

5.2   Robustness to Noise of Different Distributions

We test the robustness of our proposed model against the noise of Gaussian, Laplace, and Student noise distribution. FIGCI-J shows strong robustness given different noise distributions, achieving 100% accuracy (Table 2).

5.3   Experiments on Real-World Data

Experiments are also performed on common Cause-Effect Pairs (CEP) benchmark datasets. Because FIGCI aims at the binary causality discovery, the multivariable datasets are omitted and only 99 datasets are used. We also compare

Table 2. The results of synthetic data with different distribution of noise($\lambda = 0.1$).

Model	Gaussian noise	Laplace noise	Student noise
ANM	0.31	0.45	0.51
RECI	1.00	1.00	1.00
CAF	1.00	0.99	0.93
FIGCI-R	0.68	0.61	0.70
FIGCI-J	1.00	1.00	1.00

Table 3. The result of CEP benchmark datasets.

Model	Average accuracy
ANM	0.54
RECI	0.62
CAF	0.55
IGCI	0.59
CDS	0.67
FIGCI-R	0.66
FIGCI-J	0.58

advanced methods including CDS [11] and IGCI [16] and use the average accuracy as the final evaluation (Table 3). FIGCI-R and FIGCI-J achieve comparable performance, but the FIGCI-R is better. This is mainly because instead of the architecture of RealNVP, one-dimensional FIGCI model is based on MLP, which makes the backward gradient calculation of FIGCI-J not accurate and the performance of FIGCI-J worse than FIGCI-R.

6 Conclusion

This paper introduces FIGCI, a bivariate causal discovery method. FIGCI is based on Information-Geometric Causal Inference (IGCI), which tests the independence between the marginal distributions of X, Y and the causal function. By introducing flow-based models, FIGCI alleviates the limitation of IGCI that the causal functions must be diffeomorphism and given in advance. The discovery process of FIGCI has two stages. The first is to fit the observed samples with a flow-based model. We propose two fitting strategies. The second stage is to estimate the IGCI covariances and thus predict the direction. FIGCI demonstrates state-of-the-art performance for both synthetic and real-world data. Besides, it shows the robustness to noise of different distributions.

Acknowledgment. This paper is funded by National Key R&D Program of China (2018AAA0100703), and the National Natural Science Foundation of China (No. 62006208 and No. 62107035).

References

1. Biswas, K., Kumar, S., Banerjee, S., Pandey, A.K.: SMU: smooth activation function for deep networks using smoothing maximum technique. arXiv preprint arXiv:2111.04682 (2021)
2. Blöbaum, P., Janzing, D., Washio, T., Shimizu, S., Schölkopf, B.: Cause-effect inference by comparing regression errors. In: International Conference on Artificial Intelligence and Statistics, pp. 900–909. PMLR (2018)
3. Boyd, S., Boyd, S.P., Vandenberghe, L.: Convex Optimization. Cambridge University Press, Cambridge (2004)
4. Boyd, S., Parikh, N., Chu, E., Peleato, B., Eckstein, J., et al.: Distributed optimization and statistical learning via the alternating direction method of multipliers. Found. Trends® Mach. Learn. **3**(1), 1–122 (2011)
5. Cai, R., Chen, W., Qiao, J., Hao, Z.: On the role of entropy-based loss for learning causal structures with continuous optimization. arXiv preprint arXiv:2106.02835 (2021)
6. Chen, W., Cai, R., Zhang, K., Hao, Z.: Causal discovery in linear non-gaussian acyclic model with multiple latent confounders. IEEE Trans. Neural Netw. Learn. Syst. **33**, 2816–2827 (2021)
7. Chen, Z., Chan, L.: Causality in linear nongaussian acyclic models in the presence of latent gaussian confounders. Neural Comput. **25**(6), 1605–1641 (2013)
8. Colombo, D., Maathuis, M.H., Kalisch, M., Richardson, T.S.: Learning high-dimensional directed acyclic graphs with latent and selection variables. Ann. Stat. **40**, 294–321 (2012)
9. Dinh, L., Krueger, D., Bengio, Y.: NICE: non-linear independent components estimation. In: International Conference on Learning Representations (ICLR) (2015)
10. Dinh, L., Sohl-Dickstein, J., Bengio, S.: Density estimation using real NVP. In: International Conference on Learning Representations (ICLR) (2016)
11. Fonollosa, J.A.: Conditional distribution variability measures for causality detection. In: Guyon, I., Statnikov, A., Batu, B. (eds.) Cause Effect Pairs in Machine Learning, pp. 339–347. Springer, Cham (2019). https://doi.org/10.1007/978-3-030-21810-2_12
12. He, Y., Cui, P., Shen, Z., Xu, R., Liu, F., Jiang, Y.: DARING: differentiable causal discovery with residual independence. In: Proceedings of the 27th ACM SIGKDD Conference on Knowledge Discovery and Data Mining, pp. 596–605 (2021)
13. Hoyer, P., Janzing, D., Mooij, J.M., Peters, J., Schölkopf, B.: Nonlinear causal discovery with additive noise models. In: Advances in Neural Information Processing Systems 21, pp. 689–696 (2008)
14. Hoyer, P.O., Shimizu, S., Kerminen, A.J., Palviainen, M.: Estimation of causal effects using linear non-gaussian causal models with hidden variables. Int. J. Approx. Reason. **49**(2), 362–378 (2008)
15. Hyvärinen, A., Smith, S.M.: Pairwise likelihood ratios for estimation of non-Gaussian structural equation models. J. Mach. Learn. Res. JMLR **14**, 111 (2013)
16. Janzing, D., et al.: Information-geometric approach to inferring causal directions. Artif. Intell. **182**, 1–31 (2012)
17. Khemakhem, I., Monti, R., Leech, R., Hyvarinen, A.: Causal autoregressive flows. In: International Conference on Artificial Intelligence and Statistics, pp. 3520–3528. PMLR (2021)
18. Kingma, D.P., Dhariwal, P.: Glow: generative flow with invertible 1×1 convolutions. In: Advances in Neural Information Processing Systems 31, pp. 10236–10245 (2018)

19. Kpotufe, S., Sgouritsa, E., Janzing, D., Schölkopf, B.: Consistency of causal inference under the additive noise model. In: International Conference on Machine Learning, pp. 478–486. PMLR (2014)

20. Kraskov, A., Stögbauer, H., Grassberger, P.: Estimating mutual information. Phys. Rev. E **69**(6), 066138 (2004)

21. Nowzohour, C., Bühlmann, P.: Score-based causal learning in additive noise models. Statistics **50**(3), 471–485 (2016)

22. Peters, J., Bühlmann, P.: Identifiability of Gaussian structural equation models with equal error variances. Biometrika **101**(1), 219–228 (2014)

23. Peters, J., Janzing, D., Schölkopf, B.: Elements of Causal Inference: Foundations and Learning Algorithms. The MIT Press, Cambridge (2017)

24. Sgouritsa, E., Janzing, D., Hennig, P., Schölkopf, B.: Inference of cause and effect with unsupervised inverse regression. In: Artificial Intelligence and Statistics, pp. 847–855. PMLR (2015)

25. Shimizu, S., et al.: DirectLiNGAM: a direct method for learning a linear nongaussian structural equation model. J. Mach. Learn. Res. **12**, 1225–1248 (2011)

26. Spirtes, P., Glymour, C.N., Scheines, R., Heckerman, D.: Causation, Prediction, and Search. MIT Press, Cambridge (2000)

27. Spirtes, P., Meek, C., Richardson, T.: Causal inference in the presence of latent variables and selection bias. In: Proceedings of the Eleventh Conference on Uncertainty in Artificial Intelligence, pp. 499–506 (1995)

28. Thomas, M., Joy, A.T.: Elements of Information Theory. Wiley-Interscience, Hoboken (2006)

29. Yu, Y., Chen, J., Gao, T., Yu, M.: DAG-GNN: DAG structure learning with graph neural networks. In: International Conference on Machine Learning, pp. 7154–7163. PMLR (2019)

30. Zhang, K., Hyvärinen, A.: On the identifiability of the post-nonlinear causal model. In: 25th Conference on Uncertainty in Artificial Intelligence (UAI 2009), pp. 647–655. AUAI Press (2009)

31. Zheng, X., Aragam, B., Ravikumar, P.K., Xing, E.P.: DAGs with NO TEARS: continuous optimization for structure learning. In: Advances in Neural Information Processing Systems 31, pp. 9492–9503 (2018)

Emotional Semantic Neural Radiance Fields for Audio-Driven Talking Head

Haodong Lin[1], Zhonghao Wu[1], Zhenyu Zhang[2], Chao Ma[1(✉)],
and Xiaokang Yang[1]

[1] MoE Key Lab of Artificial Intelligence, AI Institute, Shanghai Jiao Tong
University, Shanghai, China
{icegreen,ufouso,chaoma,xkyang}@sjtu.edu.cn
[2] Youtu Lab, Tencent, China

Abstract. Generating audio-driven talking head videos is a challenging problem which receives considerable attention recently. However, the emotional expressions of the speaker are often ignored, although the emotion information is expressed in the audio signal. In this paper, we propose Emotional Semantic Neural Radiance Fields (ES-NeRF), an audio-driven method for generating high-quality and emotional talking head videos based on neural radiance fields. Our method extracts the content features and the emotion features of the audio as additional inputs to construct a dynamic neural radiance field, applies the semantic segmentation map to constrain the speaker's expression, generates a dynamic three-dimensional emotional facial semantic representation, and then synthesizes the final high-quality video through the semantic translation network. Experiments show that our method can achieve high-quality results with corresponding expressions for audios containing different emotions that surpass the quality of state-of-the-art talking head methods.

Keywords: Emotional talking head · Nerual radiance field · Semantic segmentation

1 Introduction

Synthesizing audio-driven high-quality talking head videos is a challenging problem and necessary in many practical applications, such as film-making [17], virtual video conferences and digital humans [40]. Recently, many methods have been proposed to generate high-quality talking heads, and the mouth shape is kept in synchronizing with the audio. At present, the advanced methods are divided into two categories: the methods based on generative adversarial networks (GAN) [4,14,33,35,37,39] and the methods based on neural radiance fields (NeRF) [10,13].

This work was supported by NSFC (61906119, U19B2035), Shanghai Municipal Science and Technology Major Project (2021SHZDZX0102), and CCF-Tencent Open Research Fund.

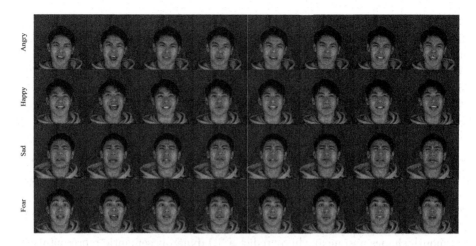

Fig. 1. Given an audio input, our ES-NeRF approach can generate high-quality emotional talking head videos. The example shows the generated talking heads with the same speech content but different emotions and poses.

Since it is difficult to directly learn the mapping from the original audio signal to the facial expression and the mouth shape, existing methods often use intermediate representations such as explicit 3D face shapes [26], 2D landmarks [31] or expression coefficients [33]. Nonetheless, there are very few works that consider the influence of the emotional factors contained in the audio signals on the expressions of the characters. The recently collected MEAD dataset [35] contains high-quality talking head videos with annotations of both emotion category and intensity.

NeRF-based methods have shown excellent results in recent years. For example, both AD-NeRF [13] and 4D facial avatar [10] can generate high-quality talking head videos with lip synchronization, and can ensure the free view direction and background switching. Nevertheless, AD-NeRF does not consider the influence of the speaker's emotions expressed on the face, and the rendering of some extreme expressions is heavily blurred, while the 4D facial avatar needs to be given the expression code of the target person and cannot be directly driven by audio signals.

To solve the problem current methods neglecting the influence of the speaker's emotion, we propose the Emotional Semantic Neural Radiance Fields (ES-NeRF), which can synthesize the high quality talking head videos with the correct expressions from emotional audio inputs, as the examples shown in Fig. 1. Different from existing NeRF-based methods, we consider to use both content features and emotional features of the input audio. For situations where it is difficult to directly learn the mapping from audio features to facial expressions and mouth shapes, we add semantic maps as additional supervisory signals. To solve the problem that dynamic neural radiance fields is difficult to handle the representation of multiple widely different expressions, we employ the generated three-dimensional semantic representation as an intermediate representation and produce the final result through a semantic translation network. The use of neural radiance fields to obtain three-dimensional semantic represen- tations can naturally and freely adjust different postures and view directions, which is impossible in traditional 2D landmarks. For generating a single expres- sion or multiple types of expressions, our model achieves better image quality, emotion accuracy and audio-visual synchronization than existing GAN-based or NeRF-based methods.

The main contributions of this work are listed as follow:

- We propose the Emotional Semantic Neural Radiance Fields, which is the first attempt to achieve emotional talking head generation in audio-driven NeRF-based methods.
- We add semantic segmentation constraints to the dynamic neural radiance fields to better learn the mapping from audio features to facial expressions and mouth shapes and meanwhile predict a 3D dynamic semantic representation.
- We propose the NeRF-to-GAN approach with adopting a semantic translation network to solve the problem of poor image quality directly rendered by dynamic neural radiance fields under multiple widely different expressions.

2   Related Work

2.1   Talking-Head Generation

Generative Adversary Network. As one pillar of the computer vision, GAN [11] contributes largely to this domain. Many researchers are inspired by this method and generate more and more realistic images and videos. Progressive GAN [15] can get high resolution results by applying the progressive training strategy on generator and discriminator. Style GAN [16] gets break through on the details and gets the ability to control the detail. Photo-realistic Audio-driven Video Portraits [37] and Neural voice puppetry [33] utilize a U-Net-based [27] GAN as a neural renderer to render 3DMM [2] parameters to realistic images and videos. Make-it-talk [39] disentangles the content feature and style feature from the audio feature, then choose landmarks as intermediary to generate final videos. Hierarchical Cross-Modal Talking Face Generation [4] proposes a cas- cade GAN with dynamic pixel-wise loss to avoid subtle artifacts and temporal discontinuities. These methods based on GAN all suffer the 3D inconsistency problem and neglect the emotional expression.

Neural Radiance Field. Since 2020, due to 3D consistency and remarkable neural rendering, Neural Radiance Field [21] has caught many eyes on it. Many methods [10,12,13,20,23,28,29] base on NeRF to set up 3D radiance fields and add additional parameters to control the generation of the results. Graf [29] combines NeRF and GAN framework to improve the quality of the image gen- eration. Giraffe [23] extracts the feature map and then feeds it into GAN for progressive training to render high-resolution image. Style-NeRF [12] solves the problem in Giraffe that cannot generate high resolution image and produces the artifacts. AD-NeRF [13] adopts DeepSpeech [1] features of audios in NeRF to catch targets' lip movements and presents torso NeRF to render the torso part of the target. Similar to AD-NeRF, 4D facial avatars [10] chooses expression code estimated by 3DMM [2] model to match the lip movements and add the latent code to improve stability. Both AD-NeRF and 4D avatars maintain the talking head pose, while GNeRF [20] predicts head poses with the use of GAN and applies the generated pose in NeRF to render the talking head video. All aforementioned works cannot reenact the emotion styles of people.

2.2 Emotion Condition Generation

Many methods focus on generating a more high-resolution picture and a clearer mouth type, which lack consideration of personal style [33,37,39] and emotional style [8,14,22,25,35]. Previous works [10,33,37] generate videos with expressions by transferring the expression from source to target. These methods are limited to the source video and cannot generate emotion videos from unrecognized audios. Emotional style methods are inspired by voice emotionally recognizing methods [7,9,19] and disentangle the emotion in the audio by the depth network to generate emotional talking head. ExprGAN [8] designs one encoder-decoder architecture to control the expression identity with an expression controller module. Wang et al. [35] propose the MEAD dataset which contains high resolution talking head videos with eight different emotions and propose a network to generate the audio-driven lower face and emotion-driven upper face. GANimation [25] proposes one conditional GAN based on Action Units to estimate continuous facial movements of a designated expression. Audio EVP [14] disentangles content encoding and emotion encoding from the audio signal, then uses landmarks as intermediary to get the edge map. Finally EVP utilizes conditional GAN to translate the edge map to high-fidelity emotion video. Our work feeds content parameters and emotion parameters into NeRF to generate semantic results with expressions. Taking full advantage of both high-resolution generated image of GAN and 3D continuity of NeRF, our method can synthesize realistic high-quality videos with arbitrary head poses and free view directions. To this end, we employ semantic results as intermediate content.

3 Method

3.1 Overview

The framework of our Emotional Semantic Neural Radiance Fields is shown in Fig. 2. In order to obtain the meaningful information in expression from acoustic signals, we extract content features and emotion features separately. Inspired by 4D facial avatars [10], we use conditional implicit function and volume rendering to model the emotional dynamic talking head (Sec. 3.2). To better learn the mapping from audio features to facial expressions and mouth shapes, we make the dynamic neural radiance field understand the semantics of the human head

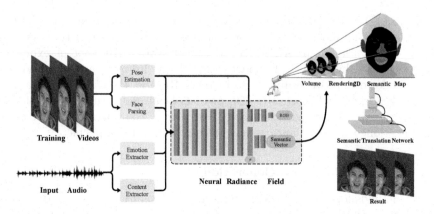

Fig. 2. Overview of our emotional semantic neural radiance fields Algorithm. We first extract content features and emotion features from the audio signal. Then we use the dynamic neural radiance field to predict 3D semantic representations. Finally, semantic translation network is applied to generate the high-quality rendering results with the corresponding emotion based on the semantic representations from the specific view direction.

and meanwhile predict its 3D semantic representation (Sec. 3.3). The NeRF-to-GAN module is designed to restore some facial details so that the model has better performance under the multiple types of emotions (Sec. 3.4). Besides, we focus on the facial emotional expression to generate natural emotional and speaking styles of the target person. Since the torso part has little relevance to the emotional expression of the characters, we process the head and torso part separately by segmenting the head and torso part and extracting a pure background, similar to AD-NeRF [13].

3.2   Emotional Neural Radiance Fields

Based on the dynamic neural rendering idea and to solve the problem of the neglect of emotion in neural radiance fields for talking heads, we employ the emotion feature and the content feature from the audio signal as additional inputs of the implicit function. In other words, spatial coordinates $\mathbf{x} = (x, y, z)$, viewing direction $\mathbf{d} = (\theta, \phi)$, content feature $\mathbf{m}$, and emotion feature e are meanwhile inputted to the implicit function which is realized by multi-layer perceptrons (MLPs) to implicitly represent the continuous 3D scene density σ and color $\mathbf{c} = (r, g, b)$. The density σ is the differential probability of a ray terminating at an infinitesimal particle at spatial coordinates x, which is only related to 3D position. The color $\mathbf{c}$ is RGB values, which can be predicted as a function of both spatial coordinates $\mathbf{x}$ and viewing direction $\mathbf{d}$. The entire implicit function can be formulated as follows:

$$F_\theta : (\mathbf{x}, \mathbf{d}, \mathbf{m}, \mathbf{e}) \rightarrow (\sigma, \mathbf{c}) \tag{1}$$

Like NeRF [21], we apply the volume rendering by numerical quadrature with hierarchical stratified sampling to compute the color of each pixel. Within one hierarchy, we mark a camera ray emitted from the center of projection of camera space through a given pixel as $\mathbf{r}(t) = \mathbf{o} + t\mathbf{d}$, where $\mathbf{o}$ is the origin of the ray, d is the view direction, and the near and far boundaries of t are t_n and t_f respectively. Then the color of this ray can be expressed as an integral (numerically estimated by quadrature):

$$C(\mathbf{r}; p, \mathbf{m}, \mathbf{e}) = \int_{t_n}^{t_f} T(t)\sigma(\mathbf{r}(t))\mathbf{c}(\mathbf{r}(t), \mathbf{d})\, dt \tag{2}$$

where $T(t)$ denotes the accumulated transmittance along the ray from t_n to t. p is the estimated head pose for transforming the sampling points to the canonical space like 4D facial avatars [10].

$$T(t) = \exp(-\int_{t_n}^{t} \sigma(\mathbf{r}(s))ds) \tag{3}$$

To extract the content feature and emotion feature, we apply the popular DeepSpeech [1] model and OpenSmile [9] model respectively to obtain the DeepSpeech features and OpenSmile features. The 29-dimensional DeepSpeech features of 16 continuous frames are then sent into a temporal convolutional network to the temporally filtered content feature where we employ the self-attention idea [33]. The high-dimensional Opensmile features of each utterance are then normalized by Min-Max and feature selection based on L2 normalization to reduce the feature size to 100 dimension [30]. The low-dimensional emotion feature and the 76-dimensional filtered content feature are used as the inputs of MLPs.

3.3   3D Semantic Representation for Talking Head

During the implementation of rendering the emotional talking head by neural radiance fields, we find that the edges of the face and facial features of the generated results often produce some serious artifacts due to the large or extreme expressions. Since semantic representation is highly correlated with geometry and radiance reconstruction [28], we consider that significant high quality semantic labelling information could feasibly improve reconstruction quality.

We assume that one 3D position $\mathbf{x}$ has one semantic attribute $\mathbf{s}$, which denotes a distribution on n semantic categories and has no relation with view directions. We introduce it into the above-mentioned dynamic neural radiance field, and map the input spatial coordinates and audio features (content features and emotion features) to semantic representation $\mathbf{s}$ through an implicit function. The specific implementation is to pass the 256-dimensional feature vector obtained after 8 fully-connected layers in MLPs through two additional fully-connected layers and a softmax normalisation layer that outputs the view-independent semantic representation. The entire implicit function can be formulated as follows:

$$F_\theta : (\mathbf{x}, \mathbf{d}, \mathbf{m}, \mathbf{e}) \rightarrow (\sigma, \mathbf{c}, \mathbf{s}) \tag{4}$$

The semantic representation of the pixels projected on the image plane through the ray can be expressed as an integral (numerically estimated by quadrature):

$$S(\mathbf{r}; p, \mathbf{m}, \mathbf{e}) = \int_{t_n}^{t_f} T(t)\sigma(\mathbf{r}(t))\mathbf{s}(\mathbf{r}(t), \mathbf{d})dt \tag{5}$$

where $T(t)$ denotes the accumulated transmittance along the ray from t_n to t.

$$T(t) = \exp(-\int_{t_n}^{t} \sigma(\mathbf{r}(s))ds) \tag{6}$$

3.4   NeRF-to-GAN

Although our method has been able to achieve the best results for rendering single-category emotions or similar emotions, when it is applied to reconstruct multiple categories of extremely different emotions, the overall clarity of the rendering results will decrease, especially the mouth part. Because semantic presentation performing better for above situation, we introduce a semantic translation network to generate corresponding image results. Following [3], we adopt a conditional-GAN architecture for the semantic translation network. We perform ray tracing on semantic occupancy field to obtain a 2D segmentation map from

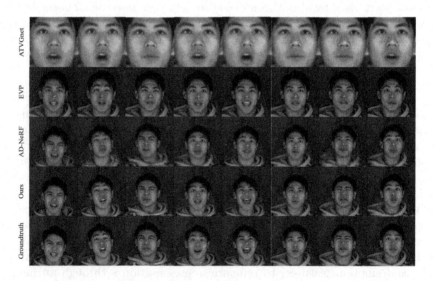

Fig. 3. Qualitative comparisons with the state-of-the-art methods. From up to down: Audio Transformation and Visual Generation Network (ATVGnet) [4], Audio-Driven Emotional Video Portraits (EVP) [14], Audio Driven Neural Radiance Fields (AD-NeRF) [13], Ours and the ground truth images. We show eight examples with different speech contents and eight different emotions. From left to right: angry, contempt, disgusted, fear, happy, neutral, sad and surprised.

a given user-specific viewpoint, then use the GAN generator to texture each semantic region from the style code sampled from the texture space. Finally we adopt a Semantic Instance Wise StyleGAN to regionally stylize the generated segmentation maps. Please refer to [3] for more details about the network architecture.

4   Experiments

4.1   Implementation Details

Dataset. We evaluate our method on the MEAD [35] dataset, a high-quality audio-visual dataset for emotional talking head generation with 60 actors and actresses and eight emotion categories. The dataset is split into the training and testing sets for models to train and test. Every emotional talking head video is converted to 25 fps and the sample rate of audio signals is set to be 16kHz.

Data Preprocessing. (1) Pose estimation. We firstly use an off-the-shelf method [38] to detect facial landmarks and align all the head part. The dynamics of the head pose are estimated by a state of-the-art face tracking approach [34] and bundle adjustment [32] approach is applied for optimization. The optimized head pose parameters are used for transforming the sampling points on the rays from the head part to the canonical space. (2) Face parsing. We use the popular face parsing method [5] to label the different semantic regions. Since we need to use the 2D segmentation result as the ground truth as supervisory signals for dynamic neural radiance fields, we cannot tolerate any obvious artifacts, such as the confusion between the left and right eyebrows. We reprocess the segmentation result by ignoring the distinction between the left and right parts to enhance the robustness to avoid the instability of the neural network training.

Training Details. We implement our framework in PyTorch [24]. Training images are resized to 512×512 for all the experiments. Neural radiance fields part are trained with Adam [18] solver with initial learning rate 5e-4. We train the neural network for 400k iterations and train the semantic translation network for 500k iterations. In each iteration of the neural network training, we randomly sample a batch of 2048 rays through the image pixels. For the target person, we choose 30 videos for each kind of emotions. We train both networks with a Tesla V100 with 32GB memory and need about 72 h with videos of single person with eight different emotions in resolution 512×512.

4.2   Evaluation Results

Evaluation Metrics. To quantitatively evaluate the expression accuracy, we extract facial landmarks from the generated videos and the ground truth videos. The metrics of Landmark Distance (LD) [4] and Landmark Velocity Difference (LVD) [39] are utilized to evaluate facial movements. LD represents the average Euclidean distance between ground truth and generated landmarks. LVD

Table 1. Quantitative comparisons with the state-of-the-art methods. We calculate the landmark accuracy, audio-visual consistency and video qualities of the results of different methods by comparing them with the ground truth images. ↑ indicates that the performance is better with higher results. ↓ indicates that the performance is better with smaller numbers.

Method/Score	LD↓	LVD↓	SyncNet score↑	PSNR↑	SSIM↑	Pose
ATVGnet [4]	3.82	1.71	4.34	28.55	0.60	static
EVP [14]	3.01	1.56	5.17	29.53	0.71	copied
AD-NeRF [13]	3.42	1.71	4.56	28.20	0.82	arbitrarily
Ours	**2.89**	**1.46**	**5.54**	**29.80**	**0.91**	**arbitrarily**

denotes the average velocity differences of landmark movements between two videos. SyncNet [6] is often used to evaluate the audio-visual consistency for lip synchronization and facial motions. To evaluate the audio-visual synchronization quality, we use a pre-trained SyncNet model to compute the audio-sync offset and confidence of audio-driven talking head videos. The performance is better with higher score. Besides, we use PSNR and SSIM [36] to evaluate the quality of the generated images.

Comparison with GAN-Based Methods. We mainly choose the EVP [14] which has the best performance for emotional talking head generations in GAN-based methods to compare with our method. From the quantitative comparison in Table 1, we can see that our method performs better. In addition, the EVP method requires simultaneous input of audio signals and the source video to generate the talking head with poses, and its head postures are copied from the source video. In contrast, the posture and view direction of the talking head generated by our method can be adjusted arbitrarily, which is due to the ability of the neural radiance field to generate semantic representation with a free perspective. Analyzing and comparing the rendering results, we can find that the rendering results of EVP cannot well reflect the expression in some emotions (such as angry and disgusted).

Comparison with NeRF-Based Methods. AD-NeRF [13] is currently one of the few audio-driven NeRF-based talking head methods, and the input conditions are the same as our method: only audio input is required. It can be seen from the quantitative comparison in Table 1 that our method catches much higher score than AD-NeRF. It can be seen from the examples in Fig. 3 that although AD-NeRF can also express the speaker's emotion to a certain extent, its robustness is very poor and the rendering results are quite blurry, especially in the mouth area.

4.3   Ablation Study

To synthesizing high quality results, we add the emotional-related part, semantic-related part and semantic translation network into the dynamic NeRF. We select

LD, SyncNet score and PSNR as metrics for the ablation study to demonstrate the necessity of these parts in our method.

Table 2. Quantitative ablation study. Emo. denotes the emotion-related part of dynamic neural radiance fields. Sem. denotes the semantic-related part of dynamic neural radiance fields. Trans. denotes the semantic translation network

Emo.	Sem.	Trans.	LD↓	SyncNet score ↑	PSNR ↑
	✓		3.36	4.75	28.5
✓			3.17	5.02	29.4
✓	✓		3.05	5.23	**30.2**
✓	✓	✓	**2.89**	**5.54**	29.8

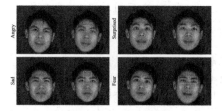 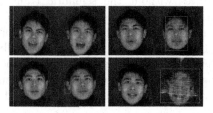

Fig. 4. Ablation study for emotional neural radiance fields. We show cases with (left) and without (right) emotion related part in neural radiance field. The red boxes show the artifacts in the generated frame. (Color figure online)

Fig. 5. Ablation study for 3D semantic representation. We show cases with (left) and without (right) semantic related part in neural radiance field. The red boxes show the artifacts in the generated frame. (Color figure online)

Emotional Neural Radiance Fields. The emotion feature as an additional input of dynamic NeRF is helpful for rendering the talking head with real emotion. In Table 2, without emotion related part in neural radiance field, all evaluation metrics perform worse. Figure 4 shows that lack of the constraints of emotional features, synthesized results are less robust in emotional representation, and often present incorrect expressions.

3D Semantic Representation for Talking Head. The semantic-related part can not only be used to correctly predict the semantic representation of the head, but also facilitate the image rendering of the NeRF. In Table 2, the result of adding the semantic part improves on all evaluation metrics. It can be seen from the Fig. 5 that the semantic part well constrains the image rendering results on the edge of each organ, making it smoother and clearer.

Semantic Translation Network. It is worthy to mention that it is difficult to generate high-quality 3D semantic representations without the emotional part or semantic part in the dynamic NeRF. Under these situations, the result with the semantic translation network is worse than directly rendered by the dynamic NeRF. Therefore, the semantic translation network is removed in the subsequent comparisons where the emotional part or semantic part in the dynamic NeRF is removed. In Table 2, both LD and SyncNet score perform worse, but PSNR improves without the semantic translation network. However, we can see from the rendered sample image in Fig. 6 that the overall clarity of the result is actually

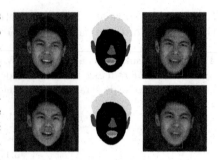

Fig. 6. Ablation study for semantic translation network. We show the cases with (left) and without (right) semantic translation network and predicted semantic representation (medium). The red box shows the artifacts in the generated frame. (Color figure online)

lower, and the image quality is not as good as the result of the complete method. Especially in the mouth area, it is difficult to recognize the mouth shape of the speaker. Therefore, the final solution adds the semantic translation network.

5   Conclusion

In this paper, we propose an audio-driven talking head method for generating high-quality and emotional portraits videos based on neural radiance fields. Our proposed emotional neural radiance field uses the content features and the emotion features extracted from the audio as inputs to reconstruct the emotional talking head. Then, we employ semantic segmentation to constrain the speaker's expression and generate the three-dimensional dynamic facial semantic representation. To improve the quality of synthesized results, we propose a NeRF-to-GAN approach and generate the final high-quality video containing different emotions through the semantic translation network. The photo-realistic generated results surpass the quality of state-of-the-art talking head methods both quantitatively and qualitatively.

References

1. Amodei, D., et al.: Deep speech 2: end-to-end speech recognition in English and Mandarin. In: ICML (2016)
2. Blanz, V., Vetter, T.: A morphable model for the synthesis of 3d faces. In: SIGGRAPH (1999)
3. Chen, A., Liu, R., Xie, L., Chen, Z., Su, H., Jingyi, Y.: Sofgan: a portrait image generator with dynamic styling. TOG **41**(1), 1–26 (2021)
4. Chen, L., Maddox, R.K., Duan, Z., Xu, C.: Hierarchical cross-modal talking face generation with dynamic pixel-wise loss. In: CVPR (2019)

5. Cheng-Han Lee, Ziwei Liu, L.W., Luo, P.: Maskgan: towards diverse and interactive facial image manipulation. In: CVPR (2020)

6. Chung, J.S., Zisserman, A.: Out of time: automated lip sync in the wild. In: Chen, C.-S., Lu, J., Ma, K.-K. (eds.) ACCV 2016. LNCS, vol. 10117, pp. 251–263. Springer, Cham (2017). https://doi.org/10.1007/978-3-319-54427-4_19

7. Cowie, R., Douglas-Cowie, E., Tsapatsoulis, N., Votsis, G., Kollias, S., Fellenz, W., Taylor, J.G.: Emotion recognition in human-computer interaction. IEEE Sig. Process. Mag. **18**(1), 32–80 (2001)

8. Ding, H., Sricharan, K., Chellappa, R.: Exprgan: facial expression editing with controllable expression intensity. In: AAAI (2018)

9. Eyben, F., Wöllmer, M., Schuller, B.: Opensmile: the munich versatile and fast open-source audio feature extractor. In: ACMMM (2010)

10. Gafni, G., Thies, J., Zollhofer, M., Niessner, M.: Dynamic neural radiance fields for monocular 4d facial avatar reconstruction. In: CVPR (2021)

11. Goodfellow, I., et al.: Generative adversarial nets. In: NIPS (2014)

12. Gu, J., Liu, L., Wang, P., Theobalt, C.: Stylenerf: A style-based 3d-aware generator for high-resolution image synthesis. arXiv preprint. arXiv:2110.08985 (2021)

13. Guo, Y., Chen, K., Liang, S., Liu, Y.J., Bao, H., Zhang, J.: Ad-nerf: audio driven neural radiance fields for talking head synthesis. In: ICCV (2021)

14. Ji, X., et al.: Audio-driven emotional video portraits. In: CVPR (2021)

15. Karras, T., Aila, T., Laine, S., Lehtinen, J.: Progressive growing of gans for improved quality, stability and variation. In: ICLR (2018)

16. Karras, T., Laine, S., Aila, T.: A style-based generator architecture for generative adversarial networks. In: CVPR (2019)

17. Kim, H., et al.: Neural style-preserving visual dubbing. TOG **38**(6), 1–13 (2019)

18. Kingma, D.P., Ba, J.: Adam: a method for stochastic optimization. In: ICLR (2015)

19. Kwon, O.W., Chan, K., Hao, J., Lee, T.W.: Emotion recognition by speech signals. In: EUROSPEECH (2003)

20. Meng, Q., et al.: Gnerf: gan-based neural radiance field without posed camera. In: ICCV (2021)

21. Mildenhall, B., Srinivasan, P.P., Tancik, M., Barron, J.T., Ramamoorthi, R., Ng, R.: NeRF: representing scenes as neural radiance fields for view synthesis. In: Vedaldi, A., Bischof, H., Brox, T., Frahm, J.-M. (eds.) ECCV 2020. LNCS, vol. 12346, pp. 405–421. Springer, Cham (2020). https://doi.org/10.1007/978-3-030-58452-8_24

22. Mittal, G., Wang, B.: Animating face using disentangled audio representations. In: WACV (2020)

23. Niemeyer, M., Geiger, A.: Giraffe: representing scenes as compositional generative neural feature fields. In: CVPR (2021)

24. Paszke, A., et al.: Pytorch: an imperative style, high-performance deep learning library. In: NIPS (2019)

25. Pumarola, A., Agudo, A., Martinez, A.M., Sanfeliu, A., Moreno-Noguer, F.: Ganimation: anatomically-aware facial animation from a single image. In: ECCV (2018)

26. Ran, Y., Zipeng, Y., Juyong, Z., Hujun, B., Yong-Jin, L.: Audio-driven talking face video generation with natural head pose. In: ICCV (2021)

27. Ronneberger, O., Fischer, P., Brox, T.: U-Net: convolutional networks for biomedical image segmentation. In: Navab, N., Hornegger, J., Wells, W.M., Frangi, A.F. (eds.) MICCAI 2015. LNCS, vol. 9351, pp. 234–241. Springer, Cham (2015). https://doi.org/10.1007/978-3-319-24574-4_28

28. S. Zhi, T. Laidlow, S.L., Daviso, A.J.: In-place scene labelling and understanding with implicit scene representation. In: ICCV (2021)

29. Schwarz, K., Liao, Y., Niemeyer, M., Geiger, A.: Graf: generative radiance fields for 3d-aware image synthesis. In: NIPS (2020)
30. Sebastian, J., Pierucci, P., et al.: Fusion techniques for utterance-level emotion recognition combining speech and transcripts. In: Interspeech (2019)
31. Suwajanakorn, S., Seitz, S.M., Kemelmacher-Shlizerman, I.: Synthesizing obama: learning lip sync from audio. TOG **36**(4), 1–13 (2017)
32. T. Baltrusaitis, M.M., Robinson, P.: Cross-dataset learning and person-specific normalisation for automatic action unit detection. In: FG (2015)
33. Thies, J., Elgharib, M., Tewari, A., Theobalt, C., Nießner, M.: Neural voice puppetry: audio-driven facial reenactment. In: Vedaldi, A., Bischof, H., Brox, T., Frahm, J.-M. (eds.) ECCV 2020. LNCS, vol. 12361, pp. 716–731. Springer, Cham (2020). https://doi.org/10.1007/978-3-030-58517-4_42
34. Thies, J., Zollhofer, M., Stamminger, M., Theobalt, C., Nießner, M.: Face2face: real-time face capture and reenactment of RGB videos. In: CVPR (2016)
35. Wang, K., et al.: MEAD: a large-scale audio-visual dataset for emotional talking-face generation. In: Vedaldi, A., Bischof, H., Brox, T., Frahm, J.-M. (eds.) ECCV 2020. LNCS, vol. 12366, pp. 700–717. Springer, Cham (2020). https://doi.org/10.1007/978-3-030-58589-1_42
36. Wang, Z., Bovik, A.C., Sheikh, H.R., Simoncelli, E.P.: Image quality assessment: from error visibility to structural similarity. TIP **13**(4), 600–612 (2004)
37. Wen, X., Wang, M., Richardt, C., Chen, Z.Y., Hu, S.M.: Photorealistic audio-driven video portraits. TVCG **26**(12), 3457–3466 (2020)
38. Wu, W., Qian, C., Yang, S., Wang, Q., Cai, Y., Zhou, Q.: Look at boundary: a boundary-aware face alignment algorithm. In: CVPR (2018)
39. Zhou, Y., Han, X., Shechtman, E., Echevarria, J., Kalogerakis, E., Li, D.: Makeittalk: speaker-aware talking-head animation. TOG **39**(6), 1–15 (2020)
40. Zhou, Y., Xu, Z., Landreth, C., Kalogerakis, E., Maji, S., Singh, K.: Visemenet: audio-driven animator-centric speech animation. TOG **37**(4), 1–10 (2018)

Multi-view 3D Morphable Face Reconstruction via Canonical Volume Fusion

Jingqi Tian[1], Zhibo Wang[1], Ming Lu[2], and Feng Xu[1(✉)]

[1] School of Software and BNRist, Tsinghua University, Beijing, China
xufeng2003@gmail.com
[2] Intel Labs, Beijing, China

Abstract. Due to the capability of easy animation and editing of faces, 3D Morphable Model (3DMM) is widely used in the task of face reconstruction. Recent methods recover 3DMM coefficients by fusing the information from a set of multi-view images via end-to-end Convolutional Neural Networks (CNNs), which alleviate the inherent depth ambiguity in the single-view setting. However, most of these methods fuse global features of all views to regress the 3D morphable face, without considering the dense correspondences of multi-view images. In this paper, we propose a novel approach to reconstruct high-quality 3D morphable faces. We first use a canonical feature volume to fuse multiple view features in 3D space, which establish dense correspondences between different views. Next, to bridge the gap between CNN regression and pixel-wise optimization and further leverage the muti-view information, we propose test-time optimization to improve the regressed results with negligible additional cost. Our method achieves the state-of-the-art performance on widely-used benchmarks, demonstrating the effectiveness of our approach. Code will be released.

Keywords: Multi-view 3D face reconstruction · 3D morphable model

1 Introduction

3D face reconstruction from images is a crucial problem in computer vision and has a wide range of applications such as face tracking [4,5], portrait relighting [41], gaze tracking [42], face reenactment [7,19,36] and so on. In order to address the difficulties in image-based face reconstruction, 3D Morphable Model (3DMM) is often adopted to provide a low-dimensional parametric representation of 3D face. Traditional methods recover the 3DMM coefficients by solving a costly nonlinear optimization problem and require a good initialization. In contrast, recent methods [9,13,15,18,30,34,35,39,43–45] adopt deep Convolutional

---

Supplementary Information The online version contains supplementary material available at https://doi.org/10.1007/978-3-031-20500-2_45.

L. Fang et al. (Eds.): CICAI 2022, LNAI 13605, pp. 545–558, 2022.
https://doi.org/10.1007/978-3-031-20500-2_45

Neural Network (CNN) to directly learn the mapping between 2D images and 3DMM coefficients. Single-view face reconstruction [13, 15, 18, 34, 35, 39, 43, 45] has been extensively studied in recent years, where an inherent difficulty is the ambiguity of depth estimation, especially in the forehead, nose and chin regions.

Compared with the single-view face reconstruction, multi-view face reconstruction [10, 27, 31, 44] can effectively resolve the depth ambiguity. However, most of existing works [27, 31, 44] simply extend the techniques of single-view reconstruction to the multi-view setting. After carefully studying the pipeline of existing methods [10, 27, 31, 44], we find that these methods mostly fuse the 2D global features extracted from different views to regress the 3D morphable face. However, the fusion of 2D global features cannot learn sufficient representation for 3D reconstruction.

In this paper, we propose a novel method for multi-view 3D morphable face reconstruction based on canonical volume fusion. Our method extracts the 3D feature volumes from multi-view images. As 3D volumes allow easy alignment of facial features in 3D space, we transform the volumes of multiple views to align with the canonical volume by the estimated head pose parameters. To fuse the transformed 3D feature volumes, our method adopt a confidence estimator to predict the confidences of the multi-view feature volumes. Therefore, the transformed feature volumes can be adaptively fused according to the estimated confidence volumes. This is essential for multi-view feature fusion since faces under different poses provide partial information of the 3D face. The fused canonical feature volume is used to regress the shape and texture coefficients. Compared with existing methods [31, 44], our work can establish better dense correspondences between different views and generate more accurate 3D reconstruction.

CNNs can directly and efficiently estimate the 3DMM coefficients, but it tends to predict reasonable but not pixel-wise accurate results, as it is trained to achieve the lowest average error over the entire dataset, not a particular sample. On the other hand, optimization fits the parametric model to multi-view images of a particular sample. However, it is sensitive to the initialization, and may fall into local minimums or take very long time without a good initialization. Therefore, the multi-view information of a particular sample may not be fully explored by the inference of the network. Directly involving multi-view constraints also in the testing rather than just in the training may further improve the results. We propose to introduce test-time optimization to CNN-based regression. Our test-time optimization can leverage the benefits of both paradigms. Specifically, we use the CNN regressed estimation to initialize the iterative optimization process, making the fitting stable and faster. We find this idea is simple but effective to bridge the gap between training and testing.

2   Related Work

2.1   3D Morphable Model (3DMM)

Since the seminal work [2], 3D morphable models have been widely used in face reconstruction over the past twenty years. [2] proposes to derive a morphable face model by transforming the shape and texture of the captured 3D faces into a latent space using Principal Component Analysis (PCA). 3D faces can be modeled by the linear combinations of PCA basis. [6] uses Kinect to capture 150 individuals aged 7–80 from various ethnic backgrounds. For each person, they capture the neutral expression and 19 other expressions. Bilinear face model is constructed by N-mode Singular Value Decomposition (SVD). [25] combines the linear shape space with an articulated jaw, neck, and eyeballs, pose-dependent corrective blendshapes, and additional global expression blendshapes. They can fit better to the static 3D scans and 4D sequences using the same optimization method compared with [2,6]. For a detailed survey of 3DMM over the past twenty years, we refer the readers to [12].

2.2   3D Face Reconstruction

With the help of 3DMM, the face reconstruction task can be formulated as a cost minimization problem [2]. Due to the nonlinearity of the optimization problem, it is time-consuming to optimize the coefficients of 3DMM. Therefore, numerous regression-based methods are proposed to employ convolutional neural network for face reconstruction. The biggest obstacle when applying deep learning to face reconstruction is the lack of training data. [45] proposes a face profiling technique which can generate synthetic images with the same identity but different face poses as the original images. They utilized their face profiling technique to create the 300W-LP database and trained a cascaded CNN to regress 3DMM coefficients. [11] utilizes publicly available 3D scans to render more realistic images. Recently, the self-supervision approaches are becoming prevailing. [15,34] enable the self-supervised training by introducing a differentiable rendering layer. This self-supervision scheme has been widely used in the following works [8,9,20,22,24,29,33,37,38].

Compared with single-view face reconstruction, multi-view face reconstruction can effectively resolve the depth ambiguity. Multi-view setting ensures that the faces in different views are geometrically consistent. There are several approaches [10,27,31,44] to study the multi-view face reconstruction. [10] proposes to address the problem using CNNs together with recurrent neural networks (RNNs). However, it is not reasonable to model the task with RNNs, and multi-view geometric constraints are not exploited in their approach. [44] adopts photometric loss and alignment loss to explicitly incorporate multi-view geometric constraints between different views. [30] further leverages multi-view geometry consistency to mitigate the ambiguity from monocular face pose estimation and depth reconstruction in the training process. However, the above methods [10,27,31,44] follow the network design of single view face reconstruction and fail to learn sufficient representation for 3D reconstruction.

3 Preliminaries

3.1 Face Model

With a 3DMM, the face shape S and texture T can be represented as a linear combination of shape and texture bases:

$$S = \overline{S} + B_{id}\alpha + B_{exp}\beta \tag{1}$$

$$T = \overline{T} + B_t\delta \tag{2}$$

where $\overline{S}$ and $\overline{T}$ are the mean shape and texture respectively. B_{id}, B_{exp} and B_t denote the PCA bases of identity, expression and texture. α, β and δ are corresponding coefficients to be estimated. All of bases are scaled with their standard deviations. In our method, $\overline{S}, B_{id}, \overline{T}, B_t$ are constructed from Basel Face Model (BFM) [26] and B_{exp} is constructed from FaceWareHouse [6]. We adopt the first 80 bases with the largest standard deviation for identity and texture, the first 64 bases for the expression bases.

3.2 Camera Model

We employ the perspective camera model to define the 3D-2D projection. The focal length of the perspective camera is selected empirically. The face pose P is represented by an Euler angle rotation $R \in SO(3)$ and translation $t \in \mathbb{R}^3$.

3.3 Illumination Model

We model the lighting by Spherical Harmonics(SH) and assume a Lambertian surface for face. Given the surface normal n_i and face texture t_i, the color can be computed as $C(n_i, t_i|\gamma) = t_i \cdot \sum_{b=1}^{B^2} \gamma_b \Phi_b(n_i)$. $\Phi_b : \mathbb{R}^3 \rightarrow \mathbb{R}$ is SH basis function and we choose the first $B^2 = 9$ functions following [34,35]. $\gamma \in \mathbb{R}^{27}$ represents the colored illumination in red, green and blue channels.

Our method can take any number of multi-view images of the same person $\{I_i\}_{i=1}^n$ as input and output the corresponding coefficients $\{x_i\}_{i=1}^n$ of these images, where $x_i = \{\alpha, \beta, \delta, P_i, \gamma_i\}$. It should be noticed that α, β, δ are shared by all images and P_i, γ_i are variant across the input multi-view images.

4 Method

Our method aims to regress 3DMM coefficients by leveraging the dense correspondences of the multi-view facial images of one subject. Therefore, we propose a Canonical Volume Fusion Network whose architectures are designed to integrate the dense information from different views. As shown in Figure 1 (a), our network first extracts 3D feature volumes from input images. Then, the dense

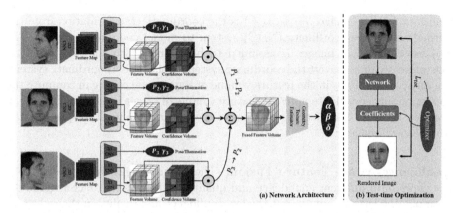

Fig. 1. Overview of our approach. (a) The network architecture of our method. (b) The test-time optimization mechanism.

feature volumes are transformed to a canonical coordinate system through feature volume alignment. Next, the aligned feature volumes are fused together in a confidence-aware manner. From the fused feature volumes, a shape/texture estimator is trained to output 3DMM coefficients. During testing, we apply test-time optimization to further improve performance, as shown in Figure 1 (b).

4.1 Canonical Volume Fusion Network

Feature Extraction. Previous methods mostly use 2D CNN backbone such as VGG-Face [32] or ResNet [16] to regress 3DMM coefficients. However, as human faces are 3D objects, it is more intuitive to model the facial correspondences in 3D space. We employ a 2D-3D feature extraction network to map a 2D face image to a 3D feature volume. Several 2D downsampling convolutional blocks extract a 2D feature map f_{2D} from the input image. Then, we utilize a "reshape" operation to project 2D feature maps to 3D feature volumes. The following 3D CNN finally extracts the 3D feature volume f_{3D}.

Volume Feature Alignment. Pose and illumination coefficients are private for each multi-view image. We regress these coefficients from f_{2D} separately. The f_{2D} is pooled to a 512-dimensional feature vector and sent through several linear layers. The 3D feature volumes extracted from multi-view images are semantically misaligned. It is unreasonable to fuse them directly and this is also the main drawback of previous work [44]. We align the 3D feature volumes extracted from multi-view images according to the estimated pose via the following equation:

$$p_d \sim T_{m \to NDC}(R_d R_s^{-1}(T_{NDC \to m}(p_s) - t_s) + t_d) \tag{3}$$

where subscript s and t represent source image and target image respectively, p is a coordinate in the feature volume, R, t are the face pose rotation and translation in the image, $T_{NDC \rightarrow m}(\cdot)$ is the coordinate transformation from the normalized device coordinate (NDC) system to model coordinate system. The f_{3D} extracted from images is assumed to be aligned with the NDC system. Therefore, we first convert the coordinate system to the model coordinate system. For any coordinate p_s in the feature volume of source image, we can compute the corresponding coordinate p_t in the feature volume of target images by Eq. (3). In practice, we align other feature volumes to the feature volume of the pre-selected frontal view image.

Confidence-Aware Feature Fusion. The input images taken from different views have different confidence and quality in the different face region. For example, the left view image has the low confidence and quality in the right face region. Therefore, we use a confidence estimator to learn the measurement of confidence and quality of the feature volume. The estimator is similar to the 3D CNN used for feature extraction but more lightweight. It outputs a 3D volume $c \in R^{h \times w \times d}$ with positive elements. c_i has the same height, width and depth as the f_{3D}. The feature can be fused via the following equation:

$$f_{3D,fuse} = \sum_i c_i \odot f_{3D,i} / \sum_i c_i \tag{4}$$

where $f_{3D,i}$ donates the 3D feature extracted from image I_i and c_i is the confidence of $f_{3D,i}$.

Coefficients Estimator. The method of estimating pose and illumination coefficients from f_{2D} has been introduced in the previous section. The shape and texture coefficients will be estimated from $f_{3D,fuse}$. Inspired by [40], we implement a similar keypoints detector, which extracts K 3D keypoints $\{x_i\}_{i=1}^K$ in feature volume. These keypoints are unsupervisedly learned and different from the common facial landmarks. The feature at the keypoint location is considered to have main contribution to shape and texture estimation. We conduct bilinear sampling operation at the keypoints locations of $f_{3D,fuse}$ to obtain the local feature f_{loc} and apply a 3D average pooling operation over the $f_{3D,fuse}$ to obtain the global feature f_{glo}. The f_{loc} and the f_{glo} are concatenated to regress the shape and texture coefficients by several linear layers.

4.2 Loss Function

Single-view face reconstruction has been widely studied. Therefore, We transfer the loss function used in single-view face reconstruction method to the multi-view setting.

Photometric Loss. The photometric loss aims to minimize the pixel difference between the input images and the rendered images, defined as $L_{photo} = \frac{1}{N} \sum_{i=1}^N \frac{1}{|M_i|} \sum_{M_i} ||I_i'(x_i) - I_i||_2$, where the $I_i'(x_i)$ is the image rendered using

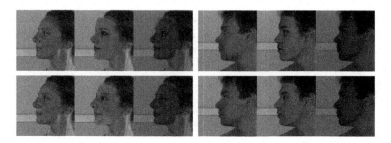

Fig. 2. Comparison of the results without (top row) and with (bottom row) using silhouette loss for training. We use the red region to mark the face region of rendered images on the input images. (Color figure online)

the face model coefficients x_i, $\mathcal{M}_i$ is the face region of $I'_i(x_i)$ and N is the number of different view images.

Landmark Loss. The landmark loss mainly contributes to the geometry of reconstructed face. We use a state-of-the-art landmark detector [3] to detect the 68 landmarks $\{q_i^k\}_{k=1}^{68}$ of input image I_i. We also can obtain the landmarks $\{q'^k_i(x_i)\}_{k=1}^{68}$ by projecting the 3D vertices on the reconstructed mesh to image plane. The landmark loss can be represented as: $L_{lmk} = \frac{1}{N}\sum_{i=1}^{N}\frac{1}{68}\sum_{k=1}^{68}\omega_k||q_i^k - q'^k_i(x_i)||_2$, where ω_k is the landmark weight. We set the weight to 20 for nose and inner month and others to 1.

Perceptual Loss. We adopt the perceptual loss L_{per} as in [9] to improve the fidelity of the reconstructed face texture. The perceptual loss measures the cosine distance between the deep feature of the input images and rendered images. With the perceptual loss, the textures are sharper and the shapes are more faithful.

Silhouette Loss. Inspired by the silhouette loss which used in human body reconstruction [14,17,21], we apply it in multi-view face reconstruction task. We use a face parsing network [23] to segment the face region from the input image. Then we detect the side view silhouette (left silhouette for left view image and right for right) of the face region. The silhouette is represented as a 2D point set $\mathcal{S}_i$ in the image plane, where i is the index of input image I_i. We can also extract silhouette from the rendered image $I'_i(x_i)$ to get another point set $\mathcal{S}'_i$. The silhouette loss is defined as the chamfer distance between the two point sets: $L_{sil} = \frac{1}{N}\sum_{i=1}^{N}chamfer(\mathcal{S}_i, \mathcal{S}'_i)$. It should be noticed that the silhouette loss will not be applied in the frontal view images. In the experiment, the face parsing network may fail due to the occlusion of the face region. Therefore, we discard the silhouette loss when its value is greater than a presetting threshold to make the training process more stable. Figure 2 illustrates the benefit of using our silhouette loss.

Regularization Loss. To ensure the face geometry and texture are reasonable, regularization loss of 3DMM is used as $L_{reg} = \omega_{id}||\alpha||_2 + \omega_{exp}||\beta||_2 + \omega_{tex}||\delta||_2$. $\omega_{id}, \omega_{exp}, \omega_{tex}$ are balancing weights of different 3DMM coefficients and are set to 1.0, 0.8, 2e-3 respectively.

To sum, the total loss function is:

$$L_{tot} = \omega_{pho}L_{pho} + \omega_{lmk}L_{lmk} + \omega_{per}L_{per} + \omega_{sil}L_{sil} + \omega_{reg}L_{reg} \tag{5}$$

4.3   Test-Time Optimization

The CNN-based approaches predict the face model coefficients x from image I by learning a mapping function $x = f_\theta(I)$, where θ is the parameters of CNNs. Assuming that the CNNs is trained on a dataset $\mathcal{D}_{train}$, the training process aims to find the optimal parameters θ^* which satisfies:

$$\theta^* = \arg\min_\theta \sum_{I \in \mathcal{D}_{train}} L_{tot}(I, f_\theta(I)) \tag{6}$$

However, when testing a particular sample I, we want to find the face model coefficients x^* which satisfies:

$$x^* = \arg\min_x L_{tot}(I, x) \tag{7}$$

There are two main gaps between Eq. (6) and Eq. (7). The first one is the test image may not be sampled from $\mathcal{D}_{train}$. This is a crucial but difficult problem caused by domain gap between datasets and is still a hotspot issue in deep learning. The second gap is neural network minimizes the loss over the whole dataset. Although we test a sample $I \in \mathcal{D}_{train}$, the neural network still can't produce a optimal result for this particular sample. Thus, we propose the test-time optimization mechanism to fill the two gaps. We take the output of neural network $x = f_\theta(I)$ as the initialization and try to find the optimal x^* by Eq. (7). Our test-time mechanism can be easily implemented in the existing reconstruction methods based on neural network, which only need to calculate derivative of $L_{tot}(I, x)$ with respect to x and conduct gradient descent algorithm.

5   Experiments

In this section, we compare the qualitative and quantitative result with both the state-of-the-art single-view and multi-view approaches. We also demonstrate the effectiveness of our approach with extensive ablation studies in the Supplementary Material. Besides, the implementation details including training strategy, datasets and hyperparameters setting will also be showed in the Supplementary Material.

Table 1. Average and standard deviation of the symmetric point-to-plane L2 errors on the MICC dataset (in *mm*).

Method	Cooperative		Indoor	
	Mean	Std	Mean	Std
3DDFA [45]	2.65	0.63	2.26	0.50
RingNet [28]	2.35	0.49	2.21	0.46
PRN [13]	2.30	0.54	2.02	0.50
Tran *et al.* [39]	2.05	0.54	2.07	0.51
MVFNet [44]	1.73	0.49	1.76	0.52
MGCNet [30]	1.71	0.47	1.73	0.48
Deng *et al.* [9]	1.69	0.53	1.70	0.51
Ours	**1.59**	**0.47**	**1.61**	**0.46**

5.1 Quantitative Comparisons

We evaluation our approaches on the MICC Florence dataset [1] which is a benchmark test dataset of the multi-view face reconstruction task. It consists of 53 identities and the corresponding 3D scans which can be regarded as the ground-truth. Each identity has two videos of "indoor-cooperative" and "indoor" respectively. We compare our methods with both multi-view methods and single-view methods. For multi-view methods, we manually select three images in each video as a triplet, where the camera viewpoints are largely different and expressions are kept neutral very well. For comparing with the single-view methods on the image triplets, we follow the method from [30,44]. We follow the data preprocessing methods and evaluation metrics from [15,44]. Then the symmetric point-to-plane L2 errors (in millimeters) between the predict 3D models and the groundtruth scan will be computed as the evaluation metrics.

We compare our method with Zhu *et al.* [45] (3DDFA), Sanyal *et al.* [28], Feng *et al.* [13] (PRN), Tran *et al.* [39], Wu *et al.* [44] (MVFNet), Shang*et al.* [30] (MGCNet), Deng *et al.* [9]. Notice that for each comparison, we use exactly the same input to test all the comapred methods. As shown in Table 1, our method outperforms all the state-of-the-art single-view and multi-view methods. Several examples of the comparison of the error maps are shown in Fig. 3. Since our method better explore the multi-view 3D information by a 3D volume-based feature fusion and a test-time optimization, it achieves lower error than the compared methods especially in the regions of forehead and chin where the z direction ambiguity is more severe.

5.2 Qualitative Comparisons

We present some visual examples from the MICC dataset. We compared our methods with RingNet [28], Deng *et al.* [9], MVFNet [44] and MGCNet [30].

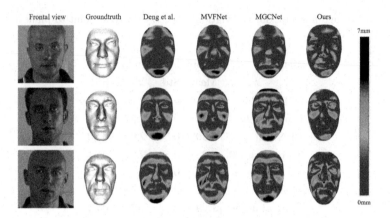

Fig. 3. The error map comparisons with Deng et al. [9], MVFNet [44], MGCNet [30] on the MICC dataset.

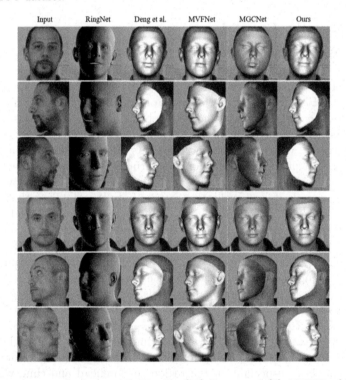

Fig. 4. Geometry comparisons with RingNet [28], Dent et al. [9], MVFNet [44], MGC-Net [30] on the MICC dataset.

From the front view images, Fig. 4 shows that the overall face shapes reconstructed by our method and Deng *et al.* [9] are more fidelity than the other methods. For the side views images, although MGCNet [30] and Deng *el al.*

[9] have achieved better pose estimation than MVFNet [44] and RingNet [28], there still exits obvious misalignment at the forehead region. While our method achieves better face alignment than the other methods by better exploring of multi-view information. More Visual comparisons in different facial expressions will be showed in Supplementary Material.

6   Conclusion

We have proposed a novel multi-view 3D morphable face reconstruction method via canonical volume fusion and demonstrated the advantages of explicitly establishing dense feature correspondences to solve the depth ambiguity in the multi-view reconstruction task. Besides, we introduced an easy-implemented and effective mechanism called test-time optimization, which refines the outputs of CNNs and obtain more accurate results. Our methods outperforms the state-of-art methods in both quantitative and qualitative.

Acknowledgement. This work was supported by Beijing Natural Science Foundation (JQ19015), the NSFC (No. 62021002, 61727808), the National Key R&D Program of China (2018YFA0704000), and the Key Research and Development Project of Tibet Autonomous Region (XZ202101ZY0019G). This work was also supported by THUIBCS, Tsinghua University, and BLBCI, Beijing Municipal Education Commission.

References

1. Bagdanov, A.D., Del Bimbo, A., Masi, I.: The florence 2d/3d hybrid face dataset. In: Proceedings of the 2011 Joint ACM Workshop on Human Gesture and Behavior Understanding, pp. 79–80 (2011)
2. Blanz, V., Vetter, T.: A morphable model for the synthesis of 3d faces. In: Proceedings of the 26th Annual Conference on Computer Graphics and Interactive Techniques, pp. 187–194 (1999)
3. Bulat, A., Tzimiropoulos, G.: How far are we from solving the 2d & 3d face alignment problem? (and a dataset of 230,000 3d facial landmarks). In: Proceedings of the IEEE International Conference on Computer Vision, pp. 1021–1030 (2017)
4. Cao, C., Hou, Q., Zhou, K.: Displaced dynamic expression regression for real-time facial tracking and animation. ACM Trans. Graph. (TOG) **33**(4), 1–10 (2014)
5. Cao, C., Weng, Y., Lin, S., Zhou, K.: 3d shape regression for real-time facial animation. ACM Trans. Graph. (TOG) **32**(4), 1–10 (2013)
6. Cao, C., Weng, Y., Zhou, S., Tong, Y., Zhou, K.: Facewarehouse: a 3d facial expression database for visual computing. IEEE Trans. Vis. Comput. Graph. **20**(3), 413–425 (2013)
7. Cao, C., Wu, H., Weng, Y., Shao, T., Zhou, K.: Real-time facial animation with image-based dynamic avatars. ACM Trans. Graph. **35**(4) (2016)
8. Chaudhuri, B., Vesdapunt, N., Shapiro, L., Wang, B.: Personalized face modeling for improved face reconstruction and motion retargeting. In: Vedaldi, A., Bischof, H., Brox, T., Frahm, J.-M. (eds.) ECCV 2020. LNCS, vol. 12350, pp. 142–160. Springer, Cham (2020). https://doi.org/10.1007/978-3-030-58558-7_9

9. Deng, Y., Yang, J., Xu, S., Chen, D., Jia, Y., Tong, X.: Accurate 3d face reconstruction with weakly-supervised learning: From single image to image set. In: Proceedings of the IEEE/CVF Conference on Computer Vision and Pattern Recognition Workshops (2019)

10. Dou, P., Kakadiaris, I.A.: Multi-view 3d face reconstruction with deep recurrent neural networks. Image Vis. Comput. **80**, 80–91 (2018)

11. Dou, P., Shah, S.K., Kakadiaris, I.A.: End-to-end 3d face reconstruction with deep neural networks. In: proceedings of the IEEE Conference on Computer Vision and Pattern Recognition, pp. 5908–5917 (2017)

12. Egger, B., et al.: 3d morphable face models-past, present, and future. ACM Trans. Graph. (TOG) **39**(5), 1–38 (2020)

13. Feng, Y., Wu, F., Shao, X., Wang, Y., Zhou, X.: Joint 3D face reconstruction and dense alignment with position map regression network. In: Ferrari, V., Hebert, M., Sminchisescu, C., Weiss, Y. (eds.) Computer Vision – ECCV 2018. LNCS, vol. 11218, pp. 557–574. Springer, Cham (2018). https://doi.org/10.1007/978-3-030-01264-9_33

14. Gavrila, D.M., Davis, L.S.: 3-d model-based tracking of humans in action: a multi-view approach. In: Proceedings CVPR IEEE Computer Society Conference on Computer Vision and Pattern Recognition, pp. 73–80. IEEE (1996)

15. Genova, K., Cole, F., Maschinot, A., Sarna, A., Vlasic, D., Freeman, W.T.: Unsupervised training for 3d morphable model regression. In: Proceedings of the IEEE Conference on Computer Vision and Pattern Recognition, pp. 8377–8386 (2018)

16. He, K., Zhang, X., Ren, S., Sun, J.: Deep residual learning for image recognition. In: Proceedings of the IEEE Conference on Computer Vision and Pattern Recognition, pp. 770–778 (2016)

17. Huang, Y., et al.: Towards accurate marker-less human shape and pose estimation over time. In: 2017 International Conference on 3D Vision (3DV), pp. 421–430. IEEE (2017)

18. Jourabloo, A., Liu, X.: Large-pose face alignment via CNN-based dense 3d model fitting. In: Proceedings of the IEEE Conference on Computer Vision and Pattern Recognition, pp. 4188–4196 (2016)

19. Kim, H., et al.: Deep video portraits. ACM Trans. Graph. (TOG) **37**(4), 1–14 (2018)

20. Koizumi, T., Smith, W.A.P.: Look Ma, No Landmarks!– unsupervised, model-based dense face alignment. In: Vedaldi, A., Bischof, H., Brox, T., Frahm, J.-M. (eds.) ECCV 2020. LNCS, vol. 12347, pp. 690–706. Springer, Cham (2020). https://doi.org/10.1007/978-3-030-58536-5_41

21. Lassner, C., Romero, J., Kiefel, M., Bogo, F., Black, M.J., Gehler, P.V.: Unite the people: Closing the loop between 3d and 2d human representations. In: Proceedings of the IEEE Conference on Computer Vision and Pattern Recognition, pp. 6050–6059 (2017)

22. Lattas, A., Moschoglou, S., Gecer, B., Ploumpis, S., Triantafyllou, V., Ghosh, A., Zafeiriou, S.: Avatarme: realistically renderable 3d facial reconstruction" in-the-wild". In: Proceedings of the IEEE/CVF Conference on Computer Vision and Pattern Recognition, pp. 760–769 (2020)

23. Lee, C.H., Liu, Z., Wu, L., Luo, P.: Maskgan: towards diverse and interactive facial image manipulation. In: Proceedings of the IEEE/CVF Conference on Computer Vision and Pattern Recognition, pp. 5549–5558 (2020)

24. Lee, G.H., Lee, S.W.: Uncertainty-aware mesh decoder for high fidelity 3d face reconstruction. In: Proceedings of the IEEE/CVF Conference on Computer Vision and Pattern Recognition, pp. 6100–6109 (2020)

25. Li, T., Bolkart, T., Black, M.J., Li, H., Romero, J.: Learning a model of facial shape and expression from 4d scans. ACM Trans. Graph. **36**(6) (2017)
26. Paysan, P., Knothe, R., Amberg, B., Romdhani, S., Vetter, T.: A 3d face model for pose and illumination invariant face recognition. In: 2009 6th IEEE International Conference on Advanced Video and Signal Based Surveillance, pp. 296–301. IEEE (2009)
27. Ramon, E., Escur, J., Giro-i Nieto, X.: Multi-view 3d face reconstruction in the wild using siamese networks. In: Proceedings of the IEEE/CVF International Conference on Computer Vision Workshops (2019)
28. Sanyal, S., Bolkart, T., Feng, H., Black, M.J.: Learning to regress 3d face shape and expression from an image without 3d supervision. In: Proceedings of the IEEE/CVF Conference on Computer Vision and Pattern Recognition, pp. 7763–7772 (2019)
29. Sengupta, S., Kanazawa, A., Castillo, C.D., Jacobs, D.W.: Sfsnet: learning shape, reflectance and illuminance of facesin the wild'. In: Proceedings of the IEEE Conference on Computer Vision and Pattern Recognition, pp. 6296–6305 (2018)
30. Shang, J., et al.: Self-supervised monocular 3d face reconstruction by occlusion-aware multi-view geometry consistency. In: Vedaldi, A., Bischof, H., Brox, T., Frahm, J.-M. (eds.) ECCV 2020. LNCS, vol. 12360, pp. 53–70. Springer, Cham (2020). https://doi.org/10.1007/978-3-030-58555-6_4
31. Shao, X., et al.: 3d face shape regression from 2d videos with multi-reconstruction and mesh retrieval. In: Proceedings of the IEEE/CVF International Conference on Computer Vision Workshops (2019)
32. Simonyan, K., Zisserman, A.: Very deep convolutional networks for large-scale image recognition. arXiv preprint. arXiv:1409.1556 (2014)
33. Tewari, A., et al.: Fml: face model learning from videos. In: Proceedings of the IEEE/CVF Conference on Computer Vision and Pattern Recognition, pp. 10812–10822 (2019)
34. Tewari, A., et al: Mofa: model-based deep convolutional face autoencoder for unsupervised monocular reconstruction. In: Proceedings of the IEEE International Conference on Computer Vision Workshops, pp. 1274–1283 (2017)
35. Tewari, A., et al.: Self-supervised multi-level face model learning for monocular reconstruction at over 250 hz. In: Proceedings of the IEEE Conference on Computer Vision and Pattern Recognition, pp. 2549–2559 (2018)
36. Thies, J., Zollhofer, M., Stamminger, M., Theobalt, C., Nießner, M.: Face2face: real-time face capture and reenactment of RGB videos. In: Proceedings of the IEEE Conference on Computer Vision and pattern Recognition, pp. 2387–2395 (2016)
37. Tran, L., Liu, F., Liu, X.: Towards high-fidelity nonlinear 3d face morphable model. In: Proceedings of the IEEE/CVF Conference on Computer Vision and Pattern Recognition, pp. 1126–1135 (2019)
38. Tran, L., Liu, X.: Nonlinear 3d face morphable model. In: Proceedings of the IEEE Conference on Computer Vision and Pattern Recognition, pp. 7346–7355 (2018)
39. Tuan Tran, A., Hassner, T., Masi, I., Medioni, G.: Regressing robust and discriminative 3d morphable models with a very deep neural network. In: Proceedings of the IEEE Conference on Computer Vision and Pattern Recognition, pp. 5163–5172 (2017)
40. Wang, T.C., Mallya, A., Liu, M.Y.: One-shot free-view neural talking-head synthesis for video conferencing. In: Proceedings of the IEEE/CVF Conference on Computer Vision and Pattern Recognition, pp. 10039–10049 (2021)

41. Wang, Z., Yu, X., Lu, M., Wang, Q., Qian, C., Xu, F.: Single image portrait relighting via explicit multiple reflectance channel modeling. ACM Trans. Graph. (TOG) **39**(6), 1–13 (2020)
42. Wen, Q., et al.: Accurate real-time 3d gaze tracking using a lightweight eyeball calibration. In: Computer Graphics Forum, vol. 39, pp. 475–485. Wiley Online Library (2020)
43. Wen, Y., Liu, W., Raj, B., Singh, R.: Self-supervised 3d face reconstruction via conditional estimation. In: Proceedings of the IEEE/CVF International Conference on Computer Vision, pp. 13289–13298 (2021)
44. Wu, F., et al.: Mvf-net: multi-view 3d face morphable model regression. In: Proceedings of the IEEE/CVF Conference on Computer Vision and Pattern Recognition, pp. 959–968 (2019)
45. Zhu, X., Liu, X., Lei, Z., Li, S.Z.: Face alignment in full pose range: a 3d total solution. IEEE Trans. Pattern Anal. Mach. Intell. **41**(1), 78–92 (2017)

DPIT: Dual-Pipeline Integrated Transformer for Human Pose Estimation

Shuaitao Zhao[1], Kun Liu[2], Yuhang Huang[1], Qian Bao[3], Dan Zeng[1(✉)],
and Wu Liu[3(✉)]

[1] Joint International Research Laboratory of Specialty Fiber Optics and Advanced
Communication, Shanghai Institute of Advanced Communication and Data Science,
Shanghai University, Shanghai 200444, China
{zhaoshuaitao,huangyuhang,dzeng}@shu.edu.cn
[2] JD Logistics, Beijing 100176, China
liukun167@jd.com
[3] JD Explore Academy, Beijing 100176, China
{baoqian,liuwu1}@jd.com

Abstract. Human pose estimation aims to figure out the keypoints of all people in different scenes. Current approaches still face some challenges despite promising results. Existing top-down methods deal with a single person individually, without the interaction between different people and the scene they are situated in. Consequently, the performance of human detection degrades when serious occlusion happens. On the other hand, existing bottom-up methods consider all people at the same time and capture the global knowledge of the entire image. However, they are less accurate than the top-down methods due to the scale variation. To address these problems, we propose a novel Dual-Pipeline Integrated Transformer (**DPIT**) by integrating top-down and bottom-up pipelines to explore the visual clues of different receptive fields and achieve their complementarity. Specifically, DPIT consists of two branches, the bottom-up branch deals with the whole image to capture the global visual information, while the top-down branch extracts the feature representation of local vision from the single-human bounding box. Then, the extracted feature representations from bottom-up and top-down branches are fed into the transformer encoder to fuse the global and local knowledge interactively. Moreover, we define the keypoint queries to explore both full-scene and single-human posture visual clues to realize the mutual complementarity of the two pipelines. To the best of our knowledge, this is one of the first works to integrate the bottom-up and top-down pipelines with transformers for human pose estimation. Extensive experiments on COCO and MPII datasets demonstrate that our DPIT achieves comparable performance to the state-of-the-art methods.

Keywords: Human pose estimation · Dual-pipeline integration · Transformer · Information interaction

© The Author(s), under exclusive license to Springer Nature Switzerland AG 2022
L. Fang et al. (Eds.): CICAI 2022, LNAI 13605, pp. 559–576, 2022.
https://doi.org/10.1007/978-3-031-20500-2_46

1   Introduction

Human Pose Estimation (HPE) has been widely investigated as a fundamental task in computer vision, which aims to localize keypoints of the human, including eyes, nose, shoulders, wrists, *etc.*, from a single RGB image. Accurate human pose estimation can provide geometric and motion information about the human, which can be widely applied in action recognition [16,17], human-computer interaction, motion analysis, augmented reality (AR), *etc.*

Early human pose estimation methods do not depend on deep learning and mainly focus on the keypoints localization of a single person, which can be roughly divided into two categories. The first category treats the pose estimation task as a classification or regression problem through a global feature [25,31]. However, this kind of method does not exhibit high precision and is only suitable for clean scenes. The other category is the methods adopt graphic model to extract the feature representation for a single keypoint [11,23]. The location of a single part can be obtained using DPM (Deformable Part-based Model) [9], and the pair-wise relationships are required to optimize the association between keypoints at the same time.

Recently, with the rapid development of deep learning, Convolutional Neural Networks (CNNs) have shown strong dominance in human pose estimation. We can roughly classify these superior networks into top-down and bottom-up methods. The top-down methods [2,5,13,21,29,33,35,36] first obtain a set of the bounding box of people from the input image through an off-the-shelf human detector , then apply a single-person pose estimator to each person. This type of method mainly focuses on the investigation and improvement of the latter pose estimation network. Different from the top-down pipeline, the bottom-up methods [3,6,8,24,40] directly predict all the joints in an image and then group them using a certain assignment strategy to achieve multi-person pose estimation.

The top-down methods rely on the result of human detection and achieve promising performance for single-person pose estimation. However, because they deal with each person individually, there is no awareness of the interaction with the other persons and the environment, which is more prevalent in real-life scenarios. When there is serious occlusion among different people, the performance of human detection becomes unreliable.   Furthermore, when the target persons are very close to each other, the pose estimator may be misled by nearby persons, e.g., the predicted keypoints may come from adjacent persons. As a result, the top-down pipeline exhibits an inherent limitation in how to explore the interaction clues among different persons. Differently, the bottom-up methods do not rely on any detection process and take all people of the image into account simultaneously. They first detect the keypoints of all people, then align them into each person by a certain grouping strategy. This pipeline leverages full-scene information to realize locating keypoints, which can observe the interactions of different people from a global perspective. However, it suffers from scale variation, i.e., different people in the image are at different scales and very unevenly distributed, which is unfriendly to the training of the network, leading to relatively poor performance. In summary, both kinds of approaches show dif-

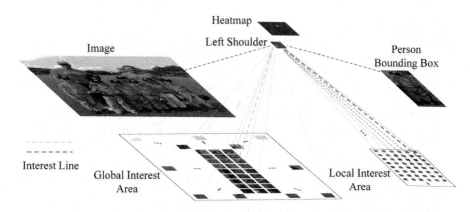

Fig. 1. Illustration of capturing information from different perspectives when predicting the left shoulder. The dotted lines point to the interest areas of the keypoint, and the thicker line indicates the more interest to the area. After the integration of different visual clues, the keypoint location is predicted by the heatmap.

ferent advantages. Consequently, integrating the advantages of the two pipelines is potential for human pose estimation.

To achieve the complementarity of two pipelines, we propose an effective network called DPIT to further promote the visual exploration of the image for human pose estimation. The proposed network integrates the advantages of the top-down and bottom-up pipelines to learn long-range visual clues with different receptive fields, which capture the full-scene and posture information of a single person. Firstly, we design two branches to extract global scene features and local features of a single person, respectively. Secondly, to fuse these features, we employ the transformer to capture different visual cues. The final output of our DPIT is predicted in the heatmap fashion.

Since the two pipelines of features contained different information are both essential for keypoints localization, our core idea is to incorporate the two pipelines into one network and perform effective information interaction. An example of how to predict the location of the left shoulder is shown in Fig. 1. Information from different perspectives can assist the network in better understanding the image scenes, and extend the interest region, which is of positive effects for human pose estimation in complex scenes. More specifically, we first employ a two-branch structure, in which the bottom-up branch captures full-scene information of the entire image, the top-down branch extracts the single-person feature of the detected human bounding box. Motivated by the great success of the recent work on Vision Transformers, the encoder of the transformer is employed as the clue interaction structure to fuse the two-branch features. In detail, we split the features into patches and take linear patch embeddings to form input visual tokens. Meanwhile, we define a set of randomly initialized embeddings as the keypoint queries, which can capture the single-person pose, full-scene visual clues, and their distributional relations from the different tokens.

Finally, we only apply the heatmap generator to the keypoint embeddings which have aggregated local and global information, and reshape them into heatmaps. To the best of our knowledge, this is one of the first works to integrate the two pipelines with transformers.

In summary, the contributions of this paper are mainly summarized as below:

- We propose a novel architecture named DPIT for human pose estimation, which is one of the first works to integrate the bottom-up and top-down pipelines in an end-to-end training manner.
- We design a Transformer-based module to capture both full-scene visual clues and posture information of a single person simultaneously, which can allocate different attention levels to different visual areas.
- We demonstrate an improvement over baselines on the widely used COCO and MPII datasets, and surpass the state-of-the-art methods.

The rest of this paper is organized as follows. In Sect. 2, we review the related works. In Sect. 3, we introduce the proposed DPIT for human pose estimation. Extensive experiments are conducted in Sect. 4 to compare the proposed DPIT with state-of-the-art methods on two benchmark datasets. The conclusion is given in Sect. 5.

2 Related Work

Our proposed method is related to the previous research on top-down human pose estimation, bottom-up human pose estimation, and applications of transformer in vision tasks.

2.1 Top-Down Human Pose Estimation

The Top-down pipeline consists of two main components: the human detector and the pose estimation network. Most of the work [2,5,13,29,33,36] focused on the design and improvement of the latter pose estimation network. CPN [5] implemented the coarse-to-fine process through a two-stage network, where the GlobalNet learns a well-defined feature representation based on a feature pyramid network to provide sufficient semantic information to locate simple keypoints. Further, the RefineNet is employed to handle the "difficult" keypoints by fusing the multi-level features of the GlobalNet. MSPN [13] performed stacking of multiple stages based on CPN's globalNet to achieve better information communication. Xiao et al. [36] employed ResNet as the backbone and added some de-convolution layers behind it, which built a simple but effective structure to produce a high-resolution representation of the keypoint heatmap. HRNet [29] started to give attention to the importance of spatial resolution. A novel high-resolution network is proposed to learn the reliable high-resolution features by connecting multi-resolution sub-networks in parallel, as well as performing repetitive multi-scale fusion. Cai et al. [2] proposed a multi-stage network where the

Residual Step Network (RSN) explores delicate local features through an effective inter-level feature fusion strategy. In addition, a new attention mechanism (PRM) was also proposed to learn different contributions for local and global features, achieving more accurate keypoint localization. Wang *et al.* [33] proposed a graph-based, model-independent two-stage network, Graph-PCNN. This framework added a localization sub-network and a graph structure pose optimization module to the original heatmap-based regression method. The heatmap regression network was employed as the first stage to provide rough localization of each keypoint. The localization sub-network was designed as the second stage to extract visual features from the candidate keypoints. Although these top-down methods can achieve satisfactory performance for the single-person bounding box, they are unreliable in obscured scenes.

2.2   Bottom-Up Human Pose Estimation

The bottom-up pipeline consists of two main stages, including the joints detection and grouping of all human keypoints in the image [3, 6, 8, 10, 20, 40]. Open-Pose [3] predicted the heatmap of keypoints to locate the position of each keypoint in the image. The Part Affinity Field (PAF) was proposed to achieve the connection of keypoints, which speeds up the bottom-up human pose estimation to a great extent. Associative Embedding [20] not only predicted the heatmaps but also output an embedding for each keypoint, aiming to make the embeddings of the same person as similar as possible. RMPE [8] proposed a two-step framework, which mainly solved the positioning error and the redundancy of the bounding box. HigherHRNet [6] provided a simple extension to HRNet [29] by deconvoluting the high-resolution heatmap to obtain the higher resolution representation. SIMPLE [40] employed knowledge distillation by treating the top-down network as a teacher network to train the bottom-up network. Both human detection and keypoint estimation were considered as unified point learning issues that complement each other in a single framework. DEKR [10] proposed a simple but effective method that employs adaptive convolution through a pixel-wise spatial transformer to activate pixels in the keypoint regions. Separate regression of different keypoints was also performed using a multi-branch structure. The separated representations can notice the keypoint regions separately so that the keypoint regression is more spatially accurate. However, the variation of the person scale in the image significantly affects the performance of these bottom-up methods.

2.3   Transformers in Vision

The amazing achievements of the transformer in natural language have attracted the vision community to explore its application to computer vision tasks. Recently, the transformer has been widely applied in different vision tasks including image classification [7], object detection [4,41], segmentation [28,37], and generation [34], *etc.*

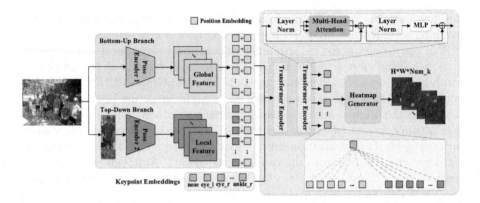

Fig. 2. The overall training architecture of our network. The image is input to the bottom-up branch to get the full-scene feature. The single-person bounding box output from the human detector is fed into the top-down branch to extract the single-human pose feature. Then the defined random embeddings are treated as the keypoint queries, which is sent into the transformer encoder together with the visual tokens in sequential fashion. The outputs of our network are the heatmaps of keypoints with the shape of $H \times W \times Num\_k$, where Num_k is the number of keypoints. All components of the network are trained together in an end-to-end manner.

ViT [7] completely abandoned CNN and applied transformer to image classification, which splits the image into fix-sized patches, each of which is expanded into sequential form and fed to the encoder of transformer by linear projection. DeiT [30] incorporated distillation into the training of ViT. It introduced a teacher-student training strategy, in which the convolution network was employed as the teacher network. DETR [4] applied transformer to the object detection. The image is processed by CNN for feature extraction, then fed into the transformer in the manner of feature sequences. The transformer architecture directly outputs an unordered set. Each element of the set contains object categories and coordinates. SegFormer [37] proposed a simple and efficient structure for semantic segmentation, consisting of a positional-encoding-free, hierarchical transformer encoder and an MLP decoder, which achieves high efficiency and accuracy.

In human pose estimation, the transformer has also received extensive attention and application [14,19,27,38,39]. POET [27] proposed an encoder-decoder structure combining CNN and transformer, which can directly regress the pose of all individuals using a bipartite matching scheme. Based on the regression manner, TFPose [19] implemented direct human pose estimation, overcoming the feature-mismatch problem of previous regression-based methods. TransPose [39] introduced a transformer-based structure to predict the location of human keypoints based on heatmaps, which can effectively capture the spatial relationships of images. Following ViT [7], TokenPose [14] divided the image into several patches to form the visual tokens, which incorporated the visual cue and constraint cue into a unified network. Swin-Pose [38] proposed a transformer-based structure to capture the long-range dependencies between pixels, using the pre-trained Swin Transformer [18] as the backbone to extract image features. In addition, the feature pyramid architecture was adopted to fuse features from different stages for feature enhancement. Different from these transformer-based methods, our method employ the transformer to integrate the top-down and bottom-up pipelines. In this way, our network can capture the global clues and local clues simultaneously.

3   The Proposed Method

The presented framework is shown in Fig. 2, where all modules are trained in an end-to-end manner. Given an image as input, a two-branch architecture is employed for feature extraction, where the bottom-up branch and top-down branch extract full-scene information and posture of a single person, respectively. Then, a transformer-based integration network is designed to jointly establish keypoint-person and keypoint-scene interactions.

3.1   Two-Branch Architecture

As shown in Fig. 2, to integrate the top-down and bottom-up pipelines into a unified network, we employ a parallel two-branch CNN for feature extraction in the first stage of our network. The two CNN backbones are pre-trained on the ImageNet classification task [26]. Specifically, an image $x_1 \in \mathbb{R}^{H_1 \times W_1 \times 3}$ is first detected by an existing human detector, from which we obtain the human bounding box $x_2 \in \mathbb{R}^{H_2 \times W_2 \times 3}$. The bottom-up encoder $\boldsymbol{E}^{BU}$ extracts the full-scene feature representation $\boldsymbol{F}^{BU} \in \mathbb{R}^{H_1' \times W_1' \times C}$ from the input image x_1. Taking x_2 as input, the top-down encoder $\boldsymbol{E}^{TD}$ outputs the posture representation $\boldsymbol{F}^{TD} \in \mathbb{R}^{H_2' \times W_2' \times C}$ of single-person. The process of feature extraction of the two branches can be represented as:

$$\boldsymbol{F}^{BU} = \boldsymbol{E}^{BU}(x_1), \boldsymbol{F}^{TD} = \boldsymbol{E}^{TD}(x_2), \tag{1}$$

where $\boldsymbol{E}^{BU}$ and $\boldsymbol{E}^{TD}$ denote bottom-up and top-down CNN encoders, respectively.

The featuremap extracted by the bottom-up encoder comes from the whole image, where we can observe the full-scene information, including the pose of all people, the interaction of different people, and the scene information of the image. The top-down branch focuses on the spatial posture information of a single person with uniform resolution. In real scenes, the environment is usually undefinable, there are various interactions among different people. As a result, capturing visual clues from different view fields can assist in locating the keypoints more effectively.

3.2   Transformer-Based Integration

Inspired by the wide applications of transformer in vision tasks, we employ the encoder of the transformer to capture and integrate the visual clues of different view fields. Together with the patch embeddings from the bottom-up and top-down branches, the keypoint embeddings are defined as input queries. In this way, our network can capture the knowledge of global fields and local fields that comes from the whole image and single-human bounding box, respectively.

Input Queries. Following the process of ViT [7], The featuremap $\boldsymbol{F}^{BU}$ and $\boldsymbol{F}^{TD}$ are split into two patch sets: $p_1 = [F_1^{BU}, ..., F_{N_1}^{BU}] \in \mathbb{R}^{N_1 \times P_1^h \times P_1^w \times C}, p_2 = [F_1^{TD}, ..., F_{N_2}^{TD}] \in \mathbb{R}^{N_2 \times P_2^h \times P_2^w \times C}$, where (P_*^h, P_*^w) $(* = 1, 2)$ is the patch size, $N_* = (H_*^{'} \times W_*^{'})/(P_*^h \times P_*^w)$ is the number of patches, C is the number of channels. The standard Transformer [32] receives a 1D sequence of the token embeddings as input. Every patch is flattened into a 1D vector with the size of $P_*^h \cdot P_*^w \cdot C$. Then, the linear projection is performed to each 1D vector, we can get the visual queries of two branches: $\mathbf{q_1} = [E_1, ..., E_{N_1}]$, $\mathbf{q_2} = [E_1, ..., E_{N_2}]$, where $E \in \mathbb{R}^{(P_*^h \cdot P_*^w \cdot C) \times D}$ and D is the embedding dimension. It is worth mentioning that human pose estimation is a location sensitive vision task, so the 2D position embeddings are added to the sequence of patches to capture positional information.

Moreover, we introduce a set of learnable keypoint embeddings: $\mathbf{kpt} = [k_1, ..., k_K] \in \mathbb{R}^{K \times D}$, where K is the number of keypoints. Each keypoint embedding is initialized randomly and assigned to a single keypoint (eyes, wrists, ...), which is employed to generate the final heatmap. Benefit from the self-attention mechanism of transformer, each keypoint embedding can capture the corresponding interest visual regions from both global and local features. In addition, it can give attention to the clues of other keypoints, which simplifies the difficulty of locating keypoints, especially in complex scenarios. The keypoint embeddings $\mathbf{kpt}$, bottom-up visual query $\mathbf{q_1}$, and top-down visual query $\mathbf{q_2}$ are put together as the input queries, which are processed jointly by the transformer encoder, as depicted in Fig. 2.

Transformer Encoder. The transformer encoder consists of multi-encoder layers, which mainly depend on the self-attention mechanism. Each encoder layer contains a multi-head self-attention (MSA) block followed by a feed-forward network (FFN). Layer Normalization (LN) is also employed before every module and residual connections after every module. Specifically, for the input sequence X, linear projections are performed to obtain Query (Q), Key (K), and Value (V):

$$Q = X * W_Q, K = X * W_K, V = X * W_V, \tag{2}$$

where W_Q, W_K, W_V are the corresponding weight matrices. The MSA process can formulated:

$$MSA(Q, K, V) = softmax(\frac{Q \times K^T}{\sqrt{d_k}}) \cdot V, \tag{3}$$

where d_k is the dimension of keys. Each query is calculated with all the keys, each (Q, K) pair is divided by d_k. Then, the SoftMax function is employed to obtain the attention scores, each score determines the attention level to the token for current query.

Heatmap Generator. The transformer encoder outputs a D-dimensional sequence. After the transformer's self-attention mechanism, the corresponding keypoint embeddings have captured the visual clues of the full-scene and single-person. We only take the keypoint queries for prediction, which are linearly mapped into $H \cdot W$ dimensions. Then the mapped 1D representations are reshaped into 2D heatmaps with the shape of $H \times W$. Finally, on output heatmaps, we find the maximum response position by channel to locate the corresponding human keypoint. In addition, between the output heatmap and the ground-truth heatmap, we adopt MSE as the loss function to train the network.

4 Experiments

4.1 Datasets

In this paper, we conducted extensive experiments on two human pose datasets, COCO [15] and MPII [1], to train and validate our network. For a fair comparison, we follow the same dataset split ratio as the comparison methods [29]. The datasets are introduced below.

COCO Dataset. COCO is a large-scale dataset in human pose estimation task, containing over 200K images and 250K person instances, annotated with 17 keypoints. The dataset is divided into a train set (118k images), a validation set (5K images), and a test-dev set (20K images). We take the train set to train our network. The validation set and test-dev set are employed to measure the performance of our network.

MPII Dataset. MPII is a well-known benchmark for the evaluation of human pose estimation, which contains around 25K images and over 40K people with annotated 16 joints.

4.2 Metrics

For the COCO dataset, the Object Keypoint Similarity (OKS) is calculated for the reported metrics, which measures the similarity between the ground truth and predicted keypoints. The OKS is defined as follows:

$$OKS = \frac{\sum_i \exp(\frac{-d_i^2}{2s^2 k_i^2})\delta(v_i > 0)}{\sum_i \delta(v_i > 0)}, \tag{4}$$

where d_i is the Euclidean distances between each corresponding ground truth and detected keypoint. v_i is the visibility flag of the ground truth. s denotes the square root of the person's proportion to the image area, δ_i is the normalized parameter of the ith keypoint. Based on OKS, the standard average precision and average recall are reported, including AP (the mean value of AP at $OKS = 0.5, 0.55, ..., 0.9, 0.95$), AP^{50} (AP at $OKS = 0.5$), AP^{75} (AP at $OKS = 0.75$), AP^M (AP of medium-scale objects), AP^L (AP of large-scale objects), and AR (mean value of AR at $OKS = 0.5, 0.55, ..., 0.9, 0.95$).

For MPII, the head-normalized Percentage of Correct Keypoints (PCKh@0.5) [1] is employed as the metric, which calculates the percentage of the normalized distance between the ground truths and detected keypoints that are lower than the setting threshold (0.5).

4.3   Implementation Details

Regarding the training scheme, all modules of our network are trained with adaptive moment estimation optimizer (ADAM) [12], whose parameters are: $\alpha = 0.001$, $\beta_1 = 0.9$, $\beta_2 = 0.999$. The initial learning rate is 10^{-3} for our network, which is trained for a total of 240 epochs. The learning rate is reduced to 10% of the previous number at the 190th and 220th epochs, respectively. For the backbones of the bottom-up and top-down branches, we adopt the models trained on the ImageNet classification task as our pre-trained models. To improve the varieties of training data, following [29], the data augmentations are conducted, including random rotation ($[-45°, 45°]$), random scale ($[0.65, 1.35]$) and flipping.

While training, for the bottom-up branch, we resize the image to a fixed size: 512×512, then fed it into the encoder of this branch. As introduced before, we split the featuremap output from the encoder into patches with the size of 8×8. On the other hand, the input of the top-down branch is also rescaled into fixed resolution. There are different settings for COCO and MPII datasets. On COCO, the patch size is set to 4×3 with input size of 256×192. On MPII, with a uniform input shape of 256×256, the feature is split into 4×4 patches. In addition, our network set up two configuration versions, DPIT-B and DPIT-L. The detailed settings of them are shown in Table 1.

Table 1. The network configurations. HRNet-W32-s and HRNet-W48-s denote the first three stages of HRNet-W32 and HRNet-W48, respectively.

Model	Backbone	Depth	Heads	Hidden_Dim
DPIT-B	HRNet-W32-s	12	8	192
DPIT-L	HRNet-W48-s	12	8	192

Table 2. Quantitative results on COCO validation set across various state-of-the-art methods with the ground-truth bounding boxes. R and H denote the ResNet and HRNet, respectively. #Params indicates the size of each model, excluding the cost of the human detection network. In each column, the best result is in bold, the second best is underlined.

Method	Backbone	Input size	#Params	AP	AP^{50}	AP^{75}	AP^M	AP^L	AR
Simple baseline [36]	R-50	256 × 192	34.0M	72.4	91.5	80.4	69.7	76.5	75.6
	R-50	384 × 288	34.0M	74.1	92.6	80.5	70.5	79.6	76.9
	R-101	256 × 192	53.0M	73.4	92.6	81.4	70.7	77.7	76.5
	R-101	384 × 288	53.0M	75.5	92.5	82.6	72.4	80.8	78.4
	R-152	256 × 192	68.6M	74.3	92.6	82.5	71.6	78.7	77.4
	R-152	384 × 288	68.6M	76.6	92.6	83.6	73.7	81.3	79.3
HRNet [29]	H-W32	256 × 192	28.5M	76.5	<u>93.5</u>	83.7	73.9	80.8	79.3
	H-W48	256 × 192	63.6M	<u>77.1</u>	**93.6**	<u>84.7</u>	<u>74.1</u>	<u>81.9</u>	<u>79.9</u>
DPIT-B	–	256 × 192	20.8M	76.9	<u>93.5</u>	83.7	73.7	81.5	79.6
DPIT-L	–	256 × 192	38.0M	**77.8**	**93.6**	**84.8**	**74.8**	**82.2**	**80.3**

4.4   Quantitative Results

To validate the effectiveness and superiority of our method, we conducted quantitative experiments on COCO and MPII datasets. The quantitative results show that our method achieves better performance on human pose estimation, the specific results are analyzed as follows:

Results on COCO Dataset. The quantitative results using the ground-truth bounding box on the COCO validation set are shown in Table 2. For the different methods, we perform quantitative comparisons based on different backbones and input resolutions. Following TokenPose [14], we do not employ the whole HRNet as our backbone, but its first three stages. In this case, the network parameters are only 25% of the original version, as indicated by HRNet-W32-s and HRNet-W48-s in Table 1. Compared to SimpleBaseline [36] and HRNet [29], it can be observed that our method achieves better performance while being more lightweight. Quantitatively, our DPIT-L achieves improvements of 0.7 AP and 0.4 AR compared to the HRNet-W48, which demonstrates the superiority of our method.

In addition, as shown in Table 3, we compare our method with the state-of-the-art methods including G-RMI [22], CPN [5], RMPE [8], SimpleBaseline [36] and HRNet [29] on COCO test-dev set. Compared with other methods, DPIT exhibits the best performance on AP and AR, achieves comparable results on other metrics.

Table 3. Comparison with various state-of-the-art methods with detected bounding boxes from the same human detector on COCO test-dev set.

Method	Input size	#Params	AP	AP^{50}	AP^{75}	AP^M	AP^L	AR
G-RMI [22]	353×257	42.6M	64.9	85.5	71.3	62.3	70.0	69.7
CPN [5]	384×288	45.0M	72.1	91.4	80.0	68.7	77.2	78.5
RMPE [8]	320×256	28.1M	72.3	89.2	79.1	68.0	**80.8**	78.6
SimpleBaseline-R152 [36]	384×288	68.6M	73.7	<u>91.9</u>	81.1	70.3	80.0	79.0
HRNet-W48 [29]	256×192	63.6M	<u>74.2</u>	**92.4**	**82.4**	<u>70.9</u>	79.7	<u>79.5</u>
DPIT-B	256×192	20.8M	73.6	91.4	81.2	70.4	79.5	78.9
DPIT-L	256×192	38.0M	**74.6**	<u>91.9</u>	<u>82.1</u>	**71.3**	<u>80.6</u>	**79.9**

Results on MPII Dataset. The PCKh@0.5 results on the MPII validation set are reported in Table 4 with a uniform input size of 256×256. DPIT-L/D6 represents the configured DPIT-L with 6 transformer encoder layers. Specifically, compared with SimpleBaseline [36] and HRNet [29], our DPIT-L/D6 achieves the best performance on the metrics reported by Elb, Wri, Ank, and $Mean$. On most other metrics, it also achieves the second-best level. In summary, the quantitative results indicate the comparable performance of our DPIT on the MPII dataset.

Table 4. Quantitative Results on MPII validation set. Experiments for all architectures are performed at the uniform input size: 256×256.

Method	Backbone	#Params	Hea	Sho	Elb	Wri	Hip	Kne	Ank	Mean
SimpleBaseline [36]	R-50	34.0M	96.4	95.3	89.0	83.2	88.4	84.0	79.6	88.5
	R-101	53.0M	96.9	<u>95.9</u>	89.5	84.4	88.4	84.5	80.7	89.1
	R-152	68.6M	<u>97.0</u>	<u>95.9</u>	90.0	85.0	<u>89.2</u>	85.3	<u>81.3</u>	<u>89.6</u>
HRNet [29]	H-W32	28.5M	96.9	**96.0**	<u>90.6</u>	<u>85.8</u>	88.7	**86.6**	**82.6**	**90.1**
DPIT-B	–	21.6M	**97.1**	95.7	90.0	84.6	**89.4**	85.9	80.7	<u>89.6</u>
DPIT-L/D6	–	31.8M	96.7	<u>95.9</u>	**90.8**	**85.9**	<u>89.2</u>	<u>86.0</u>	**82.6**	**90.1**

4.5   Qualitative Results

Our method incorporates both top-down and bottom-up pipelines, where the full-scene information of different visual fields can help capture human pose information, especially in complex scenes with multi-person interactions. Given an image, our network can accurately localize the location of keypoints for persons in the image. As shown in Fig. 3, the pose estimation results of DPIT in different scenes are demonstrated. From the first row, we can observe that for complex pose scenes of a single person, our network can achieve accurate localization of keypoints. Benefitting from the fusion of visual information from different

Fig. 3. Illustration of human pose estimation results of DPIT in different scenes on COCO validation set. The first row shows the effect of pose estimation in single-person situations with different postures. The scenes in the second row contain interactions of different people, including self-shadowing and inter-shadowing between two persons. Finally, more complex scenes with multiple people are further visualized in the third row.

receptive fields and interactions of visual clues, the network still performs well while serious occlusion among different people. In addition, our method is not affected by the scale variation of the persons in the image. It is observable that accurate human pose estimation can still be reported for scenes with large-scale

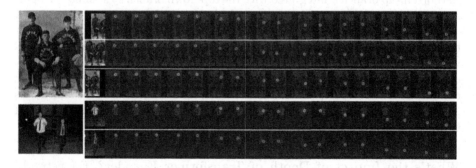

Fig. 4. Illustration of the heatmaps of all persons in the image predicted by the network. Each heatmap of the same row denotes the location response of different keypoints of one person. It can be observed that in the presence of different human distractions, our method can still accurately estimate the location of key points in the human body.

differences. As shown in Fig. 4, we further illustrate the heatmaps of keypoints, where the maximum response location represents the corresponding location of keypoints. As we can see, our network can predict precise heatmaps for different keypoints and different persons in the image. The heatmap manner effectively preserves the spatial location information.

4.6   Ablation Studies

In this section, to verify the contributions of different components and the influence of the structure parameter settings, we perform ablation experiments on the COCO dataset.

Is It Useful to Employ the Bottom-Up Branch to Capture the Full-Scene Information? The bottom-up branch extracts the full-scene information from the whole image with the encoder E^{BU}. To verify the usefulness of the bottom-up branch in locating human keypoints, we delete this branch in our DPIT, and obtain a network that does not utilize the feature of the entire image, called w/o *BU*. As shown in Table 5, we report quantitative results in the row with w/o *BU*. Without the help of the bottom-up branch, we observe degradation in the performance on different metrics. In addition, as shown in Fig. 5, the qualitative results indicate that the absence of full-scene information leads to inaccurate human pose estimation in the scenes with multi-person interaction and occlusion. As a result, both quantitative and qualitative results demonstrate the usefulness of the bottom-up branch.

Why Using Transformer Encoder? To evaluate the contribution of the transformer encoder to our DPIT, we perform another ablation experiment, i.e., removing the transformer encoder from the network. Alternatively, the featuremap of the bottom-up branch is integrated with the top-down branch by summation operation after some convolution layers, then the heatmap of the keypoints is predicted by the integrated features. It is worth mentioning that the simplified backbone no longer can capture enough information about the image in this case, which aggravates the network. In comparison, the transformer can capture long-term dependencies of the same visual field, while also integrating visual clues and posture clues from different perspectives with the help of self-attention mechanism. As shown in the row with w/o *Transformer* of Table 5, the poorer performance of the network proves the effectiveness of the transformer.

What's the Impact of Depth of Transformer Encoder? For networks equipped with transformer, the depth of the encoder is a significant setting for the performance. As shown in Table 6, to explore the impact of the different number of encoder layers, we conduct quantitative experiments on the COCO validation set. Specifically, we only change the number of encoder layers of the

Table 5. Results on COCO validation set with the input size of 256 × 192. w/o *BU*: without bottom-up branch. w/o *Transformer*: without transformer.

Model	AP	AP^{50}	AR
w/o *BU*	76.6	92.5	79.4
w/o *Transformer*	76.5	**93.6**	79.3
DPIT-B	**76.9**	93.5	**79.6**

Table 6. Ablation studies with different transformer encoder layers are performed on COCO validation dataset.

Model	Depth	AP	AP^{50}	AR
DPIT-B-D6	6	76.3	92.9	79.1
DPIT-B-D12	12	**76.9**	**93.5**	**79.6**
DPIT-B-D16	16	76.5	92.6	79.3

Fig. 5. Some qualitative results are illustrated to show the contributions of the bottom-up branch.

transformer, keeping the other configurations fixed. Three different encoder layers are validated. It can be observed that different settings have different performances on the quantitative metrics. When the depth is shallow, the network performance improves as the depth increases. The metrics, however, also exhibit a decrease with too many encoder layers. Based on the experimental validation, our final configuration of transformer encoder depth is 12 on COCO.

5   Conclusion

In this paper, we propose a novel Dual-Pipeline Integrated Transformer called DPIT for human pose estimation. To the best of our knowledge, this is one of the first works to integrate the bottom-up and top-down pipelines in one network with transformers. The proposed DPIT consists of two parts, a two-branch structure, and a feature interaction module. In our framework, the bottom-up branch and top-down branch capture full-scene information and posture visual clues with different receptive fields and perspectives, respectively. To achieve the effective integration of the two branches, the encoder of the transformer is applied to explore the long-term local-visual clues, global-visual clues, and their interactions. In addition, the defined keypoint embedding not only focuses on the different interest regions for a particular keypoint but also be allowed to concern the structural information between different keypoints. The reported quantitative and qualitative results on two public datasets demonstrate the effectiveness of our DPIT for human pose estimation.

Acknowledgement. This research was supported by the National Key R&D Program of China under Grant No. 2020AAA0103800.

References

1. Andriluka, M., Pishchulin, L., Gehler, P., Schiele, B.: 2d human pose estimation: New benchmark and state of the art analysis. In: Proceedings of the IEEE Conference on computer Vision and Pattern Recognition, pp. 3686–3693 (2014)
2. Cai, Y., et al.: Learning delicate local representations for multi-person pose estimation. In: Vedaldi, A., Bischof, H., Brox, T., Frahm, J.-M. (eds.) ECCV 2020. LNCS, vol. 12348, pp. 455–472. Springer, Cham (2020). https://doi.org/10.1007/978-3-030-58580-8_27
3. Cao, Z., Simon, T., Wei, S.E., Sheikh, Y.: Realtime multi-person 2d pose estimation using part affinity fields. In: Proceedings of the IEEE Conference on Computer Vision and Pattern Recognition, pp. 7291–7299 (2017)
4. Carion, N., Massa, F., Synnaeve, G., Usunier, N., Kirillov, A., Zagoruyko, S.: End-to-End object detection with transformers. In: Vedaldi, A., Bischof, H., Brox, T., Frahm, J.-M. (eds.) ECCV 2020. LNCS, vol. 12346, pp. 213–229. Springer, Cham (2020). https://doi.org/10.1007/978-3-030-58452-8_13
5. Chen, Y., Wang, Z., Peng, Y., Zhang, Z., Yu, G., Sun, J.: Cascaded pyramid network for multi-person pose estimation. In: Proceedings of the IEEE Conference on Computer Vision and Pattern Recognition, pp. 7103–7112 (2018)
6. Cheng, B., Xiao, B., Wang, J., Shi, H., Huang, T.S., Zhang, L.: Higherhrnet: scale-aware representation learning for bottom-up human pose estimation. In: Proceedings of the IEEE/CVF Conference on Computer Vision and Pattern Recognition, pp. 5386–5395 (2020)
7. Dosovitskiy, A., et al.: An image is worth 16x16 words: transformers for image recognition at scale. arXiv preprint. arXiv:2010.11929 (2020)
8. Fang, H.S., Xie, S., Tai, Y.W., Lu, C.: Rmpe: regional multi-person pose estimation. In: Proceedings of the IEEE International Conference on Computer Vision, pp. 2334–2343 (2017)
9. Felzenszwalb, P.F., Girshick, R.B., McAllester, D., Ramanan, D.: Object detection with discriminatively trained part-based models. IEEE Trans. Pattern Anal. Mach. Intell. **32**(9), 1627–1645 (2010)
10. Geng, Z., Sun, K., Xiao, B., Zhang, Z., Wang, J.: Bottom-up human pose estimation via disentangled keypoint regression. In: Proceedings of the IEEE/CVF Conference on Computer Vision and Pattern Recognition, pp. 14676–14686 (2021)
11. Ionescu, C., Li, F., Sminchisescu, C.: Latent structured models for human pose estimation. In: 2011 International Conference on Computer Vision, pp. 2220–2227. IEEE (2011)
12. Kingma, D., Ba, J.: Adam: a method for stochastic optimization. Comput. Sci. (2014)

13. Li, W., et al.: Rethinking on multi-stage networks for human pose estimation. arXiv preprint. arXiv:1901.00148 (2019)
14. Li, Y., et al.: Tokenpose: learning keypoint tokens for human pose estimation. In: Proceedings of the IEEE/CVF International Conference on Computer Vision, pp. 11313–11322 (2021)
15. Lin, T.Y., et al.: Microsoft COCO: common objects in context. In: Fleet, D., Pajdla, T., Schiele, B., Tuytelaars, T. (eds.) ECCV 2014. LNCS, vol. 8693, pp. 740–755. Springer, Cham (2014). https://doi.org/10.1007/978-3-319-10602-1_48
16. Liu, K., Liu, W., Gan, C., Tan, M., Ma, H.: T-c3d: temporal convolutional 3d network for real-time action recognition. In: Proceedings of the AAAI Conference on Artificial Intelligence, vol. 32 (2018)
17. Liu, K., Liu, W., Ma, H., Tan, M., Gan, C.: A real-time action representation with temporal encoding and deep compression. IEEE Trans. Circuits Syst. Video Technol. **31**(2), 647–660 (2020)
18. Liu, Z., et al.: Swin transformer: Hierarchical vision transformer using shifted windows. In: Proceedings of the IEEE/CVF International Conference on Computer Vision, pp. 10012–10022 (2021)
19. Mao, W., Ge, Y., Shen, C., Tian, Z., Wang, X., Wang, Z.: Tfpose: direct human pose estimation with transformers. arXiv preprint. arXiv:2103.15320 (2021)
20. Newell, A., Huang, Z., Deng, J.: Associative embedding: end-to-end learning for joint detection and grouping. In: Advances in Neural Information Processing Systems, vol. 30 (2017)
21. Newell, A., Yang, K., Deng, J.: Stacked hourglass networks for human pose estimation. In: Leibe, B., Matas, J., Sebe, N., Welling, M. (eds.) ECCV 2016. LNCS, vol. 9912, pp. 483–499. Springer, Cham (2016). https://doi.org/10.1007/978-3-319-46484-8_29
22. Papandreou, G., et al.: Towards accurate multi-person pose estimation in the wild. In: 2017 IEEE Conference on Computer Vision and Pattern Recognition (CVPR) (2017)
23. Pishchulin, L., Andriluka, M., Gehler, P., Schiele, B.: Strong appearance and expressive spatial models for human pose estimation. In: Proceedings of the IEEE International Conference on Computer Vision, pp. 3487–3494 (2013)
24. Pishchulin, L., et al.: Deepcut: joint subset partition and labeling for multi person pose estimation. In: Proceedings of the IEEE Conference on Computer Vision and Pattern Recognition, pp. 4929–4937 (2016)
25. Rogez, G., Rihan, J., Ramalingam, S., Orrite, C., Torr, P.H.: Randomized trees for human pose detection. In: 2008 IEEE Conference on Computer Vision and Pattern Recognition, pp. 1–8. IEEE (2008)
26. Russakovsky, O., et al.: Imagenet large scale visual recognition challenge. Int. J. Comput. Vis. **115**(3), 211–252 (2015). https://doi.org/10.1007/s11263-015-0816-y
27. Stoffl, L., Vidal, M., Mathis, A.: End-to-end trainable multi-instance pose estimation with transformers. arXiv preprint. arXiv:2103.12115 (2021)
28. Strudel, R., Garcia, R., Laptev, I., Schmid, C.: Segmenter: transformer for semantic segmentation. In: Proceedings of the IEEE/CVF International Conference on Computer Vision, pp. 7262–7272 (2021)
29. Sun, K., Xiao, B., Liu, D., Wang, J.: Deep high-resolution representation learning for human pose estimation. In: Proceedings of the IEEE/CVF Conference on Computer Vision and Pattern Recognition, pp. 5693–5703 (2019)
30. Touvron, H., Cord, M., Douze, M., Massa, F., Sablayrolles, A., Jégou, H.: Training data-efficient image transformers & distillation through attention. In: International Conference on Machine Learning, pp. 10347–10357. PMLR (2021)

31. Urtasun, R., Darrell, T.: Sparse probabilistic regression for activity-independent human pose inference. In: 2008 IEEE Conference on Computer Vision and Pattern Recognition, pp. 1–8. IEEE (2008)
32. Vaswani, A., et al.: Attention is all you need. In: Advances in Neural Information Processing Systems, vol. 30 (2017)
33. Wang, J., Long, X., Gao, Y., Ding, E., Wen, S.: Graph-PCNN: two stage human pose estimation with graph pose refinement. In: Vedaldi, A., Bischof, H., Brox, T., Frahm, J.-M. (eds.) ECCV 2020. LNCS, vol. 12356, pp. 492–508. Springer, Cham (2020). https://doi.org/10.1007/978-3-030-58621-8_29
34. Wang, X., Yeshwanth, C., Nießner, M.: Sceneformer: indoor scene generation with transformers. In: 2021 International Conference on 3D Vision (3DV), pp. 106–115. IEEE (2021)
35. Wei, S.E., Ramakrishna, V., Kanade, T., Sheikh, Y.: Convolutional pose machines. In: Proceedings of the IEEE Conference on Computer Vision and Pattern Recognition, pp. 4724–4732 (2016)
36. Xiao, B., Wu, H., Wei, Y.: Simple baselines for human pose estimation and tracking. In: Ferrari, V., Hebert, M., Sminchisescu, C., Weiss, Y. (eds.) ECCV 2018. LNCS, vol. 11210, pp. 472–487. Springer, Cham (2018). https://doi.org/10.1007/978-3-030-01231-1_29
37. Xie, E., Wang, W., Yu, Z., Anandkumar, A., Alvarez, J.M., Luo, P.: Segformer: simple and efficient design for semantic segmentation with transformers. In: Advances in Neural Information Processing Systems, vol. 34 (2021)
38. Xiong, Z., Wang, C., Li, Y., Luo, Y., Cao, Y.: Swin-pose: swin transformer based human pose estimation. arXiv preprint. arXiv:2201.07384 (2022)
39. Yang, S., Quan, Z., Nie, M., Yang, W.: Transpose: keypoint localization via transformer. In: Proceedings of the IEEE/CVF International Conference on Computer Vision, pp. 11802–11812 (2021)
40. Zhang, J., Zhu, Z., Lu, J., Huang, J., Huang, G., Zhou, J.: Simple: single-network with mimicking and point learning for bottom-up human pose estimation. arXiv preprint. arXiv:2104.02486 (2021)
41. Zhu, X., Su, W., Lu, L., Li, B., Wang, X., Dai, J.: Deformable detr: deformable transformers for end-to-end object detection. arXiv preprint. arXiv:2010.04159 (2020)

Integrative Analysis of Multi-view Histopathological Image Features for the Diagnosis of Lung Cancer

Zongxiang Pei, Yingli Zuo, Liang Sun, Meiling Wang, Daoqiang Zhang[(✉)], and Wei Shao[(✉)]

MIIT Key Laboratory of Pattern Analysis and Machine Intelligence, College of Computer Science and Technology, Nanjing University of Aeronautics and Astronautics, Nanjing 211106, China
{dqzhang,shaowei20022005}@nuaa.edu.cn

Abstract. Lung cancer is one of the most widely spread cancers in the world. So far, the histopathological image remains the "gold standard" in diagnosing lung cancers, and multiple types of pathological images features have been associated with lung cancer diagnosis and progression. However, most of the existing studies only utilized single type of image features, which did not take advantages of multiple types of image features. In this paper, we propose a Block based Multi-View Graph Convolutional Network (*i.e.*, BMVGCN), which integrates multiple types of image features from histopathological images for lung cancer diagnosis. Specifically, our method utilizes the block-based bilinear combination model to fuse different types of features. By considering the correlation among different samples, we also introduce the Graph Convolutional Network to exploit the correlations among samples that could lead to better diagnosis performance. To evaluate the effectiveness of the proposed method, we conduct the experiments for the classification of the cancer tissue and non-cancer tissue in both Lung Adenocarcinoma (*i.e.*, LUAD) and Lung Squamous Cell Carcinoma (*i.e.*,LUSC), and the discrimination between LUAD and LUSC. The results show that our method can achieve superior classification performance than the comparing methods.

Keywords: Lung cancer diagnosis · Histopathological image · Graph neural network · Multi-view fusion

1 Introduction

1.1 Related Work

Nowadays, cancer can be diagnosed through multiple imaging biomarkers, including Computed Tomography (CT), Positron Emission Tomography/Computed

This work was supported by National Natural Science Foundation of China (Nos. 62136004, 61902183, 62106104), the National Key R&D Program of China (Grant Nos.: 2018YFC2001600, 2018YFC2001602 and 2018YFA0701703), and the Project funded by China Postdoctoral Science Foundation (No. 2022T150320).

L. Fang et al. (Eds.): CICAI 2022, LNAI 13605, pp. 577–587, 2022.
https://doi.org/10.1007/978-3-031-20500-2_47

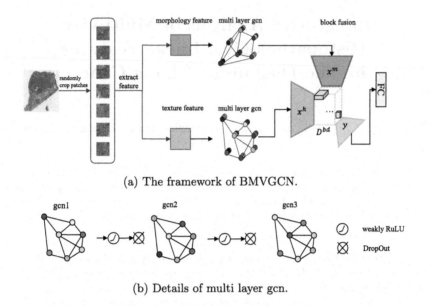

(a) The framework of BMVGCN.

(b) Details of multi layer gcn.

Fig. 1. The overall framework of the proposed method.

Tomography (PET/CT), MRI and histopathological images. Among all these imaging biomarkers, histopathological images are generally considered to be the gold standard for cancer diagnosis and prognosis since it can provide morphological attributes of cells that are highly related to the degree of the aggressiveness of cancers [1]. With the help of ever-increasing computing resources, many computational histopathological systems have been proposed to extract different types of histopathological image features to help diagnose human cancers [2–7]. For example, Gurcan et al. [3] utilized Gray-level co-occurrence matrix (GLCM) and Gray-level run length matrix (GLRLM) to extract texture features (*i.e.*, haralick features) from the histopathological images, which are proved to be sensitive to the diagnosis of brain cancer, Sparks et al. [6] presented a set of explicit shape descriptors (ESDs) to obtain morphology features for classifying gland Gleason grade in prostate cancers. Other studies include Shukla et al. [7] have extracted morphological features for accurate and reliable detection of breast cancers.

Recently, besides applying single type of image features for cancer diagnosis, several studies combined multiple types of image features for diagnosing human cancers. For instance, Cheng et al [8] proposed an 150-dimensional feature including both morphological and color information in histopathological image for diagnosing kidney cancer. Yu et al. [9] demonstrated that the combination of morphology and texture features can better predict the prognosis of lung cancer patients than using single type of features. Although the above methods indicated that the combination analysis of multiple types of image features can uncover the hidden difference between normal and cancer or different cancer subtypes that cannot be found using single type of features. Most of the studies directly combined different types of image features for the diagnosis task, which neglected the weight information for each feature type in the fusion process. As a matter of fact, different types of features may carry different task-relevant information, and fusing them by naive concatenation may limit the model's ability to dynamically determine the relevance of each type of features for the cancer diagnosis task. In addition, most of the integrative models only considered the correlation within the multiple types of features, and thus neglected to take the association among different samples into consideration that will deteriorate the cancer diagnosis performance.

Based on the above considerations, in this paper, we integrate multiple types of image features (*i.e.*, morphology and texture features) from histopathological images and propose a Block based Multi-View Graph Convolutional Network (*i.e.*, BMVGCN) for lung cancer diagnosis. Specifically, our model utilizes the block-based bilinear combiantion model [10] to fuse different types of features, which aims at automatically learning the weight for the combination of different types of image features. In addition, to better exploit the association among different samples to help lung cancer diagnosis, we introduce the Graph Convolutional Network to exploit their correlations through similarity networks. To evaluate the effectiveness of the proposed method, we conduct the experiments for the classification of the cancer tissue and non-cancer tissue in both Lung Adenocarcinoma (*i.e.*, LUAD) and Lung Squamous Cell Carcinoma (LUSC), and the discrimination between LUAD and LUSC. The results show that our method can achieve superior classification performance than the comparing methods.

2   Methods

2.1   Datasets

All the histopathological images were collected from Nanjing Medical University. Patients who received any treatment or neoadjuvant therapy before surgery/biopsy were excluded. Samples (tumor specimens, adjacent normal tissues, and peripheral blood) were obtained during surgical resection. All tissue samples were snap-frozen. HE-stained sections from each sample were subjected to an independent pathology review to confirm that the tumor specimen was histopathologically consistent with NSCLC (>70% tumor cells). For Lung Adenocarcinoma (LUAD) cohort, it contains 73 cancer and 163 normal samples. As to LUSC cohort (Lung Squamous Cell Carcinoma), 53 cancer samples and 61 normal samples are involved. We show the demographics information of these two cohorts in Table 1.

Table 1. The demographic information for different lung cancer cohorts

	Male/Female	Age	Tumor/Nontumor
LUAD	115/121	58.65 ± 10.67	73/163
LUSC	100/14	61.25 ± 8.36	53/61

2.2   Overview of Our Method

We summarize our framework in Fig. 1, which consists of the following four steps. Firstly, we extract different types of image features (*i.e.*, morphology and texture features) from pathological images. Secondly, for each type of features, we apply graph convolutional network (*i.e.*, GCN) to learn their high-level representation through sample similarity network. Thirdly, we apply the block-based bilinear combination model to fuse different types of features. Finally, we feed the fused feature into fully connected layers for the final classification task.

2.3   Feature Extraction

Before feature extraction procedure, the patches are cropped from wsi images. For each sample, we randomly crop 10 to 20 patches. Those patches with background area (brightness more than 78%) less than 30% are retained.

For morphology features, we firstly apply an unsupervised method introduced in [11] to segment the nuclei from the raw histopathological image. The utilized cell segmentation algorithm is comprised of three steps. Firstly, the color deconvolution operation is adopted to derive the gray-scale image in hematoxylin channel of the input H/E stained histopathological images. Then, the resulting grayscale image is processed with opening by reconstruction to connect close background regions to each other. Finally, a multi-level thresholding segmentation method, whose threshold can be automatically adjusted according to each input image is presented for the segmentation of cells. Then, for each segmented nucleus with their area ranging from 10 to 200, we extract five cell-level features characterizing the nuclei area (denoted as area), the major and minor axis length of cell nucleus (major and minor), the eccentricity of the nucleus (eccentricity), the ratio of major axis length to minor axis (ratio). After that, for each cell-level feature, we summarize all cell-level features into sample-level features by using a 10-bin histogram and five statistical measurements (*i.e.*, mean, standard deviation, skewness, kurtosis, and entropy). Thus, 75-dimensional morphology features can be derived for each sample. We use the same naming rule for both cell-level and sample-level features. For instance, the feature major_bin_1 represents the percentage of cells with small major axis length while major_bin_10 referred to the percentage of nuclei with long major axis. As to texture features, we extract haralick features from the histopathological images. Then, we extract 13-dimensional haralick features (i.e., Hara_1, Hara_2, ..., Hara_13) for each valid patch. Like the aggregation method for morphology features, we summarize all patch-level haralick features into 195-dimensional features for each sample. For instance, Hara_1_bin_1, Hara_1_bin_2,..., Hara_1_bin_10 represent the ten histogram features for Hara_1, and Hara_1_skewness indicates the skewness feature for Hara_1.

2.4   High-Level Feature Learning by Graph Convolutional Network

With the consideration of the correlation among different subjects can promote the classification performance, we utilize Graph Convolutional Network (*i.e.*, GCN) to extract high-level representation from each type of extracted features. The GCN model is comprised of two main parts, the first part is the node feature matrix and the second part is an adjacency matrix which can be used to describe the structure of graph.

Table 2. Results for LUAD *v.s.* nonLUAD and LUSC *v.s.* nonLUSC.

Task	Measurements	ACC	F1-Score	AUC	Recall	Precision
LUAD v.s. nonLUAD	RF	0.758	0.713	0.911	0.274	0.833
	SVML1	0.860	0.740	0.921	0.644	0.870
	SVML2	0.805	0.646	0.851	0.575	0.737
	SALMON	0.869	0.783	0.643	0.767	0.800
	GCN_BlockTucker	0.907	0.905	0.924	0.907	0.906
	GCN_Mutan	0.919	0.919	0.921	0.919	0.919
	GCN_MFH	0.919	0.918	0.909	0.919	0.919
	BMVGCN	**0.928**	**0.927**	**0.953**	**0.928**	**0.927**
LUSC v.s. nonLUSC	RF	0.877	0.865	0.934	0.849	0.882
	SVML1	0.596	0.681	0.716	0.925	0.538
	SVML2	0.868	0.860	0.958	0.868	0.852
	SALMON	0.754	0.781	0.720	0.943	0.667
	GCN_BlockTucker	0.895	0.895	0.948	0.895	0.895
	GCN_Mutan	0.939	0.938	0.879	0.939	0.940
	GCN_MFH	0.930	0.930	0.895	0.930	0.930
	BMVGCN	**0.947**	**0.947**	**0.981**	**0.947**	**0.947**
LUAD v.s. LUSC	RF	0.571	0.727	0.849	**0.986**	0.576
	SVML1	0.563	0.715	0.560	0.945	0.575
	SVML2	0.722	0.780	0.783	0.849	0.721
	SALMON	0.746	0.775	0.715	0.753	0.797
	GCN_BlockTucker	0.881	0.882	0.921	0.881	0.891
	GCN_Mutan	0.873	0.874	0.857	0.873	0.876
	GCN_MFH	0.881	0.881	0.849	0.881	0.883
	BMVGCN	**0.897**	**0.897**	**0.934**	0.897	**0.904**

Node Feature Matrix. The GCN model is comprised of two components, the first component is the node feature matrix $\boldsymbol{X}^t \in \mathbb{R}^{n \times d_t}, t \in \{m, h\}$. Specifically, let $\boldsymbol{X}^m \in \mathbb{R}^{n \times d_m}$ and $\boldsymbol{X}^h \in \mathbb{R}^{n \times d_h}$ be the extracted morphology and haralick texture features, respectively. Here, n represents the sample size, and d_m and d_h correspond to the dimensionality of the morphology and haralick texture features, respectively. By viewing each sample as a node in sample similarity network, the goal of applying GCN is to learn the function of each type of features on a graph to obtain high-level features that can capture the correlation among different samples.

Adjacent Matrix. The second component in GCN model is used to describe the graph structure, which can be represented in the form of an adjacency matrix $\boldsymbol{A}^t \in \mathbb{R}^{n \times d}, t \in \{m, h\}$. Our proposed method contains two types of features (*i.e.*, texture features and morphological features), and for each type of features, we use a graph to depict the correlation among different samples. We denote them $G_m = \{\boldsymbol{V}^m, \boldsymbol{A}^m\}$ and $G_h = \{\boldsymbol{V}^h, \boldsymbol{A}^m\}$ respectively. In the graph $G_t, t \in \{m, h\}$, each node represents a sample, the initialized adjacency matrix $\boldsymbol{A}^t$ for feature type t in GCN is constructed by calculating the cosine similarity between pairs of nodes. To control the number of edges in the adjacency matrix $\boldsymbol{A}^t$, we introduce a variable ε as a threshold, and edges with larger cosine similarity than ε are retained. Then, the adjacency between node i and node j in graph $\boldsymbol{A}^t$ can be calculated as:

$$\boldsymbol{A}_{ij}^t = \begin{cases} s(\boldsymbol{x}_i^t, \boldsymbol{x}_j^t), & \text{if } i \neq j \text{ and } s(\boldsymbol{x}_i^t, \boldsymbol{x}_j^t) \geq \varepsilon \\ 0, & otherwise \end{cases} \tag{1}$$

where $\boldsymbol{x}_i^t$ and $\boldsymbol{x}_j^t$ are the representations of node i and node j for feature type t, respectively. $s(\boldsymbol{x}_i, \boldsymbol{x}_j) = \frac{\boldsymbol{x}_i \cdot \boldsymbol{x}_j}{\|\boldsymbol{x}_i\|_2 \|\boldsymbol{x}_j\|_2}$ is the cosine similarity between node i and j. The threshold ε can be determined by a parameter k, which represents the average number of edges per node that are retained except self loops:

$$k = \sum_{i,j,i \neq j} \boldsymbol{I}(s(\boldsymbol{x}_i, \boldsymbol{x}_j) \geq \varepsilon)/n \tag{2}$$

where $\boldsymbol{I}(\cdot)$ is the indicator function and n is the number of nodes.

Construction of Graph Convolutional Network. A GCN is built by multiple convolutional layers, and each layer of specific feature type is defined as:

$$\begin{aligned} \boldsymbol{H}_{(l+1)}^t &= f(\boldsymbol{H}_{(l)}^t, \boldsymbol{A}_{(l)}^t) \\ x'x &= \sigma(\boldsymbol{A}_{(l)}^t \boldsymbol{H}_{(l)}^t \boldsymbol{W}_{(l)}^t), \end{aligned} \tag{3}$$

where $\boldsymbol{H}_{(l)}^t$ is the input of the l-th layer for feature type t, $\boldsymbol{W}_{(l)}^t$ and $\boldsymbol{A}_{(l)}^t$ refer to its corresponding weight and adjacent matrix. $\sigma(\cdot)$ denotes the non-linear activation function. In the training procedure of GCN, we follow the method introduced in [12] and modify the adjacency matrix $\boldsymbol{A}^t$ as:

$$\widetilde{\boldsymbol{A}}_{(l)}^t = (\hat{\boldsymbol{D}}_{(l)}^t)^{-\frac{1}{2}} (\boldsymbol{A}_{(l)}^t + \boldsymbol{I}_{(l)}^t)(\hat{\boldsymbol{D}}_{(l)}^t)^{-\frac{1}{2}}, \tag{4}$$

where $\hat{\boldsymbol{D}}_{(l)}^t$ is the diagonal node degree matrix of $\hat{\boldsymbol{A}}_{(l)}^t$ for feature type t and $\boldsymbol{I}_{(l)}^t$ represents the identity matrix. Then, we denote the output of the GCN with L layers as:

$$\boldsymbol{Y}_{(L)}^t = GCN_L(\boldsymbol{X}^t, \widetilde{\boldsymbol{A}}^t) \tag{5}$$

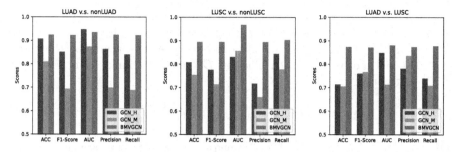

Fig. 2. The classification results by combining different types of features and using single type of features

2.5 The Block-Based Bilinear Combination Model

After applying GCN for feature learning, we derive high-level representation for both morphology and haralick features. Here, we denote the morphology and texture feature for the u-th sample as $x^{(m,u)}$ and $x^{(h,u)}$, respectively. Since different types of features may provide complementary information for the following diagnosis task, we apply block based bilinear combination model to fuse different types of features [13–17]. Specifically, let $x^{(m,u)} \in \mathbb{R}^I$ and $x^{(h,u)} \in \mathbb{R}^J$ be the input high-level morphology and haralick features of the block based bilinear combination model. The block based bilinear combination model can combine $x^{(m,u)}$ and $x^{(h,u)}$ into a K-dimensional output vector with tensor products:

$$\boldsymbol{y}^u = \tau \times_1 x^{(m,u)} \times_2 x^{(h,u)} \tag{6}$$

where $\boldsymbol{y}^u \in \mathbb{R}^K$, and $\times_1$ and $\times_2$ represents tensor products respectively. Each component of y^u ($i.e., y_k^u$) is a quadratic form of the inputs: $\forall K \in [1, K]$,

$$y_k^u = \sum_{i=1}^{I} \sum_{j=1}^{J} \tau_{ijk} \cdot x_i^m \cdot x_j^h \tag{7}$$

where I and J indicate the diemnsionality of $x^{(m,u)}$ and $x^{(h,u)}$ respectively. A bilinear model is completely defined by its associated tensor $\tau \in \mathbb{R}^{I \times J \times K}$. In order to reduce the number of parameters and constrain the model's complexity, we introduce Block model [10], which applied the block-term decomposition method to obtain τ. The decomposition of τ is defined as:

$$\tau := \sum_{r=1}^{R} \boldsymbol{D} \times_1 \boldsymbol{A}_r \times_2 \boldsymbol{B}_r \times_3 \boldsymbol{C}_r \tag{8}$$

where $\boldsymbol{A}_r \in \mathbb{R}^{I \times L}$, $\boldsymbol{B}_r \in \mathbb{R}^{J \times M}$ and $\boldsymbol{C}_r \times \mathbb{R}^{K \times N}$. $\times_1$, $\times_2$ and $\times_3$ represent the tensor products. The block-term decomposition of τ can be formulated as:

$$\tau = \boldsymbol{D}^{bd} \times_1 \boldsymbol{A} \times_2 \boldsymbol{B} \times_3 \boldsymbol{C} \tag{9}$$

where $\boldsymbol{A} = [\boldsymbol{A}_1, ..., \boldsymbol{A}_R]$ (same for $\boldsymbol{B}$ and $\boldsymbol{C}$), and $\boldsymbol{D}_{bd} \in \mathbb{R}^{LR \times MR \times NR}$ is the block-superdiagonal tensor of $\{\boldsymbol{D}_r\}_{1 \le r \le R}$. Let $\hat{x}^{(m,u)} = \boldsymbol{A}x^{(m,u)} \in \mathbb{R}^{LR}$ and $\hat{x}^{(h,u)} = \boldsymbol{B}x^{(h,u)} \in \mathbb{R}^{MR}$, we can fuse different types of features by the block-superdiagonal tensor $\boldsymbol{D}^{bd}$. Each block in $\boldsymbol{D}^{bd}$ merges chunks from $\hat{x}^{(m,u)}$ and $\hat{x}^{(h,u)}$ to generate z_r^u with size N:

$$z_r^u = \boldsymbol{D}_r \times_1 \hat{x}^{(m,u)}_{rL:(r+1)L} \times_2 \hat{x}^{(h,u)}_{rM:(r+1)M} \tag{10}$$

where $\hat{x}^{(q,u)}_{i:j} q \in \{m, h\}$ is a vector of dimension $j - i$. After concatenating all the z_r to generate $z^u \in \mathbb{R}^{NR}$. The output of the block-based bilinear combination model can be calculated by $y^u = Cz^u \in \mathbb{R}^K$.

After applying the block based bilinear combination model to integrate different types of features, a two-layer fully-connected neural network followed by the softmax function is applied to predict the label of each sample.

3 Results

3.1 Experimental Results

Our proposed method contains three graph convolutional layers. As can be seen from Fig. 1b, weakly relu layer and dropout layer are added after the first and the second graph convolutional layers. The relu ratio and dropout ratio are set as 0.25 and 0.5 respectively. The number of adjacent edges in GCN is set as 2. The dimensionality of the hidden layer of the fully connected layer is set as 100. Total epochs for training different classification models are set as 100. We use the leave-one-out strategy to evaluate the performance of different methods by the measurements of recall, precision, auc, and the f1-score. For all the samples in the training dataset, we randomly split 20% of them as validation set to tune the model hyperparameters. The experiments are conducted on a computer with 32-GB memory, Intel I9-10900X 3.7 GHz CPU, and NVIDIA GeForce RTX 3090 GPU. Moreover, the proposed method and all neural-network-based baseline models are implemented based on PyTorch 1.8.1.

3.2 Intergrating Two Types of Features Performs Better Than Only Using One Type

We first investigate the effect of using single type of features (*i.e.*, GCN_M and GCN_H) and integrating different types of features together (*i.e.*, BMVGCN) for the diagnosis of lung cancer. Here, GCN_M and GCN_H refer to the methods that only applying morphological and haralick features followed by the GCN for the classification task, respectively. We test the performance of different methods on the following three different tasks.

- LUAD *v.s.* nonLUAD: Classify LUAD samples (denoted as LUAD) and their corresponding normal samples (denoted as nonLUAD).

- LUSC v.s. nonLUSC: Classify LUSC samples (denoted as LUSC) and their corresponding normal samples (denoted as nonLUSC).
- LUAD v.s. LUSC: Classify LUAD tumor samples (LUAD) and LUSC tumor samples (LUSC).

As can be seen from Fig. 2, the combination of different types of features (*BMVGCN*) can better diagnose lung cancer than its competitors that only applying single type of features on all the classification tasks. These results strongly validate the effectiveness of integrating different types of features in distinguishing tumor and non-tumor tissues and the classification of different lung cancer subtypes. In addition, we note that GCN_H is generally superior to GCN_M across all tasks, which demonstrates that the texture features play a more important role in the classification tasks.

3.3   Comparison of *BMVGCN* and Other Methods for Lung Cancer Classification

In Sect. 3.2, We have shown the effectiveness of combining different types of features for lung cancer diagnosis. To further verify the superiority of our proposed method, we compare BMVGCN with the following 7 multi-view learning algorithms for the lung cancer diagnosis.

- RF: Concatenate haralick and morphology features at first, and then feeds the concatenated features into random forest classifier to obtain the predicted label,
- SVML1: Feed the concatenated features into support vector machine with l1 loss function,
- SVML2: Feed the concatenated features into support vector machine with l2 loss function,
- SALMON: A deep learning based multi-view learning algorithm proposed in [18],
- GCN_BlockTucker: This module correponds to Block without the low-rank constraint on third-mode slices of D_c tensors [10],
- GCN_Mutan: A GCN based multi-view learning algorithm proposed in [19],
- GCN_MFH : A GCN based multi-view learning algorithm proposed in [20].

Similar to Sect. 3.2, we conduct experiments on LUAD v.s. nonLUAD, LUSC v.s. nonLUSC and LUAD v.s. LUSC these three tasks. Table 2 shows the classification results including accuracy (ACC), F1-Score (f1-score), AUC (Area under the ROC curve), Recall and Precision. From Table 2, we can derive the following three observations: 1) The performance of deep learning based methods (*i.e.*, SALMON, GCN_BlockTucker, GCN_Mutan, GCN_MFH, BMVGCN) are superior to traditional machine learning algorithms (*i.e.*,RF, SVML1, SVML2) across all tasks, which reveals the advantages of applying deep learning algorithms for the classification of lung cancers. 2) The GCN based algorithms can better classify lung cancer patients since they consider the correlations among different patients for better representation of the input features. 3) The proposed

Table 3. Ablation study results of LUAD *v.s.* nonLUAD and LUSC *v.s.* nonLUSC and LUAD *v.s.* LUSC

	Method	ACC	F1-Score	AUC	Recall	Precision
LUAD v.s. nonLUAD	(A) AFF + FC	0.831	0.835	0.888	0.831	0.852
	(B) GCN + FC	0.860	0.852	0.911	0.860	0.865
	(C) BMVGCN	0.928	0.927	0.953	0.928	0.927
LUSC v.s. nonLUSC	(A) AFF + FC	0.833	0.830	0.819	0.833	0.849
	(B) GCN + FC	0.886	0.886	0.957	0.886	0.886
	(C) BMVGCN	0.947	0.947	0.981	0.947	0.947
LUAD v.s. LUSC	(A) AFF + FC	0.762	0.763	0.778	0.762	0.771
	(B) GCN + FC	0.786	0.785	0.880	0.786	0.785
	(C) BMVGCN	0.897	0.897	0.934	0.897	0.904

fusion algorithm can consistently obtain superior classification results than the comparing methods, which reveals the fact that the block model embedded in our method is effective since using block model can not only automatically fuse different types of features, but also reduce the complexity of the whole model.

3.4   Ablation Study

To evaluate the effectiveness of different components in the proposed method, we conduct ablation studies. Here, we conduct experiments on the following three configurations: (A) AFF + FC: Directly integrates haralick texture features and morphology features by block based bilinear combination model without applying GCN to learn high-level representations. (B) GCN + FC: Applying fully connected layers to integrate high-level haralick texture and morphology features without block based bilinear combination model after GCN. (C) *BMVGCN*: our proposed method. The results of all these three methods are shown in Table 3.

As can be seen from Table 3, our proposed method consistently achieves better classification performance than its competitors. These results show the necessity of applying GCN and block based bilinear combination model for the diagnosis of lung cancer from histopathological images. In addition, comparing (B) to (A) in all three tasks, it is worth noting that GCN + FC outperforms AFF + FC on all measurements. This demonstrates that GCN plays a more important role for the classification of lung cancer in comparison with block based bilinear combination model.

References

1. Rubin, R., Strayer, D.S., Rubin, E., et al.: Rubin's Pathology: Clinicopathologic Foundations of Medicine. Lippincott Williams & Wilkins (2008)
2. Belsare, A., Mushrif, M., Pangarkar, M., Meshram, N.: Classification of breast cancer histopathology images using texture feature analysis. In: TENCON 2015–2015 IEEE Region 10 Conference. IEEE, 2015, pp. 1–5 (2015)

3. Durgamahanthi, Vaishali, Anita Christaline, J.., Shirly Edward, A..: GLCM and GLRLM based texture analysis: application to brain cancer diagnosis using histopathology images. In: Dash, Subhransu Sekhar, Das, Swagatam, Panigrahi, Bijaya Ketan (eds.) Intelligent Computing and Applications. AISC, vol. 1172, pp. 691–706. Springer, Singapore (2021). https://doi.org/10.1007/978-981-15-5566-4_61

4. de Matos, J., de Souza Britto, A., de Oliveira, L.E., Koerich, A.L.: Texture CNN for histopathological image classification. In: IEEE 32nd International Symposium on Computer-Based Medical Systems (CBMS). IEEE, pp. 580–583 (2019)

5. Roncalli, M., Park, Y.N., Di Tommaso, L.: Histopathological classification of hepatocellular carcinoma. Dig. Liver Dis. **42**, S228–S234 (2010)

6. Sparks, R., Madabhushi, A.: Explicit shape descriptors: novel morphologic features for histopathology classification. Med. Image Anal. **17**(8), 997–1009 (2013)

7. Shukla, K., Tiwari, A., Sharma, S., et al.: Classification of histopathological images of breast cancerous and non cancerous cells based on morphological features. Biomed. Pharmacol. J. **10**(1), 353–366 (2017)

8. Cheng, J., et al.: Integrative analysis of histopathological images and genomic data predicts clear cell renal cell carcinoma prognosis. Can. Res. **77**(21), e91–e100 (2017)

9. Yu, K.M., et al.: Predicting non-small cell lung cancer prognosis by fully automated microscopic pathology image features. Nat. Commun. **7**(1), 1–10 (2016)

10. Ben-Younes, H., Cadene, R., Thome, N., Cord, M.: Block: Bilinear superdiagonal fusion for visual question answering and visual relationship detection. Proc. AAAI Conf. Artif. Intell. **33**(01), 8102–8109 (2019)

11. Phoulady, H.A., Goldgof, D.B., Hall, L.O., Mouton, P.R.: Nucleus segmentation in histology images with hierarchical multilevel thresholding. In: Medical Imaging 2016: Digital Pathology, vol. 9791. International Society for Optics and Photonics, p. 979111 (2016)

12. Kipf, T.N., Welling, M.: Semi-supervised classification with graph convolutional networks. arXiv preprint arXiv:1609.02907 (2016)

13. Gao, Y., Beijbom, O., Zhang, N., Darrell, T.: Compact bilinear pooling. In: Proceedings of the IEEE Conference on Computer Vision and Pattern Recognition, pp. 317–326 (2016)

14. Lin, T.-Y., Maji, S.: Improved bilinear pooling with CNNs. arXiv preprint arXiv:1707.06772 (2017)

15. Fukui, A., Park, D.H., Yang, D., Rohrbach, A., Darrell, T., Rohrbach, M.: Multimodal compact bilinear pooling for visual question answering and visual grounding. arXiv preprint arXiv:1606.01847 (2016)

16. Yu, Z., Yu, J., Fan, J., Tao, D.:Multi-modal factorized bilinear pooling with co-attention learning for visual question answering. In: Proceedings of the IEEE International Conference on Computer Vision, pp. 1821–1830 (2017)

17. Zhang, Y., Tang, S., Muandet, K., Jarvers, C., Neumann, H.: Local temporal bilinear pooling for fine-grained action parsing. In: Proceedings of the IEEE/CVF Conference on Computer Vision and Pattern Recognition, pp. 12 005–12 015 (2019)

18. Huang, Z., et al.: Salmon: survival analysis learning with multi-omics neural networks on breast cancer. Front. Genet. **10**, 166 (2019)

19. Ben-Younes, H., Cadene, R., Cord, M., Thome, N.: Mutan: Multimodal tucker fusion for visual question answering. In: Proceedings of the IEEE International Conference on Computer Vision, pp. 2612–2620 (2017)

20. Shah, N., Singhal, N., Singh, C., Khandelwal, Y.:Model agnostic information biasing for VQA. In: 8th ACM IKDD CODS and 26th COMAD, 2021, pp. 419–419 (2021)

Where are the Children with Autism Looking in Reality?

Xiaoyu Ren[1], Huiyu Duan[1], Xiongkuo Min[1], Yucheng Zhu[1], Wei Shen[1],
Linlin Wang[2], Fangyu Shi[1], Lei Fan[1], Xiaokang Yang[1], and Guangtao Zhai[1(✉)]

[1] Shanghai Jiao Tong University, Shanghai, China
{windkaiser,huiyuduan,minxiongkuo,zyc420,wei.shen,fangyu.shi,lei.fan,
xkyang,zhaiguangtao}@sjtu.edu.cn
[2] Shanghai Donglifengmei School, Shanghai, China

Abstract. Social difficulties are hallmarks of individuals with autism spectrum disorder (ASD), of which atypical visual attention is one of the most important characteristics. Learning and modeling the atypical visual attention of individuals with ASD have particularly important significance to related research in the fields of medical science, psychology, education *etc.*, and many studies have been conducted in the literature. However, previous studies have two weaknesses. First, all stimuli in the conducted experiments are selected by the researchers, which are not only restricted by the objective and intention of the researchers, but also limited by the subjective cognition of the photographers. Secondly, most of these stimuli are displayed on screens with restricted and relatively small field-of-view (FOV) compared with the real world. Therefore, in this paper, we conduct the first large-scale study towards better understanding and modeling the atypical visual attention of individuals with ASD in real world. To overcome the two weaknesses mentioned above, a large-scale dataset is established which includes 300 omnidirectional images with the corresponding eye tracking data collected under virtual reality (VR) environment among 15 children with ASD and 16 typically developing (TD) controls. Moreover, a vector quantized saliency prediction model (VQSAL) is applied to better learn the visual attention patterns of both ASD and TD people under the omnidirectional condition.

Keywords: Autism spectrum disorder (ASD) · Atypical visual attention · Virtual reality (VR)

1 Introduction

Autism is a complex neurodevelopmental condition, and little is known about its neurobiology [1]. Phenotype markers including social communication symp-

---

This work was supported by National Key R&D Program of China 2021YFE0206700, NSFC 61831015, 61901260, 62176159, 62101326, Natural Science Foundation of Shanghai 21ZR1432200, Shanghai Municipal Science and Technology Major Project 2021SHZDZX0102, China Postdoctoral Science Foundation 2022M712090.
X. Ren and H. Duan—Equal contribution.

L. Fang et al. (Eds.): CICAI 2022, LNAI 13605, pp. 588–600, 2022.
https://doi.org/10.1007/978-3-031-20500-2_48

toms, fixated or restricted behaviors or interests, hyper- or hypo- sensitivity to sensory stimuli, and associated features have been widely used in characterizing and diagnosing the Autism Spectrum Disorder (ASD) [2]. Among these, social difficulties are known as the hallmark features of autism. As an important aspect of social difficulties, atypical visual attention is frequently observed in individuals with autism [3] and reported in the literature [4,5]. Several possibly related visual attention traits of autistic individuals have been reported in some early studies, including reduced joint-attention behaviours [6], reduced attention to social stimuli (i.e., faces, conversations, etc.) but increased attention to non-social stimuli (i.e., vehicles, electronics, etc.) [7,8], reduced visual attention to core facial features [9,10], etc. However, the vast majority of these prior studies have used restricted or unnatural stimuli, which limited the exploration of the common characteristics underlying the ASD.

Recently, some studies have conducted large-scale experiments for characterizing the visual attention traits of ASD. Wang et al. [4] have quantified the atypical visual attention in ASD across multi-level features using natural stimuli and pointed out the preference of individuals with autism to low-level features of the stimuli. Jiang et al. [11] have presented a method to model the visual attention differences between individual with ASD and healthy people. Duan et al. [12] have established a large-scale open eye movement dataset for children with autism and fine-tuned four state-of-the-art (SOTA) visual attention models for learning the gaze pattern of autistic children [13]. Duan et al. [14] have further conducted a large-scale eye movement study for children with autism on face stimuli and proposed a model to characterize gaze pattern under this specific condition. Fang et al. [15] have studied the visual attention of children with autism on gaze-following stimuli and proposed a LSTM-based saliency model for classifying the gaze patterns between autistic children and typically developing (TD) controls. However, though these studies have conducted large-scale experiments on natural stimuli, all these stimuli were limited by the intended selections of the researchers and the restricted fields-of-view (FOVs) from the photographers, and neither of them has autism. The omnidirectional visual attention characteristics of ASD are still unknown. Furthermore, all these stimuli were displayed on the relatively small screens, while the differences between the semantic-level perception of screen images and real world still exist.

These two weakness of previous studies motivate us to conduct this study, i.e., understanding and modeling the gaze pattern of children with autism in the real world. Instead of displaying image stimuli on screens, the eye tracking experiments in this work are conducted in Virtual Reality (VR) environment. A large-scale eye movement dataset is first established, which includes 300 omnidirectional images with the corresponding eye movement data collected from 15 children with autism and 16 TD controls. Based on the dataset, we further analyze the gaze pattern differences between autistic children and healthy children under this nearly natural condition. Moreover, we also apply a saliency prediction model based on the vector quantized neural network for better modeling the visual attention of both ASD and TD people under omnidirectional condition.

To the best of our knowledge, this is the first study that analyzes and models the omnidirectional visual attention of children with autism in the literature towards better understanding the gaze pattern of them. Eye movements encode rich information about the attention, cognition and psychological factors of an individual. Thus, understanding and modeling the gaze pattern of children with autism in (virtual) reality can not only help to further understand autism, but also may contribute to related application areas, such as diagnosis [11,15] and rehabilitation [16].

2 Subjective Experiment and Analysis

2.1 Omnidirectional Image Stimuli and Displaying Apparatus

We collected 300 omnidirectional images with high-resolution from two large-scale 360 image databases, including 85 images from Salient360 [17] and 215 images from SUN360 [18]. As shown in Fig. 1, the collected images contain various scenes in indoor and outdoor scenarios. Moreover, considering the differences between the visual attention of individuals with/without autism to social/non-social stimuli, we also balanced the semantic information inside the omnidirectional images. As shown in Fig. 1, our stimuli include rich visual features with various pixel-level, object-level, and semantic-level information.

We used HTC VIVE Pro Eye[1] as the hardware apparatus to display omnidirectional stimuli and collect eye movement data [19–23]. The software system was designed using Unity3D[2] to control the experimental procedure and record all data. The resolution of the display inside HTC VIVE Pro Eye is 1440×1600 pixels per eye which covers $110°$ FOV. The refresh rate 90 Hz. The eye-tracker inside it is supported by Tobii, and the frequency to collect gaze data 120 Hz.

2.2 Subjects

We recruited 31 subjects in our experiments, including 15 children with autism and 16 TD controls. All 15 autistic children were with medium-/high- function and could cooperate with us for the experiment. The age of the participants with ASD ranged from 7 years old to 13 years old with the average age of 10.4 years old. Sixteen healthy children were recruited as controls, whose ages were ranged from 7 years old to 9.6 years old with the average of 8 years old. Besides the age, the gender, handedness, and performance IQ were also matched between two groups. Before participating in the test, the parents of subjects read and signed a consent form which explained the human study. All participants had normal or correct-to-normal visual acuity during the experiment.

---

[1] https://www.vive.com/us/product/vive-pro-eye/overview/.

[2] https://unity.com/.

Fig. 1. Sample stimuli in our database.

2.3   Experiments

Since our work is the first study that conducts eye tracking experiments under VR environment to analyze the visual attention differences between individuals with autism and TD controls. The experiments need to be carefully designed and conducted. There were three methods in the literature to conduct eye tracking experiments under VR environment. Rai *et al.* [17] conducted the eye tracking study under seated condition with free viewing. Sitzmann *et al.* [24] studied both the seated condition and standing condition with free viewing. Haskins *et al.* [25] carried out the study under seated condition while the omnidirectional image rotate at a constant speed. Considering the possible cognition and communication problems for children with autism, in this paper we conducted the experiments in two conditions.

Standing Case. We conducted the first experiment with 200 images under standing condition with free viewing, since it is hard to teach the children with autism to use swivel chairs to look through the whole image. Due to the lack of patience of ASD participants, we split the experiment into 20 recording sessions with 10 images in each session. The initial viewing direction was initialized at the center of the omnidirectional image. Each omnidirectional image was displayed in the VR device for 20 s and followed by a 1-second gray screen mask. At the beginning of each session, we re-calibrate the eye-tracker to ensure the reliability of the acquired data.

Seated Case. Since the method in [25] may cause strong motion sickness, here we propose another way to conduct the second experiment, which includes the rest 100 images. The same as the standing case, we split the experiment into 10 recording sessions with 10 images in each session. The children were seated on a fixed chair. The initial viewing direction was similarly initialized at the center of the omnidirectional image. Each omnidirectional images was similarly displayed in the VR device for 20 s but rotated 90° every 5 s. Other procedures were the same with the standing case.

2.4   Analysis

Based on the constructed database, in this section, we analyze the differences and similarities between the visual attention of autistic children and healthy controls.

Global Comparison. We first analyze the global visual attention differences and similarities over the omnidirectional space between two groups. Figure 2 demonstrates several examples under the standing case. As shown in Fig. 2(a), children with autism try to avoid the close people who are looking at them while concentrating more on other salient targets in the car. As shown in Fig. 2(b), children with autism show reduced attention to the joint-attention of the main character in the scene but spread more attention to meaningless areas. Figure 2(c), (d) and (e) indicate the core characteristic of individuals with ASD, *i.e.*, social deficits or reduced social attention. It can be observed that children with ASD try to avoid the social targets that TD groups mainly concern and tend to concentrate on marginal directions and areas which are far way from them. It is interesting that in most of the classroom conditions, as shown in Fig. 2(h), (i), (j), the global visual attentions over the whole space are similar between the ASD group and TD group. We suppose that the semantic distributions of the classroom scenes are relatively uniform over the space, while in the scenes in Fig. 2(c), (d) and (e), the semantic distributions are spatially non-uniform. This phenomenon may reveal that the atypical visual attentions of children with autism are conditionally dependent on the scene. Moreover, autistic children and TD children show similar visual attention to non-social scenes, as shown in Fig. 2(f) and (g).

We further analyze the glocal differences over the whole space under seated condition, which are demonstrated in Fig. 3. As illustrated in Fig. 3(a) and (b), children show increased visual attention to non-social objects or information, while TD children tend to pay more attention on social information. As shown in Fig. 3, similar to the standing case, children tend to look more at the directions

Fig. 2. Global differences and similarities over the whole space between the visual attention of autistic children and healthy controls (standing case).

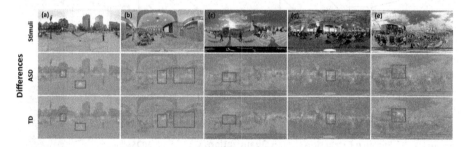

Fig. 3. Global differences over the whole space between the visual attention of autistic children and healthy controls (seated case).

far away from the social information or just trying to avoid the social scenarios near them. Moreover, children with autism seem to lack the ability of information integration and prediction, thus show reduced attention to the normally main focus in the scene as shown in Fig. 3(d) and (e).

Local Comparison. We have analyzed the global similarities and differences as above. However, we should notice that an omnidirectional image contains huge information, and even for a local FOV, the amount of information is similar to that of a regular image used in previous studies [12,13,26]. Therefore, it is also valuable to discuss the local differences between the omnidirectional visual attentions of ASD group and TD group. We show two examples in Fig. 4 to demonstrate this point. As can be observed in Fig. 4(a), in the local FOV of the yellow rectangular, children with autism tend to look more at the steering wheel,

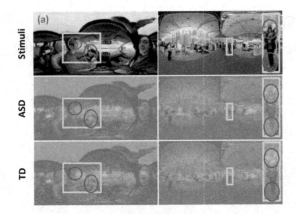

Fig. 4. Examples of local differences between the visual attention of autistic children and healthy controls for two images showed in Fig. 2 (standing case). (Color figure online)

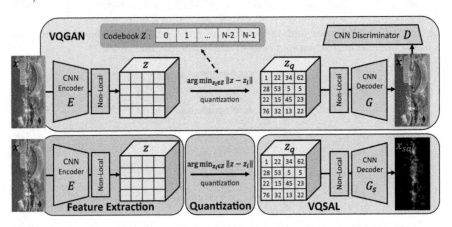

Fig. 5. Overview of the VQSAL model. Our approach uses a convolutional VQGAN to learn a context-rich codebook of the omnidirectional images, whose knowledge is then transfer to the saliency prediction.

while TD children focus more on the driver. As illustrated in the local FOV (the yellow rectangular) in Fig. 4(b), children with autism show close attention to the head and feet of the people, while TD children pay more attention to the face.

3   Omnidirectional Saliency Prediction

Our goal is to understand the context information of an image and model the visual saliency of different groups under the omnidirectional condition. In this paper, we apply a two-stage method for visual saliency prediction, which is a transfer learning framework based on a learned discrete representation model via VQGAN, as described in Sect. 3.1. We surprisingly find this approach, summarized in Fig. 5, is harmoniously consistent with the human vision model and may be useful and reasonable for modeling the visual attention of human groups with different cognitive conditions, as discussed in Sect. 3.2.

3.1   Transfer Learning for the Saliency Prediction

We first follow the VQGAN [27] to learn a discrete representation model for omnidirectional images. Through the discrete representation model learned, we can represent any image $x \in \mathbb{R}^{H \times W \times 3}$ using a spatial collection of codebook entries $z_\mathbf{q} \in \mathbb{R}^{h \times w \times n_z}$ from the codebook $\mathcal{Z}$, where n_z is the dimensionality of codes and $\mathcal{Z} = \{z_k\}_{k=1}^K \subset \mathbb{R}_z^n$ is the learned perceptually rich code book. The representation $z_\mathbf{q}$ includes the extremely compressed but perceptually rich information of the image, which can be directly used to decode and predict visual saliency information. Since visual saliency is not only related to local information, but also related to global relationship, we use the non-local neural network in VQGAN to appropriately learn the global relationship and the CNN decoder to decode local information. Moreover, we use transfer learning to the decoder of the VQGAN to decode and predict the saliency density map. The overall process of this method can be represented as:

$$\hat{x}_{\text{sal}} = G_S(z_\mathbf{q}) = G_S\left(\mathbf{q}(E(x))\right), \tag{1}$$

where G_S is the decoder for saliency density prediction. The loss function of the saliency prediction in our paper is defined as:

$$\mathcal{L} = \mathcal{L}_{\text{rec}} + \lambda \mathcal{L}_{\text{sal}}, \tag{2}$$

where $\mathcal{L}_{\text{sal}} = \mathcal{L}_{\text{CC}} + \mathcal{L}_{\text{KL}}$, CC and KL are two widely used metrics for measuring the accuracy of the predicted saliency maps. The weighting factor λ is empirically set as 0.2 in this paper.

3.2   Discussion of VQSAL

We surprisingly find that this model is harmoniously consistent with the human visual attention model and may be useful and reasonable for modeling the visual attention of human groups with different cognitive conditions. The process of neural discrete inference is similar to the process of human attention formation, i.e., encoding a given image to information, then quantifying the information with human knowledge base, and finally decoding to human visual attention activities. However, most of previous learnable saliency prediction methods have used only encoder [28] or autoencoder [29] to model the visual attention. Moreover, it seems unreasonable to finetune the whole model for human groups with different cognitive conditions since their vision perception systems are similar (i.e., encoder part) [13]. This is precisely the rationality of our method, since the discrete representation encoder is pre-trained, and it is reasonable to simulate the visual saliency of humans with different cognitive conditions using different decoders.

Table 1. Quantitative comparison results of different models for saliency prediction on ASD group (Learnable models are fine-tuned on our dataset).

Metric\Model	Itti	GBVS [30]	GBVS360 [31]	BMS [32]	BMS360 [31]	Zhu et al. [33]	Salicon [28]	MLNet [34]	SalGAN [29]	Ours
CC ↑	0.414	0.398	0.427	0.444	0.465	0.499	0.647	0.453	0.629	**0.679**
NSS ↑	0.916	0.880	0.902	0.998	1.096	1.114	1.464	1.031	1.417	**1.621**
AUC ↑	0.743	0.734	0.743	0.760	0.759	0.768	0.830	0.764	0.817	**0.833**
SIM ↑	0.452	0.444	0.452	0.462	0.468	0.464	0.571	0.476	0.576	**0.607**
KLD ↓	4.428	4.620	4.575	4.288	4.040	4.406	2.303	3.490	2.277	**1.907**

Table 2. Quantitative comparison results of different models for saliency prediction on TD group (Learnable models are fine-tuned on our dataset).

Metric\Model	Itti	GBVS [30]	GBVS360 [31]	BMS [32]	BMS360 [31]	Zhu et al. [33]	Salicon [28]	MLNet [34]	SalGAN [29]	Ours
CC ↑	0.443	0.425	0.459	0.478	0.493	0.528	0.678	0.535	0.669	**0.724**
NSS ↑	1.007	0.954	1.039	1.104	1.202	1.204	1.286	1.264	1.543	**1.797**
AUC ↑	0.764	0.752	0.764	0.778	0.781	0.790	0.841	0.787	0.834	**0.845**
SIM ↑	0.475	0.465	0.480	0.483	0.490	0.491	0.611	0.522	0.608	**0.641**
KLD ↓	3.915	4.073	3.981	3.883	3.835	3.912	1.828	2.786	1.759	**1.527**

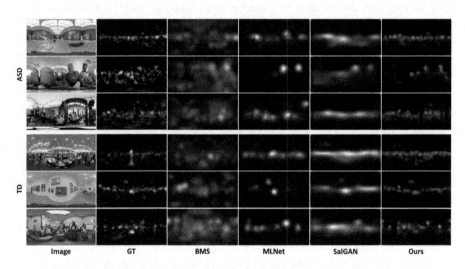

Fig. 6. Qualitative comparisons between different methods.

4   Experimental Results

4.1   Performance Evaluation on Our Dataset

We evaluate the performance of VQSAL on modeling the visual attention of different groups on our dataset. Table 1 shows the quantitative comparisons of different models for modeling the visual attention of children with ASD. It can be observed that our method acquires the best performance compared to other 9 SOTA models. As demonstrated in Table 2, towards modeling the visual attention of TD children, VQSAL also achieves the SOTA results compared with other models.

Table 3. Quantitative comparison results of different models for saliency prediction on other datasets.

Categories	Metric\Model	GBVS360 [31]	BMS [32]	BMS360 [31]	Zhu *et al.* [33]	Salicon [28]	MLNet [34]	SalGAIL [35]	Ours
Overall	CC ↑	0.590	0.557	0.714	0.727	0.511	0.589	0.742	**0.816**
	NSS ↑	0.995	0.975	1.378	1.295	0.856	1.064	1.556	**1.591**
	AUC ↑	0.766	0.758	0.841	0.821	0.757	0.784	0.853	**0.870**
	KLD ↓	0.566	0.584	0.584	0.420	0.637	0.844	0.345	**0.251**

Moreover, we further compare the qualitative results between different models for modeling the visual attention of ASD children and TD children, respectively, as shown in Fig. 6. We can observe that the predicted saliency results of our method are more consistent with the ground-truth (GT). More importantly, compared with other SOTA methods, our method can better describe the local visual attention in detail while other models can only generate a rough visual attention map over the space.

4.2   Generalization Ability on Other Datasets

VQSAL can not only be used to model the visual attention of human groups with different cognitive conditions, but also be extended to the general omnidirectional saliency prediction task. Here we demonstrate the superiority of VQSAL on another omnidirectional saliency prediction database [35]. As shown in Table 3, the overall performances of VQSAL across different metrics are better than other 7 SOTA models.

5   Discussion and Conclusion

In this paper, we present an important problem *i.e.*, where are the children with autism looking in reality? Although there were many previous studies discussing the visual attention of individuals with autism, the vast majority of prior studies not only used stimuli with restricted FOV, but also conducted experiments with relatively small and fixed FOV. To the best of our knowledge, there is no previous study conducting large-scale controllable experiments towards modeling the visual attention of children with autism in reality. Considering two factors, *i.e.*, omnidirectional free viewing and controllable experimental condition, are required to be balanced, we conduct the first large-scale visual attention study under VR environment, towards better understanding and modeling of the gaze pattern of children with autism in reality/VR.

Besides the contribution of the large-scale eye-tracking study and the database, we also apply a saliency prediction method for better modeling the human visual attention. We surprisingly find the consistence between the model and various human groups with different cognitive conditions. Quantitative and qualitative comparisons with SOTA models demonstrate the superiority of this method. Moreover, this method can also be generalized to other omnidirectional saliency prediction datasets and tasks and achieve SOTA performances.

There are many interesting phenomena can be observed from the constructed database. In this paper, though we have analyzed some omnidirectional differences between the visual attention of children with autism and healthy controls, more explorations are needed to further study the common characteristics underlying this complex neurodevelopmental condition in the future. First of all, more statistical analysis are needed to compare the differences between the gaze patterns of two groups, including the quantitative analysis of the fixations and various visual features (*e.g.*, from pixel level features to semantic level features), the relationship between head movement and eye movement, the characteristics of saccades and scanpaths *etc.* Moreover, this study can be seen as a large-scale preliminary research for future works to design specific stimuli towards diagnosis or rehabilitation application development.

References

1. Robertson, C.E., Baron-Cohen, S.: Sensory perception in autism. Nat. Rev. Neurosci. **18**(11), 671 (2017)
2. American Psychiatric Association, et al.: Diagnostic and statistical manual of mental disorders (DSM-5®). American Psychiatric Pub (2013)
3. Simmons, D.R., Robertson, A.E., McKay, L.S., Toal, E., McAleer, P., Pollick, F.E.: Vision in autism spectrum disorders. Vis. Res. **49**(22), 2705–2739 (2009)
4. Wang, S., Xu, J., Jiang, M., Zhao, Q., Hurlemann, R., Adolphs, R.: Autism spectrum disorder, but not amygdala lesions, impairs social attention in visual search. Neuropsychologia **63**, 259–274 (2014)
5. Shi, F., et al.: Drawing reveals hallmarks of children with autism. Displays **67**, 102000 (2021)
6. Osterling, J., Dawson, G.: Early recognition of children with autism: a study of first birthday home videotapes. J. Autism Dev. Disord. **24**(3), 247–257 (1994)
7. Dawson, G., Webb, S.J., McPartland, J.: Understanding the nature of face processing impairment in autism: insights from behavioral and electrophysiological studies. Dev. Neuropsychol. **27**(3), 403–424 (2005)
8. Sasson, N.J., Elison, J.T., Turner-Brown, L.M., Dichter, G.S., Bodfish, J.W.: Brief report: circumscribed attention in young children with autism. J. Autism Dev. Disord. **41**(2), 242–247 (2011)
9. Corden, B., Chilvers, R., Skuse, D.: Avoidance of emotionally arousing stimuli predicts social-perceptual impairment in Asperger's syndrome. Neuropsychologia **46**(1), 137–147 (2008)
10. Klin, A., Jones, W.: Altered face scanning and impaired recognition of biological motion in a 15-month-old infant with autism. Dev. Sci. **11**(1), 40–46 (2008)
11. Jiang, M., Zhao, Q.: Learning visual attention to identify people with autism spectrum disorder. In: Proceedings of the IEEE International Conference on Computer Vision (ICCV), pp. 3267–3276 (2017)
12. Duan, H., et al.: A dataset of eye movements for the children with autism spectrum disorder. In: Proceedings of the ACM Multimedia Systems Conference (MMSys) (2019)
13. Duan, H., et al.: Learning to predict where the children with ASD look. In: Proceedings of the IEEE International Conference on Image Processing (ICIP), pp. 704–708 (2018)

14. Duan, H., Min, X., Fang, Y., Fan, L., Yang, X., Zhai, G.: Visual attention analysis and prediction on human faces for children with autism spectrum disorder. ACM Trans. Multimed. Comput. Commun. Appl. (TOMM) **15**(3s), 1–23 (2019)

15. Fang, Y., Duan, H., Shi, F., Min, X., Zhai, G.: Identifying children with autism spectrum disorder based on gaze-following. In: Proceedings of the IEEE International Conference on Image Processing (ICIP), pp. 423–427. IEEE (2020)

16. Bellani, M., Fornasari, L., Chittaro, L., Brambilla, P.: Virtual reality in autism: state of the art. Epidemiol. Psychiatr. Sci. **20**(3), 235–238 (2011)

17. Rai, Y., Gutiérrez, J., Le Callet, P.: A dataset of head and eye movements for 360 degree images. In: Proceedings of the ACM on Multimedia Systems Conference, pp. 205–210 (2017)

18. Xiao, J., Ehinger, K.A., Oliva, A., Torralba, A.: Recognizing scene viewpoint using panoramic place representation. In: Proceedings of the IEEE Conference on Computer Vision and Pattern Recognition (CVPR), pp. 2695–2702. IEEE (2012)

19. Duan, H., Zhai, G., Yang, X., Li, D., Zhu, W.: IVQAD 2017: an immersive video quality assessment database. In: Proceedings of the International Conference on Systems, Signals and Image Processing (IWSSIP), pp. 1–5 (2017)

20. Zhu, Y., Zhai, G., Yang, Y., Duan, H., Min, X., Yang, X.: Viewing behavior supported visual saliency predictor for 360 degree videos. IEEE Trans. Circuits Syst. Video Technol. (TCSVT) (2021)

21. Duan, H., Shen, W., Min, X., Tu, D., Li, J., Zhai, G.: Saliency in augmented reality. In: Proceedings of the ACM International Conference on Multimedia (ACM MM) (2022)

22. Duan, H., Min, X., Zhu, Y., Zhai, G., Yang, X., Callet, P.L.: Confusing image quality assessment: towards better augmented reality experience. arXiv preprint arXiv:2204.04900 (2022)

23. Tu, D., Min, X., Duan, H., Guo, G., Zhai, G., Shen, W.: End-to-end human-gaze-target detection with transformers. In: Proceedings of the IEEE Conference on Computer Vision and Pattern Recognition (CVPR), pp. 2202–2210 (2022)

24. Sitzmann, V., et al.: Saliency in VR: how do people explore virtual environments? IEEE Trans. Vis. Comput. Graph. **24**(4), 1633–1642 (2018)

25. Haskins, A.J., Mentch, J., Botch, T.L., Robertson, C.E.: Active vision in immersive, 360 real-world environments. Sci. Rep. **10**(1), 1–11 (2020)

26. Wang, S., et al.: Atypical visual saliency in autism spectrum disorder quantified through model-based eye tracking. Neuron **88**(3), 604–616 (2015)

27. Esser, P., Rombach, R., Ommer, B.: Taming transformers for high-resolution image synthesis. arXiv preprint arXiv:2012.09841 (2020)

28. Huang, X., Shen, C., Boix, X., Zhao, Q.: SALICON: reducing the semantic gap in saliency prediction by adapting deep neural networks. In: Proceedings of the IEEE International Conference on Computer Vision (ICCV), pp. 262–270 (2015)

29. Pan, J., et al.: SalGAN: visual saliency prediction with generative adversarial networks. arXiv preprint arXiv:1701.01081 (2017)

30. Harel, J., Koch, C., Perona, P.: Graph-based visual saliency (2007)

31. Lebreton, P., Raake, A.: GBVS360, BMS360, ProSal: extending existing saliency prediction models from 2D to omnidirectional images. Signal Process.: Image Commun. **69**, 69–78 (2018)

32. Zhang, J., Sclaroff, S.: Exploiting surroundedness for saliency detection: a Boolean map approach. IEEE Trans. Pattern Anal. Mach. Intell. (TPAMI) **38**(5), 889–902 (2015)

33. Zhu, Y., Zhai, G., Min, X.: The prediction of head and eye movement for 360 degree images. Signal Process.: Image Commun. **69**, 15–25 (2018)

34. Cornia, M., Baraldi, L., Serra, G., Cucchiara, R.: A deep multi-level network for saliency prediction. In: Proceedings of the IEEE International Conference on Pattern Recognition (ICPR), pp. 3488–3493 (2016)
35. Xu, M., Yang, L., Tao, X., Duan, Y., Wang, Z.: Saliency prediction on omnidirectional image with generative adversarial imitation learning. IEEE Trans. Image Process. (TIP) **30**, 2087–2102 (2021)

Study on Practical Utility of Image Dehazing Algorithms Based on Deep Learning in Computer Vision Scene Understanding

Linhui Li[1,2], Xinliang Zhang[1(✉)], Jing Lian[1,2], Yifan Zhang[3], and Yan Zhao[3]

[1] Dalian University of Technology, Dalian 116081, China
1843476299l@163.com
[2] Key Laboratory of Energy Conservation and New Energy Vehicle Power Control and Vehicle Technology, Dalian 116081, China
[3] Hualu Zhida Technology Co., Ltd., Dalian, China

Abstract. Deep learning-based methods have achieved remarkable performance for single image dehazing. However, previous studies are mostly focused on the dehazing of human-perspective images without considering the practical application in the field of computer vision. Whether the image dehazing of deep learning-based methods(IDDL) can be applied in the field of computer vision will determine the research direction of computer vision dehazing scenes. This work presents a comprehensive study that the feasibility and reliability of applying IDDL from human vision to practical computer vision scenarios. An approach for practical utility and portability evaluation of the IDDL based on human vision, including the comparison regarding the detection accuracy, model running time, and model scale of the detection method, is proposed. Our research focuses on re-evaluating the applicability of image dehazing algorithms based on a computer vision perspective, including evaluation method and evaluation index. To better verify the detection effect of the dehazing algorithm, we use the synthetic dataset method as a control experiment and make a comparison with 6 state-of-the-art dehazing methods on a real-world hazy scene. Additionally, investigate the proportion of synthetic hazy images in the training dataset used, including object detection and semantic segmentation algorithms. Extensive experiments demonstrate that the poor practical utility and portability of IDDL in computer vision are verifiable, and the IDDL solution should be extensively paid attention to concerning the computer vision domain rather than leveraging the IDDL based on human vision. Finally, We provide some methods to solve the hazy scene.

Keywords: Computer vision scene understanding · Dehazing network · Practical utility analysis

Supported by the National Natural Science Foundation of China under Grant Nos. 51775082,61976039,52172382 and the China Fundamental Research Funds for the Central Universities under Grant Nos. DUT19LAB36, DUT20GJ207, and Science and Technology Innovation Fund of Dalian under 2021JJ12GX015.

L. Fang et al. (Eds.): CICAI 2022, LNAI 13605, pp. 601–612, 2022.
https://doi.org/10.1007/978-3-031-20500-2_49

1 Introduction

The existing recommendation methods based on deep learning mainly address single image dehazing using human vision as an image evaluation criterion. However, computer vision has become an active research topic in the multi-field and has been widely used in many industries, including intelligent driving environment perception [14], medical image segmentation [25], human-computer interaction [31], and robot vision [28]. Additionally, it is emphasized that application scenarios of computer vision need to achieve all-weather working capabilities to ensure its safety and reliability. Since adverse conditions are unavoidable in real outdoor scenarios, stable and reliable methods are urgently required to identify and corresponding research programs are quickly provided. This research focuses on hazy scenes of computer vision.

Note that deep learning-based methods have achieved considerable success on single image dehazing in recent years. It is worth considering applying dehazing methods to the field of computer vision. The successful application of the scheme will also lead to research in other scenarios, such as rain, snow, and night. Thus, the IDDL portability issue should be analyzed because it can determine how dehazing research direction on computer vision will evolve in the future, whether the IDDL based on human vision or the new scheme of computer vision will be used. However, there has been a lack of reasonable evaluation and suggestions for dehazing methods development under the computer vision scenes.

Considering the variability and complexity of natural hazy environmental conditions, different hazy images can affect the dehazing effect of the IDDL. It will directly affect the detection effect of computer vision. To overcome these problems, we design a computer vision detection accuracy comparison including object detection and semantic segmentation, model scale, and real-time analysis.

Considering the measure the degree of the improvement of dehazing methods in object detection and semantic segmentation, we train the network with the synthetic hazy dataset for comparison. Real-world hazy datasets are greatly limited due to the difficulty of obtaining hazy images and their annotations, while the rational and scientific solution of using the synthetic fog dataset to replace the real hazy dataset [4]. The generalization and robustness of detection networks can be improved by using image dataset-based methods [24]. Additionally, synthesis approaches based on the standard optical model have been developed [19,20], and various public datasets have been selected to synthesize hazy datasets to avoid the contingency error of a single dataset.

To provide a reasonable and reliable conclusion, this study performs a series of contrast experiments for portability evidence. The main contributions of the paper can be summarized as follows:

- Compared the performance of the original detection network, detection network based on synthetic hazy dataset and detection network based on the different IDDL in real hazy environment.
- Comprehensive evaluation of image dehazing methods from three aspects of detection network model improvement performance, model scale and running time.

- Propose appropriate proportions of synthetic blurred images in the training dataset according to the object detection and semantic segmentation results of different synthetic image ratios in the dataset.

2   Related Work

Image Dehazing Methods. Since the hazy environment can cause blurring and sharpening of the visual image information, a large number of studies on dehazing algorithms have been conducted. These algorithms can be roughly categorized into three types: prior-based methods [18,34], fusion-based methods [6,29], and deep learning-based methods. The studies on the dehazing algorithms have been considering different dehazing scenes [23,26]. Currently, the IDDL-based methods can achieve a better dehazing effect than the other two methods, so they have become a research hotspot in the domain of image dehazing. This paper selects six representative advanced hazing networks as validation criteria networks. For instance, Qin et al. proposed an end-to-end feature fusion attention network (FFA-Net) to restore the image information of a single image effectively [21]. Hang Dong et al. proposed a multiscale boosted dehazing network as a part of boosting and error feedback modules, which were used to boost the overall structure of the encoded decoder to restore the haze-free image progressively [7]. Zhang et al. designed an end-to-end gated context aggregation network to help to remove the Gridding artifacts and to fuse the features from different levels, thus directly restoring the final haze-free image [2]. Yu et al. developed fully end-to-end generative adversarial networks with fusion-discriminator for image dehazing, which uses frequency information as additional priors [8]. Xiao et al. introduced a trainable convolutional neural network (Grid-Net), which effectively solve the bottleneck problems of the traditional multiscale estimation methods and can reduce dehazing work [17]. Chen et al. proposed the patch-map-based hybrid learning dehazed net (PMHLD), which integrates the strategies of using a hybrid learning technique involving the patch map and a bi-attentive generative adversarial network to achieve better reconstruction [3].

Detection Networks. The object detection and semantic segmentation algorithms of CV scenes have been extensively studied. Numerous mature network models can achieve real-time detection and high accuracy in many application scenarios [10,16]. The object detection algorithms can be divided into two categories [30]: the object detection algorithms based on the target candidate region and the object detection algorithms based on regression. Semantic segmentation algorithms can be divided into two categories [32]: the semantic segmentation algorithms that are based on region classification segmentation and the semantic segmentation algorithms that are based on pixel classification. In order to ensure the reliability and rationality of the comparison methods, we select each object detection and semantic segmentation methods. Faster RCNN [22] and YOLOv5 [13] networks are selected as representatives of the two-stage and one-stage algorithms and SegNet [1] and Mask R-CNN [11] networks are selected in this study as representatives of the segmentation algorithm based on the pixel classification and region classification to evaluate the effect of dehazing methods.

Evaluation Indexes. The image quality evaluation methods for dehazing methods can be categorized into two groups, including the subjective image quality evaluation methods and the objective image quality evaluation methods. The subjective image quality evaluation methods is use human visual perception as an evaluation standard for subjective evaluation [33]. The objective image quality evaluation methods is to obtain the evaluation results by utilizing different evaluation indexes, such as PSNR [12], SSIM [27]. However, using human vision as the criterion for judging image quality algorithms is different from computer vision. Thus, the evaluation indicators of object detection and semantic segmentation algorithms should be used to measure the image quality evaluation methods [30]. In this study, mAP@.5 and mIoU are used as quantitative indicators of object detection and semantic segmentation, respectively.

3   Methods

3.1   Dataset

To ensure the rationality of the study, we select some public datasets, including PASCAL VOC 2007 and 2012, Microsoft COCO 2017 and RTTS. This study used PASCAL VOC [9] and Microsoft COCO [5] for training and validation, and RTTS [15] are used as testing datasets to ensure the diversity and scale difference of the images and the scientific and objective results of experiments.

To ensure the evaluation authenticity of the semantic segmentation scenario, the semantic segmentation annotation is provided on the RTTS dataset using the image application LabelMe, including person and car. In addition, the PASCAL VOC and Microsoft COCO datasets are randomly divided into the training dataset (80%) and the validation dataset (20%).

3.2   Data Pre-processing

The synthetic hazy datasets can improve the generalization and detection precision of network models. Due to the difficulty of collection and annotating hazy images, the synthetic hazy on real images that depict clear-weather public image sets and leverage the synthetic data for computer vision by employing a standard optical model. The standard optical model has been widely used for dehazed and synthetic hazy images, and it can be expressed as [19, 20]:

$$I(x) = J(x)t(x) + L(1 - t(x)) \tag{1}$$

where $I(x)$ denotes the hazy image, and $J(x)$ denotes the clear image; x denotes a pixel position in the image, L denotes the global atmospheric light, and $t(x)$ denotes the transmission map. In a homogeneous scenario, the transmission map can be represented as $t(x) = e^{-\beta d(x)}$, where β and $d(x)$ denote the atmosphere scattering parameter and the scene depth, respectively.

3.3 The Proposed Architecture

We have been comprehensively considered about IDDL from human vision to computer vision. Our studies focuses on three aspects, including the detection accuracy of different detection networks, the running times and model scales based on the different IDDL. The contents of the structure, which present the validation process of IDDL portability, are demonstrated in Fig. 1.

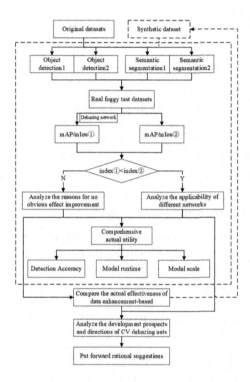

Fig. 1. The validation process of IDDL portability. The dehazed images and hazy images are respectively denoted as ① and ②.

4   Results

4.1   Experimental Configuration

All the experiments were performed on an Intel Xeon E5-2620 v4 @ 2.10 GHz graphics TITAN Xp/PCle/SSE2 server. The initial parameters of the network model remain in the initial state.

As a comparison of the effect of the dehazing algorithms, we select the synthetic dataset for reference and verify the reliability of using the data-driven method. The data enhancement-based method is proposed to improve the detection effect of the dehazing network by applying this method to the synthetic datasets. The conclusion is crucial for other researchers in the study of hazy scenes. For the specific network training set and testing set refer to Table 1, including the original dataset and the synthetic dataset.

Table 1. Network and dataset information.

Network	Dataset type	Training dataset	Training number		Test dataset	Test number
			Original	Synthetic		
YOLOv5	Public	VOC2007+12	22,136	0	RTTS_4332	4332
	Synthetic	VOC2007+12	17,125	5,011	RTTS_4332	4332
Faster RCNN	Public	VOC2007	5,011	0	RTTS_4332	4332
	Synthetic	VOC2007	2,511	2,500	RTTS_4332	4332
Mask R-CNN	Public	MS COCO	123,287	0	RTTS_200	200
	Synthetic	MS COCO	93,287	30,000	RTTS_200	200
SegNet	Public	VOC2012	11,355	0	RTTS_200	200
	Synthetic	VOC2012	9,355	2,000	RTTS_200	200

4.2 Experimental Results and Analysis

Object Detection. To ensure the rationality and reliability of the conclusions, we selected six advanced dehazing models and two efficient object detection networks to verify the accuracy of the detection effect. The object detection results are shown in Table 2 and Table 3.

Table 2. The evaluation result of the Faster RCNN for the five-class. The three best results are marked in bold

Method	AP (%)					mAP (%)
	Person	Car	Bicycle	Motorbike	Bus	mAP@.5
Original	56.8	32.5	44.8	34.1	18.7	37.38
Synthetic	**60.0**	**35.9**	46.8	**40.7**	**25.8**	**41.85**
FD-GAN	**58.4(1)**	33.7	**47.1(1)**	34.6	21.4	**39.04(1)**
FFA-Net	57.4	33.0	44.6	**34.7(2)**	19.9	37.90
GCA-Net	57.8	**34.1(2)**	**46.1(2)**	33.6	**21.7(1)**	38.67
Grid-Net	**58.2(2)**	**33.4(1)**	**45.8(3)**	**34.9(1)**	**21.6(2)**	**38.78(3)**
MSBDN-DFF	**58.2(2)**	**33.4(1)**	**45.8(3)**	**34.9(1)**	**21.6(2)**	**38.82(2)**
PMHLD	58.0	33.3	45.1	33.8	20.4	38.12

The mAP@.5 is chosen as the main criterion for model performance comparison. Our experiments compare the effect of dehazing image detection using the different dehazing algorithms and demonstrate the improved effect of image dehazing in actual hazy scenes. Three points can be seen in Table 2 and Table 3.

- The preprocessing method using the dehazing networks can improve the detection effect of Faster RCNN and YOLOv5.
- Different dehazing networks have a different effect on the detection effect of the detection network, which the difference of about 3 times in maximum and minimum of detection index improved.
- The synthetic dataset can effectively improve the detection accuracy and has the best index. Compared with the detection result of the best dehazing algorithms, this method improves the mAP@.5 by 2.81% and 1.9% on Faster RCNN and YOLOv5.

Table 3. The evaluation result of the YOLOv5 for the five-class.

Method	AP (%)					mAP (%)
	Person	Car	Bicycle	Motorbike	Bus	mAP@.5
Original	79.6	66.0	47.2	39.3	28.6	52.1
Synthetic	79.7	66.8	**54.2**	**47.1**	**31.9**	**56.0**
FD-GAN	79.0	**68.2(2)**	47.3	**43.1(1)**	30.2	53.6
FFA-Net	79.9	66.9	47.6	40.6	29.3	52.8
GCA-Net	79.9	**68.5(1)**	**48.3(2)**	**42.7(2)**	**31.4(2)**	**54.1(1)**
Grid-Net	**80.3(1)**	68.0	**48.6(1)**	42.1	**31.3(3)**	**54.1(1)**
MSBDN-DFF	**80.0(2)**	67.8	**47.8(3)**	**42.7(2)**	31.2	**53.9(2)**
PMHLD	**80.0(2)**	**68.2(2)**	46.7	41.9	**31.6(1)**	53.7

Semantic Segmentation. To ensure the rationality and reliability of the conclusions, we selected six advanced dehazing models and two efficient semantic segmentation networks to verify the accuracy of the segmentation effect. The semantic segmentation results are shown in Table 4 and Table 5.

For this experiment, the mIoU is chosen as the main criterion for model performance comparison. It is of great help to the judge the effect of the segmentation effect and a commonly used evaluation index. Three points can be seen in Table 4 and Table 5.

- Semantic segmentation is more affected by hazy images than object detection.
- Most of the dehazing networks can improve the accuracy of semantic segmentation, and others may reduce the accuracy, such as using GCA-Net is more accurate than not using GCA-Net in SegNet and Mask RCNN.
- The synthetic dataset can Significantly improve the semantic segmentation accuracy and has the best index. Compared with the segmentation result of the best dehazing algorithms, this method improves the mIoU by 1.87% and 1.33% on SegNet and Mask RCNN.

Table 4. The evaluation results of the SegNet on the two-class

Method	IoU (%)		mIoU (%)
	Person	Car	
Original	41.0	50.4	45.70
Synthetic	**48.2**	52.7	**51.35**
FD-GAN	39.1	52.4	45.76
FFA-Net	38.6	**54.2(2)**	46.42
GCA-Net	39.2	49.6	44.39
Grid-Net	**43.2(3)**	52.0	**47.58(3)**
MSBDN-DFF	**44.4(1)**	**54.1(3)**	**49.24(2)**
PMHLD	**43.8(2)**	**55.2(1)**	**49.48(1)**

Table 5. The evaluation results of the Mask RCNN on the two-class

Method	IoU (%)		mIoU (%)
	Person	Car	
Original	69.5	66.0	67.71
Synthetic	73.1	**67.6**	**70.35**
FD-GAN	66.7	**64.8(3)**	65.76
FFA-Net	72.0	**65.8(1)**	**68.88(2)**
GCA-Net	68.9	64.1	66.47
Grid-Net	**73.1(2)**	64.7	**68.88(2)**
MSBDN-DFF	**73.6(1)**	63.8	68.65
PMHLD	**73.1(2)**	**65.0(2)**	**69.02(1)**

5   Synthetic Data Studies

5.1   Synthetic Data Contrast and Analysis

According to the analysis of dehazing methods, we choose to compare three aspects:

- In Sect. 4.2, the testing accuracy of the synthetic hazy method is significantly better than that of the dehazing methods.
- The real-time requirement of a detection network plays a vital role in the actual application in the computer vision field. The running times of the six methods are analyzed, and the average single-image running times of different dehazed networks on the RRTS dataset are given in Table 6. The IDDL cannot meet the real-time detection requirement of the computer vision scenario due to the high running time cost. However, the synthetic hazy method does not increase the model running time significantly.
- The scales of different dehazing network models are listed in Table 7. The network model with a better dehazing effect in computer vision is large in scale.

A large models scale occupies storage memory and puts higher requirements on the chip process during the application process, which will increase the difficulty of model deployment. The main reason is that the dehazing requirement depends only on the image effect and ignores the scale of the dehazing model. However, the synthetic dataset method does not increase the model scale of the dehazed network.

Table 6. Comparison of the average runtimes of the six dehazing networks.

Dehazing Network	MSBDN-DFF	FD-GAN	FFA-Net	Grid-Net	PMHLD	GCA-Net
Average Time (s)	0.3623	0.4014	0.764	0.4757	10.8642	0.5604

Table 7. Model scale results of the image dehazing methods.

Dehazing Network	FD-GAN	FFA-Net	GCA-Net	Grid-Net	MSBDN-DFF	PMHLD
Model Scale (MB)	56.4	26.6	2.8	3.9	125.6	198.4

5.2   Improved Data Comparison Results and Analysis

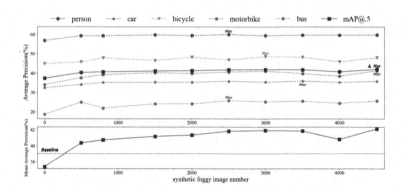

Fig. 2. The average class detection precision of differing numbers of hazy images under the Faster RCNN. The baseline represents the best detection effect of the dehazed network.

The above-presented results demonstrate that the synthetic hazy method can significantly improve the effect of object detection and semantic segmentation, generalization performance, and robustness of a detection network. Due to the synthetic dataset being composed of the synthetic hazy images instead of the original images, the percentage of hazy images in the synthetic dataset is an important influencing factor. The performances for 10 proportions of synthetic datasets based on Faster RCNN and SegNet are presented in Fig. 2 and Fig. 3. We can find that low proportions of synthetic hazy images decline the detection accuracy, and high proportions of synthetic hazy images result in a limited detection effect of the clear weather. Therefore, the proportion of synthetic images should be adjusted to about half synthetic images to achieve the best effect of object detection and semantic segmentation.

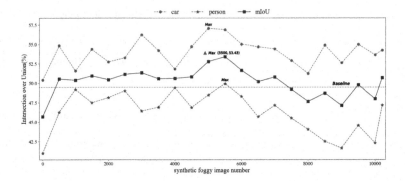

Fig. 3. The average class detection precision of differing numbers of hazy images under the SegNet. The baseline represents the best detection effect of the dehazed network.

6 Conclusion

This article analyzes the practical utility and portability of the IDDL from human vision to computer vision. The poor adaptability and portability of the IDDL are demonstrated according to the subjective evaluation indexes of mAP and mIoU in object detection and semantic segmentation. Compared with the synthetic hazy scheme, the dehazing network scheme has a poor detection effect. Furthermore, the IDDL is cost-consuming in terms of the model running time, occupies a certain space in the processor, and increases memory consumption. In contrast, the synthetic dataset method can achieve an excellent detection effect based on the time and model of original detection networks. Overall, the dehazing work still has a great development prospect in the computer vision scene understanding.

In future work, more methods will be studied to achieve hazy scenes in computer vision. In the view of datasets, the researcher could realize the collection of real haze images. By training the network with a large number of real haze images, the detection of haze images can be improved, and the robustness, stability, and effectiveness could also be further improved. In the view of sensors, utilizing multi-device sensors could perform efficiently in adverse weather environments, For example, the use of infrared sensors can effectively reduce the impact of hazy scenes. In the view of hardware, using high-performance hardware equipment could mitigate the concerns about the running time and scale.

References

1. Badrinarayanan, V., Kendall, A., Cipolla, R.: SegNet: a deep convolutional encoder-decoder architecture for image segmentation. IEEE Trans. Pattern Anal. Mach. Intell. **39**(12), 2481–2495 (2017)
2. Chen, D., et al.: Gated context aggregation network for image dehazing and deraining. In: 2019 IEEE Winter Conference on Applications of Computer Vision (WACV), pp. 1375–1383. IEEE (2019)
3. Chen, W.T., Fang, H.Y., Ding, J.J., Kuo, S.Y.: PMHLD: patch map-based hybrid learning DehazeNet for single image haze removal. IEEE Trans. Image Process. **29**, 6773–6788 (2020)
4. Chum, L., Subramanian, A., Balasubramanian, V.N., Jawahar, C.: Beyond supervised learning: a computer vision perspective. J. Indian Inst. Sci. **99**(2), 177–199 (2019)
5. COCO: Common objects in context dataset (2020). https://cocodataset.org/#overview
6. Devi, L.M., Wahengbam, K., Singh, A.D.: Dehazing buried tissues in retinal fundus images using a multiple radiance pre-processing with deep learning based multiple feature-fusion. Opt. Laser Technol. **138**, 106908 (2021)
7. Dong, H., et al.: Multi-scale boosted dehazing network with dense feature fusion. In: Proceedings of the IEEE/CVF Conference on Computer Vision and Pattern Recognition, pp. 2157–2167 (2020)
8. Dong, Y., Liu, Y., Zhang, H., Chen, S., Qiao, Y.: FD-GAN: generative adversarial networks with fusion-discriminator for single image dehazing. In: Proceedings of the AAAI Conference on Artificial Intelligence, vol. 34, pp. 10729–10736 (2020)
9. Everingham, M., Eslami, S., Van Gool, L., Williams, C.K., Winn, J., Zisserman, A.: The pascal visual object classes challenge: a retrospective. Int. J. Comput. Vis. **111**(1), 98–136 (2015)
10. Hao, S., Zhou, Y., Guo, Y.: A brief survey on semantic segmentation with deep learning. Neurocomputing **406**, 302–321 (2020)
11. He, K., Gkioxari, G., Dollár, P., Girshick, R.: Mask R-CNN. In: Proceedings of the IEEE International Conference on Computer Vision, pp. 2961–2969 (2017)
12. Huynh-Thu, Q., Ghanbari, M.: Scope of validity of PSNR in image/video quality assessment. Electron. Lett. **44**, 800–801 (2008)
13. Jocher, G.: YOLOv5 (2020). https://github.com/ultralytics/yolov5
14. Kuutti, S., Bowden, R., Jin, Y., Barber, P., Fallah, S.: A survey of deep learning applications to autonomous vehicle control. IEEE Trans. Intell. Transp. Syst. **22**(2), 712–733 (2020)
15. Li, B., et al.: Benchmarking single-image dehazing and beyond. IEEE Trans. Image Process. **28**(1), 492–505 (2018)
16. Liu, L., et al.: Deep learning for generic object detection: a survey. Int. J. Comput. Vis. **128**(2), 261–318 (2020)
17. Liu, X., Ma, Y., Shi, Z., Chen, J.: GridDehazeNet: attention-based multi-scale network for image dehazing. In: Proceedings of the IEEE/CVF International Conference on Computer Vision, pp. 7314–7323 (2019)
18. McCartney, E.J.: Optics of the Atmosphere: Scattering by Molecules and Particles. New York (1976)
19. Narasimhan, S.G., Nayar, S.K.: Contrast restoration of weather degraded images. IEEE Trans. Pattern Anal. Mach. Intell. **25**(6), 713–724 (2003)

20. Nayar, S.K., Narasimhan, S.G.: Vision in bad weather. In: Proceedings of the Seventh IEEE International Conference on Computer Vision, vol. 2, pp. 820–827. IEEE (1999)
21. Qin, X., Wang, Z., Bai, Y., Xie, X., Jia, H.: FFA-Net: feature fusion attention network for single image dehazing. In: Proceedings of the AAAI Conference on Artificial Intelligence, vol. 34, pp. 11908–11915 (2020)
22. Ren, S., He, K., Girshick, R., Sun, J.: Faster R-CNN: towards real-time object detection with region proposal networks. In: Advances in Neural Information Processing Systems, vol. 28 (2015)
23. Ren, W., Liu, S., Zhang, H., Pan, J., Cao, X., Yang, M.-H.: Single image dehazing via multi-scale convolutional neural networks. In: Leibe, B., Matas, J., Sebe, N., Welling, M. (eds.) ECCV 2016. LNCS, vol. 9906, pp. 154–169. Springer, Cham (2016). https://doi.org/10.1007/978-3-319-46475-6_10
24. Shaaban, A.M., Salem, N.M., Al-atabany, W.I.: A semantic-based scene segmentation using convolutional neural networks. AEU-Int. J. Electron. Commun. **125**, 153364 (2020)
25. Sravya, V.J., Sb, M.: Deep learning for multi grade brain tumor classification in smart healthcare systems: a prospective survey. Smart Intell. Comput. Commun. Technol. **38**, 321 (2021)
26. Wang, S., Zhang, L., Wang, X.: Single image haze removal via attention-based transmission estimation and classification fusion network. Neurocomputing **447**, 48–63 (2021)
27. Wang, Z., Bovik, A., Sheikh, H., Simoncelli, E.: Image quality assessment: from error visibility to structural similarity. IEEE Trans. Image Process. **13**(4), 600–612 (2004)
28. Wu, Q., et al.: A novel underwater bipedal walking soft robot bio-inspired by the coconut octopus. Bioinspiration Biomimetics **16**(4), 046007 (2021)
29. Wu, X., Liu, X.Y., Yuan, F.: Fast dehazing method for improving the image quality in pellet size measurement. Comput. Ind. **128**, 103438 (2021)
30. Wu, X., Sahoo, D., Hoi, S.C.: Recent advances in deep learning for object detection. Neurocomputing **396**, 39–64 (2020)
31. Xue, K., et al.: Robotic seam tracking system based on vision sensing and human-machine interaction for multi-pass mag welding. J. Manuf. Process. **63**, 48–59 (2021)
32. Zhang, R., Li, J.: A survey on algorithm research of scene parsing based on deep learning. J. Comput. Res. Dev. **57**(4), 859 (2020)
33. Zhao, S., Zhang, L., Huang, S., Shen, Y., Zhao, S.: Dehazing evaluation: real-world benchmark datasets, criteria, and baselines. IEEE Trans. Image Process. **29**, 6947–6962 (2020)
34. Zhu, Q., Mai, J., Shao, L.: A fast single image haze removal algorithm using color attenuation prior. IEEE Trans. Image Process. **24**(11), 3522–3533 (2015)

Benchmarking Deep Reinforcement Learning Based Energy Management Systems for Hybrid Electric Vehicles

Wu Yuankai[1]([✉])[ORCID], Lian Renzong[2], Wang Yong[3], and Lin Yi[1]

[1] Sichuan University, Chengdu 610065, Sichuan, China
wuyk0@scu.edu.cn
[2] Tsinghua University, Shenzhen 518055, China
lianrz21@mails.tsinghua.edu.cn
[3] Beijing Institute of Technology, Beijing, China

Abstract. Energy management strategy (EMS) is important for improving the fuel economy of hybrid electric vehicles (HEVs). Deep reinforcement learning techniques have seen a great surge of interest, with promising methods developed for hybrid electric vehicles EMS. As the field grows, it becomes critical to identify key architectures and validate new ideas that generalize to new vehicle types and more complex EMS tasks. Unfortunately, reproducing results for state-of-the-art deep reinforcement learning-based EMS is not an easy task. Without standard benchmarks and tighter metrics of experimental reporting, it is difficult to determine whether improvements are meaningful. This paper conducts an in-depth comparison between numerous deep reinforcement learning algorithms on EMSs. Two different types of hybrid electric vehicles, which include an HEV with planetary gears for power split and a plug-in HEV, are considered in this paper. The main criteria for performance comparison are the fuel consumption, the state of batteries' charges, and the overall system efficiency. Moreover, the robustness, generality, and modeling difficulty, which are critical for machine learning-based models, are thoroughly evaluated and compared using elaborate devised experiments. Finally, we summarize the state-of-the-art learning-based EMSs from various perspectives and highlight problems that remain open.

Keywords: Deep reinforcement learning · Energy management · Hybrid electric vehicles

1 Introduction

The decline of global oil inventories and the serious concern for air quality have caused several challenges for the vehicular industry. These challenges have encouraged the development of hybrid electric vehicles (HEVs), which have been considered the most feasible and immediate choice by automakers. HEV is a structure that includes two or more energy sources with their associated energy

© The Author(s), under exclusive license to Springer Nature Switzerland AG 2022
L. Fang et al. (Eds.): CICAI 2022, LNAI 13605, pp. 613–625, 2022.
https://doi.org/10.1007/978-3-031-20500-2_50

converters. As a result, HEVs have lots of flexibility in the powertrain configuration, the size of its components, and how vehicle power demand is split. These flexibilities allow HEVs to reduce overall fuel consumption by enabling hybrid powertrain to operate its components, such as electric motors and internal combustion engines, close to their fuel-efficient spot.

Crucial to achieving improved fuel economy is an efficient energy management strategy (EMS) for HEVs. The EMS concept emerges in the early 1990s, intending to reduce ICE fuel consumption and emission [2]. In general, the availability of energy storage makes the EMS a decision-making/control problem over the driving cycle horizon. Both short and long-term avails in the EMS should be considered, which is significantly different from traditional vehicle control problems that can be solved instantaneously. To better address the energy management problem, a plethora of EMSs has been proposed in the past.

In recent years, reinforcement learning-based approaches have attracted significant attention as a possible solution to address the limitations associated with traditional EMSs. RL learns the optimal action not from a label created by the optimization model but from trials and errors. In RL, the optimal strategy is learned by sampling actions and then observing which one leads to our desired outcome. Several works [12,13,24] demonstrated that RL algorithms is able to achieve effective EMS for numerous types of HEVs. In recent years, the rise of deep learning, which utilizes the powerful function approximation properties of deep neural networks, has dramatically improved RL [1,5]. Thus attempts have applied DRL algorithms to numerous real-world applications [6,20].

In EMS, DRL is mainly used to address the errors caused by state (inputs) and action (outputs) discretization in the traditional RL approach [18]. Current research on DRL-based EMSs is mainly focused on two kinds of algorithms. The first one is popularized by the Deep Q-Learning algorithm [4,7,15,22], which approximates the values of each action with deep neural networks. DQL can only handle discrete and low-dimensional action spaces. The task of EMS has continuous (ICE power) action spaces. Therefore the researchers using DQL have to incorporate well-designed action discretization rules. In [22], the action A on changing engine power is defined by $A = [-1\,\mathrm{KW}, 0, 1\,\mathrm{KW}, 20\,\mathrm{KW}, 40\,\mathrm{KW}, set0]$. Second main direction of DRL based EMS research is to use the deep deterministic policy gradient (DDPG) method [8–10,18,23], which is a model-free, off-policy actor-critic algorithm using deep neural networks that learn deterministic policies in high-dimensional, continuous action spaces. Therefore it can directly output continuous actions such as ICE power, torque, and wheel speed.

In theory, both DQL and DDPG belong to the so-called off-policy algorithm, which reuses past experiences by storing them in a memory replay buffer and trains a value function or Q-function with off-policy updates. This improves data efficiency, but often at a cost in ease of use. For EMS of HEVs, an off-policy algorithm makes the real-time update and driver adaption difficult. Moreover, it is reported that off-policy algorithms are brittle and sensitive to hyperparameters. In order to make the algorithms more stable, Haarnoja et al. [3] proposed a soft actor-critic (SAC) algorithm, which combines the reward maximization objective with an entropy maximization term. Improvements in both performance and efficiency were reported in this paper. Traditionally, the on-policy methods, which require new experience to be collected for each learning step, are data-inefficient but relatively easy to use. Recently, some researchers have sought to eliminate these issues with approaches such as Trust Region Optimization (TRPO) [16] and Proximal Policy Optimization (PPO) [17] by a surrogate objective and optimizing an update's size. The improved on-policy algorithms can update the agent in real-time and minimize the cost function while ensuring the deviation from the previous policy is relatively small.

With various DRL-based models and tools in hand, it is very crucial for a researcher to determine which model is applicable to the EMS of HEVs. In current studies on the learning-based EMS, where limited driving cycles and simple scenarios are often evaluated, we argue that the current results fail to provide comprehensive improvements. We also note that the diversity of metrics and lack of standardization in building the agent and environment of the learning-based systems creates the potential for misleading reporting of results. Systematic evaluation and comparison will further our understanding of the strengths of existing algorithms and reveal their limitations, and suggest directions for future research. To fill those gaps, we conduct a systematic benchmarking studies on DRL-based EMSs in this paper.

2 HEV Models

In this paper, we conduct comparisons on two different types of HEVs, including a Prius and a plug-in series hybrid tracked vehicle (SHTV). The powertrains of those two HEVs are listed in Fig. 1. We choose Prius for the case study because Prius is one of the first commercial and the most classical HEVs, whose EMS has been extensively studied. Conversely, the SHTV is only used under special conditions. As a result, it exhibits significantly different attributes, i.e., a large battery pack and a stronger lateral force. We only briefly introduce the HEV powertrains in this section. More details of those two powertrains can be found in [10] and [4].

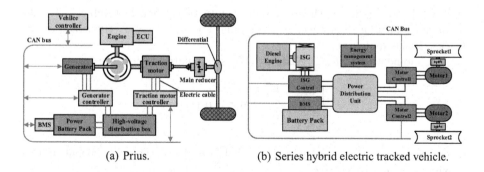

(a) Prius.   (b) Series hybrid electric tracked vehicle.

Fig. 1. Schematic graph of two types of HEV powertrain architectures.

Prius HEV [14] belongs to the second generation of the Toyota hybrid system. As shown in Fig. 3(a), the core power-split component is a planetary gear, which is utilized to realize power coupling among the engine, motor, and generator. In addition, Prius is equipped with a small capacity lithium battery, which is used to drive the traction motor and generator.

The SHTV [4] is driven by dual motors independently, and its powertrain configuration is shown in Fig. 3(b). In this structure, the power sources are composed of the engine-generator set and the battery pack, where the engine works as a generator to power the electric motor or to recharge the battery.

2.1   Power Request Model

In the aspect of power request model, the vehicle longitudinal dynamic is modeled by longitudinal force (F_r) balance equation in Eq. (1) which mainly consists of four parts: rolling resistance F_f, aerodynamic drag F_w, gradient resistance F_i and inertial force F_a.

$$\begin{cases} F_r = F_f + F_w + F_i + F_a \\ F_f = W_f = G \cdot f \\ F_w = \frac{1}{2}\rho \cdot A_f \cdot C_D \cdot v^2 \\ F_i = G \cdot i \\ F_a = m \cdot a \end{cases} \tag{1}$$

where G is the gravity force of HEV, f the rolling resistance coefficient, ρ the air density, A_f the frontal area, C_D the coefficient of air resistance, v the longitudinal vehicle velocity without regard to wind speed, i the road slope (road slope is not considered in this paper), m the vehicle mass, a the acceleration.

Hence, the power request P_{req} of wheeled vehicles is calculated by the production of longitudinal resistance F_r and longitudinal velocity v. Based on the vehicle-terrain theory in [21], the power request P_{req} can be calculated as follows:

$$\begin{cases} P_{req} = F_r v + M_r \omega \\ v = \frac{v_1 + v_2}{2} \\ \omega = \frac{v_1 - v_2}{B} \end{cases} \tag{2}$$

where v is the speed of the center of gravity of the tracked vehicle, M_r the moment of turning resistance, ω the angular speed, v_1 and v_2 the speed of two tracks, B the vehicle tread.

The moment of turning resistance M_r is calculated as follows:

$$\begin{cases} M_r = \frac{\mu G L}{4} \\ \mu = \mu_{max}(0.925 + 0.15\frac{R}{B})^{-1} \\ R = \frac{V}{|\omega|} \end{cases} \tag{3}$$

where μ and μ_{max} are the empirical-based lateral resistance coefficient and its maximum value, respectively, L is the length of track on ground and R is the turning radius.

2.2 Power Source Model

The battery pack is modeled by an equivalent circuit model in Eq. (4), wherein the impact of temperature change and battery aging are not considered in this research.

$$
\begin{cases}
P_{batt}(t) = V_{oc}(t) - R_0 \cdot I^2(t) \\
I(t) = \frac{V_{oc}(t) - \sqrt{V_{oc}^2(t) - 4 \cdot R_0 \cdot P_{batt}(t)}}{2R_0} \\
SoC(t) = \frac{Q_0 - \int_0^t I(t)\,dt}{Q}
\end{cases}
\tag{4}
$$

where SoC is the state of charge (SoC), V_{oc} the open-circuit voltage, I_t the current at time t, R_0 the internal resistance, P_{batt} the output power in the charge-discharge cycles, Q_0 the initial battery capacity, Q the nominal battery capacity.

3 Comparing Methods

3.1 Energy Management Objective

In this paper the energy management of HEV is modeled as a long-term sequential decision process target to minimize the total energy consumption, while maintaining the battery state of charge (SOC) within reasonable limits. The optimization objective can be formulated as Eq. (5):

$$
J = min \sum_{t=0}^{T} (fuel_t + \alpha f_s(SoC(t)))
\tag{5}
$$

where T is the total length of the trip, $fuel_t$ the fuel consumption, $f_s(SoC(t))$ the SoC maintaining function, α the tradeoff between fuel consumption and SoC maintaining.

3.2 Optimization Control Methods

In optimization control methods, the EMS of HEV is framed as a nonlinearly constrained optimization formulation minimizing the objective function given in Eq. (5). **Dynamic Programming (DP)** is the widely used global optimization method, which obtains the minimum cost function of every grid at every stage backward in time. DP utilizes future driving cycles, which are not available in practice. In this study, DP acts as the global optimum, which provides upper limits. We also include another optimization baseline-**Model Predictive Control (MPC)**. In MPC, we utilize some algorithms to predict the future driving cycle and minimize a series of cost functions over the prediction horizon using DP. In our experiments, we assume that the prediction accuracy of MPC is 100% accurate.

3.3 Supervised Learning

In EMS, the global-optimization approaches like DP are acted as the instructor, which is used to generate the optimal energy management trajectories. The learning objective of supervised learning is to mimic the behavior of DP. The learning objective can be formulated as follows:

$$\min_{\theta} \sum_{t=0}^{T} error(a_t^{DP} - \pi_\theta(s_t)) \tag{6}$$

where π_θ is a machine learning model parameterized by θ, a_t^{DP} is an optimal action at time point t produced by the DP algorithm, s_t is some state factors such as acceleration, speed, battery SOC, trip length, trip duration, etc. The main challenge in supervised learning is that the generalization performance of the trained model to previously unseen inputs.

3.4 Deep Reinforcement Learning

Off-Policy RL Deep Q Network (DQN): The DQN algorithm is the earliest work that combines the classical Q-learning algorithm with a deep neural network. DQN uses a deep neural network named target network to represent the action-value function. The target network can be learned by updating the parameters to minimize the error in the Bellman equation. By approximating the Q-function at each iteration,

Double DQN (DDQN) [19]: The DDQN can be regarded as an improved DQN algorithm that tends to overestimate action values. In DDQN, there are two networks that are parameterized by two sets of weight. The first network is referred to as the online network, which is used to choose the action from the maximum Q-value. Besides that, the target network is used to estimate the Q-value that remains the same as DQN.

Deep Deterministic Policy Gradient (DDPG) [11]: The DDPG algorithm is proposed to overcome the issue of continuous action space. The DDPG algorithm uses two neural networks. One acts as the Actor-Network and the other acts as the Critic Network. For the Actor, it learns a deterministic target policy by mapping states to a specific action. The Critic part is used to estimate the Q-value of a state-action pair.

Soft Actor-Critic (SAC) [3]: SAC is based on the maximum entropy RL framework that the actor aims to maximize expected return and entropy simultaneously. SAC concurrently learns three functions: soft value function, soft Q-function, and policy function. The soft value function is trained to minimize the squared residual error. The loss function for the soft Q-function is to minimize the difference between the estimated Q value and the truth. The policy network is optimized by minimizing the expected KL-divergence.

On-policy RL: Unlike off-policy algorithm, all of the policy updates of on-policy algorithm are made using data that was collected from the trajectory distribution induced by the current policy of the agent. In this work, we use **PPO** as the on-policy baseline.

For the above algorithms, the states include velocity, acceleration and state of charge (SoC). For algorithms with discrete action space, such as DQL and DDQL, the action space needs to be discretized. For example, the motor torque increment or decrement in value is set as action, including 21 options: remain unchanged, set 0 Nm (shut down electric motor), increase 10 Nm, decrease 10 Nm, increase 20 Nm, decrease 20 Nm, increase 30 Nm, decrease 30 Nm, etc. Unlike the algorithms with discrete action space, the algorithms with continuous action space can output continuous actions directly (DDPG) or the probability of actions accordingly (SAC, PPO). To sum up, the states and actions are set as follows:

$$\begin{cases} state = \{SoC, v, acc\} \\ action = \{T_{eng}, W_{eng}, T_{mot}\} \end{cases} \tag{7}$$

where v is the velocity of HEV, acc the acceleration of HEV, T_{eng} the engine torque, W_{eng} the engine speed, and T_{mot} the motor torque (only for SHTV).

4   Experimental Results

4.1   Driving Cycle Dataset

In many DRL-based EMS studies, the training and test driving cycles are not separated. As a result, the results of those studies are not convincible since DRL agents might be overfitted to training driving cycles, and thus the generalization capability can not be guaranteed. In this benchmark study, we separate training and test driving cycles. For Prius, the training data consists of standard driving cycles (CTUDC, NEDC, etc.) and driving cycles collected from real HEVs. Two driving cycles, the HEB driving cycle and Guiyang City driving cycle are used as the testing data. For SHTV, the Driving cycle 2 and Driving cycle 3 are the training data, and Driving cycle 1 is the testing data. Details about Dataset can be obtained in the Github project (https://github.com/lryz0612/DRL-Energy-Management).

4.2   Evaluation Metrics

To evaluate the performance of these algorithms on the energy management tasks, several evaluation metrics are defined particularly:

1. Fuel economy: the overall fuel and electricity consumption of HEVs are calculated in a specific driving cycle. For comparison purposes, the energy consumption of dynamic programming (DP) serves as the global optimum.
2. Generalization performance: the performance that the algorithms are generalized to new unseen driving cycles. This is often neglected by existing studies.

3. Performance robustness: to evaluate the robustness of the DRL model to different driving cycles, robustness is introduced as follows:

$$
\begin{cases}
\mu = \sum\limits_{i=k}^{k+N} ((f_{eco})_i)/N \\
\sigma = \sqrt{\frac{1}{N} \sum\limits_{i=k}^{k+N} ((f_{eco})_i - \mu)^2}
\end{cases}
\tag{8}
$$

where f_{eco} represents the fuel economy, k is the convergence step, and μ and σ represent the mean and standard deviation of fuel economy respectively.

Tuned hyperparameters play a large role in eliciting the best results from all the DRL algorithms. The best hyperparameters are chosen using the Tree-structured Parzen Estimator (TPE) on the training driving cycles. The structure of all neural networks are shown in Fig. 2, and the number of neurons in hidden layers decreases layer by layer.

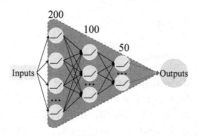

Fig. 2. Structure of all neural networks used in the deep reinforcement learning algorithms.

4.3   Performance Comparison of Algorithms

The main evaluation results are presented in Tables 1 and 2. We only show the results of the best possible hyperparameters. A detailed analysis of each method is given below:

MPC: Despite its simplicity, MPC is an effective algorithm for optimizing energy management strategies. It gives the best fuel economy on Prius and the second one for SHTV. Moreover, the SoC generated from MPC is stable. It should be noted that we assume that the prediction accuracy of MPC is 100% accurate, which means it can always achieve the global optimum in its rolling horizon. Unfortunately, 100% accurate prediction is impractical in the real world. Still, the experimental results suggest that an MPC model with accurate prediction algorithms can outperform the deep reinforcement learning ones. Another thing worth mentioning is that MPC uses an optimization algorithm to find the best action, which is far more computationally expensive than DRL algorithms.

Table 1. Comparison on prius.

Algorithm	Driving cycle	Fuel economy	Terminal SoC	Best fuel economy and terminal SoC	Fuel economy and terminal SoC of DP	Energy ratio(%)	Performance robustness
MPC	CTUDC×3	0.513	0.547	N/A	0.497/0.547	96.9	97.0 ± 1.1
	NEDC	0.392	0.592	N/A	0.385/0.592	98.2	
	HEB driving cycle	1.228	0.56	N/A	1.173/0.56	95.5	
	Guiyang City	0.321	0.58	N/A	0.31/0.58	97.4	
DNN	CTUDC×3	0.610 ± 0.027	0.567 ± 0.070	0.592/0.540	0.494/0.540	83.4	91.2 ± 5.5
	NEDC	0.413 ± 0.025	0.586 ± 0.061	0.410/0.590	0.384/0.590	93.7	
	HEB driving cycle	1.227 ± 0.030	0.552 ± 0.065	1.268/0.565	1.161/0.565	91.6	
	Guiyang City	0.346 ± 0.028	0.619 ± 0.069	0.325/0.582	0.312/0.582	96.0	
DQL	CTUDC×3	0.589 ± 0.098	0.547 ± 0.11	0.549/0.568	0.521/0.568	94.8	90.1 ± 3.68
	NEDC	0.455 ± 0.09	0.568 ± 0.142	0.426/0.56	0.372/0.56	87.3	
	HEB driving cycle	1.335 ± 0.137	0.549 ± 0.11	1.267/0.55	1.154/0.55	91.1	
	Guiyang City	0.381 ± 0.06	0.557 ± 0.08	0.347/0.558	0.302/0.558	87.0	
DDQL	CTUDC×3	0.651 ± 0.055	0.520 ± 0.074	0.558/0.563	0.504/0.563	90.3	89.9 ± 0.9
	NEDC	0.483 ± 0.041	0.590 ± 0.094	0.446/0.614	0.395/0.614	88.6	
	HEB driving cycle	1.415 ± 0.122	0.541 ± 0.057	1.272/0.541	1.152/0.541	90.6	
	Guiyang City	0.388 ± 0.038	0.522 ± 0.087	0.336/0.558	0.303/0.558	90.2	
DDPG	CTUDC×3	0.559 ± 0.029	0.544 ± 0.008	0.526/0.547	0.497/0.547	94.5	94.5 ± 1.4
	NEDC	0.410 ± 0.007	0.603 ± 0.013	0.403/0.592	0.385/0.592	95.5	
	HEB driving cycle	1.350 ± 0.087	0.537 ± 0.013	1.248/0.547	1.154/0.547	92.5	
	Guiyang City	0.323 ± 0.005	0.556 ± 0.007	0.318/0.558	0.303/0.558	95.3	
SAC	CTUDC×3	0.616 ± 0.029	0.555 ± 0.008	0.616/0.574	0.506/0.574	82.2	86.15 ± 3.66
	NEDC	0.434 ± 0.002	0.600 ± 0.003	0.429/0.599	0.388/0.599	90.4	
	HEB driving cycle	1.324 ± 0.005	0.568 ± 0.005	1.327/0.574	1.165/0.574	87.8	
	Guiyang City	0.369 ± 0.009	0.569 ± 0.004	0.366/0.572	0.308/0.572	84.2	
PPO	CTUDC×3	0.754 ± 0.034	0.589 ± 0.013	0.720/0.607	0.521/0.607	72.4	79.9 ± 5.31
	NEDC	0.483 ± 0.022	0.575 ± 0.030	0.478/0.591	0.384/0.591	80.3	
	HEB driving cycle	1.397 ± 0.015	0.579 ± 0.013	1.376/0.577	1.166/0.577	84.7	
	Guiyang City	0.390 ± 0.009	0.574 ± 0.015	0.376/0.575	0.309/0.575	82.2	

DNN: The DNNs are trained with label data from the global optimization algorithms. However, DNN achieves a competitive overall fuel economy. However, it can not keep the SoC within an acceptable range. The final SHTV SoC of DNN is below 0.3 for all driving cycles, which is not desirable for the battery of SHTV. It indicates that supervised learning algorithms can not learn semantic features (keep SoC in an acceptable range) underlying EMS tasks purely from the expert demonstrations. Another reason might be that the number of label data in this study is limited.

DQL and DDQL: Both DQL and DDQL provide competitive performance. However, compared to DQL, DDQL offers better energy management strategies on SHTV. In addition, it indicates that DDQL can reduce the observed overestimations for SHTV.

DDPG: DDPG is the only algorithm generating continuous and deterministic actions. It achieves the best performance among all DRL algorithms, and its performance is stable and robust. Moreover, it generalizes to test driving cycle very well. Compared with DQL and DDQL, it avoids the errors resulting from action discretization. Compared with SAC and PPO, its output is a deterministic value rather than a distribution, making its performance more stable.

SAC: SAC also provides acceptable results. Its fuel economy is more stable than DQL and DDQL on Prius and is higher than on SHTV. SAC outputs a probabilistic action rather than a deterministic one. Thus its robustness is relatively lower than DDPG. The standard deviations of SAC are 3.66 and 3.18 for Prius and SHTV, respectively. They are higher than the ones of DDPG, which are 1.4 and 1.25, respectively. It indicates that the deterministic action is more suitable for EMS tasks.

PPO: Surprisingly, the on-policy PPO algorithm can not achieve satisfactory results on EMS tasks. Its results are significantly poorer than other off-policy DRL algorithms. The problem might be that the on-policy approach can only learn a near-optimal policy that still explores. This strategy is not fitted for the energy management of HEVs.

Table 2. Comparison on SHTV.

Algorithm	Driving cycle	Fuel economy	Terminal SoC	Best fuel economy and terminal SoC	Fuel economy and terminal SoC of DP	Energy ratio(%)	Performance robustness
MPC	Driving cycle 2	20.6	0.31	N/A	19.6/0.31	95.2	95.76±0.81
	Driving cycle 3	21.3	0.31	N/A	20.6/0.31	95.4	
	Driving cycle 1	18.3	0.31	N/A	17.7/0.31	96.7	
DNN	Driving cycle 2	16.30 ± 0.35	0.131 ± 0.018	16.64/0.150	15.75/0.150	94.7	96.20 ± 1.37
	Driving cycle 3	18.57 ± 0.55	0.140 ± 0.032	19.17/0.177	18.67/0.177	97.4	
	Driving cycle 1	16.67 ± 0.65	0.201 ± 0.036	17.30/0.236	16.69/0.236	96.5	
DQL	Driving cycle 2	24.28 ± 1.97	0.381 ± 0.065	24.02/0.373	19.10/0.373	79.5	81.90 ± 2.10
	Driving cycle 3	26.58 ± 1.64	0.374 ± 0.090	24.90/0.310	20.62/0.310	82.8	
	Driving cycle 1	22.31 ± 1.72	0.355 ± 0.060	21.57/0.325	17.99/0.325	83.4	
DDQL	Driving cycle 2	22.31 ± 1.80	0.324 ± 0.057	21.88/0.325	18.40/0.325	84.1	85.67 ± 1.46
	Driving cycle 3	24.63 ± 1.66	0.319 ± 0.057	24.40/0.333	20.96/0.333	85.9	
	Driving cycle 1	21.15 ± 1.57	0.326 ± 0.053	20.57/0.320	17.90/0.320	87.0	
DDPG	Driving cycle 2	20.64 ± 0.35	0.334 ± 0.007	20.14/0.334	18.55/0.334	92.1	93.33 ± 1.25
	Driving cycle 3	22.91 ± 0.32	0.333 ± 0.007	22.37/0.330	20.88/0.330	93.3	
	Driving cycle 1	19.33 ± 0.33	0.319 ± 0.015	19.13/0.330	18.10/0.330	94.6	
SAC	Driving cycle 2	21.48 ± 0.25	0.307 ± 0.006	21.30/0.311	18.13/0.311	85.1	87.80 ± 3.18
	Driving cycle 3	23.64 ± 0.24	0.297 ± 0.004	23.48/0.301	20.42/0.301	87.0	
	Driving cycle 1	19.21 ± 0.19	0.300 ± 0.009	19.71/0.324	17.99/0.324	91.3	
PPO	Driving cycle 2	27.05 ± 0.72	0.348 ± 0.010	26.06/0.339	18.60/0.339	71.4	76.43 ± 4.37
	Driving cycle 3	27.31 ± 0.74	0.302 ± 0.013	25.74/0.293	20.39/0.293	79.2	
	Driving cycle 1	23.17 ± 0.68	0.308 ± 0.010	21.97/0.282	17.30/0.282	78.7	

Figure 3 presents the Prius and SHTV SoC curves of MPC, DNN, DQL, DDQL, DDPG, SAC, and PPO. Apparently, the SOC curves of DNN-based and MPC-based EMSs are different from DRL-based EMSs. For MPC-based EMS, SOC depletes very slowly within the acceptable SoC ranges. On the other hand, DNN-based EMS fails to maintain the SOC curves within the acceptable SoC ranges on SHTV driving cycle 1, despite achieving strong fuel economy in

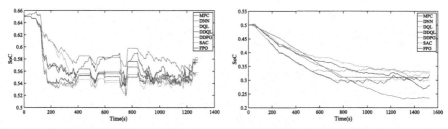

(a) Prius SoC curve on Guiyang City driving cycle.

(b) SHTV SoC curve on Driving cycle 1.

Fig. 3. SoC curve of algorithms.

Tables 1 and 2. For all DRL-based EMSs, relatively sharp drops are found during the early stage of Guiyang City driving cycle, which is the major difference from MPC-based EMS. In the final stage of Guiyang City driving cycle, SoC oscillations around 0.54 SoC are observed from all DRL-based EMSs. For SHTV, all EMSs' SoC curves are more stable. Those results indicate that DRL algorithms can learn various energy management strategies, however, their stabilities require further studies.

5   Conclusion

In this work, a benchmark of hybrid electric vehicle energy management problems for reinforcement learning is presented, covering two different types of vehicles and a variety of driving cycles. We implemented several deep reinforcement learning algorithms and compared them with optimization and supervised learning algorithms. Results show that among the implemented algorithms, on-policy algorithms such as DQL, DDQL, DDPG, and SAC are effective methods for training deep neural network-based energy management strategies. Still, the poor performance of the on-policy algorithms calls for new algorithms to be developed. Implementing and evaluating existing and newly proposed algorithms will be our continued effort. In the future, we will provide an open-source release of the benchmark and encourage other researchers to evaluate their algorithms on the hybrid electric vehicles used in this paper.

References

1. Arulkumaran, K., Deisenroth, M.P., Brundage, M., Bharath, A.A.: Deep reinforcement learning: a brief survey. IEEE Sig. Process. Mag. **34**(6), 26–38 (2017)
2. Biswas, A., Emadi, A.: Energy management systems for electrified powertrains: state-of-the-art review and future trends. IEEE Trans. Veh. Technol. **68**(7), 6453–6467 (2019)
3. Haarnoja, T., Zhou, A., Abbeel, P., Levine, S.: Soft actor-critic: off-policy maximum entropy deep reinforcement learning with a stochastic actor. In: International Conference on Machine Learning, pp. 1861–1870 (2018)

4. Han, X., He, H., Wu, J., Peng, J., Li, Y.: Energy management based on reinforcement learning with double deep q-learning for a hybrid electric tracked vehicle. Appl. Energy **254**, 113708 (2019)
5. Henderson, P., Islam, R., Bachman, P., Pineau, J., Precup, D., Meger, D.: Deep reinforcement learning that matters. In: Proceedings of the AAAI Conference on Artificial Intelligence, vol. 32 (2018)
6. Hilleli, B., El-Yaniv, R.: Toward deep reinforcement learning without a simulator: an autonomous steering example. In: Proceedings of the AAAI Conference on Artificial Intelligence, vol. 32 (2018)
7. Hu, Y., Li, W., Xu, K., Zahid, T., Qin, F., Li, C.: Energy management strategy for a hybrid electric vehicle based on deep reinforcement learning. Appl. Sci. **8**(2), 187 (2018)
8. Li, Y., He, H., Khajepour, A., Wang, H., Peng, J.: Energy management for a power-split hybrid electric bus via deep reinforcement learning with terrain information. Appl. Energy **255**, 113762 (2019)
9. Li, Y., He, H., Peng, J., Wang, H.: Deep reinforcement learning-based energy management for a series hybrid electric vehicle enabled by history cumulative trip information. IEEE Trans. Veh. Technol. **68**(8), 7416–7430 (2019)
10. Lian, R., Peng, J., Wu, Y., Tan, H., Zhang, H.: Rule-interposing deep reinforcement learning based energy management strategy for power-split hybrid electric vehicle. Energy, 117297 (2020)
11. Lillicrap, T.P., et al.: Continuous control with deep reinforcement learning. In: ICLR (Poster) (2016)
12. Liu, T., Hu, X., Li, S.E., Cao, D.: Reinforcement learning optimized look-ahead energy management of a parallel hybrid electric vehicle. IEEE/ASME Trans. Mechatron. **22**(4), 1497–1507 (2017)
13. Liu, T., Wang, B., Yang, C.: Online Markov chain-based energy management for a hybrid tracked vehicle with speedy q-learning. Energy **160**, 544–555 (2018)
14. Prokhorov, D.V.: Toyota Prius HEV neurocontrol and diagnostics. Neural Netw. **21**(2–3), 458–465 (2008)
15. Qi, X., Luo, Y., Wu, G., Boriboonsomsin, K., Barth, M.: Deep reinforcement learning enabled self-learning control for energy efficient driving. Transp. Res. Part C: Emerg. Technol. **99**, 67–81 (2019)
16. Schulman, J., Levine, S., Abbeel, P., Jordan, M., Moritz, P.: Trust region policy optimization. In: International Conference on Machine Learning, pp. 1889–1897. PMLR (2015)
17. Schulman, J., Wolski, F., Dhariwal, P., Radford, A., Klimov, O.: Proximal policy optimization algorithms. arXiv preprint arXiv:1707.06347 (2017)
18. Tan, H., Zhang, H., Peng, J., Jiang, Z., Wu, Y.: Energy management of hybrid electric bus based on deep reinforcement learning in continuous state and action space. Energy Convers. Manag. **195**, 548–560 (2019)
19. Van Hasselt, H., Guez, A., Silver, D.: Deep reinforcement learning with double q-learning. In: Proceedings of the AAAI Conference on Artificial Intelligence, vol. 30 (2016)
20. Won, D.O., Müller, K.R., Lee, S.W.: An adaptive deep reinforcement learning framework enables curling robots with human-like performance in real-world conditions. Sci. Robot. **5**(46), eabb9764 (2020)
21. Wong, J.Y.: Theory of Ground Vehicles. Wiley, Hoboken (2008)
22. Wu, J., He, H., Peng, J., Li, Y., Li, Z.: Continuous reinforcement learning of energy management with deep q network for a power split hybrid electric bus. Appl. Energy **222**, 799–811 (2018)

23. Wu, Y., Tan, H., Peng, J., Zhang, H., He, H.: Deep reinforcement learning of energy management with continuous control strategy and traffic information for a series-parallel plug-in hybrid electric bus. Appl. Energy **247**, 454–466 (2019)
24. Zou, Y., Liu, T., Liu, D., Sun, F.: Reinforcement learning-based real-time energy management for a hybrid tracked vehicle. Appl. Energy **171**, 372–382 (2016)

Self-attention Based High Order Sequence Features of Dynamic Functional Connectivity Networks with rs-fMRI for Brain Disease Classification

Zhixiang Zhang, Biao Jie$^{(\boxtimes)}$, Zhengdong Wang, Jie Zhou, and Yang Yang

School of Computer and Information, Anhui Normal University, Wuhu, China
jbiao@ahnu.edu.cn

Abstract. Dynamic functional connectivity networks (dFCN) based on rs-fMRI have demonstrated tremendous potential for brain function analysis and brain disease classification. Recently, studies have applied deep learning techniques (*e.g.*, convolutional neural network, CNN) to dFCN classification, and achieved better performance than the traditional machine learning methods. However, previous deep learning methods usually perform successive convolutional operations on the input dFCN to obtain high-order brain network aggregation features, extracting them from each sliding window using a series split, which may neglect non-linear relations between different regions and the sequentiality of information. Important high-order sequence information of dFCN, which could further improve the classification performance, is ignored in these studies. To address these issues, we propose a self-attention-based convolutional recurrent network (SA-CRN) learning framework for brain disease classification with rs-fMRI data. The experimental results on a public dataset (*i.e.*, ADNI) demonstrate the effectiveness of our proposed SA-CRN method.

Keywords: High order · Self-attention · Time series analysis · Brain disease classification

1 Introduction

Functional connectivity network (FCN) calculated from resting-state functional magnetic resonance imaging (rs-fMRI) has been widely used to identify brain disorders automatically, such as Alzheimer's disease [1]. The majority of FCN research focuses on two aspects: stationary FCN (sFCN) and dynamic FCN (dFCN). Currently, for sFCN, studies have been dedicated to the longitudinal study of brain disease diagnosis, using rs-fMRI data from multi-time points. For example, Huang *et al.* [2] proposed to add both Pearson correlation correction (PCC) and modular structure to the sparse low-rank brain network (SLR), obtaining the PCC-related SLR brain network features for ASD diagnosis. Yang *et al.* [3] proposed a fusion sparse network (FSN) method to extract longitudinal

L. Fang et al. (Eds.): CICAI 2022, LNAI 13605, pp. 626–637, 2022.
https://doi.org/10.1007/978-3-031-20500-2_51

features for detecting MCI phases. However, they only focused on sFCN, thus neglecting the dynamic patterns of interaction between brain regions. Another serious problem with the longitudinal study is the need for years-long accumulation of clinical data, which can be detrimental to early diagnosis of brain disease. Therefore, changing characteristics of dFCN may provide better prospects for clinical applications in early diagnosis of brain diseases and personalized medicine, while facilitating a better understanding of the pathological basis [4].

To investigate changes of dFCN over time, existing studies often use analysis of sliding window correlations between regional brain activity to estimate correlations of brain activity across multiple, possibly overlapping, time-series segments. For example, Chen *et al.* [5] extract the root-mean-square features of dFCN for automatic diagnosis of mild cognitive impairment (MCI) via ensemble support vector machine (SVM). Zhao *et al.* [6] proposed to employ a central-moment method to extract temporal-invariance properties, fusing the features extracted from conventional FCN, low-order dFCN, and high-order dFCN, to explore the higher level and more complex interaction among brain regions for the autism spectrum disorder's (ASD) diagnosis. However, all these studies neglect the change patterns of dFCN sequence information, which may further improve the performance of brain disease diagnosis.

As a new paradigm for scientific study, deep learning methods have shown applicable potential in the field of medical imaging, such as computer-aided diagnosis [7–9] and detection [10–13]. In recent years, deep learning techniques (*e.g.*, convolutional neural network, CNN) have been applied to the diagnosis of brain diseases, and dramatically improve the performance compared with traditional machine learning methods. For example, Jie *et al.* [4] proposed a novel method that used a weight correlation kernel model for effectively constructing a dFCN from rs-fMRI, obtaining impressive performances in comparison to previous methods such as SVM.

In addition, convolutional recurrent network (CRN) has been applied to brain disease analysis with rs-fMRI data, and yields outperformance in processing spatial-temporal sequence information. For example, Wang *et al.* [14] proposed to learn the spatial-temporal dependency of brain regions for an MCI diagnosis. Recently, Lin *et al.* [15] extract the changing patterns of the dFCN for brain disease diagnosis, which achieved one of the state-of-the-art classification performances on different classification tasks. However, important high-order sequence information of the dFCN has been ignored in these studies.

To address these problems, we proposed a self-attention based CRN (called SA-CRN) learning framework to extract high-order sequence features of brain regions from the dFCN as features for brain disease classification.

2 Method

2.1 Subjects and fMRI Data Preprocessing

We use rs-fMRI data for 174 subjects, including 48 normal controls (NC), 50 early MCI (eMCI), 45 late MCI (lMCI) and 31 Alzheimer disease (AD), which

Table 1. Characteristics of the studied subjects (Mean ± Standard Deviation). MMSE: Mini-Mental State Examination.

Group	AD	lMCI	eMCI	NC
Male/Female	16/15	27/18	20/30	20/28
Age	74.7 ± 7.4	72.3 ± 8.1	72.4 ± 7.1	76.0 ± 6.8
MMSE	21.8 ± 3.3	27.1 ± 2.1	28.1 ± 1.6	28.8 ± 1.4

are derived from the ADNI database. Of these, 154, 165, 145, and 99 scans obtained from each of the nine different periods are for AD, lMCI, eMCI and NC subject groups, respectively. Nevertheless, data of the eMCI and AD groups are unfilled from month 48 to month 84. The scan parameters for data are as follows: the echo time (TE) is 30 ms, 2.2–3.1 s for the repetition time (TR), 2.29–3.31 mm for the in-plane image resolution and 3.31 mm for slice thickness. The demographic and clinical information of these subjects is summarized in Table 1. From Table 1, we can see that the first point is that the number of subjects in the different disease groups and the gender ratio are well balanced. Besides, the second point is that our subjects are mainly aged between 64 and 83, which suggests that our findings hold more pertinence and significance for an older population who are at high risk of brain disease.

Following the previous study [16] approach, we adopt a standard processing flow with the FSL FEAT software package: (1) Remove the first three volumes of sampled data. (2) Do slice timing. (3) Correct head motion. (4) Do bandpass filtering. (5) Regress white matter, CSF, and motion parameter covariates. We divide the subject's brain space of rs-fMRI scans into 116 regions of interest (RoI) by the specified automated anatomical labelling (AAL) template and the non-parametric registration method. At last, we treat the average time series calculated from BOLD signals in each specific RoI as the input.

2.2   The Self-Attention (SA) Mechanism

Before proposing the use of the SA mechanism, we scrutinized the approach of the feature extraction phase in previous deep learning methods for the diagnosis of brain diseases. They usually perform successive convolutional operations on the input FCNs to obtain higher-order brain network aggregation features. However, if you further observe the nature of convolution, you will find that convolution is a linear feature aggregation method, which ignores the non-linearity of information superimposing, as multiple brain regions interact with others [17]. Additionally, according to the latest research, a key feature of the SA mechanisms is their data specificity, rather than long-range dependency [18], exploring the spontaneous correlation of data, which in brain science is mainly reflected in the complex pattern of low-order as well as high-order information interaction between brain regions.

As a significant improvement in the non-linear interactivity of features from multiple regions, the original SA mechanism [19] comprises the following process.

Given the input $I \epsilon R^{m \times n}$, where m indicates the number of features on the input, and n denotes the dimension of features on the input. We employ linear transformations to create the query vector $Q = IW_Q$, the key vector $K = IW_K$, the value vector $V = IW_V$, where $W_Q, W_K, W_V \epsilon R^{n \times p}$, p refers to the dimension of the features after embedding, and then we obtain the score vector through dot-product of Q and the transpose of K. Then, the score vector is divided by $\sqrt{d_k}$ ($d_k = n$) and normalized by Softmax function. At last, we get the output $O \epsilon R^{p \times p}$ through multiplying the score vector by the value vector, obtaining the cumulative weighted features. The SA mechanism can be summarized as:

$$O = \text{Soft} \max \left(\frac{QK^T}{\sqrt{d_k}} \right) V \tag{1}$$

where Q, K, V are the query vector, key vector and value vector, individually.

To make the SA mechanism more applicable to few-shot learning, we introduce the following two points of adjustment: On the one hand, we employ the SA mechanism based on linear transformations by 1×1 convolution, reducing the weight parameters that need to be trained for one SA calculation from $3 \times n \times p$ to $3 \times 1 \times 1$. On the other hand, we adopt the residual network structure, where the input vector O and the output vector O are added, aggregating both the original features and the updated features calculated by attention weights, as shown in Fig. 1 (d).

2.3   Proposed SA-CRN Learning Framework

As shown in Fig. 1, our proposed SA-CRN learning framework consists of three parts: (a) dFCN construction, (b) spatial feature and temporal feature extraction, and (c) classification. We will cover the details of these three parts in the following subsections.

dFCN Construction. As shown in Fig. 1 (a), dFCNs based on continuous and overlapping time windows are constructed by using average time series of the specified N RoIs. For every subject, we first segment his or her all rs-fMRI time series into T consecutive and overlapping time windows of constant L length. Next, we construct the dFCN: $F^t \epsilon R^{N \times N}$ ($t = 1, \cdots, T$) with Pearson's correlation coefficients between BOLD signals of paired RoIs at the t-th time window, as shown below:

$$F^t (j, k) = \frac{\text{covr} \left(x_j^t, x_k^t \right)}{\sigma_{x_j^t} \sigma_{x_k^t}} \tag{2}$$

where *covr* denotes the covariance of two vectors, $\sigma_{x_j^t}$ and $\sigma_{x_k^t}$ represent the standard deviation corresponding to the vectors x_j^t and x_k^t respectively. The vector x_j^t refers to the BOLD signals of the j-th RoI at the t-th time window as well as x_k^t.

According to Eq. 2, F^t is correlation coefficient matrix for all RoIs at the t-th time window. Further, each row or column of the matrix F^t represents the

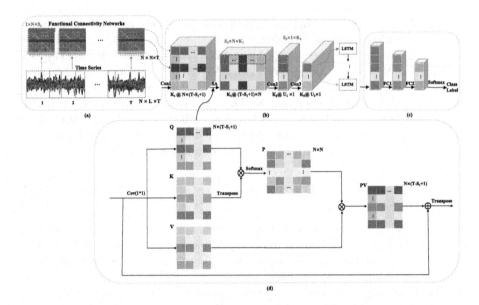

Fig. 1. Illustration of the proposed SA-CRN learning framework for sequential feature extraction and classification with rs-fMRI data, including three parts: (a) dFCN construction, (b) spatial feature and temporal feature extraction, and (c) classification. Of these, (d) represents the complete course of the SA mechanism.

degree of correlation between the specific RoI and the all RoIs at time window t. Thus, a group of FCNs $\mathbf{F} = \{\mathbf{F}^1, \mathbf{F}^2, \cdots, \mathbf{F}^T\} \epsilon \mathbf{R}^{\mathbf{T} \times \mathbf{N} \times \mathbf{N}}$ work on transmitting dynamic brain information of these subjects.

Spatial Feature and Temporal Feature Extraction. Similar to Jie's method [4], we first use consecutive convolution layers to further extract higher-order brain network features, as shown in Fig. 1 (b). In detail, we set the kernel size of the first convolution layer **Con**1 to $1 \times \mathbf{N} \times \mathbf{S}_1$, where $1 \times \mathbf{N}$ represents the size of the convolution kernel in the spatial dimension and $\mathbf{S}_1$ indicates the size in the temporal dimension, and set the stride to $(\mathbf{N}, \mathbf{S}_1)$ along the spatial dimension and the temporal dimension, mainly to aggregate information from separate ROIs across $\mathbf{S}_1$ adjacent time windows. Then, we respectively update features from all ROIs with the SA mechanism on a channel-wise basis, as shown in Fig. 1 (d). The SA layer operates by the following process:

We perform a linear transformation of the input $\mathbf{I} \epsilon \mathbf{R}^{\mathbf{N} \times (\mathbf{T} - \mathbf{S}_1 + 1)}$ from one channel through thrice independent 1×1 convolution, where $\mathbf{N}$ denotes the amount of ROIs and $(\mathbf{T} - \mathbf{S}_1 + 1)$ refers to the total length of time windows. So far, we obtain the vectors $\mathbf{Q}, \mathbf{K}, \mathbf{V} \epsilon \mathbf{R}^{\mathbf{N} \times (\mathbf{T} - \mathbf{S}_1 + 1)}$, where $\mathbf{Q}$ is used as the query vector, $\mathbf{K}$ as the key vector and $\mathbf{V}$ as the value vector, as shown in Fig. 1(d).

Next, the query vector $\mathbf{Q}$ is multiplied by the transpose of the key vector $\mathbf{K}$, acquiring the score vector $\mathbf{P} \epsilon \mathbf{R}^{\mathbf{N} \times \mathbf{N}}$, which refers to the dynamic degree of correlation between all ROIs. Then, the score vector is divided by $\mathbf{d_K} = \mathbf{T} - \mathbf{S}_1 + 1$

and normalized by Softmax function, as in equation $\mathbf{P} = \mathbf{Soft}\max\left(\frac{\mathbf{QK^T}}{\sqrt{\mathbf{d_k}}}\right)$. Unlike Pearson correlation which constructs relevant degree for paired ROIs in a complex calculation (Eq. 2), it is more efficient to get dot-product of $\mathbf{Q}$ and the transpose of $\mathbf{K}$ in much cheaper time complexity. Moreover, contrary to traditional convolution that linearly performs feature aggregation, the vectors $\mathbf{Q}$ and $\mathbf{K}$ are learnable so that the score vector $\mathbf{P}$ can be non-linearly updated as the input changes, constructing correlation information for different brain regions in the higher-order spatial features.

For the final step of the SA layer, we introduce the residual network to the output, aggregating both the input and updated features, as expressed in equation $\mathbf{O} = (\mathbf{PV} + \mathbf{I})^{\mathbf{T}}$, where $\mathbf{PV}$ indicates the value vector $\mathbf{V}$ should be updated with the score vector $\mathbf{P}$, and $(\mathbf{T} - \mathbf{S_1} + 1) \times \mathbf{N}$ stands for the output. After features from all channels have been updated with the $\mathbf{SA}$ mechanism, layer normalization (LN) serves as the activation function.

Hence, the convolution layer $\mathbf{Con2}$ and $\mathbf{Con3}$ are utilized to better aggregate higher-order features from different ROIs along the spatial dimension, and the kernel size of the layer $\mathbf{Con2}$ equals to $\mathbf{S_2} \times \mathbf{N} \times \mathbf{K_1}$. Similarly, the kernel size of the layer $\mathbf{Con3}$ is $\mathbf{S_3} \times 1 \times \mathbf{K_2}$. We set the stride of the layer $\mathbf{Con2}$ and $\mathbf{Con3}$ along the time dimension and the space dimension to (1, 1) and (2, 1), respectively. Each convolutional layer ($\mathbf{Con1}$, $\mathbf{Con2}$, $\mathbf{Con3}$) is followed by batch normalization (BN), rectified linear unit (ReLU) activation, and 0.25 dropout.

At the end of the spatial feature and temporal feature extraction stage, to capture the sequence change patterns and dig deeper into the different contributions between time series of dFCN, we choose LSTM (containing 48 neurons) network followed by RELU activation and 0.5 dropout.

Classification. As shown in Fig. 1 (c), we employ two fully connected layers and a softmax layer for prediction with the output of LSTM as input. In particular, we set up 32 neurons and 16 neurons for the first fully connected layer and the second fully connected layer, respectively. There are 2 and 4 neurons in the last fully connected layer for binary and multi-class classification, separately. It is worth noting that we adopt L2 regularization in the last fully connected layer for better parameter optimization.

Implementation. For our proposed network shown in Fig. 1, we empirically set the parameters as follows: $\mathbf{N} = 116$, $\mathbf{T} = 34$, $\mathbf{L} = 70$, $\mathbf{S_1} = 2$, $\mathbf{S_2} = 1$, $\mathbf{S_3} = 8$, $\mathbf{K_1} = 5$, $\mathbf{K_2} = 16$, $\mathbf{K_3} = 32$, $\mathbf{U_1} = 33$, $\mathbf{U_2} = 13$. The Adam optimizer with recommended parameters is used for training, and the number of epochs and batch size are empirically set as 150 and 16, respectively.

3   Experiment

3.1   Experimental Setup

In the study, a 5-fold cross-validation (CV) strategy is utilized to ensure that the training set and test set do not overlap with each other. We perform both binary

Table 2. Performance of five methods in two binary classification tasks, *i.e.*, eMCI vs. NC and AD vs. NC classifications. ACC = Accuracy.

Method	eMCI vs. NC (%)			AD vs. NC (%)		
	ACC	SPE	SEN	ACC	SPE	SEN
Baseline	57.1	48.1	65.6	73.3	77.8	66.7
SVM	63.6	50.0	75.0	75.0	80.0	66.7
DFCN-mean	67.7	47.3	84.7	76.4	**100.0**	33.3
CNN	80.8	88.4	78.6	87.8	95.0	88.1
CRN	84.2	84.7	88.3	92.8	95.0	93.8
SA-CRN (OURS)	**87.8**	**89.7**	**88.7**	**97.5**	**100.0**	**96.7**

and multi-class classification experiments, including 1) eMCI vs. NC classification, 2) AD vs. NC classification, and 3) AD vs. lMCI vs. eMCI vs. NC classification. Each subset in turn is selected as the test set, while the remaining four subsets are joined together to construct the training set. Further, we select one-fifth of the training set as validation data to find the best empirical parameters for the optimal model. It's worth pointing out that each scan of each subject is treated as an independent sample to enhance the model's generalization ability, but all scans of the same subject have the same class label.

We compare our method with the following five methods. (1) **Baseline**: The stationary FCN is constructed by computing the Pearson correlation coefficient between the time series of each ROI at the start. Next, the connectivity strengths of the stationary FCNs are set to the features. After feature selection with the t-test method (i.e., $p - value < 0.05$), a linear SVM with default parameters is used for classification. (2) **CC**: Contrary to the Baseline, local clustering coefficients of the stationary FCNs from each subject are extracted as features. Then, the t-test method and a linear SVM with default parameters are also used for feature selection and classification, respectively. (3) **M²TFS**: The dFCN is first constructed for each subject. Next, the temporal and spatial mean features of the dFCN are extracted. The manifold regularized multi-task feature learning (M2TFL) and multi-kernel SVM are used for feature selection and classification, respectively. (4) **CNN**: The dFCN is constructed for each subject as the input. Then, consecutive convolution layers and an average pooling layer are used to extract features. Finally, fully connected layers and a softmax layer are used for classification. (5) **CRN**: As a variant of CNN, this method has a similar network architecture, but replaces the LSTM layer with an average pooling layer with considering the temporal dynamics along with time steps.

3.2   Classification Performance

Table 2 and Table 3 depict the comparison results of all methods for the two binary classification tasks and the multiclass classification task. As can be seen from Tables 2 and 3, our proposed SA-CRN method outperforms the competing methods in almost all the three classification tasks.

Table 3. Performance of five methods in the multi-class classification task, *i.e.*, AD vs. lMCI vs. eMCI vs. NC classification. ACC = Accuracy.

Method	AD vs. lMCI vs. eMCI vs. NC (%)				
	ACC	ACC_{NC}	ACC_{eMCI}	ACC_{lMCI}	ACC_{AD}
Baseline	30.6	20.0	38.9	30.0	33.3
SVM	35.0	22.0	69.5	21.0	6.7
DFCN-mean	44.0	36.0	**87.6**	22.0	0.0
CNN	62.2	21.4	74.8	52.0	60.0
CRN	67.4	52.7	74.8	64.0	**66.7**
SA-CRN (OURS)	**69.6**	**64.7**	78.1	**65.0**	**66.7**

For instance, our proposed method yields the accuracy of 87.8% and 97.5% for eMCI vs. NC classification and AD vs. NC classification, respectively, while the best accuracies obtained by the competing methods are 84.2% and 92.8%, respectively. For the challenging AD vs. lMCI vs. eMCI vs. NC classification task, our proposed method achieves the overall best accuracy of 69.6%, while the second-best overall accuracy of four competing methods is 67.4%. These results suggest the effectiveness of our proposed method in rs-fMRI-based brain disease classification.

From Table 2 and Table 3, we provide certain interesting new findings. First, as compared to traditional methods, models using CNN structures can achieve better performance in terms of accuracy, sensitivity and specificity. Second, the performance of the SA-CRN model using the SA mechanism is further improved by capturing feature correlations in the spatial dimension. Third, the SA-CRN model is the only one to test above 60% accuracy on each multiclass classification task, which is a meaningful breakthrough for the use of brain network features in the task of Alzheimer's disease prediction.

To verify the generalization ability of the SA mechanism, we use four different convolution kernel sizes for the layer **Con**1 to check the testing accuracy of our model. Our SA-CRN model maintains state-of-the-art performance at four different kernel size settings. Complementarily, we also give a comparison of the accuracy of the SA-CRN model for each of the multiclass classification tasks at different kernel sizes, as presented in Fig. 2.

3.3   Visualization Analysis

We visualize the t-SNE the output features of the feature extraction stages in CRN and SA-CRN in Fig. 3, where the data for visualization belongs to the 5-fold cross-validation. From Fig. 3, we observe that the features trained with CRN present a distribution which is locally clustered and globally separated, however, features trained with SA-CRN are more uniformly distributed, which facilitates our method to be more sensitive to hard samples and boosts the classification performance [20], especially for the classification of AD vs. NC classification.

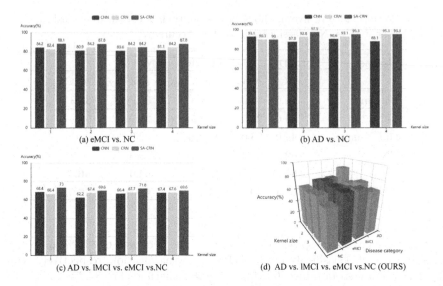

Fig. 2. (a), (b), (c): The classification accuracy of the SA-CRN and CRN and CNN method under different convolution kernel sizes on tasks of the eMCI vs. NC classification, the AD vs. NC classification, and the AD vs.lMCI vs. eMCI vs. NC classification. (d): The influence of kernel size of our model SA-CRN in the AD vs. lMCI vs. eMCI vs. NC classification.

Specially, we extract the high order sequence features after the **SA** layer in SA-CRN to explore discriminative regions that contributed to the specific classification tasks and the most important connectivity between them. It is noteworthy that the obtained feature vectors are different in each fold of cross-validation. The output features are tested in a separate t-test (**p** < 0.05) significance groups by channel. Figure 4 depicts the most discriminative regions on the 5th, and 1st channels for (a) eMCI vs. NC group and (b) AD vs. NC group, respectively.

As shown in Fig. 4, for eMCI vs. NC classification, the most brain regions we selected have been proved to have important correlations with eMCI, including the lobule III of the vermis and the lobule IV, V of the vermis, the left inferior frontal gyrus, the left orbitofrontal cortex, the right orbitofrontal cortex, the right middle occipital gyrus [15,21]. The top ROIs with an impact on AD vs. NC classification include the left middle frontal gyrus, the right inferior frontal gyrus, the left orbitofrontal cortex, the left hippocampus, the left superior occipital gyrus, and the right thalamus, which are also consistent with previous studies [15,21].

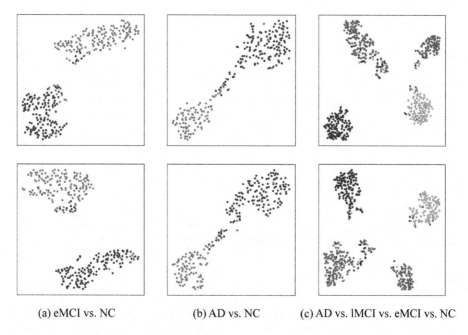

(a) eMCI vs. NC   (b) AD vs. NC   (c) AD vs. lMCI vs. eMCI vs. NC

Fig. 3. The t-SNE visualization for output features of the feature extraction stage for different detection tasks, where the first row is CRN and the second row is SA-CRN.

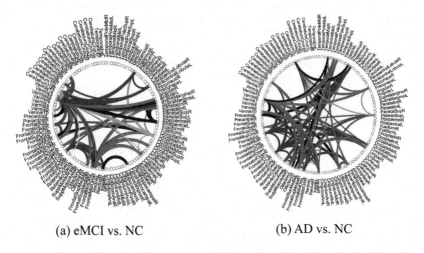

(a) eMCI vs. NC   (b) AD vs. NC

Fig. 4. Discriminative functional connectivities for (a) eMCI vs. NC and (b) AD vs. NC classification. Each arc shows the selected connectivity between two ROIs, where colours are randomly allocated for better visualization, and the thickness of each arc indicates its discriminative power that is inversely proportional to the corresponding p-value in the t-test.

4   Conclusion

In this paper, we developed a SA-based convolutional recurrent network (SA-CRN) learning framework of rs-fMRI time series data for brain disease diagnosis. In SA-CRN, we construct dynamic high-order connectivity networks from time-series using an overlapping sliding window. Then these networks are fed into three convolutional layers with a SA module for extracting high-level features and preserving the sequential information of extracted features. Finally, the subjects' features from typical convolution layers are classified through three fully connected layers. Experiment results on ADNI data demonstrate the effectiveness of our proposed framework compared with state-of-art methods.

Acknowledgement. Z. Zhang, B. Jie, Z. Wang, J. Zhou and Y. Yang were supported in part by NSFC (Nos. 61976006, 61573023, 61902003), Anhui-NSFC (Nos. 1708085MF145, 1808085MF171) and AHNU-FOYHE (No. gxyqZD2017010).

References

1. Duc, N.T., Ryu, S., Qureshi, M.N.I., Choi, M., Lee, K.H., Lee, B.: 3D-deep learning based automatic diagnosis of Alzheimer's disease with joint MMSE prediction using resting-state FMRI. Neuroinformatics **18**(1), 71–86 (2020)
2. Huang, F., et al.: Self-weighted adaptive structure learning for ASD diagnosis via multi-template multi-center representation. Med. Image Anal. **63**, 101662 (2020)
3. Yang, P., et al.: Fused sparse network learning for longitudinal analysis of mild cognitive impairment. IEEE Trans. Cybern. **51**(1), 233–246 (2019)
4. Jie, B., Liu, M., Lian, C., Shi, F., Shen, D.: Designing weighted correlation kernels in convolutional neural networks for functional connectivity based brain disease diagnosis. Med. Image Anal. **63**, 101709 (2020)
5. Chen, X., Zhang, H., Zhang, L., Shen, C., Lee, S.W., Shen, D.: Extraction of dynamic functional connectivity from brain grey matter and white matter for mci classification. Hum. Brain Mapp. **38**(10), 5019–5034 (2017)
6. Zhao, F., Chen, Z., Rekik, I., Lee, S.W., Shen, D.: Diagnosis of autism spectrum disorder using central-moment features from low-and high-order dynamic resting-state functional connectivity networks. Front. Neurosci. **14**, 258 (2020)
7. Larrazabal, A.J., Nieto, N., Peterson, V., Milone, D.H., Ferrante, E.: Gender imbalance in medical imaging datasets produces biased classifiers for computer-aided diagnosis. Proc. Natl. Acad. Sci. **117**(23), 12592–12594 (2020)
8. Karar, M.E., Hemdan, E.E.D., Shouman, M.A.: Cascaded deep learning classifiers for computer-aided diagnosis of Covid-19 and pneumonia diseases in x-ray scans. Complex Intell. Syst. **7**(1), 235–247 (2021)
9. Koo, C.S., Dolgunov, D., Koh, C.J.: Key tips for using computer-aided diagnosis in colonoscopy-observations from two different platforms. Endoscopy (2021)
10. Repici, A., et al.: Efficacy of real-time computer-aided detection of colorectal neoplasia in a randomized trial. Gastroenterology **159**(2), 512–520 (2020)
11. de Groof, A.J., et al.: Deep learning algorithm detection of Barrett's neoplasia with high accuracy during live endoscopic procedures: a pilot study (with video). Gastrointest. Endosc. **91**(6), 1242–1250 (2020)

12. Jarnalo, C.M., Linsen, P., Blazís, S., van der Valk, P., Dickerscheid, D.: Clinical evaluation of a deep-learning-based computer-aided detection system for the detection of pulmonary nodules in a large teaching hospital. Clin. Radiol. **76**(11), 838–845 (2021)

13. Misawa, M., et al.: Development of a computer-aided detection system for colonoscopy and a publicly accessible large colonoscopy video database (with video). Gastrointest. Endosc. **93**(4), 960–967 (2021)

14. Wang, M., Lian, C., Yao, D., Zhang, D., Liu, M., Shen, D.: Spatial-temporal dependency modeling and network hub detection for functional MRI analysis via convolutional-recurrent network. IEEE Trans. Biomed. Eng. **67**(8), 2241–2252 (2019)

15. Lin, K., Jie, B., Dong, P., Ding, X., Bian, W., Liu, M.: Extracting sequential features from dynamic connectivity network with rs-fMRI data for AD classification. In: Lian, C., Cao, X., Rekik, I., Xu, X., Yan, P. (eds.) MLMI 2021. LNCS, vol. 12966, pp. 664–673. Springer, Cham (2021). https://doi.org/10.1007/978-3-030-87589-3_68

16. Jie, B., Liu, M., Shen, D.: Integration of temporal and spatial properties of dynamic connectivity networks for automatic diagnosis of brain disease. Med. Image Anal. **47**, 81–94 (2018)

17. Bronstein, M.M., Bruna, J., Cohen, T., Velivcković, P.: Geometric deep learning: grids, groups, graphs, geodesics, and gauges. arXiv preprint arXiv:2104.13478 (2021)

18. Park, N., Kim, S.: How do vision transformers work? arXiv preprint arXiv:2202.06709 (2022)

19. Lin, Z., et al.: A structured self-attentive sentence embedding. arXiv preprint arXiv:1703.03130 (2017)

20. Wang, F., Liu, H.: Understanding the behaviour of contrastive loss. In: Proceedings of the IEEE/CVF Conference on Computer Vision and Pattern Recognition, pp. 2495–2504 (2021)

21. Lei, B., et al.: Diagnosis of early Alzheimer's disease based on dynamic high order networks. Brain Imaging Behav. **15**(1), 276–287 (2021)

Author Index

Printed in the United States
by Baker & Taylor Publisher Services